THE SHAPING OF MODERN BRITAIN

Identity, Industry and Empire, 1780–1914

Eric J. Evans

Longman
is an imprint of

Harlow, England • London • New York • Boston • San Francisco • Toronto
Sydney • Tokyo • Singapore • Hong Kong • Seoul • Taipei • New Delhi
Cape Town • Madrid • Mexico City • Amsterdam • Munich • Paris • Milan

PEARSON EDUCATION LIMITED

Edinburgh Gate
Harlow CM20 2JE
United Kingdom
Tel: +44 (0)1279 623623
Fax: +44 (0)1279 431059
Website: www.pearsoned.co.uk

First published in Great Britain in 2011

ISBN: 978-1-4082-2564-6

British Library Cataloguing in Publication Data
A CIP catalogue record for this book can be obtained from the British Library

Library of Congress Cataloging in Publication Data
Evans, Eric J., 1945–
   The shaping of modern Britain : identity, industry and empire,
1780–1914 / Eric J. Evans. – 1st ed.
      p. cm.
   Includes bibliographical references and index.
   ISBN 978-1-4082-2564-6 (pbk.)
   1. Great Britain–Social conditions–18th century.   2. Great Britain–Social
conditions–19th century.   3. Great Britain–Social conditions–20th century.
4. Great Britain–Politics and government–18th century.   5. Great Britain–Politics
and government–19th century. 6. Great Britain–Politics and government–20th century.
7. Great Britain–History–18th century.   8. Great Britain–History–19th century.
9. Great Britain–History–20th century.   10. Ireland–Social conditions.
11. Ireland–Politics and government.   I. Title.
   DA505.E94 2011
   941.081–dc22

                                                              2011006096

10 9 8 7 6 5 4 3 2 1
15   14   13   12   11

Set by 35 in 11.25/13pt StonePrint
Printed and bound in Great Britain by Henry Ling Limited, at the Dorset Press, Dorchester, DT1 1HD

Contents

List of boxes

Boxes: list of terms and concepts

Boxes: list of people

Preface

This book has been long in the gestation although relatively short in the writing. It reflects a teaching and research career spent in a British academic environment and a primary concentration on British history in the eighteenth and nineteenth centuries. Those familiar with my *Forging of the Modern State* will notice some similarities of approach. In particular, this book, like its predecessor, is structured into a large number of short thematic chapters which introduce readers to the key aspects of important topics, including recent historiographical debates and emphases. This book is also accompanied by a substantial 'Compendium of Information', although here not in the form of a series of appendices but as an interactive website (www.pearsoned.co.uk/evans) which will be regularly expanded and revised at need and in the light of the comments made by users.

The detailed information available on the website aims to mirror the thematic range of the book. Thus, readers will find information on all the governments in office during the period, results and analysis of general elections and on the impact of parliamentary reform. Other sections cover the key legislative changes concerning work, health, welfare, poverty and education. Users will also find material on the economy, including trade, taxation, prices and incomes, on the size and structure of the UK population, on diplomacy, treaties and wars and on religion.

In no sense is this book a 'fourth edition' of *The Forging of the Modern State*. First, its chronological span is almost a half-century longer. This enables me to cover the entire period during which Britain was, in effect, the world's only super-power. The book, therefore, begins with the quickening of that process still conventionally called the Industrial Revolution (though the validity of that description of economic change has been challenged) and ends with the outbreak of the First World War. It explains how Britain developed into a modern state whose economic, political and cultural dominance was felt in every continent of the world. It studies the process whereby the nation's political structures at home were reformed and modernised and why its influence overseas was so substantial. The book explains how, in the process of pursuing predominantly commercial ambitions, Britain acquired the largest empire the world has ever seen. British dominance was, however, subject to increasing challenge in the latter part of the nineteenth century and the book analyses how effectively these challenges were met. Finally, it explains how, in 1914, Britain and its empire came to be involved in a world war the winning of which would so sap its energies and diminish its resources that British power and influence would never fully recover.

Secondly, in order to take account of the wealth of new research and fresh historiographical approaches undertaken during the last thirty years or so, I decided that it was better to start afresh than to try to pour yet more wine into a venerable bottle. This, therefore, is an entirely new book which attempts to engage with the historical thinking of the early twenty-first century. For example, previously dominant interpretations which explained nineteenth-century social change within the inflexible context of hostility between classes have come under challenge. Since the 1980s, the influence of Marxism has been in rampant retreat both in contemporary world politics and historical writing. Greater emphasis is now placed on complex social interactions in a range of different contexts and on how people construct and experience their own 'multiple' identities within a variety of political, social and cultural contexts. This is one of the most valuable historical by-products of that protean, yet strangely slippery, intellectual movement known as 'Postmodernism' and this book makes some use of its insights for the benefit of the general reader. It would be ungenerous and inappropriate to dilate at any length here on postmodernism's most obvious downsides: academic reductionism grounded in an often unsophisticated and overly present-minded evaluation of historical evidence and simple findings too often expressed in ungainly, obscurantist and jargon-laden prose.

Partly because of shifts in the intellectual world, 'grand narratives' of political and social change, in which the rich and powerful are the principal actors, have become less fashionable. It is the author's hope that readers of this book will conclude that the reaction against what is sometimes dismissively referred to as 'top–down history' has gone too far. It is extraordinary, for example, how little serious academic research in the diplomatic history of a period when Britain exercised world-wide influence is now being undertaken by the younger generation of scholars. Although most institutions of higher education in Britain offer degrees in History, conventional political history figures in their curricula far less than it did. The appearance in 2004 of the new *Oxford Dictionary of National Biography* has also provided ample evidence – should it be needed – of the necessity to study important and powerful people. This book tries to strike a balance between treatment of changing social and cultural structures and the specific influence of key individuals in public life. Also, and perhaps especially in an age when so many influential contemporaries minded little if the adjectives 'English' and 'British' were used more or less interchangeably, it is important to give attention to the development of what was known from 1801 as the United Kingdom of Great Britain and Ireland.

Many debts are owed by any author who is painting on so broad a canvas. Any attempt to list the huge number of colleagues who have been so generous with their time and who have, either directly or inadvertently, provided valuable suggestions, approaches and insights would be invidious. Reluctantly, therefore, since my indebtedness to so many is so substantial, I shall not reproduce here what could not be more distinctive than a long sequence of names. I do, however, wish to acknowledge my profound gratitude to those archivists and librarians up and down the country who have placed their specialist skills so generously at my disposal. A special debt is owed to the staff of the Lancaster University Library. Never, over a period stretching now over more than forty years, have my requests for materials both basic and arcane been met with anything less than courtesy and good humour while the responses have invariably been characterised by immense professionalism. I owe them a huge amount.

The most valuable help I have received in planning and writing this book, however, has come from the students I have taught. Their enthusiasm, good humour and general tolerance towards my historical whims have made most of my teaching an enormous pleasure. From them, I hope I have also learned something of what threatens to turn students off serious historical study as well as what – with often heart-warmingly effective results – engages them. I hope that this book never disengages the reader. Whatever merits it may have derive in significant part from the enthusiasms which have been so generously shared with me. I hope that a new generation of readers may find in the pages which follow something to sustain and to stimulate them in their study. I hope also that I have given them enough to pause over, reflect on – and also to challenge, since only through engaged, informed and lively debate and reinterpretation can the discipline of History be nourished, renewed and progressed.

Finally, this Preface is written at a time when the arts and humanities community in Britain is being forced to defend its right even to exist in both school and higher education curricula. Historians, in particular, need to make the powerful argument that a nation ignorant of how its past has been shaped must fight for its future having thrown away some of its most important weapons. These include: a critical awareness of lessons learned from precedent and experience; an understanding of how constructive communal activity develops; and, perhaps above all, a complex and informed sense of identity grounded in informed understanding of, and tolerance towards, the diversity of humankind. If this book plays but a small part in persuading readers of the crucial importance of studying the past, it will have served its purpose.

Eric J. Evans
Lancaster
December 2010

Publisher's acknowledgements

We are grateful to the following for permission to reproduce copyright material:

Dowlais Ironworks, 1840 (w/c on paper) by Childs, George (1798–1875), © National Museum Wales/The Bridgeman Art Library; Engraving depicting the Last Charge of Napoleon's Old Guard at the Battle of Waterloo, captioned 'The Chasm of Death at Waterloo,' June 18, 1915, © Kean Collection/Getty Images; Cato Street (3), City of Westminster Archives Centre; Edwardian infant children in classroom circa 1910 – Walton Lane School (UK) infants dept., thislife pictures/Alamy; William Ewart Gladstone (1809–1898) was Prime Minister of the United Kingdom from 1869–1874, © Michael Nicholson/Corbis; Blind Man's Buff, 1788–9 (tapestry cartoon) (for sketch see 61070) by Goya y Lucientes, Francisco Jose de (1746–1828), Prado, Madrid, Spain/The Bridgeman Art Library; View of the London Stock Exchange, London, England, United Kingdom, engraving, DEA/A. DAGLI ORTI/Getty Images; The Doctor's Consultation, 1815–1820 (pen and ink and w/c over graphite on paper) by Rowlandson, Thomas (1756–1827), Yale Center for British Art, Paul Mellon Collection, USA/The Bridgeman Art Library; The King of Brobdingnag and Gulliver, published by Hannah Humphrey in 1803 (hand-coloured etching) by Gillray, James (1757–1815), © Courtesy of the Warden and Scholars of New College, Oxford/The Bridgeman Art Library; The sailors poled, © Trustees of the British Museum. All rights reserved; A View of Government House from the Eastward by Robert Havell, Jr. Havell's print is after an original work by James Baillie Fraser, © Stapleton Collection/Corbis; Minton Floor, © Pete Carr; George IV, 1829 (oil on canvas) by Wilkie, Sir David (1785–1841), The Royal Collection © 2010 Her Majesty Queen Elizabeth II/The Bridgeman Art Library; Queen Victoria's Diamond Jubilee Procession through London, passes down Mansion House Street, watched by waving crowds, © Hulton-Deutsch Collection/Corbis; The window of Swan and Edgar's was smashed by suffragettes, © Hulton-Deutsch Collection/Corbis; Indian troops in Orleans, France, guarding boxes of ammunition in September 1914, © Mirrorpix; The Empire Needs Men! recruitment poster by Arthur Wardle, © Swim Ink 2, LLC/Corbis.

In some instances we have been unable to trace the owners of copyright material, and we would appreciate any information that would enable us to do so.

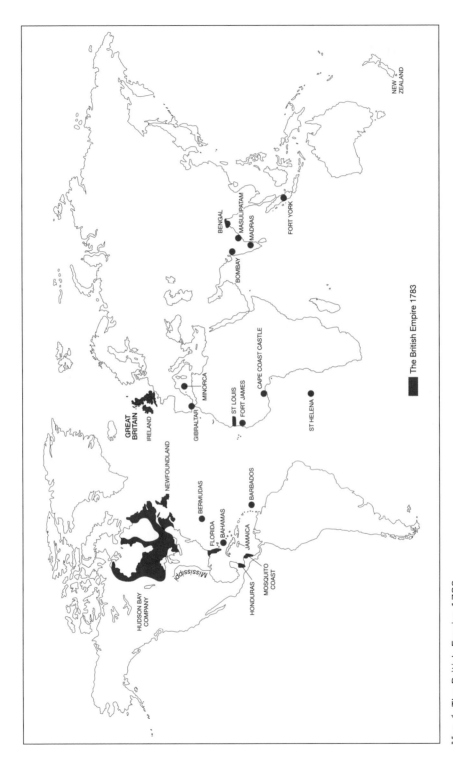

Map 1 The British Empire 1783

Map 2 Early Industrial Britain c1850

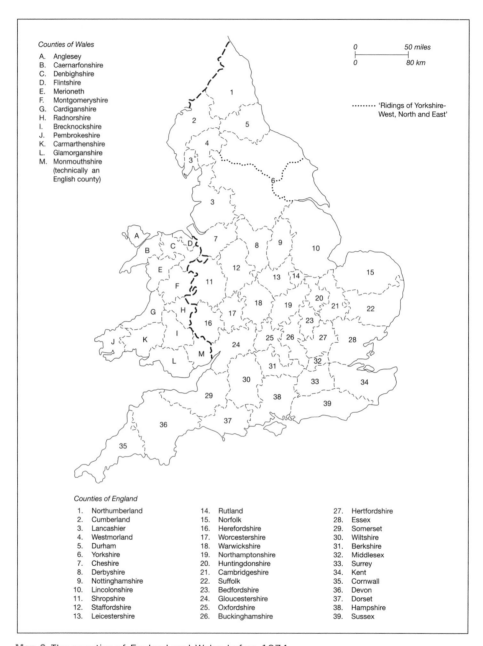

0   50 miles
0   80 km

········ 'Ridings of Yorkshire–
West, North and East'

Map 3 The counties of England and Wales before 1974

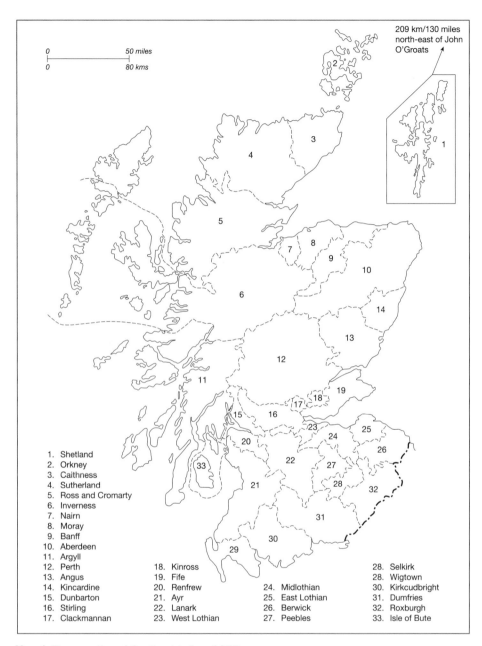

209 km/130 miles north-east of John O'Groats

0 ___ 50 miles
0 ___ 80 kms

1. Shetland
2. Orkney
3. Caithness
4. Sutherland
5. Ross and Cromarty
6. Inverness
7. Nairn
8. Moray
9. Banff
10. Aberdeen
11. Argyll
12. Perth
13. Angus
14. Kincardine
15. Dunbarton
16. Stirling
17. Clackmannan
18. Kinross
19. Fife
20. Renfrew
21. Ayr
22. Lanark
23. West Lothian
24. Midlothian
25. East Lothian
26. Berwick
27. Peebles
28. Selkirk
28. Wigtown
30. Kirkcudbright
31. Dumfries
32. Roxburgh
33. Isle of Bute

Map 4 The counties of Scotland before 1975

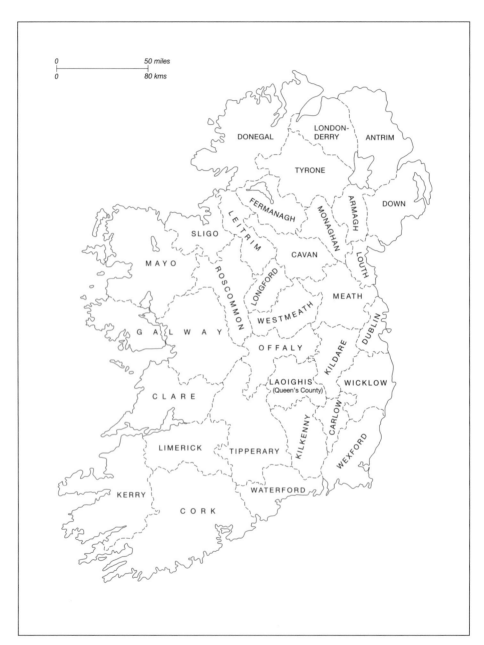

Map 5 Ireland, 1801–1922

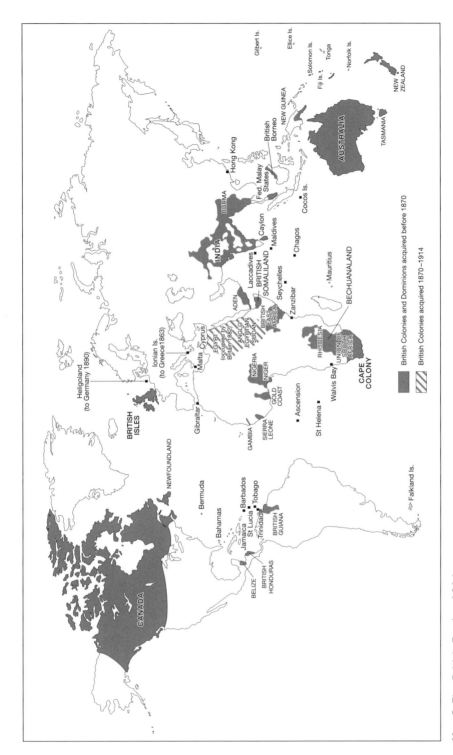

Map 6 The British Empire, 1914

Gilbert Is.

Ellice Is.

•Solomon Is.

Tonga

Fiji Is.

•Norfolk Is.

NEW
ZEALAND

New Guinea

TASMANIA

AUSTRALIA

Hong Kong

British
Borneo

Fed. Malay
States

Cocos Is.

BURMA

Ceylon

Maldives

INDIA

•Chagos

Laccadives

BRITISH
SOMALILAND

Mauritius

Seychelles

ADEN

BECHUANALAND

Zanzibar

BRITISH
EAST
AFRICA

ANGLO
EGYPTIAN
SUDAN

RHODESIA

EGYPT
(occupied by
Britain 1882)

Cyprus

UNION OF
SOUTH
AFRICA

Malta

NIGERIA

Ionian Is.
(to Greece 1863)

NIGER

CAPE
COLONY

Heligoland
(to Germany 1890)

Gibraltar

GOLD
COAST

Walvis Bay

BRITISH
ISLES

SIERRA
LEONE

St Helena

Ascension

GAMBIA

British Colonies and Dominions acquired before 1870

British Colonies acquired 1870–1914

NEWFOUNDLAND

•Bermuda

Barbados

Bahamas

•Tobago

Jamaica

St Lucia

Trinidad

BELIZE

BRITISH
GUIANA

BRITISH
HONDURAS

CANADA

Falkland Is.

Section 1

Early Industrial Britain, *c*1780–1850

A watercolour by George Childs of the Dowlais Ironworks, Merthyr Tydfil, in 1840

The Dowlais iron works near Merthyr Tydfil in South Wales, originally established in 1759, was by 1845 the largest iron works in the world. Its eighteen blast furnaces were producing almost 90,000 tons of iron a year. It employed almost 9,000 men, most of them, as this picture implies, working in dangerous and unhealthy conditions. Dowlais seems to epitomise the speed of change which transformed Britain in the late eighteenth and early nineteenth centuries.

To understand the extent to which both society and economy in Britain changed in these years, it is necessary to put such dramatic examples of industrial transformation into a wider context. This Section attempts to explain the factors involved. It begins by discussing (Chapter 1) how the three countries, England, Scotland and Wales, which comprised late eighteenth-century Britain had developed and the extent to which, culturally, they remained separate nations. Chapter 2 discusses the reasons why British population was growing so fast. A growing population was vital for industrial growth, which needed a healthy supply of labour not just for the new factories but also to meet the need for unskilled and semi-skilled labouring tasks. The social and economic roles of the landed aristocracy, which invested heavily in urban development at this time, are examined in Chapter 3, while Chapter 4 explains how, and why, the middle classes became an increasingly important element in British society, even challenging the dominance of the aristocracy in some areas.

Chapters 5 and 6 are concerned with the nature of Britain's industrial and urban growth. The industrial revolution did not transform all of Britain in this period. Even by 1850 more people worked on the land than in the towns and cities. So, is it appropriate to talk of an 'industrial revolution' at all? Perhaps the main changes were evolutionary rather than revolutionary. Towns had very diverse functions. In addition to the great factory communities of south-east Lancashire, the West Riding of Yorkshire and the central valley of Scotland, this was a time of growth and increased prosperity for towns such as Bath and Brighton, whose main economic rationale was leisure and social interaction. Older regional centres such as Bristol and Norwich and market and cathedral towns of England, such as Oxford and Shrewsbury, were also growing significantly.

Chapter 7 examines the continued importance of agriculture. No study of industrial change should ignore the rural sector of the economy, not least because significant changes in agricultural organisation and production were needed to feed a growing population, a smaller proportion of which was growing food. Whether 'revolutionary' or 'evolutionary', industrial change was massively disruptive. The final chapter of this Section discusses the nature of this disruption. It examines the extent of social conflict in this period and investigates whether, by 1850, Britain had become a society riven by class antagonisms.

1

A 'Greater Britain' in 1780?

I. A costly war

During the period covered by this book, Britain, or the United Kingdom of Great Britain and Ireland, its official title after the Act of Union in 1800, was the wealthiest and the most powerful nation in the world. In the first half of the nineteenth century, Britain became not just the workshop but the manufactory of the world, using new technologies to produce a range of manufactured goods, especially textiles, much more quickly and efficiently and also at prices which no competitor could match.

We begin in 1780 because, although strict chronological precision is not attainable, a consensus exists that the pace of Britain's commercial activity and industrial production, the prime agents of its nineteenth-century supremacy, substantially quickened in the last quarter of the eighteenth century. If supremacy is a key theme in this story, however, 1780 might seem a perplexing date from which to begin. Contemporaries saw it as a time of humiliation abroad and dangerous political conflict at home. Britain had been at war with its thirteen North American colonies since 1775. It was at war with France and Spain from 1778 too, as those countries weighed in on the colonies' side, once it became clear that British arms would not bring about the rapid victory which had been widely assumed. By 1780, a series of reverses had brought it close to defeat. That defeat, and consequent American independence, would be confirmed by decisive reverses on the battlefield during 1781 and then, formally, by the Treaty of Versailles in 1783. The assumption was that the loss of the colonies would severely damage Britain's trade routes and commercial activity. One provincial newspaper suggested that the combined might of France and the American colonies would destroy Britain as a naval power.[1]

The war was also costly. British governments had to find about £80m, which they did by raising loans and substantially increasing the National Debt. Crucially, it also raised taxes, including those on salt, soap and alcohol which fell disproportionately heavily on the poor. Despite this, **excise duties**, substantially the largest source of government income, fell during the later stages of the war as consumption was squeezed. Over-taxed, poorly governed, resentful and defeated in war, the country appeared to be at its lowest eighteenth-century ebb in the early 1780s.

Excise duties

These are taxes raised on goods sold in the country, in contrast to customs duties which are levied on goods coming into it. These are indirect taxes. This means that they are added to the price of the goods when sold, irrespective of the ability of the purchaser to pay. In the eighteenth century, excises were levied on a wide range of basic items, including salt, beer, soap and candles as well as luxury items such as wine or gold.

The country in question, of course, was 'Great Britain', but Britain was a relatively recent creation, comprising the nations of England, Scotland and Wales formally brought together by the Act of Union passed in 1707. It is worth a brief introduction to the nations which comprised Great Britain. England was, of course, the largest of the three nations both geographically and, in particular, demographically. In 1780, it comprised about 78 per cent of Britain's population, compared with Scotland's 16 per cent and Wales's 6 per cent.[2] A century later, after substantial industrial development in all three countries, the overall demographic proportions showed little change: England 82 per cent, Scotland 13 per cent, Wales 5 per cent.

England's overall wealth and current level of economic activity were also much higher, although both the central lowlands of Scotland and parts of South Wales experienced significant commercial and economic development in the second half of the eighteenth century. Critically, the development of agriculture, which employed the majority of the population, proceeded more rapidly during the eighteenth century in England than in either Wales or, allowing for a few exceptions in the Lowlands, Scotland. Many economic historians speak of an English agricultural revolution in the eighteenth century (see Chapter 7). This had significant social consequences. **Subsistence farming** by small peasant proprietors had been almost eliminated from England by the last quarter of the eighteenth century. By contrast, central and North Wales and the Highlands of Scotland both retained significant numbers of small landowners engaged in subsistence farming. As we shall see, England's superior overall levels of prosperity persuaded many of its well-heeled citizens that the inhabitants of Wales and Scotland were backward and their countries a deadweight on England.

Subsistence farming

This might best be considered as 'domestic farming', as it was usually practised by small proprietors or 'smallholders' known as peasants. Its purpose was to provide sufficient food for the family. This form of farming contrasted starkly with agriculture designed to produce crops and animals for the market and, therefore, for profit.

The Scots – more numerous, better educated and a more obvious presence in influential London society than the Welsh – bore the brunt of this opprobrium. For much of the century, the dominant English perception of Scotland was of a barren, backward, poverty-stricken nation. James Boswell, the Edinburgh-born biographer of Dr Samuel Johnson, frequently felt the force of his biting anti-Scottish wit. The definition of oats in Johnson's 1755 Dictionary as 'a grain, which in England is generally given to horses, but which in Scotland supports the people' is famous. Boswell was also briskly told that 'the noblest prospect which a Scotchman ever sees, is the high road that leads him to England' and that 'much may be made of a Scotchman, if he be caught young'. Its superior education system notwithstanding, the image of Scotland as an unworthy supplicant at the rich Englishman's table was widely accepted as plain truth.[3] Metropolitan hostility to the Scots was real enough.

II. Wales

Wales had been yoked to England for almost five centuries, having been dominated by the larger country since Edward I's conquests in the early 1280s. It was formally joined to England by an Act of Union passed in 1536, although it retained some separate legal courts and practices until the Council of Wales was abolished in 1689.[4] The judicial system of Wales would finally be assimilated with the English in 1830. Precise calculations of Welsh population are not available but most estimates suggest that it was not greater than half a million in 1780.[5]

Welsh society revolved around the influence of the few prosperous gentry families who often established links by marriage with English landowners. Most were Tory supporters throughout the eighteenth century, when the government was, until the 1760s, Whig and in the hands of large, and mostly English, landowners.[6] Sir Roger Mostyn (1673–1739), for example, married the daughter of Daniel Finch, second Earl of Nottingham, and represented Flintshire in parliament. Sir Watkin Williams Wynn (1693–1749) became the largest landowner in Wales on the occasion of his marriage in 1715 into another prominent Welsh family, the Vaughans. He entered parliament the following year as a staunch Tory who opposed the Hanoverian succession and supported the return of the Stuarts.[7] He remained an MP until his death in 1749 and was for a time perhaps the most prominent Tory in the House of Commons during the period of the so-called 'Whig supremacy'.

Wynn's elder son (1749–89) – also named Watkin Williams – was a prominent patron of the arts who helped further the London career of the composer George Frederick Handel. In the Commons from 1772, he kept up the family tradition of opposition – in his case to Lord North in the 1770s and the Younger Pitt in the 1780s. Unlike many landowners from the Principality, Wynn made a point of stressing his support for 'Welshness' and the upholding of Celtic traditions. He was a generous patron of the London Welsh charity school, which was supported by the Society of Ancient Britons, of which Wynn became Vice-President in 1772.

By 1780, Wales, unlike Scotland or Ireland, had long ceased to be regarded as a threat to England. It retained its own language, of course, but only the lower orders made much use of it. The English dismissed Welsh as a barbarous language befitting only the uncivilised – and then mostly forgot about it. Celtic history, ballads and literature were little studied by the propertied classes and remained to be practised safely by the lower orders on the western side of Offa's Dyke. Ordinary Welsh working families in the late eighteenth century had few links with their English counterparts. Not until well into the nineteenth did Welsh workers migrate in significant numbers to the larger cities of England – Liverpool, Birmingham and London in particular – to pose any kind of threat to the earning power of their English counterparts.

The Church of England was the established Church of Wales also, although Welsh bishops had low status in the episcopal hierarchy and, in consequence, some of the lowest incomes. During the course of the eighteenth century, nonconformist Churches, particularly Baptist and Methodist, were establishing themselves at the expense of the established Church.

Welsh politics, too, had long since been thoroughly assimilated into the English-dominated parliamentary structure. As the Wynns demonstrated, Welsh MPs might oppose the government of the day, and many Welsh MPs were Tories in an age dominated by the so-called **Whig Oligarchy**. Some might even be seditious. However, the Welsh gentry did not produce firebrands or tub-thumping orators either capable of, or much interested in, exciting public opinion and raising a crowd. Eighteenth-century Wales did not produce a David Lloyd George (see Chapter 38). Likewise, Welsh nationalism mostly slumbered. In any case, the Principality returned only twenty-four MPs to the House of Commons, less than 5 per cent of its total complement. Few issues indeed turned on what the Welsh thought.

Whig Oligarchy

An oligarchy is a form of government in which a small number of privileged men dominate affairs. This phrase relates to the long period of political dominance exercised over almost half a century by great landowners (most were titled aristocrats) in the Whig party, from the death of the Tory-inclined Queen Anne in 1714 down to the accession of George III in 1760. There was no hard-and-fast ideological or social division between Whigs and Tories in the eighteenth century, although Whig politicians tended to own more land and to have more aristocratic titles than did Tory ones.

III. Scotland

Scotland was different. Its relationships with England had frequently been fractious. Disputes over territory on either side of the border were frequent in the early medieval period, not infrequently spilling over into war. Edward I threatened to do to Scotland what he had done to Wales and might well have succeeded had he not died near Carlisle in 1307 while preparing an invasion of Scotland. Not surprisingly, Scotland established what it called an 'auld alliance' with France for much of the early modern period, seeing it as an effective safeguard against a much more powerful neighbour. Relations improved somewhat when James VI of Scotland was named as the successor to Elizabeth I. He united the two thrones as James I of England from 1603. United crowns did not make for a united British nation. Charles I attempted to recover his fortunes in the Civil Wars of the 1640s by making an alliance with Scotland against the English parliament.

The so-called 'Glorious Revolution' of 1688–89, which saw the ejection of James II and the installation of the Dutch William III on the throne, catapulted England into wars against Louis XIV of France. These lasted, with a brief break, for more than twenty years. The strains of war and the ever-present fear of a French invasion made the prospect of a united British nation to combat the threat much more attractive – at least south of the border. Proposals for Union raised little excitement in England. Not so in Scotland, where opinion was bitterly divided. The decision to agree to an Act of Union (1707) was taken by influential Scottish landowners and merchants, some of whom were well rewarded for bringing their influence to bear when it mattered.[8] There was, of course, a strong Scottish argument for Union. It was pressed hard by improving landlords and bankers who had most to lose from being perpetually tied to what they considered a partially feudal society and an almost stagnant economy destined always to be on the wrong side of commercial competition with England. Thanks to the Union, eighteenth-century Scots became part of the largest, and most buoyant, trading economy in Europe.

The Union created a greater Britain, and helped set its course in an imperial direction. It did little to heal historic wounds of suspicion and nothing to create a new amity between England and Scotland. Many north of the border felt that their negotiators in 1707 had been either incompetent or corrupt and had sold out to English interests and power. Nevertheless, the terms of the Union were far from draconian. The Union deprived Scotland of its own parliament and thus of its political independence. However, both its legal system and its Presbyterian Church survived intact. Scotland received a sum just short of £400,000 for agreeing to bear its share of responsibility for England's (now Britain's) **National Debt**. The larger, richer nation did, of course, hold the upper hand. In 1713, the new British parliament imposed what had previously been an exclusively English malt tax on the Scots to anguished, but impotent, cries of betrayal from Edinburgh.

National Debt

In its simplest terms, this is the amount of money borrowed by governments since 1691 and not yet paid off. A new system for raising government loans was instituted in 1693, when the English parliament voted in support of a proposal by King William III to raise £1m on annuities with an interest rate payable at 10 per cent. Linked to the Bank of England, formed in 1694, the National Debt became a linchpin of national finance during the eighteenth century, providing the country with a more formal and genuinely 'national' structure for raising loans. It represented a financial revolution, albeit one which was disliked by many landowners. They argued that it lined the pockets of financiers and encouraged excessive, and expensive, involvement in European affairs. The National Debt fell into two categories. So called 'funded debt' was that for which the interest payments were covered by additional taxation of whatever kind; 'unfunded debt' took the form of 'bills' raised by the government departments or by the armed forces which the Bank of England exchanged for money, anticipating that revenue shortly to be raised by those departments would pay them off. The great majority of the Debt was 'funded'.

Scotland was an overwhelmingly rural country; most of its population of about 1.5m in 1780 were peasants tilling hard, unproductive land to win a very basic living for their families. Only one person in eight lived in towns in 1750, even if we, rather generously, allow every community of more than 4,000 people to rank as a town.[9] Both agricultural efficiency and living standards were substantially lower than those of England. Many also resented the influence of the forty-five MPs who were allocated to the new British parliament under the arrangements of 1707. The Scottish peer, the Earl of Bute, was ridiculed when George III appointed him Prime Minister in 1762. John Wilkes, the leading satirical journalist of his day, used his journal *North Briton* (the title itself a riposte to the government's propaganda sheet *The Briton*) to attack all things Scottish with a pungent mixture of wit and vulgarity.

Educated Scots were increasingly attracted to London for its wealth, society and for the employment opportunities which it offered. Scottish lawyers and Scottish doctors soon established themselves there. In response Englishmen, resenting unwelcome competition, were easily persuaded that the Scots favoured their own kith and kin when contacts were made and contracts drawn up. Naked prejudice also played a part. **Lord Shelburne** called the Scots 'a sad set of innate, cold-hearted, impudent rogues'.[10] **Henry Dundas**, one of the ablest of the Younger Pitt's ministers and the first Scot to enjoy a long period in high office in a British government, was nevertheless an outsider at Westminster and attacked in the 1780s for unconstitutionally ingratiating himself into the Prime Minister's confidence.[11]

William FitzMaurice, second Earl of Shelburne, 1737–1805

Shelburne was born in Dublin as William FitzMaurice, the son of an Irish peer. His early years were spent in Ireland before he saw service during the Seven Years War. He briefly served in both the Irish and the British Houses of Commons before succeeding to his peerage as the second Earl in 1761. He served in the ministries of Grenville and the Elder Pitt in the 1760s but his sympathy for the American colonists' cause earned him the enmity of George III and he was out of office from 1768 until the ministerial instability of the early 1780s, when he served as Secretary of State for the Home Department under Rockingham in March 1782, succeeding him as Prime Minister on Rockingham's death four months later. His own government lasted for only nine months and he did not return to office. The Younger Pitt created him Marquess of Lansdowne in 1784.

Henry Dundas, 1742–1811

Henry Dundas, first Viscount Melville, came from a distinguished Scottish legal family and his career was in Scotland, where he served as Solicitor-General. He was elected an MP in 1774 and rose to prominence in the Younger Pitt's long administration. He was influential in imperial affairs in the 1780s and 1790s and especially those of India. He became Home Secretary in 1791 and Secretary of State for War in 1794, during the early stages of the French Revolutionary Wars. He was impeached by parliament in 1806 for maladministration of naval finances. He was acquitted but the notoriety which the charges against him entailed in effect ended his ministerial career.

Anti-Scottish hostility persisted, especially in London and among the English elite, at least until the need for a genuinely British defence against the French revolutionaries in the 1790s[12] (see Chapters 12 and 13). Only in the first half of the century did Scotland pose a direct threat, in the form of two attempts, in 1715 and 1745–46, to overthrow the newly established Hanoverian monarchy and restore the Stuart dynasty. The second came closer to success than is often recognised. These so-called Jacobite Risings cannot be characterised as eighteenth-century examples of old-style Anglo-Scottish hostility. Neither rising was truly pan-Scottish; both relied disproportionately for support from the Highland clan chiefs. In general, the more productive, wealthier and in most respects more progressive Lowlands of Scotland favoured George of Hanover over the son (the so-called 'Old Pretender'), and then the grandson (the 'Young Pretender'), of the deposed James VII and II. At the decisive Battle of Culloden in April 1746, more Scots fought against Charles Edward Stuart the 'Young Pretender' than fought for him.[13]

IV. A commercial culture

We have so far concentrated on what the English thought about their Scottish and Welsh neighbours. They had views about the Irish too, which are considered separately later (see Chapter 14). What of England and English culture in the later eighteenth century? It was increasingly commercial. These commercial and cultural developments should not be seen as distinctively 'English', however. Many of the elite classes in England considered themselves as readily 'British' as English. In the case of its great landowners, this was often literally the case, since marriages across English, Scottish and Welsh families were common. It is hardly surprising that a kind of 'assimilationist' model held sway. Britain was, too readily perhaps, assumed by the middle and upper classes to be a kind of greater England.

Scotland's attempts to establish itself as a significant trading nation in its own right had met with only limited success. The 'Darien Scheme' of 1698 established a colony – 'New Caledonia' – in an ambitious development designed to secure Scotland as a world trading nation. Its disastrous failure convinced many that continued competition against superior English resources was doomed to failure. Controversial though it was in other respects, the Union of 1707 helped create a formidable commercial force. By the middle of the eighteenth century, Britain was firmly established as the world's largest, and most successful, trading nation. For most of the sixteenth and seventeenth centuries, England's basic export trade had been of woollen cloth to Northern Europe. From the late seventeenth century lighter fabrics – the so-called 'new draperies' – were being manufactured and exported to Southern Europe. During the eighteenth century, imports to Britain were increasingly of raw materials, particularly cotton, and foodstuffs such as sugar, tea and tobacco. These came from outside Europe, especially the Americas and India. From 1700 to 1780, the total values of both imports and exports more than doubled, while exports to the Americas (mostly to the thirteen colonies and to the Caribbean) increased by a factor of eight.[14]

At the heart of mercantile profits from trade with the Americas was the slave trade. During the eighteenth century, British ships conveyed over half of all the slaves transported as the famous 'triangular trade' grew massively. Slaves were taken on hazardous, insanitary journeys from West Africa, through Britain and across to the Americas. Not surprisingly, mortality levels on slave ships were high. It was the slave plantations of Virginia and the West Indies which supplied Britain with its sugar and tobacco. Britain was much the most important slave-trading great power by the middle of the eighteenth century. As Professor Walvin says, 'Atlantic slavery was driven forward by British commercial and political forces.'[15] The trade was to reach its peak in the 1780s, during which decade about 900,000 slaves were removed from Africa.

The slave trade contributed substantially to the development of west coast ports, especially Bristol, Liverpool and Glasgow. The population of Liverpool grew from a mere 5,000 in 1700 to 40,000 in 1780, at which point it was the fourth largest city in England after London, Bristol and Birmingham. It has been estimated that about

40 per cent of Bristol's wealth in the middle of the eighteenth century derived from the slave trade.[16] Tobacco transformed Glasgow. By 1760 Scottish imports of tobacco from Virginia, Maryland and North Carolina exceeded those coming in to all English ports combined. As Professor Devine notes, the profits of the tobacco trade 'fed into a very wide range of industries, funded banks and financed agricultural improvement through merchant investment'.[17] Glasgow's population increased more than fivefold during the eighteenth century. At 62,000 in 1791, it was the third largest city in Britain, behind only London and Edinburgh.[18]

The growth of towns, and with it the development of a distinctive urban culture, was a key feature of Britain's eighteenth-century advance. In 1600, a mere 8 per cent of England's inhabitants lived in towns. That had increased to 17 per cent in 1700 and to 21 per cent in 1750, more than twice the proportion of town dwellers in France.[19] As they grew, towns established distinctive cultures. Much the most famous of the many associations formed at this time was the Lunar Society which met regularly in Birmingham from 1775. Its members included some extraordinarily able men: Erasmus Darwin, the botanist who would pioneer ideas of evolution, Matthew Boulton the engineer, James Watt, the Scottish inventor and Boulton's business partner, Joseph Priestley the research chemist who discovered oxygen and Josiah Wedgwood, the immensely successful Staffordshire potter.[20] The Lunar Society was, of course, exceptional in its scope and influence. However, most sizeable English towns had organisations which brought together leading citizens for social, business and intellectual purposes. Literary and Philosophical Societies were the most numerous. A strong sense of civic identity also developed. Merchants and traders often dominated local corporations and were, from the 1750s, building fashionable squares for domestic residence, following London's lead.[21]

The other important change in the years before 1780 was what some have called an 'Agricultural Revolution'. In the late seventeenth and eighteenth centuries, new technology made little impact on these changes. Productivity changes were much more important. They enabled a rapidly growing population to be fed without damaging inflation of food prices. By 1750, output per English worker considerably outpaced that of every other European country.[22] The structure of landownership contributed substantially to this increasing productivity. The average sizes of estates increased as smaller freeholds were sold by yeomen farmers (often under considerable duress) to bigger landowners. A recognisably modern structure of landholding resulted. Wealthier landowners increasingly delegated estate-management to a new breed of professional land stewards. Owners and estate stewards leased out most of the land to tenant farmers at market rates. Tenants were generally able to renew their leases only if their land management had been productive. In their turn, tenant farmers employed agricultural labourers to work the land. This was an agrarian structure geared as never before towards profit and farming for the market (see Chapter 7).

Critically, and in stark contrast to the situation in Scotland, Ireland and much of the rest of Europe, England was, by the middle of the eighteenth century, a country with very few peasant subsistence farmers. Despite a growing population, England – traditionally a food importing country – was a net exporter of wheat. It is important to note that most of the main changes which made English agriculture profitable and successful took place in the century or so *before* 1780. As we shall see (Chapters 7 and 23), the agricultural sector fell behind the pace of industrial and commercial change after 1780. Indeed, in the years to 1914, it was – or perhaps more accurately felt itself to be – in crisis more often than not.

It is clear that developments in Britain in the century or so before 1780 do much to explain why, despite the gloomy prognostications, the country successfully weathered the various storms which blew up during the war with the American colonies. More, it was able to maximise the opportunities for profitable expansion which arose thereafter. By 1780, Britain had already developed much of the infrastructure of a modern state and an unprecedentedly profit-conscious and commercial society was emerging in response.

2

The demographic revolution in Britain and Ireland

I. How great a change?

A nation's population is its prime resource. When the size, or the structure, of population alters, then significant developments almost always ensue. A nation whose population is declining will face problems in sustaining economic growth and prosperity. A rising population does not necessarily bring improved living standards or economic growth, however: more mouths must be fed and a nation may not have sufficient resources to meet the challenge. The structure of a population matters too. A population whose average age is declining usually also means a larger number of economically active citizens, if opportunities exist for young people to work. A population whose average age is increasing, as is the case with many European populations in the early twenty-first century, is likely to present problems. In that case, the economically active section of the population will need to support a larger number of the economically inactive, while medical and social support for the elderly takes up a larger proportion of a nation's budget. Trends in population, therefore, are critical indicators for the historian to follow. They underpin many of the changes with which this book is concerned.

> ### Demography
>
> Demographers study human population, analysing especially rates of birth, death and migration and their effect on communities and social structure.

In recent years, historians have been much more cautious in their use of the word 'revolution'. Changes once considered self-evidently dramatic and sufficiently short-term to earn the description have been downgraded as historians have increasingly emphasised longer-term trends (see Chapter 5). No such danger for historians studying European population trends in the eighteenth and nineteenth centuries. In the space of not more than a century and a half, from c1750 to c1900, long-term trends were disrupted and populations grew with unprecedented rapidity. Before the middle of the eighteenth century, the broad pattern was one of long-term, gentle population growth, interrupted by short-term crises. The most dramatic of these was the so-called Black Death, a worldwide pandemic of plague, which, beginning in Asia in the late 1320s, killed roughly one-third of England's population in the space of two to three years when it reached the country from continental Europe, probably through the port of Bristol in 1348.

Over the four centuries since *c*1350, England's post-plague population probably increased – there are no real indicators, such as parish registers, for demographers to work with until the 1530s – from around 3.5m to 5.9m. The reason was probably greater job opportunities for survivors and relatively buoyant wages leading to rising living standards. Long-term upward trends, however, were interrupted by short-term declines, so-called '**Malthusian** checks'. The last of these probably occurred in the late 1720s when the population fell by about 3 per cent, probably as the result of an influenza epidemic. Thereafter, the English trend was not only remorselessly upwards but at a faster rate than ever before. Between 1751 and 1801, the population increased by 46 per cent. Between 1801 and 1851, it grew much more quickly, by 94 per cent. Over the century from 1750 to 1850, England's population almost trebled, from 5.9m to 16.8m. Thereafter, the pace slackened, though only a little. In the period 1851–1901, England's population increased by 81 per cent.

Thomas Malthus, 1766–1834

Malthus was both an Anglican clergyman and a student of economics. His fame derives from his book *An Essay on the Principle of Population as it Affects the Future of Society*, first published in 1798. In it, he argued that populations had a general tendency to increase but growth could not continue indefinitely since a population's size would outgrow the capacity of food resources. Population would decline (or 'check' itself) until size and food needs got back into balance. Much of this chapter explains how these 'Malthusian checks' were circumvented in modernising societies.

The rate of growth in Scotland and Wales over this period was, in general, similar to that of England. Scotland had a population of approximately 1.5m in 1781, which had grown to 2.9m by 1851. Wales's population stood at about 0.6m in 1781 and had doubled to 1.2m by 1851.[1] In the second half of the century, Scotland's population increased by 55 per cent and Wales's, buoyed by the success of the iron and coal industries concentrated in the south of the Principality, by 74 per cent. The overall consequence was that, on the eve of the First World War, Great Britain's population had reached approximately 39m, more than four times greater than the total of 9m in 1780.[2]

It is also interesting to compare Britain's changing share of the overall population of western Europe. The comparison is useful because western Europe as a whole was much more developed than eastern Europe, with a higher population density and a larger proportion of that population living in towns. Population grew across western Europe as a whole during the course of the eighteenth century. In 1680, it has been estimated that the population of Britain comprised about 7.5 per cent of the overall western European population. By 1850, this had risen to 11 per cent.[3] It seems clear that, with the partial exception of Scandinavian lands, Britain's population was growing faster than elsewhere in Europe.

The demographic history of Ireland (which is not technically part of Great Britain anyway) does not conform to this pattern. It is worth noting, however, that for much of the eighteenth century, Ireland experienced significant economic growth, the benefits of which were enjoyed by landlords from the ruling so-called 'Protestant Ascendancy'.[4] Ireland experienced a demographic crisis in 1740–41 when the winter was especially severe and the potato crop failed. Almost half a million people starved and about 150,000 emigrated. The population, which had been growing steadily in the first half of the eighteenth century, suffered short-term decline. Recovery was swift, though. The available data are limited in various ways[5] until the first official census in 1801, but Ireland's population seems to have risen from approximately 2m in 1700, to almost 2.5m in 1750 and with greater acceleration thereafter to approximately 4.4m in 1790, to 6.8m in 1821 and to an unsustainable 8.2m in 1841.[6]

These bald statistics seem to support the surprising conclusion that the population of predominantly rural Ireland was, in the years 1780–1810, increasing faster than that of rapidly urbanising England and much faster than that of Scotland or Wales. Ireland's apparent population explosion seems the more surprising if one leans on stereotypes rather than the more complex reality. Late eighteenth-century Ireland was not all impoverished Catholic peasants eking out a miserable living from the land and continually exploited by a wealthy Protestant elite. Dublin was one of the larger, most prosperous, civilised and educated cities in Europe. Belfast in the north-east and Cork in the south were already substantial towns. Also, Ireland, like England, had a flourishing textile industry, albeit one based more on a 'domestic industry' model than on the factories then springing up in such numbers in England and Scotland. Competition from factory production in Scotland and north-west England, however, did not hit Ireland's weaving trade until early in the nineteenth century.

It seems that Irish population matched, or exceeded, that of Britain until the 1820s after which it slackened. Tellingly, it grew by only 5 per cent in the 1830s, after three decades during which the growth rate was never less than 14 per cent.[7] There were two main reasons for this. The first was that a declining textile industry led to substantial emigration from the country before the 1840s, not least to England. Although the statistics are fallible, it seems likely that least 1m people left Ireland in the period 1815–45.[8] The second reason was a now massively over-stretched agricultural sector, in which at least a third of the population was dependent on a single crop: the potato.

The short-term cause of the Irish famine, which began in 1845, was the failure of this crop. The longer-term social and economic context is also important and is discussed in more detail elsewhere (see Chapters 14, 23 and 30). Briefly, in the years after 1815 when arable prices dropped sharply, much more of Ireland's land was converted to pasture cultivation. About three times as many cattle were being profitably exported from Ireland in the mid-1840s than in the mid-1820s. Sheep exports doubled at the same time. The vicious irony is that what brought greater prosperity to Irish landowners brought disaster to the majority of the peasant population. More people were now expected to subsist on land where fewer crops were grown. The Famine, or 'Great Hunger', one of the greatest demographic disasters to occur anywhere in nineteenth-century Europe, was the result. The south and west of the country were worst hit but this was a national catastrophe. More than a million Irish died as a direct result of the famine, while more than a million emigrated in the late 1840s and early 1850s.

The disaster proved long-term. Emigration, particularly to England and the United States, did not end in the 1850s. Almost as many were leaving Ireland in the 1860s and 1880s as in the late 1840s and early 1850s.[9] After the Famine, the population history of Ireland diverged spectacularly from that of Great Britain. The Irish population continued its decline during the second half of the nineteenth century, and beyond. At 5.4m in 1871, it was 3m lower than at the peak of the early 1840s. By the turn of the twentieth century, it was less than 4.5m. Even at the beginning of the twenty-first century, the population of Ireland, at 5.2m, was three million less than on the eve of the Famine. Only Ulster, in the north-east, experienced any substantial industrial development in the mid-nineteenth century. In stark contrast to the general trend, Belfast's population did not decline in the 1840s; it increased by more than five times between the Famine and the First World War.[10]

II. The mechanics of population change

Since it is clear that the later eighteenth and nineteenth century represented the most startling discontinuity yet seen in demographic history, this presents obvious questions: why, and how, did populations grow so rapidly at this time? Only three factors can be in play. Increases happen because birth rates increase, because death rates decrease or because of inward migration. Demographic historians of Britain discount the last explanation. Much migration occurred in the later eighteenth and nineteenth centuries, not least because means of long-distance transportation increased, but there seems to have been as much out of Britain, particularly to the colonies, as into it. In the British Isles, only the substantial emigration from Ireland seems to have contributed significantly to long-term population change and, although much of that was eventually to North America, a larger proportion came to settle in industrial England and Scotland.

Attention has therefore concentrated on factors influencing changes in the birth and death rates. The issue used to be framed in simple terms: was a rising birth rate or a declining death rate the main cause of population growth? The answer to it also seemed to be clear. As the most influential study of the early twentieth century argued, 'a remarkable decrease in the death rate' was the primary cause, with a birth rate 'rising steadily' over the death rate as a subsidiary factor.[11] In the last forty years or so, the techniques available to students of population history have advanced mark-edly. As a result, and despite the fallibility and fragility of the available evidence before official censuses were taken in Britain from 1801, more statistically based and less impressionistic conclusions have emerged.[12] These have switched the emphasis from 'death rate' to 'birth rate'. On E. A. Wrigley's calculations, 'fertility accounted for about 64 per cent of the increase in the intrinsic [population] growth rate' for England in the years 1680–1840.

A number of factors are relevant. First, fertility rates among married women increased significantly between the late seventeenth century and the mid-nineteenth, and especially so in those who married young, as an increasing number did. Early marriage seems to have been more frequently precipitated by pregnancy towards the end of the period under study. The increase in the number of illegitimate births was also noticeable. At the end of the seventeenth century, about 7 per cent of births in marriage were conceived before marriage and the same proportion of births were illegitimate. By the early nineteenth century, the proportion of births in both cat-egories had risen to 25 per cent.

The time interval between live births also decreased from 31.7 months in the first thirty years of the eighteenth century to 30.5 months in the years 1790–1819. Such a change is estimated to have accounted for about a seventh of all the population growth over the period. It is possible that the most important single reason for this difference was a decline in the number of stillbirths which, in its turn, probably reflected better nutrition available to mothers as the eighteenth century progressed.

Perhaps the most important single variable explaining rises in the birth rate is the age of first marriage. This fell in almost identical proportions for both men and women. In 1700, the average age for a man's first (and usually only) marriage was 27.4 and for a woman 26.0. This fell with remarkable consistency. Only the 1820s witnessed a very small movement in the opposite direction. By the 1830s, the relevant ages were 24.9 and 23.1 respectively. Such a fall probably resulted in a 20 per cent rise in a married couple's fertility. The decline in stillbirths linked to the reduction in the mean age of first marriage for women probably explains three-quarters of the change in fertility rates.

Death rates, in general, declined over the period. As with birth rates, however, the picture is complicated by substantial variations, the most significant of which was the different picture in respect of infant and child mortality, compared with that of adults. The rates of infant and child mortality declined, especially in the second half of the eighteenth century. Infant mortality (considered as rates of death in the first year) was always considerably higher than later childhood mortality (i.e. from age 1 to 15) and it declined by about 16 per cent in the second half of the eighteenth century and by a further 13 per cent in the first forty years or so of the nineteenth. Children fared worse than infants, especially in the late eighteenth and early nineteenth cen-turies. Overall, the impact on the rising population made by changes in infant and child mortality was limited.

Changes in death rates among the adult population were much more dramatic. Deaths of women in childbirth more than halved between the mid-eighteenth and mid-nineteenth centuries. Life expectancy for those surviving infancy had also increased significantly by the end of the eighteenth century. It now approached forty years. Death rates for those who survived into their fifties and early sixties declined substantially in the second half of the eighteenth century, but greater longevity here had a limited impact on population change since few in this age range (and no women) would still be producing children. Of greater significance were changes in death rates among fertile adults during the eighteenth century. Between the later seventeenth and the later eighteenth centuries, mortality rates among those in their later twenties declined by almost 30 per cent. For those in their early thirties, the decline was 34 per cent.

Although a strong consensus now exists that rises in the birth rate were the more important factor explaining dramatic population growth from about 1750 to 1850, falling death rates also played a significant part. It is more difficult to find hard evidence explaining these changes than it is to quantify them. Demographers have proved exceptionally skilful at finding valid means of compensating for the absence of official census evidence before the early nineteenth century. They do, however, have to admit methodological difficulty in reaching their conclusions. Evidence of deaths or of burials is only rarely accompanied by evidence about causes of death, although more is known about the increasing numbers (still a tiny proportion of the total) who died in hospital. Even here, what is said by doctors may not necessarily be true. Diagnoses in the eighteenth and early nineteenth centuries were notoriously fallible. Furthermore, then as now, doctors are loath to admit that infections contracted, or errors made, in hospital have deprived the patient of the bleak comfort of dying from the disease for which he or she was admitted.

It seems plausible to argue, however, that environmental factors were more important in explaining falling death rates than were institutional ones. A small number of hospitals were founded in eighteenth-century England. Some, such as the London Foundling Hospital for orphan children, the brainchild of the philanthropist **Thomas Coram** and bankrolled by the large numbers of wealthy governors he had corralled in its support, and Addenbrookes in Cambridge (founded in 1767), were justly famous, though not always for the quality of their medicine. Only a couple of dozen hospitals had been founded outside London before 1780.[13] The development was, of course, important but they were neither numerous enough nor efficient enough to make any difference to death rates. The likelihood is that lower death rates were the consequence of agricultural improvements, and the associated transport developments which brought the crops and cheeses to market (see Chapter 7), more than any single factor. Diets became somewhat more varied and diverse. Sugar from the colonies was consumed in ever greater quantities. A better-fed population is a healthier population. After about 1730, also, infectious diseases went through a less virulent phase.

Thomas Coram, _c_1668–1751

Coram was a philanthropist who made his money building ships in New England, from investment in colonial developments in the New World and from commerce through London. He is best known for creating a hospital for Foundling Children in London which opened in 1741. The hospital also became a centre for music and the arts. Both the artist William Hogarth and the composer George Frederick Handel were governors.

Higher birth rates resulted from changes to economic opportunity. The eighteenth-century economy became both more productive and diverse. Many of the new opportunities thus created reduced or removed some of the constraints which militated against early marriage. The rapid growth of towns in the later eighteenth and early nineteenth centuries afforded opportunities for young people to become more mobile and independent at an earlier age. Doubtless, the greater opportunities for meetings and liaisons which urban society afforded had something to do with the growing number of illegitimate births.

Too comfortable a picture of British population growth must not be painted. As the pace both of economic growth and of urbanisation accelerated, many in Britain experienced the downside. Many of the new industrial towns which expanded so rapidly in the first half of the nineteenth century (Chapter 6) were desperately unhealthy places: overcrowded, insanitary breeding grounds for disease. Excessively long hours of work also ground populations down. Very high birth rates characterised early industrial towns but, especially in the 1820s and 1830s, death rates were frequently even higher. Cholera epidemics ravaged unprepared populations in the 1830s and 1840s, but the death rates from typhus, diarrhoea and dysentery, those regular, insidious visitors of doom, ran higher.[14] Not surprisingly, as the middle of the nineteenth century approached, death rates differed ever more widely across the country. London and the new industrial towns revealed the most rapidly rising death rates, while rural areas, especially the pastoral sector (see Chapter 7), showed little change.

Unhealthy towns would not inhibit population rise. After all, they continued to provide jobs and, for many at least, a regular wage alongside the dangers, depravities and squalor. The demographic revolution would not be halted in its tracks. However, the evidence of the 1830s and 1840s suggests that students of population history in Britain should pay attention to the impact of short-term demographic crises on the death rate as well as to the long-term significance of factors which encouraged earlier marriage and greater fertility.

3

···················

Aristocracy rampant?

I. Land and marriage

'If powers are put into the hands of a comparatively small number, called an **aristocracy** – powers which make them stronger than the rest of the community, they will take from the rest of the community as much as they please of the objects of desire. They will thus defeat the very end for which government was instituted.'[1] As he well knew, **James Mill**, who offered this view in the 1820s, was not making a merely theoretical observation. Government and social leadership in Britain for most of the period covered by this book remained firmly in the hands of Mill's 'comparatively small number'. This chapter examines the truth of Mill's assertion that the aristocracy were merely 'takers' from the rest of the community.

Aristocracy

This is a word which has a number of meanings. It comes from the Greek for 'the best' and William Gladstone used it in this sense when he stated that he wished to see an aristocratic government in the sense of government by its best citizens – though Gladstone was not specific in how he defined 'the best'. More commonly, it used to describe those with titles (mostly inherited). Aristocratic government is that by a small ruling body usually comprising the most wealthy and privileged men in society. This is the sense in which the word is used in this chapter.

James Mill, 1773–1836

Mill was a philosopher and a political economist who wrote much on the nature of government and about legitimate sources of power. He was much influenced by the ideas of Jeremy Bentham and became a member of a group known as the 'Philosophical Radicals'. His *Essay on Government* called for a democratic system of government, with frequent elections so that the governed could hold their governors to account and, if necessary, change them. He was the father of the better-known John Stuart Mill.

If we restrict ourselves to the peerage, those with inherited titles who sat in the House of Lords, English peers numbered only 189 in 1780. Scottish and Irish peers were generally considered (at least by their English counterparts) to be of lower status and were, for the most part, considerably less wealthy. They numbered 78 and 145 respectively. William Pitt the Younger found it politically useful to urge George III to increase the size of the House of Lords in the 1780s and 1790s and ninety-four new peerages were created in consequence. This was something of a radical departure; more than 40 per cent of the eighteenth century's new peerages were created in its last two decades. New creations did not usually mean new blood. The number of English and Welsh peers had risen to 267 by 1800, but only 7 per cent of Pitt's new creations, and 10 per cent of peerages created over the eighteenth century as a whole, went to people who were not related to the existing aristocracy. The most common category, indeed, was sons of existing peers.[2] Peerage creations expanded more quickly again in the early nineteenth century. By 1850, the English and Welsh peerage totalled 399, although titles still went overwhelmingly to those with land, albeit increasingly to landowners whose family fortunes were grounded in commerce, the forces or the professions.[3]

Small in numbers as it was, the aristocracy dominated land holding throughout the United Kingdom. We lack precise evidence before the 1870s, when thirty-five great landowners each owned 100,000 acres or more and 0.2 per cent of landowners owned 43 per cent of the land.[4] A significant process of land consolidation went on during the eighteenth century, often accelerated by the desire of the aristocracy and other landowners owning more than about 3,000 acres to bring their estates together in order to facilitate land improvement. The overall size of farms increased. Whereas only a fifth of all farms in Staffordshire and Shropshire were larger than 200 acres in 1700, for example, by 1780 this proportion had increased to a third.[5] It is very likely that the aristocracy owned a larger proportion of land in Britain in 1800 than it had done in 1700. Certainly, that was the case in the counties of Northamptonshire and Bedfordshire, which were increasingly seen as 'aristocratic territory'. However, in an active land market, an increasing proportion of buyers were successful bankers and overseas traders. They saw the purchase of land as an essential adjunct to the enhancement of status which their increasing wealth encouraged (see Chapter 4).[6]

Although some spectacular exceptions can be found, the eighteenth- and nineteenth-century aristocracy generally kept things firmly within the wider family of wealthy landowners. Daughters of wealthy London bankers or coming from other hyper-successful commercial families might be acceptable as recruits to an aristocratic family. Indeed, some were strategically sought as a means of repairing family fortunes threatened by excessive gambling, debauchery or debt. Thus, the second Viscount Bolingbroke was reported in 1777, according to the waspish comment of the Whig politician George Selwyn, 'gone down to Bath in pursuit of a lady, who he proposes should retrieve his finances. Her name is Curtis: she is about thirty years of age, and has a fortune of forty-three thousand pounds.'[7] Otherwise, prudent aristocrats sought marriages for their children or other close relatives which either sustained or reinforced a titled connection.

When peers themselves married, they looked to marry their own kind. An effective marriage strategy paid lucrative benefits for the Bedford family and was an essential element in its rise to the eminence it reached in the eighteenth and nineteenth centuries. In the second half of the eighteenth century, some 125 English peers married for the first time. Of these marriages, roughly a third were to daughters of English peers. Another third were made with those who had strong aristocratic connections. Virtually all the other peers married women who, if from non-titled families, were at least wealthy enough to bring with them a substantial dowry.[8]

Perhaps the most striking beneficiary of marital bounty is the splendidly named George Granville Leveson-Gower (1758–1833). By the middle of the eighteenth century, the Leveson-Gowers were already established as one of the most substantial landed families in the counties of Staffordshire and Shropshire. In 1785, George married Elizabeth Sutherland, who had been Duchess of Sutherland in her own right since her father died when she was one year old. Gower therefore became, at the age of 27, owner of most of the Scottish highland county of Sutherland. He succeeded his father as Marquess of Stafford in 1803. Both Staffords and Sutherlands were involved in considerable commercial activities which enhanced their wealth. The new Marquess inherited the revenue of the Bridgewater Canal from his uncle in 1803. In 1825, he bought one-fifth of the shares in the new venture to build a railway from Liverpool to Manchester. In the 1820s, his annual income was estimated at £200,000 a year (nearly £14m in early twenty-first-century prices). The leading diarist of the day called him 'the leviathan of wealth'.

He is best, and for some notoriously, known for his improvement of the massive, but under-developed and under-capitalised, Sutherland estates. Hundreds of thousands of pounds were spent on transport improvements and on harbour construction on the north and east coasts to reduce the county's isolation. Inland, thousands of acres were leased out to commercial sheep farmers, most of whom were enticed northwards from England and southern Scotland by the promise of profit which was, in most cases, amply realised. The losers were the thousands of peasant proprietors removed from their smallholdings in two concerted campaigns in 1812–15 and 1819–21. Houses and outbuildings were burnt to prevent those evicted from attempting to resettle. A legacy of bitterness continued throughout the nineteenth century. Stafford was created a Duke in the last year of his life and adopted the Sutherland title already owned by his wife.[9]

II. Urban development

The apex of British society, therefore, was occupied by men of substantial property and extraordinary wealth. When William Cavendish became the fifth Duke of Devonshire in 1764, he inherited large landed estates in Derbyshire, Yorkshire and

County Waterford (Ireland). Their value alone was estimated at £36,000 a year (more than £4m at early twenty-first century equivalences). That was not the end of the matter. He also inherited Chatsworth House and Hardwick Hall in Derbyshire, a castle in Ireland and highly desirable properties in, or near, London, including Chiswick House, Devonshire House and Burlington House.[10]

The Russells, the family name of the Dukes of Bedford, owned land in no fewer than eleven counties. Successive Dukes demonstrated the wide range of profitable landed and commercial interests which aristocrats could embrace. The fifth Duke (Francis Russell, 1765–1802), although he died young, made a substantial contribution to the agricultural improvements of the late eighteenth century. He was a founder member of the Board of Agriculture and invested heavily to increase crop yields and in experiments to improve animal breeding (see Chapter 7). He was also one of the most ambitious urban improvers, employing the architect James Burton to develop Bloomsbury Square, Tavistock Square and Russell Square in central London. Rents from the family's London properties provided half the Russell income by 1820.[11] His brother, the sixth Duke (John Russell, 1766–1839), was a minor politician who maintained the family tradition for well-funded land management. He re-established Woburn Abbey as one of the great fashionable country houses and as a focal point for Whig politicians to meet and discuss great affairs of state during weekend shooting parties.

He was, however, extravagant on an Olympic scale. Less prudent than his unmarried elder brother, he fathered thirteen children and bought whichever pieces of artwork took his fancy, running up debts of £500,000. His eldest son Francis (1788–1861), the seventh Duke, ruefully admitted that his father 'had not the power or resolution to hold his hand, whenever money was within his reach' – thanks to the family's accumulated fortunes, either it, or ready credit, invariably was.[12] At all events, Francis inherited enough money and, with a great deal more business acumen than his father, became a major estate developer. In the 1840s and 1850s he remodelled, in fashionable Gothic style, much of the centre of the west Devon town of Tavistock, largely owned by the family since the dissolution of its monastery in 1539. A new Town Hall and Pannier Market were constructed. He also built a reservoir to improve the town's water supply and promoted developments instrumental in the arrival of the Great Western and London and South Western Railways in 1859. The proprietorial stamp was reinforced in the building of a hundred miners' houses – the Bedford Cottages – to accommodate workers in the tin and copper mining industries.[13]

Aristocratic families needed to be urban developers, especially in London. During the eighteenth century, parliament met more frequently, requiring the presence of members of parliament for five or six months of the year. This, together with the rapid development of London as a commercial centre, encouraged the growth of exclusive housing developments for peers and their retinues. It is not surprising that a 'London season' developed during the winter months. Families visited each other's residences, held lavish balls at which marriage prospects might be gauged, and attended theatres, subscription concerts and operatic performances. In 1791 and 1794, the Austrian composer Joseph Haydn (1732–1809) made visits to London, where he was treated lavishly, bowled over by the city's wealth and enjoyed for the first time a celebrity lifestyle. He composed twelve of his greatest symphonies – six for each visit – to mark the occasions. Collectively, and appropriately, they are known as the 'London Symphonies'.

The influence of the aristocracy was especially apparent in central and west London. Aided by the genius of **Robert Adam**, Westminster, St James's and Mayfair were all transformed in the second half of the eighteenth century. When in 1746, John, first Earl, Spencer inherited estates of 100,000 acres and an annual income of £35,000, he spent upwards of £50,000 in hiring the architect John Vardy to build Spencer House. It became the grandest aristocratic house in London.[14] In the early nineteenth century, the work of the landscape gardener **Humphry Repton** and the architect **John Nash** was particularly prominent in and around London.

Robert Adam, 1728–1792

Born in Fife and the son of the architect William Adam, Robert was the greatest, and most celebrated, British architect of his day. He was much influenced by Italian architecture, especially classical Palladian architecture, on two visits to Italy in the 1750s and 1760s. In London he was particularly famous for his work in transforming Derby House in Grosvenor Square and Wynn House in Berkeley Square, occupied by the Earl of Shelburne. He both built and radically extended a number of country houses for the aristocracy, including Chiswick House for Lord Burlington and Luton Hoo for the Earl of Bute.

Humphry Repton, 1752–1818

Repton, who was born in Suffolk and spent most of his early years in East Anglia, became the most celebrated landscape gardener of his age. His career flourished under the patronage of the third Duke of Portland, who was twice Prime Minister, and he made a point of ingratiating himself with landed, including royal, society. He is particularly well known for his work at the beginning of the nineteenth century at the country estates of Longleat (Wiltshire, for the Marquess of Bath) and Woburn (Bedfordshire, for the Duke of Bedford) and the Brighton Pavilion.

John Nash, 1752–1835

Nash came from a humble background. His father was a millwright from South Wales. Nash came to prominence as an architect designing public buildings in Wales. His career in London was helped by his business association with Humphry Repton. Their partnership ended in 1800, but Nash rapidly established himself as the most fashionable architect of the age. He is best known for the works which derived from his association with the Prince Regent (later George IV) and particularly for the creation of the Brighton Pavilion in exotic Oriental style and, in London, for a number of important developments, including Regent's Park and buildings along the Regent's Canal. He was also responsible for the creation of the classically-designed Regent's Street (1813–25) which connected Regent's Park with St James's Park and Whitehall.

Many provincial towns owed their prosperity in significant part to aristocratic patronage. The example of Bath is, of course, exceptional. Largely designed in the early and middle years of the eighteenth century by the architects John Wood Senior (1705–54) and his son John Wood Junior (1732–82), it became the most fashionable resort in England, attracting the wealthy to take its spa waters, arrange marriages and just to be seen. During the course of the second half of the eighteenth century, its population grew from 2,500 to 40,000. Not surprisingly, considerable aristocratic money was invested in the town's development. The property developer Sir William Pulteney (1729–1805), who married into the Earl of Bath's family, engaged Robert Adam to design the Pulteney Bridge and was responsible for the erection of properties in what became known as Great Pulteney Street.[15]

Several industrial towns also owed their success to aristocratic investment. The so-called Black Country towns north-west of Birmingham increasingly underpinned the large fortunes of the Legge and Ward families, the former Earls of Dartmouth and the latter Earls of Dudley. Both reaped huge profits from mining, quarrying and property development in West Bromwich, Dudley and Bilston. One late nineteenth-century commentator encapsulated the profitable symbiosis of land with industry: 'The fact that the great country landlord is also, in many cases, the great proprietor of mines and factories, is at once a guarantee and a sign of the fusion between the different elements of English life, and the diverse sources of our national power.'[16] Similarly, it is certain that the rapid growth of Cardiff, as much the largest port for the export of iron manufactures and of coal from South Wales, would not have been possible without the investment and the despotism, sometimes benevolent, of the Bute family in developing both its Cardiff estate and its interests in Glamorgan. Especially prominent was John Crichton Stuart, the second Marquess (1793–1848), who developed a new masonry dock in Cardiff. The family also owned the Dowlais iron works – the largest in the world in the 1840s – and extensive coal deposits in the Rhondda valley. Cardiff increased in size from a village of 1,900 people at the first census in 1801 to more than 39,000 in 1871, by which time it was much the largest town in Wales.[17] On a smaller scale, but important in, and perhaps more typical of, landowning and industrial partnership in the early nineteenth centuries, is the role of the Derby family in the development of Preston (Lancashire). The family bought up property in the town for industrial development towards the end of the eighteenth century. It was richly rewarded when rental values increased more than fourfold in the years 1796–1801. The Derbys also patronised social events, including horse-racing and cock-fighting. The family also held one of the two parliamentary seats from 1802 to 1826 in usually harmonious conjunction with a member of the Preston cotton manufacturing firm Horrocks, Miller and Company.[18]

III. Political power

The political power of the aristocracy was dominant throughout the eighteenth century and almost all of the nineteenth. Indeed, the House of Commons was misleadingly named. Only in a technical sense was it a house of 'commoners' until the last third of the nineteenth century. With surprising consistency, the most numerous social category of members was the sons of peers and Irish peers. Professor Cannon's calculation of the Commons elected in 1784 suggests that sons and near relatives of the peerage account for almost a third of the members. At least a third more were wealthy, if untitled, landowners. At its peak in 1826, they comprised 25 per cent of the total. By 1841, the proportion had declined to 19 per cent and had drifted downwards further to 14 per cent by 1874.[19] These statistics nevertheless indicate the abiding influence of the aristocracy over the political process. If one includes less close relatives and in-laws, grandsons, nephews, those married to a peer's daughter and the like, then the results are yet more striking. Until the 1860s, a third of all members of the House of Commons had clear aristocratic connections and in the parliament elected in 1868, 62 per cent of members came from families owning more than 2,000 acres of land.[20] A significant decline in landed participation began only in the 1870s.

A House of Commons dominated by large landowners was in a strong position to determine the outcome of the many so-called '**private members' bills**' which came before it. Most concerned economic matters, in particular bills to make new arrangements for land by enclosure or to sanction the building of a canal or, a little later, a railway. Since many landowners had extensive mining interests, they would have an interest to promoting bills which would make the transportation of coal or tin more efficient. It is hardly surprising that bills to enable canal construction generally had an easier passage through parliament when its purpose was to carry coal. Aristocratic sponsorship mattered. Bills lacking landowner support might well fail. A bill's success could often be traced back to an agreement between commercial proprietor and great landowner. The owners of the Dudley canal were wise to pass a specific resolution thanking Lord Dudley for his 'very powerfull and successful Exertion in Parliament in support of the Extension of this Canal'.[21]

Private members' bills

These are bills brought into either House of Parliament which were not introduced by the government or any opposition grouping but by members acting either on their own initiative or to support a measure favoured by their constituents.

This picture of aristocratic pre-eminence is confirmed by the status of Prime Ministers. Over the Period 1780 to 1866, twenty-seven British governments were formed, headed by nineteen different Prime Ministers. Of those nineteen, twelve were members of the House of Lords when they first became Prime Minister. One (Lord John Russell) was created an Earl before becoming Prime Minister for a second time in 1865 and was anyway the son of the Duke of Bedford. Lord North (Prime Minister 1770–82) sat in the House of Commons but was the eldest son of the Earl of Guilford and succeeded to the earldom just before his own death in 1790. Spencer Perceval (1809–12) was the second son of the Earl of Egmont. Sir Robert Peel inherited a baronetcy from his industrialist father. Baronets are the lowest hereditary titled British order and sit in the House of Commons. Only two Prime Ministers came from a non-titled background. Henry Addington (1801–4) was the son of a doctor. George Canning came from a modestly wealthy Irish landed family, though his own father, a minor writer and frequently indebted, renounced any rights to the family estates in order to have his father redeem his debts. Addington was elevated to the Lords as Viscount Sidmouth in 1805, from where he served as Lord Liverpool's Home Secretary for ten years (see Chapter 16). Thus, only one of the nineteen Prime Ministers had no direct or close family connection with the peerage.

Not surprisingly, the peerage also dominated the Cabinets. Down to the 1870s, the majority of Cabinet members sat in the House of Lords. William Pitt, as the second son of an Earl, did not succeed to the peerage and sat in the Commons throughout his political career. All of the Cabinet colleagues in his first ministry of 1783–94, however, were either peers or directly connected to the peerage. Only he and Henry Dundas of the ten members of the Cabinet formed in December 1783 did not bear a title. Although the number of commoners did modestly increase from the 1830s, the first Cabinet in which members of the House of Commons outnumbered those in the Lords was Palmerston's of 1859, and then only by eight to seven. For another twenty years, this was the exception rather than the rule. Gladstone's first government, formed at the end of 1868, included important positions for the commoners Robert Lowe, Edward Cardwell, Henry Bruce and the redoubtable Quaker John Bright. Nevertheless, eight of fourteen Cabinet members were peers or the eldest sons of peers, including four earls and a duke.

IV. Abusing their power?

How beneficial in this period was the aristocratic influence which the previous sections of this chapter have identified? For intellectual radicals like James Mill and for self-appointed spokesmen of the underprivileged like Thomas Paine, Thomas Hardy, William Cobbett and 'Orator' Hunt (see Chapters 11 and 16), the answer was obvious. Members of the aristocracy inherited both wealth and dominant social position. For the Paines and the Hunts what had not been earned was not deserved. On one level, there is little to be said: you either accept hereditary succession as a legitimate social device or you do not. Paine had asserted in his famous polemic *The Rights of Man* (1791–92) that 'the idea of hereditary legislators is as inconsistent as that of hereditary judges or hereditary juries; and as absurd as an hereditary mathematician'.

The radicals did not, of course, leave it there. They made a fair job of ascribing all the ills of society to misgovernment and corruption by a small, unrepresentative elite. Great landowners controlled both houses of parliament and were the leaders of those Whig and Tory family groupings which gradually emerged as coherent political parties (see Chapters 15–17). They fixed jobs for their relatives and lackeys, irrespective of merit. They had taken Britain into a number of expensive wars paid for by raising loans at interest rates which crippled the country and by increasing taxes and disproportionately burdening the poor. Radicals branded the whole squalid system 'Old Corruption'. Their remedy for its manifold sins and wickednesses was root-and-branch parliamentary reform.

A powerful historiographical tradition developed in the 1970s and 1980s which was broadly sympathetic to analyses such as these.[22] While Paine and Hunt concentrated on the abuse of power at national level, many historians studied its impact on the countryside. Great landowners exercised huge, and often unchallengeable, authority in their localities. Their influence often extended well beyond the broad acres which they directly owned. Justices of the Peace administered the law at local level and their appointment was usually on the basis of a recommendation by the Lord Lieutenant. By the later eighteenth century, Lords Lieutenant had few administrative functions but they remained the monarch's representative in the countryside. The majority of Lords Lieutenant were peers or other great landowners. Conscientious Lords Lieutenant could exercise a strong influence on how the law was administered.

It has been contended that this influence was used to extend property rights and to come down hard on ordinary folk who either asserted the primacy of local customs or whose poaching activities involved highly risky attempts to outwit the gamekeepers employed by the larger landowners. Historians have noted the increasing use of severe sentences – including execution – as punishment for relatively trivial property crimes. In particular, the so-called Black Act, passed in 1723 but not repealed until 1827, was designed to deter trespass, attacks on cattle and poaching by ordinary folk. Poachers who blackened their faces in order to make identification by gamekeepers more difficult were described in the words of the Act as 'Wicked and

Evil-Disposed Persons Going Armed in Disguise, and Doing Injuries and Violences to the Persons and Properties of his Majesty's Subjects'.[23]

The rural poor had to rely on custom and practice, validated by long and undisputed usage, to assert their rights. Such rights included gleaning, the collection of corn or other produce left on the ground after the harvest, and grazing of animals on rough pasture. These were of considerable importance to the domestic economy of villagers. It is not surprising that agricultural improvement not infrequently provoked hostility and riot from the lower orders (see Chapter 7). Decisions in the redistribution of land through parliamentary enclosure, which took place between *c*1760 and *c*1845, were made on the basis of proportions of property ownership. Hostile critics alleged that this enabled the elite to ride roughshod over the rights of the lower orders.[24] They contended that attacks on customary rights constituted a class war between the haves and the have-nots which the haves were bound to win. Since the aristocracy were the greatest property owners, their 'crimes' against the people were the most heinous.

Some corrective is surely necessary. Pressure for new legislation against what contemporaries considered to be a serious crime wave was by no means the preserve of the aristocracy or even **gentry** landowners. Much came from the towns, and especially from London, where pickpocketing and what would now be called 'mugging' had been on the increase since the early seventeenth century.[25] Perhaps ferocious legislation was an admission of weakness. For an elite facing the challenges of rapid urbanisation and even faster population growth, forms of awesome deterrence seemed the only weapon. This was not the same thing as class war.

Gentry

The name collectively given to independent landowners with lower status and income than the aristocracy whose property was sufficient to produce a comfortable income. Estimates of their wealth and the extent of their land holdings at the beginning of our period differ widely, but most landowners who were called 'gentlemen', which was then a clear indication of superior status, would have incomes from their estates which ranged from £200 to £1,000.

Similarly, the use of formal contracts was a necessary part of what many have seen as the 'commercial revolution' of the eighteenth century. Almost inevitably, they privileged the propertied and the literate, but they were also part of a massive economic expansion which generated new jobs for a rapidly growing population (see Chapter 2). As we have seen, extensive aristocratic involvement in mining, agricultural improvement, urban development and trading ventures was also a crucial feature of Britain's early industrial success (see Chapter 5) and its growing prosperity.

Certainly, the great landowners wanted their own way. As Professor Cannadine argues, 'it was the landed elite which remained in control of a landed polity, boasting a power and a coherent sense of its own self-identity which neither middle nor working classes could rival'.[26] The Duke of Sutherland brooked no argument as he cleared the Highlands to enable sheep-farming to transform the Highlands and, in doing so, further enhance his phenomenal fortune. The Duke of Bedford took no heed of local opposition when he cleared the centre of Tavistock in the 1840s to foster the urban improvements he wanted. Yet aristocratic entrepreneurial activities, whether driven by greed, vanity or dedication to a family interest, generally went with the grain of British economic development. Aristocrats were not a dead weight on change. A strong hypothesis can be constructed on the premise that the huge investments and political clout of a wealthy, interconnected and entrepreneurial aristocracy were the main reason why Britain's economy and society developed so far and so fast in the late eighteenth and early nineteenth centuries.

4

The role and impact of the middle classes

I. Wealth and influence

The middle classes are not easy to define. Shine the historical torch on any segment of society which is neither selling its labour for wages nor farming a small patch to feed the family, on the one hand, nor living – usually very well – from the value of rents paid by others for working **hereditarily owned land**, on the other, and you identify 'the middle classes' or 'the middle ranks'. This, however, is a definition by default. Identifying a social group by indicating what it is not invites imprecision. Yet two broad categories are discernible. The first covers those whose living depended on making profits, whether in trading or in manufacturing activities. The phrase most commonly used for them is 'the commercial middle classes'. The income of the second group came from the selling of specialist services. The range of occupations is wide but all depended, to a greater or lesser extent, on education, training, literacy and the acquisition of specialist skills. These are 'the professional middle classes'. Both the numbers and the status of lawyers, doctors and journalists increased substantially during the eighteenth century. The clergy also fit into this category, given their specialist knowledge of scripture and religious doctrine.

> ### Hereditarily owned land
>
> Technically, this refers to any land which has been passed down to its present owner because of a family connection. In eighteenth- and nineteenth-century Britain, this usually meant an estate passing in its entirety to the eldest son, since land was held under the system of primogeniture – or inheritance by the first born, although this almost invariably meant the first-born male.

A distinctive urban culture developed in the later eighteenth and early nineteenth centuries, reflecting the developing attitudes, beliefs and lifestyles specifically associated with town living. The middle classes as a whole are considered to be predominantly town-based, but it is important to recognise that rural society had its own middle class. In terms of the specialist services, the most important were those provided by land, or estate, stewards. Their role in managing the process of agricultural improvement on some of the largest estates in the county was pivotal (see Chapter 7). Some increased their status through service to eminent local families. In Lincolnshire, for example, the expertise of the Parker family in making itself indispensable to the Dukes of Ancaster in the late eighteenth and early nineteenth centuries enabled them to become established landowners themselves at Hanthorpe (near Spalding) by 1815.[1] The most famous estate steward of the period was James Loch (1780–1855), from 1812, commissioner to the huge estates of the Dukes of Sutherland. Loch came from a Scottish landowning background and was a law graduate from Edinburgh. His was no rags-to-riches story, but his professional work for the Sutherlands, which included the hugely controversial Highland Clearances (see Chapter 3), substantially increased his status. Among many other public offices, he was elected as a Fellow of the Geological, Statistical and Zoological Societies. He was also a Whig MP continuously for twenty-five years, from 1827 to 1852. Able, determined and flexible, his 'upper-middle-class' status was clear. Indeed, he qualified as a member of the early nineteenth century's 'great and good'.[2]

Tenant farmers might also be considered as members of the middle classes. Some were small landowners in their own right but, as tenants, their relationship with the land depended on the profit they could extract from it. When they took up, or renewed, a lease they were entering into a business transaction with the landowner; their aim was to make a profit by selling their produce for more than they paid for the lease. Increasingly, that objective depended upon their demonstrating a high degree of both professionalism and enterprise: skills usually associated with the middle classes.

Tenant farmers

Those who rented land owned by others. The amount of rent to be paid was usually set out in a lease, which would include conditions governing the farming of the land. During the eighteenth century, the number of tenant farmers increased as larger landowners brought their estates together and leased them out in parcels of land to tenants.

It is a historical truism that, whatever the period being studied, the British middle classes are always on the rise. The truism results from the fact that, massive natural demographic catastrophes such as the Irish potato famine (see Chapter 2) or extreme examples of genocide apart, the general trend in society over time is not only for population growth but also for a growing diversity of economic activity. The trend is usually called 'progress'. The growing importance of the middle classes reflects the natural ingenuity of humankind. Of course, developments occur at different speeds. What sets the eighteenth and early nineteenth centuries apart is the sheer pace of change. The key factors are a rising population, much more extensive commercial activity (see Chapter 1) and a growing appetite for consumption, at least among the middle and upper classes.

Specific indicators of middle-class income are problematic. Income and rental values varied across the country. They were higher in London than elsewhere and, in general, higher in the larger and most rapidly developing provincial towns such as Liverpool and Leeds where land was at a premium, than in county or cathedral towns such as Shrewsbury or Salisbury. It has become conventional, though, to suggest that the minimum income for someone of middling rank in the eighteenth century was £50 a year.[3] By the early nineteenth century, the threshold had moved up – certainly in London – to about £120.[4] On these figures, about 20 per cent of the English population could claim to be middle class in the 1760s and 25 per cent by 1800. Most estimates of the amounts needed to provide food and clothing at basic subsistence levels were at roughly half of the middle-ranks threshold level. It follows that those in the middle ranks had surplus income and could afford at least some fashionable or luxury items. Making every allowance for fluctuations in economic circumstances among the middle ranks in the years *c*1780–1850, it is clear that disposable income for such purchases increased over the period. The middle ranks comprised the engine room of a new 'consumer society'.

If £100–£120 (roughly £85,000 in terms of early twenty-first-century earnings) was regarded as the threshold for membership of the middle ranks at the beginning of the nineteenth century, then secure status within what Boyd Hilton calls the 'upper middle class' required at least twice that, probably as much as £300 a year. According to Colquhoun's calculations, not more than a third of the middle ranks would reach this higher status. At this level, they had sufficient capital assets to invest significant sums in the money markets.[5] A substantial investment profile was becoming a more reliable indicator of status in early nineteenth-century urban society than was the ownership of land.

As in all societies experiencing very rapid economic expansion, early industrial Britain witnessed huge disparities of income. This was particularly noticeable at the apex of the middle ranks where a few highly successful traders with profitable overseas connections and the most eminent lawyers representing wealthy aristocratic clients could earn as much as £10,000 a year (nearly £8m in early twenty-first-century equivalences). Of the very wealthy, who left more than £100,000 in personal property (not including land) in the years 1809–39, merchants and financiers accounted for 43 per cent of the total as against 22 per cent for wealthy landowners and only 9 per cent for manufacturers and industrialists.[6]

The career of Sir Francis Baring (1740–1810) is instructive on three levels.[7] It indicates how immense fortunes could be accumulated in commerce and banking. It exemplifies the importance of personal contacts both at home and abroad in exploiting new opportunities in developing markets. Finally, it demonstrates the dependence of governments on ready sources of finance during wartime. Several merchant bankers enjoyed exceedingly profitable wars, none more so than the Barings.

Baring was born in Exeter, the son of a successful textile merchant-manufacturer who had emigrated from northern Germany at the beginning of the eighteenth century. With initial capital of £10,000, he established the London merchant house of Barings in 1762. Initial losses notwithstanding, Baring benefited from sitting on the court of a leading insurance company in London in the 1770s, where he made numerous valuable contacts, especially in international trade with Europe, the West Indies and North America. Through his brother and brother-in-law, who were both MPs, Baring gained access to government in the early 1780s and was close to the Earl of Shelburne when he was Prime Minister. This access led to substantial commissions for financial services rendered and opened doors for further profitable contacts both national and international. Baring was influential in rebuilding profitable trade between Britain and the United States in the years after the War of Independence.

Baring's links with the great families of England were further enhanced when he became an MP, by buying the Cornish seat of Grampound in 1784. His continuing relationship with Shelburne saw him nominated for parliamentary seats in Oxfordshire and Wiltshire from 1796 to 1806. He was Chairman of the East India Company in 1792–93, which earned him a baronetcy from the Younger Pitt, and remained on its board until his death. The wars with Revolutionary and Napoleonic France (see Chapters 12 and 13) provided more opportunities. His firm was the leading supplier of loans to the government. Baring also acted as intermediary for the transmission of subsidies to Britain's European allies. By the end of his life he was also, in effect, acting as banker to the United States government.[8] Baring used some of his immense wealth in traditional ways. He bought substantial properties in London, Surrey and Hampshire. At death, his fortune totalled just over £600,000 (roughly £407m in early twenty-first-century values).

The growth of the middle classes also loosened formal divisions of status. Titles usually associated with 'gentility' tended to be less reliable indicators of a family's status in the early nineteenth century than they had been half a century earlier. The term 'esquire' had always indicated someone with recognised, and usually landed, property. The title Mr or Mrs was in the eighteenth century an indication of status. By 1780, it was already being used by town dwellers to denote ownership of their own property, however modest, or a family which employed servants. By the middle of the nineteenth century, it was in common use in virtually all towns in order to identify those whose occupation and income clearly placed them above apprenticed craftsmen and other skilled workers.

II. The commercial middle class

In 1780, the value of Britain's exports was about £10m and its exports about £14m. By the middle of the nineteenth century, the value of imports had increased to nearly £80m and exports to £124m. Imports were predominantly of foodstuffs and raw materials for the growing textile industry (see Chapter 5). Together, these accounted for about 70 per cent of the total. By 1850, 85 per cent of Britain's exports were of manufactured goods and of iron. The manufactures in their turn were overwhelmingly of textile goods.[9] Similarly precise figures for domestic trade do not exist but information from trade directories, advertisements in newspapers, domestic accounts and **probate inventories** all tell a similar, if less dramatic, story of growth and diversity.

Probate inventories

Lists of goods left by a person at death. They represent an official record for inheritance purposes. However, these inventories have been a prime source of information for social and cultural historians since they enable inferences to be made about changing consumption patterns and the impact of fashion on purchases.

In general, only the richer, more established members of the commercial middle classes were involved in overseas trade. They also benefited most from the so-called 'Fiscal-Military State'. This is the phrase coined to describe Britain's increasingly centralised system of eighteenth-century parliamentary government. At its heart was a powerful Treasury which managed the National Debt by raising loans, from which the upper middle classes profited through interest payments. The Treasury also imposed new taxes to finance its many wars.[10] Britain also levied tariffs to protect goods such as tobacco, sugar and muslins in the colonies. It ensured that trade in such goods came through British ports. In this way, London established itself as the world's financial capital well before the end of the eighteenth century. The wealthiest members of the commercial middle classes were not hit by the higher tax regime which the Younger Pitt imposed on Britain in the late 1790s. A petition sent to the Commons from the inhabitants of Shoreditch during the economic crises which afflicted London in that decade (see Chapter 12) complained of the 'unbounded wealth which is acquired by factors and speculatists with ease and expended with profusion'.[11] These 'money men' bought land, invested in town houses, entertained lavishly and, perhaps most importantly, developed their connections with the leading politicians and administrators.

Few of those in what we might call the lower middle classes owned their own homes; rental of property was almost universal. Nevertheless, the home was the focus of middle-class life. One of the most numerous middle-class occupations was shopkeeping and many in the lower middle classes would have domestic accommodation on the back of, or over, the shop. For more prosperous mercantile families, property would not only be larger but, increasingly, situated out of the centre of the cities, away from the smells and effluent which emanated from workshops and overcrowded slums. London was a partial exception to this but only because of its size. The newly built squares towards the north and west of the capital provided much-sought-after terraced accommodation for business and professional families. For the higher **bourgeois family**, Bloomsbury was desirable. For those in slightly more modest, but still comfortable, circumstances, Islington a mile or so further north was eligible enough. Both were at reassuring and comforting distance from Bow or Shoreditch in London's East End. In the provinces, spacious accommodation was put up by speculative builders in suburbs such as Edgbaston on what was in 1850 the outskirts of Birmingham or Victoria Park in Manchester. For those involved in the coal or shipping industries who found Newcastle upon Tyne too dirty or too crowded, a detached villa in Low Fell, just to the south of the Tyne, was an ideal retreat.[12] The trend towards 'Villadom' grew more quickly in the second half of the nineteenth century but it was already established by 1850.

Bourgeoisie

This term of French origin is an alternative name for 'middle class', although its use is often restricted to owners of capital in mercantile or manufacturing, thus excluding the professional middle class. The term has also often taken on a derogatory connotation. For Marxists, a 'bourgeois' is the owner of the means of production and uses the power this gives to oppress workers by low wages and long working hours in poor conditions. Culturally, the term is often applied to people with conventional, unimaginative, and overly materialistic lifestyles. The 'petit bourgeoisie' are otherwise known as the 'lower middle class'. They have less capital, less power and often less education than the 'bourgeoisie'. The term is used pejoratively to denote defensiveness, narrow-mindedness and limited cultural horizons.

Much was spent on domestic accoutrements. The middle classes bought clocks, china, jewellery, pewter, linen and much else. So the consumption patterns of shopkeepers, smaller merchants, manufacturers who employed, say, half a dozen journeymen and apprentices provided work for others in the growing population. They also fuelled a consumer revolution. When the first trade directories were published at the beginning of our period, the full range of commercial activity could be gauged. Except in the most fashionable places, individual shops and 'manufactories' were small in scale. Overall, however, towns were offering an increasingly extensive range of products.[13]

The commercial middle classes also bought books. Like most below them in the social scale, their worlds were generally bounded by home and workplace. For many small manufacturers these might be the same place. The most basic workforce unit was the family. It had defined tasks, for example in the manufacture of woollen clothing, for men, women and children. A very high premium was put upon the acquisition of education. This was partly a question of snobbery. The middle classes wanted to put recognisable distance between themselves and the labouring masses. As Peter Borsay says, education was both a 'socially selective process' and 'a fundamental tool of improvement'.[14] It was socially selective because until well into the nineteenth century relatively few in the working classes could read, at least with any fluency. For the middle classes who wished to entertain and thus to acquire the skills of polite conversation, the need to read the newspapers and magazines which were being produced in ever increasing numbers was of paramount importance. It was a tool of improvement also, because the middle classes wished to ensure that their children were provided with the means of acquiring the kinds of knowledge, understanding and perspective which would open doors to a range of careers.

The range of educational provision was extensive, though more so for boys than for girls. Some middle-class children might go to grammar schools, many of which had been founded in the Tudor period, but which might have a curriculum rooted in the classics, when the middle classes wanted learning of a more obviously practical bent, such as science, mathematics and the new subject of '**political economy**'. A large number of day schools and private academies were established in the eighteenth century to cater for what was a rapidly growing demand. Many were deliberately designed (unlike their Tudor predecessors) to emphasise social distinction. As Langford puts it, 'the social priority of education' was the need 'to make good connections by placing one's child among the rich, the powerful and the privileged'.[15] Families which could afford it made a much more thorough job of this by sending their male children to the so-called public schools which were growing substantially in number by 1850. Middle-class girls were much more likely to be taught at home, where the emphasis was on 'domestic accomplishments' such as sewing, needlework and music (usually singing and the piano). Not until the middle of the nineteenth century did the long, and frequently frustrating, march towards equality of educational opportunity for women begin (see Chapter 25).[16]

Political economy

A branch of the social sciences dealing with the production and distribution of consumer goods and services. It is a slightly misleading phrase, since although it is the forerunner of the modern subject Economics, it is concerned with politics only in its broadest sense. In our period, it was associated with some of the new thinking about the economy, particularly the new ideas being published by Adam Smith (*The Wealth of Nations*, 1776), Thomas Malthus (*Essay on the Principle of Population*, 1798) and David Ricardo (*On the Principles of Political Economy and Taxation*, 1817).

The middle classes also joined things. As usual, an ulterior motive beyond enjoyment and staving off loneliness in advanced years lay behind this 'associational activity'. It too provided opportunities for what we now call 'networking': the making of profitable connections as an aid to 'getting on'. For many, the key association was the church or the chapel. Baptist congregations were particularly strong in Wales. A disproportionate number of the middle classes belonged not to the established Church of England but to a nonconformist community. They were often called religious 'dissenters'. The Church of England was not fleet-footed in adapting to the challenges of rapid urban population growth. Nonconformist churches filled the resultant gap. Large numbers of Congregational and Baptist churches were erected. The cheek-by-jowl woollen towns of Leeds and Bradford were particularly prominent centres of religious nonconformity. Business links were also strongly associated with religious nonconformity in Lancashire. Families associated together and, as with the aristocracy, marriages among the business classes strengthened a sense of cohesion and loyalty.[17] In business, this encouraged a culture of collective risk-taking based on mutual trusts (see also Chapter 6).

The largest nonconformist grouping, however, was the Methodists, who more than doubled their membership in the thirty years from 1820 to 1850. They claimed almost half a million members in 1851, by which time Britain's only dedicated religious census revealed that nonconformist churches had rather more of the faithful through their chapel doors on census Sunday than did the Church of England.[18]

Many other organisations established in the late eighteenth and early nineteenth centuries might broadly be called 'improving'. These included subscription libraries, where newspapers were available, and subscription concerts. Menfolk might attend local Literary and Philosophical Societies. There they might discuss the great political or intellectual issues of the day and perhaps debates the views of a visiting speaker. Many were also involved in charitable work. The link between nonconformity and Evangelicalism (see Chapter 10) was strong, especially through its emphasis on 'Christianity by good works', rather than merely faith. Middle-class women, in particular, would undertake charitable work, such as that for the Society for Bettering the Condition of the Poor, founded in 1796. They might also help out in one of the new urban hospitals or 'public dispensaries', which provided medicines for the poor.[19]

III. The professional middle class

The influence of the professional middle classes grew markedly. By the middle of the nineteenth century, a leading barrister offered this almost lordly view of their worth:

> The importance of the professions, and the professional middle classes can hardly be over-rated, they form the head of the great English middle class, maintain the tone of its independence, keep up to the mark its standard of morality, and direct its intelligence.[20]

Such high-minded generality almost begs to be pricked by specific examples of less than either moral or intelligent professional behaviour. Visual and literary cultures abound with them. Cartoonists portrayed lawyers as duplicitous and venal, charging fees for services either not rendered or skimped. Doctors were represented as charlatans and priests either as other-worldly or as compliant tools of a harsh, repressive state, particularly in their role as clerical magistrates.[21] As a young man, Charles Dickens worked as a clerk in a solicitor's office, an experience he detested. His representation of the law in the novels is not flattering. The interminable Jarndyce *v*

Jarndyce case in *Bleak House* (1853), which eats up the Dedlock family fortune, is often cited as an example of the lawyers' desire to rack up fees by using every stratagem of delay. The lawyer Tulkinghorn is scheming and manipulative. Mr Jaggers in *Great Expectations* (1860) is precise, mechanical and detached.[22]

Satire, of course, is often a mask for reluctant respect, which it is difficult to deny the professional classes had earned. They became increasingly organised and regulated as their numbers grew and they met a growing demand for their professional services in an increasingly complex society. The Law Society was established in 1792 from a 'Society of Gentlemen Practisers in the Courts of Law and Equity'. It 'vetted candidates for enrolment in the law courts, monitored legal changes that affected the profession and lobbied parliament on a wide range of legal issues'.[23] More than 14,000 barristers and attorneys were practising in England and Wales in 1851; their numbers had more than tripled since 1780.

It proved more difficult to regulate the medical profession, at least until the formation of the General Medical Council in 1858. A much larger proportion of the population needed medical than legal services and the degree of professional expertise available was roughly proportional to the ability to pay. A hierarchy within the profession had physicians at the apex. Their concern was diagnosis and prescription, but at a distance from the patient. Below them stood the surgeons, who studied anatomy and who treated patients. On the lowest rung were the apothecaries, who sold drugs. Increasingly, however, as hospitals grew in number, this older hierarchy was replaced by one led by hospital consultants, university trained, linked to a wide range of general practitioners. By 1850, it was clear that, as Professor Corfield puts it, hospitals were 'the secular cathedrals of the emergent medical sciences'. Within these, 'the great teaching hospitals . . . formed the heartland of medical training'.[24] London had eleven in the mid-century; eleven provincial towns also had medical schools. The provision of medical care was an area with many opportunities for women, virtually all of them on the lower rungs of the hierarchy. Of the 32,000 women in the United Kingdom listed in the 1851 Census as working in medicine, 88 per cent were nurses and a further 11 per cent midwives.

In Boyd Hilton's words, 'Urbanization spawned a hugely expanded salariat':[25] those who earned fees for their work. Salaries may differ little from wages in basic meaning but 'being in receipt of a salary' screamed 'higher status'. Workers earned wages which could be variable and were liable to be withdrawn during trade depressions or when a firm went bankrupt, as many did in the first half of the nineteenth century. The attraction of a salary was that it was normally a fixed and permanent form of income. It gave, and was intended to give, a sense of security.

Specialist professional societies developed rapidly in this period. These aimed to safeguard standards by restricting entry to those who could demonstrate professional competence. They also tried to ensure that users of those services would pay the going rate to skilled practitioners. The Royal Society of Surgeons received its charter in 1800. In 1832, the Provincial Medical and Surgical Association met in

Worcester; it was the forerunner of the British Medical Association. The growth of towns and the expansion of transport generated more engineers and architects. The Institution of Civil Engineers was established in 1818, that of Mechanical Engineers followed in 1847. Architects were particularly anxious to establish their respectability and set themselves apart from semi-trained builders who produced houses and commercial buildings to no particular specification and with no concern for permanence. The Institute of British Architects was founded in 1835. Its aim was to ensure that buildings constructed by its members would be sound in structure and responsive to contemporary taste.[26]

IV. The growth of influence

By 1800, few doubted the increased importance of the middle classes. For Lord John Russell in 1819, the 'middling orders of society' were showing 'curiosity, intelligence, boldness and activity of mind. A much greater proportion of the collective knowledge and wealth of the nation has thus fallen to their lot'.[27] The **Unitarian** minister and medical practitioner Thomas Southwood Smith saw them as 'that portion of our people to whom every thing that is good among us may with certainty be traced . . . the middle class . . . which gives to the nation its character'.[28] For the petitioners of Shoreditch complaining about high prices and increased taxation at the end of the eighteenth century, the 'middling classes of society' were 'the life's blood of the country, who encourage arts, patronize improvements, create the resources and support the burthens of the nation'.[29]

> **Unitarians**
>
> Description given to those who believe that God is one 'person' and who reject the Christian doctrine of the Holy Trinity: equality of God, Jesus Christ and the Holy Spirit. Unitarianism's influence grew during the eighteenth-century Enlightenment, with its emphasis on reason and rational enquiry rather than an acceptance of tradition. In England, a separate Unitarian denomination began in the 1770s and gained many adherents among intellectuals, scientists and writers.

Why did the middle classes seem to have such clout in the late eighteenth and nineteenth centuries? The answer lies partly in numbers. If about a quarter of the population of Britain could consider itself to be 'middle class', then they numbered about 2.7m at the time of the first census in 1801. By 1851, when urbanisation, with its associated industrial and commercial developments, had developed apace, the middle class probably numbered about 5.5m.

There was considerably more to it than numbers, however. The middle classes mattered wherever they congregated. They had adequate incomes. They were

God-fearing. Their families were generally stable and law-abiding. They paid their taxes. Such respectability earned regard. By 1850, also, the middle classes controlled local government in most of Britain's industrial and commercial towns. More pertinently, the upper classes – however much they might disdain regional accents, a lack of 'breeding' and an over-zealous commitment to the acquisition of wealth – saw in the middle classes a shield and protection from the rough ways and revolutionary potential of the lower orders. As we shall see (Chapters 11, 15 and 20), early industrial Britain experienced much popular protest. When complaints by the lower orders about food shortages and high taxation merged with the articulation of 'The Rights of Man' and implicit social 'contracts' between governors and governed, the aristocracy became alarmed. In the 1830s, a British revolution was by no means out of the question.

It was hardly surprising, therefore, that the landed classes paid due respect to commerce and the professions. It helped that roughly a hundred bankers, merchants and lawyers sat in the House of Commons in the early nineteenth century. The latest estimates suggest that about 17 per cent of MPs sitting in the Commons in the years 1820–32 had business and professional backgrounds. Service with the East India Company was a particularly prominent route to recognition. Over the same period, however, only fifteen MPs came from the new textile manufacturing industries.[30]

This significant, and confident, minority kept consciousness about middle-class attitudes and concerns well to the fore in a landowners' parliament. Intermarriage between the wealthiest bourgeois (see Chapter 3) and landowners further reduced social barriers. However much some might resent it, there was also an increasing awareness among the aristocracy that the middle classes were generating an ever larger proportion of the nation's wealth. Much of it – albeit rather less than the advocates of parliamentary reform suggested – was first-generation wealth. Aristocrats owed their wealth, privileges and political position to the accident of birth and were therefore vulnerable to attacks based on any meritocratic view of the world. Perhaps most significantly, the landed interest recognised that what they had most in common with the middle classes was property. If they deferred, or seemed to defer, to the virtues of middle-class acquisition and the respectability which accompanied it, then they could hope to build a secure position against revolution from below. Allowing that the middle classes mattered and deserved respect and representation would prove to be one of the most successful accommodations of the age.

5

....

Industrial revolution or industrial evolution?

I. Explaining Britain's pre-eminence

During the period 1780–1850, Britain underwent the most radical economic and social transformation in its history. For more than a century, since the phrase was coined by an eminent historian of the late nineteenth century, we have been calling this transformation an 'industrial revolution'.[1] This was a period characterised by the development of purpose-built factories, particularly in the textile industry, and of the much more intensive use of mechanisation, both to increase the rate of production in that industry and to reduce unit costs, making prices more competitive. More or less contemporaneous with the textile revolution, and caused in part by it, came important developments in transport: new **turnpike roads**, the emergence of a canal network and, from the 1820s, steam-powered railways.[2] These required radical change to the infrastructure: more bridges, more houses, more commercial and industrial workshops, more ships – and much more besides. Demand for iron, in particular, increased hugely at this time. All of these demands required a response from the extractive industries. More power meant boom time for coal owners. In the North-East, a major centre of the coal industry, the amount of coal shipped from both Newcastle and Sunderland increased by a factor of 2.5 between 1750 and 1820.[3] Nationally, coal output increased at least five times during the course of the eighteenth century.[4] All of this meant plenty of gruelling, dangerous work for those who spent most of their, often brief, working lives underground.

Turnpike roads

A turnpike is a fixed barrier, usually in the form of a spike, placed across a road. Turnpike roads were run by 'turnpike trusts'. They levied tolls on most passengers and goods which passed along the road and these tolls paid for road improvements. The early turnpikes, authorised in the early eighteenth century, were mostly for only short distances but much longer routes soon followed. A network of well-constructed roads was in place by the end of the eighteenth century and proved vital for the conveyance of heavy goods, particularly in the new industrial areas. By the 1830s, more than 900 turnpike trusts had been set up.

This hurried sketch of key changes is enough to indicate why historians have found the phrase 'industrial revolution' so useful. Social historians, in particular, see something more in the developments of the late eighteenth and early nineteenth centuries. Harold Perkin called them 'the more than industrial revolution': 'a revolution in men's access to the means of life, in control over their ecological environment, in their capacity to escape from the tyranny and niggardliness of nature'.[5] More than forty years on, and against a background of apparently remorseless climate change, these words may have a hollow ring. As a historical judgment on the period under study, however, they capture the sense of limitless opportunity which opened up before nations which industrialised.

Another historian has usefully identified four different aspects of change with which historians have been concerned when they use the phrase 'industrial revolution'. Brief reference to each will help to explain why the phrase has excited controversy. The first emphasises the increasing dominance of market forces as determinants of change. Far less reliance was placed on customary practice and restrictive regulations such as tariffs. Competition ruled. The second concentrates on the structure and scale of industrial enterprises – factories, mines, railways and the rest. The third might be called the quantitative school. Its concern is with numbers: population growth, the rate of growth in the national income, the scale of investment and the rest. The fourth aspect relates to changes in technology, the organisation of an industrial workforce and with understanding how goods were distributed and sold.[6]

All four aspects are pertinent and separating them enables us to understand why the concept of an industrial revolution has excited considerable debate over the last thirty years. There is, however, no debate over which nation was the first to experience the intoxicating cocktail of interlocking change and very little over its impact on Britain's enhanced power and status in the world during the nineteenth century. It is, therefore, worth considering why Britain established this lead. This is not to explain why Britain became the world's first industrial nation, because such a complex phenomenon defies simple causal explanation. Some historians have argued that it is not even a sensible question since industrial change took place in regions, not across nations. As has been pointed out, we cannot neglect 'the fact that the "industrial revolution" came much earlier . . . to south Lancashire and the Black Country than it did to Lincolnshire or Kent'.[7] While this is perfectly true (see Chapter 6), it hardly invalidates a crucially important dimension. First, the impact of changes in south Lancashire and south Staffordshire was felt nationally soon enough. Secondly, the fact that an industrial revolution occurred first in particular regions within Britain had immense consequences for Britain's status as a great power during the nineteenth century. Industrial change had political as well as social, economic and cultural impact.

Some factors which help to explain why Britain was first are geographical. Britain is a small nation with relatively few extremes of climate or topography. It is, therefore, relatively easy to get around, partly because it has a large number of readily navigable rivers and particularly because it does not have an Alpine, or similarly elevated, mountain range to surmount. The ease with which goods could be moved around the country during the eighteenth century was considerably enhanced by substantial investment in road and canal transport. It also helped that nowhere in Britain is as much as a hundred miles from the sea. Britain is a group of small islands, dominated by one relatively large land mass which covers almost all of England and Wales and the substantial bulk of Scotland. The development of overseas trading links, necessitating an emphasis on shipbuilding and navigation skills, was a prerequisite for such a nation. The development of long-distance overseas trade routes, particularly to India and the Americas, was a natural progression in the late seventeenth and earlier eighteenth centuries. Britain is also a nation rich, in proportion to its size, in mineral resources, particularly coal, iron and tin. British coal was the cheapest in the world and its rich seams enabled Britain to develop as a cheap energy economy, with huge consequences for the nature of its economic growth and the success of its industrial revolution.[8]

Other predisposing factors included an advanced agricultural system geared to profit and high productivity, from which peasant farmers were very largely absent (see Chapters 1 and 7) and a growing population. These two were beneficially linked. Britain's population grew at least as rapidly as anywhere else in Europe in the years after 1740. More importantly, it urbanised quicker. It has been estimated that England accounted for more than half of the overall rise in Europe's urban population during the eighteenth century.[9] The efficiency of Britain's agriculture enabled its growing population to be fed and, in most years, for there to be a surplus for export. An improved distribution network kept the growing towns efficiently provided with food. The labour force was therefore highly productive both in the countryside and in the towns.

It also helped that some of the wealthiest landowners were so heavily involved in commercial investment. The British aristocracy was the most entrepreneurially minded in Europe. Since, in contrast to much of Europe, landowners (rather than the monarch) had rights to the exploitation of minerals under the ground, large landowners could make fortunes from mining. Many, like the Bridgewater, Stafford and Marlborough families, invested heavily in canal development, not least because their own business interests, as overseas traders, urban developers and agricultural improvers, stood to benefit from an enhanced transport system. By 1820, 4,000 miles of navigable waterways were open for trade. Some of the new canals provided effective water routes linking Britain's major rivers, such as the Trent, Severn and Mersey.

The role of the state was also of critical importance. The development of the so-called 'Fiscal-Military State' (see Chapter 4) benefited the moneyed interest, helped to provide stability and security for England's banking system and thus encouraged both investment and what is now called an appropriate '**risk appetite**'. During the early eighteenth century, London took over from Amsterdam as Europe's, and therefore at that time the world's financial capital. Additionally, Britain's frequent involvement in wars helped to stimulate both the iron and the shipbuilding industries. Not only that; most of the wars were won. The outcome of the Seven Years War, in particular, secured for Britain commercial pre-eminence over the French in India and the Americas. The Union of England, Wales and Scotland also represented a huge commercial advantage (see Chapter 1). After 1707, the new Great Britain operated as the largest integrated market in Europe.

Risk appetite

This is a piece of jargon imported from the world of finance. It is used, particularly by managers and auditors, to describe the extent to which a business, or other organisation, is willing to take risks. The business world thrives on risk-taking, for example in pursuit of new markets. However, a high 'appetite' for risk may be unwise, since it may not be appropriately balanced against the likely rewards and could lead to over-commitment and even bankruptcy. Similarly, in certain organisations, or at certain times (as during a financial depression), a low-risk appetite may be preferable since firms are looking to consolidate, or to survive adverse trading conditions.

It seems likely that the nature of the British state in the eighteenth century conveyed further advantages. Britain was not an absolute monarchy. Its commercial and financial policies did not depend either on individual whim or on the constraining prejudices of a hidebound, or inward-looking, court. Particularly in the reigns of the 'German' Hanoverians, George I (1714–27) and George II (1727–60), commercial policies were much more the preserve of parliament than of the monarch. As we have seen (see Chapter 4), significant numbers of MPs had extensive commercial interests.

Above all, perhaps, Britain in the eighteenth century was secure and mostly stable. It had surmounted the many constitutional crises of the seventeenth century and, although few would have predicted it at the time, the so-called Glorious Revolution of 1688–89, which removed the Catholic James II and secured both a Protestant succession and a Protestant state, ushered in a long period of domestic tranquillity. The significance of the Jacobite risings of 1715 and 1745–46 (see Chapter 1) should not be lightly dismissed but, in the broader eighteenth-century context, they were only pebbles which briefly disturbed the otherwise calm waters of a constitutional nation. It is over-egging the pudding to call England or Britain 'a Land of Liberty'[10] in the eighteenth century, but neither was it an **autocracy**. It was ruled by a monarch whose powers were statutorily limited from 1689 onwards[11] and by a parliament which represented a wide range of landed and other propertied interests.

Autocracy

The name given to a regime in which total power is in the hands of one ruler.

In explaining why Britain won the race to industrialise, it is necessary to relate 'favourable factor endowments' to a political context. One economic historian has argued that conditions in France, a larger country and one in 1780 with a population almost three times that of Britain, were at least as favourable for industrial advance.[12] While this is true, such an analysis ignores the fragility of the French political regime under Louis XVI and the desperate struggle for fiscal stability which would contribute to its downfall in 1789. The British fiscal-military state also operated under the rule of law, as defined by the **Revolution Settlement**, which provided firm protection at least for its propertied citizens. Great Britain was both a state itself well set up for business and a state with which many others wished to do business.

Revolution Settlement

This was the arrangement by which the constitution was settled after the ejection of James II at the end of 1688 and the installation of his daughter, Mary, and her husband, William of Orange, as joint monarchs. The so-called Bill of Rights in 1689 listed a number of things which the monarch was not permitted constitutionally to do 'without consent of parliament'. These included the power to suspend the operation of laws, the keeping of any standing army, and the levying of money for the use of the crown. Elections to parliament were to be free of any constraint and, when elected, members were to enjoy absolute freedom of speech. The Act of Settlement, passed in 1701, confirmed that the monarch had to be a member of the Church of England and that monarchs could not marry a Roman Catholic. Foreigners were not allowed to be privy councillors, who advised the monarch. The monarch could not leave the country without the consent of parliament. Also, judges were to hold office for life. They could be removed only for proven misdemeanours and then only by both Houses of Parliament, not by the monarch. Although these Acts were passed almost a century before the beginning of the period covered by this book, their impact was long-lasting and their influence substantial. They provide an important context for understanding many key developments.

II. The debate on 'revolution'

With the benefit of hindsight, it is not difficult to identify advantages which cumulatively made it likely that it would be Britain, rather than one of its continental west European competitors, which first underwent the economic and social transformation associated with industrialism. How valid is it to describe this process as a 'revolution'? The answer lies in what, precisely, is being counted and over what period. The narrower the frame of historical reference, the more dubious the word 'revolution' can be made to appear.

Until the 1980s, a consensus existed that the pace of British industrial growth increased sharply during the last quarter of the eighteenth century. This apparent advance fitted neatly with near-contemporaneous technological developments. James Hargreaves's spinning jenny, which made possible mechanised spinning of cotton cloth, was developed in 1764. Richard Arkwright had patented a spinning frame powered by water in the same year and established the first water-power spinning mill at Cromford (Derbyshire) seven years later. In 1779, Samuel Crompton invented the spinning mule, which brought together the inventions of Hargreaves and Arkwright. In 1775, James Watt had invented an engine powered by steam. The first power loom, which mechanised the weaving process of textile manufacture, was built in 1785. These inventions, famously called by the historian T. S. Ashton, allegedly quoting a schoolboy's essay, 'a wave of gadgets',[13] were assumed to have contributed substantially to a growth in industrial output from about 2 per cent a year in the period 1700–80 to one of 3–4 per cent a year from 1780 onwards.[14] Such an increase justified the use of the phrase 'take off into self-sustained growth'. Professor W. W. Rostow argued that the process of economic growth 'can usefully be regarded as centering on a relatively brief time interval of two or three decades when the economy and the society of which it is a part transform themselves in such ways that economic growth is, subsequently, more or less automatic'.[15]

Such a substantial discontinuity would clearly justify the use of the phrase 'an Industrial Revolution'. However, the figures have been challenged by economic historians using sophisticated new quantitative techniques. They calculated that, although national income statistics indicated steady growth during much of the eighteenth century, any changes from the 1780s were relatively smooth and did not justify the use of any phrase such as 'take-off'. The rapid growth which Rostow and Deane and Cole thought that they were observing in the 1780s seems to have been delayed until after the end of the Napoleonic wars in 1815.[16] A range of data relating to economic growth – those concerning industrial output and gross domestic product, productivity and investment levels – all seem to indicate gradual, rather than especially rapid change during the last quarter of the eighteenth century. The figures produced by Professor Crafts suggest an annual growth in industrial production of about 2 per cent a year in the last decade of the eighteenth century, in contrast to Deane and Cole's 3.4 per cent a year.[17] Even Crafts's figures, however, do show an increase from 1.5 per cent a year in the years 1760–80 to 2.1 per cent in the years 1780–1801. The overall implication of these figures is that Britain was already an advanced society, experiencing significant industrial development, by 1760. More or less consistent growth had been a feature of the British economy since quite early in the early eighteenth century but 'modern economic growth only became fully established in Britain in the railway age': i.e. from the 1830s onwards.[18]

The evidence of technological advance can also be drawn upon to press the case for an industrial evolution. The key innovations referred to above did not revolutionise the whole of industry over a period of thirty years or so. Rather they concentrated industrial production in well-defined areas. Older forms of production continued, in some cases side by side with mechanised ones. According to Professor

McCloskey, as late as 1860 only about 30 per cent of jobs were in sectors which 'had been radically transformed in technique since 1780'.[19]

Proponents of the view that industrialism was a relatively gradual process can readily demonstrate that the new machines did not change everything during the period of the 'take-off into self-sustained growth'. This has not proved enough to persuade historians to abandon 'the industrial revolution' as a viable description of economic and social change. The defence has come from two main quarters. First, historians have revisited the data. Much detailed attention has been paid to the validity of different kinds of available economic data, to their typicality and thus their fragility as indicators of the rate of overall economic growth. As one historian put it, 'the data are fragile, incomplete and relate only indirectly to the problem in hand'.[20] The reworking of this fragile material appears to show that the reduced estimates of growth were themselves insufficiently well grounded and that industrial activity did indeed grow faster from the 1780s onwards. On quantitative grounds, the question of whether the last quarter of the eighteenth century should be seen as a turning point on the road to the emergence of an industrial society remains open.

The second defence of the 'industrial revolution' comes from historians who emphasise the importance of context. National economic growth statistics give, at best, a partial perspective. A strong case exists for concentration on the diverse regional picture, which helps us the better to understand the importance of structural change. It has been argued that 'dynamic industrial regions generated a social and economic interaction which would have been absent if their component industries had not been spatially concentrated and specialized'. This regional specialisation generated 'dynamism which was unique to the period and revolutionary in its impact'.[21] Macro-economic calculations at a national level thus miss a key element in structural change. It is also dangerous to assume that mechanised industries, especially textiles, experienced revolutionary change whereas sectors of the economy not so directly affected by technological change were relatively stagnant. A number of studies have demonstrated how effectively 'traditional' industries could often adapt. In the metal trades, dominated by small workshops rather than large factories, for example, the early nineteenth century saw many innovations in the organisation of production and in the use of cheap alloys rather than refined metals. Goods of somewhat lower quality could find their market on grounds of price competitiveness. As with textiles, employers could substitute child and women's labour for men's in some parts of a given manufacturing process since men claimed higher wages. In such ways, parts of the metal trade had adapted to the demands of a mass market by 1850 without wholesale technological change. It is clear that mass markets – which had been developing since the eighteenth century – had become dominant in many trades by 1850, almost irrespective of whether they were at that stage factory-based or not.[22] Only in production for local, and often rural, markets, which provided fewer incentives for innovation, do growth rates appear to have been static rather than increasing.

Even if we accept that the last quarter of the eighteenth century was a period of less hectic economic growth than had previously been thought, the perceptions of contemporaries suggested novelty, progress and growth. They considered that they were living during a period of profound change. **Patrick Colquhoun** stated in 1814 that it was 'impossible to contemplate the progress of manufactures in Great Britain within the last thirty years without wonder and astonishment. Its rapidity, particularly since the commencement of the French revolutionary war, exceeds all credibility.'[23] A visitor to the Darby family iron works at Coalbrookdale in 1776 spoke of the immense changes brought to a previously rural area by iron-smelting. The furnace 'continues to vomit out its Flames and emit a vast Column of Smoak. The great Number of Buildings for the Furnaces, Forges, Founderies, Warehouses etc and the habitations of the workmen . . . compose a little City.'[24] It is also possible to trace how, from about 1760 onwards, members of the middle classes associating in local philosophical and scientific societies discussed the magnitude of the economic and social changes they were experiencing.[25]

Patrick Colquhoun, 1745–1820

Born in Dumbarton into a comfortable family, Colquhoun, having been sent as a young man to Virginia to learn the tobacco trade, became a successful Glasgow merchant who made his fortune in tobacco and cotton. He was Lord Provost of Glasgow from 1782 to 1784 and one of the founders of the Glasgow Chamber of Commerce. He moved to London in 1789 where he became a magistrate and interested himself in many social questions. He wrote pamphlets on the police in London and was instrumental in the foundation of a police force to deter crime on the River Thames. He founded a charity school in Westminster and wrote extensively on how to deal with poverty. He is best known among social and economic historians for his calculations on the social structure of England and Wales in 1801–3. His estimates, along with those by Gregory King (1688) and Joseph Massie (1759), have been a starting point for enquiries about the numbers and wealth of the population.

It is probable that, in discussing the industrial revolution, too much emphasis has been placed both on the period c1780 to c1800 and also on the concept of a 'take-off'. Stand back from these, and there is no real debate surrounding the assertion that 'over the period 1750–1850, the growth of the British economy was historically unique and internationally remarkable'.[26] Nor do historians any longer contest the proposition that this growth was vitally dependent on a long period of commercial expansion in the eighteenth century to which the British state had decisively contributed through its willingness to fund wars. These were usually won, and the outcomes were an increased colonial presence and expanded market opportunities. The political origins of the industrial revolution are now inescapable.

The industrial revolution, therefore, is a phrase which earns its place because it brought about unprecedented economic growth. It changed everything: population size and distribution, urban life, the nature of markets, social relationships and how people related to government, both local and central. As David Landes pithily expressed it, 'the basis of wealth, hence power, had been transformed'.[27] It is worth remembering, finally, that even the main revisionists are quite happy to use the phrase 'industrial revolution' if its context is clarified. They agree that 'though industrial innovations had a more modest impact on economic growth than was previously believed, they did create a genuine industrial revolution reflected in Britain's economic and social structure'.[28] To understand how this happened, it is necessary to adopt a regional perspective on change in the later eighteenth and early nineteenth centuries.

6

·················

Urban growth, industrial development and regional diversity

I. The pattern of urban growth

Over the years covered by this book, Britain became a predominantly urban society. The process, however, was long in the gestation. In 1600, only about 8 per cent of England's population lived in towns with 2,500 inhabitants or more. That proportion more than doubled over the course of the seventeenth century. The 17 per cent of urban dwellers in England in 1700 had become 23 per cent by 1750, half of whom lived in London. The rate of urbanisation accelerated markedly from the second half of the eighteenth century onwards.[1] By 1801, the proportion had risen to 34 per cent. Over the next half-century it grew to 54 per cent. By 1900 almost four in every five British citizens (according to the 1901 census, 78 per cent) were town dwellers.[2]

Britain also became the most urbanised country in Europe. Whereas England and France had much the same proportion of urban dwellers in 1600, England had pulled ahead by 1700. By 1850, almost two and a half times as many English folk lived in towns as did the French. The Dutch had been much more urbanised than either the English or the French in 1700 and retained more town dwellers as late as 1800. They had, however, been decisively overhauled by 1850. Nevertheless, even after at least half a century of unprecedentedly hectic commercial and industrial expansion, more English folk lived and worked in hamlets and small communities, if not necessarily as rural labourers, than did so in urban areas. Both the rate of urban growth and the absolute decline in numbers of those farming the land would be much greater in the second half of the nineteenth century than it had been in the first (see Chapter 23).

The pattern of urban growth in Britain was also distinctive (see Chapter 2). Whereas the largest half-dozen towns in the most urbanised countries of western Europe tended to be the same places in 1700, in 1800 and still in 1850, British urban growth was characterised much more by change than by continuity. London, however, remained the largest city – not only in Britain but in Europe. Its population lead over the second city in Britain, whichever that might be at any given time, has nearly always been by a factor of approximately ten. Until well into the nineteenth century, its pre-eminence was such that when people said that 'they were going to town', it was generally assumed that they were going to London, just as, from the earliest days of the railway, 'up lines' went to London and 'down lines' away from it. If London is taken out of the equation, furthermore, then a majority of Britain's population were not town dwellers until the early 1870s.[3]

In 1700, the largest towns in England after London were Norwich, Bristol, York and Newcastle upon Tyne. None made it into the 'top five' by 1800, when the leading urban communities were Liverpool, Manchester, Birmingham and Leeds, all of them either major manufacturing centres or, in the case of Liverpool, a port. Liverpool's massive recent growth and prosperity depended upon overseas trade, particularly imports of raw materials, exports of manufactured goods and the buoyant inhumanity of the slave trade, much of which was brokered through the port.

In Scotland, the situation was different. There, Edinburgh and Glasgow were always substantially the biggest cities in the country. In 1800, about 60 per cent of Scotland's entire urban population lived in one or the other.[4] Even so, a remarkable shift in balance is discernible. In 1700, Edinburgh, the Scottish capital, had an estimated population of 60,000 – which made it, after the Union of 1707, much the largest British city after London. Glasgow's population at that time was less than 15,000. By 1800, Glasgow, with a population of 77,000, had almost caught up with Edinburgh (83,000). The latter remained the second largest city in Britain, just ahead of Liverpool (82,000) and followed by Glasgow, then Manchester (75,000) and Birmingham (71,000).

In 1801, Ireland became part of the United Kingdom (see Chapter 14). Its capital, Dublin, whose population was about 60,000 in 1700, dominated Ireland in much the same way as London did England. Over the course of the eighteenth century, Dublin had developed as a major European capital city and its population grew much more quickly than that of Edinburgh. It is often forgotten that its population of 170,000 made it not only the second city of the United Kingdom in 1801 but more than twice as large as Liverpool, its closest English rival.[5]

II. Diversity and function

Making sense of urban development in the late eighteenth and early nineteenth centuries requires awareness of the extent of diversity, regionally, functionally and also between the constituent countries of the United Kingdom. Mention has already been made of the urban role of the aristocracy (see Chapter 3), especially in London. This represented only one facet of the capital's growth, albeit the most refined. London grew in this period, not primarily as a factory town but as a capital city and a port, although, as transatlantic trade grew, so its proportion of overseas trade declined somewhat under challenge from the west-coast ports. London factories built in the early nineteenth century tended to be small-scale affairs used for calico printing, flour-milling and snuff manufacture.[6] London's dockland grew in absolute terms and the East End of London witnessed spectacular growth of wharves, timber yards, small workshops and cheap housing. Population density was greatest in this part of London and, as a direct result both of overcrowding and poor nutritional standards, so were death rates. Although the overall London death rate was only slightly lower than the national average in 1841, this masked substantial specific variations. The population in the west of the capital was considerably wealthier than in the south and east. It also lived longer and enjoyed lower rates of infant mortality.

In general, London south of the River Thames was less prosperous than was the north, a trend which intensified as the capital expanded outwards. Thus, Clapham had been a village separate from London in 1780 and many prosperous merchants lived there. It was also the centre of the religious evangelical revival (see Chapter 10). Its exclusivity was diminished by a spate of building in the 1810s and 1820s. Soon Clapham, and many other erstwhile villages in east Surrey, were absorbed into London as suburbs. The prosperous merchants moved out, seeking secluded, semi-rural accommodation a few miles from the capital.

Movement out of town centres had significant social implications in the provinces as well as the capital. Nottingham, in the north of the East Midlands, was a lace-making and hosiery centre and was considered a genteel town during the eighteenth century. In 1801 its population was 28,000. That more than doubled in the next fifty years, standing at 58,000 in 1851. The expansion was poorly managed. As new houses were speedily erected with insufficient attention paid to factors such as sanitary provision, water supplies and street lighting, so the 'respectable' moved out to increasingly fashionable villages within commuting distance of the town. A report published in 1845 described Nottingham as an extended slum. A large mass of inhabitants were crowded into alleys and courts 'of the worst possible construction [and] wretched in the extreme'. The town was 'hardly to be surpassed in misery by anything to be found within the entire range of our manufacturing cities'.[7]

Towns were not invariably or immediately changed by the arrival of industry. Some benefited, at least environmentally, from an accession of wealth from nearby. In Chesterfield, for example, new iron works brought enhanced prosperity to the north of Derbyshire but these works stood mostly outside the town, which grew only slowly, having a population of just 7,000 in 1851. It continued to function into the 1830s as a well-appointed market town, increasing in prosperity. Its period of rapid change began only with the coming of the railway from 1840.[8]

III. Textiles and the towns

Much of the textile trade was revolutionised by machinery but its growth was asymmetrical. Spinning machinery developed quicker than weaving machinery, since most spinning machines were both simpler in design and more robust. In Scotland, as in Lancashire and Yorkshire, the use of the power loom was not common before the 1820s. As a trade, coarse weaving was easily learned and was taken up by migrants from the rural areas of Scotland, both lowland and highland, and also by Irish immigrants. Well before mechanisation, an excess of labour supply drove down wages in competitive markets. The number of weavers in Scotland, 25,000 in 1780, had more than doubled to 58,000 by 1800, reaching a peak of almost 80,000 by the 1820s, a level from which it did not fall until the 1840s.[9] By the 1830s, the bulk of spinning in Scotland was done in factories, whereas weaving remained largely a domestic trade, practised by skilled workers at home or in small workshops.

New opportunities for employment in the mills of Lancashire and in the docks of Liverpool and Birkenhead acted as a magnet for immigrants from elsewhere in the United Kingdom. By 1851, the populations of Lancashire and Cheshire combined totalled about 2.4m, of whom 1.9m (79 per cent) had been born in the two counties. Many of this substantial majority had moved relatively small distances from agricultural to urban areas in order to find work. Of those born elsewhere, roughly equal numbers had migrated from within England or from post-famine Ireland. By 1861, 9 per cent of Lancashire's population was Irish-born. In the main urban centres the proportions were higher: 19 per cent in Liverpool and 10.5 per cent in Manchester and Salford. At the same census, only 50 per cent of Manchester, and 37 per cent of Liverpool, residents had been born in Lancashire.[10]

Factory spinning came later to the Yorkshire woollen industry than to Lancashire cottons but it was established by the 1820s, after which it grew faster than the pioneer industry west of the Pennines. In the years 1835–50, the number of power looms in operation in the woollen industry increased from 5,000 to 42,000 and the number of factory workers increased tenfold. Towns grew spectacularly, none faster than Bradford, which increased from a population of 4,000 in 1781 to 104,000 in 1851, by which time it was the tenth largest town in Britain. Although, in 1841, a rather lower proportion (44 per cent) of Yorkshire woollen operatives worked in factories than did cotton operatives in Lancashire (53 per cent), the imbalance was being swiftly redressed.[11] Some weavers did, however, maintain a much older way of Yorkshire life by twinning part-time textile work, carried on at home, with work on the land.[12]

Even in the textile industry, however, technological innovation did not necessarily produce a short-term revolution in productivity. Nor did large increases in productivity necessarily require large factories. Certainly, the explanation that factories were erected primarily to house the new machinery is altogether too simple. When demand was increasing, factories located in larger towns offered owners considerable benefits. A workforce concentrated in a central location, rather than dispersed as in domestic industry, produced savings on transport costs. When, as so often with mass production, the need was for reliably uniform quality, factory production also offered advantages in terms of training and discipline. Centralised production facilitated closer supervision of the entire process. This in turn might reveal areas in which technical improvements were possible or where labour might be more productively deployed.[13]

Another reason for factory production was the changed nature of work. Some contemporary commentators considered English workers lazy, disorganised, ill-disciplined and tenacious in the defence of outmoded customs such as '**Saint Monday**'. When economic conditions were favourable and the demand for manufactured goods buoyant, it suited factory owners to have their employers work set, regular hours in an environment in which a worker's performance could be monitored and punishments imposed on those who were considered to be working, inefficiently. This system of '**time orientation**' was much easier to operate within the closed environment of the factory. It was, however, fiercely challenged by workers, who considered that it deprived them of any influence over their working environment. Not surprisingly, this led to a number of labour disputes. Women and children, coerced and often intimidated as they often were, proved much more amenable to the disciplines of factory production. This, combined with the considerably lower wages which they received, helped to explain why roughly two-thirds of employees in textile factories were women and children by the 1830s.[14]

Saint Monday

The custom of observing Monday as a holiday in the form of an extension of the week-end. It was widely practised among English workers, particularly those used to working to complete particular tasks, rather than according to prescribed hours. Employers resented the widespread absenteeism which it entailed and tried to put a stop to its observance. They were largely successful by 1850, although some trades were able to resist the general trend. The observer Thomas Wright noted in 1867 that tailors remained 'among its most ardent devotees' (*Some Habits and Customs of the Working Classes*). It is worth pointing out that the observance of Saint Monday did not usually mean that workers were in employment on only four days a week. Most would work on Saturdays, at least until lunchtime.

Time orientation and task orientation

Phrases used to describe two different forms of work organisation. Time organisation has been much the more common since the Victorian era. Here, workers are employed to work set hours. Work under 'task orientation' is more flexible and was characteristic of much domestic production. Workers would be given assignments of work to be completed by a given date. So long as the employer, or the 'putter out', of the work could collect it as arranged, workers could arrange their time to suit themselves. Not surprisingly, workers (and, we could note, contemporary undergraduates) preferred the relative freedom which 'working to the task' allowed; employers increasingly preferred to discipline their workers to set hours.

IV. Mines and metals

It is not possible to envisage a British industrial revolution without extractive industries, and particularly coal mining. Together with water and steam, they provided its motive power. Coal was also the pre-eminent fuel for domestic heating, accounting for 42.5 per cent of all coal consumption (8.9m tons) in 1775, almost identical to the usage made by industry (42.4 per cent). By 1850, the overall consumption of coal had increased to 30.4m and the share taken by industry had risen slightly to 46 per cent.[15] The proportion used in iron production had increased over the same period from 2.3 per cent to 18.6 per cent, appropriately reflecting iron's increased importance in the British economy.

The organisation and scale of iron-based industries were revolutionised in the period from 1780 to 1850 and the impact was rapidly apparent in the towns which became centres of production or distributors of the product, or both. It was, however, possible for a region to experience 'both revolutionary change and a high degree of continuity in the organisation of production'.[16] The West Midlands is perhaps the best example. Over a period hardly exceeding thirty years (c1780–c1810), iron smelting by charcoal was replaced by coke. Steam power was found much more effective than water power in producing the necessary 'blast'. New forms of refinement were introduced to convert pig iron into more malleable forms. Much of the industry also relocated to be near the Staffordshire coalfield, the main source of power.

Some industries expanded effectively without requiring much technological change. The glass industry was one such. New glass houses were established, particularly beside the canals, in order to benefit from convenient supplies of coal. Neither the basic technology involved in heating and reheating the glass nor the size of the manufacturing workforce underwent significant change during the first half of the nineteenth century. Lock-makers found themselves in greater demand as both the number of businesses and the need to secure them grew. The number of nail and chain makers grew. All three trades benefited from some improvements in technology but these were not complex. They could readily be incorporated in existing workshops, or even in the home. Much of the industrial West Midlands' 'Black Country' – the area running north-west from Birmingham to Wolverhampton – remained workshop-based during a period of major expansion. In 1840, only four of the one hundred and fifty locksmiths working in Wolverhampton had premises larger than a single shop.[17]

Britain rapidly established a clear lead in coal production. In 1800, it produced five times more coal than any other European nation[18] and, although other nations had begun to claw back some of the collective disadvantage by 1850, the coal industry remained central to Britain's industrial revolution and would expand still faster in the second half of the century under the stimulus of more rapid mechanisation of transport and the metals trades (see Chapter 23).

Coal mining was concentrated in six main regions. In roughly descending order of size of output, these were: the North-East of England, the West Midlands, South Wales, west Lancashire, central Scotland and south Yorkshire. In each, miners and their families lived in small communities – 'pit villages' – away from the main centres of population, for fairly obvious reasons related to risks from subsidence wherever deep shafts were sunk. Mining communities thus developed a strong sense both of identity and of 'otherness'. Many believed in 'keeping themselves to themselves'; it was not unusual for mining families to live and work in the one small community all their lives. In this respect, if few others, they operated like agricultural villages. Few mining communities had strong links with the Church of England. Methodism and other forms of evangelical religion were much more influential.

The North-East coalfield, centred on County Durham and the south of Northumberland, had been serving the rest of the country, and especially London, since the thirteenth century. Coal was mostly shipped around the coast, a key reason why Newcastle upon Tyne developed as a successful port in the early modern period. By 1750, commercial organisation in the North-East was able to meet the substantially increased demand for fuel generated elsewhere. It has been estimated that about 10 per cent of the region's economically active population were coal miners in the second half of the eighteenth century, a proportion which rose to about 15 per cent by 1851.[19] By then, the iron industry of the North-East was developing fast. It was stimulated by railway transport, including the Stockton–Darlington line opened in 1825, the first passenger railway in the world. Shipbuilding in the region was still little developed in 1850, a situation which would change dramatically with the emergence of iron ships and the growth of Middlesbrough over the next twenty years.

In some respects, Wales's coal mining industry followed the opposite path to that of the North-East since the exploitation of metals preceded that of coal. The immensely rich seams of the South Wales coalfield were not fully exploited until after 1850. Copper-smelting near the coalfield's south-west tip led to the expansion of Swansea in the early nineteenth century. Iron-smelting on the north-east of the coalfield, boosted by substantial investment from English entrepreneurs, especially the Guests and the Crawshays, transformed the economic prospects of the region, creating new urban communities and paving the way for the development of Cardiff, a distribution point for iron as well as coal, as the major port of the principality. In 1851, however, the iron town of Merthyr Tydfil – home to the huge Dowlais iron works – was almost three times as large as Cardiff. Its population had grown from 8,000 to 46,000 over the previous half-century.

Mining was, of course, an especially dangerous occupation. It became more so as shafts were sunk ever deeper. This increased the problems of securing adequate ventilation and avoiding flooding. Sedimentary rocks often contained methane gas and thus the additional danger of explosions. In the recently developed Lancashire coalfield, an average of 215 miners a year lost their lives in the early 1850s.[20] In Yorkshire, mining was relatively safe until deeper pits were sunk from the end of the eighteenth century. Explosions, and consequent fatalities, became common, especially from the 1840s to the 1860s. Inquiries regularly urged the installation of proper ventilating equipment. The priority of most coal owners, however, was profit rather than safety and the disasters continued. In 1866, 361 miners, men and boys, were killed in an explosion at the Oaks Colliery near Barnsley, the second disaster at the same colliery owned by Messrs Firth, Bamber and Co.[21]

V. Scales of production

Many accounts of the industrial revolution have concentrated on explaining how, and why, mechanised production and the extractive industries came to dominate the world of work. Although recent studies have redressed the balance somewhat, it is less commonly noted that hand-crafts held their own in many trades well into the second half of the nineteenth century. Simpler forms of machinery, then technologically almost obsolete, also continued in widespread use. There are many reasons for this. Sometimes, the available technology could not produce mechanised goods of appropriate quality. This was the case when finer, fashion-targeted, weaving was necessary or for producing cloths when purity or complexities of colour were essential to meet market demand. Then, as now, consumers of fashionable items took the view that purchasing a particular line, or being seen wearing a particular fabric or design, was the objective. Price was a secondary consideration. Manufacturers were happy to sustain hand-production if demand was secure and profit margins remained high. For products which did not need a skilled workforce, master manufacturers might calculate that the abundant supply of labour caused by massive population increase made speculative investment in machinery an unattractive option, especially when contingent infrastructure costs were added to the equation. In some cases, also, the introduction of new technologies was halted, or significantly delayed, by opposition from workers who believed that new technology threatened either security of employment or the wage premiums they had previously enjoyed (see Chapter 8).

Innovation always entailed risk. Would market demand justify outlay? Had any wider adjustments to the productive process been properly costed? It is not surprising that what appeared to be an unstoppable tide of mechanised innovation often looked rather different on closer inspection. Even in south and east Lancashire, the world's first industrialised region, the size of factories in the 1830s was surprisingly small. Only 25 of the 975 identified (3 per cent) had a workforce of more than a thousand; only sixty (6 per cent) employed between five hundred and a thousand. Modally, the Lancashire factory was small; 43 per cent had fewer than a hundred employees.[22] By 1851, the average number of workers in a woollen mill was 59, in a **worsted** mill 170 and in a cotton mill 167.[23] The trend, it is true, was towards larger factories but these came more as a result of business mergers during the period of mature capitalism in the second half of the century. Earlier, it was often difficult to recruit factory workers and the more regimented conditions usually attracted a wage premium.

Worsted

Worsted is a woollen fabric made from closely twisted yarn spun from long, fine combed fibres of wool. Worsteds were originally developed in Norfolk, but the West Riding of Yorkshire had become the main centre of production by the second half of the nineteenth century, especially around Huddersfield and Halifax.

In the Midlands, many industries expanded almost exclusively on the basis of small workshops rather than large factories. In addition to the metal trades (see below), Worcester had become the leading glove manufacturing centre by the early nineteenth century. Coventry, in relative decline by the 1830s in the face of developments in Birmingham and the Black Country, remained an important centre for ribbon manufacture. The hat industry was located in the predominantly rural counties of Bedfordshire, Buckinghamshire and Hertfordshire. Industrial revolutions may require machines, but the majority of industrial workers did not operate them.

VI. Leisure and urban culture

Many important towns contributed little or nothing to Britain's commercial and industrial growth but were, in Peter Borsay's words, 'attractive and fashionable places' and helped to develop a new sense of urban culture. The 'idea and ideal of the town came to occupy a new prominence in people's minds'.[24] Population size was not a crucial consideration. Even smaller towns developed distinctive cultures, especially if they included as residents a significant proportion of gentry, commercial and professional families. Some, of course, were not small. Norwich, England's pre-eminent worsted town in the seventeenth and early eighteenth centuries, remained its third largest manufacturing centre as late as 1780, when it housed 39,000 inhabitants. Its wool trade was rapidly eclipsed by developments in the West Riding. Population growth slackened in consequence but the importance of Norwich as, in effect, the regional capital of East Anglia continued. The presence of prosperous mercantile families in the city presented numerous cultural and associational opportunities. An Assembly House was built in the 1750s, where the middle classes met, read newspapers – Norwich's first local paper was produced in 1721 – and gambled. The town hosted many balls and concerts. It also had a well-established and thriving theatre, one of a hundred established in the provinces by 1815.[25]

The single adjective covering the various forms of urban culture was 'polite'. Polite society comprised those from the middle ranks who observed behavioural and cultural conventions designed at least as much to exclude 'the vulgar' who lacked education, financial resources and refined taste. A small population was no bar to the development of a polite culture. Salisbury, the county town of Wiltshire and home to one of England's finest Gothic cathedrals, had been an important centre of the wool trade in the fifteenth century. Thereafter, both its economy and its population (about 7,500 in 1780 and almost static over the next seventy years) had stagnated. However, a number of gentry, merchants and members of the professional classes still lived in the centre of the town. Gentry and even aristocratic presence in the town was guaranteed by its cathedral status. The bishopric of Salisbury was one of the most eminent in the country. Its bishops, and many of its other senior clergy, were almost invariably drawn from gentry, higher professional and mercantile or aristocratic families.[26] Like much larger communities, Salisbury demonstrated all the characteristic social attributes and amenities demanded in 'polite society' by 'persons of quality'.

Spas and seaside towns only became fashionable from the middle of the eighteenth century onwards. Their fortunes were transformed by aristocratic and royal patronage. Bath (see Chapter 4), rebuilt and extended at huge expense, exceeded all expectations. The wealthiest and most socially eligible could hardly afford not to be seen there during the summer months. Cheltenham's architectural development in the first half of the century was much influenced by that of Bath. The scale was more modest but the town's population nevertheless increased from 3,000 in 1801 to 20,000 in the mid-1820s.[27] Scarborough on the Yorkshire coast was also a spa before it developed into a seaside resort attracting large numbers of visitors from the inland woollen towns. Buxton, in North Derbyshire's upland Peak District, was hardly more than a village in the 1780s. It had fewer than a thousand residents but strong aristocratic connections. Its fortunes were transformed by the fifth Duke of Devonshire. He commissioned a new crescent in the Georgian style that began a process of urban development which established Buxton as one of the most fashionable resorts in Victorian Britain.

Sea bathing, previously considered an eccentric activity far from the world of high fashion, received a major boost in 1789. George III, recovering from porphyria, a disease often accompanied by bouts of mental instability, was persuaded to visit the south-coast resort of Weymouth (Dorset) to enjoy the benefits of salt water and sea air. Fashionable society followed him to Weymouth and other south-coast resorts. What George III did with reasonable decorum, his eldest son developed to excess. Arriving at Brighton, on the Sussex coast, in 1783 with his usual ill-assorted entourage of genuinely aristocratic friends, political toadies, pleasure seekers, gamblers, and other chancers, the Prince of Wales (later Prince Regent and from 1820 **George IV**) took to the place and transformed it within thirty years. Fashionably expensive new buildings jostled for space with much more modest accommodation as Brighton struggled to keep up with a population which rose from 3,500 in the early 1780s to 40,000 at the time of George IV's death in 1830. Everything on the sea front was dwarfed by the Regent's hugely exotic 'Royal Pavilion' built in the Oriental style.

George IV, 1762–1830

Born in London, the eldest of George III's fifteen children, he was educated privately at Kew. He was intelligent but inclined to laziness and lack of attention. His father was disappointed both by his application and, a little later, by his choice of friends, whom George III considered idlers and wastrels. The two were rarely close. From his late teenage years, he developed a reputation both for sexual licence and wasteful expenditure. He contracted an illegal marriage to Maria Fitzherbert in 1785 and a legal, but loveless and latterly scandalous, one to Princess Caroline of Brunswick. He was Prince Regent, with royal powers taken from his mentally incapacitated father, from 1811 to 1820, when he succeeded to the throne. In his youth, he supported the Whigs and was a great friend of Charles James Fox. When Regent and then monarch, he supported Tory ministries in office. His reputation and attitudes did not inspire respect and his attempt to divorce Caroline in 1820 brought the monarchy into contempt. He was not without aesthetic taste but he indulged his tastes with characteristic excess. In addition to building the ornate Brighton Pavilion in Oriental style, he also refurbished Buckingham Palace and largely rebuilt Windsor Castle.

We began this chapter by asserting that, over the period 1780–1914, Britain became an urban society. That is an over-simplification. There was no one, coherent 'urban society'. As we have seen, towns had different dominant functions – commercial, industrial, administrative, leisured – and those functions often over-lapped. In the late eighteenth and early nineteenth centuries, however, they were all associated, in one way or another, with the idea of progress: economic growth, ways of making money, a range of new opportunities. As we shall see, Victorian society would have to grapple with a substantial downside to this optimistic picture: environmental deterioration, extremes of wealth and poverty, the rapid spread of disease in confined spaces and the need to devise ways of governing and controlling confined spaces with high population densities.

7

·················

Agriculture in the early industrial age

I. Growing productivity

It might seem paradoxical to suggest that the key to the success of Britain's industrial revolution lay in the changes occurring in rural society. Yet an efficient agricultural sector was critical in Britain's successful transition to a predominantly urban society whose prosperity depended on trade and on its rapidly expanding manufacturing industries. The explanation is straightforward. First, Britain's population was growing rapidly from the second half of the eighteenth century onwards (see Chapter 2) and Britain had more mouths to feed. Eleven million more people lived in Britain in 1850 than in 1750. Although this required increasing dependence on food imports, it is still remarkable that about six and a half million extra mouths were being fed by British agriculture at the latter date.[1] An agricultural sector geared predominantly towards subsistence farming would not have kept pace with demographic change after 1750. Secondly, an urban population needed access to efficient supplies of food, growing very little of its own.

Many historians have called the process which enabled this transition an 'agricultural revolution', although the term is now used much more cautiously than it was.[2] A number of studies have cast doubt on the extent to which agriculture was revolutionised in the later eighteenth and nineteenth centuries. It has long been recognised that the process of significant mechanisation did not get under way on the land until the 1850s. If an agricultural revolution occurred, then it did so – in stark contrast to the Industrial Revolution – with very little assistance from mechanisation. Literally speaking, agricultural change on the ground was effected by hand craft and horse power. A general assumption held, however, that farming became much more productive in the eighteenth century, largely because of higher levels of investment, greater regional specialisation and, encouraged by tenants anxious to make the most profitable use of the land they leased, increased labour productivity. A host of regional surveys on agricultural productivity has failed to confirm a picture of steady growth in productivity over the eighteenth century as a whole. It seems likely that the productivity of rural labour was considerably greater in the late seventeenth and early eighteenth centuries than it was from the 1760s onwards.[3] In the second half of the eighteenth century, and under the stimulus of parliamentary enclosure (see below), increases in productivity depended upon extensions of land use, particularly by bringing previously waste land into cultivation. During the period 1770–1850, the acreage under cultivation increased by about 50 per cent, from 10m to 15m. The acreage sown with wheat, normally the most profitable crop, went up by about 36 per cent, from 2.8m to 3.8m.

Although historians are hampered by a dearth of reliable quantitative information, by most measurements, agriculture became much more productive in the first half of the nineteenth century rather than earlier. However, if the term 'agricultural revolution' is used, it now seems safer to apply it to a longer period: one beginning towards the end of the seventeenth century and continuing into the era of so-called 'high farming' (see Chapter 23) in the 1850s. For some historians, this is evolutionary, rather than revolutionary, change. As the most authoritative study of agriculture in this period concluded, 'the achievements of the hundred years after 1750 were remarkable. It could hardly be said that they amounted to an agricultural revolution.'[4]

What is not in dispute is that British farming became more commercial during the eighteenth century and particularly so from about 1760 onwards. Commercial farming was underpinned by two linked developments: more specialised practice and a change in the structure of landholding. Landowners increasingly attempted to consolidate their holdings in central, convenient locations. The consolidation of land was also accompanied by its concentration in fewer hands. By the last years of the eighteenth century larger landlords owned about 75 per cent of Britain's cultivated land and smaller freeholders not more than 20 per cent. Nevertheless, the extent to which farming was dominated by a few great aristocratic landowners (see Chapter 3) can easily be exaggerated. By 1850, the South-East of England was almost certainly the most modernised agricultural region, dominated by farming to meet the needs of urban markets, especially that of London. Even here, however, land consolidation had not swept away a substantial number of landowners and tenants working small farms and more or less impervious to modern methods.[5]

II. Profits and wages

The great spur to agricultural improvement was, of course, profit. A landed hierarchy was well developed and, in its higher reaches, jealously guarded. Below the great aristocracy (see Chapter 3) came the gentry, which can be divided into two categories. Many in the higher gentry, which comprised about seven hundred families, would have minor titles as baronets or knights. Their landed income in the middle of the eighteenth century did not normally fall below £3,000 a year – the equivalent of about £450,000 in early twenty-first-century values. The lesser gentry comprised almost four thousand families with an annual income between £1,000 and £3,000 a year. Increasingly, gentry and aristocratic families rented out the bulk of their land to tenants. A few tenant farmers, especially in productive arable counties like Norfolk, might have control of hundreds, or even thousands, of acres. Most tenants were much humbler, both in income and aspiration. All, however, were attempting to make a profit on the deal they had cut. Their livelihoods depended most on their own efficiency.

It is probable that, by the later eighteenth century, enterprising tenant farmers and smaller gentry were more responsible for agricultural improvement than were the greater landowners, whose attentions became increasingly fixed on exploiting mining wealth, overseas trade, colonial development and, particularly, the very considerable profits and perquisites of government office.[6]

Tenants, therefore, were looking for what today's unlovely jargon would call 'efficiency savings'. Unlike so many in our own day, however, these savings were real and were made at the expense of the lower orders in rural society. The main change here was a shift in the terms of employment. Farm servants, who generally 'lived in' with the farmer's family, had some security of employment. Many were engaged at hiring fairs, usually for a continuous period of a year or more. Most were young, unmarried workers. Most left farm service either when they married or when their first child was born. In the later eighteenth century, they comprised up to a third of the labour force, but their prized job security was coming under ever greater threat.

Landowners and tenant farmers on arable estates employed a core of reliable, trusted labourers on a more or less permanent basis. The specialist skills of good ploughmen and shepherds were highly prized. These workers gained a double premium in the form of regular employment and higher wages.[7] To this core, they added casual labourers as the rhythms of the seasons dictated. Labour was particularly in demand at haymaking and harvest time. By contrast, winter work was scarcer and poorly paid. With little or no job security, agricultural labourers were vulnerable to economic change. Wage levels held up reasonably well during the period of the French wars (1793–1815) when demand for agricultural produce was buoyant and prices high. Moreover, recruitment to the armed forces even meant labour shortages in some areas, despite the obstinate rise in population.[8] A male labourer might then earn ten to twelve shillings (50–60p) a week at harvest time. In the winter, this could fall to seven or eight shillings (35–40p) a week.

The return of peace in 1815 changed the picture dramatically. For both landowners and tenants, the easy profits of the war years came to an abrupt halt. Many found themselves strapped for cash, particularly when – as was frequently the case – they had taken out loans to finance improvements during a period of easy credit and were now faced with crippling repayment bills just as their own incomes were squeezed by falling agricultural prices. The landed interest did not lack for influential spokesmen in parliament, and Select Committees on Agricultural Distress were established in 1821, 1833 and 1836. These produced compelling evidence that many property owners were indeed 'distressed'. Some sold up and others survived only because creditors were accommodating or the family had other sources of income. Parliamentary committees exaggerated the bleakness. Some areas did much better than others. Farmers fared worse on heavy clay soils, where agricultural productivity was always hard-won, than they did on the lighter soils, where adaptable farmers could turn to produce whose prices had fallen less far. Pastoral areas did better than arable ones. Livestock prices generally held up well and, in some counties of the north and west, it is doubtful if there was much of an agricultural depression at all.

Most agricultural labourers, however, worked on arable farms. It is easy to see why the general trend of agricultural wages was downward in the first half of the nineteenth century, despite modest improvements in the later 1830s and 1840s. Farmers found labour costs easiest to cut, not least because demography produced an ever greater imbalance between labour supply and demand. Between 1811 and 1851, the population of the predominantly rural counties of England increased by 53 per cent.[9] The return to the land of thousands of demobilised soldiers and sailors from 1815 only exacerbated the problem. Agricultural wages fell by about a third in the years 1814–22, leaving families in a state of almost continuous dependence on charity and the poor law.[10]

Such estimates conceal substantial regional variations. Wages held up best in pastoral areas where demand for labour – particularly for those tending animals – was less seasonal. In industrialising counties such as Lancashire, where alternative labour opportunities were relatively plentiful, wage levels were consistently higher than in southern and eastern counties. In the south and east, where arable counties predominated, rural wage levels ran higher in areas close to London's apparently insatiable demand for labour. Elsewhere in the south-east, lack of labour mobility contributed both to low agricultural wages and also to structural inefficiencies in the overall labour force.[11]

Even then, men's agricultural wages were higher than those of women. Women worked in the fields in labour 'gangs' and, in the pastoral sector, as dairymaids and cheese-makers with some fruit-picking in the autumn. Economic historians assert that the employment of women and children on the land declined in the first half of the nineteenth century.[12] While this is probably true, we should note that women's employment was considerably under-recorded in nineteenth-century censuses. Their contribution to the agricultural labour force, particularly before the widespread introduction of agricultural machinery, remained significant, if subordinate.[13]

Agricultural labourers were not among the groups most prone to disturbance, still less to riot or rebellion. The small parishes characteristic of arable England were controlled by the local landowner, usually abetted by the Church of England clergyman, who might well be a local magistrate, or related to the landowner – or both. In such circumstances, labourers learned to respect their betters and to count their blessings. In any case, even if such lessons were forgotten, a dispersed and fragmented labour force is difficult to organise, still less to politicise.

Nevertheless, the voice of 'Hodge' – the disparaging name often attached to the agricultural labourer – was heard in this period. A rapid rise in food prices provoked riots in East Anglia during 1816. The most substantial disturbance took place at Littleport, near Ely (Cambridgeshire), where labourers armed with clubs and pitchforks gathered in the main street, demanding higher wages. They broke shop windows and confronted the vicar, Revd J. Vachell, who was also a magistrate, looting the vicarage when he threatened them with a pistol. It took the arrival of troops to end the disturbance. The rioters were speedily tried. Five were hanged and nine transported to Australia. Revd Vachell was awarded more than £700 to compensate him for the damage done to the vicarage.[14]

Still more serious disturbances occurred throughout the south-east of England in 1830–31. The so-called Swing Riots, named after their supposed but mythical leader 'Captain Swing', had their origins in protests against high food prices, inadequate wages and the introduction of threshing machines, which threatened one of the few sources of winter work for agricultural labourers. The main targets of threatening letters and other forms of abuse were authority figures: farmers who paid below the going wage rate; clerical magistrates ('Parson justasses', as one letter termed them) likely to compromise their pastoral role in the harsh administration of justice; poor law overseers known to be mean or uncharitable. The riots were real and genuinely threatening. Much damage was done – not least to threshing machines, the wide-spread introduction of which the rioters probably delayed by a generation. But this was selective, and considered, hostility rather than blind hunger protest. In some villages the rioters carried slogans calling for parliamentary reform and an end to 'corruption'. It is also noticeable that some tenant farmers and gentry sympathised with the labourers, valuing the continuance of mutually respectful rural communities.

The Swing Riots overlapped with, and in some cases supported, the political agitation for parliamentary reform (see Chapter 20). Authorities already alarmed by the extent of popular agitation were unlikely to be lenient with the rioters, however genuine their grievances. The full majesty of the law was cranked up. A large num-ber of capital sentences were commuted, to avoid provoking further agitation. Only nineteen rioters were hanged. However, five hundred were transported to Australia and a further six hundred imprisoned.[15]

III. Innovation and improvement

Agricultural improvement, both in the arable and the pastoral sectors, was a pro-nounced feature in the development of a national market for goods. The use of what used to be called '**new crops**' actually began in the sixteenth and seventeenth centuries. Their main purposes were to restore fertility to soil weakened by consistent crop farming and to provide fodder for livestock. The new crops were much more exten-sively farmed from the later eighteenth century onwards as rising prices and general agricultural prosperity encouraged greater landowner investment.

New crops

These included clover, lucerne and sainfoin, forms of grass mostly grown for animal fodder. Turnips and swedes, in essence a hardier variety of turnip, were also grown for fodder but also formed part of the human diet. Many new crops were 'leguminous'. Legumes, a family of plants including peas and beans, have pods and nodules on their roots which fix nitrogen in the soil, thus increasing its fertility.

Varying forms of crop rotation were also introduced in the eighteenth century. Their main purpose was to reduce the amount of time during which land was unproductive, or 'fallow', while it recovered from the process of bearing crops. Increased productivity was necessary to keep up with growing demand. The most famous of these rotations was the so-called 'Norfolk system', a four-year cycle of wheat, turnips, barley and clover, but there were many variants, adapted to different types of soil.

Many accounts of agricultural improvement stress the importance of key individuals, such as Charles ('Turnip') Townshend (1674–1738), who gave up a highly successful political career to pursue agricultural experiments on his Norfolk estate in the last years of his life, **Thomas Coke** and **Robert Bakewell**. These men were important, even if the number of innovations for which they can claim personal credit has been exaggerated. There were very many 'agricultural improvers'. It is more helpful to see the Cokes and the Bakewells as symptomatic of opportunities grasped and of innovations implemented in response to new market opportunities. Agricultural improvements were well publicised by a number of influential writers. The best known was **Arthur Young**, who wrote indefatigably, and always optimistically, on the subject for more than forty years. He was appointed Secretary to the Board of Agriculture in 1793. The Board was founded with government money to provide advice on agricultural improvement. In the years 1793 and 1817, the Board, headed by Sir John Sinclair, published a series of accounts, county by county, of the state of agriculture in England. Young's writings were more enthusiastic than reflective and he was more interested in innovation than in celebrating established methods which had been proven to work. An altogether cooler, empirically grounded, approach was taken by **William Marshall**. How influential these publications were is difficult to estimate. It could be argued that the landed interest required little incentive to invest and improve when the price of wheat almost doubled, as it did during the 1790s. However, publications such as *Farmers' Journal* and *Farmers' Magazine* kept up the pressure for change and probably contributed to keeping agricultural improvement fashionable even when, as after 1815, it was not especially profitable. Altogether weightier ballast was provided when the Royal Agricultural Society was founded in 1838.[16] By 1850, a number of county agricultural societies were in existence, providing social networking and practical advice in more or less equal measure.

Thomas Coke, 1754–1842

Born in London into an established Norfolk landowning family, Coke became a Whig MP soon after he inherited a large estate at Holkham (Norfolk) in 1776. Here, with the help of the many practical agriculturalists he gathered around him, he conducted experiments to improve the quality of his land. Coke's personal importance has probably been exaggerated since some of the changes he claimed as his own had been practised in Norfolk for several years before he took them up and much of the practical work done during

▶

his own time relied on efficient and skilful tenant farmers. Nevertheless, Coke managed the process of granting long leases to good, improving tenants and both his personal involvement – he claimed to have invested half a million pounds in agricultural improvements – and his conscientious oversight deserve to be recognised. He was created first Earl of Leicester in 1837.

Robert Bakewell, 1725–1795

Born near Loughborough, Bakewell worked for most of his life on a 450-acre farm at Dishley Grange, near his birthplace. He conducted extensive breeding experiments and was responsible for the development of 'Leicester sheep' and Leicestershire longhorn cattle, both remarkable for the meat they yielded. He also developed a new breed of black horses noted for their strength. He improved grass yields by irrigation, flooding meadows and building a canal for the purpose. Recent research has suggested that his fame depends at least as much on the publicity he received from influential contacts like Arthur Young and William Marshall as on breeding methods, some of which were already being used by others in the Midlands.

Arthur Young, 1741–1820

Young was born in London and apprenticed to a wine merchant in King's Lynn (Norfolk) before trying his hand at practical farming in Hertfordshire, where he was unsuccessful. His writings on the need for improvement of agricultural land and the cultivation of wastes included *The Farmer's Guide in the Hiring and Stocking of Farms* (1770), *Political Arithmetic . . . Policy in the Encouragement of Agriculture* (1773). He founded the magazine *Annals of Agriculture* in 1784, which survived, albeit on low sales, until 1815.

William Marshall, c1745–1818

Marshall, the son of a yeoman farmer, was born Yorkshire's North Riding. He is best known for his series of publications on rural economy in England, beginning with a volume on Norfolk, published in 1787. He was a thorough and painstaking researcher and he resented what he saw as the more cavalier pronouncements of his rival, Arthur Young. In the last decade of his life, he devoted himself to rearranging the Board of Agriculture county reports into consolidated regional form.

In strictly numerical terms, agriculture remained the most important employer in Britain until the 1860s. Rural populations increased less fast than urban ones but they still increased substantially. During the period 1789–1815, for example, they went up by 26 per cent.[17] It has been estimated that more than a third of the population in 1800 was engaged in farming of one kind or another.[18] Such a concentration necessarily required an infrastructure of specialist craftsmen: wheelwrights, saddlers, blacksmiths, carpenters, masons, thatchers and the like. Links between land and industry were also much closer than a surface appraisal might suggest. The drink industry is perhaps the best example of this. Merchants acted as middlemen supplying brewers with barley for conversion into malt. As population grew, so the drink trade expanded to meet demand. Barley became a specialist crop grown in much of East Anglia, Hertfordshire and south Nottinghamshire.[19] Likewise, hops were farmed extensively in Kent. The abiding importance of links between urban and rural society was emphasised annually in the south-east of England in September and early October when hordes of migrant workers, most of them normally resident in London's East End, descended on the county to work as hop-pickers.

By the early nineteenth century, the largest factories in London were breweries, with Southwark at the centre of the trade. The Anchor Brewery in Southwark's Park Street was owned from 1781 by the firm of Barclay and Perkins. Producing more than 330,000 barrels of beer a year in the early nineteenth century, it was then the largest in the world, exceeding the output even of the mighty Whitbreads and Trumans.[20] Few provincial towns lacked a brewery. Burton-on-Trent (Staffordshire) became the brewing capital of the Midlands, but its population grew slowly, from 4,600 in 1800 to only 8,500 in 1850.[21] Market towns, such as Horsham in Sussex, Banbury in Oxfordshire and Hoddesdon in Hertfordshire, all had breweries which thrived on supplying the ever-expanding needs of the larger towns. Aping developments in manufacturing industry, however, smaller breweries were, by the middle of the nineteenth century, either closed down or consolidated into larger, and much more integrated, enterprises. They involved barley and malt merchants, the manufacturing process itself and also, at point of sale, an increasing number of 'tied' public houses supplying beer only from a particular brewer.[22]

In Scotland, similarly, many breweries in the early nineteenth century were small-scale, rural and vulnerable to competition from larger firms in Glasgow and Edinburgh. Among the smaller towns, Alloa, situated in the even smaller county of Clackmannanshire, stood apart. Despite having a population barely over 6,000 in 1850, it was home to no fewer than nine major breweries. It was known locally as Scotland's 'beeropolis'. As in England, the process of consolidation quickened with the more rapid expansion of the brewing trade from the 1850s.[23]

IV. Parliamentary enclosure

For many years, the most intensively studied aspect of agricultural change in this period was the enclosure movement, particularly **enclosures of land**, effected by Acts of Parliament. In the years 1750–1850, more than 4,000 separate Acts of Parliament were passed which sanctioned the enclosure of land in villages throughout England. Together they enclosed almost 7 million acres, just over a fifth of the then cultivated acreage of England. Both the chronology and the purpose of parliamentary enclosure need some refinement, however. Enclosing previously open fields had been going on for centuries. We should see parliamentary enclosure as the culmination of a long process. Much of the land enclosed by parliament after 1760 had not been previously enclosed by landowner agreement because holdings were complex, disputed or awkwardly scattered. On one level, parliamentary enclosure was a process of rationalisation and tidying up. On another, its social and economic consequences were both important and controversial.

> ### Enclosure of land
>
> The process whereby the limits of separate pieces of land were formally divided, usually by hedges, fences or ditches. The ownership of enclosed land could readily be identified and recorded. Enclosures are usually contrasted with 'open-field' farming, where a large number of proprietors own, and usually themselves farm, narrow strips of land with fewer, if any, obvious boundaries. These strips were normally scattered across the field rather than consolidated as a block. Typically, a village would have two or three such fields.

Enclosure was undertaken for a variety of reasons. The ending of open fields might create more efficient farming since landholdings would be more convenient to work. Enclosure gave owners greater freedom to make the improvements they considered most appropriate. As Arthur Young declaimed in 1808, 'By giving an exclusive property to the soil, the owner has his industry unfettered . . . his talents, his energy, and his capital are free to be employed for his own benefit; he thrives and national prosperity follows in his train.'[24] Enclosure of common and waste was undertaken to increase the area of land under cultivation. Enclosure also afforded an opportunity for getting rid of **tithes**, a complex and vexatious form of property.[25] At enclosure, tithe owners, who might be either laymen or clergy, received an allocation of land in lieu of their tithe rights. Different factors influenced the decision to pursue enclosure but the prime agitators for change were the greater landowners. They knew by 1800 that enclosed land could be let out for substantially greater sums than unenclosed, in some cases four times as much. It has been estimated that the landowner's gross return on his investment in enclosure was between 15 and 20 per cent. As such, it was 'by far the most profitable use of capital in connection with land'.[26]

Tithes

Tithe means 'tenth', in this case a tenth of the produce of the land, originally payable to the Church. Tithe owners were entitled to collect tithes 'in kind' (a tenth of the corn, every tenth pig, etc.), although they increasingly accepted cash payments in lieu. Tithes were a contentious property, not least because the tithe owner was legally entitled to a tenth of the gross, not the net, produce. Tithe owners therefore benefited from the investment and effort put in by others.

Although profitable once the job was done, parliamentary enclosure could be a very expensive business. The Board of Agriculture estimated that the average cost was £1 8s 0d (£1.40) per acre in the 1790s.[27] A strict average is not helpful, however. In larger parishes where land holdings were contested, or where open-field farming had been unduly complex, the cost could run to several pounds per acre.

In 1750, open fields remained most common in the English midlands, and particularly in the arable lands of the south midlands and the central southern counties. The two counties where parliamentary enclosure was most extensive were Oxfordshire (54 per cent of land thus enclosed) and Northamptonshire (50 per cent).[28] Enclosure of waste land and rough common pasture was much more common in the north and east of England, particularly the counties of Yorkshire, Derbyshire, Lincolnshire and Norfolk.[29]

The overall impact of parliamentary enclosure has provoked considerable debate, polarising historians across an ideological divide. Historians on the left have considered it, in Edward Thompson's famous phrase, 'a plain enough case of class robbery'.[30] On this analysis, smaller landowners, unable to pay the costs of enclosure, were forced to sell up, some becoming mere labourers. Those who subsisted on common land lost out and 'squatters' were turned off land which became, quite clearly and as never before, private property. The picture which is painted is of the rich taking from the poor, depriving them of their common rights. These included keeping cows on common land, 'gleaning' the remnants of harvested corn or other crops, collecting wood for winter fuel and many other small, but cumulatively crucial, benefits deriving from common ownership.[31]

On the other side of the argument, territory occupied mostly by economic rather than social historians, parliamentary enclosure has been seen as a necessary process of rationalisation. It helped improve the quality of the land, and contributed to the feeding of a rapidly growing population. Both the practical process of enclosing land, and the greater productivity which followed it, created and sustained jobs. Without enclosure, the risk of famine and demographic disaster would have been much higher.

As is usually the case with such extreme positions, detailed research tends to reveal the virtues of occupying some middle ground. Parliamentary enclosure did indeed invalidate common rights on thousands of acres of English farmland. It is not difficult to point to examples of extreme hardship created by enclosure. On Otmoor (Oxfordshire), proposals for parliamentary enclosure were furiously contested for almost half a century and the process was not completed until 1829. The number of folk denied direct access to land then increased by 70 per cent.[32] But were such examples typical? If the rural labour force was 'proletarianised', the process was well under way before parliamentary enclosure began. Relatively few agricultural labourers retained common rights by the 1780s.[33] Perhaps too much has been made of the very real plight, acknowledged by Arthur Young among others, of relatively few.

The impact of parliamentary enclosure was hardly the watershed its apologists believed. Enclosure of waste land brought more land into cultivation, but open-field arable enclosures produced fewer benefits. It has been estimated that open-field enclosure increased the productivity of English and Welsh agriculture by only about 3 per cent, when the overall productivity increase in the period 1700–1850 was about 50 per cent.[34] Similarly, while enclosure put pressure on the smaller landowners, it is not easy to demonstrate that the process was particularly significant in the much longer-run process which consolidated land in fewer hands.

Parliamentary enclosure was important since it significantly altered farming practices on the land to which it was subjected. It also directly and adversely affected the lives of a small proportion of the rural population. Overall, however, historians have been beguiled into investing an extremely well-documented process with disproportionate significance. Longer-term developments, rather than specific short initiatives, were the more important in explaining agricultural change in the late eighteenth and early nineteenth centuries.

8

....

Industrialism: impact and conflict

I. The organisation of work

Industrial revolutions generate more fundamental and long-lasting changes
than any other man-made phenomena. Preceding chapters have examined broad
changes in demography, social structure, urbanisation and agriculture. This chapter
looks more directly at the impact of industrialism on work and attempts to explain
why this fundamental transformation engendered so much social conflict.

The extent to which the nature of work changed depended upon the occupation.
The agricultural sector was little changed by mechanisation until the 1850s but
the organisation of work altered as more was done by waged labourers rather than
farm servants. Farm service declined partly because tenant farmers found it more
economical to pay for agricultural work as and when needed. By the middle of the
nineteenth century, women were finding significantly less work in the fields, except
at haymaking and harvest time (see Chapter 7). Farm service also declined because
younger men and women were moving away from the village in larger numbers to
seek employment in the expanding manufacturing and commercial sectors.

Gender differentials for waged work were substantial. Women were rarely paid
more than half the wages earned by men doing similar work. It was, therefore, very
difficult for women to be financially independent.[1] Prostitution might provide
larger short-term rewards but at immense risk to health, safety and, of course,
reputation. Younger women in search of respectable urban employment often found
it living in as domestic servants. Here they earned little pay, and had less free time,
but they did gain some security. A key indicator of middle-class status and
respectability in nineteenth-century urban Britain was the ability to employ domestic
servants. Census evidence shows that about 40 per cent of the female workforce in
1851 was occupied as domestic servants. This is almost certainly an over-estimate.
The extent of women's work was frequently under-recorded by census enumerators,
who were much more likely to capture in their notebooks workers who 'lived in' with
respectable families than they were women who did part-time work and who moved
about. They were certainly not encouraged to record prostitution as an occupation.
On the other hand, in respectable society – which by the middle of the nineteenth
century included upper-working-class families headed by skilled men in regular
employment – it was considered inappropriate for women to do waged work. The
emphasis was on duties in the home. A 'respectable' wife might well be an unpaid
domestic manager, responsible for the family budget. She might do charitable work;
she would be expected to master 'domestic accomplishments' such as needlework and
musical performance. She would not go out to work.

The biggest shift in the overall balance of work was from agriculture to manufacturing. In 1850, manufacturing and mining accounted for almost 43 per cent of the labour force. Given the emphasis which used to be given to the textile industry in explaining change, it might be assumed that the main impetus for this substantial shift was mechanised production and the concentration of the workforce in large factories. We have examined both the importance of non-textile employment in this period and also the tenacity of hand-craft even in the textile industry (Chapters 5 and 6). As one historian puts it, 'it is hardly much of a distortion to suggest that the manufacture of finished consumer goods down to the mid-nineteenth century was for the most part small-scale and un-mechanised'.[2] Small enterprises using older forms of organisation and production played a crucial role in the industrial expansion of nineteenth-century Britain.[3]

Changes in the organisation of work were most dramatic in the new factories. Time-discipline was tightened (see Chapter 6) through clocking in and out. Fines for lateness were commonplace. This was an aspect of a broader phenomenon: the greater control which many employers sought over their workers' lives. The cotton magnate **Henry Ashworth** attacked Lord Shaftesbury's proposals for a maximum ten-hour working day in cotton factories. He noted that factory owners whose businesses were in the country enjoyed 'many opportunities of controlling the habits and ministering to the comforts of those in their employ'. They should take every opportunity of introducing disciplines which would conduce to the happiness of poor families. For many, work in the mills had been a release from debt and low-paid, uncertain improvement. His employees enjoyed 'The feeling of discipline and good order' which beneficent superintendence by the factory owner was able to secure.[4] Ashworth asserted that the 'control and superintendence' which he and his brother exerted over their employees conduced to 'their moral and social improvement'. He clearly thought nothing of inspecting the labourers' bedding and furniture and stated that 'their income and habits of life' were 'carefully enquired into, and remarks thereon are entered in books which are kept for the purpose'.[5]

Henry Ashworth, 1794–1880

Born in Bolton, Ashworth became one of the most prominent cotton masters in Lancashire. Like many, he was a nonconformist. His Quaker background made him wary of, and often overtly hostile to, the landed classes. He was proprietor of the New Eagley Mill, near Bolton. Here he built a cotton community including, in addition to a large factory employing more than 700 men, women and children, cottages for his workmen, schools and a library. His primary objective was undoubtedly profit but he demonstrated how a well-run community could enhance the self-respect and self-discipline of his workers. He engaged in numerous controversies in the 1830s and 1840s, notably over child labour in factories, the new poor law and the repeal of the Corn Laws. He opposed the activities of trade unions and especially strike activity.

II. Luddism

The nonconformist conscience, of which Ashworth's is a good example, was actuated by a belief that order, regularity and discipline were the sure route not only to economic progress but also eternal salvation. His prescriptions left little room either for doubt or denial. If they disagreed, however, his workers had limited weapons at their disposal. Nevertheless, their fight for jobs, decent wages and conditions was both impressive and sustained.

The word 'Luddism' has acquired a wholly misleading modern usage. It implies the use of violence and destruction to oppose any form of progress. The early nineteenth-century Luddites, who took their name from their almost certainly mythical leader Ned Ludd, were no vandals. They were highly skilled textile and hosiery oper-atives whose job security and high wages were threatened by the introduction of new machinery. Luddites operated in well-defined areas of the country, particularly the old craft woollen textile districts of Wiltshire and Gloucestershire, the East Midlands, particularly Nottinghamshire and Leicestershire, and the West Riding of Yorkshire. Their attacks were carefully selected and their activities supported, more often than not, by a community which had developed a strong sense of craft-identity. It was that identity which was being threatened. Thus, the attack on cloth-finishing machinery by Wiltshire craftsmen in 1802 was accompanied by calls to have such machinery declared illegal and by petitions to parliament to uphold craft traditions and practices.[6]

Elsewhere, and particularly in the hosiery industry of the East Midlands in 1811–12, protests concentrated on new machinery producing stockings of inferior quality which were woven, cut up (the short name was 'cut-ups') and stitched, in contrast to the fine stockings knitted by craftsmen. Skilled workers were threatened not only by machinery but by the government's so-called 'Orders in Council' (see Chapter 13) which damaged the export trade to the United States and thus employ-ment opportunities. Since 1799, when peaceful 'combinations of workmen' were declared illegal, non-violent trade union activity had not been an option (see Chapter 12). Master manufacturers in the hosiery trade took the opportunity to reduce the prices they paid to knitters, thus provoking violence against the machines. It has been estimated that about a thousand stocking frames were destroyed in the year from March 1811 to February 1812.[7] In Yorkshire, skilled workers protested against the introduction of shearing frames from 1812 to 1816. Again, machines were broken and some larger woollen mills experienced arson attacks. Physical violence was used on some mill owners known to be particularly unsympathetic to their employees and to skilled out-workers. One, William Horsfall, the owner of Ottiwell Mill in Marsden near Huddersfield, was killed.

The authorities, concerned also by growing radical activity, reacted sternly. Machine-breaking was declared a capital crime; seventeen Luddites were executed for it in 1813. Substantial troop reinforcements were moved to the affected areas.

It is not clear to what extent the Luddites were also political radicals calling not only for parliamentary reform but also for the overthrow of a corrupt government.[8] It does, however, seem probable that the response of the authorities played a part in radicalising many from 1812 onwards. The spies employed by the government and local magistrates naturally played up whatever evidence they could cobble together of secret meetings, drilling with live weapons on remote Yorkshire moors and even plans for violent revolution. However, the rumours of such activity, inevitably patchy and usually unsubstantiated as they were, were extensive enough to discount pure fabrication. Whether they posed any real threat to the existing order is, of course, another question and must be doubtful.

III. Standards of living

Any evaluation of the impact of the industrial revolution in the late eighteenth and early nineteenth centuries should take into account its effect on the standard of living of those who lived through it. For nearly half a century now, a debate has raged on whether the majority of the population benefited from the changes. For many years, what seems now to be a false argument went on between economic historians using quantitative data (wage and price levels etc.) and social historians relying much more on qualitative information related to working conditions, the state of towns and contemporary accounts.[9] Economic historians used to be confident that wage data confirmed what their training encouraged them to believe anyway: that substantial economic growth fed its way, not equally but significantly, into greater job opportunities, higher wages and thus improved living standards. Social historians concentrated on long working hours, the abuses of child labour, and the high levels of mortality produced by the desperately unhealthy state of accommodation in overcrowded towns.

The danger was that a crucial question would default to a dialogue of the deaf. Fortunately, in the last thirty years, attempts have been made to bring quantitative and qualitative issues together and also to try to compensate for the inevitable gaps in, and possibly the distorting nature of, much of the evidence. The task is undeniably difficult. Wage data do not reliably equate to earnings. We know much more about men's wages than about women's and we have more data about men in continuous employment than we have about casual labourers. Regional wage variations add a further complication. Workers moved into, and out of, urban employment with bewildering rapidity. Many experienced periods of short-term working and of unemployment. Reliable quantitative information about unemployment before the middle of the nineteenth century is virtually absent. Some optimists attempted to correct this while reaching broadly similar overall conclusions. One influential contribution from the 1980s concluded that 'material gains were even bigger after 1820 than optimists had previously claimed' and that the low wage levels of the troubled years 1815–19 were followed by a long, and more or less unbroken, period of improvement down to 1850. It concludes that 'pessimists must retreat to the pre-1820 era where workers' net gains look as elusive . . . as in past studies of single occupations'.[10]

This proved to be the high-water mark of the optimists' case. Since then, most protagonists have come to the debate bearing caveats. Discussion of earnings and wage levels has run into the sand as historians have failed to get to grips with the complexities both of regional variations and the structure of income. How much weight should be given to the contribution of women and children? While this varied, most estimates suggest that women and children in early-industrial Britain contributed between a quarter and a third of the family income. In any case, 'income' – even it could be precisely calculated – does not usually encompass **payments in kind** or the food and fuel which common rights provided for many rural workers. Since common rights were coming under attack at this time (see Chapter 7), it is likely that such customary or traditional family enhancements were not making the same contribution by the end of the eighteenth century: precisely the time when, as economic historians generally agree, prices were going up. Estimates of consumption suggest that there was a pronounced downwards movement from the 1770s to the early 1820s, when a modest rise began. Over the period from 1780 to 1850, consumption of such previously luxury imports as sugar and tea, which were now more widely available, increased by only a modest amount, although some acceleration is observable from the 1830s onwards.[11] New work on prices suggests that these declined less after 1815 than previous studies had calculated, thus helping to offset at least some of the optimistic projections about the rapidity with which real wages increased from the 1820s onwards.[12]

Payment in kind

This phrase relates to payments made by providing goods or food in lieu of cash. They were an important element in the economy of most families at least until the early nineteenth century.

Other indicators, such as rising infant mortality, point in a similarly pessimistic direction. Three children out of every twenty born in the 1840s died in the first year of life. Any idea that the optimists have 'won' the standard of living debate is at best premature and at worst plain wrong. No amount of sophisticated manipulation of inadequate data makes that data more useful in itself and too many optimists have made too much of inadequate, unreliable or just plain duff figures. Historians are perhaps wiser to take a step back from quantification and to reflect on the nature of social change during this period. It was an exceptionally volatile age. Ever more people moved from countryside to towns. The rate of population growth – one of the few relevant areas for which statistics are reasonably reliable – was unprecedentedly high. It shifted the balance between labour supply and demand and also, in general, pushed up prices.

Economic circumstances also lurched uneasily and uncontrollably between boom and slump. Although boom years comfortably outnumbered slumps in the first half of the nineteenth century, the consequences of a slump were severe. Slumps were invariably accompanied by wage-cuts, short-time working and rising unemployment. In boom years, most of the indicators suggest that employers required their workers to toil for longer hours than had been the case in the eighteenth century. Urban living conditions in those areas occupied by most working people were appalling. Population surge and consequent overcrowding meant inadequate basic amenities and further risks to health. As the physician to the Sheffield Infirmary noted in 1843: 'We have no hesitation in asserting that the sufferings of the working classes, and consequently the rate of mortality, are greater now than in former times.'[13]

No one doubts that, over time, an industrial revolution increases living standards. In the shorter term it also increases inequality. Some skilled workers, such as engineers and printers, did very well out of economic change in the late eighteenth and early nineteenth centuries. Most, even those in regular employment, experienced only small increases in real wages which needed to be set against substantial environmental deterioration. Sustained improvements in working-class living standards had to wait for the last quarter of the nineteenth century.

IV. A new working class?

There is no doubt that the period 1780–1850 was characterised by substantial conflict. Change brought destabilisation both at home and abroad. The American Revolution had developed a new type of state, with power and authority based on a system of checks and balances with no deference given to hereditary privileges. The new United States had no monarch. The French Revolution made warring flesh of what had previously been rather rarefied ideas about 'liberty' and 'equality'. It is possible to see both the French Revolutionary and Napoleonic Wars (see Chapters 12 and 13) as a conflict between old and new systems of government. The Industrial Revolution, linked to huge population growth, produced arguably the most radical changes of all. It gave rise to a series of conflicts threatening to established hierarchies and it could easily be represented as 'class conflict'. It increased the power and influence of the middle classes (see Chapter 4), some of whom were challenging the very right of the aristocracy to rule. If industrialism transformed patterns of work, putting greater distance between employers and workers, while emphasising that, for the owners of the new factories, the purpose of industrial production was profit, then it followed that the interests of worker and owner were diametrically opposed. Employers believed that paying high wages threatened profitability and competitiveness; workers felt that their employers exploited their labour – the only property they had to sell. The basis seemed to have been laid for the emergence of a mutually antagonistic three-tier class system comprising aristocracy, middle class and working class.

This, in simplified form, was the argument of Karl Marx and his collaborator Friedrich Engels. It surfaced most powerfully in their *Communist Manifesto* of 1848, which, drawing on evidence from the world's first industrial nation, looked forward to a new social order to be controlled by the numerically superior workers. This was the so called '**dictatorship of the proletariat**'. Analyses of social change in early industrial Britain have been heavily influenced by this class-based approach. By no means all the historians writing on the topic were themselves Marxists, but the historiography of the 1960s and 1970s was dominated by discussions of how, and when, the English working class was made.[14] How valid is the assertion that the numerous political and social conflicts in Britain at this time were examples of 'class consciousness'?

Dictatorship of the proletariat

This phrase is much used but not so often explained. Karl Marx intended it to describe a transitional period during which wage-labouring workers (the 'proletariat') would need to take over power in the state in order to eliminate the old, and immensely damaging, relations of production between 'capital' and 'labour'. As the Communist Manifesto put it '. . . the first step on the path to the workers' revolution is the elevation of the proletariat to the position of ruling class'. Marx and Engels saw all hierarchies as oppressive. Class distinctions would thereafter be abolished and new, benign and above all 'classless' social organisations and arrangements would take their place. It never happened.

It is not difficult to demonstrate hostility between different ranks in society and beguiling to conclude that they derive from different economic perspectives. Many landowners, whose incomes were not rising as fast as those of bankers and merchants, considered that the new 'money men' were getting too big for their boots. They had a number of articulate mouthpieces in parliament. **Edmund Burke**'s critique of the follies of the French Revolution contained within it a stinging attack on what he called 'a great moneyed interest' which had 'insensibly grown up, and with it a great power'. He was concerned that 'Nations are wading deeper and deeper into an ocean of boundless debt'. A moneyed interest which did not share the principles and attitudes (Burke's word was 'manners') of the established elites threatened the stability of the state.[15] Many examples of attacks on the moneyed classes might be cited, more from landed, Tory-supporting groups, than from political radicals, although journals such as *Black Dwarf* tended to portray them as merely in league with the aristocracy to keep down the poor.[16]

Edmund Burke, 1729–1797

Burke was a leading Whig politician and thinker, born in Ireland and educated at Trinity College Dublin. He became an MP in 1766 and made a name for himself as an eloquent and persuasive speaker. He supported most of the Whig causes, including support for the American colonists in the 1770s, but always distanced himself from abstract principles of the Enlightenment. He argued that established political traditions reflected not only practical wisdom but also the will of God. He is best remembered for his *Reflections on the Revolution in France*, which prophesied that the Revolution, in defying the established order, would end in bloodshed and chaos. He broke with most of his Whig allies and supported the government of Pitt the Younger from 1792 until his death.

Yet hostility between the upper and middle classes was hardly a defining characteristic of social relations in early nineteenth-century Britain. There were, of course, numerous individual differences and antagonisms but much more bound them together than separated them. As we have seen (see Chapter 4), the middle classes both owned, and had a healthy respect for, property. At the upper end of the stratum, bankers and merchants shared seats in the Commons with prosperous landowners. Mutual respect, modified by intermittent exasperation, characterised the relationship. It was also the case, of course, that aristocratic wealth was being enhanced during the industrial revolution by commercial activities and mining (see Chapter 3).

Perhaps more importantly, the lower middle classes had an acute sense of the importance of their property, however meagre, as setting them apart from the lower orders. They looked to protection from the authorities when mass demonstrations tipped over into violence. On such occasions, after all, it was the windows of small shopkeepers in the towns which were most likely to be broken and their shops ransacked if things got out of hand. It may be that the middle classes' propensity for joining voluntary societies broke down occupational barriers and enhanced a sense of separate urban identity.[17] Such a sense could be enhanced when nonconformists met together, in or out of the chapel. Nonconformists were still subject to discrimination. Until 1868, they had to pay church rates to support the Church of England, of which they were not members. They were also debarred from attending the universities of Oxford and Cambridge. Campaigns to change this situation were hard fought, but a sense of rooted class antagonism against the aristocratic elite was not an especially prominent feature.

It might be thought more likely that working people would develop a sense both of separateness and of antagonism both from the middle classes and from their aristocratic rulers. From the former, they might expect dire working conditions and poor pay, from the latter high taxes. The period saw much protest activity: food riots, labour disputes, mass meetings and ever more insistent calls for parliamentary reform (see Chapters 11 and 16). For E. P. Thompson, 'the outstanding fact of the period between 1790 and 1830 is the formation of *the* working class'. Harold Perkin's calculation was more precise. For him, the working class was born in the hectic, disturbed years of 1815–20.[18]

What *can* be discerned in the years before the passing of the Great Reform Act in 1832 (see Chapter 20) is a well-supported and strongly focused attack on the old power structure. Increasingly, these protests attracted substantial middle-class support. They represent another example of a long-established phenomenon: protest against a privileged, hereditary and mis-governing elite. They were not in themselves instances of class conflict.

The main argument against the emergence of a coherent working class in this period is the fragmentation of occupations and the tenacity of older forms of production, both hand-craft and workshop-based, at least until 1850 (see Chapter 6). It is plausible to see the riots in 1831 at Merthyr Tydfil against wage-cutting by the dominant Crawshay family as indicating a 'working class identity' in South Wales.[19] Both the Crawshay works at Cyfarthfa and the Guest concern at Dowlais were expanding rapidly. Operatives were working on nine furnaces in Cyfarthfa by 1830 and the production of pig-iron there had trebled in twenty years.[20] The strike showed an example of proletarian solidarity, although it is ironical that William Crawshay (1788–1867), the business head at Cyfarthfa, was a radical in politics and even favoured universal manhood suffrage. The scale and nature of the largest factories in south Lancashire, the West Riding of Yorkshire and in central Scotland might also conduce to proletarian consciousness. However, most textile firms were not large and many small industrial villages survived in Lancashire and Yorkshire. Beyond the iron and textile trades, workers were fragmented and lacked a common identity. A plethora of radical newspapers and journals might urge workers to act collectively to achieve improvements in wages and working conditions but the wide variety of experiences of work generally militated against combined action. Attempts at a General Union of the Working Classes failed in 1834 and most trade unions remained small, single-trade based, regional and the preserve of skilled workers.[21]

Even Chartism, much the most impressive movement of working people in nineteenth-century Britain, had both multiple targets and a divided leadership (see Chapter 21). For some Chartist leaders, like George Julian Harney and Ernest Jones, Chartism was a means of bringing working people to understand and embrace socialist principles. Harney said that his aim was to increase 'the happiness, prosperity and independence . . . of that class whose labour produces the wealth of the country'. For others, the objective was primarily political: to end the political dominance of the existing elite by extending the franchise to working men. One of their number, Thomas Cooper, ruefully remarked that it was necessary to 'get the people out to fight . . . they must be irresistible, if they were united'.[22] He was rightly sceptical of the possibilities for united action. For all its impressive cultural associations – Chartist concerts, Chartist co-operative shops, Chartist schools and the like, unprecedentedly strong support from women – the movement was more attractive to the skilled and literate working classes, except at times of deepest depression, and it was much stronger in some parts of the country than others.

Although industrialism produced profound social changes, clearly defined class consciousness was not one of them. Almost half a century on, it seems strange that so much ink was spilled in trying to explain the emergence of mutually antagonistic classes. Despite E. P. Thompson's ferociously articulate advocacy, no integrated working class ever was 'made'. In the three theoretical Marxist social constructs – aristocratic landowners, middle class and working class – there were usually greater social and cultural divisions within a class than there was economically driven 'class' antagonism. A larger gulf probably separated upper- and lower-middle-class group-ings than divided the commercial from the professional middle class (see Chapter 4). Within the working classes, divisions of skill, literacy and permanence of work opportunities were of paramount importance. The respectable artisan was more likely to view the casual dock labourer with disdain, even contempt, than to recognise an ally in a class war. British society in 1850 remained resolutely hierarchical, its population acutely aware of status, obligations and proprieties. Its intricate filigree required consciousness of many things – but rarely of class.

Section 2

Britain at War and Peace, 1780–1815

An engraving depicting the charge of Napoleon's Old Guard near the end of the Battle of Waterloo, 18 June 1815

The period covered by this Section is one of the most momentous in Britain's history. The country was at war for almost half of the period from 1690 to 1815. The Battle of Waterloo, pictured here, was a true watershed. It ended more than twenty years of almost continuous warfare with France and it established Britain's status as the dominant power in Europe. That status was hardly ever militarily challenged over the period covered by the remainder of this book. After Waterloo, and with the brief exception of the Crimean in the 1850s, Britain fought no further European wars until 1914. This Section explains why Britain and France renewed hostilities in the early months of 1793 and why, eventually, Britain emerged triumphant from the conflict (Chapters 12 and 13).

Before then, however, Britain had to come to terms with the loss of the thirteen American colonies. Failures during the American War of Independence led to prolonged political crisis in Britain and to a substantial increase in the size of the national debt (Chapter 9). Contemporaries considered the commercial advances made during the eighteenth century to be at risk, and the national mood when the American conflict ended in 1783 was decidedly pessimistic. How Britain recovered during the peacetime administration of the Younger Pitt and why Pitt himself dominated the politics of the 1780s and early 1790s are the key themes discussed in Chapter 10.

The French Revolution, which began in 1789, had a significant impact on Britain quite apart from being a contributory cause of the French wars which began in 1793. Revolutionary ideas were a divisive factor in British politics since they caused the break-up of the old Whig party, leading to a coalition which strengthened Pitt's position. Even more importantly, ideas concerning liberty, rights and citizenship energised political groups outside parliament. Tom Paine's *Rights of Man*, published in 1791–92, proved to be an immensely influential text, which educated and galvanised both middle-class radicals and artisan workers to press for parliamentary reform. The conflict of ideas between reformers and 'conservatives' is the dominant theme of Chapter 10. Radical activity and labour disputes continued after 1800 and are discussed in Chapter 15, as are developments towards modern political parties after the deaths of Pitt and Fox in 1806.

The period covered by this Section is also a critical one in the history of Ireland (Chapter 14). It witnessed a separate, if never independent, Irish parliament which lasted from 1782 to 1800. Events in France also had a considerable significance for Ireland. Revolutionary ideals acted as a stimulus on movements for independence from Britain. Also, once Britain was at war with France, Ireland was seen as a useful launch pad for a French invasion. The need to secure Ireland was one of the most important factors in the Pitt government's drive for a political Union. The Act of Union, which nationalist politicians considered to have been imposed on Ireland by a hostile power, was to become the touchstone for resistance to British rule throughout the nineteenth century.

9

····················

Government in crisis: the impact of the war for America

I. A war lost

On 3 September 1783, Great Britain endured an unusual experience. It signed a peace settlement, the Treaty of Versailles, to end a war it had lost.[1] Any prospect of retaining the thirteen north American colonies within the British empire had gone almost two years earlier when Brigadier-General O'Hara, representing General Cornwallis, presented a sword to the French commander General Rochambeau to symbolise the surrender of British forces at Yorktown to the American colonists. Contemporaries considered the likely consequences to be severe. As one historian has put it, 'The American Revolution was the first successful rebellion in modern history, and this considerably increased its contemporary impact and the damage it did to British prestige.'[2]

The war had, however, dragged on, allowing Britain to reassert its naval supremacy over France and Spain, the colonies' allies, during 1782. Britain was able to retain control of Gibraltar and also to prevent a combined Franco-Spanish attack on Jamaica. British recovery against these older foes enabled the country to sign a peace which was considerably less humiliating than it might otherwise have been. The thirteen colonies were, of course, lost but the other essentials of Britain's empire of trade were preserved. The French took the West Indian islands of Tobago and St Lucia, while Spain recovered the Mediterranean island of Minorca, captured by the British in 1708 during the War of the Spanish Succession. These losses were readily absorbed.

The real damage of the American war had been done not to Britain's armed forces, tactically outmanoeuvred though they had been, but to the authority of **King George III**. Failure to win a war in which victory had initially been assumed put greater pressure on the unpopular, but long-lived, government led by **Lord North**, the King's favourite and trusted adviser of. North had been Prime Minister since 1770. Once expected victories in America failed to materialise, opposition groups in parliament increasingly echoed public opinion, particularly among country gentlemen, when they attacked the government on the grounds of waste, inefficiency and corruption.

George III, 1738–1820

He was the son of Frederick, Prince of Wales (who died in 1751) and the grandson of George II, whom he succeeded to the throne in 1760. He came to the throne during the Seven Years War and his reign was punctuated by wars, notably that against the American colonies and the French Revolutionary and Napoleonic wars. For much of the latter part of his reign he was mentally ill and was declared medically unfit to govern after 1810, when his eldest son assumed royal duties as Prince Regent.

Frederick, Lord North, 1732–1792

Born in London the son of the third Baron Guilford (later first Earl of Guilford), he was educated at Eton and Oxford University and became an MP in 1754. He served in most of the short-lived governments of the 1760s before being appointed Prime Minister by the King in 1770. He remained in office until 1782 with the King's support. His ministry was controversial and he attracted special criticism – much of it exaggerated and some of it unfair – for his handling of the American war. He returned briefly to government in 1783 as Secretary of State in the brief Fox–North coalition, which, since the King hated Fox and his Whig supporters, ended both his friendship with the King and his ministerial career. He remained an opponent of Pitt throughout the 1780s. His political reputation has enjoyed partial rehabilitation in recent years, with his abilities as a finance minister and an administrator increasingly recognised.

Support for reform policies had been growing since the early 1760s, not least because leading politicians were concerned about the King's increasing influence over politics. Aristocratic Whig landowners had been the dominant force in British politics since 1714. This so-called 'Whig Oligarchy' lasted pretty much unchallenged until the early 1760s for two reasons. The first two Hanoverian monarchs, George I (1714–27) and George II (1727–60), had been persuaded that many in the Tory party, the opponents of the Whigs, wanted to restore the Stuart monarchy. Also, apart from strong views on foreign policy, European diplomacy and military matters, the first two Georges had little liking for, or interest in, the intricacies of domestic politics in Britain. Until the accession of George III, therefore, the Whigs had the field pretty much to themselves.[3]

The accession of George III in 1760 changed matters. The new King was the first Hanoverian monarch to have been born in Britain and he made it clear that he intended to assert the considerable rights which remained in royal hands after the deposition of James II in the so-called Glorious Revolution of 1688–89. He would play an active role in government, showing that the monarchy had much more than ceremonial functions. It was for the monarch to choose the Prime Minister and George's choice was always likely to fall upon men who respected his own powers. While it was, of course, necessary for the Prime Minister to command majorities in **parliament**, particularly the House of Commons, which had the sole power of voting taxes, George wished his Prime Minister to acknowledge the monarch's role as an equal partner in the business of government[4] and that ministries were genuinely his to choose. The politics of the 1760s were less stable than before largely because of the difficulty the King had in finding Prime Ministers both satisfying to him and also with a stable majority in parliament. When, in Lord North from 1770, he found one, he clung to him like a limpet.

Parliament

Then, as now, parliament consisted of two Houses, Commons and Lords. The House of Commons comprised 558 members (658 after the Act of Union with Ireland in 1801). Its members were elected by constituencies divided into counties and boroughs, although in practice many eighteenth-century elections went uncontested. The House of Lords comprised members of the aristocracy, who sat there either because they had inherited their titles or because they had been granted a peerage by the monarch, and the twenty-six bishops of the Church of England. In the 1780s, the House of Lords had much more power in its own right than now. Prime Ministers often sat in the Lords and it was normal for Cabinets to have a substantial majority of peers.

Some of the leading Whigs, having lost their grip on government, responded by claiming that the King was relying on 'secret advisers' and that what lay behind his claim to influence over government was a desire to reimpose autocratic rule. Since 1689, the Whigs had seen themselves as guardians of the people's liberties. This claim was as far-fetched as the idea that, given half a chance, George III would reveal himself as James II reincarnate. Still, it was a useful rallying cry for men deprived of power for the first time in two generations. The Whigs were not a political party in the modern sense, rather an association of family groupings who broadly agreed on a set of principles. It is too cynical to claim that these principles boiled down to the belief that Britain's government was safe only in their hands, but the assertion has more than a grain of truth. Certainly, their aversion to the exercise of royal influence was a constant factor.

In the late 1760s and early 1770s, however, many Whigs, led by the **Marquess of Rockingham** found a major policy issue – America – on which to attack both government and monarch. Many in the Whig opposition had taken up the cause of the American colonists. They argued that government attempts at increased taxation were ham-fisted, the means of governing the colonies from a distance ineffective and that damaging conflict was bound to ensue. Prominent among them was Edmund Burke.

Charles Watson-Wentworth, second Marquess of Rockingham, 1730–1782

Born in Yorkshire, he succeeded to his father's title in 1750. He therefore sat in the House of Lords throughout his career and was one of the richest aristocrats in Britain. He was Prime Minister in 1765–66, when his ministry asserted the right of Britain to tax the American colonies. He emerged as the leader of the main opposition Whig group in the 1770s and, as such, criticised the government's conduct of the war against the colonies and also attacked it for waste and for being subject to undue monarchical influence. The King reluctantly appointed him as Prime Minister in succession to North in March 1782. Before his death in early July, his ministry passed 'Crewe's Act', which excluded government revenue officers from sitting in the House of Commons, and 'Clerke's Act', which similarly barred government contractors.

The American issue also focused opposition on political rights. If the conflict with America turned on the right of British ministers to raise taxes on colonies which were not directly represented in parliament, how different was the position of that vast majority of the British adult population in the 1770s which did not have the right to vote? 'No taxation without representation' was a sound-bite which resonated almost as clearly in Great Britain as across the Atlantic. By no means all of those who supported the American colonists in parliament favoured an extension of the franchise in Britain but the two causes became ideologically linked.

II. Government in crisis, 1780–83

In 1780, the pressure on North's government intensified. He faced attacks from MPs favouring 'economical reform'. This was a predominantly Whig stratagem to cut out waste. Economical reform would save money but would also deprive government of much of its power to reward supporters with those offices, pensions and 'perks' carrying few, if any, duties beyond loyal, unreflective support for the government. The means of rewarding loyalty rested directly in many cases with the Crown. North's critics condemned him not only as ineffective but also as a pawn in the hands of the monarch. In February, the jurist and politician **John Dunning** introduced his famous resolution that the 'influence of the Crown has increased, is increasing and ought to be diminished'. 'The saving of money is but a secondary object. The reduction of the influence of the Crown is the first.'[5] His resolution passed by 233 votes to 215. In the following month, opposition Whig politicians followed the lead of **Revd Christopher Wyvill** in calling for parliamentary reform. The primary objective of Wyvill's so-called County Association Movement was to launch petitions against **sinecures** and government pensions.

John Dunning, 1731–1783

Dunning was born in Ashburton (Devon), the son of a lawyer. He made his reputation defending the East India Company against its Dutch counterpart in the 1760s and remained a highly regarded lawyer. He came to the attention of Shelburne, who found him a parliamentary seat in 1768. He remained a consistent opponent of North's American policies during the 1770s and supported 'economical reform' from 1778 onwards. He was created a peer as Baron Ashburton in 1782 and served as Chancellor of the Duchy of Lancaster in both Rockingham and Shelburne's administrations of 1782–83. Despite their disagreements over America, the King regarded him highly.

Christopher Wyvill, 1738–1822

Wyvill was born in Edinburgh, the son of a revenue officer. He was ordained into the Church of England in 1763 and was appointed rector of a parish in Essex but neglected his clerical duties. He inherited a substantial landed estate in north Yorkshire in 1774. He came to prominence as the leader of a group of country gentlemen who, in 1779–80, put pressure on government to reduce expenditure and to pass measures of reform. His 'County Association' movement called for moderate parliamentary reform, stopping far short of universal manhood suffrage, and petitioned parliament to this end. He hoped that the Younger Pitt would be able to secure reform, but after the failure of Pitt's second attempt in 1785, the County Association movement lost momentum. Wyvill remained a supporter of moderate parliamentary reforms in the 1790s.

Sinecures

These were jobs which were either entirely unnecessary or which required very little work. They were sometimes given as a form of pension to those who had performed long service, for example in government or in the Church. In the late eighteenth century, however, the word was normally used to describe 'non-jobs' offered in return for political loyalty.

North had lost credibility by 1780. His government, fatally wounded, remained on life support. He survived throughout 1781, including the disaster of Yorktown, only because the King refused to accept his repeated offers of resignation. No stable or competent ministry was ready to step into the breach, not least because the King had no trusted candidate who could also command a majority in parliament. The consequence was that, from the eventual resignation of North in March 1782 to the appointment of William Pitt the Younger in December 1783, the country endured five unstable ministries in twenty-one months as the King flailed around in a desperate search for stability. As a free agent, he would have appointed none of them. All were headed by men who had both opposed his American policy and, albeit to varying degrees, supported economical reform as a direct challenge to royal authority.

The first of the Prime Ministers George III would much rather not have appointed during this crisis was the Marquess of Rockingham. He brought into government with him two equally troublesome Whigs, Shelburne at the Home Department and Charles James Fox as Foreign Secretary. The ministry began the process of enacting economical reforms but came to an abrupt end with Rockingham's death in July. Shelburne, hardly more to the King's liking, succeeded him. It is true that Shelburne had recently stated that he 'would never, under any possible given circumstances . . . acknowledge in the independency of America'.[6] His pronounced preference was for the emergence of a new form of transatlantic empire based on free-trade principles.[7] However, he had been a leading critic of North's government for much of the 1770s and, once Prime Minister, had to accept that American independence was unavoidable. The ministry, which did not include Fox, was in general short on talent. The great exception was the Younger Pitt, who became a minister for the first time as Shelburne's Chancellor of the Exchequer. The absence of Fox, now leader of the Rockingham Whigs, however, was to prove decisive. His debating abilities and effective leadership had their effect. In any case, Shelburne proved a poor leader. He was unpopular with his colleagues, some of whom left a demonstrably sinking ship a few weeks before his ministry resigned in February 1783 when it suffered two defeats in the House of Commons at the hands of an opposition grouping in which supporters of North and Fox, previously outright enemies, voted together.

For the next two months, the identity of the new government remained uncertain. The King well knew that, in the volatile political situation, the new alliance between North and Fox represented much the largest grouping in parliament. He was, however, reluctant to return either man to office. The former he considered a betrayer, the latter a dangerous reformer, an opponent of royal power and, overall, the sharpest thorn in his side. It did not help either that Fox was a close friend, and epic drinking companion, of his eldest son, Prince George, whom – in time-honoured Hanoverian tradition – the King hated. During this period, the King attempted to persuade the 23-year-old William Pitt to head a ministry. It is a measure both of George's desperation that he made no fewer than four such overtures in 1783 and of the precocious young man's assurance and high self-regard that Pitt felt able to reject the first three and, in effect, choose his own time to accept the fourth.

By April 1783, the King had to bow to the inevitable. Fox and North were brought back as leading members of a government which, George insisted, was nominally headed by the **Duke of Portland**. Fox was, however, the dominant figure in the coalition and the next few months can be interpreted as a struggle for constitutional supremacy between the King and the Foxite Whigs. It seemed at the outset that the Coalition must win, since its majority in the House of Commons was secure and the King seemed to have run out of alternatives. The most lustrous of them, Pitt, went on holiday to France – the only foreign trip of his life – in the late summer, sure that the Coalition had now established itself.[8] Matters were not so straight-forward. From the outset, the King made it clear that he wished to rid himself of that 'most infamous coalition' at the first opportunity and he refused to grant peerages to nominees the government brought forward.[9] Moreover, in both the House of Lords and among the significant numbers of independent MPs in the Commons, residual loyalty to the institution of monarchy remained strong and unease at the King's predica-ment was growing. His open hostility to his latest ministry weighed with them.

William Henry Cavendish-Bentinck, third Duke of Portland, 1738–1809

Born into one of the best-connected and wealthiest families in England, he inherited his title on the death of his father in 1762. He became associated with court politics almost immediately, but in the late 1760s he became a follower of the Marquess of Rockingham and, as such, a consistent opponent of Lord North's government during the 1770s. He served briefly as Lord Lieutenant of Ireland under Rockingham but, like most Rockingham Whigs, refused to serve under Shelburne. George III insisted that he head the government which became known as the Fox–North coalition (1783) but his leader-ship was purely nominal. After the fall of the ministry, he headed the opposition to Pitt before breaking with Fox over the French Revolution in the early 1790s and joining Pitt as Home Secretary in a coalition government formed in 1794. He became Prime Minister again in 1807 when the King dismissed the so-called 'Ministry of All the Talents' but he was ill and unable to stand up to the more assertive ministers in his Cabinet. He resigned office for the last time in September 1809 and died the following month.

In any case, the Coalition was encountering difficulties of its own. Having attacked Shelburne's peace plans in respect of America, the Foxites found themselves signing up to much the same arrangement in September 1783, leaving the Coalition open to charges of opportunism and inconsistency. The future government of Ireland was also problematic (see Chapter 14). By the early autumn, parliamentary support for the coalition was considerably lower than it had been in the spring.

The Coalition's decisive difficulty, and one which would have significant constitu-tional implications, was with the administration of India. The East India Company, still massively influential and the source of much patronage, was nevertheless bend-ing under the strains of war and in need of financial help. No government was likely to act as a beneficent banker without imposing new constraints and administrative structures. The Fox–North solution was to remove all political and military control from the Company, vesting it instead in the hands of a Board to be nominated by parliament, and to bring the Governor-General of India and his council of advisers under much more direct supervision of Commissioners working from Britain. On one level, this was a sensible plan. Given the importance of India to Britain's commer-cial interests, greater direct government involvement was a necessity. However, the proposed solution left Fox – perhaps unfairly – open to the charge that, in having parliament nominate the controlling Board, he was putting substantially enhanced patronage in the hands of ministers. At the very least, this was a maladroit move from someone who had been consistently calling in the 1770s and early 1780s for royal patronage to be curbed. Pitt, back from his brief sojourn in France in late October 1783, quickly got the lie of the land. He described Fox's India Bill 'the boldest and most unconstitutional measure ever attempted, transferring . . . the immense patronage and influence of the East to Charles Fox, in or out of office'.[10] He further predicted that the bill 'can never succeed' in the House of Lords. He also perceived that here was an ideal opportunity to advance his own career.

In late November and early December a plot was hatched by opponents of the Coalition and supporters of the Crown to ambush Fox's Indian proposals in the House of Lords. By mid-December, the King was convinced that a defeat for Fox's bill in the Lords would enable him to dismiss his detested ministers. He let it be known that whoever voted for the India Bill 'was not only not his friend, but would be considered by him as an enemy'.[11] It was enough. The Lords threw out the India Bill by a majority of nineteen votes on 17 December 1783. On the evening of 18 December, George required his ministers to hand back their seals of office. They were out. On the following morning, Pitt was installed as Prime Minister. It was a carefully staged, brutal coup. Fox complained about royal chicanery: 'We shall certainly lose our liberty . . . by the illegal and extraordinary exertions of **prerogative**.'[12]

> ### Prerogative
>
> This word now usually means a special privilege or right claimed by particular groups. Fox was using it here in its older sense as relating to special rights exercised by a monarch. He believed, not without some evidence, that he had been brought down by a royal conspiracy.

There was some truth to Fox's charge. The backstairs manoeuvres from which Pitt, an active participant, was the ultimate beneficiary were of dubious constitutional validity since they involved giving the Crown secret advice. Their political significance, however, was to be massive.[13]

III. A commercial accommodation

Never far from politicians' minds in these years was the fear that the loss of the American colonies would be a commercial disaster. William Grenville later remembered sharing 'the deep despondency of my country in the sacrifice of that immense territory . . . I partook of those apprehensions of distress and ruin which so great a loss had universally diffused.'[14] Those territories which would shortly form a new 'United States of America' had become by the 1760s the focal point of British overseas commerce. As Judith Williams put it, the withdrawal of the thirteen American colonies violently disrupted an arrangement which was 'widely regarded as the mainstay of Britain's prosperity and security'.[15] This was hardly surprising. Migration had advanced so rapidly in the late seventeenth and the eighteenth centuries that, by 1770, the ratio of British settlers in North America to the population of England and Wales was roughly one to three. A century earlier it had been one to a hundred.[16] This was a huge, and disproportionately wealthy, overseas market. As early as the 1770s, the export of woollens, previously the basis of British overseas trade, was being overtaken in both volume and value by other manufactured goods, especially cottons. About two-thirds of these new industrially based exports went to America. Britain's American colonies supplied ever-increasing quantities of tobacco, sugar and cotton, grown in the West Indies and in the southern colonies of the American mainland, Virginia, the Carolinas and Georgia in particular. Not only was the direction of British commerce increasingly transatlantic, America was providing an ever larger proportion of the ships in which it was carried. When the war for independence began, almost one-third of Britain's sea-going merchant fleet had been built in the shipyards of the eastern seaboard colonies.[17]

Trade within the British Empire was subject to protective legislation. 'Navigation Acts', dating originally from the middle of the seventeenth century and intended at first to protect English shipping from Dutch competition, allowed goods to be imported into Britain and also British colonies only in British ships. Although evasions were frequent, these Acts did create and sustain important economic ties between Britain and its colonies.[18] Naturally, the independence of the thirteen colonies threatened this relationship.

Recognising the importance of sustaining what was a mutually advantageous trading relationship, some British politicians sought to extend to an independent America that freedom of trade which the colonies had enjoyed before independence. The Earl of Shelburne attempted to negotiate a settlement whereby the Americans would be granted their independence and would in return allow Britain to continue trading with them on a duty-free basis. The colonists, who had already in effect won their independence, insisted on legal recognition of that fact before any commercial talks began. Negotiations on the point broke down. Relations worsened further in December 1783, when Britain prohibited North America from trading directly with the West Indies. In 1786, a new Navigation Act tightened regulations designed to ensure that all ships trading within the British empire were built either in Britain or the colonies. The President of a new Committee (later Board) of Trade, **Charles Jenkinson**, indicated its importance: 'if proper means could be devised to secure the navigation trade to Great Britain, though we had lost a dominion [the American colonies], we might almost be said to have gained an empire'.[19] The new Act was clearly aimed at preventing the independent colonies from sustaining their trade links with Canada and the West Indies.

Charles Jenkinson, 1729–1808

Born at Winchester, the son of an army officer from an Oxfordshire gentry family, he was educated at Charterhouse and Oxford University. He became an MP in 1761 and came to prominence as a supporter of the Earl of Bute in the early 1760s. He was a supporter of Lord North in the 1770s and became Secretary at War at the end of 1778. His close relations with George III were widely criticised by Whig opponents of North's ministry. They considered his influence at court to be excessive. He was accused of buttressing royal power at the expense of politicians in the House of Commons. Jenkinson served under William Pitt the Younger as the first President of the Board of Trade from 1786. He was created Baron Hawkesbury at the same time and became the first Earl of Liverpool in 1796. He was the father of Lord Liverpool, who became Prime Minister in 1812.

Over the next few years, pressure on the government from British merchants disadvantaged by heavy duties on goods brought into the United States in British ships yielded nothing. The situation worsened after Britain declared war on France in 1793 (see Chapter 12). It seized a number of American ships carrying produce to France. The United States came close to declaring war on Britain. For its part, Britain was anxious to avoid fighting Franco-American forces for the second time in less than twenty years. Thus, at the end of 1794, Britain signed a commercial agreement, known as the Jay Treaty. The United States agreed not to increase duties on British imported goods, while Britain accepted American rights to trade in the British East Indies.[20] The British also granted access for smaller American ships to trade in its West Indian markets in molasses, sugar, coffee, cocoa and cotton, but the US Congress refused to ratify this clause, considering the concession inadequate.[21]

The Jay Treaty may have been an expedient dictated by the needs of war but it reflected a delayed, if genuine, recognition of mutual interests. When the details were known to parliament, they provoked little comment and less criticism. After all, the United States represented one of Britain's most important manufacturing markets. For their part, the New England states of the north had few exports beyond fish and agricultural produce with which to pay for the cheap manufactured goods which Britain could now provide in such quantity. US exports went disproportionately to Canada and the West Indies, which Britain still controlled. It is easy to see why the United States saw the value of strong commercial connections with the British Empire surviving the political upheaval of the American revolution. With the Jay Treaty in place, the value of British exports to the United States more than doubled, from £3.3m in 1793 to £6.7m in 1800. At the turn of the century, more than 20 per cent of all British exports were going to the United States.[22] For good reason 'the United States survived as a great market for British industrial production'.[23]

10

National revival? Britain, 1783–1793

I. Pitt and the consolidation of power

Asking the stripling **William Pitt** to form a government in December 1783 represented George III's last throw of the dice. His 'project' to restore royal authority to a pivotal position in British political affairs hung in the balance. Not for the first time, he contemplated abdication. Despite the strong impression the younger Pitt had made in debates, he was only twenty-four years and seven months old when he became Prime Minister and his ministerial experience extended to only eight and a half months as Chancellor of the Exchequer in Shelburne's administration of 1782–83. Quite apart from his age and inexperience, George had further reasons for reservation since Pitt had announced himself from the beginning of his parliamentary career as a reformer. He had asserted in May 1782 that 'the people were loud for a more equal representation, as one of the most likely means to protect their country from danger, and themselves from oppressive taxes'[1] and, after discussions with Wyvill, he introduced a parliamentary reform bill in May 1783 whose purpose was 'to renew and invigorate the spirit of the Constitution'.[2] For the always suspicious King, invigorating the spirit of the Constitution could easily be translated as 'working to undermine it in general, and me in particular'. That he turned to this immature reformer at such a critical juncture is evidence of the weakness of the King's position.

William Pitt the Younger, 1759–1806

Pitt was born in Kent, the fourth child of William Pitt the Elder (later Earl of Chatham). His birth occurred at a time of great success for his father as Prime Minister during the Seven Years War. He was educated at home before going to Cambridge University. He entered parliament in 1781 at the age of 21 and was Prime Minister less than three years later. He always considered himself an 'independent Whig' despite his reputation as a Tory opponent of reform after 1789. Like his father, however, he was not a strong 'party man' anyway. He believed that Britain had a strong constitution which did not depend on the playing out of narrow party struggles. He preferred to emphasise his 'independence' of action rather than his 'Whiggery'. He held office continuously for almost eighteen years which spanned both peace, economic and diplomatic recovery (1783–93) and war, threat of invasion and economic crisis (1793–1801). He resigned in 1801 because the King would not permit him to introduce Roman Catholic Emancipation as part of the package of measures associated with the Union of Ireland with Great Britain (see Chapter 14). He returned as Prime Minister in 1804, dying in office at the beginning of 1806. He was a highly competent minister, a good debater and a master of detail, especially in respect of administrative and financial affairs. Overwork and excessive drinking seem to have contributed to his early death.

Certainly, the supporters of **Fox** considered that the ultimate prize was almost theirs. Pitt was nowhere near a majority in the House of Commons and the Foxites believed that they could choose their moment to bring him down. That done, and the King defeated, they could impose parliamentary and administrative reforms which would preclude independent action by the monarch.

Charles James Fox, 1749–1806

Fox was born in London, the second son of Henry Fox (later Baron Holland) and Lady Lennox, daughter of the Duke of Richmond. His aristocratic connections were crucial to his career. He held minor offices under Lord North in the early 1770s before resigning. He increasingly committed himself to the Rockingham Whigs, particularly in their opposition to North's government and to what they saw as the excessive influence of the Crown in parliamentary affairs. In his political ideas, he was also much influenced by Edmund Burke. He became, in practice, leader of the largest Whig grouping in parliament after the death of Rockingham in 1782. He was Foreign Secretary three times: under Shelburne in 1782, in the Fox–North coalition in 1783 and, in the last year of his life, under Grenville. He was a very able politician but was the main loser of the great constitutional struggle of 1782–84, spending virtually all of his mature years in opposition to Pitt. Unlike many of his Whig colleagues, he continued in opposition after war broke out with France in 1793 (see Chapter 11), leading what was now a small group committed to parliamentary reform and to curbing monarchical power.

Pitt was playing for high stakes himself. He had been cautious in refusing office hitherto but he knew that he risked losing credibility if he were to be forced from office in such circumstances. Certainly, a triumphant Whig grouping headed by Fox and North would have no need of his talents. Pitt would not have survived without the deployment of substantial royal patronage on his behalf but he was determined to be his own man in the House of Commons. His selection of ministers was bold. He calculated that, although he was not spoiled for choice in possible Cabinet members, he could still do without the able but unpopular Shelburne. He deliberately stuffed his Cabinet with peers, in part so that he could shine in the Commons where the real conflict would be played out. All of Pitt's six initial Cabinet colleagues sat in the Lords.

In the short term, Pitt's strategy for retaining office consisted of three prongs. First, in the Commons he would maintain a cool head and a mastery of detail in debate, winning first the respect and then the support of the significant number of MPs independent of the Fox–North connection. Commons defeats did not matter so long as the size of the opposition's majorities began to dwindle, since Pitt had no intention of resigning. Secondly, he knew that he could rely on the King's agreement to the creation of peers; Pitt was adept at offering ennoblement to the politically useful. Sir James Lowther, who had furnished Pitt with his first parliamentary seat at Appleby in 1781, became the first Earl of Lonsdale. A younger son of the Duke of Northumberland received a peerage, whereupon the MPs who sat in the Commons under the Duke's patronage switched allegiance from Fox to Pitt. The young Prime Minister's political exigencies decisively burst the dam which had been holding back peerage creations for much of the eighteenth century. Horace Walpole sardonically noted: 'They are crying peerages about the streets in barrows.'[3]

The third prong of the strategy was at least as much the King's as Pitt's. The convention was that once a new House of Commons was elected, it should run at or near its full course of seven years. Since the Hanoverian dynasty began, the only parliament which had lasted less than six years was that automatically ended by the death of George II in 1727. Now, if the parliamentary wind was seen to be blowing in Pitt's sails, the option was open for the King to dissolve the parliament elected in 1780 and call for fresh elections. Drawing on the advice of his supreme parliamentary fixer **John Robinson** as majorities for Fox dwindled from more than fifty in January 1784 to single figures two months later, George dissolved parliament in late March. Only half its allotted course had run. The reason was clear: an election would give Pitt opportunity to capitalise on his growing popularity.

John Robinson, 1727–1802

Born in Appleby (Westmorland), the son of a wealthy merchant, he became prominent as a supporter of Sir James Lowther, the largest landowner in the area, for whom he arranged elections. He became MP for Westmorland himself in 1764 and, during the 1770s, was a political manager and election organiser for Lord North, in which capacity he became close to George III, who gave him a handsome pension when he left office in 1782. He deserted North at the end of 1783 and organised the general election in 1784 which gave the Younger Pitt a handsome majority. He remained an MP for the remainder of his life, most of which he devoted to consolidating his family's political and financial future.

More than £30,000 of treasury money was spent on supporting pro-Pitt candidates in the 1784 election, mostly in the boroughs with small numbers of voters, where bribery and 'treating' had long proved effective. Pitt's victory was spectacular and some of the most surprising reverses for Fox occurred in the larger boroughs and the county seats, where public opinion swung decisively Pitt's way. Up to a hundred of Fox's supporters lost their seats. They were dubbed 'Fox's Martyrs' by wits who recalled the pro-Reformation *Acts and Monuments of the British Martyrs* compiled by

John Foxe in 1563 which listed those who had suffered Catholic persecution. That Pitt's position was now unchallengeable was demonstrated by his majority of 168 in the vote on the King's speech held in May 1784.[4]

Why was Pitt able to turn the situation around so completely and so quickly? His evident abilities and generally calm authority under pressure impressed the independent MPs but that does not explain why he did so spectacularly well in seats with the largest electorates. The 1784 election was highly unusual in that it was one of the very few before the 1830s which turned on major national issues. Almost all eighteenth-century elections had a predominantly local focus. When contests were held at all – and on average only about one-third of the seats were – electors generally voted for individuals rather than for a party. The constitutional issues raised by this election were obvious. Many electors seem to have considered that Fox had overplayed his hand. His attacks on the monarch went far beyond the dubious use of court patronage into territory uncharted since the Civil Wars of the 1640s. He was challenging the monarch's prerogative to use patronage, to choose his own ministers, to dissolve parliament and call a general election on his own initiative. The unreformed electorate was not prepared for such radicalism. Some of the more reflective electors might also have concluded that Fox was close to claiming the same privileges for his aristocratic cronies that he wished to deny to George III. He was to pay dearly for this presumption.

Pitt's India Act rubbed the point home. Pitt agreed with Fox that Indian administration needed a thorough overhaul to reduce the powers of the East India Company (see Chapter 9). Pitt had been narrowly defeated in the Commons on an India bill a couple of months before the election. A very similar measure, largely formulated by Henry Dundas (see p. 9), reappeared immediately afterwards. Pitt's solution and Fox's were in many respects similar. However, the Board of Control which Pitt set up was to be appointed by the Crown, not parliament. All its six members were **privy councillors** and two would be serving Cabinet ministers. Both routine administration and most patronage in India remained with the East India Company, as did commercial decisions. Pitt's solution was less confrontational and less radical than Fox's. Crucially, it left the King to exercise the kind of influence which had not normally been seen as controversial.

Privy councillor

A privy (or private) councillor is an adviser of the monarch. The role developed from the medieval King's Council, and the privy council operated from the sixteenth century as a small committee which advised the monarch and had executive roles in government. The privy council lost its specifically executive functions to the Cabinet in the seventeenth century but the idea that its members, as senior and distinguished figures, were free to offer the monarch advice remained. All Cabinet members were privy councillors, retaining that title after they left the Cabinet.

II. Dealing with debt

While the 1784 general election ended what had become an increasingly bitter parliamentary and constitutional crisis, the calmer waters into which Pitt now sailed
buoyed by reliable parliamentary majorities were still being buffeted by economic
turbulence. All of the indicators which later generations have learned to scrutinise
carefully, if not always comprehendingly, seemed to indicate a crisis. Over the,
largely wartime, decade 1775–84 the National Debt (see Chapter 1) had increased
by 91 per cent and, as Boyd Hilton has noted, high levels of public debt in the late
eighteenth and early nineteenth centuries were 'almost universally thought to por-
tend calamity . . . a harbinger of national bankruptcy, social collapse and even religious apocalypse'.[5] Exports had also declined by about 12 per cent during the same
period and some considered that the nation stood on the verge of bankruptcy in 1783.
Looking back from the vantage point of the early 1820s, William Grenville recollected
that 'the nation gave way . . . to an almost universal panic on this subject'.[6]

In this situation, Pitt not unnaturally decided that cutting the debt had to be his
government's first priority. Not far behind it, however, came the need to restore order
and efficiency to the process of revenue-raising. In 1786, he introduced a new sinking fund. The idea of a **sinking fund** was not new. It had been advocated as recently
as 1783 by the Commissioners for Examining the Public Accounts.[7] The priority which
Pitt gave to implementing one and the efficiency with which the fund was then administered were, however, distinctive. Both paid off. By the end of 1793, the amount of
the nation's funded debt had been reduced by £10m.

Sinking fund

This is the term given to a financial device in which money is set aside in a separate
fund for the reduction of debt. Pitt's 1786 plan was to allocate £1m of tax revenues
every year for specially appointed commissioners to use in buying government stocks.
These were to be invested in a fund. The ultimate aim was to accumulate a fund worth
£4m a year, massively to reduce, or even eliminate, the debt.

The revenue to support the fund came from a bewildering range of excise taxes,
including new or reimposed levies on windows, hackney carriages, servants, trade
licences, horses, wig-powder and wills. The list is extensive and might seem random.
Many raised disappointing sums since, then as now, ingenious means were available
to conceal or evade tax liabilities. There was, however, an overall method in what
a cursory glance might suggest was the madness of Pitt's fiscal fidgeting. His list appears
bizarre because it was intended to be socially selective. He wished to avoid adding
to the burdens laid on the poor, whose complaints about both excessive taxation and
corruption were insistent at times of economic dislocation, and whose propensity
for rioting and other forms of public disturbance was well established. Food riots

were endemic, and some of the largest parliamentary constituencies, including Westminster and Liverpool, had seen riots during the recent general election. Further taxes bearing heavily on these were best avoided. As has been said elsewhere, 'the poor could not afford equestrian transport, were not conveyed in carriages, did not wear wigs . . . [or] follow fashion'.[8]

Knowing that punitively high levels of taxation invited evasion, Pitt turned his attention to the revenue from customs and, in particular, to smuggling, which, as William Hague has said, was 'a way of life in many coastal areas of Britain'.[9] Many towns, especially in Devon and Cornwall, had developed a 'counter-culture' grounded in tolerance of smugglers and mutual antagonism to the activities of revenue men acting for wealthy landowners sitting in parliament more than three hundred miles away. Some revenue officers found it safer to run with the smuggling hares as well as hunting (or pretending to hunt) with government hounds. Smuggling was immensely lucrative and made more so by the levels of duty which governments had set. Tea duty was famously 119 per cent, making its price in British shops almost six times higher than those in continental Europe.

Pitt's response was to reduce duties and to improve the administration of revenue collection. By a 'Commutation Act' in 1784, he reduced the tea duty to a uniform 25 per cent. Duties on rum, wine and brandy were reduced in 1785–87; collection of some items was transferred from customs to the more efficient excise officers. A 'Hovering Act' (1784) extended the authority of customs officers to search ships for contraband. Although smugglers fought back and the battle was not quickly won, Pitt's combination of carrot and stick saw customs revenue increase by about £1m by 1792.[10] An overall increase in government income over expenditure, small but steady, had been established by 1787. It continued until 1792 – the last year of peace.

III. Administrative reform

'Efficiency savings' have received a deservedly bad press in the late twentieth and early twenty-first century as a clichéd cover for lazy, mendacious and badly supervised policy to curb government expenditure. In the late eighteenth century, the governmental machine was both less complex and the amount of 'waste' – in the form of sinecures and pensions rewarding political loyalty – even more overt. Pitt had railed in opposition against the costs and inefficiencies of government departments. In office, he was determined to reduce them. Caution was required, of course. Appointments to the government bureaucracy were on the basis of patronage, and the preservation of patronage powers was a key element explaining the bitterness of George III's conflict with the Fox–North coalition.

Pitt characteristically advanced by stealth. He took great care to discover how government departments worked and carefully scrutinised the reports of the Public Accounts Commissioners, who were not slow to identify inefficiencies. In 1786, they urged Pitt to abolish 180 redundant sinecure offices. He did not comply. Very few government officials were sacked outright during his time as Prime Minister. However, many were not replaced when they retired or died. The case of Edward and Horace Walpole, sons of the early eighteenth-century Prime Minister Robert Walpole, is indicative of Pitt's methods. Unsurprisingly, both brothers were well connected and had accumulated a significant number of sinecures on the way. When Edward died in 1784, his share of the collectorship of customs died with him. Horace survived until 1797, an unreconstructed Foxite Whig who considered the 'light and juvenile' Pitt 'a tool' in the hands of a monarchy bent on 'aggrandizement' rather than on presiding over 'a great and puissant free kingdom'.[11] He retained the title of Usher of Exchequer Receipts, a post which carried an income but no duties, until his death.

Pitt's policy on sinecures, therefore, worked slowly but safely. George III was largely unaware of what was going on and, in consequence, of the risk to his power 'to reward services'. And Pitt was a very long-serving Prime Minister. By the time he left office in 1801, few of the sinecures identified by the Commissioners fifteen years earlier remained a charge on the public purse.

The other side of Pitt's administrative policy concerned the promotion of able men into positions of influence. He translated talented administrators like Richard Frewin and William Stiles onto a revitalised Customs Board. Stiles later became its Secretary. He and Frewin undertook an investigation of the fee system with the intention of replacing fees, with professional salaries. They proposed the abolition of fees, which would save the revenue more than £60,000 a year, but the necessary legislation was delayed by the outbreak of war.[12]

The reform of the armed services was given even higher priority. Pitt did not forget that the navy had for a time lost control of the Channel during the recent war. It was also the case that the cost of the army, navy and ordnance was two and a half times greater than that of all civilian administration combined. Some economies were made and waste tackled in the 1780s, but efficient administration of a programme of expansion, particularly in the navy, was more important. In the decade 1783–93 forty-three new ships of the line were built and another eighty-five thoroughly repaired. The naval complement was also increased from 15,000 to 18,000.

The senior administrator on whom Pitt relied heavily for this work was Charles Middleton, Comptroller of the Navy, a post to which he had originally been appointed during Lord North's administration. An observer at the Navy Board stated that 'the load of business he gets through . . . is astonishing, and what I am confident no other man will be able to execute'.[13] Pitt could observe this for himself. It was part of his working method to visit relevant offices, be that in the City of London or the army or navy and to acquire detailed knowledge of how things worked. He was thus able to judge the quality of Middleton's work for himself and to back him against the First Lord of the Admiralty, Admiral Richard Howe, when the two men differed. Middleton was in significant measure responsible for ensuring that, by 1790, the British navy had regained its European pre-eminence and the potential for deterrence which went with it. These attributes would be critical in the impending struggle with France.

IV. International relations

The lesson which politicians took from America's successful revolution was that it was foolhardy to fight a war without allies. Britain had already been involved in three major eighteenth-century wars before 1775 and a feature of each was the attention given to acquiring, co-operating with and sustaining European allies. Not surprisingly, therefore, Pitt sought foreign allies. Inexperienced in foreign affairs, he followed the advice of diplomats such as Sir James Harris, whose view was that 'judicious alliances' were necessary 'to recover our weight on the continent'.[14] He needed to proceed cautiously, however, since the King was concerned that the signing of alliances could be interpreted as a declaration of warlike intent at a time when Britain could not afford to fight yet another war.

France, sunk deep in debt after 1783 and poorly governed for years, was nevertheless still considered the main threat to British interests, not least because it was trying to recover its trading position in Asia.[15] Britain's main objective was to deter expansionist activity and, in particular, to challenge any incursions into the Netherlands which could threaten Britain's trade routes into Europe through the River Scheldt. Aided by Sir James Hague, Britain's envoy to the United Provinces (Netherlands), Pitt supported William V, Prince of Orange in 1787, when he was threatened by a pro-French 'patriotic' party. The Prussians, Britain's ally during the Seven Years War in Pitt's father's time, harboured similar concerns about French ambitions in Holland and massed troops on the Dutch border. It was they who invaded Holland in September 1787 on behalf of William V and restored his authority. Britain had, however, informed the French court that it was prepared to send troops to oppose any aggressive action on behalf of the pro-French patriots. The French backed down, suffering a significant diplomatic defeat. The immediate benefit for Britain was the signing in 1788 of a new Triple Alliance with Holland and Prussia. Notionally, its purpose was to help preserve the peace of Europe. In practice, it signified that Britain's European isolation was over.

Britain enjoyed further diplomatic success when Spain, a long-term ally of France not least because both powers were ruled by members of the Bourbon family, attempted to upset the balance of power in North America by asserting what it considered to be its ancient rights on the western seaboard. A Spanish warship captured a British vessel off the western coast and then occupied Nootka Sound, west of Vancouver in what is now British Columbia in July 1789. The isolated area was of little immediate value, being occupied by only a few British fishermen and fur traders. However, the developing whaling industry in the north-west Pacific showed its potential. Pitt demanded Spanish withdrawal. As an earnest of British intent, the navy was mobilized. The Spanish were forced to withdraw from Nootka Sound in 1790 and to pay compensation for damage caused.

It is difficult to find any explanation for the so-called Ochakov crisis of 1791 beyond British over-confidence and Pitt's acceptance of unreliable advice from Joseph Ewart, the British envoy to Prussia. During a war between Russia and Turkey, which lasted from 1788 to 1792, the Russians captured Ochakov, a fishing port and fortress on the Black Sea in present-day Ukraine. Pitt was concerned that its acquisition would encourage Russia's ambitions in south-eastern Europe and thus clash with British interests. Pitt attempted to use his closer links with Prussia via the Triple Alliance to demand Russian withdrawal. The Russian Empress, Catherine the Great, ignored the British demand and eventually made her own peace with the Turks. Pitt found that the main effect of his Black Sea initiative was to increase the confidence of his Whig opponents in parliament. Fox made some effective speeches, and the Commons as a whole could see no compelling reason to threaten war over a trivial place in which the British seemed to have no significant interest. The Cabinet was divided. The Foreign Secretary, the Duke of Leeds, who supported Pitt's policy, felt betrayed when the Prime Minister backed down. Leeds resigned, claiming that his authority had been undermined. He was replaced by William Grenville, one of Pitt's closest colleagues. Ochakov was, in itself, unimportant. Pitt's reputation quickly recovered; Fox's always optimistic hopes of taking over as Prime Minister fell as quickly as they had risen. Ochakov did, however, provide the earliest indicator of one of the great diplomatic conflicts of the nineteenth century: whether to challenge Russian advances in south-east Europe and, if so, to what lengths Britain was prepared to go (see Chapters 34 and 35).

Diplomacy in the 1780s was broadly anti-French. Commerce was another matter. As part of the Treaty of Versailles (see Chapter 9), Britain and France agreed to later negotiations designed to reduce the protective tariffs employed by both countries. Pitt was anyway anxious to move, if cautiously, in the direction of greater freedom of trade between states. He had read **Adam Smith**'s famous *Wealth of Nations* and he had been influenced also by Shelburne, a much more doctrinaire free-trader than Pitt, when the latter was Chancellor of the Exchequer in 1782–83. In the years 1784–92, Pitt's envoys opened trade negotiations with eight European countries. Few came to much, but the attempts demonstrate Pitt's belief that encouraging trade might help to compensate for the loss of the American colonies. Trade agreement with France was reached in 1786 with the so-called Eden Trade Treaty, after William Eden who conducted the negotiations. It was a surprisingly liberal agreement, providing for freedom both of navigation and trade between the colonies of the two nations and allowing citizens of each country to visit the other without passports or taxation. It also significantly reduced tariffs on a wide range of goods. French wine came into Britain at preferential rates. During the brief period of its operation before the beginning of war in 1793 (see Chapter 12), the Eden Treaty worked to Britain's advantage. It was, of course, agreeable for society hostesses to have good French wine available for their entertainments at cheaper prices. However, access to French markets for a wide range of manufacturing goods, and particularly textiles, was of much more commercial significance.

Adam Smith, 1723–1790

Born in Kircaldy (Fife), he became Professor of Logic and of Moral Philosophy at Glasgow University in 1751. He travelled to France in the 1760s, where he met, and was influenced by, many of the leading figures of the European enlightenment. He published on ethics, including a work on justice, *The Theory of Moral Sentiments* (1759), but he is best known for *The Wealth of Nations* (1776). Many have seen this book as the most influential contribution to the widespread adoption in the nineteenth century of free-trade policies. Smith argued that the activities of individuals operating in a free market benefit society as a whole, even if the motives of individuals are predominantly selfish. He believed that free trade imposed important disciplines and efficiencies on manufacturers and capitalists, since if they were not efficient they would not meet the needs of the market and go out of business. Despite the frequency with which his views are misrepresented, Smith's prime concern was for the needs of the consumer, not the producer.

V. Revival and constitutional crisis

How effective were Pitt's peacetime policies? Historians have in general been kind, and there used to be a fashion for contrasting them with the inadequacy of Pitt's wartime leadership (see Chapter 12). One early twentieth-century assessment argued that the difficulties he inherited in 1783 were 'enormous' and Pitt's response to them characterised by 'financial genius'.[16] More recent assessments have also been appreciative, if less fulsome. Michael Turner notes that Pitt saw himself as 'a selfless and dependable public servant' and argues that his successes before 1793 were not merely 'a victory of style over substance'.[17] William Hague believes that he 'helped to restore faith in the British state after a period in which it had been discredited among its own people'.[18]

Pitt did, however, enjoy much good fortune. Britain recovered quickly from the American war in large part because its economy was booming. Between the mid-1780s and the mid-1790s, the value of British exports increased by 90 per cent.[19] The American need for manufactured textile goods mitigated the adverse commercial effects of independence. Well before 1783, Britain had an extensive commercial infrastructure in place to benefit from new opportunities. Despite Pitt's cautious moves over trade liberalisation, the performance of the economy in the 1780s and early 1790s owed relatively little to government agency.

Britain in the 1780s was still at least half a century away from the emergence of a clear two-party system. However, the continued, and to many surprising, coherence of an opposition in which Fox and North remained the key figures made the lines of political division clearer, especially as Pitt could increasingly rely on the loyalty of large numbers of independent members in most of the big votes. It is true that he failed to pass a modest bill for parliamentary reform in 1785 but Pitt knew of the King's 'unalterable sentiments on any change in the constitution'[20] and told him that the bill was merely consistent with his stated position during the general election in the previous year. In presenting proposals for increasing the electorate and redistributing the seats of some of the smallest parliamentary boroughs to the counties and to London, he was acting almost as a private member of parliament who just happened to be the Prime Minister. No one considered his substantial defeat, by 74 votes, to be a resigning issue.

Only once was Pitt's grip on power seriously threatened and that accidentally. In October 1788, George III succumbed to what his doctor called a condition 'nearly bordering on delirium'.[21] It was the first indication of what medical historians are now sure was the presence of the inherited ailment known as porphyria. One of the most obvious symptoms is an altered mental state. Talking to himself, and others, incessantly and inconsequentially, the King was clearly unfit to discharge his royal duties. With no immediate improvement in his condition, thoughts turned to the need for a Regent to act for him. The obvious problem for Pitt was that the Regent would necessarily be the King's eldest son, George, Prince of Wales. His relations with his father were bad. Worse, his links to Charles James Fox and his Whig allies were close. If the Prince became Regent, he would dismiss Pitt and install Fox as his Prime Minister. Whether that ploy would have been successful, it is impossible to know. Probably not, since the House of Commons by late 1788 was loyal to Pitt and many county MPs were appalled by the Prince's character and behaviour, which they considered (not without cause) to be reckless, wasteful and libidinous. Fox would have had real difficulty in securing majorities.

Pitt used the only weapon at his command. He skilfully played for time in the hope of royal recovery. The Commons were informed that there was no need for haste. Pitt also made use of the informed opinion of Francis Willis, the King's doctor, that his patient would make a full and fairly speedy recovery. In fact, it took until February 1789, by which time Pitt was running out of delaying tactics. By the late winter, however, George was writing rationally to his Prime Minister. What he called his 'tedious illness' was over and he resumed normal service. The Regency Crisis was over. The general election which followed in the following year was relatively quiet. The usual third of constituencies saw contested elections. Pitt strengthened his position in the Commons with an overall majority estimated at about 120 seats.

Pitt's peacetime administration was undoubtedly successful. By the time Britain went to war again, the country's financial system was more professionally administered. Pitt appointed a number of new functionaries and was usually vindicated in his choice by the effectiveness of their performance. He also promoted others who had survived from earlier regimes because he valued their abilities more than he worried about their prior political allegiances. The stability of the government contrasted with the near chaos of 1780–83. By 1793, Henry Dundas (see Chapter 1) and William Grenville (see Chapter 13), who had been Pitt's closest advisers since the early days of his ministry, were both in prominent Cabinet positions. The less able were removed or shunted to the sidelines. As we have seen, the debt had been reduced and the sinking fund appeared to be working well. Pitt's attention to detail ensured that the figures were inspected carefully and policy initiatives followed up.

We should not, however, give the Younger Pitt too much credit. The general tendency of Hanoverian governments was towards longevity, as Walpole, Pelham and North had all demonstrated. The independent country gentlemen who sat in the House of Commons preferred security to excitement and usually voted to keep long-serving ministries in place when they faced difficulties. Once Pitt had his feet firmly under table, they were likely to remain there. In any case, his inheritance proved to be a good deal less sickly than had been assumed in 1783–84. Pitt's peacetime administration was also cautiously reformist. He was anxious not to travel faster than the temper of the House of Commons, naturally conservative, would allow. So, while he absorbed new economic ideas from Adam Smith and Shelburne, he was careful not too push them too far. Finally, he was not averse to using promotion and financial inducement to secure loyalty as well as to reward competence. His was no new broom used to sweep away the encrustations of sleaze, patronage and undercover dealings which stuck fast to all Hanoverian administrations. Perhaps Pitt's peacetime administration was the more successful because he worked with the grain of eighteenth-century politics rather than because it anticipated a more open and more accountable era.

11

....

Britain in the 1790s: the impact of the French Revolution

I. The contagion from France

The French Revolution took Europe unawares. Reform ideas had, of course, been given a good airing, not least by the so-called *Philosophes* in France. However, Enlightenment ideas had been seen almost as the plaything of the intellectual and propertied classes. It was one thing to use coffee houses and other resorts of polite society to debate how ideas of citizenship might be advanced and a properly representative system of government framed, quite another to see one of the great powers of Europe rocked by revolution. Within six weeks of the fall of the Bastille prison in Paris, widely seen as the symbol of royal tyranny, the French National Assembly had abolished both the feudal privileges of the nobility and the ancient property rights of the Church. It also approved a Declaration of the Rights of Man, which stated that 'men are born free and remain free and with equal rights'. In Britain, the initial response was favourable. Known reformers expressed mingled astonishment and delight. Charles James Fox offered perhaps the most celebrated response. A fortnight after the fall of the Bastille in July 1789, he wrote to Richard Fitzpatrick, his close friend and Whig colleague: 'How much the greatest event it is that ever happened in the world! And how much the best!'[1]

Britain could, of course, point to its own reformist tradition, dating back at least to the 1640s and 1650s. It encompassed a more or less bloodless revolution in 1688 and, as we have seen (see Chapter 9), came to the surface during the attacks on the alleged corruption and inefficiency of North's government in the late 1770s and early 1780s. Reform issues went beyond the political. Nonconformists were agitating for equality of civil and religious rights with the established Church of England. Their mounted campaigns for the repeal of the **Test and Corporation Acts** in the 1780s received considerable support.[2] Many reformers welcomed the French Revolution in 1789–90 as evidence that Catholic absolutism had been given a much-needed jolt into the modern world, that Enlightenment ideas were bearing fruit and that France was at last trying to catch up with Britain's 'advanced' representative system of government. Perhaps the French Revolution could act as a stimulus to further reform in Britain. The assumption was that the propertied classes would continue to control both the pace and direction of any such changes.

Test and Corporation Acts

These were pieces of legislation discriminating against those who did not conform to the doctrines of the Church of England (hence 'nonconformists'). They were passed soon after the restoration of King Charles II to the English throne in 1660. The Corporation Act (1661) required all members of 'corporations' (agencies of local government) to take Holy Communion according to the rites of the Church of England and to acknowledge the monarch as the Supreme Head of that Church. The Test Act (1672) required holders of any civil or military office to conform to the Acts of Supremacy and Uniformity – in essence swearing allegiance to the Monarch and the Church of England – and also to deny the Roman Catholic doctrine of transubstantiation.

Such patronising reflections were soon outmoded. One of the most remarkable consequences of the French Revolution was the emergence of new reformist political societies, strongly influenced by events across the Channel, and composed of skilled workers. Pre-eminent among them was the London Corresponding Society, which was founded by **Thomas Hardy** in January 1792, but a number of corresponding societies were established in many provincial towns at much the same time. Sheffield, whose Society for Constitutional Information, founded in 1791, seems to have been first in the field, Norwich, Derby and Nottingham all contained a significant proportion of skilled workers in the metals, woollen textile and hosiery trades. Many were literate and had been politically active before 1789 whether they had votes in parliamentary elections or not. They formed the vanguard of what is known as 'artisan radicalism'.

Thomas Hardy, 1752–1832

Born in Larbert (Stirlingshire), the son of a merchant seaman, he was apprenticed as a shoemaker and left Scotland for London in 1774. He founded the London Corresponding Society with a small number of friends. The Society was organised to correspond with others and to agitate for universal manhood suffrage and parliamentary reform. The Society also discussed forming a Convention which could claim greater popular authority to govern than parliament. Hardy was arrested in 1794 and charged with high treason but found not guilty by a London jury. His business was ruined by this affair and he never properly recovered. His house was attacked by a loyalist crowd in 1797. Hardy then retreated from political engagement but maintained contact with leading propertied radicals including Edmund Cartwright and Sir Francis Burdett.

The most influential publication for these artisans was **Tom Paine**'s *Rights of Man*. Its title was taken directly from the French 'Declaration' of August 1789 (see above). *Rights of Man* was an extended polemic grounded in the rationalism of the

Enlightenment. It was anti-aristocratic: 'That . . . which is called Aristocracy . . . arose out of the governments founded upon conquest . . . Aristocracy is kept up by family tyranny and injustice . . . Aristocracy has a tendency to degenerate the human species.'[3] The book was also egalitarian. Paine was no socialist. He believed in equality of opportunity rather than of income or property and his racy prose precisely targeted its intended audience. *Rights of Man* was the Bible of British radicalism and was hugely influential in the political education of the skilled working classes in the 1790s. Above all, Paine offered a practical, if dangerous, way forward. Parliament had refused to reform itself. Paine therefore considered further application to parliament to be 'a worn-out, hackneyed subject'. The wider nation should determine the entitlement to vote. Since parliament represented a narrow range of interests, that responsibility should be taken 'by a national convention, elected for the purpose by all the people'.[4]

Thomas Paine, 1737–1809

Born in Thetford (Norfolk), the son of a Quaker corset manufacturer and tenant farmer, he became a government excise officer in the 1760s. He went to America from where he published *Common Sense* (1776), which supported colonists' arguments for independence. His *Rights of Man*, published in two parts in 1791 and 1792, advocated democracy and republican forms of government. The second part put forward plans for a range of welfare benefits, including family allowances, which the nation would be able to afford once the monarchy, the aristocracy and their hangers-on were no longer funding expensive wars. He was granted honorary French citizenship and sat as a Deputy in the National Convention. He was arrested during the Terror and narrowly escaped execution. He wrote *The Age of Reason* (1793), an anti-Christian, though not thoroughgoing atheist, work, and *Agrarian Justice* (1796), in favour of the forcible redistribution of land on the principle of equal shares. In 1802 he returned to America, where he owned a farm, but encountered frequent financial difficulties. He died in Greenwich Village, New York.

From 1792, radical societies increased both in the number and range of their activities. In Scotland, radical groups took Paine at his word. Thomas Muir, member of the so-called 'Scottish Friends of the People', summoned a Convention to meet in Edinburgh, with members drawn from eighty radical societies. By early 1794, the London Corresponding Society was also calling for a representative Convention to be held. During 1795, with food prices rising sharply and signs of economic distress obvious in most large towns, mass meetings were calling for reform. Mass meetings were to play a critical role in popular agitation from the 1790s down to the end of the Chartist movement in the late 1840s (see Chapters 16, 20 and 21). They became a focal point for peaceable assembly at which reformist speeches were delivered by articulate, impassioned reformers. These gatherings, in the necessarily restricted spaces of growing towns, also implied unity of purpose. Their sheer size represented a threat to the authorities. The meetings were increasingly republican and anti-aristocratic in temper. They also asserted the validity of ancient political rights. Radical crowds heard much about the 'free-born Englishmen' whose liberties were being wantonly subverted by an unrepresentative elite.[5]

Many of the arguments employed by artisan radicals echoed those of their middle-class counterparts. Both advocated political liberty and a range of reforms; not infrequently, they worked together. The lines of communication remained open at least until 1795. Thomas Fysshe Palmer, active at the Edinburgh convention, was the son of a Bedfordshire landowner and had been educated at Eton and Cambridge University. Maurice Margarot's father was a successful wine merchant and Margarot himself owned property in the West Indies and in Portugal.[6] Not surprisingly, however, few middle-class radicals wanted anything to do with plots, revolutionary schemes or any other forms of direct action.

Whig radicals, through their own Society of the Friends of the People, attempted to control radical enthusiasms. Two developments militated against this. First, the progress made by artisan radical organisations from 1792–95 suggested that skilled workers were finding their own voice. Men like Hardy willingly acknowledged the importance of middle-class support by radicals like Cartwright, while rejecting the idea that working people should be led by them. Secondly, from 1792 the French Revolution careered off track. Its predominantly constitutional phase ended with the arrest and subsequent execution of the King and Queen. The Revolution lurched into a Terror phase in 1793–94, the dimensions of which alarmed most of the propertied classes in Britain.

The government's response reflected both heightened concern about radical threats at home and the dangerous turn taken in France. In May 1792, in a move primarily directed at Paine, it banned the publication of 'seditious publications'. It also subsidised newspapers like *The True Briton* and *The British Critic* to pump out loyalist propaganda. In December, responding to almost certainly exaggerated rumours of French spies on a mission to attack the Bank of England and the Tower of London, the government issued a Royal Proclamation summoning the **militias** of ten counties to be prepared to resist rebellion.[7] By early 1793, Britain was war with France (Chapter 12) and the authorities increasingly saw support for radical activity grounded in 'French principles' as potentially treasonable. Spies were employed to monitor developments and to identify key agitators and possible ringleaders. By 1793, a string of reports, some luridly exaggerated but cumulatively worrying, were reaching the Home Office concerning secret meetings, plots and threats of revolution. The authorities dispersed the Edinburgh Convention in 1793, and arrested its leaders, Thomas Muir, the Unitarian (see Chapter 4) minister, Thomas Fysshe Palmer and Maurice Margarot. They were sentenced to transportation for fourteen years. Further arrests were made, and charges of high treason brought against leaders of the English reform movements in 1794, although London juries refused to convict Hardy and his colleagues. The operation of **Habeas Corpus** legislation was also suspended.

Militia

This was a formal military force comprising a mixture of full-time and part-time soldiers. Many were volunteers; others were chosen by local ballot. They stood ready for service and particularly to defend the nation against invasion or to suppress rebellion. Militiamen received training but were not considered part of the regular forces. They were, however, more organised and generally better trained than the numerous 'volunteer corps' hastily assembled during the French Wars.

Habeas Corpus

This Latin phrase literally means 'You shall have the body'. Its origins date back to Magna Carta (1215) but its modern implementation relates to the requirement that those accused of a crime and arrested must not be detained against their will without specific charges having been brought against them. These they then have the right to answer in a court of law. The Habeas Corpus Act of 1679 was the most important of several acts giving legal protection to the accused person. Governments suspended the operation of the Act when they believed that national security was threatened.

Finally, in response to increased activity during 1795, which included an attack on the King's coach as he went in procession to the state opening of parliament, two restrictive pieces of legislation were passed. The Treasonable Practices Act defined treason much more broadly. The Seditious Meetings Act prohibited the holding of any political meeting attended by more than fifty persons without a magistrate's licence. These two pieces of legislation became known as 'The Gagging Acts'. Their purpose was to suppress debate and deter potentially threatening crowd behaviour, rather than to create martyrs. In this, they were largely successful.

II. Whig divisions

The French Revolution also had a significant effect on political allegiances at Westminster. While most Whigs initially saw the Revolution as broadly progressive, one foresaw the dangers of the Revolution almost from the outset. Edmund Burke's *Reflections on the Revolution in France*, published in 1790, anticipated revolutionary excess: 'Those who attempt to level, never equalize . . . The effect of liberty to individuals is that they may do what they please: we ought to see what it will please them to do before we risk congratulations, which may soon be turned to complaints.'[8] This brought him into conflict with Fox. The two men, allies over America, had drifted apart during the 1780s, but their disagreement over events in France, which Fox was in 1791 still calling 'a most stupendous work',[9] had damaging consequences for the party. Burke could be marginalised in the earlier stages of the Revolution but, from 1792 with the King arrested and France at war with Austria and Prussia, his prophecies seemed vindicated by events. At the same time, the younger Whigs, including Grey and Sheridan, had formed an Association to press for parliamentary reform, a policy which seemed wildly inappropriate in a party which believed in the primacy of property. Nevertheless, Fox, ever the party's most consistent advocate for 'liberty', allowed his name to be linked to this new grouping, but its activities placed him in a quandary. Many of the wealthiest and most aristocratic Whigs, not least Portland and Fitzwilliam, were deeply alarmed by events in France, especially the increasing hostility shown by the revolutionaries to the aristocracy. They were prepared to consider coalition with Pitt to demonstrate national resolve against the new threat. Fox continued to bang the liberty drum, announcing at a meeting of the Whig Club in early December 1792 that he remained 'an advocate for "The Rights of the People"'. His toast to the 'equal liberty of all mankind' could not have been more provocative – or, to his own political ambitions, more damaging.[10] When France declared war on Britain in February 1793, Fox complained about a monarchical conspiracy against liberty-loving France and declared that war was unnecessary. **William Windham** immediately severed relations with him and formed a 'Third Party' numbering about thirty adherents. By then, Loughborough had already become the first member of the Fox–North opposition grouping to accept office under Pitt, becoming Lord Chancellor in January 1793.

William Windham, 1750–1810

Born into an East Anglian landowning family, he became MP for Norwich in 1784. Associated with Fox's Whigs, he was at first a supporter of the French Revolution but became converted to Burke's view and was by the summer of 1792 arguing strongly against parliamentary reform. His conflict with Fox deepened at the end of 1792, when he refused to recognise the French Republic as a valid government. In February 1793, he resigned from the Whig Club and formed what was, in effect, a 'third party'. He joined Pitt's government as Secretary at War in the coalition formed in 1794. He became reconciled to Fox late in life and became Secretary for War in the 'Ministry of All the Talents' in 1806–7.

Pitt, of course, happily exploited Whig divisions. He put out feelers for a coalition at various points in 1793 and made it clear that he would be happy to include Fox. Fox refused to give precedence to Pitt as Prime Minister and rebuffed all offers. Most established Whigs believed that coalition at a time of emergency was the proper course. Protracted negotiations finally resulted in a deal sealed in July 1794. Portland, Fitzwilliam, Windham and Spencer all accepted office under Pitt. Portland, the most senior defector, became Home Secretary. Pitt now presented himself as a national leader at the head of a coalition government formed in the interests of national security.[11] Fox was left with a rump of socially extremely well-connected but relatively inexperienced politicians. Many were close personal friends. Numbering about fifty-five in all, they were bereft of all influence. They consoled themselves only with bleak adherence to principle. They favoured parliamentary reform; they saw no reason for Britain to be fighting the French. Above all, they hated royal influence which cheated the people of their liberties. It was fanciful, self-indulgent stuff.

III. Dealing with sedition

Repressive legislation drove radicalism underground after 1795. While this deprived radical leaders of mass support, it arguably increased their danger. An underground movement must act secretly and secrecy implies plots. Radical activity after 1795 is difficult to research. Three things are clear, however. First, the pursuance of war resulted in economic strain, the main impact of which was borne by the lower orders. Hunger feeds desperate measures and the high food-price years 1798–1803 were particularly difficult. The years 1799–1801 saw many food riots and protests against high taxes.[12] Secondly, the government behaved as if threats of revolution were both real and imminent. It had to deal with two naval mutinies in the spring of 1797. In a year of major crisis for the war effort (see Chapter 12), these were serious affairs. It may have suited the government's purpose to exaggerate such threats since they helped to justify more repressive legislation. There was little difficulty in rounding up the leading suspects. Its opponents denounced fresh attacks on Englishmen's liberties. Increased regulation of, and taxes on, newspapers were introduced in 1798, in an attempt to put 'dangerous' publications out of reach for the lower orders. The Combination Act of 1799 outlawed trade unions – 'combinations' of working people to raise wages. In the same year, the London Corresponding Society and the United Irishmen were formally banned. In 1801, Habeas Corpus was suspended again.

Thirdly, much of the revolutionary activity which reaches the surface in these years has Irish involvement. Irish nationalist leaders saw the war as an opportunity to call on French aid to mount an invasion in support of a war of liberation. James O'Coigly, an ordained Catholic priest, seems to have been the leader of a plot in 1797–98 which included recent Irish migrants to England who were working in Manchester and London. Some members of the London Corresponding Society, including its Secretary, Thomas Evans, were also involved. O'Coigly was arrested in Kent as he tried to make his way to France and hanged in 1798. In 1802 Colonel Edward Despard, an Irish landowner, ex-army officer and probably a member of the London Corresponding Society, was involved in a plot which involved taking the Tower of London and the capture, and possible execution, of the King.[13] He was captured in 1802 and executed in 1803. Both O'Coigly and Despard worked with a shadowy organisation known as the United Englishmen, of which no record seems to exist before

1796. To what extent its objectives differed from those of the United Irishmen (see Chapter 14) is unclear but it included Irish personnel and had close links with a break-away wing of the London Corresponding Society committed to violence. After the execution of Despard, however, rumours of insurrectionary plots fall away.[14]

IV. Loyalism

Scholarly interpretations from the 1960s and 1970s concentrated on the rise of artisan radicalism in the 1790s and on the government's 'repressive' response to revolutionary threats. They fitted neatly into a progressive story charting growing pressure for reform in the years before the Reform Act of 1832 (see Chapter 20). This is a slanted view. It was not just a fearful landowners' parliament which opposed reform. Parliament spoke for many, at least down to the level of the shopkeeping classes, who thought that ideas about liberty were bought at too high a price. During 1792, the newly established Association for the Preserving of Liberty and Property against Republicans and Levellers recruited in large numbers. One historian has claimed that opposition to radicalism in the 1790s won the key arguments and that conservative attitudes and beliefs were 'widespread among large sections of the population'.[15] This view has not won wholehearted acceptance. The conservatism flowing through the Association movement has been described, albeit tendentiously, as 'vulgar' and much of the propaganda put out by the Association movement was not so much in defence of a coherent conservative position as an alert to the middle classes that they should 'fear the ignorant and violent character of their social inferiors'.[16]

Determining which 'side' won the argument in the 1790s is not straightforward. It is easy to understand why many in the middle classes should see the defence of property as essential to the maintenance of status. The phrase 'liberty and property' was more than an easy slogan. The educated eighteenth-century mind held that the defence of property rights was essential to the appreciation of liberty. It involved free-dom to take responsibility, freedom to trade and take risks, the confidence to make informed decisions in a complex, rapidly changing world and above all the absence of interference from established hierarchies. Thus, many property owners saw no con-tradiction between a broadly anti-aristocratic, reformist view of the world and resistance to theoretical speculation and to lectures about abstract rights from mere 'citizens'. Large numbers joined Volunteers Companies, the formation of which the government sanctioned in 1794. By 1805, about 400,000 men had enlisted. They had diverse reasons for doing so but, as Linda Colley has said, the motivation of most was 'quite simply [the threat of] invasion'.[17]

It is more difficult to gauge popular opinion when the evidence is limited and opaque. Artisan radicals could attract large crowds to pro-reform meetings in the cities, especially when economic conditions were poor. It is probable, however, that the largest gather-ings reflected hunger politics rather than considered support for political reform. The more skilled the workers, the more secure their employment and the higher their levels of literacy, the more they adopted a Painite position. The lower down the social scale, the less 'political' the response. Many of the poor believed that politics were not their sphere. Some continued to respect their betters for their greater education and understanding and followed their lead. Perhaps the main influence, though, was straightforward patriotism. An English nation so easily be roused to anti-Scottish sentiments a little earlier in the century (see Chapter 1) would respond to calls to defend Britain against threats from France. War bred patriots and, revolutionaries or not, the French remained both natural enemy and 'Catholic other'. France threatened British liberties, however imperfectly that notion was understood. Cartoonists and propagandists also took a predominantly patriotic line. **James Gillray**, in particular, frequently reinforced the message that the French threat took precedence over all other considerations. His loyalty secured with a pension from William Pitt, he characterised 'French principles' as abhorrent. He denounced political radicalism in general, and Charles James Fox in particular, as 'unBritish'.

James Gillray, 1756–1815

Perhaps the most gifted practitioner during what was a golden age of political caricature, Gillray was born in London, the son of a soldier who fought in the War of the Austrian Succession. He was apprenticed first to a lettering engraver and then attended the Royal Academy Schools. He did not commit himself to caricature work until the later 1780s, but then revealed an extraordinary talent for visual characterisation, especially of Pitt, Fox and Burke. Although he did work for the government, he was not a political partisan, seeing the self-interested and the potentially corrupt in almost any given situation. His satire on the Ministry of All the Talents (1806–7), representing ministers as pigs – a 'new litter of happy grunters' – is particularly celebrated.

It is not easy to gauge the effectiveness of government and other propaganda in favour of the status quo. Certainly, the authorities considered it necessary to keep the pressure up in the second half of the eighteenth century. George Canning, later Prime Minister, first came to prominence as a waspishly effective journalist on the *Anti-Jacobin*, a pro-government newspaper edited by the Devonshire verse-satirist William Gifford, and published in 1797 and 1798. Canning's clever rhyming couplets frequently punctured their targets, as here in a denunciation of Foxite Whig foreign policy:

> A steady patriot of the world alone
> The friend of every country but his own.[18]

The Evangelical religious revival also played its part. Evangelicalism aimed at moral reformation, promoting vital Christianity, as opposed to paying religion lip-service.

It stressed the importance of a practical Christian life in action. Evangelicalism was activated by humanitarian considerations, as both its contribution to the anti-slavery movement (see Chapter 15) and the generous charitable donations made by its most prominent supporters attest. Particularly as interpreted by the so-called 'Church Evangelicals' operating within the Church of England, rather than as nonconformists, it was also socially quietist. Very few supported parliamentary reform. The general drift of the evangelical message was twofold. First, the wasteful and lecherous habits of the upper classes set a poor example to the lower orders. What was called 'polite society' created some desperately inappropriate role models. Secondly, radical politics were misguided in themselves. They undermined the cohesion of society and led the lower orders astray. It was a general Evangelical tendency to wallow in sinfulness – particularly the sinfulness of others. For them, the French Revolution was 'both . . . a manifestation of evil and . . . a divine punishment for the sins of everyone'.[19]

William Wilberforce considered his 'vital Christianity' to be the solution. It made 'the inequalities of the social scale less galling to the lower orders, whom he also instructs, to be diligent, humble, patient; reminding them that their more lowly path has been allotted to them by the hand of God'.[20] Wilberforce's Evangelical colleague **Hannah More** produced more insidious anti-reform propaganda. For *Village Politics* (1792), directed at 'mechanics, journeymen, and day labourers', she created the character of 'Will Chip', a country carpenter who epitomised the virtues of sobriety, hard work and honesty. In her tales, Chip was always on hand to warn labourers about the dangers of heeding ideas about equal rights and citizenship. *Cheap Repository Tracts*, a collection of more than a hundred morality tales written by herself and her sisters Sarah and Martha, followed. The messages of the *Tracts*, aimed at ordinary honest workmen, were unremittingly loyalist. Employers bought multiple copies for distribution around their labour force. More than two million sales were made in one year alone.

William Wilberforce, 1759–1833

Born in Hull into a prosperous trading family, he was educated at Hull Grammar School and then at Cambridge University, where he met, and became a lifelong friend of, the Younger Pitt. Pitt's political influence was of use to him at various stages of his career. He experienced a religious conversion in the mid-1780s and thereafter devoted himself to good causes. In particular, he became the parliamentary leader of the movement to abolish the slave trade. During the 1790s, he failed in a number of attempts to pass legislation to this effect before an abolition bill was passed by the Grenville ministry in 1807. Wilberforce was associated with a number of other humanitarian causes, including prison reform, and he was an active member of the Society for Bettering the Condition of the Poor. His charitable bequests were substantial. In 1798, he donated more than £2,000, more than £170,000 at early twenty-first-century values.

Hannah More, 1745–1833

Hannah More was born in Bristol, the daughter of a schoolmaster. With her sisters, she ran a boarding school before establishing a reputation as a playwright in Bath and London in the 1770s. She wrote a number of works particularly for women, including *Essays Principally Designed for Young Ladies* (1777) and *Strictures on the Modern System of Female Education* (1799). She became an evangelical Christian in the 1780s and campaigned with Wilberforce for the abolition of the slave trade. Many of her publications in the 1780s and 1790s were designed to improve the morals of social elites. In the 1790s, she established schools for the poor in and around Cheddar (Somerset). To counteract the influence of the French Revolution on the poor, she produced *Village Politics* (1792) and *Cheap Repository Tracts* (1795–98). Her publications reached a wide audience, both among the lower orders and the propertied classes. She had a substantial effect on the moral climate of the age.

Debate about the impact of the French Revolution continues. It is clear that the French Revolution radicalised an important section of the working population. Although support for political reform continued within the middle classes, it is difficult to deny that most property owners became much more wary. For many, the execution of the French King and Queen, the wider bloodlust of the Terror and the establishment of a republic offered sufficient evidence that a revolution originating in Enlightenment ideals had developed a malign, aberrant and aggressive momentum of its own. Looked at from the perspective of 1793, the Revolution had spiralled out of control. For most, the key development was not ideological but visceral. The outbreak of war between Britain and France polarised opinion along lines of patriotism and national identity. France had long since been established as the national enemy and its defeat was widely seen as the key priority. By the turn of the century, the political reform issue had been sidelined and many of its advocates either took up other causes or were operating in the shadows. As we shall see, however (Chapters 15 and 16), even before the French wars were over, the reformers' agenda had moved centre-stage once again.

12

....

The French Revolutionary Wars, 1793–1801

I. The road to war

It took contemporaries some time to appreciate the significance of the French Revolution. In the summer of 1789, British eyes were on events in the Netherlands, where, although French interests had been thwarted in 1787 (see Chapter 10), the situation remained uncertain. In 1789–90, Pitt commented little on events in France, though he would shortly regret a statement in February 1790 that 'the present convulsions' must 'terminate in harmony and regular order' and that the Revolution might make France 'less obnoxious as a neighbour' since the country 'would enjoy that just kind of liberty which he venerated'.[1]

Although the roaring success of Burke's polemic (see Chapter 11) on the French Revolution concentrated many propertied minds, it did little to alter diplomatic relations between Britain and France in 1790–91. Events moved more speedily in 1792, partly because of the radicalisation of the French Revolution and the declaration of a republic, but mainly because of the outbreak of war between Austria and France in April. Britain remained neutral and, like most European powers, anticipated a crushing French defeat. Events turned out very differently. In early November the French general Charles Dumouriez won a crushing victory at the Battle of Jemappes. The French took control of the Austrian Netherlands, territory which equates to that of modern Belgium. It was these developments which most alarmed Pitt. The French decision to open the estuary of the River Scheldt to all navigation, anyway contrary to a series of international agreements dating back to 1648, threatened Britain's trading interests in the Low Countries. Even more importantly, the southern Netherlands in French hands represented a significant threat to the United Provinces in the north. By mid-November 1792, the government had agreed that it would be prepared to go to war to protect both British commerce and the Dutch.[2] Even so, as late as the end of December, frantic diplomatic activity was in progress to avoid war. Had it been successful, and despite the perilous plight of Louis XVI of France, who was about to be put on trial for his life, Britain would have acknowledged France's status as a republic.

Louis's execution on 21 January 1793 ended any lingering hopes of continued peace. Pitt called it the 'foulest and most atrocious deed'.[3] Britain hired 13,000 Hanoverian troops to help defend the Dutch against France.[4] Even so, it was the French

Convention which declared hostilities against Britain on 1 February, deciding at the same time to launch an attack on the Dutch Republic. Though war was inevitable, and revulsion at the execution of the French King widespread, at least among the propertied classes, Britain, unlike France, was not launching an ideological war. It aimed to defend its own commercial interests while also attempting to maintain the existing balance of power in western Europe which France's attack on the Low Countries directly threatened.

II. Coalitions and subsidies

Pitt's optimism about the outcome of the war was ill-founded. Ever inclined to see all aspects of political life in rational and quantitative terms, his judgment was based on two factors. First, the French economy had virtually collapsed before the Revolution. Nothing since then suggested to him that France could sustain an expensive war for any length of time. Secondly, Britain would not be fighting alone. Within a month of the declaration of war, an apparently powerful coalition was in place. Britain, Prussia and Holland were already allies (see Chapter 9); Austria, Prussia and Sardinia were already at war with France. Spain, ruled by the Bourbon King Charles IV, was also readily recruited. The so-called First Coalition fell naturally into place.

Pitt's optimism was quickly quenched. Revolutionary governments rarely play by conventional rules and the French response to the enlarged coalition it now faced was both impressive and effective. The armies of the main European powers traditionally relied on the use of **mercenaries**. The French reacted to this major threat to their revolution by issuing a *levée en masse*: in effect, conscription into the armed forces. As a result, France could put large forces into the field. The general quality of French commanders, even before the emergence of Napoleon Bonaparte, was also high. To meet a desperate shortage of cash, 'assignats' had been issued since the end of 1790 as a form of paper currency. Albeit at the cost of substantial inflation, assignats did their short-term job. The financial system did not collapse. It was military success, however, which kept France economically afloat until early 1797 when the country was forced to go back to a metal-based currency.

Mercenaries

Soldiers, often from another country, who are hired for fighting. During the eighteenth and early nineteenth centuries, Britain often recruited into its army soldiers from one of the German states. Some of these were hired individually or in groups; others were provided by a ruler in larger numbers in return for payment.

Britain's war strategy showed unsurprising similarities to that so successfully employed by the Elder Pitt in the 1750s. It had two prongs: continental alliances supported by British subsidies and a naval 'blue-water' strategy which defended existing commercial interests and captured enemy colonies. Since Britain had no territorial claims in continental Europe, it made sense to pay allies to engage the enemy there. Britain made tactical forays in support either of their allies or of French royalists plotting to destroy the Revolution from within. The first three years of the war followed a familiar pattern. Subsidies paid to German states and to Sardinia increased from £833,000 in 1793 to £5.7m in 1795. It has been estimated that, over the course of the two wars from 1793 to 1815, Britain provided more than £46m in subsidies and loans to European allies great and small. Even Morocco, on the North African coast, appeared on the government's payroll in 1812 and 1813 – to the tune of £16,000.[5]

Britain's direct involvement in European warfare during the 1790s achieved little. In August 1793, a detachment from the Mediterranean fleet under Alexander Hood occupied Toulon in support of counter-revolutionaries, but the French army had forced its withdrawal by Christmas. The King's second son, the **Duke of York**, substantially over-promoted to head British forces in Flanders (southern Netherlands), fought the French in alliance with Austrian troops under the Prince of Coburg. After early successes, the allies suffered major military defeats at the hands of a remodelled French army in the autumn of 1793 and spring of 1794.

Prince Frederick, Duke of York and Albany, 1763–1827

Frederick was born in London, the second, and favourite, son of George III and his wife, Queen Charlotte of Mecklenburg-Strelitz. He entered the army in 1780 and spent most of the following decade in Hanover. His leadership of British forces in the southern Netherlands in 1793–95 was widely criticised, giving rise to the ironic nursery rhyme 'The Grand Old Duke of York' who 'had ten thousand men. He marched them up to the top of the hill, and he marched them down again.' His father created him a field marshal and Commander-in-Chief of the British army in 1798. This led to a further humiliating reverse in the Low Countries in 1799. He was, however, instrumental in attempting to raise army morale and in getting rid of incompetent officers and replacing them with men of greater talent. This initiative led to a scandal in 1809. The Duke's mistress from 1803 to 1806, Mary Ann Clarke, promised promotion to army officers in return for payment. The Duke was himself accused of trading army office for payment. Although the House of Commons dropped the charges, the Duke had, at the least, been incautious and unwise in his dealings. He was heir to the throne from 1820 until his death from dropsy leading to heart failure.

The intrinsic weaknesses of the First Coalition were ruthlessly exposed during 1795. Two British naval attempts to support French counter-revolutionary royalist émigrés, first at Quiberon Bay, north-west of Nantes, and then further south at La Vendée, were easily repulsed. There would be no immediate restoration of the Bourbon monarchy. By the end of April 1795, the French had overrun Holland. British troops had to be hastily evacuated. France's formal annexation of Holland was complete by the autumn. In one of many instances of French revolutionary thraldom to classical provenance, Holland was transmuted into 'the Batavian Republic'. Dutch or Latin, it declared war on Britain. Prussia had already made peace with France in April. French forces successfully invaded Spain and Piedmont, in modern north-west Italy. Spain agreed peace terms with France in July. With only Austria and Sardinia still in the field at the end of the year, the First Coalition had in effect collapsed.

What had gone wrong? The Coalition was never coherent since the Allies squabbled among themselves, not least about their objectives. Prussia and Austria had far greater interests in central and eastern Europe than did Britain. From a British perspective, the partitions of Poland in 1792 and 1795 represented an irritatingly significant diversion. Austria proved a particularly troublesome ally. It complained about the terms under which Britain proposed to make further loans and did nothing to support British plans in La Vendée. The Foreign Secretary, Lord Grenville, complained in September 1795 about the 'Timidity and Uncertainty' of Austria.[6] Harassed in parliament by MPs who considered expensive subsidies merely wasteful, the British government's thoughts increasingly turned to peace. Grenville and Pitt continued to hope that the increasingly burdensome costs of war would bring revolutionary France to the conference table. The ending of the 'Terror' phase of the revolution, the establishment of a new constitution and the emergence of the so-called Directory in November 1795 were all considered as hopeful signs.

Events in Europe in 1796–97 required such hopes to be deferred. In August 1796, Spain signed an offensive alliance with France. Two months later, it declared war on Britain. Meanwhile, Napoleon, now commander of French forces in Italy, enjoyed spectacular success. Defeats were inflicted on Sardinia, which hastily declared its neutrality. A series of French victories in Italy led to substantial territorial gains at Austria's expense. By the Treaty of Campo Formio of October 1797, Austria made peace with France and pro-French client states were established in northern Italy. Peace negotiations with France having broken down in 1796, Britain continued the war without allies.

III. Sea power and naval strategy

The second prong of Britain's war strategy – sea power – played to Britain's strength as a maritime nation. The aim was to eliminate France as an effective commercial or imperial competitor. The strategy also had a more defensive purpose. Captured French colonies might prove a useful bargaining counter in later peace negotiations. As in previous eighteenth-century wars, particular attention was paid to the navy.

A complement of 16,000 in 1792, the last year of peace, had risen to 120,000 by 1798, when the cost to the Exchequer at that point had spiralled to £13.5m.[7]

Henry Dundas, as Secretary for War, held primary responsibility for the colonies. He looked first to the French West Indies. Martinique and St Domingue, reputedly the richest colony in any European empire, were in British sights in 1793. The British enjoyed some early successes in America and Asia. Some smaller French possessions in Newfoundland and India were taken in 1793. The island of Tobago, ceded to France at the Treaty of Versailles ten years earlier, reverted into British hands. The following year, a fleet under **Sir Charles Grey** captured Martinique, Guadeloupe and St Lucia in the spring. However, insufficient supporting forces were available to defend these gains. All were back in French hands by the summer of 1795, by which time the British were tied down by slave uprisings, aided by the French, especially in Jamaica.[8]

Sir Charles Grey, 1729–1807

Born at Howick (Northumberland), the son of a baronet, he owed his early army promotion to his father's influence. He served in the Duke of Cumberland's army at the Battle of Culloden. He fought in both the Seven Years War and the American War of Independence before going into partial retirement. He was recalled to service at the outbreak of war with France and led the expedition to the West Indies which captured French sugar islands in 1794. He was promoted General in 1796 and was in charge of British defences against invasion in 1797. His high competence as an army officer was compromised by a number of accusations both of cruelty to captives and of enriching himself by harsh fines levied on property owners in captured colonies. He was the father of Earl Grey who passed the Reform Act in 1832.

Grey's mission eventually failed because Pitt gave priority to landing a decisive blow on the French in European waters. Thirty-two French ships were captured here between early 1793 and early 1794. A breakthrough looked imminent when **Admiral Howe** defeated the French in the Atlantic on 1 June 1794, capturing six ships and returning with them to Portsmouth amid much jubilation. This engagement was quickly, though erroneously, dubbed 'The Glorious First of June'. It was no knockout blow. The French fleet had been protecting a massive shipment of grain from the United States. Though ships were lost, the grain got through. Howe's success was not followed up and by 1795 France was rebuilding its navy. The Dutch and Spanish were now allies of France and both possessed significant navies. By 1796, the balance of power in the Mediterranean had shifted. Britain was forced to reduce its operations there to give priority to defending its own shores against invasion and to protecting both commerce and colonies in the West Indies. The British did, however, take control of Ceylon from the Dutch early in 1796.

Richard Howe, 1726–1799

Born in London, the son of an Irish peer, Howe had a long and distinguished naval career. He was first enlisted at the age of 13 and saw action in the War of the Austrian Succession, the Seven Years War and the American War of Independence. His activities in America drew considerable criticism but he outmanoeuvred the Franco-Spanish fleet in relieving Gibraltar and returning it to British hands in 1782. He was MP for the naval constituency of Dartmouth continuously from 1757 to 1782, when the Rockingham administration promoted him full Admiral with a peerage. He was First Lord of the Admiralty from 1783 to 1788 and was Commander of the Channel Fleet during the French Revolutionary Wars. His intervention prevented the naval mutiny at Spithead in 1797 from spiralling out of control. He was a formidable organiser, a master of detail and was respected by those serving under him. He was influential in promoting the efficiency and professionalisation of the British navy in the eighteenth century.

Renewed efforts in the Caribbean met with mixed success at best. A huge expeditionary force, eventually totalling 35,000 men, shored up Britain's hold on Jamaica in 1795–96 and captured the Dutch South American colonies of Berbice, Demerara and Essequibo. The operation secured Britain's commerce in the Americas. However, the French were not ejected from Guadeloupe or St Domingue and the British lost 14,000 troops to yellow fever and malaria in 1796 alone.[9] Probably 40,000 naval and army personnel died and as many were incapacitated in the West Indies in the years 1793–96. The capture of Trinidad from Spain in February 1797 was only limited compensation.

IV. Struggle for survival

In the years 1797–1802, Britain faced a struggle for survival. The last chance for a negotiated peace appeared to have gone in September 1797 when the so-called Coup d'État of Fructidor increased the influence of the French military and the more radical revolutionaries at the expense of the moderates. Pitt now had to find cash to pay the ever increasing bills. Government borrowing had risen almost tenfold since the war began, from £4.5m in 1793 to £44m in 1797, which represents £3,784m in early twenty-first-century values. This led to fiscal crisis. The Bank of England suspended cash payments in February 1797. With cash running out, the government found it almost impossible to raise new loans. In response, Pitt substantially increased **assessed taxes** in the so-called Triple Assessment Bill and, when this failed to produce sufficient income, introduced Britain's first direct tax on income in 1799. His tax proposals were vigorously opposed in parliament, especially by Foxite Whigs, who claimed that they placed unsupportable burdens on the middle ranks in society.[10] The finance bills passed, however. The ability of an increasingly prosperous middle class to pay its taxes proved to be a critical factor in Britain's ability to outlast France in what would turn into a war of attrition (see Chapter 13).

Assessed taxes

This term referred in the eighteenth century to taxes raised on commodities, especially on goods which could be defined as luxuries. These included horses and carriages, dogs, windows and even inhabited houses.

Naval unrest and the threat of invasion also contributed to make 1797 a crisis year. True, the invasion was the dampest of damp squibs. A small, ill-trained French force, led by a 70-year-old Irish-American, Colonel William Tate, was bound for Bristol. Blown off course, it landed at Fishguard (Pembrokeshire) in February. The invasion force, as bemused by unfamiliar geography as it was befuddled by familiar brandy, was easy meat for the local militia. The lesson, however, was that even a small force can make a landing on British soil. Effective naval and coastal defence against a larger, better-disciplined force was considered to be a priority.

Against a background of increased economic distress, the navy experienced two mutinies near to the English coast. One at Spithead, off Portsmouth, against conditions on ship and low pay, lasted from mid-April to mid-May 1797; the other, at The Nore, in the Thames Estuary, began in mid-May. The Nore was the more overtly radical. Its mutineers called for the dissolution of parliament and immediate peace with France. They won some concessions on pay and the replacement of unpopular officers but discontent within the navy continued. This was hardly surprising since so many sailors were forcibly 'impressed' into service during the 1790s. Further unrest was experienced both in the West Indies and off the coast of Ireland.

Discontented and occasionally mutinous the British seaman may have been. Incompetent he was not. The numerical naval superiority available to the French after the accession of the Dutch and Spanish fleets did not last long. British victories against the Spanish fleet off Cape St Vincent in February and the Dutch fleet at Camperdown, north-west of Amsterdam, in October rectified the imbalance. A number of enemy ships were captured during both engagements. These victories provided renewed evidence of the superior tactical awareness of British naval commanders – Jervis at St Vincent and Duncan at Camperdown. The most celebrated naval commander of the age, Horatio Nelson (see Chapter 13), won an even more decisive victory in August 1798 against the French fleet in Aboukir Bay, near Alexandria in Egypt. Eleven of the thirteen French warships were destroyed. This foiled the plans of Napoleon Bonaparte, who had led a French force into Egypt in 1798 as part of an ambitious strategy to disrupt profitable British trade through the Mediterranean and on to India. The French navy never recovered from this mauling. Malta, an island in the eastern Mediterranean of considerable strategic importance which Napoleon had captured on his journey to the Middle East in 1798, came under British control in 1800 after a British naval blockade helped a Maltese uprising against French rule.

Further diplomatic negotiations came to fruition in late December 1798 when a second coalition against France, comprising Britain, Austria, Russia, Naples and Portugal, was formed. British subsidies were again a potent inducement to participation, although Prussia remained aloof. Hostilities were formally declared at the beginning of March 1799. Grenville had been especially active in the negotiations. His aim was a grand coalition to overwhelm France. Like the First Coalition, the Second achieved some initial success, especially in Italy. However, Grenville had made a double miscalculation. The new coalition was one of convenience not conviction. All felt threatened by rampant French expansionism. There the similarities ended. Russia and Austria had been suspicious of each other for years and early Russian successes in Italy alarmed the Austrians. To Grenville's fury, they refused to co-operate in the Anglo-Russian attempt to wrest control of the Netherlands from France. The direct involvement of British troops, commanded again by the Duke of York, was restricted to three months' nugatory activity in the Low Countries from August to November 1799.

Grenville's other miscalculation was Napoleon Bonaparte. He was not only a commander of genius. By the end of 1799, Bonaparte was also First Consul of France and, in effect, its ruler. He put his new power to quick effect, winning a comprehensive victory over the Austrians at the Battle of Marengo in June 1800. General Jean Moreau inflicted a further defeat in December at Hohenlinden in southern Germany. By this time, Russia had already withdrawn from the coalition. Austria had little option but to come to terms with France at the Treaty of Luneville in February 1801. Although Britain's war with France spluttered on until early 1802, grand plans for a combined allied victory had long since crumbled to dust.

Hard-pressed and war-weary, British opinion during 1801 strongly favoured peace. The new administration of Henry Addington (see Chapter 14) conducted negotiations which led to the Treaty of Amiens in March 1802. It helped Britain little. Both Britain and France agreed to let Egypt revert to Turkish rule; France also gave up claims to southern Italy. France did, however, retain most of its European gains further north while, from its full quiver of colonial conquests, Britain retained only two: Ceylon in the east and Trinidad in the west. The Cabinet ministers with foreign and colonial responsibility under Pitt were bitterly critical of the new government. Windham melodramatically asserted that the Treaty represented 'the death warrant' of the country. Grenville was alarmed that so much territory 'on which our security in a new contest may principally depend' had been so lightly sacrificed.[11] Their concerns, and also Grenville's prescience about the likelihood of a 'new contest', were buried under massive public expressions of joy at the return of peace.

V. A failure of strategy?

The French Revolutionary wars were a failure. How critical of Pitt's wartime strategy should the historian be? By 1797, the country – in dire financial straits – was hanging

on for dear life and Pitt must bear his share of the blame. He did not take to governing in wartime. Its contingencies and uncertainties of armed conflict more often grated
on than stimulated his orderly mind. Nevertheless, despite lacking appropriate
experience, he was determined always to give a lead. His response to a setback was
to work yet harder. Hard pressed, and with almost no domestic diversions, his
judgment was tested and frequently found wanting. Against mounting evidence, it
proved impossible to dissuade him from the view that France would be overcome
if attacked on several fronts at once. Britain's two-pronged strategy worked better
in theory than in practice. In 1794–95, for example, the navy was pinched for
resources because of Britain's commitments on the continent. Grey's expedition to
the West Indies suffered as a result. The so-called Glorious First of June would have
been useful as well as glorious if resources had been made available to follow it up.
Operational activities sat awkwardly within the overall strategy. Pitt often misread
the Allies' priorities and intentions and was slow to react to changing circumstances. Diplomatic initiatives were often heavy-legged. When things went badly, as
they increasingly did from 1794, Pitt was prone to bouts of depression.[12] Much of
the subsidy money was wasted and the subsidy policy contributed significantly to
the financial crisis of 1797. Britain limped thereafter towards a messy, inadequate
and, above all, insecure peace.

Yet, given the hand he was dealt, would any other leader have done better? Pitt
failed to foresee how effectively revolutionary power and direction could be harnessed
to defend France and its revolution – but so did everyone else. The French
Revolution, even as its Terror phase gripped the nation, made its own weather. Its
military organisation was impressive from late 1792 onwards, and the revolution threw
up effective commanders even before Napoleon's genius transformed the scene.
Even as it passed through bewilderingly rapid stages, the revolution was creating
a new, and much more inclusive, sense of national identity. Eighteenth-century conventions both of war and diplomacy, dictated by royal and aristocratic elites, were
ill-equipped to cope with it.

Pitt also had troubles not entirely of his own making at home. The sealing of the
coalition between himself and Portland in 1794 provided impregnable parliamentary majorities but it did not make for easy government. Pitt led a divided Cabinet,
several of whose members he did not trust. Some – and particularly the Secretary
at War William Windham – were as determinedly, and impractically, driven by the
desire to destroy all things revolutionary as were the monarchs and emperors of continental Europe. Ironically, since they had been close allies of Fox until the early 1790s,
more anti-French fanatics came from the old Foxite Whig camp than from Pitt's own
supporters. The fact that Grenville and Dundas, his closest political allies, occupied
critical positions in the administration was partial compensation. He used them as
a sounding-board for ideas and as kind of privileged inner Cabinet. Unsurprisingly,
though, this irked other Cabinet members.

In any case, Grenville and Dundas disagreed on war strategy. Grenville, who wanted to see the French Revolution destroyed, favoured every 'big push' in Europe. Dundas, less ideologically driven, favoured the 'blue-water strategy': colonial expansion (including the capture of French and Spanish colonies) and overseas commerce backed by naval might. Pitt did not take a decisive direction. Thus, the Cabinet remained divided on whether seeking an honourable peace was preferable to waging ideological war in defence of that civilisation in which all of its members were steeped.

It is also worth stressing the positive attributes which Pitt brought to the task. He was an effective speaker in the Commons and frequently won over members initially critical of his policies. He also persuaded MPs to vote continued supplies and new taxes. Building up the navy brought longer-term benefits. Above all, his financial grasp equipped Britain to face the rigours of a long war. It is a considerable irony that, while Pitt was persuaded only with the greatest reluctance that the war with France would not be short, his financial policies were instrumental in ensuring that Britain would be able to fight the long one which would be won, albeit not until a decade after his death and at immensely high cost.

13

....

The Napoleonic Wars, 1803–1815

I. War resumed

The Peace of Amiens, so wildly celebrated in Britain, lasted less than fourteen months. The main reason for this was Napoleon's restless dual quest to consolidate French military dominance in Europe and also to continue the export of French revolutionary principles – at least those principles as interpreted by him. Thus, French troops continued to occupy Holland after the Peace was signed. Napoleon reoccupied Switzerland at the beginning of 1803 and continued to dominate northern Italy. He also tweaked George III's nose by occupying Hanover, of which the King was also ruler. Napoleon invested in naval reconstruction aimed at mounting a fresh challenge on Britain's naval supremacy while also casting a covetous eye towards India. This represented a direct challenge to Britain, which, increasingly wary, did not quit Malta as the Amiens Treaty had required. Recognising that peace was unsustainable in the face of Napoleon's provocations, the Prime Minister, **Henry Addington**, took the initiative and declared war on France in mid-May.[1] This second French war would last longer and prove to be much more costly even than the first.

Henry Addington, first Viscount Sidmouth, 1757–1844

Born the son of a physician from a minor gentry family in Oxfordshire, he was educated at Winchester College and Oxford University. He became an MP in 1784 and supported Pitt. He was elected Speaker of the House of Commons in 1789, a post he held until 1801 when the King asked him to form a government. Though a poor speaker in the Commons, he was a generally competent minister and he improved on Pitt's income tax by halving the rate at which it was levied but collecting it at source. He resigned in 1804 after Pitt withdrew his support. He accepted a peerage in 1805, being known thereafter as Viscount Sidmouth, and joined Pitt's government. He was Home Secretary under Liverpool (see Chapter 16) from 1812 to 1822 but after that did not hold office during the remaining twenty-two years of his life.

Addington ordered a blockade of French ports. The aim, as in the 1790s, was to make maximum use of sea power and also to provoke Bonaparte to attack one of the greater European powers, thus making it easier to rebuild an anti-French coalition. Bonaparte reacted by moving troops to Boulogne to threaten immediate invasion of Britain. This was hardly realistic given the state of the French navy in 1803.

Nevertheless, news of French troop movements caused alarm in Britain. Addington's government passed an Act enabling it to call up males between the ages of 17 and 55 for military training. Addington's appeals for patriotic service in 1803 proved far less divisive than Pitt's had been in the 1790s, when French Revolutionary ideals still had some purchase in Britain. Cartoonists now represented Bonaparte either as an arrogant, vainglorious warlord or, thoroughly implausibly, as a puny midget in the control of Britain. Volunteers came forward in droves. By the beginning of 1804, 85,000 men had been recruited for service in the official militia, placing themselves under military law. More than 400,000, activated by a heightened sense of patriotism, became Volunteers. They received military training but were also free to resign. Many were ordinary working men and many did later resign, validating Windham's calculation that a permanent volunteer system 'was very near a contradiction in terms'.[2] In 1804, however, a heightened sense of patriotism contributed substantially to recruitment in the struggle against France.

By the spring of 1804, Addington was facing political difficulties in the form of lower majorities in the Commons and loss of control in the Lords. With the unlikely combination of Pitt, Grenville and Fox voting against him, the Prime Minister increasingly talked of resignation. When Addington threw in the towel in May, Pitt replaced him and would have formed a coalition government of national unity had not George III, by now a practised and exemplary nurser of long-term grudges, refused point-blank to allow Fox to join it.

Pitt was Prime Minister for the last twenty months of his life. He was joined in government by six members of Addington's Cabinet, including the Duke of Portland, Dundas (now ennobled as Viscount Melville) and Viscount Castlereagh.[3] The new government was neither distinguished nor secure. The King would rather Addington had stayed as Prime Minister and more or less forced Pitt to give him office in January 1805. Furthermore, Pitt showed signs both of strain – immoderately moderated by drink – and ill health. Nevertheless, this ministry witnessed developments which would determine the course of the remainder of the epic struggle against France. In April 1805, Russia and Britain agreed to an alliance. There was a mutual interest here. Russia was increasingly concerned about French aggression in northern Europe. Anything which promised greater security for Hanover would go down well with George III. Three months later, Austria joined the association – with the inevitable *douceur* of a British subsidy, this time of £3m. The so-called 'War of the Third Coalition' resulted.

Subsidy or no subsidy, Austria soon rued its decision. In September, the French Grand Army crossed the Rhine and in October the Danube. After the Battle of Ulm the Austrian general Mack surrendered, along with 25,000 men. Napoleon marched into Vienna in November and inflicted a yet more crushing defeat on a combined Austro-Russian force at Austerlitz at the beginning of December. With Napoleon apparently unchallengeable on land, the coalition was dead within a year. Prussia and Austria made rapid alliances of convenience, if not preservation, with Napoleon. The only benefit for Britain was that his military campaigns forced Napoleon to withdraw potential invasion forces from Boulogne.

The fortunes of war were spectacularly reversed at sea. After chasing the French fleet to the West Indies and back, a British fleet under **Horatio Nelson** decisively defeated a larger Franco-Spanish fleet off Cape Trafalgar, near Cadiz, on 21 October 1805, the day after the Battle of Ulm. Only five ships of the original fleet returned to the Spanish port in seaworthy condition. Nelson, whose last words apparently were 'God and my country', had, in a little under two hours, done more to save that country than any other individual during the French wars. Napoleon would never again challenge Britain's naval supremacy, in effect rendering a French invasion impossible. Nelson's funeral at St Paul's Cathedral was an apotheosis at which the British nation was encouraged to immortalise a glorious military hero, preserving the ideal of service and sacrifice for the inspiration of later generations.[4] Trafalgar decisively changed the nature of the Napoleonic wars.

Horatio Nelson, 1758–1805

Born the son of a country rector in Norfolk, Nelson joined the navy at the age of 12 and saw service in the East and West Indies during the American War of Independence. Like many able young naval officers during wartime, he was rapidly promoted. He earned a reputation as a commander for swift and decisive, if sometimes foolhardy, action. He was raised to the rank of Commodore in 1796, distinguished himself in the Battle of St Vincent in 1797 and was raised to the peerage after his victory at the Battle of the Nile in 1798. His personal courage led to severe injuries. He had lost an eye in Corsica in 1794, his right arm during an engagement in the Canaries in 1797 and received a severe head wound, which had long-term effects, at the Battle of the Nile. He won another important victory at the Battle of Copenhagen in 1801, when he defied the orders of his superior officer, Vice-Admiral Hyde-Parker. Ends justifying means, Nelson was promoted to a Viscountcy on his return. His reputation already unchallengeable, he commanded the Mediterranean fleet in the summer of 1805, which led to his victory at Trafalgar, during which engagement he was mortally wounded. Nelson was not an easy colleague. He could be both hot-tempered and insubordinate. His open, long-standing affair with Emma Hamilton, the wife of the British ambassador to the Two Sicilies, caused scandal and produced much evangelical outrage. He did, however, have great charisma and basked in the adulation his successes encouraged. For his long-standing reputation, he probably died at exactly the right time.

II. Commercial warfare

The year 1806 was one of almost complete triumph for Napoleon. He contemptuously rejected overtures for peace from Britain's new government, the so-called 'Ministry of All the Talents'. Back in office again as Foreign Secretary, after more than twenty-two immensely frustrating years, his peace plan proved to be Charles James Fox's last important initiative – and yet another failure.[5] By July, he knew that his peace plan was dead; his own death followed in September. Perhaps he could claim one minor, if unintentional, achievement. The failure of peace helped resolve a question which had perplexed Whig aristocrats: how were they to regard Napoleon? 'Boney' was both a man of enormous ability and also, after a fashion, a man of the people. He had embarked in France on a series of legal and administrative reforms which the Whigs applauded. Self-nominated Emperor or not, he was far more enlightened than those monarchs against whose tyrannous activities the Whigs convinced themselves they were defending the British people. But if Napoleon had the temerity to turn down Charles James Fox, then perhaps they needed to re-think. Napoleon was clearly an inveterate warmonger. Was he also an enemy of the strangely skewed, and often contradictory, beliefs which Whigs held dear? The third Baron Holland, social leader of the clan, made the definitive judgment eight years later. He wrote to his sister, Caroline Fox, in 1814: I 'hate and detest Bonaparte'.[6] Clearly, the Emperor's fate was sealed!

Meanwhile, Napoleon continued both to snaffle territory and, as with Joseph Bonaparte in Naples and Louis Bonaparte in Holland, make his brothers into Kings. The King of Prussia, not unnaturally, saw the newly created Confederation of the Rhine – 'Protector' Napoleon Bonaparte – as a threat to his territories. Prussia declared war on France in early October 1806 but was defeated within a week at the Battles of Jena and Auerstadt. A swift, almost unchallenged invasion of Prussia resulted and Napoleon was in Berlin by the end of October. The following month, with his usual theatrical sense both of place and timing, he issued his Berlin Decrees from the Prussian capital. This formally inaugurated economic warfare against Britain. In May 1806, Britain had announced a blockade of French-controlled ports from Brest in the south to the mouth of the Elbe in the north, but this had damaged the economy of Prussia more than it did that of France. Now Napoleon returned the compliment with interest. Using his almost complete territorial domination of western and central Europe, Napoleon declared Britain to be in a state of blockade. All ports in France and in territories allied to France were closed to shipping from Britain or its colonies. All British goods in French territory would be confiscated and British citizens captured in French-held territory were liable to indefinite imprisonment.

Napoleon intended to starve Britain by stifling its commerce. The stakes were as high for France as for Britain. In January 1807, Britain retaliated with its 'Orders in Council', prohibiting trade between any two ports controlled by France. Portland's government (see Chapter 15) published further, more draconian Orders in November. Any port from which the French had excluded British trade was to be blockaded. All neutral ships trading in Europe were required to put in at a British port; favourable commercial terms then encouraged them to re-export from Britain.

For his universal embargo to do its intended job of commercial strangulation, Napoleon needed to sustain control over the entire coastline of western Europe. His grip on Europe tightened further in 1807, when he made peace with Russia and Prussia in July by the Treaties of Tilsit. Again, the treaties were imposed on the back of defeats. Napoleon harried Russian forces into bloody near-defeat at Eylau in February 1807 and complete defeat at Friedland a few months later. Russia was now driven out of Poland. Prussia lost roughly half its territory, some of which was rechristened Westphalia. Unsurprisingly, yet another brother of Napoleon became its King.

Britain responded in September with a long and unprovoked bombardment of Copenhagen. It wreaked havoc, not only destroying the Danish fleet but many public buildings too. The specific purpose – to prevent Napoleon from taking over Denmark's fleet and using it to secure the Baltic against Britain – was achieved, though at the cost of Danish entry into the war on Napoleon's side and a lowering of Britain's reputation through flagrant breaches of the rules of war. British ministers were unconcerned. Although a French navy enhanced by Danish ships was hardly likely to reverse the outcome of Trafalgar, Britain needed no lessons in flouting the conventions of war from Napoleon Bonaparte.

III. The 'Spanish ulcer'

Over one important western European coastline, the Iberian Peninsula, Napoleon lacked full control. He was rightly suspicious about Spain's continued commitment to alliance with France, particularly after the Trafalgar disaster. Portugal was Britain's oldest ally and British goods were still entering Europe from both Portugal and Spain. Napoleon aimed to close this substantial loophole in his blockade and, more generally, to strengthen France's position in the Peninsula by modernising loyal governments of both Spain and Portugal along Napoleonic lines.[7] In the autumn of 1807, aided by Spain's pro-French government, French troops attacked Portugal and captured its capital, Lisbon. Napoleon's forces then turned east to establish control over Spain. By the end of March 1808, Madrid was also in French hands. Two months later, the popular King Ferdinand VII, who himself had only recently succeeded the abdicated Charles IV, was himself replaced, in the now conventionally nepotistic fashion, by King Joseph Bonaparte.

Napoleon's initiative had strategic rationality. Success would have reduced Britain's chances of winning the economic war to which Napoleon was now committed. His error, more critical than seemed likely in the first part of 1808, was failure to anticipate Spanish reaction to the deposition of their King. A rebellion in Madrid was put down but at the cost of fomenting more widespread revolt. This determined Britain's response. Expeditions against the French in Egypt and the Spanish in Buenos Aires in 1806–7 having proved unsuccessful, an initiative in southern Europe to support nationalist upsurge seemed attractive. **Arthur Wellesley** was despatched to Portugal at the head of an expeditionary force in August 1808, while **Sir John Moore** left Lisbon for Spain in October.

Arthur Wellesley, first Duke of Wellington, 1769–1852

Born in Dublin, the son of an Irish peer, Wellesley entered the army in 1787 and first saw active service in the Netherlands in 1794 under the Duke of York. His reputation was enhanced by service in India in the years 1797–1806 when he played an important role in the capture of Mysore. He became an MP in 1806 and was Chief Secretary for Ireland in the years 1807–8. He was commander of the British forces in the Iberian peninsula in the years 1808–14, where he proved to be a resiliently effective defensive general, often gaining success against numerically superior forces. He gained a peerage as Viscount Wellington after his victory at Talavera in 1809. In 1812 was promoted first Earl, then Marquis, in rapid succession. The victory in Spain achieved, he was created a Duke in May 1814. His most famous military victory, also his last, was Waterloo in June 1815. It won him honours from almost all of the allied powers and he was an influential figure at the peace negotiations which restored the Bourbon monarchy. Wellington had a long political career after Waterloo. He joined Liverpool's government in 1818 and acted as adviser on all military, imperial and diplomatic matters. He stayed in office until Liverpool resigned in 1827, returning as Prime Minister (1828–30 and 1834), then Foreign Secretary (1834–35). Under Peel, and at the age of 72, he served as Minister without Portfolio (1841–46), again fulfilling an advisory, almost honorific role, on defence and the Empire, especially India. Neither Wellington's temperament nor his military experience matched the subtler, and perhaps more devious, requirements of a politician. A natural high Tory by conviction and used by experience and authority to having his orders unthinkingly obeyed, he often spoke without full consideration of the implications of his words. As Prime Minister, he bears responsibility for the break-up of the Tory party and for his opponents' passage of the 'Great' Reform Act, which he hated.

Sir John Moore, 1761–1809

Born in Glasgow, the son of a physician, he enlisted in the army at the age of 16. He was an MP from 1784 to 1790 but determined on a permanent career in the army. He saw much active service during the French Revolutionary wars, especially in Corsica and the West Indies. He was promoted Brigadier-General in 1795, and was a popular officer who inspired the loyalty of his troops. He served in Ireland, where he helped to put down the nationalist rebellion in 1798, and then in Egypt. He is best known for his role in the early part of the Peninsular War, when he was despatched with a force from Portugal into northern Spain with the objective of linking British forces with Spanish nationalists and driving the French out of Spain. Spanish support was inadequate and in January 1809 Moore was left to defend a position at Coruña against much superior French forces. British troops managed to evacuate Coruña successfully but Moore was killed in action.

It is not necessary to follow all the twists and turns of the Peninsular War, though it witnessed generalship of the highest order, particularly from Wellesley (later Duke of Wellington) on the British side and by Napoleon himself, Soult and Massena on the French. For Wellesley, the objective until the very end of the war was defensive.[8] Portugal must not be overrun. Wellesley was frequently forced onto the back foot, although successful offensive initiatives, such as those at Talavera (July 1809), Fuentes d'Onoro (May 1811) and Badajoz (April 1812), frustrated Napoleon's overall objective. Victories also afforded the opportunity for some incursions into Spain. Wellesley's decisive offensive was delayed until 1812. The decisive victory at Vitoria (June 1813) drove Joseph Bonaparte out of Spain and left the way open for Wellesley to cross the border into France itself.

The Peninsular War achieved Britain's key objective. French forces found themselves tied up in Spain and Portugal, frustrating Napoleon, who wanted to deploy them elsewhere. Wellington's understanding of the terrain and his ability to adapt his forces to harsh, mountainous conditions were critical to British success. So, as Wellington himself later acknowledged,[9] was the unflagging hostility of the Spanish to a French army of occupation. There was a psychological point too. Before the Peninsular War, Napoleon had achieved his military objectives decisively, and usually quickly, confirming his reputation as a military genius. Events in the Peninsula broke the spell. Reflecting later on his military career, he called his Spanish policy in 1807 one of the worst of his mistakes: his 'Spanish ulcer' never healed.

Beyond the Peninsula, however, Napoleon still enjoyed more or less unchallenged success. When, in 1809, Austria attempted to recoup earlier losses, it was defeated at the Battle of Wagram and forced to sign a treaty from which it lost yet more territory and to pay an indemnity to France. Britain's part in what is sometimes called the War of the Fifth Coalition was brief and inglorious. At the end of July, the government sent the largest British expeditionary force yet mounted to the island of Walcheren on the estuary of the River Scheldt. Almost forty thousand men arrived, charged both with taking Antwerp and destroying the French fleet anchored there. Indecisive leadership permitted Franco-Dutch troops time to prepare. Antwerp, well-defended, was never attacked. Instead, several thousand British soldiers and seamen on Walcheren were lost to disease, mostly to malaria and typhus which flourished on the damp, ill-drained flatlands. A further eleven thousand remained unfit for service in early 1810.

The Peninsula apart, Europe saw relatively little fighting in 1810 and 1811. Napoleon's empire was at its zenith. The only European powers not formally incorporated within it, or operating as client states, were Britain, Russia and, critically, part of Portugal. Napoleon's territorial dominance, however, was threatened by growing economic troubles. By 1810, he had realised that his 'Continental System' would not close off Europe to British trade. Worse, French industry was losing markets, not least because British ships had captured so many of France's colonial bases. Supply difficulties brought increased prices, which severe winters in Europe in 1809 and 1811 only exacerbated. French dominance was less securely grounded than it seemed.

Meanwhile, mutual disenchantment was growing between Russia and France. Tsar Alexander I gained far less from alliance with Napoleon than he had hoped and he feared remorseless French expansion. For his part, Napoleon was concerned that Russia was threatening his Continental System, which, by hook or very fragile crook (see Chapter 15), Britain was evading. He probably also feared a fresh Russian attack on Poland. Frustrated in the Peninsula, he felt that another spectacular victory would raise morale in France. He withdrew 27,000 crack troops from Spain at the beginning of 1812, intending to employ them against Russia. This cut French forces in the Peninsula by a quarter,[10] presenting Wellington with an opportunity he would not miss.

Without declaring war, Napoleon invaded Russia with a massive force of 650,000 men in June 1812. The next month, Britain, Sweden and Russia signed a treaty of alliance against France. Events now moved more quickly and almost all against Napoleon. He forced the Russian army to retreat after the Battle of Borodino in September but found Moscow, which he entered unopposed, deserted and without provisions. Napoleon's formidable *Grande Armée* could not follow its usual practice of provisioning itself from the land it conquered. It also faced the full rigours of a Russian winter during its retreat from Moscow. Well over a half of the French army perished.

Britain had no difficulty in persuading Spain and Portugal to join the new coalition. In February 1813, Prussia also joined, declaring war on France in March. Austria joined the coalition shortly afterwards. Napoleon won significant victories against Prussians, Russians and Bavarians in 1813. However, he lost the critical one: the so-called 'Battle of the Nations' near Leipzig in October. His troops were heavily outnumbered by combined forces from Austria, Prussia, Russia and Sweden numbering more than 360,000 and Napoleon was at last forced back west of the Rhine.

France was invaded from the east and the south-west early in 1814. Britain's Foreign Secretary, Viscount Castlereagh, masterminded a final agreement between mutually suspicious allies at the Treaty of Chaumont in March, backed once again by British subsidies. Austria, Prussia, Russia and the United Kingdom offered Napoleon an immediate ceasefire whereupon French borders would revert to those of 1791. Napoleon refused and fought on against hopeless odds. Paris having already fallen, he surrendered unconditionally in April. The following month Louis XVIII entered Paris as King of France.

The romantic coda of the 'Hundred Days' began with Napoleon's escape from exile on the Isle of Elba in late February 1815. He landed on the French Mediterranean coast, near Frejus, on 1 March and successfully appealed to the loyalty of his old comrades. The old magic still cast its spell and he was triumphantly back in Paris on 20 March. The Chaumont alliance held, however. Each of its signatories agreed to keep 75,000 men under arms until a final peace settlement was agreed. Thus it was that Napoleon, trying to pick off the allies one by one, found himself at Waterloo, eight miles south of Brussels, on 18 June at the head of an army of 68,000 men to be confronted by an allied force of 72,000 under the Duke of Wellington. The battle was long, bloody and evenly contested until the arrival of Prussian forces under General

Blucher in the late afternoon. By early evening, the French army's resistance had crumbled. The capture, and despatch to remote St Helena, of Napoleon ensured that Waterloo ended more than twenty years of almost continuous European warfare.

IV. Victory

The Duke of Wellington called the Battle of Waterloo 'the nearest run thing you ever saw in your life'.[11] He is also reported to have said to fellow officers as the battle proceeded: 'Hard pounding this, gentlemen; let's see who will pound longest.'[12] Wellington's observations might well act as a synecdoche: as with Waterloo, so with the French wars as a whole. Napoleon might easily have won. There were times, particularly in the months before Trafalgar, when he almost did. Britain and France were evenly matched opponents whose contrasting strengths dictated a long, debilitating conflict. Napoleon's Empire controlled most of central and western Europe for almost a decade. Trafalgar gave Britain unchallengeable control of the sea. After 1805, the spectre of invasion receded and the long slog continued. Why did Britain and its allies emerge triumphant, with consequences which would shape the course not only of European but of world history for almost a century?

Many historians emphasise Britain's superior economic power. Napoleon's alternative strategy to invasion – economic warfare – engaged his most tenacious enemy at its strongest point. Britain used its naval supremacy to sustain its own transatlantic trade routes and also, by picking off its overseas territories, to put France at commercial disadvantage. Also, though the strain was considerable in the later years of the war, Britain could, by increasing taxation and drawing on its relatively strong credit with the bankers (see Chapter 15), raise enough to pay subsidies to continental allies. It was an expensive strategy. The average annual cost of subsidies in the years 1807–11 was £2.65m and much of the money was wasted. Nevertheless, Napoleon did have to face a string of coalitions. Some historians have argued that his treatment of defeated nations – particularly Prussia and Austria – amounted to subjugation not accommodation and that this enabled Britain, never remotely popular with its notional allies, to keep stitching alliances together. And, of course, it was a coalition which eventually brought Napoleon down, making the £26m Britain spent in the last three years of the war a bargain.[13] Since subsidies accounted for only 8 per cent or so of Britain's total wartime expenditure, it is easy to exaggerate their burden on the public purse.[14]

West Indies ports retained strategic importance while the French wars raged. They acted as an **entrepôt** for British manufactured goods.[15] Meanwhile, new opportunities were being exploited in central and south America and the importance of India was increasing substantially (see Chapter 19). Naval supremacy enabled Britain to pick off colonies almost at will. During the Napoleonic Wars, Britain acquired in Africa Cape Colony (1806), Sierra Leone (1808) and Mauritius (1810), in the Americas Trinidad (1797), Tobago and St Lucia (1803), Demerara, Essequibo and Berbice (1814). It also increased its control in India in both Bengal and Poona. Important though European trade obviously was, disruption of European markets could be compensated elsewhere. In a literal as well as a metaphorical sense, France had less room to play with.

Entrepôt

A term used to describe a commercial centre which both receives imports and also acts as a distribution point to send received goods on to another port. Thus, goods manufactured in Britain might be sent to an 'entrepôt' port in the West Indies, from where they might be sent on either to southern America or to the United States.

The Peninsular War was critical. It began as just one of a number of short-term stratagems to shore up opponents of French expansionism. It ended by depriving Napoleon of resources elsewhere. The Peninsula also brought out the best in Wellington, a general who, if he could not rival Napoleon's military genius, stood head and shoulders above other British commanders. After a long and formative stint in India, he was in the Peninsula at the right place and, from 1809–14, at the right time.

It is important not to place too strong an emphasis on the struggle between Britain and France. In the final analysis, Napoleon, whose unprovoked decision to invade Russia in 1812 must rank as the most spectacular mistake of an extraordinary career, was defeated not by the United Kingdom but by an alliance of great powers. After several unsuccessful – even pathetic – attempts, this alliance held together from 1813 to 1815 to inflict comprehensive defeat on one country whose economy was close to collapse and which could no longer recruit the numbers of troops required to stave off disaster. Much has been made both of the distinctiveness and extraordinary achievements of the French revolutionary army and, of course, of the genius of Napoleon. In the final analysis, though, Napoleon's vision was clouded by illimitable ambition. Whether that ambition was personal or for the greater glory of revolutionary France is beside the point.[16] France was ultimately defeated by sheer weight of numbers. Even had Wellington failed at Waterloo, fresh Russian and Austrian armies stood ready to deliver the knock-out blow to a severely weakened French army. It took purblindness of a high order to create common purpose in a coalition largely comprising autocratic states with separate ambitions and conflicting agendas, but Napoleon managed it after 1812. In doing so, he handed ultimate victory in 1815 to the armies, and the rulers, of the *ancien régime*.

14

....

John Bull's other island: Ireland, conflict and Union, 1780–1815

I. The Protestant Ascendancy

Throughout the eighteenth century, Ireland was an important resource for Britain. It was also a deeply divided society. Almost 80 per cent of its rapidly growing population was Roman Catholic and Roman Catholics had been the principal losers from James II's unavailing struggle to regain his throne in Ireland in 1690. The Battle of the Boyne, still controversially commemorated on 12 July each year, resulted in a decisive victory for the troops commanded by the new Protestant (indeed Dutch Calvinist) King, William III. This cemented what became known as a 'Protestant Ascendancy': an ascendancy which was both political and cultural. Ireland was ruled by a social elite who were members of the Church of Ireland, the Irish equivalent of the Church of England. Although numbering less than 10 per cent of Ireland's population they exercised a dominant hold on its land. At the time of the Glorious Revolution, they owned about three-quarters; by 1776, this had increased to 95 per cent.[1]

Nearly all of the remaining non-Catholic citizens of Ireland were Presbyterian. They constituted about 12 per cent of the population and congregated mostly in Ulster, the most northerly of the four historic provinces of Ireland. Many were of Scottish origin and an increasing number became involved in the growing linen trade around Belfast, whose population increased from barely more than 2,000 in 1700 to 20,000 in 1800.

The influence of the historic Catholic nobility and gentry classes in Ireland was already declining long before the eighteenth century. The Protestant victory in the 'Glorious Revolution' of 1688–89 reduced it still further. Some Catholic gentry emigrated; more converted to Anglicanism in order to retain their lands and social influence. Most political offices and other indicators of social prestige and esteem were closed to Catholics. Consequently, the overwhelming majority of Ireland's Catholic population were either tenant farmers or, more commonly, landless labourers. In the towns, some Catholics enjoyed modest prosperity in trade. Overall, however, the Catholic community was powerless and dependent on agricultural prosperity to eke out a marginal living from the land.

Most members of the Ascendancy descended from English landowning families and were themselves extensive landowners. However, the Ascendancy also encompassed professionals, especially lawyers, businessmen and manufacturers – particularly of beer.[2] It accommodated Protestant Irishmen and those originally from Scottish families. The Ascendancy was not an ethnic construct and it helped to make eighteenth-century Dublin one of Europe's most civilised, and architecturally attractive, cities. With a population approaching 175,000 in 1800, it was also by some distance the largest city in the British Isles, London excepted, and larger than the cities of Glasgow and Edinburgh combined.

The Irish cattle trade became increasingly important to the British economy. Landowners developed large herds, especially in the counties of Tipperary and Limerick, and specialist breeds primarily for the British market. In 1700, imports from Ireland constituted less than 5 per cent by value of Britain's total imports. By 1780, their value had increased sixfold and imports from Ireland constituted almost 11 per cent by value of Britain's. Exports to Ireland increased sevenfold over the same period and constituted 10 per cent of the British total by 1780.[3]

Ireland had long had its own parliament, but, by the British parliament's 'Declaratory Act' of 1720, the right of the Westminster parliament to make laws binding on the people of Ireland was re-asserted. While the change was largely cosmetic, it signalled that Britain saw Ireland as, in effect, its nearest and most immediately profitable colony. The Act provoked predictable hostility among Irish MPs resenting not only Britain's control over Ireland but also the corrupt politics which underpinned it. The rapidity with which offices changed hands, not least the office of **Lord Lieutenant**, was regularly criticised. Such criticisms were the stock-in-trade of the so-called Patriot movement, which gained more adherents in the second half of the century. 'Patriotism' gained a clear focus from the American Revolution. Not only did the American slogan of 'no taxation without representation' find sympathetic ears in Ireland, but fighting the war involved the British government in actions which antagonised the Irish. The withdrawal of troops from Ireland was resented and the closing, first, of American and, from 1778, French and Spanish markets to Irish trade was alleged to be a prime cause of Ireland's economic difficulties at the time.[4]

Lord Lieutenant

The title of the chief governor of Ireland. The Lord Lieutenant was invariably a British politician and the post carried with it membership of the British government. Until the late 1760s, the Lord Lieutenant came to Ireland only every second year to attend sessions of parliament. In his absence, day-to-day government business was discharged by leading Irish politicians and landowners, known as 'undertakers', who also manipulated patronage, often to their own advantage. Viscount Townshend, Lord Lieutenant from 1767 to 1772, introduced a number of reforms, which involved the occupant of the office being a permanent resident who directly managed both government business and its accompanying patronage.

France and Spain's declaration of war on Britain in 1778 added to the pressure for change. Public opinion in Ireland predominantly supported Britain, but the Volunteer movements which sprang up to defend the country against invasion quickly made common cause with the 'Patriotic' movement. Mainly Protestant anyway, and often raised by local gentry, Volunteer forces sought to express a quintessentially Irish patriotism. They wanted to see off the French but, equally, they claimed to speak for Ireland. As one historian has put it, volunteering was 'a great psychological affirmation: of citizenship, of "patriotism", of exclusive identity'.[5] It gave enhanced impetus for re-negotiating the constitutional relationship with Britain.

At the end of 1779, against a background of Volunteer parades, patriotic placards and a large demonstration in Dublin, **Henry Grattan** carried a bill through the Irish parliament declaring that it was 'inexpedient' to grant new taxes until the British government redressed Irish political and economic grievances.[6] The majority was almost four to one. Grattan gained another majority in 1780 for a declaration of rights, asserting that only the Irish parliament could pass laws which bound the people of Ireland. With Irish political opinion overwhelmingly in favour of immediate peace with the Americans, the fall of Yorktown in 1781 (see Chapter 9) proved decisive. As British politicians knowledgeable about Ireland, like **William Eden**, were aware, Irish grievances could readily be translated into a coherent political programme. It began with the demand to repeal the Declaratory Act, but Volunteers and Patriots also wanted a demonstrably independent judiciary and trading rights which favoured Irish merchants and manufacturers.

Henry Grattan, 1746–1820

Born the son of a Dublin lawyer, he trained for the same profession and was called to the Irish bar in 1772. He entered the Irish parliament in 1775, soon taking the lead in the movement for a free and independent Irish parliament. When this was achieved, parliament voted him £50,000 to buy a landed estate. In the 1790s, he was an opponent of the French Revolution and of the United Irishmen who supported it. He was also critical of British government policy, however, and returned to public life in 1799 to oppose Pitt's bill for political union. He became a member of the British House of Commons in 1804, where he supported Whig policies on increased political liberties for Roman Catholics.

William Eden, Baron Auckland, 1744–1814

Born in County Durham, the son of a baronet, he was educated at Eton and Oxford University and also trained for the law. He was interested in legal and penal reform and accepted minor office in Lord North's government in 1772. He entered parliament in 1774 and served as Chief Secretary for Ireland from 1780 to 1782 with a seat in the Irish parliament. There, he developed a professional interest in commercial matters. He opposed

Pitt's commercial proposals on trade with Ireland in 1785, but Pitt, recognising Eden's talents, employed him on negotiations with France for a commercial treaty in 1786. He was also involved in diplomatic negotiations with the United Provinces and Spain in the later 1780s. He gained an Irish peerage as Baron Auckland in 1789 and sat in the British House of Lords with the same title from 1793. He was heavily involved in the negotiations preceding the Act of Union from 1798 to 1800. His final government post was as President of the Board of Trade in the 'Talents' ministry of 1806–7.

Rockingham's brief Whig government acceded to Irish demands in 1782. The repeal of the Declaratory Act in June was followed by confirmation that Irish judges would be independent of British jurisdiction and that the Irish House of Lords was to be the final court of appeal. It seemed that an era of legislative independence had begun.

II. A 'free people'?

Grattan famously rhapsodised on the constitutional settlement in 1782, claiming that he was about to address 'a free people' and asserting that 'Ireland is now a nation'.[7] The legislature which was then constituted, and which survived only until 1800, is commonly known as 'Grattan's parliament'. To what extent was the eponym deserved and how far, in reality, was Ireland 'free'?

Substantial changes did take place. The Catholic Relief Act (1778) allowed Catholics who had sworn an Oath of Allegiance to take out long leases on land and bequeath property rights to a single heir. In 1782, further relief legislation permitted Catholics to buy land and also removed restrictions on Catholic education. During the 1770s also, despite pressure from Protestants fearing that Catholics-in-arms would lead to a re-match of the Battle of the Boyne, more Catholics were being re-cruited into the army. By the time of the Napoleonic wars (see Chapter 13), between a quarter and a third of troops in the regular army were Catholic Irishmen. North's government approved a resolution in 1778 which would have given Ireland unrestricted access to trade with Britain's colonies. Howls of protest from British commercial centres such as Liverpool, Manchester, Preston and Glasgow promoted a retreat from such unselective liberality but a compromise was reached which freed up trade while restricting the export of some Irish goods, particularly wool, cottons and coal.[8]

However, Grattan's triumphalist pronouncement of 1782 proved optimistic. Ireland had shaken off only British parliamentary shackles, not Britain's wider influence. The British privy council's rights over Irish legislation remained intact. So did the requirement that royal assent to Irish bills needed the formal confirmation of a British 'Great Seal'. Only very rarely, however, was either sanction used. In effect, though the Irish parliament was not a fully sovereign body, it could, for many practical purposes, act as if it were. Nothing was specifically said in 1782 about imperial or foreign policy, although it would have been rash for the Irish parliament to send an Irish ambassador to a foreign power – particularly to the United States. More significantly, the Irish administration was still subject to British constraints. The Lord Lieutenant and **Chief Secretary** were Crown appointees, were invariably British, and their roles remained unchanged.

Chief Secretary for Ireland

The government officer responsible for managing government business. This was a more executive post than that of Lord Lieutenant and was often taken by British politicians at an early stage of their careers. The Chief Secretary also managed the key government offices.

Until the late 1780s, however, the main constraints were internal. Grattan's parliament, more than half of whose seats were controlled by landowners and patrons – both British and Irish – was elected wholly by Protestants. It spoke not for Ireland but, as before, for the Protestant Ascendancy. Henry Grattan was as good an exemplar of Ascendancy attitudes and beliefs as any. Both cultural and political links with Britain remained strong and the two parliaments behaved in similar ways. Events in Dublin often reflected developments in Britain. Changes of government at Westminster mattered as much in Dublin as they did in London or Edinburgh.

Even party allegiances replicated one another. Debates in Dublin over the Regency Crisis in 1788–89 were between an Irish government which wanted to follow Pitt's line and an Irish opposition which, like Fox and the Whigs at Westminster, wanted the Prince of Wales to take over from his father. The assumption seemed to be that replicating British processes in Dublin added authority and weight to the activities of the Irish parliament. This would not have been tenable in a parliament which represented Irish people as a whole. It was, however, appropriate for a cultivated Protestant elite who thought that representation meant giving the people what they ought to want. Aristocratic Whigs across the Irish Sea thought much the same.

Economic considerations emphasised Ireland's continued subordination to Britain. William Pitt's more ambitious scheme of 1785 to rationalise Anglo-Irish commercial affairs raised hackles within the Ascendancy. Pitt proposed a substantial realignment of trade between Britain and Ireland based on an assessment of reciprocal interests and mutual reduction of tariffs. He explained to the Lord Lieutenant, the Duke of Rutland, that he wished to 'open to Ireland the chance of competition with ourselves, on terms of more than equality'.[9] The scheme was unpopular with British manufacturers who – fancifully – imagined themselves swamped by cheap imports of Irish manufactured goods produced in a low-wage economy. They formed a General Chamber of Manufacturers to protest against Pitt's proposed 'customs union'. Pitt appropriated the disparaging remarks of Adam Smith to bemoan the 'evils of a nation dominated by shopkeepers'.[10] He might also have reflected, with Smith, that most manufacturers only support free trade when they can see the profit in it. The Irish parliament resented Pitt's requirement that, since both nations stood to profit from these proposals, Ireland should contribute to the cost of imperial defence. This was construed in Dublin as a British attempt to circumvent Ireland's legislative independence. Having extracted a favourable compromise from Pitt on financial contributions, Grattan argued that Ireland should accept Pitt's policy. Even with the Irish government propaganda and patronage machines cranked up to full volume, its parliament would not grant the secure majority needed for success with the more detailed proposals which would follow. Pitt's plan foundered, in part at least because of Irish suspicion of the larger neighbour's motives.

III. Resistance

Events in France from 1789 necessarily broadened the focus of Irish politics beyond the narrow concerns of the Protestant elite. As in Britain, the French Revolution energised Irish reformers. Ideas about citizenship and the Rights of Man were widely debated, especially in the towns. A Society of United Irishmen was founded in Belfast in 1791. Its most impressive figure was the Protestant lawyer, **Theobald Wolfe Tone**. He argued for a reduction of British influence in Irish affairs for all Irishmen, irrespective of religion, to claim full political rights. A branch of the United Irishmen, founded in Dublin by **Napper Tandy**, quickly followed.

Theobald Wolfe Tone, 1763–1798

Born in Dublin, the son of a prosperous tradesman, Tone qualified as a lawyer. An excellent speaker and a reflective, democratic thinker, he was a leading figure both in the United Irish movement and in the radicalised Catholic Committee. He persuaded the Directory in France to support a rebellion in Ireland to be used as springboard for a French invasion of Britain. He was captured while sailing to Ireland to start an insurrection. While awaiting execution for treason, he committed suicide.

Napper Tandy, 1737–1803

He was a small tradesman influential in the Volunteer movement in the late 1770s and early 1780s. He supported parliamentary reform, protection for Irish trade and political relief for Roman Catholics. During the 1790s, he was active in the United Ireland movement and linked up with the pro-Catholic secret society of 'Defenders'. He was accused of treason and fled Ireland, spending time both in the United States and in France. He enlisted in the French army in 1798 with the rank of Brigadier-General and was involved in French invasion plans. His arrival with a small force in Donegal did not attract widespread support and he was forced to flee. He was arrested in Hamburg, tried for treason in Dublin and sentenced to death but reprieved. He was shipped to Bordeaux in 1802 and died in France a year later.

The United Irishmen presented a new challenge to the Protestant Ascendancy. It aimed to unite artisans, many of them politically aware Presbyterians, with mostly rural Catholics in a movement of protest against the Irish elite. The objectives of the radical reformers were frequently deflected, however, by sectarian clashes between Catholic 'Defenders' and Protestant 'Peep O'Day boys', especially in rural areas in the north of Ireland. The authorities increasingly recognised the need for a response to calls for further concessions to Catholics. Both Westminster and Dublin were also alarmed about plans for a French invasion to be launched from Ireland.

Few examples of continued British dominance over Ireland are more telling than the Catholic Relief Act of 1793. The Catholic Defenders approached the British government directly, asking for redress. Pitt responded by instructing the Chief Secretary, Robert Hobart, to introduce a Relief Bill. The British administration used its considerable powers of patronage to drive the bill through the Irish parliament, where Grattan was only a reluctant convert to the proposals. The preamble to the Act commended Catholic citizens for their 'peaceful and loyal demeanour', making it fit that the 'restraints and disabilities' placed upon them should 'be discontinued'.[11] Roman Catholics were permitted to vote in parliamentary elections. They were also entitled to hold most civil and also military offices up to the rank of Colonel. They could not, however, be members of parliament and remained debarred from holding the key legal and political offices. Even so, Roman Catholics in Ireland from 1793 to 1829 enjoyed more 'emancipation' than did their counterparts in England.

Granting Catholics political rights did not reduce sectarian strife, which continued to increase in many places. Nor were United Irishmen dissuaded from their view that British-dictated reforms were a sham and that the struggle for a democratic Ireland should continue. The purpose of the Relief Act, of course, was to dampen down protest and to win the allegiance of all propertied, right-thinking Irishmen. As the future Lord Lieutenant Viscount Bayham (Earl Camden from 1794) told Viscount Castlereagh in 1793, the aim of Pitt's government was to 'quiet and satisfy the minds of the moderate men'.[12]

The problem, however, was that events after 1793 worked against moderate solutions. As the United Irishmen plotted, so the government prepared to meet a dual threat: insurrection and a French invasion. A full-time Irish militia was formed in 1793. It numbered over 12,000 troops by 1795. Its officers were mostly Protestant, the rank and file Catholic. A Yeomanry corps, raised by officers commissioned by the Crown, was established in 1796. Its numbers had reached 40,000 by 1798. Administering illegal oaths became an offence punishable by death under the Insurrection Act of 1796, which remained in force until 1802. The Act also permitted the authorities to declare any area 'disturbed' and impose a curfew on it. Magistrates gained increased powers of search and detention. Trial by jury was frequently suspended.

These extensive preparations were dictated by Pitt's government, and often by Pitt himself, but the driving force behind their implementation was Irish. **John Beresford** was able, experienced and committed to the preservation of a Protestant

Ascendancy. Strong support was also provided by John Foster, Speaker of the Irish House of Commons, and John Fitzgibbon, the Lord Chancellor from 1789 to 1802. Fitzgibbon, created Earl of Clare in 1795, thought that strong economic and political links with Britain were the only route to continued prosperity in Ireland. Fitzgibbon was also a convert from Catholicism and, like many converts, implacable in his hostility to the grouping he had left.

John Beresford, 1738–1805

Born in Dublin, the son of the Earl of Tyrone, Beresford came from a highly political family. He became MP for County Waterford in 1761 and retained that seat until his death. From an early age, he hitched his political course to serving British interests in Ireland. This brought rapid dividends and he became First Commissioner for Revenue in 1780. His power grew partly because he proved himself a diligent and able administrator, increasing the revenue substantially, and partly because of personal friendship with Pitt. His influence led to the sardonic description of 'King of Ireland'. He survived the Whig Lord Lieutenant Earl Fitzwilliam's attempt to sack him in 1795. In the wake of the Irish Rising in 1798, Beresford advised Pitt that political union was the only way to secure Ireland in the British interest. After the Union, he advised Addington on Irish financial management. Always loyal to Pitt, however, he used his group of MPs personally loyal to him to help destabilise the Addington administration in 1803–4.

No punches were pulled in resisting both rebellion and invasion. General Gerard Lake was charged in 1797 with breaking up organisations of United Irishmen which had proliferated in Ulster. Following the Lord Lieutenant's message that the army intended 'to strike terror' into the hearts of its opponents, Lake discharged his duties – which involved arson, mass arrests and torture – with efficient relish.[13] His reward was promotion to Commander-in-Chief of the Irish army in 1798. In this capacity, he repeated the dose in southern Ireland. Forcible entry and other strong-arm measures uncovered a considerable quantity of arms in readiness for a rebellion which eventually began in Dublin in May and spread south-east into Counties Wicklow and Wexford. Lake broke up the rebellion in Wexford with a bloody victory at the Battle of Vinegar Hill in June.

The 1798 rebellion was not controlled by the United Irishmen. Any hope it had of asserting the primacy of republican idealism and thus of restraining sectarian division had disappeared a year or two earlier. 1798 witnessed the popular uprising of Catholics against the hated Protestant ascendancy.[14] It was also motivated by antagonism to Protestant landlords and accompanied by calls for a more equitable land distribution. Short-lived and wholly ineffective as it was, the rebellion ineluctably pointed the way towards nineteenth-century Ireland in which protest was the province of Roman Catholics. The targets were continued Protestant domination and British rule.

French attempts at invasion were disastrous. The Directory sent 15,000 troops to Ireland under the command of General Hoche in December 1796. The invasion fleet was damaged by a storm and when it arrived at Bantry Bay (County Cork) it found little evidence of indigenous support for a rising. No landing was attempted. In August 1798, General Humbert landed at Killala Bay (County Mayo) with a much smaller force. It succeeded in recruiting about three thousand Irish volunteers and won an initial engagement at Castlebar. However, denied promised reinforcements from France, these scratch troops were encircled by Lake at Ballinamuck in early September. Despite Humbert's formal surrender, Lake's forces – obeying government instructions to 'take no prisoners' with implacable literalism – massacred about two thousand Irish Catholics anyway.

IV. Union

The events of 1798 finally convinced Pitt the constitutional arrangement of 1782 would no longer serve. He had long believed that legislative independence for Ireland was unsustainable both on economic and political grounds. However, he had paid little attention to Irish affairs until then, trusting to the efficiency of the administration in Ireland, if not to the Irish parliament, to keep things on an even keel. As soon as he heard of the rebellion, he wrote to Camden: 'Cannot Crushing the Rebellion be followed by an Act appointing Commissioners to treat for an Union?'[15] Pitt supported Union in the Commons in January 1799, arguing that Ireland was 'subject to great and deplorable evils . . . [which] lie in the situation of the country itself'. He called for the Irish parliament to be replaced by 'An imperial legislature standing aloof from local party connexion, sufficiently removed from the influence of contending factions . . . That is the thing which is wanted for Ireland'.[16]

What Pitt did not say was that the 'thing' wanted for Ireland left its Protestant-dominated and British-influenced administration intact. As Foster puts it, 'The new system abolished the Irish parliament, while retaining the castle government.'[17] A proposal which preserved an administration which Britain could readily control while ditching a parliament which it sometimes could not was bound to be contentious. Pitt's proposals for Union reduced three hundred Irish MPs to one hundred who would appear in Westminster as members of a new parliament for 'the United Kingdom of Britain and Ireland'. Opposition was particularly strong in Dublin among the capital's professional and mercantile classes. When the Irish administration presented the Union bill in parliament, wrecking amendments by anti-Unionists were passed by small majorities.

The task of reversing this outcome was deputed to the Lord Lieutenant, Earl Cornwallis, and his new Chief Secretary, Viscount Castlereagh. Their methods excited considerable controversy, both at the time and among historians since. The facts are that a small anti-Union majority (111–106) in January 1799 was converted to a much larger pro-Union majority (158–115) when the bill returned in January 1800. In the meantime, a mixture of rational argument, gentle arm-twisting and outright bribery was applied. Some historians consider that the process exemplified the arrogant use of power by Britain. On this argument, Britain rarely noticed Ireland, except when it became a nuisance, and these Union proposals should be seen as a means of bolstering Britain's security and alliance systems. Others have noted that the task of persuasion fell much more on Irish politicians like Beresford and Castlereagh than it did on British ones like Cornwallis.

Certainly, significant sums of money were expended on persuading anti-Unionist politicians into early retirement, suitably compensated with cash and titles, and on securing jobs, perks and influence for the many Irish politicians who, cannily, had abstained first time round, anticipating that government representatives would come again, not only calling but bearing gifts. Notice that the numbers of Irish MPs voting on the Union increased by more than 26 per cent when the bill returned in 1800.

Some gifts were substantial indeed. The value of a borough seat slated for dis-appearance under the terms of Union was set at £15,000. Some of the most entrenched opponents of Union were paid handsomely to quit politics and, as often as not, return to the land. But it is difficult to maintain that such bribes were out of line with standard political practice. Inducements were part of eighteenth-century political life and anti-Unionists were also making them.

There was an argument to be won too. Castlereagh found that promising Ulster's linen merchants and manufacturers greater prosperity as part of an expanded, and commercially prosperous, 'United Kingdom' fell on receptive ears. In the south and west of Ireland, however, antagonism to the Protestant Ascendancy had deep roots. It was difficult for Grattan's parliament to claim significant benefits for the local popu-lation. There the suggestion that a United Kingdom parliament would respond more sympathetically to Catholic pleas for political equality was warmly received.

The problem, however, was that Protestant politicians could not deliver on **Catholic Emancipation**. Pitt, Cornwallis and Castlereagh strongly favoured it but residual opposition in Ireland was both strong and vocal. Furthermore, Pitt's government was divided over the war and not amenable to resolving what many members considered a controversial side issue.[18] Even more importantly, the King was unpersuadable on Emancipation. Relations between monarch and Prime Minister had recently become strained, not least over war policy. Pitt could also have been more attentive to the court, less consumed by the exigencies of war and also, unluckily for him, in better health.[19] Closer contact in 1798 and 1799 might have persuaded the King to compromise. As it was, George III noted that Pitt had given little attention to Ireland until 1798 and had then suddenly immersed himself in a major constitutional change. Now, with minimal preparation of the ground, Pitt told him that Catholic Emancipation would strengthen the Union. George III would have taken some persuading anyway but he specially resented the fact that Pitt's efforts had been so perfunctory. Above all, and as a conscientious if limited monarch, he hated being sidelined. Catholic Emancipation thus became the occasion, if not the direct cause, of Pitt's resignation in March 1801.

Catholic Emancipation

The name given to the movement to remove political discrimination against Roman Catholics, especially in Ireland. Catholics could not be elected as members of parliament or hold most of the senior political and administrative offices. It was a controversial issue in British as well as Irish politics from the time of the Act of Union. The Irish political leader Daniel O'Connell (1775–1847) re-focused attention on discrimination when he founded the Catholic Association in 1823 to press for the removal of all discrimination and the repeal of the Act of Union. Catholics were permitted to become members of parliament as a result of the Catholic Relief Act of 1829. However, they had to subscribe to a special oath in order to be individually exempt from penal statutes. These discriminatory statutes were not repealed.

The Act of Union, minus Catholic Emancipation, had come into effect two months earlier. Castlereagh was one of many who considered Union a job only half done – indeed dangerously half-baked. Catholic support for the Union had been critical, yet it confirmed the large Roman Catholic majority as second-class citizens.[20] It left work for secret societies to do and therefore bequeathed a tradition of violence for Catholics, including the peasantry, to exploit. Meanwhile, the Yeomanry and Volunteers became indistinguishable from the Protestant cause, which increasingly translated as loyalty to the Union with Britain. The quarter-century after the Union, when Irish politics seemed 'placid', revolving once again around the activities of wealthy Protestant landlords, proved illusory (see Chapters 17 and 20).[21] Irish politics were close to completing their narrowing progress to a position of entrenched sectarian hostility. The Catholic majority, which had been critical of the passage of Union, focused its later struggles on destroying it. The course for Ireland's bitter, and frequently violent, relations with the rest of the new United Kingdom had already been set.

15

Parties, politics and religion in early nineteenth-century Britain

I. Paying for the war

Britain was used to fighting expensive eighteenth-century wars. The conflict against France from 1793, however, dwarfed all, both in length and cost. The total expenditure over the twenty-two mostly wartime years was nearly £672m, almost six times as much as the war against the American colonists.[1] In consequence, governments demanded ever more from the taxpayer. In the 1780s, 11 or 12 per cent of national income had been taken in taxes. By 1802, this had risen to 14 per cent, but it was the Napoleonic, rather than the French Revolutionary, war which hit the nation hardest. By 1806, 19 per cent of national income was being taken in taxes.[2] Likewise, the government was raising ever more via loans and bonds. The National Debt, at £902m in 1816, was almost four times as high as in 1793 and more than double the output of Britain's industrialising economy. Britain's over-dependence on paper money led to a fall in the value of sterling.

Not surprisingly, government policy was heavily criticised. The stock market had experienced a major boom in the years 1805–7[3] but the value of stocks and shares fell precipitously in 1810–11 as bankruptcies reached unprecedented levels.[4] Bankruptcies brought higher levels of unemployment in their wake. Even established, successful banks, like Baring's, lost heavily in the slump which followed a recommendation from the Commons' Bullion Committee for the nation to return to cash payments as soon as possible. This gave an opportunity for the Jewish financier Nathan Rothschild to raise large amounts of cash in Germany, France and Holland and then, using some highly irregular connections, convey it for Wellington's direct military use in Portugal. Rothschild later called this transaction 'the best business I ever did'. By 1814, he had loaned nearly £1.2m to the British government. His shrewdness and risk-taking established him as Europe's leading banker: the Napoleon of finance.[5]

Wheat prices were rising rapidly, reaching a peak of 126 shillings and sixpence (£6.33) in 1812:[6] the highest price reached in the entire nineteenth century. Widespread unemployment and high bread prices stimulated a resurgence of radicalism in the later years of the war.[7] As already suggested (see Chapter 8), Luddite outbreaks were yet another indicator of discontent and disaffection. So was the flood of petitions from the leading manufacturing towns, organised in 1811–12 with Whig support, against Britain's Orders in Council. These, the petitioners maintained, were keeping mills idle and inflicting woeful damage on overseas trade not only with Europe but also to the Americas.[8]

Those who had never trusted the 'money men' and who believed in plain dealing – preferably between honest, upright landowners – were particularly vocal in their attacks on ministers for getting too close to 'funny money'. An anonymous 'Merchant' in 1810 argued that the stock exchange had 'gangrened our hearts'. He attacked financial speculators: 'Woe to the people who obtain wealth without labour.'[9] In an attack which bears an eerie similarity to that on the Labour government almost two hundred years later, a correspondent to the *Liverpool Mercury* noted:

> The government of this kingdom has been long and closely associated with the commercial interest; and, I am sorry to say, with the worst part of the commercial interest. The ministers are, at length, sensible of the difficulties which have grown out of the former . . . negotiations with those money brokers who both lent and borrowed a subornation [implying illegality] of fictitious credit, which can no longer be supported . . . The reign of bank credit is, in my opinion, nearly at an end and while many may expect ruin . . . I . . . console myself that the good of the country will certainly be the ultimate consequence.[10]

II. Political parties and ministerial instability

The later years of the French wars saw rapid changes of government. Pitt's first ministry had lasted for more than seventeen years (1783–1801). Lord Liverpool's, which began in the spring of 1812, would survive for almost fifteen. In between, Britain had five governments, none of which survived as long as four years. It would be wrong to infer, however, that politics were especially unstable. Two of the five ministries were ended by the Prime Minister's death: Pitt in January 1806 and **Perceval**, assassinated by a deranged, unsuccessful and grudge-bearing commercial agent, in May 1812. A third ended because of severe illness: Portland's stroke in 1809. Additionally, the strong anti-revolutionary consensus which had been cemented by the Pitt–Portland coalition in 1794 (see Chapter 11) held firm in the age of Napoleon. Parliament remained conservative in temper and the small number of radical MPs in the House of Commons could find themselves under considerable pressure. In 1810, for example, the aristocratic radical, **Sir Francis Burdett**, spent almost three months in the Tower of London for accusing the Commons of attacking press freedoms and making arbitrary use of its privileges when it cleared the public gallery during a debate.[11]

Spencer Perceval, 1762–1812

Born in London, the son of the second Earl of Egmont, he was educated at Cambridge University and practised as a lawyer in London. He was a strong opponent of the French Revolution and assisted in the prosecutions of Thomas Paine and John Horne Tooke in

1792. Family connections eased entry into parliament in 1796. He was successively Solicitor-General and Attorney-General before becoming Chancellor of the Exchequer in 1807 in Portland's administration. Here he drafted the Orders in Council, responding to Napoleon's Berlin Decrees. He succeeded Portland as Prime Minister in 1809 and proved a steady, if unimaginative, Prime Minister. He secured sufficient funds for the Peninsular campaign, which was moving towards a successful conclusion at the time of his assassination. Unusually among leading politicians, he was a firm supporter of the Evangelical wing of the Church of England. Like most Church Evangelicals, he was equally opposed to political radicalism and to Roman Catholic Emancipation.

Sir Francis Burdett, 1770–1844

Born in Derbyshire, the grandson of a baronet whose title he inherited in 1797, he was educated at Westminster School and Oxford University, and entered parliament in 1796 for a seat controlled by the Duke of Newcastle. In the Commons, he supported issues relating to liberty and free speech. He also advocated improved conditions for prisoners. After leaving parliament for a few years, he was elected for the open borough of Westminster in 1807 on a programme of radical reform. He spoke in favour of parliamentary reform and the restoration of trade union rights. He also supported the establishment of a non-sectarian University of London. He became increasingly disenchanted with what he saw as the rabble-rousing of populist radical leaders in the 1820s and 1830s.

Short-lived ministries may not linger long in the memory. The names of Addington, Grenville, Portland and Perceval resonate only with specialists in early nineteenth-century political history. Nevertheless, significant developments were taking place in the structure of politics at this time which help to explain how a two-party system came to dominate modern British political life. The roles of monarch and Prime Minister were evolving, and relatively cohesive groups were identifiable in the House of Commons which can be called 'government' and 'opposition'.[12]

George III's political role had always been important and sometimes pivotal. The King expected not only to be consulted about the composition of a ministry but to take the lead in determining who would head it. One important reason for his detestation of the Fox–North coalition in 1783 – which converted his previous suspicion of Fox into unshakeable hatred – was that he felt that it ignored his constitutional rights (see Chapter 9). When a ministry fell, which senior politician had the best credentials to lead its successor was rarely clear. Loose, frequently shifting groupings of politicians were much more common than were coherent and disciplined parties. Addington was George's choice to succeed Pitt (see Chapter 12) but the King resented the way Addington was undermined in 1803–4. Pitt was not welcomed back with open arms in 1804, despite George Canning's propagandist characterisation of him as 'the Pilot that weathered the Storm'.[13] In any case, Pitt's second ministry was not successful. Accusations of sleaze and financial irregularity against Henry Dundas (now Viscount Melville) as First Lord of the Admiralty led to conflict within, and defections from, the government. Its Commons majorities dwindled accordingly. When Pitt died in office, and with his supporters demoralised and in disarray, the King asked **Grenville** to form a government. This was at some cost to George's own principles. Grenville had not been a minister since 1801 and had become much closer to Fox's Whigs. Grenville insisted that any government he led must have Fox in it. The King, with no plausible alternative from within Pitt's supporters, was forced to give way. The so-called 'Ministry of All the Talents' lacked Pitt's followers from his last administration, but was otherwise a coalition across family and party groupings. A general election held in 1806 increased the new government's supporters by about forty.

William Wyndham Grenville, 1759–1834

Born in Buckinghamshire, the son of George Grenville, Prime Minister from 1763 to 1765, he was educated at Eton and Oxford University before studying for the law. He became an MP in 1782. His career was advanced by his friendship with the Younger Pitt and he served him as Home Secretary (1790–91) and Foreign Secretary (1791–1801). He also resigned with Pitt over Roman Catholic Emancipation. He attacked Addington over the Peace of Amiens and headed the 'Talents' ministry of 1806–7 but never held office after resigning as Prime Minister. Instead, he became the head of a family grouping of Whigs and became, in effect, leader of the opposition, where he continued to support Roman Catholic Emancipation. He gave up active politics in 1817 when the Whig leadership passed to Grey, with whom he had never been close.

The 'Talents' ministry was even less successful than the Pitt ministry it replaced. Peace proposals foundered (Chapter 13) and its domestic policies were unpopular. Nevertheless, it could usually rely on secure majorities in the Commons. When, sensitive to the Whig reformers in the coalition and particularly to the recently deceased Fox's legacy, it proposed to allow Roman Catholics to hold higher commissioned rank in the army, the King's implacable hostility to any such liberality (see Chapter 14) resurfaced. He required that his ministers pledge never to revive 'the Catholic question' again. The Whigs would not be held to ransom by the King and Grenville's resignation rapidly followed. The King asked the Duke of Portland, Pitt's ally from 1794, to replace him. Portland's government was dominated by ministers who had served, and in many cases grown to political maturity under, Pitt. Another election followed, in which the King contributed £12,000 to support candidates favourable to his new government. A year earlier, he had not helped the Talents one whit.[14] Although Portland's ministry was never confidently established, and was weakened both by further reverses in the war and by the damaging personal rivalry of Viscount Castlereagh and George Canning, the origins of a more explicit and cohesive political party can be discerned in this administration. It was also confronted by a larger, and more coherent, opposition. Foxites and supporters of Grenville stuck together, numbering more than two hundred anti-ministerial MPs in the new parliament.[15] This did not deter the King. In appointing Spencer Perceval to replace the terminally ill Portland, he was confirming his trust in another essentially Pittite ministry. It was his last important act before the shadow of mental illness closed over him for the last time in 1810.

The replacement of the King in 1811 by his eldest son, who held the title 'Prince Regent' until the old king finally died in 1820, was of considerable significance. He had taken an active, if quixotic, interest in politics from the 1780s. He tended to see it as a game which formed part of his inordinately expensive and self-indulgent lifestyle. Gambling friends in his youth had been mostly Rockingham Whigs and he was a strong supporter of the opposition Whigs until Fox's death in 1806. That Fox's friends were opponents of his father he saw as a further justification for his political allegiance. As he aged and his dissolute friends either died off or settled down, he became less interested in politics. He disappointed old friends who thought that he would bring them back into office. The Regent had a quite different view of monarchy from that of his father. He much preferred putting on a show – preferably at lavish expense – to putting in the hours. Important papers often went unread and his knowledge of politics, never securely grounded, became scanty. He was not stupid and could rouse himself to response when he felt his interests were being threatened. However, he was not suited to the task of defending monarchy against increasing incursion from parliament or Cabinet.[16] That the powers available to the monarchy were considerably fewer in 1830, when George IV died, than they had been in 1810, when he prepared to become Regent, is no accident.

By 1815, a changing political configuration, more dependent on coherent political parties, can be discerned. Its appearance remained clouded by the adverse, if anachronistic, connotations which still clung to the description 'Tory': Jacobitism, disloyalty, support for 'absolute monarchy'. The 'Whig Supremacy' of the early and mid-eighteenth century cast a long, opprobrious shadow. Thus, both before and after his alliance with the Duke of Portland in 1794, the Younger Pitt always called himself an 'independent Whig'. When, after much prevarication and failed negotiations with other candidates, the Prince Regent finally asked **Liverpool** to replace Spencer Perceval in 1812, the incoming Prime Minister informed the Prince that he was constructing his ministry on 'Whig principles'. As Boyd Hilton reminds us, the term 'Tory' was not regularly used as a descriptor of political attitudes until the late 1820s.[17]

Robert Banks Jenkinson, second Earl of Liverpool, 1770–1828

Born the son of Charles Jenkinson, later first Earl of Liverpool, politician and adviser to George III, he was educated at Charterhouse and Oxford. He witnessed the storming of the Bastille when staying in Paris as a 19-year-old. He became an MP in 1790 and became a strong supporter of Pitt and opponent of reform. Most of his adult life was

▶

spent in office, first as President of the Indian Board of Control (1799–1801), and then Foreign Secretary under Addington (1801–4), Home Secretary under Pitt and Portland (1804–6 and 1808–9) and Secretary for War and the Colonies. His Cabinet colleagues recommended him to the Prince Regent as Perceval's successor in 1812, but the Prince investigated other options before turning to him with some reluctance. Liverpool stayed in office until forced to resign on grounds of ill-health in 1827. He had many useful political skills: he was diligent, efficient and not tainted by the scandals which afflicted many of his contemporaries. In essence, a loyal follower of the Younger Pitt, he remained a firm opponent of political reform but was increasingly attracted to trade liberalisation and administrative reform. There is little doubt that he supported the more liberally minded ministers against the 'high Tories' in his remodelled Cabinet after 1822. He demonstrated considerable skill in keeping his Cabinet together on most issues and he showed good judgment in keeping Catholic Emancipation off the Cabinet agenda for as long as possible.

Nevertheless, family groupings were becoming less important. In the years 1812–15, Sidmouth's personal group in parliament put its allegiance pretty consistently behind Lord Liverpool. So, a good deal more capriciously, did Canning's friends. The French Revolution had necessitated ideological introspection. The break-up of the old Rockingham Whigs over citizenship and revolutionary principles led to a painful, personal rift between Burke and Fox (see Chapter 11), but the secession of the so-called 'Portland Whigs' to Pitt in 1794 was of greater long-term significance. Most of them never returned to any Whig grouping. The appearance of new journals also helped define the divide. While heavyweight publications, almost by their nature, do not march to any unwaveringly regular political drum, the emergence of the Whig *Edinburgh Review* in 1802 and the *Quarterly Review*, launched in 1809 as a ministerial (if not yet quite 'Tory') riposte, were significant indicators of the growing importance of party. By the mid-1820s, *Blackwood's Edinburgh Review* and the *Westminster Review*, respectively extreme (or 'Ultra') Tory and 'Radical', had sharpened divisions further.

Party allegiance was far from watertight either on specific policies or on personal loyalties. Whigs solidly favoured Catholic Emancipation but most had reservations about parliamentary reform. They could not agree on either when or how much. On the other side, Liverpool's governments were split almost down the middle over Catholic Emancipation (see Chapter 17). Though Huskisson, Robinson and Peel (see Chapters 16 and 17) had firm views about the general direction of economic policy, only rarely did clear water appear between government and opposition in this area. Economics proved too recondite and esoteric an area for party slanging matches. We should note also that contemporary political managers found it exceedingly difficult to tell how many individuals were likely to support them on any given issue, let alone ascribe permanent party loyalties to them. Published lists of party support after general elections, at least until the 1830s, have strong elements of speculation and *post hoc* rationalisation about them.[18]

Party allegiance was neither fixed by 1815 nor strongly disciplined. Still, what one might call 'distinguishing indicators' increasingly mark out Whig from Tory. The Whigs were, in general, the more reform-minded in both politics and religion. Their leaders were more likely to be 'old-aristocratic', tracing their origins back to family political interests grounded in great wealth and broad acres. Perhaps anachronistically by the early nineteenth century, they remained wary of royal power. They were particularly hostile to the use of royal patronage to support and sustain ministries, perhaps because, after 1783, that patronage was so rarely deployed in their favour. The Whigs also attracted more support than did the Tories, especially in growing urban areas, from the professional, business and mercantile classes. Nonconformists also disproportionately voted for Whig candidates.

The Tories also had aristocratic support. However, the gentry (see Chapter 3) were much more likely to vote Tory than Whig. Tories were much more vigorous in their support of the old order, especially when challenged by 'reform' or by theoretical and 'speculative' opinion. They saw themselves as practical men of affairs, relying on a curious, yet potent, mixture of experience, instinct and pragmatism to respond appropriately to whatever political challenges faced them. They forged a strong, almost umbilical, alliance with the Church of England and their support tended to be strongest in the English counties. Many Tories were also bigotedly anti-Catholic.

III. A new American war

Economic war against Napoleon had the unintended, and distinctly unwelcome, consequence of worsening relations with the United States. The British Orders in Council of 1807 aimed to disrupt French trade (see Chapter 13). France had been America's ally in its war for independence and its trade remained an important element to the commerce of the United States. The United States challenged Britain's right to use its naval strength to define terms of trade in the Americas. It was also irked by British support for native American Indians resisting US settlements in the so-called Northwest Territory. A series of specific incidents ratcheted up tension. The navy attacked the US frigate *Chesapeake* in 1807 in search of British deserters and it employed less than fastidious methods of enlistment, as a result of which many American citizens found themselves reluctant recruits on British warships.

The basic problem, however, was mutual misperception. Commercial interests notwithstanding (see Chapter 9), diplomatic relations between Britain and the United States had been fragile, going on frosty, since 1783 anyway. During the French wars, Britain saw the Atlantic almost as its personal playground and its need to do so increased after Napoleon's Berlin Decrees. In the Atlantic, Britain already had dominance in Canada, was extending its empire in the Caribbean at the expense of France, Spain and the Dutch (see Chapter 13) and was forging ever more profitable trading links with southern America. The long strip of land running down from Maine to Georgia, which had claimed its independence in 1783, was an irritation in the way of transatlantic territorial and commercial dominance. This was thinking which saw the rest of the world as an extension of Europe. Not unnaturally, the United States saw things differently. Central to the objectives of the 'Founding Fathers' was the establishment of an independent state standing proud and entirely separate from the dynastic and territorial squabbles afflicting Europe. In particular, they bitterly resented the British navy's transportation of a European theatre of war to the boundaries of the USA.

In any case, the United States had its own territorial ambitions to satisfy, not least in Canada, which remained under British rule. Its so-called Macon Act of 1810 quickly elicited a declaration from France that it would respect the neutrality of the United States. The United States was thereupon declared closed to British trade and President Madison declared war on Britain in June 1812. During the conflict neither side gained a decisive advantage. Britain, heavily involved both with war in the Peninsula and with negotiations for a new coalition against Napoleon, would much rather not have been fighting and deployed only limited forces. US troops were at first poorly organised and indifferently led. Their incursions into British north America had limited success, although the United States did achieve dominance around the Great Lakes by the end of 1813. In August of that year, a British force in the north under Major-General Robert Ross defeated the Americans at Bladensburg (Maryland), which led to the capture and partial destruction of Washington, the US capital. Peace was agreed at the Treaty of Ghent in 1814. This returned affairs to the situation before the war broke out. It was characteristic of a messy conflict that two significant engagements – Andrew Jackson's successful defence of New Orleans against British troops and a defeat for the Americans at Fort Boyer – took place early in January 1815. Word had not reached the combatants that peace had already been declared.

IV. Nonconformity and the Evangelical Revival

Arguably, the French wars required as much spiritual as physical resilience. The Church of England was ill-equipped to respond to the new challenges posed by urbanisation and social change. Increasingly, it was seen as a rural Church. At the turn of the nineteenth century, for example, Norfolk had more than seven hundred ecclesiastical parishes, industrialising Lancashire only seventy, although some of them were very large. Birmingham had a mere five parish churches in 1821 to accommodate a population growing by more than 30 per cent a decade.[19] Not surprisingly, nonconformist sects made significant strides. By the middle of the nineteenth century, they had almost three million adherents, representing 17.2 per cent of the whole population.[20]

Long-established nonconformist congregations grew more slowly in the early nineteenth century than did the more recently founded sects which formed a key part of the Evangelical Revival. Much the largest was Methodism. By 1851, it could claim almost a million and a half adherents, albeit split into a number of often warring factions. Some, like the Calvinistic Methodists, were dutiful, diligent and dour; others, like the 'magic Methodists' of Cheshire's Delamere Forest or the 'Kirkgate Screamers' of Leeds were incongruously exotic. Dominant, however, were the Wesleyan Methodists, who preserved both the organisation and the conservative principles of its founder, **John Wesley**. Wesley was a firm loyalist during the American Revolution and, in the very last years of a long life, hostile to the French Revolution as well. He stated that 'a republican spirit is injurious to Methodists: as I find most fallen Methodists . . . are Republicans'.[21]

John Wesley, 1703–1791

Born in Epworth (Lincolnshire), the son of the Church of England rector of the parish, he went to Oxford University, where he studied classics. He had a distinctive conversion experience in 1738 which made him determined to bring the word of God directly to the people, particularly those not well served by the Church of England. He began missionary work with open-air preaching in Wales and the north of England in the late 1730s and 1740s and his followers were quickly called 'Methodists', reflecting the methodical and orderly ways in which Wesley organised and supported his followers. His greatest successes were with isolated communities separate from the Church of England but with their own distinctive cultures, such as miners in the North-East and far South-West. His system depended on the extensive use of 'lay preachers' He always said that he had no intention of breaking away from the Established Church, though many of his converts felt pushed out of it by hostile Anglican clergy and gentry. He worked in partnership with his brother Charles (1707–88), who is best remembered for his hymn writing.

In the 1820s, Wesley's successor, Jabez Bunting (1779–1858), tried to maintain both his predecessor's organisational abilities and his political conservatism. This led to many defections from Wesleyanism. A 'Primitive Methodist' grouping had already been forced out in 1810 for importing American-style open-air revivalist 'camp meetings'. The 'Prims' grew rapidly with strong working-class support. They developed close links with trade unionism, especially among agricultural labourers and to the fury of the gentry. Several union leaders learned about effective organisation and persuasive public speaking from their experience as **lay preachers**. By 1851, Primitive Methodism claimed more than 330,000 adherents.

Lay preachers

Literally, this refers to preaching done by members of the 'laity', in other words those who had not been ordained into a ministry. Lay preaching was common in many nonconformist sects and the subject of much criticism and condemnation by the Church of England.

Most Wesleyan Methodists came disproportionately from lower-middle-class or skilled working-class backgrounds. Fruitful alliances were forged between sections of the community known for their hard work, thriftiness and independence. They were also self-disciplined, sober and anxious to ensure that their children had a decent education.[22] They attended formal services in sturdily built Wesleyan churches. Above all, they were 'respectable'. The Victorians would draw a line which distinguished respectable working people, working with the grain of an improving society, from the 'roughs' who, in their view, subverted it by anti-social behaviour, petty crime and fecklessness. Wesleyanism worked hard to earn 'respectability'.

Despite Wesley and Bunting, many Wesleyans were political radicals who called for parliamentary reform and an end to political discrimination against nonconformists. Conflict between Methodists and Anglicans was particularly sharp in the years 1790–1820. Anglicans saw dissent from the Established Church as destabilising to society and, for some, even potentially treasonable since the nation should be united to defeat the French.

Evangelicalism was neither a unified cause nor an integrated 'movement'. Some of the sharpest divisions of both attitude and belief were between the so-called 'Church Evangelicals' (members of the Church of England) and the more radically inclined nonconformists. All Evangelicals in Britain, however, shared a commitment to salvation by faith, renewal and 'vital' Christianity. Although Evangelicals defined and prioritised them differently, 'practical Christianity' required their support for humanitarian causes. Church Evangelicals were strong on the heavy-duty moralism embodied in Societies against Vice and Immorality, and those for Promoting the Religious Instruction of Youth (see also Chapter 11). Although there are important exceptions, nonconformists tended to be rather less interested in such societies and rather more committed to supporting personal journeys of faith.

Both wings considered the slave trade an abomination. The story of William Wilberforce's leadership of the campaign to abolish it is well known. From 1788 onwards, few parliamentary sessions lacked a debate on the subject initiated by Wilberforce. The extent of nonconformist involvement in the campaign is less frequently emphasised. Yet Quakers had set the ball rolling in the late seventeenth century. Six of the nine inaugural members of the London Committee for the Abolition of the Trade in 1787 were Quakers.[23] By the 1790s, petitions against the trade were supported not only by the middle-class Evangelicals, some of whom had an economic, as well as a religious, motivation, but also by skilled workers, many of whom saw the anti-slavery campaign as a logical extension of their own struggles for political enfranchisement.[24]

Legislation abolishing the slave trade throughout the British Empire was passed in February 1807. It was widely welcomed, but why was it so long delayed? After all, the Commons had agreed fifteen years earlier to abolish the trade in stages. Furthermore, outside pressure for abolition was less extensive in 1807 than it had been during the 1790s. The delay had several causes. Black rebellions in the West

Indies from 1791 to 1795 caused bloodshed and revulsion among the propertied classes in Britain. The House of Lords was much less sympathetic to abolition than was the Commons and could delay its passage. Sugar planters proved more effective lobbyists against abolition than their numerical strength suggested. They set up smokescreens and used delaying tactics. Also, the wave of petitions demonstrating strong support for abolition outside parliament came forward more in the 1790s, when parliament was not receptive to external pressure groups.

Practical, unheroic reasons explain abolition in 1807. For the first time since 1783, Foxite Whigs were in government and Fox was a staunch abolitionist. His death at the end of 1806 concentrated supporters' minds on passing legislation to which he had been committed for so long. That, though, hardly explains the huge size of the majorities: 283 to 16 in the Commons and 100 to 34 in the Lords. Perhaps the most persuasive explanation is that the West Indian colonists now considered the trade less important. The slave population in the Caribbean was almost self-sustaining as death rates fell.[25] Commodity prices in the West Indies were also falling sharply. Britain's Caribbean colonies were shifting their emphasis away from slave-based primary production to establishing themselves as profitable entrepôts for the onward transmission of British manufactured goods, mostly to Latin America. Fewer slaves were needed and an unpopular slave trade was no longer worth fighting for. Enough West Indian colonial plantation owners felt able just to let it go. The slave trade was abolished, although slavery itself remained in British dominions for another generation (see Chapter 21).

Section 3

A New Political Era, 1815–1846

An engraving showing the execution of the Cato Street consipirators outside Newgate Prison, London, on 1 May 1820

Source: City of Westminster Archives Centre

The dominant theme of this Section is 'reform'. The first major parliamentary Reform Act was passed in 1832 and the causes, consequences and overall significance of this measure are considered in some detail (Chapters 16, 20 and 21). The extent to which this Reform Act changed the nature of politics in Britain is evaluated, as is reaction to it outside parliament, not least in the Chartist movement. How far did the development of radicalism in these years suggest the presence of more engaged and informed extra-parliamentary political activity (Chapter 21)?

However, 'reform' has often been interpreted too narrowly. This was a period of considerable change both in economic policy and in the role of government. The Tory government's response to economic and political challenges in the troubled years after the end of the Napoleonic Wars is evaluated (Chapter 16), as are the objectives of so-called 'Liberal Toryism' (Chapter 17). It is also argued that the Tory party, which dominated politics in the first thirty years of the nineteenth century, was by the 1820s divided on major issues, particularly religious reforms and the value of trade liberalisation. Those divisions help to explain the 'implosion' of the Tory party in 1830 and also its formal break-up over repeal of the Corn Laws in 1846 (Chapters 20 and 22). The role and importance of Sir Robert Peel, the ablest politician of his generation, is also considered. Is it justifiable to think of the 1830s and 1840s as 'the age of Peel'? The objectives and achievements of the Whig governments of the 1830s are considered. How far, by 1846, had older Whig groupings evolved and coalesced into a rather more inclusive 'Liberal' party?

This is also an important period for British foreign and imperial policy. Britain emerged from the Napoleonic Wars in 1815 as the world's most powerful nation. Traditionally, Britain's foreign policy and defence objectives for most of the eighteenth century had been driven by commercial interests and by reliance on its navy. Chapter 18 considers how far Castlereagh's diplomacy in 1814–15 committed Britain to a more interventionist role in European affairs. Britain's involvement in the so-called 'Congress Diplomacy' which followed is assessed, as is the question of how far British interests diverged from those of the other Congress powers. Canning's foreign policy has often been characterised as having fundamentally different priorities from those of Castlereagh. This Section discusses the extent to which differences should be ascribed to changing circumstances rather than differences of basic principle. British reaction in the 1820s both to the emergence of nationalist movements and to new commercial opportunities is also evaluated.

Although Britain, like other European great powers, did not wish to acquire new territories as an indicator of national aggrandisement, this was a period of considerable colonial expansion and development. Chapter 19 analyses the reasons for this. Attention is given to how new colonies were governed, to cultural developments in the Empire and to differences in the administration of 'white' and other colonies. Special attention is paid to Britain's increasing involvement in India, which was becoming the 'jewel' in the imperial crown. Relations between Britain and Indian princes are analysed and the reasons for the changing relationship between the British government and the East India Company are also explained.

16

The age of Lord Liverpool I: radicalism, reform and repression, 1815–1822

I. An uneasy return to peace

The peace which followed Napoleon's defeat at Waterloo proved to be long-lasting. On the domestic front, however, it was exceedingly uneasy. Within a year, Britain faced a barrage of economic difficulties. The harvest of 1816 was deficient, causing shortages and higher food prices. The 1810s saw the highest average price of wheat in the nineteenth century.[1] Inevitably, food prices rose sharply. Trade was also depressed, bringing short-time working and unemployment. The products of those industries which had been in high demand during a long war, particularly the iron industry in the English Midlands and shipbuilding especially in the North-East, were particularly hard hit. The demobilisation of about 300,000 soldiers and sailors as Britain moved onto a peacetime footing added surplus labour to an already depressed job market.

The government's responses to these problems were not fleet-footed and they elicited considerable criticism from the established political classes. Liverpool's government itself suffered an important reverse in 1815 when the House of Commons refused to renew the income tax, arguing that Pitt (see Chapter 12) had introduced it solely as a wartime emergency measure and that there was therefore now no moral warrant for its continuance. The government also gave up the lucrative tax on malt and these two changes left it seriously short of the means of reducing the National Debt. In the years 1816–20, interest charges on the National Debt averaged almost £32m, the highest level in the century. The government had no coherent policy to deal with the problem. **Nicholas Vansittart**, who had been Chancellor of the Exchequer since 1813, pursued short-term policies, which included heavy borrowing from the City and the Bank of England, linked to investment in stocks to keep prices and confidence high.

Nicholas Vansittart, first Baron Bexley, 1776–1851

Vansittart was born in London, the son of the then Governor of Bengal. He trained as a lawyer and became an MP in 1796. He was a Tory politician best known as Liverpool's Chancellor of the Exchequer from 1812 to 1823. He failed to keep the income tax in 1816, while his attempts to raise revenue did little to alleviate Britain's financial problems, and he lost the confidence of many of his colleagues and also of the Bank of England. He accepted a peerage in 1823 and remained in government office for all but five of the years 1801–28.

William Huskisson did not think much of what he called 'expedients and ingenious devices'.[2] More weighty, permanent solutions were required. The 'income tax revolt' of 1816 was an early indication that parliament was prepared to finance neither high levels of government expenditure into peacetime, nor, perhaps especially, the sinecures, patronage appointments and waste which went with them. Radicals called the system supporting all of this 'Old Corruption'. Over the next thirty years or so what has been described as the 'Fiscal-Military State', which had financed massively costly eighteenth-century wars, was dismantled. It was replaced by policies geared towards retrenchment, low taxation and greater professionalism in government administration.[3] The road to the low-cost, limited-function *laissez-faire* regimes which characterised early Victorian Britain was paved not so much with good intentions as with efficiency savings.

William Huskisson, 1770–1830

Born in Worcestershire, the son of a country gentleman, he became an MP in 1796 and his early career was much influenced by support for William Pitt and, after Pitt's death, George Canning. As a Tory politician he developed a special expertise in financial policy. He was President of the Board of Trade under Liverpool from 1823 to 1827 but he was an influential adviser for several years before that and was the brains behind the decisions to return to the **gold standard** and to resume cash payments. He was also strongly in favour of free trade policies rather than relying on government tariffs. He was MP for Liverpool, to whose commercial interests he was sympathetically alive, from 1823 until his death. Huskisson might well have become Prime Minister had his career not been cut short. In September 1830, when attending the ceremonial opening of the railway line between Liverpool and Manchester, he was hit by a train and became the world's first railway fatality.

Gold standard

This involves setting the value of paper money (bank notes and the like) and gold against an agreed fixed rate. The purpose was to tie a nation's currency to a stable commodity (gold) in order to prevent unforeseen fluctuations in the value of money. Britain was 'off the gold standard' from 1797 to 1821, during which time the government was, in effect, printing money by allowing the Bank of England to issue notes which were not tied to any external value.

Fidgety finance was one controversial area of government policy. The imposition of a new Corn Law in 1815 was another. Corn Laws were not new devices. Putting tariffs on the import of corn to England and offering bounties to those who exported English grain to continental markets had been a standard tactic since the medieval era. Governments wanted to ensure that English farmers had the incentive to keep growing crops – especially wheat – which formed the staple diet of most citizens. The immediate reason for passing a new Corn Law was poor harvests in the years 1810–12 which reduced supply and increased prices. The government now had, via its censuses of 1801 and 1811 (see Chapter 2), the first hard evidence of British population growth. The 1811 figures revealed a much higher increase (around 14 per cent) than had been predicted and the government was worried.

It is easy to see the stringency of the 1815 Corn Law as a government over-reaction. Under it, no foreign corn could be imported until the domestic price reached the famine level of 80 shillings (£4) per quarter. Colonial imports were permitted at prices above 67 shillings. Liverpool defended the measure on the traditional protectionist ground of incentives to domestic producers. His assertion that the 'great object was the interest of the Consumer'[4] cut no ice at all outside Westminster. The new Corn Law was received with such hostility precisely because protesters believed that the interests of consumers were being sacrificed to those of landowners. Where Liverpool and his ministers saw a means of providing steady and regular food prices, his extra-parliamentary opponents saw naked class legislation. Parliament, after all, was dominated by landowners. Were they not just passing laws in their own interest? Radical newspapers inveighed against the new law on grounds of landowner self-interest and also because of the high taxes which still oppressed the people – taxes also sanctioned by a landowners' parliament. Tenant farmers were usually exempted from blame. They would be capable of producing sufficient corn, were it not for, as one correspondent put it, 'the enormous load of taxes with which we are oppressed'.[5]

II. The revival of radicalism

It was the upsurge of political protest outside Westminster which most concerned the government. The target of radical writers like **William Cobbett** was 'Ministers' and the 'settled ministerial majorities' which enabled them to ignore the protests and petitions of honest Englishmen. It is not surprising that the passage of the Corn Law Bill occasioned riots in London. Radicals were increasingly arguing that laws passed by unrepresentative parliaments lacked legitimacy and that the only route to non-corrupt government was the passage of a measure to reform 'the Commons House of Parliament'.[6]

William Cobbett, 1763–1835

Born at Farnham (Surrey), the son of a publican and farmer, Cobbett developed into per-haps the most gifted, and certainly one of the most influential, radical journalists of the age. He was largely self-taught and read voraciously in his youth. He attacked what he saw as corrupt ministers in his *Weekly Political Register*, a publication which easily outsold

▶

journals produced for the propertied classes and became an immense commercial success. In *Cobbett's Parliamentary Register* he provided his readers with an alternative version of parliamentary debates to that available in the more orthodox *Hansard*. Perhaps his best-known work is *Rural Rides*, first published in 1830. It is an extended polemic, based on the author's extensive observations, against the evils and excesses of modern, profit-driven farming methods. A Hampshire farmer himself and coming from a rural background as a ploughboy and gardener in Surrey, he hated London ('the great wen'). He wrote especially sympathetically about the plight of rural labourers and of paupers. He was elected as MP for the Lancashire town of Oldham in 1832.

Levels of popular unrest with aristocratic government reached a new pitch in the years 1815–20. It is, of course, worth remembering that radical agitation for reform attracting mass support had been challenging the authorities for almost twenty-five years (see Chapter 11). However, two features distinguished the agitation in this period. First, it was more widespread geographically; secondly, it made a much greater impact in Britain's rapidly growing industrial towns and cities, especially those in Lancashire and Yorkshire. When the Lancashire weaver Samuel Bamford recalled the years 1815–16 in his famous memoir *Passages in the Life of a Radical* published twenty-five years later, he saw them as years of riot. In Bridport (Dorset) and Dundee the trigger was the high price of bread; in Barnstaple (North Devon) to prevent grain being exported up the River Taw. In Bury (Lancashire) and Nottingham protests were held against the introduction of machinery threatening skilled workers' jobs. In Merthyr Tydfil (South Wales) there were riots against wage reductions and in Birmingham the unemployed took to the streets.[7] In Glasgow, serious rioting led to bloodshed.

The most famous disturbances took place in London at the end of 1816. On 15 November, the radical **Henry (Orator) Hunt** addressed a meeting attended by about 10,000 people. He called for parliamentary reform as the only way to prevent 'the people' being burdened by high prices and higher levels of taxation. A second meeting was held on 2 December but, before Hunt could address it, the protest was hijacked by followers of **Thomas Spence**, who, engaging some sailors in the crowd to help them, marched off to take control of the Tower of London.[8]

Henry Hunt, 1773–1835

'Orator' Hunt was born into a prosperous Wiltshire farming family and developed into one of the most exciting speakers in early nineteenth-century Britain. He was an innovative gentleman farmer in his youth and was a loyalist in the early stages of the French Wars. He absorbed radical ideas while serving a short prison sentence for insubordination to his commanding officer in the local Yeomanry. His key targets were established in 1805: a corrupt, incompetent government which oppressed the people. These never varied. His oratory was put at the service of what he called 'the operative manufacturer, the mechanic and the labourer'. He helped to develop the so-called 'Mass Platform' with the intention of converting the maximum number of people to the idea of radical parliamentary reform. He addressed the meeting at St Peter's Fields in 1819 and was later arrested and imprisoned. He was elected MP for Preston in 1830 but lost his seat at the first elections for the reformed parliament in December 1832.

Thomas Spence, 1750–1814

Spence was born into a poor working family in Newcastle upon Tyne. Self-educated but widely read, he moved to London and by the early 1790s was acting as a seller of radical literature. He also developed his long-established sympathies for the poor into a political philosophy grounded in the need for the destruction of the aristocracy, the establishment of a democratic republic and, particularly, the nationalisation of land. He was not an active political agitator himself but he inspired many who were. Known as the 'Spencean Philanthropists', Arthur Thistlewood and James Watson became leading figures in the Cato Street Conspiracy of February 1820.

Although this episode came to nothing, and the protagonists were acquitted when it was revealed at their trial that the main witness for the prosecution was a government agent, ministers took note. It remains a moot point whether the government reacted as it did because it genuinely feared revolution or because it suited its strategy for handling discontent to emphasise episodes of violence and quote from hot-headed speeches in order to alarm the propertied classes with the spectre of revolution and thus justify harsh legislation. At all events, it hastily established a 'Secret Committee' to enquire into the distressed state of the country. Its report to parliament in February 1817 asserted that the current 'distress' of the labouring and manufacturing classes had been used by dangerous radicals to attempt 'a total overthrow of all existing establishments'.[9] The solution was repression. As in 1795 (see Chapter 11), Habeas Corpus was suspended. As in 1795 also, a Seditious Meetings Act was passed, giving magistrates enhanced powers to prevent the holding of political meetings.

The government's moves to shore up the old order against radical attack brought an important political benefit at Westminster. William Wyndham Grenville, who had been prime minister in 1806–7 and had led the Whigs in opposition since then (see Chapters 11 and 15), resigned his position, handed over to Earl Grey and, in effect, retired from active politics. His influence had been waning since 1812. Although he opposed the new Corn Law, he supported the general direction of the government's economic policies. Unlike many Whigs, he was also fundamentally opposed to parliamentary reform and he considered the government's policies to subdue extra-parliamentary radicalism sensible and measured.[10] Although the number of his personal supporters in parliament was not large, Grenville's resignation strengthened Liverpool's position. The number of Whig supporters returned to the Commons in the general election of 1818 was reduced by about forty.[11] Perhaps more importantly, Grenville's retirement made it easier for parliamentary supporters of the existing order to coalesce behind the Pittite Lord Liverpool as head of the 'party of order'.

III. From Pentrich to Cato Street, 1817–1820

Radical activity continued into 1817. With the trade depression and consequential unemployment still continuing, in March unemployed Lancashire weavers began a protest tramp from Manchester to London which got no further than the seven miles to Stockport, where the local **Yeomanry** discouraged any furtherance of the adventure. The so-called 'March of the Blanketeers' gained its name from the blankets worn by the weavers which were intended to serve as bedding on the long march to the capital.

> **Yeomanry**
>
> A force of volunteers, formed in 1794, which was trained by, and attached to, the army. It was established to provide support for local magistrates, particularly in resisting popular protests. Most of the volunteers were comfortably off and expected to discharge their duties on horseback. Being a 'cavalryman' implied status and a natural predisposition to defend the established order. Not surprisingly, therefore, the Yeomanry were viewed with suspicion, and usually antagonism, by radical reformers. The Yeomanry was eventually integrated into the Territorial Army, founded in 1908.

The precise extent of the preparations for a direct assault on government is hard to determine, partly because conspirators embarked on illegal activity generally take care not to advertise their plans and partly because the government employed a large number of spies and *agents provocateurs*. Such employees, paid to discover plots and revolutions, were anxious to deliver. They were all too likely to maximise, often beyond credibility, the extent of any threat to the authorities. Nevertheless, it is clear that parts of west and south Yorkshire were involved with weavers in the East Midlands in plans for a general rising of the distressed. The only outcome was a march in June from Pentrich (Derbyshire) to Nottingham, led by the unemployed framework knitter Jeremiah Brandreth. It involved only a hundred or so workers from the hosiery industry. The plot had been revealed in advance, probably by 'Oliver the Spy'. On arrival in Nottingham, Brandreth found a group of hussars armed and ready to deal with the by now bedraggled group. Forty-five men were arrested and three, including Brandreth himself, were executed at Derby in November 1817.

The government's response to economic distress in 1817 was not purely repressive. It passed a 'Poor Employment Act', the mechanics of which were dear to Vansittart's heart. Once again, government powers to print money were exercised, this time in the form of exchequer bills, with a total value up to £1.75m, to individuals or to public corporations willing to invest in employment-generating public works schemes. Within two months, more than half of the fund had been subscribed. The money was mostly spent on canal- and road-building and on draining marshes to bring more land into effective cultivation. These were the most extensive and ambitious public works schemes yet seen in Britain, and although, as Boyd Hilton has noted, its practical effects were limited, this Act 'marked a considerable extension of the scope of government'.[12]

A good harvest in 1817 and a trade revival combined to make 1818 a year attended by much less radical activity, although new pro-reform newspapers like the *Manchester Observer* appeared and enjoyed good sales. Meanwhile, petitions calling for parliamentary reform were still being presented in large numbers. The year 1819 nevertheless saw a much greater polarisation of views for, or against, parliamentary reform. The fulcrum event was the so-called 'Peterloo Massacre'. The context for this was the return of economic distress with attendant short-time working and unemployment. This gave greater purchase to radical claims that the only solution to the nation's difficulties was a concerted attack on the 'tax eaters', 'placemen' (lackeys on the government payroll who were employed for their loyalty rather than their expertise) and the whole unproductive paraphernalia which was being called 'Old Corruption'.[13]

Orator Hunt had addressed a successful pro-reform meeting in Manchester in January 1819. Other mass meetings, confirming Hunt in his belief that 'the Platform' was the way forward, were held in Birmingham, Leeds and London. Hunt was invited back to Manchester for a reform meeting to be held on 16 August. It attracted at least 60,000 people against a background of rising tension and spies' reports that industrial Lancashire was to be the focus for another attempt at revolution. The local Yeomanry forcibly broke up the meeting, injuring about six hundred of the crowd in the process. Estimates vary, but between eleven and seventeen were either killed outright or died of their wounds shortly afterwards.[14] These 'martyrs' to the reform cause became vital propaganda tools. Privately, many in the government believed that the Yeomanry had over-reacted; publicly they had to support those who upheld public order and property rights.

The consequences were dramatic. The radical cause became truly national for the first time. Pro-reform political unions were established in areas, such as Staffordshire, which had been relatively unengaged before. Rioting in the second half of 1819 was commonplace. Radicals soon named the event 'The Peterloo Massacre', in satirical recollection of the Duke of Wellington's victory at Waterloo. The effect of this wordplay was heightened by the knowledge that the Duke was one of the most forthright opponents not only of parliamentary reform but of any activity critical of the established order. Cartoonists and satirists had a field day. The most gifted of them, George Cruikshank, created the image of a Peterloo Medal which showed a member of the Yeomanry attacking an undernourished, unarmed man with an axe. Such visual attacks were particularly potent when circulated among the lower orders in the industrial areas, since many were, at best, semi-literate.[15]

The government responded to widespread disaffection and not a little violence in anticipated fashion. They resurrected some of the old repressive legislation and found a few new things to ban. The Six Acts (quickly dubbed the 'Whip with Six Strings') were in place by the end of 1819. Among other things, the holding of political or religious meetings which more than fifty people were expected to attend had to be approved by a magistrate, laws against sedition and libel were strengthened, local magistrates were given powers to search any private property for weapons and many newspapers were subject to taxation and stamp duties for the first time. The purpose of this last measure was to tax radical newspapers out of the means of working people. Professor Hilton considers the Six Acts 'in the circumstances quite mild'.[16] Few contemporaries thought them so and most historians since have generally thought them harsh.[17] Nevertheless, as in previous instances, the government intended quietly to withdraw, or ignore, these new Acts when the political temperature reached acceptable levels and spies stopped reporting dastardly revolutionary plans or drilling with weapons on those remote moorlands situated conveniently outside many northern towns and cities. We should also remember that an assassin's bullet needs to hit the intended target only once, or a *coup d'état* by a small, unrepresentative group to succeed, for events to spiral out of control and disproportionate consequences to ensue, as the assassination of Archduke Franz Ferdinand at Sarajevo in 1914 or the Bolshevik seizure of power in Moscow and St Petersburg in 1917 amply demonstrate.

In any case, a genuinely revolutionary attempt in 1820 needed no exaggeration by a spy anxious to nail down his reward, since the spy, George Edwards, pretended to be part of a plot which would be called the 'Cato Street Conspiracy'. He revealed its progress to the authorities at every stage. In London, a so-called 'Committee of Two Hundred' was planning to launch a nationwide rebellion immediately after the assassination of all of Liverpool's Cabinet as it assembled for dinner in Grosvenor Square. The moving force, Arthur Thistlewood, was a follower of Thomas Spence and already known to the authorities for his involvement in the projected attack on the Tower in 1816. The details of the conspiracy have been graphically set out. One conspirator, James Ings, stated that he would personally cut off the heads of Castlereagh, the Foreign Secretary, and Sidmouth, the Home Secretary, put them in a bag and take them to Westminster Bridge for impaling. The assassination was planned for 23 February and the conspirators hoped to benefit from a time of transition, the aged and demented King George III having died less than a month before. The stillborn plot ended with the arrest of the conspirators. Five of them, including Thistlewood and Ings, were executed for high treason on 1 May.[18]

IV. The Queen Caroline affair

The King's death at the end of January 1820 precipitated the final public outburst of these crowded few years. It brought to the throne the vain, unprepossessing, self-indulgent, solipsistic George IV, who had been exercising royal power as Prince Regent since 1811. He had an estranged wife, Caroline of Brunswick-Wolfenbüttel, whom he had married in 1795. She shared many of her husband's unattractive characteristics and added a distinctive few more. The pair loathed each other. Caroline was cut out of royal engagements when George became Regent and had spent most of the five years before 1820 travelling in Europe in the company of a servant, Bartolomeo Pergami, who was almost certainly her lover.

In 1820, George had been preparing to divorce his wife for almost two years, but his accession to the throne placed the issue in full public gaze. George was determined that Caroline would not be crowned or in any way treated as his Queen. Caroline, however, returned to England determined to enjoy the rights to which she believed her status entitled her. Worse, from the King's and the government's point of view, the Queen was making highly political statements. To proclaim, against all the evidence of her wilful life over the past quarter century, that 'All classes will ever find in me a sincere friend to their liberties, and a zealous advocate of their rights'[19] was further to polarise opinion between loyalists and conservatives on the one hand, and radicals and much popular opinion on the other. Her proclamation could also be read as an early statement of support for women's independence of political action and as a rebuttal of the notion that a wife became, on marriage, her husband's property (see Chapter 25).[20] For loyalists to George, his Queen's immorality and immodesty of lifestyle debarred her from assuming the role of 'the first woman of the most loyal nation . . . the patroness of female virtue and domestic decency'.

When the Queen, having refused an offer of the enormous sum of £350,000 (almost £25m in early twenty-first-century values) to stay away, arrived in London in June 1820, she found huge welcoming crowds on the streets. Both in public and in the radical press, Queen Caroline was represented as the people's champion. In the House of Lords a 'Bill of Pains and Penalties', as precursor to a divorce, ran into severe opposition, not least because many peers considered the King's conduct at least as reprehensible as the Queen's.[21] When the bill passed the Lords by only nine votes in November 1820, Lord Liverpool withdrew it. He knew that it was sure to fail when it was debated in the Commons and was anxious to dampen down public protests. The King was furious. He considered dismissing his ministers before the reflection dawned that any administration which took Liverpool's place would be less sympathetic to him. In London, the streets were illuminated as radicals and their supporters celebrated a great triumph. Petitions supporting the Queen, which had been tumbling into Westminster over the past four months, seemed to have been vindicated.

For both the Whigs, who had organised many of the petitions, and the radicals, who saw the events as a means of consolidating public opinion incontrovertibly against

'Old Corruption' and in favour of the people's rights and reform, it proved a false dawn. The King was implacably opposed to any rapprochement with his wife. The Queen was in no way the defender of liberties that her supporters wanted her to become. In March 1821, she accepted a pension of £50,000 from the King, thus depriving herself at a stroke of any chance of reclaiming the moral high ground. On 19 July, the King was crowned in a wildly overblown, extravagant and vulgar ceremony at Westminster Abbey. The loyalist press took the opportunity to trumpet its allegiance to monarchy as the symbol of national unity. The Queen was forbidden to attend and made herself a laughing stock by tramping from door to door and shrieking for admittance. A month later, she died quite unexpectedly. It is true that rioting in London forced the funeral cortège to make a detour on its way to Harwich and thence to burial in Brunswick, but this was little more than a gesture. Queen Caroline, that most implausible champion of liberty, had ceased to matter.

The events of 1820–21 have been called 'the storm before the calm'.[22] It is difficult to disagree, although the ensuing 'calm' would not last long (see Chapter 20). At the time of George IV's coronation, *Blackwood's Edinburgh Magazine* was announcing with relief that 'quiet times have come'.[23] It seems clear that, as in the 1790s (see Chapter 11), the radical press and radical crowds were inclined prematurely to claim that they spoke for the nation. Whether the political left (championing 'liberty') or the right (claiming the virtues of 'legitimate authority' and 'order') could properly occupy the patriotic high ground was a matter of furious contention. It is often forgotten that a number of loyalist journals with evocative names such as *John Bull*, *True Blue* and *The British Freeholder* were successfully launched during the Caroline crisis.

Radicals often found it difficult to coalesce around a single reformist theme. They disagreed not only about the means of achieving reform but also about what kind of reform it was most desirable to promote. The Caroline affair, for example, brought to the surface implicit disagreements about the role of women in politics. In simple terms, the right had only to find the most effective language and registers to support and defend what *was*. The left had the much more complex task of achieving consensus around a political programme which *might be*. It is not surprising that radicalism fared best when the economy fared worst. Radicalism and 'hunger politics' were close allies. By the summer of 1821, the economy was reviving and more jobs were being created. It was not a propitious moment to anticipate a radical reform of the Commons House of Parliament.

17

The age of Lord Liverpool II: 'Liberal Toryism', 1822–1827

I. Liberal Toryism and the mechanics of government

The phrase 'Liberal Toryism' should be used with care. It is seductive, but misleading, to see the suicide of Castlereagh and the resignations of Sidmouth and Vansittart in 1822–23 as initiating a new, more enlightened form of Tory government. Liverpool had not reconstructed his ministry to that end. Rather he was concerned about the number of defeats the government had suffered in the Commons in 1820–21. He also knew that few of his experienced ministers in the Commons were effective performers. Liverpool therefore promoted men he knew to be abler and more creative than those they replaced. William Huskisson, though only in a minor office, was already widely recognised as Liverpool's key adviser on economic policy. Peel had made an impact as Chairman of the Bullion Committee in 1819. Canning was an awkward colleague but extremely able and perhaps the best speaker in parliament. Castlereagh's suicide presented an opportunity, however unfortunate, to strengthen the lower house while giving Canning the promotion he coveted. Liverpool was also glad to include Charles Wynn in his Cabinet. Wynn was not especially able but his appointment had political importance. He had led the remnants of the Grenvillite faction (see Chapter 16) in the Commons. His acceptance of office in 1822 ended the role of the Grenvillites as an independent group.[1] In effect, and despite the remaining coolness of Grenville himself, they had joined the Tories. Collectively, Liverpool's 'new men' felt that they could do a better job than the old guard. Huskisson was highly critical of what he saw as Vansittart's unsystematic approach to financial management. He called him 'the real blot and sin of the government'.[2]

The government reshuffle was, therefore, likely to produce change. Canning, the new Foreign Secretary, **Peel** at the Home Office, Huskisson (who accepted the Presidency of the Board of Trade in February 1823 but was not promoted to Cabinet rank until November) and **Robinson** (Chancellor of the Exchequer) all imposed a distinctive stamp their ministries. Canning placed less reliance than Castlereagh on treaties with Europe's autocratic rulers (see Chapter 18). Huskisson and Robinson lowered the tax burden, attacked the navigation laws, reduced tariffs and generally encouraged a less restrictive attitude to trading agreements between states. Peel initiated major administrative and legal reforms. These promotions, however, did not mark any intentional transition from 'repressive' to 'liberal' Toryism. All the 'new' men were experienced, while Liverpool himself experienced no cathartic, short-term conversion to enlightened attitudes and policies. Liberal Toryism did not imply 'reform', pure and simple. Nor were the ministers sitting in Liverpool's Cabinet after 1822 all of one mind over the direction of policy.

Robert Peel, 1788–1850

Born in Bury, the son of a highly successful textile manufacturer, Peel became an MP in 1809 and a junior minister a year later. His whole career was spent at, or near, the centre of power. He was Chief Secretary for Ireland from 1812 to 1828, Home Secretary from 1822 to 1827 and 1828 to 1830, Prime Minister in 1834–35 and 1841–46. His early career suggested that he was a 'high Tory' and he was an ally of Wellington, whom he persuaded to grant political emancipation to Roman Catholics in 1829. He was thereafter regarded as a traitor by many of his colleagues. They gave him only grudging support when he led the Tory party and felt vindicated when he repealed the Corn Laws, widely seen as essential to the preservation of the landed interest, in 1846. Corn law repeal was very popular outside parliament, since repeal aimed to keep food prices down. Peel was very able and immensely hard-working but widely regarded as cold, aloof and arrogant. He left office in 1846, taking a group of those who had served in his government into opposition with him as 'Peelites'. He died as the result of a riding accident.

Frederick Robinson, Viscount Goderich, 1782–1859

Born in Yorkshire, the son of a diplomat, landowner and serving Member of Parliament, he became an MP in 1806, thanks to the patronage of Viscount Castlereagh. He held a number of government offices, most notably Chancellor of the Exchequer, when he helped to reduced trade tariffs and lowered taxes. He accepted a peerage in 1827 and became Prime Minister in 1827 after the sudden death of Canning but his ministry lacked authority and, uniquely among Prime Ministers, he resigned office in 1828 without ever attending a sitting of parliament in that capacity. He did not join Wellington's administration but served in Grey's Whig-led coalition of 1830–34. He was created Earl of Ripon in 1833. After leaving the Whig government in 1834, he rejoined the Conservatives and served as a Cabinet minister throughout Peel's administration of 1841–46.

It is more fruitful to explain the differences in terms of understanding what government was *for* rather than in comparing and contrasting the policy achievements of key office-holders before and after 1822. An important ideological division existed over the proper role of government in a rapidly changing world. 'High Tories' (a more useful phrase than 'repressive Tories') and 'liberal Tories', while they agreed on many important areas of policy, had different attitudes to the role of government. High Tories, like **Lord Eldon**, the Duke of Wellington and Viscount Sidmouth, believed that the efficient functioning of government required interventionism, careful management and supervision. They believed both in landed property and the established Church of England as the legitimate agencies of authority. High Tories believed in the landed interest's almost divine right to rule, sanctioned by custom, practice and even the Church. The existing social structure was geared to producing men from privileged backgrounds; with their usually extensive education, they had almost been 'bred for rule'.

John Scott, first Earl of Eldon, 1751–1838

Born in Newcastle upon Tyne, the son of a prosperous coal merchant, Scott trained for the law and became an MP in 1783. While continuing his legal career, he was also a strong supporter of Pitt. He was appointed Solicitor General in 1788. During the 1790s, he was an unyielding opponent of political radicalism and prosecuted a number of leading radicals. The King thought very highly of both his abilities and his loyalty to the monarchy. He became a peer as Baron Eldon in 1799. In 1801 he became Lord Chancellor in Addington's government and served continuously (with the sole exception of the 'Ministry of All the Talents', 1806–7) in that capacity until 1827 in the administrations of Pitt, Portland, Perceval and Liverpool. He was created an Earl in 1821. Eldon was regarded by his many opponents as the sternest opponent of reform. He opposed religious reforms in the 1820s and also, with Wellington, led resistance to the Reform Act in the House of Lords. He maintained his reputation for unbending conservatism by opposing Whig plans for Church reform in Ireland in 1834.

The 'liberal' Tories preferred to see government functioning as a kind of machine operating for the benefit of society as a whole. The more the machine was 'self-acting', the better it worked. As Peel put it, a well-ordered government should beat 'with a healthful and regular motion – animating industry, encouraging production, rewarding toil, correcting what is irregular, purifying what is stagnant and corrupt'.[3] It is no coincidence that two of the most prominent 'liberals', George Canning and Robert Peel, came from non-landed backgrounds. Canning's father was a lawyer without a fortune and Peel's father was a highly successful cotton manufacturer. Neither took on trust the high Tory view that landowners were born to rule. Though the dividing lines are not clear cut, in the 1820s a battle for supremacy was going on between those who mostly adopted a 'liberal' and those who took a 'high' Tory position.

Definitions are both difficult and contentious. The 'liberal Tories' did not agree on all issues. However, they lived in a period of revolutionary political, social and economic change and sought to achieve a practical balance between the 'conservatives' who instinctively opposed change and the 'radicals' who wanted to pull down the established order and construct a new one based on theoretical principles, including equality of representation if not of property.[4]

It is also important to note that economic conditions for much of the 1820s were far more benign than in the years immediately following the French Wars (see

Chapter 16). A prescient commentary written in 1824 argued that the progress of British commerce since the 1770s would have seemed incredible to an observer from the period of the American wars: 'A whole hemisphere of the globe has, within the last ten years, been in a manner opened to our industry – an event of magnificent promise, and which may ultimately change the aspect of the civilised world.' It looked forward to the 'progressive expanding development of the unrestricted energies of our trade'.[5] Increased commercial revenues enabled the government to reduce excise taxes on windows, servants and carriages. Of greater significance to more people were reduced import duties on wool, linens, coal, silk and a range of other commodities. The aim was to wring the malign effects of war out of the system and return the government's revenue-raising operations to something like the situation in the last years of Pitt's peacetime administration. Huskisson, however, could not forbear to add a liberal ideological twist. He told the House of Commons in June 1823 that it 'was high time, in the improved state of the civilisation of the world, to establish more liberal principles; and show, that commerce was not the end, but the means of diffusing comfort and enjoyment among the nations embarked in its pursuit'.[6]

At the Board of Trade, Huskisson aimed to maximise the advantage of Britain's early lead in industrial production by removing restrictions on the growth of domestic industry and by providing incentives for exports. This meant further moves towards free trade, drawing on principles articulated by Adam Smith and David Ricardo. His Reciprocity of Duties Act in 1823 broke with the principle of protection enshrined in the Navigation Acts. It offered equality of duties on both goods and ships to any nation which would offer the same to Britain. Trade treaties were signed with Prussia and France. By 1830, most European states, unwilling to be left out of interchange with such a powerful economy as Britain's, had signed up.[7] In 1824–25, tariffs on imports, including raw materials, were reduced and the whole duty system was rationalised under only eight headings. Over one thousand customs Acts were repealed. Huskisson explained in 1825 why a low-duty regime would advantage British manufacturers: 'We furnish, in a proportion far exceeding the supply from any other country, the general markets of the world with all the leading articles of manufacture.' Foreign manufactures would, of course, be allowed in, but 'they will not interfere with those articles of more wide and universal consumption, which our own manufacturers supply cheaper and better'.[8] In general, manufactured imports were of luxury items intended for a restricted market. British exporters were capturing the larger and more profitable mass markets. Statistics suggest that Huskisson was right. The value of imports to Britain during the 1820s was 33 per cent higher than in the first decade of the nineteenth century. The value of British exports, however, was 81 per cent higher. Of those exports, 74 per cent in the 1820s were manufactured textile goods. Britain's **Gross National Product** increased by almost 17 per cent during the 1820s and earnings from foreign investment increased by 60 per cent.[9]

Gross National Product (GNP)

GNP is a term used to cover the total value of all goods and services produced in a nation's economy. It is usually expressed as the total value produced over a one-year period. Because it describes the totality of economic activity within a nation, the value of all imported goods and services are included in the calculation. Conversely, the total value of the goods and services which leave the country as exports is subtracted from the total.

This benign position was rudely interrupted by the severe banking crisis of 1825–26. It brought both the export and stock-market boom to a shuddering halt. The basic difficulty was that the Bank of England, attempting to stimulate investment in agriculture, had permitted excessive loans to the country banks which in their turn lent unwisely. Too much went to newly formed companies with links to highly speculative new projects, especially in Latin America, some of which were specious. Share prices, which had quadrupled since 1821, were checked in the spring of 1825. Many undercapitalised companies failed. Worse followed in the autumn when a number of country banks failed. This led directly to the failure of London banks, including such reputable and established names as Pole, Thornton and Co. For a week in mid-December, it seemed probable that the Bank of England itself might become insolvent and that the Exchequer itself would be saddled with insupportable levels of unfunded debt. The Bank was saved by an influx of gold bullion, embarrassingly for the government from the Banque de France. This enabled a return to some kind of stability when the government persuaded the Bank to lend on the security of goods rather than exchequer bills. The fall-out was substantial. Eighty more country banks failed in the early months of 1826, while 500 or so of the 624 companies formed during the 'bubble' of 1824–25 had collapsed by 1827.[10] The role of the Bank of England as a **lender of last resort** was called into question, though a viable solution to the problem would be almost twenty years in coming (see Chapter 22).

Lender of last resort

This technical term refers to a bank, normally a country's central bank, which offers loans to other banks or to large companies which cannot meet their commitments and which would otherwise fail. The aim is to have a secure fallback both to protect investors and also to prevent panic withdrawals from other banks, precipitating a domino effect of banking failures and national financial collapse. In 1825, it is clear that the Bank of England acted too late in making rescue funds available.

II. Peel and administrative reform

Peel's changes at the Home Office were not motivated by humanitarianism. As perhaps the most 'technocratic' of all Liverpool's ministers, he wanted to see English law work better. He was concerned that English law, lacking proper codification, was complex and, in parts, chaotic. He was even more worried about the range of savage sentences available to judges after convictions on relatively minor offences. Early nineteenth-century judges were not noted for their exercise of leniency. Consequently, juries often acquitted on the basis of the likely sentence rather than on the evidence. Peel noted that some of the most draconian sentences were passed for crimes against property. Such crimes, including petty theft and poaching, were always more prevalent at times of depression, such as had afflicted Britain after the end of the Napoleonic Wars. Many Englishmen felt that they were living through a crime wave in the decade after 1816. Commitments for trial on criminal offences were 97 per cent higher in the period 1818–25 than they had been in the period 1809–16[11] and theft accounted for almost 87 per cent of crimes in 1825. When he examined the problem, Peel found that no fewer than ninety-two separate statutes related to theft, some passed as far back as the thirteenth century.[12] With pressure for parliamentary reform growing on the grounds that the existing system of electing MPs was anachronistic and profited only the rich, a system which saw laws passed by wealthy landowners zealous to preserve their property rights was intrinsically dangerous. Peel's legal reforms aimed to bring much needed stability and efficiency to the process.

Peel looked for consolidation and rationalisation. His Gaols Act of 1823 enabled the emergence of a national policy on prisons, although prison inspectors were not appointed until 1835. Each county and large town was required to maintain its own gaols out of local rates. Gaolers now received proper pay, rather than charging the families of felons for the privilege of incarcerating them. Prisoners were to be visited by chaplains and the use of irons and manacles to restrain prisoners – previously common – was banned. Peel noted the evidence presented by reformers such as **Elizabeth Fry** and **Sir James Mackintosh**, but his legislation was designed to be efficient and practical, while not being too 'liberal' to gain majorities in parliament.

Elizabeth Fry, 1780–1845

Born in Norwich, the daughter of the prosperous merchant and banker John Gurney, her Quaker faith led her to support humanitarian causes, particularly prison reform and female education. She used the evidence gained from studying insanitary and overcrowded conditions experienced by women prisoners to press for reforms. She introduced a more humane, although regimented and supervised, regime for women prisoners and demonstrated that, under appropriate conditions, prisoners would respond and could be reformed.

James Mackintosh, 1765–1832

Born near Inverness, the son of a Scottish army officer, he moved to London in 1788, where he made a reputation as a writer and intellectual. In 1791 he wrote *Vindiciae Gallicae* in defence of the French Revolution, a work he later repudiated. He associated with the Whig Friends of the People (see Chapter 11). After training for the law, he was appointed as a judge in Bombay, where he attacked corruption in the operation of the law and opposed capital punishment. On return from India, he entered parliament in 1813 as a Whig supporter. He argued consistently for parliamentary reform and wrote extensively on political and philosophical subjects.

In 1823, Peel introduced five statutes which greatly reduced the number of crimes for which judges could impose the death penalty. This consolidation, however, brought no decrease in the number of executions – and intentionally so. Peel argued that greater respect would be shown towards laws which no longer prescribed execution for relatively trivial crimes, although horse-stealing, for example, remained a capital offence. Therefore, the prerogative of mercy to those under sentence of death should be exercised more sparingly. The Lord Chancellor, Lord Eldon, wished to leave sentencing discretion with the judges; Peel did not. He preferred consistency. Potential felons should know with greater certainty what punishment awaited them if they committed a given crime. In Boyd Hilton's words, Peel wanted 'citizens to make rational prudential calculations on the disutility of criminal behaviour'.[13] Such calculations needed to include the likelihood of transportation. It has been calculated that by the late 1820s, almost a third of those convicted of serious crimes were sentenced to transportation, usually to Australia and often for life.[14] Conditions on convict ships were such that, for many, transportation operated as a delayed death sentence.

Peel's Jury Act of 1825 rationalised more than eighty existing statutes and made the process of jury selection much clearer. Greater clarity also lay at the heart of his great 'consolidating' statutes of 1826 and 1827. The first aimed at improving the administration of central justice. The second replaced ninety-two confusing and repetitive statutes on theft with just five. Together, these two Acts covered more than 80 per cent of the most common offences.

Combinations of workers had been illegal since 1799 when anti-union legislation had been rushed through parliament at the peak of anti-radical hostility (see Chapter 11). With the return of prosperity and the apparent decline of threatening political gatherings, it seemed safe to decriminalise trade unions. The experienced radical politician **Francis Place** organised a campaign for repeal which was supported in parliament by **Joseph Hume**. Place argued to a House of Commons Select Committee, somewhat implausibly but apparently convincingly, that trade unions only developed in response to employers' own 'combinations' to reduce wages. As he wrote to Francis Burdett, 'Men have been kept together only by the oppression of the laws; these being repealed, combinations will lose the matter which cements them into masses, and they will fall to pieces.' The Combination laws were repealed in 1824 during a trade boom. Newly legalised trade unions rushed to exploit their opportunity at a time when the skills of respectable working men were at a premium. A series of strikes for higher wages and better working conditions resulted in 1825. When some turned violent, Huskisson asked a new Select Committee to frame fresh recommendations. These took back most of the gains unions had won in the previous year. Unions could continue to exist – but little else. The usual means of pressurising employers – obstruction of their works, persuading other workers to strike, the issuing of threats – were declared to be conspiracies 'in restraint of trade' and thus illegal.[15]

Francis Place, 1771–1854

He was born into a poor family and was apprenticed as a tailor. He helped to found the London Corresponding Society in 1792 and supported a wide range of radical causes. Well-read himself, he believed that the vote had to be earned by education, organisation and respectable behaviour. He masterminded the repeal of the Combination Acts in 1824. He also helped to draft the petition which became the People's Charter in 1838. His personal fortune increased and he became a prosperous London shopkeeper and tailor.

Joseph Hume, 1777–1855

Born in Montrose (Scotland), the son of a shipmaster, he studied medicine at Edinburgh and was employed by the East India Company at the beginning of the nineteenth century to practise surgery in Bengal. On his return to Scotland, a business venture to supply army uniforms prospered. He became a Director of the East India Company and entered parliament in 1812. He quickly associated with Whig politicians and intellectuals. He was particularly influenced by the ideas of David Ricardo, James Mill and Jeremy Bentham. Over a long career, he supported many reformist political and religious causes. He attacked the government over Peterloo, helped in the repeal of the Combination Acts and pressed for more extensive parliamentary reform after 1832, including a secret ballot and an enlarged electorate. Unsurprisingly, he also supported the Chartist petitions to parliament.

III. Catholics, contention and division

The disparate collection of individuals who occupied Cabinet positions in Liverpool's government both before and after 1822 had agreed to disagree about religion. The issue of Catholic Emancipation was particularly toxic. It divided colleagues, like Peel and Huskisson, who agreed on most other issues and it had united those, like

Castlereagh and Canning, who had otherwise been at daggers drawn. To keep the government together, Liverpool had extracted from colleagues the undertaking that ministers would not discuss the Catholic question in Cabinet, or raise it with the King – whose opposition to Emancipation was predictably iron-clad. Unfortunately for the government, debates on 'the Catholic question' soon became unavoidable.

It is not easy to explain why those who had advocated Catholic Emancipation in Ireland so persuasively during debates on the Union (see Chapter 14) took so long to regroup after Union was implemented without Emancipation. The eventual regrouping was sectarian. Daniel O'Connell's Catholic Association was founded in 1823. It created what one Church of Ireland bishop called 'a complete union of the Roman Catholic body' in favour of the political emancipation of Catholics.[16] By 1824, Marquess Wellesley, the Lord Lieutenant, was writing to Canning that 'The Roman Catholics of Ireland are now a *Nation*, a *People*'. Note his perceptive assessment of the significance of O'Connell's movement: the Irish majority saw itself as '*a People without a Government*'; while the Protestant power is a '*Government without a People*'.[17]

Resolving this paradox would take almost a century. In the much shorter term, it brought to the surface tensions in Liverpool's government previously hidden by prosperity and secure majorities in the Commons. In 1825 the pro-Catholic Whig Henry Brougham got parliamentary support for a Catholic Relief Bill. Peel and Liverpool both considered resignation. When the Lords threw the Emancipation Bill out, the Duke of Wellington, with characteristic lack of both political acumen and sensitivity, suggested that this would be an ideal moment to call a general election and exploit growing 'No Popery' feeling in the country at large.

Wellington did not get his 1825 election but the Catholic question increasingly dominated Cabinet discussion. Ministers were troubled that both pro- and anti-Emancipation Tory candidates would stand at the next election, thus emphasising the Tory party's deep divisions. At the general election held in June and July 1826, fewer than 30 per cent of constituencies were contested: more than in 1820 but roughly par for the course before 1832. The Catholic question was the most important issue but by no means the only one. In several county seats, many agriculturalists expressed frustration at being tricked by the minor amendment made in 1822 to the 1815 Corn Law. This had failed to produce the hoped-for rise in corn prices. In 1825, Huskisson had also allowed Canadian wheat into Britain for two years on payment of only a minimal import duty.[18] That rubbed salt into arable farmers' wounds. This press, however, concentrated on the Tories' strife over religion. This was embarrassingly displayed at Cambridge University, where only support from opposition Whigs enabled Lord Palmerston to hold his seat against a challenge from two 'anti-Catholic' junior ministers. Overall, the number of 'Protestant' supporters in the Commons went up by about thirteen.[19]

The result of the election did not threaten Liverpool's Tories as much as the recognition that the Catholic question was dominating political debate and would shortly require resolution. Any such resolution risked splitting the Tories from top to bottom. Furthermore, 'pro-Catholics' in the Cabinet now found themselves closer to the Whig opposition than at any time since the French Revolution. The Whigs strongly favoured emancipation and they also broadly supported the liberal Tories' policies on commerce, administration and law reform. Most liberal Tories – Peel was the outstanding exception – were pro-Catholic. This was no bad basis for political realignment. It was the position reached in February 1827 when Liverpool suffered the stroke which removed him from public life. The Tory hegemony, which had survived since the mid-1790s, was no longer so securely founded as mere longevity would suggest.

18

....

Congresses, commerce and conflicts: foreign policy, 1815–1830

I. Castlereagh and Congress diplomacy

After the Battle of Waterloo in June 1815, peace finally returned to Europe. A peace treaty had already been signed. After the collapse of Napoleon's armies in the spring of 1814, the United Kingdom, Russia, Austria, Sweden, Portugal and Prussia agreed by the Treaty of Paris that France's territorial boundaries should revert to those of 1792. France was also required to recognise the independence of the Netherlands. The River Scheldt, free navigation of which had been the specific objective causing Britain to declare war on France in 1793, was confirmed once more as a river open to navigation and Antwerp, at its mouth, was declared in future to be 'solely a Commercial Port'. Britain therefore secured a key British trading route from the North Sea into northern Europe.

This treaty, negotiated on Britain's behalf by **Viscount Castlereagh**, is worthy of comment even though, thanks to Napoleon's 'Hundred Days', it had limited immediate effect. First, Britain now accepted free navigation in the Netherlands. Castlereagh agreed to the principle that 'the Navigation of the Rhine, from the point where it becomes navigable unto the sea, and vice versa, shall be free, so that it can be interdicted [prohibited] to no one'.[1] In the 1790s, Britain had opposed free navigation, believing that its vessels needed protection. Secondly, the great powers had agreed, albeit with varying degrees of reluctance and thanks in large part to Castlereagh's insistence, that France should neither be humiliated by large losses of territory nor destabilised by fines or other financial penalties. The victorious allies of 1814–15, therefore, avoided the mistakes of their successors at Versailles in 1919.

Robert Stewart, Viscount Castlereagh, 1769–1822

Born in Dublin into a Presbyterian landowning family, he entered the Irish parliament in 1790 and became a British MP as member for a small Cornish borough in 1794 on the recommendation of William Pitt, the Prime Minister. He took the **courtesy title** of Viscount Castlereagh in 1796 when his father was created Earl of Londonderry. As he indicated himself, his career was largely shaped as a follower of Pitt, who appreciated his clear-headed approach to issues and his capacity for hard work. He came to prominence as the Chief Secretary for Ireland who brokered Irish Union with Great Britain

▶

(see Chapter 14). He was involved in Indian affairs from 1802 to 1809, when he served as President of the Board of Control with responsibility for oversight of the East India Company. He was Secretary for War and the Colonies from 1805 to 1809 and Foreign Secretary from 1812 to 1822. His diplomatic skills were widely admired, especially during negotiations for what emerged as the Congress System. His overall aim as Foreign Secretary was to secure both a workable balance of power and peace in continental Europe, so that Britain would not again be deflected by European wars from its commercial and colonial priorities. He succeeded to the title of Marquess of Londonderry on his father's death in 1821. Castlereagh had ambitions to be Prime Minister, but a mental breakdown, probably precipitated by overwork, led to his suicide in 1822.

Courtesy title

Courtesy titles are one reason why names of the aristocracy undergo sometimes frequent, and usually confusing, changes. These are titles used by children, wives and other close relatives of a peer of the realm. Thus, a peer from one of top ranks – in descending order Duke, Marquess, Earl – may nominate his son to use one of them, as the formal phrase has it, 'by courtesy'. It is not uncommon for the eldest son of a Duke to be known by the title Earl or Marquess, although he would not be entitled to sit in the House of Lords. Younger sons of Dukes and Marquesses may also adopt the courtesy title 'Lord'. Names also change on the first granting of a title and on any subsequent granting of a higher one.

The powers met again at Vienna in June 1815 and Paris in November. The need to make any new peace settlement permanent, recognised anyway by war-weary and impoverished combatants, was reinforced by Napoleon's attempt to recover his position. Should the settlement be a pan-European one, or should it concentrate on how to bring stability back to France and its neighbours? Would it be safer, as far as territories and national aspirations went, just to turn the clock back to 1789, or would it be more prudent to recognise that the French Revolution had raised important, and insistent, questions relating to citizenship, political rights and national identities? Such questions could not be resolved merely by signatures on treaties made by representatives of what was still, after all, the old, pre-Napoleonic, political order. A more radical and imaginative approach was required.

The outcome was that France gave up more territory on its eastern and southern borders. An allied army of occupation was sent to France for five years to ensure that the re-establishment of the Bourbon monarchy was secure and unchallenged. The victorious powers also agreed to act together to repel any French attempt to subvert this settlement. One of the main beneficiaries of the settlement was Prussia, which gained much of Saxony and the coal and iron-ore rich Ruhr in North Rhine-Westphalia. Inadvertently, the allies provided Prussia with many of the raw materials necessary to follow Britain's path to industrial development and eventually to become its main European rival and competitor (see Chapters 35 and 42). The main innovation, however, was the decision of the victorious powers to hold regular meetings designed to resolve any issues of European diplomacy which might threaten peace. Thus was born the so-called **Congress System**.

Congress System

This was the name given to the arrangement whereby the Great Powers held regular conferences to discuss matters of dispute and concern. The intention was to settle problems between nations without resort to war. The first was held at Vienna in 1815 in order to confirm peace treaties ending the Napoleonic Wars. Five further Congresses were held as follows:

1818: *Aix-la-Chapelle*: France was re-admitted to the congress of nations and the army of occupation was withdrawn two years early. With the addition of a fifth great power, the Quadruple became the Quintuple Alliance.

1820: *Troppau*: the Quintuple Alliance (United Kingdom, Prussia, Russia, Austria and France) discussed how to deal with a revolution in Naples against Austrian rule. Britain objected to taking any action against Naples.

1821: *Laibach*: this confirmed Britain's basic disagreement with the right of intervention, claimed by the other allies as international peacekeepers, to intervene to suppress nationalist revolts. The Congress endorsed Austria's right to intervene in Naples.

1822: *Verona*: here the great powers faced further issues relating to nationalist uprisings: in Northern Italy against Austrian rule; in Greece against Ottoman Turkish rule; in Spain against continued Bourbon rule. Only the last was discussed. Prussia, Russia and Austria agreed to help France to maintain its influence in Spain if called upon. Wellington, representing the United Kingdom, withdrew from the Congress. The UK maintained the principle of non-intervention, clearly separating it from the other great powers.

1825: *St Petersburg*: attended by only Austria, Prussia and Russia. Austria and Prussia disagreed, nothing was decided and no further Congresses were held.

It might seem surprising that Britain, the one power which was neither defeated by France nor forced to sign a submissive peace with Napoleon, claimed relatively modest territorial rewards. Many of Britain's colonial conquests from France, Spain and the Dutch were handed back in 1815–16. However, those which were retained were significant (see Chapter 19). They confirmed British dominance in the West Indies and gave easier access to the developing South American market. Above all, the end of the war confirmed the decline of France, Spain and the Dutch as commercial rivals. The formal acquisition of territory from the Dutch on the southern tip of Africa was confirmed in 1815. It was thereafter called 'Cape Colony' and had been in British hands since 1806. In Europe, Britain retained Malta as its Mediterranean sentinel and also took Heligoland from Denmark with an eye to enhancing already well-developed trading links in northern Europe. In 1815, Britain also established a protectorate over the Ionian Islands, off the west coast of mainland Greece. Overall, however, Britain wished to signal that it had not fought against the French to make large territorial conquests in Europe.

Strategically, British political leaders – and particularly Castlereagh – were already aware of the dangers of what a later generation would call 'imperial over-stretch'. Britain aimed to make its naval supremacy pay a substantial commercial dividend. It had large quantities of high-quality, but cheap, manufactured goods – particularly textiles – to sell worldwide. For this it needed strategic staging posts and good relations with the trading nations. Taking substantial chunks of territory would arouse suspicions of ulterior British motives. Also, crude 'empire building' was expensive and probably counter-productive. What was taken had to be defended, some-times hundreds, even thousands, of miles away from a base. Thus, Castlereagh looked to nurture an 'informal commercial empire'. Looked at from this perspective, the territories gained in 1815 were to be important in sustaining Britain's pre-eminent position during the nineteenth century.

Though Castlereagh won high praise for his diplomacy in 1814–15, Britain did not obtain all that it wanted from the peace settlements. Castlereagh would have liked to see Prussia, a natural ally of Hanover, obtain more territory in Saxony in order to counterbalance Russian ambition in eastern and central Europe and Austria further south. On the other hand, the reorganisation of German lands into a new Confederation of thirty-nine states offered greater prospects of stability in central Europe. Prussia, which gained territory in the Rhineland, was soon establishing itself as the dominant state in this new Confederation. Britain, however, continued to see Prussia as a less threatening proposition than Austria.

Castlereagh wanted to re-create a truly independent Poland after its progressive dismemberment between 1772 and 1795. As it was, although a so-called 'Congress Kingdom of Poland was created', its King was Tsar Alexander I of Russia. Russia's control over Poland was tightened after an abortive uprising in 1830–31, when the Polish army was disbanded. British fears that Russia was becoming the major threat to its interests were in no way allayed (see Chapter 34).

The period of Congress Diplomacy promised much but delivered relatively little. The idea of regular meetings to air differences and defuse crises was pushed hard, and successfully, by Castlereagh in 1814–15. In doing so, he was making a reality of the path to lasting peace identified by his mentor, William Pitt. Pitt wrote a Memorandum in January 1805 in which he identified the key principles of foreign policy. One of these was 'to form, at the restoration of peace, a general agreement and guarantee for the mutual protection and security of different powers'.[2] Like Pitt, Castlereagh believed in bringing the great powers together. His objective was to rebuild Europe on the basis of broadly conservative principles, with Britain taking a much more interventionist role than had been the case in the eighteenth century. This partly reflected ideology. Castlereagh, though a reformer in some respects, was basically a conservative who believed that the blame for the French wars lay with speculative ideology run disastrously out of hand. It also reflected hard-headed pragmatism. Britain was, without doubt, now a leading great power, if not the greatest power. It could not work from the periphery. It became in 1814–15 an unequivocally European presence.[3]

In 1815, Castlereagh brought the great European powers together in what he called 'a just equilibrium' and his influence helped to secure a united Netherlands, including what had been until 1792–93 the Austrian south, and some westward expansion of Prussian territory to provide a secure bulwark against future French incursions into an area important for British trade routes. Both the Congresses of Vienna and Aix-la-Chapelle had successful outcomes from a British perspective. Alexander I's Holy Alliance, comprising Russia, Austria and Prussia, has been characterised as a reactionary league whose purpose was explicitly to crush rebellion, although one historian has recently argued that it reflected 'the application of Christian principles to politics'.[4] Castlereagh dismissed it as a piece of 'sublime mysticism and nonsense'.[5]

Only from 1820 did Castlereagh's system begin to fail and then not on grounds of irreconcilable international rivalry but because of internal challenges to established authority. These were motivated by a mixture of nationalist aspiration and a desire for more representative government. The British government's view was clear: the Congress System had not been put in place to sanction great-power intervention in the internal affairs of states. Castlereagh's famous State Paper of May 1820 called such interference by force 'a question of the greatest possible moral as well as political delicacy'.[6] This was diplomatic language meaning, in plain English, that it should not happen. Accordingly, the United Kingdom refused to sign the so-called Troppau Protocol by which the other great powers agreed not to recognise the legitimacy of any regime coming to power as a result of an internal revolution. Castlereagh did not appear at the re-convened Congress of Laibach in 1821 but briefed his half-brother Lord Charles Stewart that Britain would support great-power intervention only if that power's 'immediate security or essential interests' were threatened.[7] This would permit Austria, in control of much of Italy, to intervene in Naples while not allowing blanket great-power interventions. At the Congress of Verona in 1822, attended by Wellington after Castlereagh's death, the focus had shifted to the right of France to intervene in Spain. Britain invoked its principled stance against such intervention, although the new Foreign Secretary, George Canning, was more concerned about possible French invasion threats from Cadiz and even a re-run of the Peninsular conflict ten years earlier (see Chapter 13). After Verona, Britain permanently detached itself from Congress diplomacy; the whole system rapidly fell apart.

It is pointless to deny that fundamental disagreements, especially those between Britain and the other great powers, led to the break-up of the Congress System within a decade. The system was, however, rather more successful than it might seem. Major wars in continental Europe had been frequent in both the seventeenth and the eighteenth centuries; the first half of the twentieth would witness the unprecedented carnage of two world wars. The nineteenth century was different. There were nationalist uprisings, internal rebellions and colonial challenges aplenty. However, wars between the major European powers were rare. Even the most significant were brief and usually decisive. The United Kingdom was directly involved in only one: the Crimean War of 1854–56. Despite its failings, the Congress System did, as intended, provide a structure for debate. In doing so, it also afforded the great powers an opportunity to reflect on the risks of renewed conflict.

II. Canning and diplomacy in the Peninsula

Canning was no fan of his Congress diplomacy. He judged 'that system of periodical meetings of the . . . great powers, with a view to the general concerns of Europe, new, and of very questionable policy'.[8] He was no fan of Castlereagh either. The two men had been personal enemies who had fought a duel in 1809. They were also temperamental opposites and political rivals. It might be thought that Canning would oppose any Castlereagh initiative on principle. We should not conclude, however, that the foreign policies of the two men were fundamentally different. In the words of E. L. Woodward, 'he agreed more with Castlereagh's decisions than with his methods'.[9] It was under Castlereagh, not Canning, that Britain's involvement in Congress diplomacy had died a death. Canning was determined only that it should not be resurrected. In his own words, from now on: 'Every nation for itself and God for us all.'

George Canning, 1770–1827

Born in London of Irish-born parents, his father was a lawyer in modest circumstances and his mother became an actress after his father's early death. His education was paid for by an uncle whose fortune came from merchant banking. He was educated at Eton and Oxford University, excelling academically in both places. He came to the attention of Pitt, who provided him with initial political support and found him a seat in the House of Commons in 1793. Canning was an excellent speaker and a witty writer. He used both talents to attack opponents of the government in the 1790s. He wrote to great effect for the loyalist journal *Anti-Jacobin* in 1797–98. His career stalled after Pitt resigned in 1801, not least because he used his waspish talents to sting Addington. A combination of snobbish disdain at his relatively humble origins and dislike of his talent for personal abuse and invective earned Canning many enemies, not least Viscount Castlereagh and the Prince Regent. This helps explain why he was only in the Cabinet for two years (1807–9) before he became President of the Board of Control, with responsibility for India, in 1816, a position he held until 1821. He became MP for Liverpool in 1812 and his links with the commercial classes there were close and influential. He was associated as Foreign Secretary with 'liberal' policies, including support for peoples in South America struggling to free themselves from Spanish rule. He became Prime Minister in April 1827 but died only four months later.

Political disturbance in Spain soon gave Canning a perfect opportunity to match deeds to the words of which he had already proved himself such a master. King Ferdinand VII had never accepted the constraints imposed on him by the liberal constitution of 1812. A pro-liberal coup in 1820 increased Spain's political instability and led to the King's deposition in 1822. Canning was able to prevent great-power intervention at the Congress of Verona but not the successful unilateral invasion by France which brought about Ferdinand's restoration. When France invaded in 1823, Canning openly expressed the view that the liberals in Spain 'would come triumphantly out of this struggle'.[10] The speech excited much adverse comment, because of its undiplomatic language, because the Cabinet did not know what Canning was going to say on a controversial subject, and because it raised the suspicion that the Foreign Secretary intended to intervene against France anyway.

Canning had no such intentions. His position over Portugal three years later was very different. Portugal had experienced similar political instability. King John VI had reluctantly accepted a liberal constitution in 1821, which was overthrown two years later by an army coup led by the King's younger son. Canning feared further instability and especially intervention by Spain with behind-the-scenes support from France. He sent a naval squadron to the mouth of the River Tagus to keep a watching brief. The death of King John in 1826 led to a more direct threat to British interests when his heir, Pedro, immediately abdicated in favour of his daughter. Conservatives in Portugal wished to secure the return of authoritarian rule under Pedro's brother, Miguel. Canning immediately despatched 4,000 troops to dissuade Spain from invading in support of Miguel. Canning's defence of British intervention was that Portugal was an ally in need of support. As he put it: 'We go to Portugal, not to rule, not to dictate, not to prescribe constitutions, but to defend and preserve the independence of an ally.'[11] This was far from the whole truth. The constitutional position was so confused and the political situation so unstable that it was far from clear whose 'independence' was being safeguarded. The plain fact was that Canning was using the force of a great power to block the intentions of France and Spain. Both states were now back in the hands of authoritarian rulers, seeking to challenge Britain's influence in southern Europe and, in particular, its commercial dominance. Some of Canning's critics also believed that he was committing Britain to intervention, not to defend its own interests but to shore up a liberal regime. British protection was time-limited. When he became Prime Minister, Wellington ordered the removal of troops, whereupon Miguel was free to exercise the powers of a despotic ruler.

III. Canning and 'informal empire' in the Americas

Canning's foreign policy is perhaps best remembered for activity in the Americas. The situation was dramatically altered by most of Latin America's repudiation of rule from Spain. Buenos Aires, Colombia, Chile and Mexico claimed recognition as independent nation states. As Canning argued to Wellington in November 1822: 'the American questions are out of all proportion more important to us than the European . . . if we do not seize and turn them to our advantage in time, we shall rue the loss of an opportunity never, never to be recovered.' He could see obvious, and probably immediate, advantage from recognising the independence of the new states of South America. The policy seemed to bear fruit. As a French agent working from Colombia reported in 1823: 'The power of England is without a rival in America, no fleets but hers to be seen; her merchandises are bought almost exclusively.'[12]

Canning's policy in America was controversial on both sides of the Atlantic. It threatened to fall foul of the new '**Monroe Doctrine**', articulated in the United States in December 1823. At home, it deepened the rift between 'liberal' and 'high' Tories. Wellington disliked nationalism anyway and thought that Canning's policy would further weaken European alliances. For George IV, who hated the idea of ill-bred nationalists taking territory away from European monarchs, it provided further evidence that his Foreign Secretary was not only personally unpalatable but politically unsound. Even Earl Grey, the Whig leader, had reservations, expressed in typically snobbish fashion. In South America, 'we but too plainly show that we have no views but to our trading interests. In short the whole policy of our Ministers is that of stock-jobbers and commercial speculators.'[13] But then, Grey's view was that Canning, as the son of a mere actress, had no business interfering in high politics at all.

Monroe Doctrine, 1823

The policy, articulated by President James Monroe in his 'State of the Union' message to the United States Congress, that further colonisation by European powers of any part of the Americas was unwelcome and would not be tolerated. The Doctrine attempted to establish separate spheres of influence for America and Europe.

Canning pressed on. In the House of Commons, he called himself an 'enthusiast for national independence' and made sure that his enthusiasms received maximum publicity outside Westminster. His almost confessional relationship with the British public in general, and his constituents in the commercial city of Liverpool in particular, was in stark contrast to his refusal to follow normal diplomatic channels for informing other powers of his intentions in the Americas. The independence of Buenos Aires was recognised in 1824, that of Colombia and Mexico in 1825. During Canning's propaganda blast in support of 'nations struggling to be free', he waxed overly lyrical about the likely immediate benefit to be expected from these new commercial opportunities. The value of British exports to Latin America had doubled in the decade 1815–25. Ironically, once independence had been recognised, this market all but stagnated over the next ten years. The English banking crisis in

1825–26 (see Chapter 17) did not help, but it had been precipitated in part by the wild overselling of South America as a market with illimitable opportunities. The new states lacked the population, the communications infrastructure and particularly the consumer-orientated society to support an export market on the scale of Britain's. The initial reaction of Liverpool, Bristol, Manchester and Birmingham to the opening up of South America was one of considerable disappointment. By contrast, trade with the much richer and much more populous United States boomed. Britain's 'informal' policy in the Americas did not fall foul of the Monroe Doctrine and relations with the USA at last began to thaw. By the 1840s, the United States was taking roughly 60 per cent of all Britain's exports.

IV. Canning, Wellington, and the impact of the Greek Revolt

Canning's foreign policy frequently clashed with the judgments and prejudices of the Duke of Wellington. Whereas Wellington was more concerned with developments in the East, Canning's preoccupation was with the West, where, he believed, the most immediate threat to Britain's commercial and imperial interests lay. Wellington had no special sympathy for 'nations struggling to be free', not least because he believed their struggles to be informed by malign 'French principles' and dangerously democratic ideas. He was much keener to preserve links between the great powers, although he worried about the implications of Greece's struggle for independence from the Ottoman Empire. The Greek revolt of 1821 had begun in modern-day Romania. After initial successes, it spread to southern Greece. The Greek cause attracted many sympathisers in Britain, where a classically educated elite empathised with Greek culture and civilisation while having no love for, and little understanding of, Islamic culture. There was outrage when the Turks attacked and massacred Greek communities. Canning insisted that Britain must remain neutral in the struggle but did recognise the Greeks as legitimate 'combatants' rather than mere rebels. He refused to discuss the matter as part of Congress Diplomacy, but he was concerned about the general volatility of south-east Europe, particularly how Russia might exploit the opportunities which this climate of uncertainty could provide. Wellington was sent to St Petersburg in 1826 to negotiate a protocol whereby Britain and Russia jointly agreed to act as honest brokers with the Turks, on the basis that the Greeks would receive a measure of self-rule.

Just as the Turks were on the point of breaking Greek resistance, an Anglo-Russian agreement was formalised under the Treaty of London in July 1827. Britain, Russia and France agreed to confirm Greece's autonomy over internal affairs, while Turkey retained limited overall control (or 'suzerainty'). The treaty lapsed after Canning's death, however, and a combined British, Russian and French fleet under Sir Edward Codrington was despatched to the Ionian Sea to protect the Greeks while their struggle continued. It defeated the Turks at the Battle of Navarino in October

1827. The Greek independence campaign continued but the Anglo-Russian accord was soon shattered. When the Sultan proclaimed a jihad (holy war) against the European powers in 1828, Russia declared war on Turkey. Its rapid success alarmed Wellington, who feared the consequences of a substantially enhanced Russian presence in south-east Europe. His fears were justified. When the Russians signed a favourable peace with the Turks by the Treaty of Adrianople in September 1829, Wellington, now the British Prime Minister, wrote to his Foreign Secretary, the Earl of Aberdeen: 'It will be absurd to think of bolstering up the Turkish Power in Europe. It is gone . . . and the Tranquillity of the World . . . along with it'.[14] Wellington was prone to see things in black and white. A more nuanced perspective on recent events was possible. However, when the London Protocols of February 1830 finally confirmed the independence of Greece, it was at the cost of enhanced Russian influence in the Balkans. British desire to curb Russian expansionism would dominate British foreign policy for half a century (see Chapters 34 and 35).

Matters imperial, *c*1780–*c*1850

I. Empire, markets and commerce

The nineteenth century has rightly been called 'Britain's Imperial Century'.[1] Territorial expansion during the eighteenth century had been predominantly transatlantic. The loss of the thirteen American colonies in 1783 caused a rethink. Although their diplomatic relations remained tense – or worse – the commercial self-interest of both the United Kingdom and the United States ensured that no long-term damage was done to trading links (see Chapter 9). However, it is possible to argue that the loss of America produced what one historian has called 'a fundamental reordering of the Empire' with a first, predominantly transatlantic, empire 'giving way to a second one' in which the East played a much more significant part.[2] One historian argued that this shift to the east represented nothing less than the founding of 'a Second British Empire'.[3]

Few now accept this and, as with so many historical explanations, it is important to separate effect from intention. We shall search in vain for any government-level debate in the late eighteenth or early nineteenth centuries about the value, or otherwise, of a 'swing to the east' as such. However, the search for new markets was never-ending and, if the long conflict with France had proved nothing else, it had demonstrated that Britain's commercial, diplomatic and political interests were worldwide. As developments were to show, also, the relative economic and commercial value of colonies in the west declined substantially in comparison with those in the east during the nineteenth century. Against this, trade with the United States, over which Britain had no control – formal or informal – after 1783 remained immensely important.

The value of the Empire as an economic resource was clearly signposted from the 1820s onwards, when William Huskisson, as President of the Board of Trade, anticipated a 'great change in our colonial system', broadly in the direction of trade liberalisation.[4] This view was supported by those in the colonisation front line. **Sir Stamford Raffles** emphasised that Britain's interest in the East Indies 'ought to be purely commercial' and that it was 'of the first importance that the nature of this commerce should be . . . directed . . . to the preservation of a free and unrestricted commerce, and to the encouragement and protection of individual enterprise and the interests of the general merchant'.[5] By 1828, Britain's colonies could conduct trade using their own shipping, as could foreign powers trading directly with those colonies.[6]

Stamford Raffles, 1781–1826

Born not only the son of a sea captain but actually at sea off Jamaica, he worked for the East India Company from the age of 14. His abilities won him rapid promotion and he became Lieutenant-General of Java from 1811 to 1815. He explored the East Indies and recommended in 1819 that Singapore be purchased. He organised its administration in 1822–23 before sailing back to England in 1824. He was a leading scholar of botany and anthropology and he supported much Christian missionary work and the freeing of slaves owned by the East India Company.

The belief that colonial markets should be 'closed' to outsiders was abandoned during the 1840s. Peel reduced the level of protection given to colonial trade in his budgets of 1842 and 1845 and the Corn Laws were abandoned in highly controversial circumstances in 1846 (see Chapter 22). Of greater significance to the colonies and to other trading partners, however, was the final repeal of the Navigation Acts enacted by Russell's Whig–Liberal government in 1849. This produced a significant increase in the amount of foreign shipping entering Britain's ports. As in so many instances, however, British free-trade policies worked in harmony with Britain's commercial dominance. The mercantile marine was able to meet the challenges it now faced and most colonial links also remained profitable.

No clear-cut, still less centralised, model of colonial governance or administration was developed. From 1801 to 1854, a Secretary for War and the Colonies had overall responsibility and the post invariably carried Cabinet rank. Once international peace was restored, however, it was rarely a high-profile posting and attracted few high-profile political leaders. The amiably ineffective Earl Bathurst occupied it for the full fifteen years of Lord Liverpool's government, from 1812 to 1827, but was invariably overshadowed either by Castlereagh, by Canning – or simply by events. Operational activity was divided, sometimes awkwardly, between Westminster and a particular colony. India's administration under the East India Company was famously distinctive (see below) but the relationship between Britain and its colonies was diverse and often relaxed. It could involve, in whatever combination, colonial governors, ambassadors, consuls and, not infrequently, the Foreign Office and the Admiralty. Only rarely did the metropolitan leash tug tightly. In the so-called 'white colonies' – Canada, Australia, New Zealand and South Africa – long, and often little-used, lines of communication proved effective, if unintentional, preparation for internal self-government in the later nineteenth and early twentieth centuries.

II. Canada and the Antipodes

After 1783, Canada proved an attractive haven to American colonists loyal to the Crown. Britain was keen to formalise constitutional arrangements which secured stability and thus the opportunity to develop trade, especially in fish and furs. The potential difficulty was the strong French-Catholic presence in Quebec. Canada was divided into two provinces in 1791: 'Upper Canada', overwhelmingly British, was based around the Great Lakes; 'Lower Canada' was situated around the St Lawrence river with its French-speaking majority based in Quebec. Both provinces had representative government through an elected legislative assembly.

This constitutional settlement worked well enough for a time, although substantial immigration to Montreal increased the proportion of British colonists in Lower Canada. Migrants were also claiming land which French-Canadians considered as their own. Rebellions in 1837, largely on the issue of revenue-raising powers and the provinces' ability to provide adequate services, alarmed Britain, which continued to fear United States ambitions on their northern border. The rebellions were put down easily enough but they caused the Whig government to ponder the formulation of a constitution more acceptable to the colonists. Under the prompting of the grandly titled new 'Governor in Chief of North America', **Earl Durham**, whose Report on the position appeared early in 1839, the Canada Act created a unified Province out of Upper and Lower Canada. It had a single parliament and limited powers of self-government. These were extended in 1847 when Lord Grey, Secretary to the Colonies and a strong supporter of colonial self-government, in effect confirmed that the result of elections in Canada should determine the political complexion of a ministry which would be responsible to the local assembly. This became the prelude to the granting of so-called 'Dominion' status for Canada under the Dominion Act of 1867 and thereafter a working model for internal self-government in other 'white colonies'. Most of the Australian colonies obtained internal self-government in the 1850s. A federal system was established later, when the Commonwealth of Australia Constitution Act was passed in 1900.

John Lambton, first Earl of Durham, 1792–1840

He was born in London, the son of a substantial landowner in County Durham. His father was a supporter of Charles James Fox, and the son inherited his father's radical Whig sympathies. He became an MP in 1813 and came into contact with the second Earl Grey, the Whig leader, whose daughter he married. His radical reputation was cemented by the proposal of parliamentary reform bills in 1819 and 1829. He became Lord Privy Seal in Grey's government formed in November 1830. He played a major role in drafting what became the Great Reform Act. Once the Act had been passed, he resigned and accepted an earldom from his father-in-law. He is best known for his report recommending the creation of a unified province of Canada, with substantial internal powers of its own. The Canada Act of 1840 followed most of his recommendations, though historians have cast doubt on how securely grounded in knowledge of the province these were. Durham was a difficult man, quick to anger, arrogant and frequently at odds with his Whig colleagues.

The first British settlers in Australia arrived at Sydney Cove in January 1788. They were mostly convicts, transported to a remote land for hard labour over several years. The incentive of land grants existed on the expiry of their sentence but significant numbers of hardened criminals never qualified. By 1800, about 5,000 inhabitants were eking a basic living from rough agriculture while Sydney, one of the great natural harbours of the world, developed as a centre for the whaling trade and supplies to Europe and America.[7] Under the leadership of Lachlan Macquarie, a Scottish ex-army officer, Governor of New South Wales from 1810, Sydney became a civilised city with impressive public buildings built in European style. Macquarie insisted that 'emancipists', ex-convicts whose sentences had run their course, should have equality of treatment with free settlers. Some were even appointed to government posts.

Success in New South Wales encouraged further colonisation. Van Diemen's Land (Tasmania) had been settled as a convict colony from 1803. Other settlements developed around the Brisbane River (Queensland) from 1824, the Swan River (Western Australia) from 1829, Melbourne (Victoria) from 1835 and Adelaide (South Australia) in 1836. Convicts were not allowed to settle in South Australia but, although transportation survived until 1867, free migrants substantially outnumbered convict settlers as early as the 1820s.

British settlers first arrived in New Zealand in 1840 under a scheme devised by **Edward Gibbon Wakefield**. In the same year, the Treaty of Waitangi declared British sovereignty but with undisputed Maori rights to lands and fisheries on North Island. A New Zealand constitution was adopted in 1852 and the colony became self-governing four years later. It was, of course, a constitution for white settlers. Maoris were frequently deprived of their land and other property rights. A series of tribal rebellions in the 1840s were followed by war against the North Island settlers. It ended with Maori defeat in 1872.

Edward Gibbon Wakefield, 1796–1862

Born into a Quaker family in London, the son of the philanthropist and economist Edward Wakefield, his early career was troubled. He was imprisoned for three years in 1827 for abducting an heiress. In prison, he developed his ideas about the value of encouraging emigration both to support under-populated colonies and to reduce over-population in Britain. His favoured method was to sell colonial land and to raise a land tax to fund the transportation of labourers at no charge to themselves. He formed the National Colonisation Society on his release from prison in 1830. The passing of the South Australia Act in 1834 enabled the first settlers to leave England in 1836. Wakefield's work also encouraged emigration to New Zealand and Canada, both of which he visited. In the 1850s he served on the New Zealand general assembly. The settlements founded under Wakefield's plans were small but his overall influence was considerable, especially in his belief that well-run colonies should become self-governing.

III. India

For Britain, 'India remained of paramount importance in any assessment of imperial assets'.[8] Many saw its commercial development as a necessary counterbalance to the loss of the American colonies. Pitt told the House of Commons in 1784 that India's significance had 'increased in proportion to the losses sustained by the dismemberment of other great possessions'.[9] British interest in India was more than two centuries old by the early nineteenth century. For almost all of that time its public face had been that sprawling financial, administrative and political entity known as the East India Company. The Company's primary purpose was trade but it had increasingly taken on governing responsibilities. Its relationship with Indian princes in the Mughal Empire was complex. Many individual arrangements were made and mostly kept. These gave the princes local autonomy. Increasingly, however, the key economic decisions were taken by the Company.

Conflict with the French from the middle of the eighteenth century increased the level of British political control in India. However, instability in the Mughal Empire also contributed since the Emperor could no longer impose his authority. Indian princes increasingly acted as if they were independent. Internal rivalries and growing instability resulted. To this, the East India Company, now acting as a regional power in its own right, contributed not a little since its remit was being extended from mere trading company into effective military aggressor. Its administration was also often heavy-handed and not infrequently corrupt. East India Company power was used from the 1750s to see off the challenge of France during the Seven Years War. Success brought direct control over ever more Indian territory. All of Bengal, Bihar and Orissa, in the north-east of the subcontinent, was in Company hands by the mid-1760s. Over the period to 1830 or thereabouts, the Company was turning into 'a militarised, state-subsidised and controlled organ of the British government'.[10]

British power was further consolidated in the 1790s and early 1800s, when, during the next French wars, policy emphases shifted from accommodation to control. During **Richard Wellesley**'s Governor-Generalship, many territories were annexed while other Indian states paid subsidies to ensure protection from the East India Company's troops. A series of conflicts culminating in a decisive battle at Seringapatam in 1799 left Mysore, in southern India, in the Company's control. In the first years of the nineteenth century, on the pretext that they had made an arrangement with the French, the Company's troops attacked the Marathas, the most powerful federation of Hindu peoples, based in the west around Poona. The so-called 'Second Marathas War', lasting from 1803 to 1805, resulted in complete victory for the Company, and the occupation of Delhi.[11] It did, however, triple Company debt, to which Wellesley's personal extravagance further contributed. Government House in Calcutta was extended in opulently expansive style. Wellesley was anxious to convey the symbolic message that, as the King's representative, Indians should see how a King lived. Not surprisingly, the Company's credit on the Indian money markets was exhausted by 1805. Army pay arrears mounted dangerously and general mutiny threatened for a time.[12] One brief, but for the British unnerving, mutiny did occur, at the fortress of Vellore in 1806. Indian **sepoys** revolted against the recent requirement that beards should be shaven and Hindu religious marks removed from foreheads. The mutiny lasted only a day or two but two hundred British troops were killed before it was put down.[13] It was a harbinger of much more serious disturbance half a century later (see Chapter 36).

Richard, Marquess Wellesley, 1760–1842

Born in County Meath into a prosperous Irish Protestant landed family, he was educated at Harrow and Eton. He succeeded to the title of Earl of Mornington on his father's death in 1781. He aligned himself with Pitt in the 1780s, supporting moves towards trade liberalisation and the abolition of the slave trade. He gained knowledge of Indian affairs as a member of the Board of Control from 1793 and was appointed Governor-General of Bengal in 1797. With the help of his brother, Arthur (later Duke of Wellington), he defeated the Marathas. His victory did not gain him popularity with the directors of the East India Company, who considered him aloof, arrogant and a spendthrift. They were also suspicious of his free-trade policies, which threatened their often heavily protected markets. He was Foreign Secretary (1810–12) in Perceval's government but was out of office thereafter until 1820, when he became Lord Lieutenant of Ireland. As a long-standing supporter of Catholic Emancipation, he attempted to introduce measures, including the reduction of tithe burdens, which showed his sympathy for Ireland's majority population. However, he supported the continued dominance of the Protestant Ascendancy (see Chapter 14). He resigned the Lord Lieutenancy in 1828 when his fiercely pro-Protestant brother became Prime Minister, although he returned to the post under Earl Grey from 1832 to 1834.

Sepoys

Indian soldiers serving in military forces commanded by Europeans. By the early nineteenth century, they were enlisted almost entirely into the East India Company's army.

The Marathas war irrevocably changed Britain's position in India. It was now the unchallengeably dominant power on the subcontinent, in practice even controlling the Mughal emperor himself. Power was backed by huge numbers. By 1815, the East India Company's armies totalled a quarter of a million men, only 30,000 or so of whom were Europeans. With the possible, but unquantifiable, exception of China's, this was much the largest military force operating in Asia and it had grown extremely fast. In 1790, the army had numbered only 90,000 men.[14] After 1815, its influence was felt, not just within the subcontinent, but across Asia, not least in Burma, Singapore and Afghanistan. Along with the British navy, the army of the East India Company played the critical role in the expansion of the Empire in the east.

Well before 1815, however, the real power in India lay not with the East India Company but with the British government. A combination of financial scandals and reduced profits from the 1760s compelled action. Lord North's Regulating Act of 1773 established ultimate government authority over the Company and created the new post of Governor-General. Judges in the new Supreme Court sitting in Calcutta were appointed from London and not by the Company. Pitt's India Act of 1784 strengthened the powers of the Governor-General and established a 'Board of Control', the President of which was always a government, and usually a Cabinet, minister. The East India Company Charter was also renewed with some reluctance in 1813, since indebtedness and the frequent examples of exploitation and corruption had severely damaged the Company's reputation. Its monopoly of the Indian trade was brought to an end. Only continued monopoly of the tea trade from China enabled it to pay shareholders their dividends.[15] As the work of the two dominant Governors-General of the period, the reform-minded **Lord Cornwallis** (1786–93) and the spectacularly unpopular, inflexible and arrogant Marquess Wellesley (1798–1805), demonstrates, the British government was increasingly exercising direct control.

Charles, second Marquess Cornwallis, 1738–1805

Born in London into an aristocratic family, he was educated at Eton and decided as a youth on a military career. He was also an MP, taking his seat for a borough owned by his family in 1760. He inherited the family's earldom in 1762 and thereafter sat in the Lords. He fought against the American colonists in the war for independence and proved himself an efficient tactician, though less effective as an overall strategist. His surrender at Yorktown in 1781 effectively ended the war. He became India's first Governor-General in 1786. He spent much time in India trying to root out systemic corruption in the East India Company but was also active in military matters, defeating the forces of Tipu Sultan in southern India (1790–92). After returning to England, he joined Pitt's coalition Cabinet as Master General of the Ordnance, bringing his considerable practical military skills to this post. He was Lord Lieutenant of Ireland from 1797 to 1801. During the rebellion of the United Irishmen, he also acted as commander-in-chief. After the rebellion was put down, he played a key role in the negotiations to unite Ireland with Great Britain in a 'United Kingdom'. Like Pitt, he had wanted Catholic Emancipation to be part of the Union process. Like Pitt, he resigned from the government when this did not happen. He was the leading negotiator for peace with France which resulted in the Treaty of Amiens (1802). He returned to India as Governor-General in 1805 to negotiate peace with the Marathas but died two months after his arrival.

This process continued after 1815. The Maharatas Confederation was finally defeated in 1818 and the Company assumed control of significant chunks of territory in central India. Sir Charles Napier, fresh from his duties in facing down Britain's Chartists (see Chapter 21), captured Sind in the far west in 1843, a conquest which was widely criticised in Britain and by East India Company directors both on grounds of dubious morality and the future cost of administering the territory.[16] Napier, who had gone to India, as he put it, 'to catch the rupees', made about £70,000 from his military exploits there.[17] He governed Sind personally until 1847. Further territorial acquisitions followed. Punjab, abutting Afghanistan and Kashmir in the far north-west of the subcontinent, was taken over in 1849 after a long struggle with Sikh rulers whose objective had been to drive the British out of India. When Nagpur (1853–54), in central India, and Oudh (1856) on its northern border with Tibet fell, British control appeared to be complete.

What impact had British rule had on India by 1850? Much emphasis has been placed on the incorporation of British law, governmental systems and even the trappings of royalty. A new school – Haileybury – was established by the East India Company at Hertford in 1805 to train those who would run India's civil service. The period of Lord William Bentinck's Governor-Generalship (1828–35) is associated with land reforms, with the abolition of suttee (the practice of Hindu women placing themselves – or being forcibly shoved – onto their dead husband's funeral pyre), with the forbidding of infanticide (many Indian female babies were killed at birth) and with attempts, albeit half-hearted, to privilege the use of English and to Westernize Indian education. When, on his death in 1835, a statue to Bentinck was erected in Calcutta, the historian Thomas Babington Macaulay, who was in India from 1834 to 1838 helping to establish the new Supreme Council, wrote that the late Governor-General had 'infused into Oriental despotism the spirit of British freedom' and 'never forgot that the end of government is the happiness of the governed'.[18]

This characteristically optimistic assertion of the virtues of rationality and enlightenment exported to distant, and of course less developed, lands by an able, sophisticated and beneficent British aristocrat naturally invites challenge. By 1850, India was controlled by the British but Indian society had not been much modernised, still less Westernised. Its social structure remained overwhelmingly rural. The agricultural economy remained peasant-based. India's rigid caste system experienced little change and it was protected by British laws. Above all, with the partial exception of Bengal, India was in practice under military rule in the first half of the nineteenth century. As the Scottish solider turned Indian administrator, Sir John Malcolm, put it in the 1820s 'Our government . . . is essentially military and our means of preserving and improving our possessions through the operation of our civil institutions depend upon our wise and politic exercise of that military power on which the whole foundation rests.'[19] More British rulers in this period interpreted 'wise and politic' to mean working, as far as possible, with the grain of traditional peasant communities and showing respect for indigenous religion than saw military dominance as an opportunity to force-feed modern Western ways.

IV. Emigration

Britain's rapidly expanding empire needed immigrants and it got them – in huge numbers. Over the period 1815–1914 as a whole, 22.6m UK citizens emigrated.[20] They did not all go to the colonies. At least three-quarters of emigrants from the British Isles went to the USA rather than to the Empire.[21] Most did not leave because the British government ordered them to, although the forcible transportation of felons was a critical factor in the early development of Australia. Almost 160,000 convicts were transported to New South Wales and Van Diemen's Land (Tasmania) between 1788 and 1853.[22] Admiral Arthur Phillip, the first Governor of New South Wales, sounded a warning note to Whitehall as early as 1790: 'Men able to support themselves, if intelligent and industrious, I think cannot fail; but if people come out . . . who are indolent and, having nothing to lose, want [lack] that spur to industry, they may become a burthen to the settlement because they cannot be left to starve.'[23]

In any case, governments were chary of prescribing emigration as an eligible policy, although the implacable evidence of unprecedentedly rapid population growth, especially in the 1810s and 1820s, made a persuasive case on its own. Most emigrants made their own decisions to leave the British Isles. By 1850, they were persuaded more or less equally by 'pull' factors, mostly the persuasive advocacy of already emigrant relatives and friends, and 'push' factors associated with declining job opportunities, inadequate wages and the environmental deterioration and health hazards all too evident in Britain's industrial cities. Pull factors were particularly persuasive in the United States, which appeared in 1850 to be a nation of boundless opportunity and almost limitless land.

V. An imperial ethic?

Finally, did any coherent idea of Empire emerge in Britain in the first half of the nineteenth century? Expansion afforded opportunities aplenty for aristocratic families to export their perception of benevolent rule, be it the Irish Moiras and the English Cavendish-Bentincks in India or the Somersets in South Africa. It also provided career opportunities for gentry family members. The East India Company, whatever its frequently dire financial situation, provided an established career structure and diverse opportunities – many of them legal – for wealth creation.[24] It may also be that, since most attractive judicial and administrative jobs in Britain went disproportionately to English families, 'making good' in the empire seemed a particularly attractive option for Scots, Irish and Welsh. Highland Scots, in particular, looked to the Empire to rebuild family fortunes. It is, however, difficult to discern a clear and common understanding of what the British Empire should be. Leading politicians like Canning paid so much attention to the superiority of an 'informal' empire based on mutual commercial interest that it was easy to forget how powerfully the preservation of that interest required ever greater 'formality' in the links between Britain and its colonies. Paradoxically, fighting European wars accelerated this process, nowhere more extensively than in India. Overall, Britain had forty-three colonies in 1816 compared with only twenty-six in 1792, although the land masses thus acquired were not in general extensive.

One recent explanation of the motives for imperial acquisition argues that 'the engine of British expansion . . . was the chaotic pluralism of private and sub-imperial interests: religious, commercial, strategic, humanitarian, speculative and migrational'.[25] Clearly, no one cause predominated, and the difficulty involved in judging the relative importance of numerous interlocking factors may be explained by the plasticity of the Empire itself. The Empire incorporated: large areas dominated by white settlement, particularly Canada, Australia and New Zealand; a controlled Indian subcontinent; and a mass of diverse smaller conquests and expropriations, often acquired in wartime. Thus, 'the Empire often merged imperceptibly into a wide range of global interests which transcended any narrow territorial view of the world and the sources of power or wealth'.[26] In recent years, a different perspective on the growth of empire has been advanced. It emphasises weakness rather than strength, seeing Britain's imperial journey as a defensive one: unplanned, halting, contingent on other structures and forces over which the British had little control.[27] A 'bottom-up' analysis of the development of Empire stresses the relative limitations of Britain's resources. Britain was a collection of small islands ruling unprecedentedly large territories. To do so, the British needed at least some support from within those territories. This required racial and cultural accommodations.

Colonial acquisition involved defeats as well as victories. The story of those who were either captured or deserted and thereafter lived in other cultures indicates how inadequate is any account of British colonialism which plays up the remorseless onward march of a Protestant Anglo-Saxon empire bent upon 'civilising' the globe. Forty per cent of all British troops in the 1830s were Irish, and therefore predominantly Catholic. In India, the proportion was in excess of 50 per cent. Any 'Protestant' account risks underplaying both necessary cultural accommodations and also Britain's frequent weakness. In India, sepoys were often treated better and paid more regularly than white troops. Partly, this was merited. Sepoys proved good, sober, reliable and disciplined soldiers; British troops were not invariably models either of sobriety or self-restraint. Mostly, however, it was because without a loyal indigenous force, British control in India would have collapsed.

Despite the image of Empire presented to British citizens at the end of the nineteenth century (see Chapter 36), the imperial journey did not result from any sense of a 'manifest destiny'. Territories were acquired for commercial and strategic purposes and for defence. Only later were questions such as 'What is the British Empire for?' asked. Once asked, rationalisations were readily available. It could be seen as a repository of Britain's 'surplus' population and as a route, if things went well, for that surplus to make the journey from dependency to sturdy independence, security and even riches. The Empire provided reliable sources of raw materials and foodstuffs and it took ever larger proportions of British manufactures as exports. Furthermore, properly administered, the colonies did what the North Americans had refused to do in the 1760s and 1770s: pay taxes in support of imperial defence. By the 1840s, however, politicians were coming to see colonies as an extension of the British nation and spent large sums on their defence. To lose colonies was to lose not only prestige but international influence. Since no other state acquired remotely as much overseas territory as Britain, its Empire emerged as the distinctive symbol not only of its worldwide influence but also of Britain's status as the world's leading power. Little of this was planned. Once perceived, however, Empire was stoutly – sometimes brutally – defended and increasingly celebrated.

20

···················

The crisis of Toryism and the road to Reform, 1827–1832

I. Tory travails, 1827–1828

By the beginning of 1827, Lord Liverpool had held a broad coalition of Tories together in government for almost fifteen years. As we have seen (Chapters 16 and 17), his administration endured several bumpy periods, some caused by outside events and some by personal rivalries within the government. Liverpool survived them all and, by keeping a lid on the particularly fractious question of Catholic Emancipation, secured what must have seemed to his Whig opponents almost a permanent lease on power. Politics, however, are never as stable as they seem and they remain subject to the contingency of unexpected 'events'. Also, Liverpool's health was not robust. For much of the 1820s he suffered from what would now be called 'stress-related disorders'. At home in central London on 17 February, he suffered a severe cerebral haemorrhage. It was quickly clear that full recovery was not possible. Though few could have predicted it, his resignation precipitated a series of events which undermined the Tory hegemony and utterly changed the political landscape.

How much of this was due to the absence of Liverpool's own political skills? He had considerable strengths, not least in economic policy. He was an effective co-ordinator of government business and Cabinet colleagues usually respected his sensitive, informed leadership, if never his dynamism.[1] More than anything, he was the most senior Pittite still standing and Pitt's reputation still counted for much. Disraeli's famous assessment, in his novel *Coningsby*, that Liverpool was 'the Arch Mediocrity who presided over [a] Cabinet of mediocrities', is preposterously, if characteristically, wide of the mark. However, Liverpool, though he had tried to bury it, had not resolved the Catholic question and it was religion which would tear the Tories apart.

As ever in politics, personalities count for much, and George IV's invitation to Canning – with whom he had latterly, if oddly, become reconciled (see Chapter 17) – revealed how fragile Tory unity had become. Half of Liverpool's Cabinet refused to join a Canning government. Wellington was the most famous absentee, Eldon and Westmorland perhaps the most hostile to it. All the 'refuseniks', with the solitary exception of Peel, were 'high Tories' who rejected not only Catholic Emancipation but almost everything which smacked of 'reform'. To fill the gaps, Canning recruited Whigs, most notably **George Tierney** and the **Marquis of Lansdowne**. His unexpected death brought Canning's government to a premature end after only four months. It passed no significant legislation but it was portentous just the same. It demonstrated how, even after an apparently stable administration which had lasted for fifteen years, political allegiances remained fluid. However annoyed Grey and Russell were to have their colleagues thus plundered for a new Tory-led ministry, party allegiances were far from solid. Canning's government was also the harbinger of a new Liberal–Tory/Whig political alignment which was to carry the Great Reform Act.

George Tierney, 1761–1830

Born in Gibraltar, son of an overseas trader from Ireland, he first became an MP in 1789. He joined the Whig Club in 1791 but fell out with Fox which impeded his political progress. After Fox's death, however, he was always at, or near, the centre of Whig affairs. He served as President of the Board of Control in the 'Talents' ministry of 1806–7 and became leader of the Whigs in the Commons in 1818, though his relations with Earl Grey were often poor. The two were never reconciled after Tierney accepted a Cabinet post first in the Canning and then in the Goderich governments (1827–28). After the Goderich government fell, he did not hold office again.

Henry Petty-Fitzmaurice, third Marquess of Lansdowne, 1780–1863

Born into an aristocratic family and the son of the Earl of Shelburne (Prime Minister, 1782–83), his career operated near the heart of Whig politics for half a century. He became an MP in 1802 and was a fervent supporter of Charles James Fox. He was Chancellor of the Exchequer during the 'Talents' administration. He became Marquess of Lansdowne in 1809, with a seat in the Lords, on the death of his half-brother. During the 1810s and 1820s, he was a leading Whig opponent of Liverpool's government, although he served Canning and Goderich as Home Secretary (1827–28). In 1830, he refused the King's offer to become Prime Minister and refused again before Melbourne became Prime Minister in 1834. He served as Lord President of the Council in the Whig governments of 1830–34 and 1835–41. He led the Whig party in the Lords after Melbourne's stroke in 1842, resuming as Lord President when Russell became Prime Minister in 1846. He retired from public life in 1852, but was still being pressed to become Prime Minister as late as 1855. Although his family background and extensive landed connections determined lifelong Whig allegiance, he was always inclined to compromise and to work with political opponents whenever he thought it in the national interest.

After Canning's death, the King invited Goderich to form a government, which he did with no reluctance but no success either. His ministry was undermined by the King, who insisted that a high Tory, John Herries, be appointed as Chancellor of the Exchequer. Herries had long been a firm ideological opponent of Huskisson's liberalising financial policy and it was quickly clear that the two men could not work together. Attempts failed to shore up the government by bringing in Wellington, from the high Tories, and Holland, from the aristocratic Whigs, in what would have been an even more unlikely coalition. Goderich told George IV that the burdens of office were making it difficult for him to function efficiently. The King, already disenchanted with his new Prime Minister, smartly relieved him of that burden. In January 1828, he turned to Wellington instead.

II. Wellington and Catholic Emancipation

Wellington was in office for almost three years. He was not a good Prime Minister and he knew it. Neither by temperament nor by experience, which, despite his being in the Cabinet continuously from 1819 to 1827 remained overwhelmingly military, was he fitted for the perpetual negotiations, accommodations and compromises which are part and parcel of high politics. He knew his duty and he worked extremely hard both at superintending the work of government departments and reading the position papers of colleagues. His speeches in the Lords were direct, sometimes overly blunt and usually out of tune with the times. Command of parliament and command in the field required very different skills. He seems to have believed that, having been appointed by the King, he had no need to curry favour with colleagues or to build up party support for his leadership. Above all, he genuinely wished that he were doing something other than running the country. He wrote confidentially to a fellow officer who had served with him in the Peninsula: '. . . if people think I like this station they are mistaken . . . my line was to command the army but if I think I can do any good by being [prime] minister, I am willing to sacrifice my time & habits & do what I can'.[2]

His beliefs were old-fashioned and unwavering. He saw his duty as preserving the prerogatives of the Crown and also the privileges of the Church of England since it was an essential support for the state. He believed in the right of property owners to rule in the interests, as they interpreted them, of the nation as a whole. It was a sign not only of weakness but of misguidedness to change policy in the face of public pressure. Thus, at the height of the agitation for parliamentary reform in November 1830, he told the House of Lords that he knew of no reform proposals which could put representation 'on a footing more satisfactory to the people of the country than it now is'.[3]

If Wellington lacked political skills, he also inherited a highly problematic legacy. The monarch, to whom he owed unswerving allegiance, was a capricious, interfering nuisance who got it into his head after Liverpool's departure that the nation needed him to exercise greater influence both on the selection of ministers and the direction of policy. He was wrong, but Wellington would not tell him so. Party politics had been in flux since 1827 and the making of ministries required both more patience and more political finesse than either George IV or Wellington possessed. Religious questions loomed ever larger and ever more divisively. Within a year, parliamentary reform would return as a key issue 'out of doors'. Maintaining political stability and effective government in such circumstances would have tested the skills of a much subtler politician than the victor of Waterloo.

Wellington did at least have Peel, probably the ablest politician of the day, in office with him as Home Secretary. Peel now led the Tory party from the Commons. Peel agreed to serve only on condition that his erstwhile 'liberal' colleagues, led now by Huskisson, also came back. He told his wife: 'I cannot undertake the business . . . without more assistance than the mere Tory party . . . would afford me'.[4] Peel was perfectly content that the Whigs Lansdowne, Carlisle and Tierney be excluded but he had one further stipulation. He did not feel that the temper of the times would stand the reintroduction of the most implacably reactionary of the 'high' Tories. He strongly, and successfully, urged that neither Eldon nor Westmorland (respectively Lord Chancellor and Lord Privy Seal under Liverpool) should return. Thus, Wellington's Tory government largely reverted to the party-political situation of the earlier 1820s, although with a slightly more 'liberal' tinge than Liverpool's in 1827.

Political harmony did not last. Wellington and Peel were taken unawares when in February 1828 Lord John Russell introduced a bill from the Whig benches to repeal the Test and Corporation Acts after the so-called Protestant Dissenters had stirred themselves in pamphlets and other propaganda to revive agitation which had last been substantial forty years earlier (see Chapter 11). The bill was carried in the Commons by forty-four votes. Peel squared the higher clergy by getting them to agree to a form of words whereby each office-holder now needed only to pledge not to do anything in office designed to weaken the Church of England.[5] The Lords, where much visceral opposition still lurked, did not press the point. In any case, the Acts had been a dead letter in most places for many years. Russell argued that forcing Peel to abandon what had been a firm sticking point for the Tories represented a turn of the tide. More reforms could now be introduced with greater prospect of success.

Opinion in parliament was divided on the implications. Would largely theoretical advances for the Dissenters embolden those who wanted to tackle the much more contentious issue of Catholic Emancipation or would they convince majority opinion that one religious reform per parliament was plenty? Before that issue could be tested, however, Peel's idea of a balanced government was thrown into disarray in the spring of 1828 by the departure of most of the 'liberal Tories'. Wellington had been outmanoeuvred in Cabinet by Huskisson and his liberal colleagues over the amendment to the Corn Law which passed in 1828. Wellington resented what he saw as a slight. So, when Huskisson later wrote a courtesy letter to the Prime Minister to explain why he had voted against the majority in Cabinet on the trivial issue of how to distribute two parliamentary seats recently disfranchised for corruption, Wellington deliberately misinterpreted the missive as a letter of resignation – and promptly accepted it. The three other Huskissonites in senior government posts – the Earl of Dudley, Viscount Palmerston and Charles Grant – walked out in protest.

At a stroke, Wellington had lost the balance which Peel considered vital for the ministry's survival. He also lost substantial debating talent in the Commons, a matter of no little consequence when Catholic Emancipation forced itself centre-stage in July 1828. The law of unintended consequences links the departure of the Huskissonites with Catholic Emancipation. Peel suggested that Wellington replace Grant as President of the Board of Trade with Vesey Fitzgerald, who had worked closely with Peel in the 1810s when the latter was Chief Secretary for Ireland. By the convention of the times, MPs accepting ministerial office had to submit themselves to their constituents for re-election. This was normally a formality, but Fitzgerald's parliamentary seat was in Ireland, where, thanks to rising support for Daniel O'Connell's Catholic Association, politics were not normal. O'Connell himself stood against Vesey Fitzgerald (who, ironically, supported Catholic Emancipation) in the County Clare by-election and won a resounding victory. As a Catholic, O'Connell was not permitted to take his seat in parliament, thus creating a *cause célèbre* and the ideal focus for renewed agitation.

Peel and Wellington, who had given some consideration four years earlier to resolving the Catholic question,[6] thought it unlikely that Emancipation could be blocked. A protracted parliamentary battle would heighten tensions in Ireland. The next general election could well see many more 'County Clares' or even the emergence of an unofficial Catholic 'counter-parliament', thus subverting the Union. Protest in Ireland might tip into a new rebellion. In hindsight, it would have been better to concede straight away. Whenever managed, however, political dangers lurked. The King was resolutely opposed and might dismiss ministers who tried to force his hand. Both Wellington and Peel had been strong 'Protestants'. Their change of policy would be interpreted as treachery and split the Tory party still further. Wellington got the worst of both worlds. He delayed, thus encouraging mass Catholic demonstrations in Ireland in opposition to which Protestant, pro-Unionist and often violently inclined 'Brunswick clubs' responded. Wellington failed to mollify either the King or his 'Protestant' followers.

The Emancipation Act of 1829 satisfied neither side. 'Protestants' screamed 'betrayal', mostly at Peel, whom the Ultras never fully trusted again (see Chapter 22). A few even converted to parliamentary reform, believing that a House of Commons elected on a wider franchise would never have emancipated Catholics. Tory unity was shattered. The Catholics believed that what Emancipation had granted with one hand had been taken away with the other. Not only were some lofty positions in government still 'Protestant only' but existing penal statutes were maintained, with 'exemptions' for individuals who took a special oath. Also, many political societies, including O'Connell's Catholic Association, were specifically banned. Most provocatively of all, smallholders with land worth 40 shillings (£2) or more lost their votes since the threshold was raised to £10. Daniel O'Connell and his supporters still had much to fight for.

III. Parliamentary reform revived

The last twenty months of the Wellington administration were dominated by parliamentary reform. The issue seemed to come, if not out of a clear blue sky, then from one clouded by other issues. Religious differences still reverberated around Westminster. Landowners were worried about the implications of lowering levels of agricultural protection. Evangelicals and others were pressing for the abolition of slavery in the British Empire. Until 1829, religion occupied far more newspaper space than did parliamentary reform. Ironically, reform revived in part because of an initiative by one of the most viscerally anti-reformers of the lot. The **Marquess of Blandford** introduced two bills in the autumn of 1829 and the spring of 1830, the first to abolish the so-called 'rotten boroughs' and the second, more radically, to transfer all small borough seats to the counties and large towns. He also advocated that male ratepayers should have the vote and that members of parliament should be paid.[7] Blandford's targets were both Roman Catholics, who should not be allowed to buy seats in parliament, and the allegedly corrupt 'money system' run by 'loan-mongers and borough-mongers, wallowing in the stagnant and unproductive accumulations of their joint and several monopolies'. Blandford hoped that all right-thinking Englishmen, with the power of an extended franchise behind them, would put the funny-money fiddlers, stock-jobbers and Jewish deal-brokers firmly in their place.

George Spencer-Churchill, Marquess of Blandford and sixth Earl of Marlborough, 1793–1857

Born in Surrey into an aristocratic family, he was educated at Eton and Oxford and became an MP in 1818. His Tory beliefs were emphatic and he consistently supported the rights of landowners against the 'moneyed interest'. He is best known for his attacks on Wellington's government in 1829–30, when he argued that the improper influence of the executive, as deployed both by ministers and in a growing administration, was weakening the political system by giving elected MPs too little scope. His famous motion for parliamentary reform was defeated by 160 votes to 57 but showed the extent of the disillusionment of many Ultra-Tories with the leadership of Wellington and Peel. He inherited the Dukedom of Marlborough from his father in 1840. At first he supported Peel's Conservative administration of 1841–46 but opposed both the grant to the Roman Catholic College at Maynooth (see Chapter 22) and the repeal of the Corn Laws.

Since the Radicals paid little heed to Blandford's rantings, it is not entirely clear why the reform cause revived when it did. Although food prices rose after a bad harvest, no sharp, new economic crisis broke in 1829–30. The effects of the Banking Crisis (see Chapter 17) did linger, however, delaying the return of investor confidence and stunting economic growth. Rising unemployment provoked strikes in Lancashire. Also, the passage of economic and religious reforms in 1828–29 raised expectations both outside parliament and, among Huskissonites and Whigs, inside. By early 1830, parliamentary reform was being pressed with greater confidence and insistence than at any time since Peterloo (see Chapter 16).

Opinion is divided on whether the passage of the First Reform Act owed more to extra-parliamentary pressure or to rapidly changing fortunes at Westminster. In recent years, the pendulum has swung more towards emphasis on the travails of the Tories.[8] Wellington's government was in what Professor Hilton calls 'terminal disarray'.[9] It never recovered from the divisions opened up over religion. The electorate got a chance to pass its own judgment in the summer of 1830 when George IV's death necessitated a general election. It was widely agreed that the government had done badly, but only a proportion of wider propertied public opinion could be tested since in two-thirds of constituencies members of parliament were returned unopposed. The government's net losses were modest, perhaps fifteen seats. It did worse, however, in Ireland, where the number of contests was greater. The lingering unpopularity of Peel over Catholic Emancipation did no favours for members of his family. One brother lost his seat at Norwich, another at Newcastle-under-Lyme and his brother-in-law was defeated in Ireland.[10] A noteworthy feature of the election was the number of seats in which the traditional loyalties of deference to wealthy landowners failed to hold. This affected Whigs as well as Tories. Lord John Russell, from one of the most powerful Whig families of all, lost his seat on the home territory of Bedford.

The bigger picture was that, by the autumn of 1830, Wellington could not count on the loyalty of members who were notionally his supporters. The second half of 1830 was disturbed by the Swing Riots at home (see Chapter 7) and rebellions abroad, most notably a new French Revolution resulting in the overthrow of another Bourbon monarch, King Charles X. The parliamentary mood was jittery in consequence, although nothing directly threatened Wellington's government. Indeed, by the early autumn, he was negotiating to bring liberal Tories back into his government, thus healing at least one side of the Tory breach.

Then, early in November, Wellington torpedoed his own government. Just as extra-parliamentary pressure for reform was building, he declared insouciant opposition to the whole idea. He told the Lords that 'He had never read or heard of any measure . . . which could in any degree satisfy his mind that the state of the representation could be improved, or rendered more satisfactory to the country at large'.[11] This was a government woefully out of touch. A fortnight later, it was defeated in the Commons on a finance bill. Wellington resigned immediately. Even at the last, more sympathetic lobbying of members – an activity which the Prime Minister disdained – would probably have brought around the fifteen or so defectors needed to pass the bill.

The consequence was the first Whig-led government for more than twenty-three years. Wellington was soon telling the Duke of Buckingham that 'the country was in a state of insanity about Reform'.[12] If so, the new Prime Minister shared the affliction, making it clear from the outset that he would only accept office on condition that his government would introduce a parliamentary reform bill. Grey's government was a coalition. Brougham, Lansdowne and Holland were, like Grey himself, committed, lifelong Whigs. But the government also included the leading Canningite Tories: Palmerston, Goderich and Grant, and for distinctive, if not good, measure the Ultra-Tory Duke of Richmond. Public opinion generally welcomed the change of government. *The Times* newspaper stated that ministers 'accede to office by capitulation [making an agreement] with the people – they must redress our grievances, or be for ever ruined'.[13] A year later, it was urging people to form themselves 'into political societies throughout the whole realm' to clinch reform.[14]

IV. The crisis of reform, 1830–1832

It is probable that, had he not made his famous November gaffe, Wellington could have continued in office. He retained an enormous residual reputation as a war hero and could have used it to pass measures he deemed to be in the national interest – which would not have included parliamentary reform. Grey had not anticipated the call to office. However, this does not clinch the argument that reform came about because of developments inside parliament. Although comfortably more than half the MPs arriving at Westminster after each general election had not had to face an electoral contest themselves, they were responsive to public opinion 'out of doors'. Their interpretation of the nature of representation almost required this, and in 1830 and 1831 extra-parliamentary pressure for parliamentary reform reached unprecedented heights.

Skilled working men were forming themselves into organisations, including the grandly titled 'National Association for the Protection of Labour' in 1829. Its leader, John Doherty, used the pages of his trade union journal *Voice of the People* to press for parliamentary reform. Around 130 'Political Unions' were established in the years 1830–32. Some, like the Birmingham Political Union, advertised themselves as 'a general political union between the Lower and the Middle Classes of the People' to press for reform. Political Unions were diverse organisations, however, which often reflected the social structure of the towns in which they were based. 'Middle' and 'lower classes' might more naturally combine on a political programme in towns, such as Birmingham and Sheffield, dominated by small workshops and which offered reasonable opportunities for social mobility. In factory towns, the political priorities of textile labourers and manufacturers usually differed.[15] The years 1830 and 1831 also saw the return of those large, and potentially threatening, political meetings last seen in 1819–20. Invariably, their objective was parliamentary reform.

Whether these numerous, but disparate, forces of protest were capable of provoking national revolution in 1831 is unlikely. Some radical leaders themselves doubted it. Many parliamentary reformers would have recoiled in horror at the very idea. What mattered, however, was what the social elite feared. It was important to the success of reform that in 1831–32 enough MPs were persuaded that resistance to extra-parliamentary pressure was now the most dangerous course of action. Previous governments since the early 1790s had consistently resisted, but parliamentary reform was now government policy. The Whigs hoped that a combination of fear and fealty to the established order, as represented by an overwhelmingly aristocratic Cabinet which nevertheless proposed to extend the franchise, would do the trick.

Like Waterloo, it proved a damned close-run thing. The details of the bill were drawn up by Whig ministers, particularly Durham and Russell. When the Commons assembled in March 1831 to learn from Russell that the government proposed to eliminate 168 borough seats from 108 boroughs and to replace them with 43 newly created borough seats in larger centres of population and a much increased number of county seats, there was consternation. Many of these seats were, in their occupants' perception, pieces of property for which either good money had been paid or which had been in an aristocratic family's gift from time immemorial. The proposal to introduce a standard voting qualification for all men occupying property worth at least £10 a year excited less hostile comment. Self-preservation was one reason why the **second reading** of the bill passed by only a single vote when Grey had anticipated a much larger majority. Knowing that the bill would be emasculated in Committee, Grey asked the bemused new monarch, **William IV**, to dissolve parliament, although the present one had been elected only months earlier. The ensuing election of 1831 resulted in a landslide majority for the government.

'Second reading' of a parliamentary bill

Proposed legislation goes through several formal processes before becoming law. 'Second reading' is that relatively early stage at which the overall principle of a bill is voted upon. Only after the principle has been approved are the specific details considered, usually by a parliamentary committee established for the purpose.

William IV, 1765–1837

William was the third son of George III and, as such, not expected to come to the throne. However, of his elder brothers, neither George IV nor the Duke of York, who died in 1827, left surviving legitimate heirs. William was created Duke of Clarence in 1788. Most of his career was spent in the navy, where he rose to the rank of Admiral of the Fleet in 1811 and Lord High Admiral in 1827. He inherited the throne just before the Reform Act crisis, which he did not handle well. After the Lords rejected the Reform Bill, he at first agreed to create sufficient peers to produce a pro-reform majority but then changed his mind, precipitating Grey's resignation. In November 1834, he dismissed Viscount Melbourne and became the last monarch to get rid of a government which had a parliamentary majority. He never developed insight into, or tactful handling of, difficult political matters and was not widely respected.

With a Commons majority assured, attention turned to the Lords, who rejected the bill in October 1831. This precipitated howls of protest from the Political Unions and also the most sustained violence of the period. Numerous riots occurred. In Bristol, where rioters targeted an unsympathetic Tory town corporation, the troops could not restore order for over three days. In Nottingham, which, like many towns, had a tradition of hearty, and often drunken, disorder at election times, rioters directed their efforts to harassing known anti-reformers. Famously, the Duke of Newcastle's castle was burned to the ground. Rioting in Derby led to fatalities.[16] The excitable Princess Lieven, wife of the Russian ambassador, told her brother: 'We too, in England, are just on the brink of a revolution.'[17] Even the normally sanguine Viscount Melbourne was said to have been 'frightened to death' by the events in Bristol.[18]

Order was eventually restored. A third Reform Bill was introduced the following spring. It enjoyed smooth progress, including second-reading approval in the Lords in April, until wrecking amendments there three weeks later threatened the return of chaos. Grey resigned. William IV asked Wellington to return as Prime Minister and precipitated the crisis known as 'the Days of May'. Leading radicals, including the ubiquitous Francis Place (see Chapter 17) and the wealthy Birmingham banker, political radical and currency theorist Thomas Attwood, called mass meetings, supported strikes and urged pro-reform middle classes to withdraw their savings from the banks. The aim was to provoke economic and financial anarchy, thus blocking the King's plans and seeing Grey reinstated on terms which would ensure the passage of reform. Wellington was unable to form a government. Grey returned. Finally, and for many resentfully, the Lords capitulated. The Reform Act became law on 7 June 1832.

21

The reality of Reform: the new order and its critics

I. Whig objectives

The Reform Act of 1832 was the creation of a government dominated by Whig landowners. Although popular pressure in 1829–32 played an important part in its passing, the measure itself was not designed to satisfy radicals outside parliament who wanted the new system to be representative of all interests and not merely of the propertied. The Whigs' aim was to get the lower middle classes out of the clutches of just those radicals by bringing them within what William Gladstone would later call 'the privileged pale of the Constitution'.

So, when Grey told the King's private secretary in October 1831, 'It is . . . undeniable that the middle classes . . . are activated by an intense and almost unanimous feeling in favour of the measure of reform'[1] he was not just trying to screw William IV's courage to the sticking place, though that would later prove necessary (see Chapter 20). He was discharging what Whigs from the Glorious Revolution onwards believed to be their main political task in life: interpreting the wishes of propertied Englishmen and legislating them into beneficent life. By design, the Act contained no provision for universal male, or even a ratepayer, suffrage, for equal electoral districts or for a secret ballot. As Grey had told fellow peers in November 1831: 'there is no one more decided against annual parliaments, universal suffrage, and the ballot, than I am. My object is not to favour, but to put an end to such hopes and projects.'[2]

The Reform Act was intended to recalibrate and reinforce an old system rather than to create a new one.[3] It was about ensuring the appropriate representation of 'interests', not of individuals. Though the Whigs hoped that the Act would defuse tensions and avert revolution, their approach was not cynical or specially self-serving. As Professor Parry has said, their interest in reform was 'genuine and long-standing',[4] though it had brought them precious few benefits during the long years in opposition before 1830. The new electorate, however, rewarded their Whig benefactors at the general election held at the end of 1832. Those MPs supporting reform, most of whom acknowledged the label 'Whig', held a majority over the Tories of more than three hundred seats.

Thereafter, although the Whigs remained in power for all but three months of the nine years to 1841, their position after 1832 weakened steadily. Their own redistribution of seats worked against them. While most of the newly enfranchised large cities returned Whig, or '**Liberal**', members to parliament, the situation in the counties was very different. The Reform Bill increased the number of county seats in England and Wales by 73 per cent – from 92 to 159. This was done partly to acknowledge that most county seats before 1832 had far more electors than most borough seats. The Whigs also felt that county seats were least prone to 'manipulation', influence or outright purchase.

Liberal party

The Liberals emerged from inside the Whig party over the period from about 1835 to 1860. Definitions are not precise but, whereas the power and wealth of the Whigs derived directly from the land they owned, those who called themselves 'Liberals' were more likely to come from an urban background, either from the manufacturing or the professional classes, as lawyers, doctors, writers or intellectuals. Over this period, the political importance of the towns grew. Reflecting this, the term Whig/Liberal, or even Liberal, was increasingly used to describe the party which opposed the Tories. The influence of the Whigs, though still substantial especially among the party leadership, began a long period of decline. Many 'Liberals' advocated free trade and the Liberal Party was also a much more natural home for nonconformists. Within the broad Liberal group were a number of so-called 'radicals' calling for more extensive parliamentary reform and who wished to see the influence of landowners decline, since society was becoming increasingly urban. Not surprisingly, this caused growing tensions within the party as a whole.

Mainly, though, the Whigs just got it wrong. They believed that their gains in county seats in the elections of 1830 and 1831 betokened a welcome, if much delayed, return of the gentry to their old Whig loyalties after a long flirtation with Pittite Conservatism. Since both elections were held in unusual circumstances, and the second was largely a **plebiscite** on parliamentary reform anyway, this was a substantial misjudgment. It derived from the damaging Whig propensity to look backward for justification – in this case to the so-called Whig Oligarchy during which the Tories were marginalised – rather than forward to seize new political opportunities in a rapidly urbanising society.

Plebiscite

In strict terms, a plebiscite is a vote of the entire electorate to decide a single important issue, such as whether one state should unite with another. In that sense, it resembles a referendum. The election of 1831 was not technically a plebiscite but the issue of parliamentary reform was so central to its outcome that it was probably as close as the United Kingdom has come to a 'one-issue' general election.

It had the bizarre consequence that the immediate beneficiaries of the new political system were landowners and the larger tenant farmers – the so-called '£50 **tenants-at-will**'. Whereas the number of voters in county seats increased by 55 per cent after 1832 those in the boroughs went up by only 41 per cent. The English counties were the heartland of Tory support. The Tories recovered quickly after their disastrous loss in the 1832 general election, when they won only 175 of the 658 parliamentary seats. In 1835 they won 273 seats, in 1837 313 and in 1841 367, when the Tories won an outright majority. As the number of Tory MPs increased, so did the party's stranglehold on the counties.[5] The Whigs and their radical associates had won 104 of the 144 county seats in the 1832 election; in 1841, they won a mere 20, the Tories taking 124.

Tenants-at-will and copyhold

Tenants-at-will held property from a landowner under a lease for which they paid rent. The phrase 'at will' meant that the lease could be terminated by either side at any time. As a result of the so-called 'Chandos Amendment', the 1832 Reform Act gave the vote in county constituencies to tenants paying a lease worth at least £50 a year. Most historians believed that this change strengthened landowners' political hold over their tenants. The requirement to vote according to the landowner's wishes could be backed up by the withdrawing of the lease. 'Copyhold' tenure covered land originally held under the custom of the Lord of the Manor, the leading landowner in a village. Many copyhold properties by the early nineteenth century were considered, in effect, as freehold property. 'Copyholders' of land to the value of £10 a year or more were entitled to vote in county constituencies.

II. The impact of parliamentary reform

How great an impact did the Reform Act have? Historical opinion remains divided. In the early twentieth century, when many historical accounts were written with the intention of charting, and celebrating, progress, 1832 represented a national turning point. It was said to have 'placed the feet of the nation . . . in the direction of democracy'. Having harnessed 'the power of the whole nation, enfranchised and unenfranchised', it had been 'carried by the popular will against the strenuous resistance of the old order entrenched in the House of Lords'.[6]

Later generations tended to concentrate on what they saw as the Act's limitations. It left the same social groups in charge at Westminster. The nation continued to be ruled by aristocrats. The social composition of the House of Commons did not change very much before the 1860s. A slightly larger number of professional men found their way into parliament, but 'professionals', journalists, intellectuals, bankers and the like, had been effective participants in pre-1832 parliaments as well. Significant numbers of constituencies, though fewer than before, remained at the disposition of large landowners. One of them, the Duke of Newcastle, provided the young W. E. Gladstone with his first parliamentary seat – Newark, which the Duke in effect owned – at the general election of 1832.[7] Uncontested elections remained common after 1832. Contests took place on average in 40 per cent of constituencies before the Reform Act. Between 1832 and 1867, the proportion increased, but only to 60 per cent, and even that proportion was inflated by the keenly contested election of 1832 itself.[8]

Recent research has also revealed how 'participatory' the unreformed electoral system could be. Elections provided an opportunity for active participation, vigorous debate and political theatre. Candidates would usually be expected to explain their attitudes, policies, social connections and patronage links, in public. Only a few pre-1832 boroughs operated on the basis of virtual manhood suffrage but, even where the franchise was more restricted, it was not necessary to be a voter in order to have a voice, and to have it listened to.[9] The Reform Act curbed the more boisterous activities associated with elections. A respectable electorate tended to behave respectably.[10]

Those who were entitled to vote before 1832 kept their votes during their lifetimes. This was the Reform Act's only concession to a non-propertied electorate. It meant, however, that the size of electorates in what had been the more 'open' boroughs before 1832 dwindled over time as voters died off. Preston had an electorate of 5,300 in 1832; almost 90 per cent of its adult males were entitled to vote. By 1857, its electorate had fallen below 2,000. Between 1832 and 1851, the proportion of adult males entitled to vote in Gloucester fell from 51 per cent to 18, that in Northampton from 65 per cent to 24.[11] In one sense, these reductions were counterbalanced by substantial increases in the new industrial constituencies such as Birmingham and Leeds, of course. However, the new voters in Birmingham, for example, had a necessary property qualification which most in the 'open' boroughs before 1832 did not.

Overall, the English electorate increased by about 49 per cent and roughly 20 per cent of adult males had the vote. In Scotland, which had resembled a vast national rotten borough since 1707 (see Chapter 1), the increase was much greater: 4,600 voters became more than 64,000 after 1832. In Ireland, the restricted franchise which had been established at the time of Catholic Emancipation (see Chapter 14) was retained, although leaseholders could now vote in county seats. The county electorate increased from 37,000 to 60,000 but only 5 per cent of adult males in Ireland were enfranchised.

III. Reform: a psychological shift?

Although it is possible to argue that the Great Reform Act changed little, such a conclusion is misleading. Despite Whig assertions that it represented 'the final solution to a great constitutional question', the Great Reform Act's very passing was critical. It undermined a key anti-reform argument, much used by high Tories, that the pre-1832 system should not be altered because, in use over many centuries, it acquired a mystical, almost divine, significance. Many Tories saw the hand of God supporting the United Kingdom's constitutional arrangements. Once a major Reform Act was on the statute book, then cases for further change could be debated on their merits. This is what John Bright meant when he offered the initially puzzling judgment that the Great Reform Act was 'not a good bill . . . [though] a great Bill when it passed'.[12] Whatever its shortcomings, and whatever its consequences, the Act finally surmounted opposition which had blocked change for over half a century. Since that opposition was most fervent in the House of Lords and the Whigs had faced it down in May 1832, the passage of parliamentary reform accelerated the long and tortuous process whereby the influence of the Upper House *vis-à-vis* the Commons declined.

Reform also shifted the focus of politics. Robert Peel referred to 'a change in the position of parties and in the practical working of public affairs'.[13] Intending voters after 1832 had to be registered and registration required organisation. This was done by local party agents and nationally through political clubs: the Tory Carlton and the Whig Reform, established in 1832 and 1836 respectively. Politics became a more professional game and, during the 1830s at least, the Tories, guided by Francis Bonham and Granville Somerset, learned its rules more quickly. The frequency of general elections steepened the learning curve, especially at local level. Four elections were held under the new rules in the years 1832–41, against a normal average of two per decade. More candidates now found it useful to sport a label other than 'independent' when they presented themselves before their constituents. For their part, electors, having two votes to cast, were increasingly unlikely to 'split' them between the parties. Voters displayed increasing loyalty to one party or the other. Between 1832 and 1865, fewer than 30 per cent of all votes cast were split between the parties. It seems that debates and agitation over reform in 1830–32 polarised opinion and helped to increase awareness of party allegiance. At all events, far more 'voters became consistent partisans'.[14]

Party discipline at Westminster, however, was far from watertight. Many MPs continued to act independently, much as they had done before 1832. In the years 1835–41, more than 70 per cent of Whig, Liberal or Radical members voted against Melbourne's government in up to 10 per cent of divisions and up to a fifth voted against it more than 10 per cent of the time.[15] Of course, many radical MPs did not consider themselves Whig supporters anyway. They were just more fervently anti-Tory. From a different perspective, Sir Robert Peel, after 1832 the acknowledged leader of the Tories, was hardly the epitome of partisanship. He continued his propensity for voting in the national interest, as he saw it. Though he flayed the Whigs over economic policy in the years 1839–41, he had earlier supported a number of Whig measures, not least the Poor Law Amendment Act in 1834 (see Chapter 22). Although there is abundant evidence of greater partisanship not only after, but in significant part because of, parliamentary reform, a two-party system was far from fully established by the 1840s.

The true significance of the Great Reform Act is not to be measured by calculating the numbers of men it enfranchised or the parliamentary constituencies it removed or redistributed. Its decisive impact was psychological. The Great Reform Act changed how property owners thought about the system of government. As has been said, it confirmed that 'the electorate had an undeniable role in the political life of the country'.[16] In acknowledging this role, members of the House of Commons could experience a heightened sense of their own legitimacy. As radicals like J. A. Roebuck noted, the substantial reduction in the number of 'rotten' boroughs' further reduced the extent of government patronage. Many parliamentary radicals believed that the House of Commons could now act as a more effective brake on what they saw as the excessive power of the executive, not least in the careful scrutiny of public expenditure.[17]

Still, the government had forged what proved to be a powerful propertied alliance against 'mere numbers'. MPs could speak with greater confidence as representatives of the propertied interest, be it landed, commercial or industrial. It is difficult to imagine a pre-1832 parliament having either the confidence or the will to embark on the range of reforms enacted by both Whigs and Conservatives in the years 1832–46. The Municipal Corporations Act (1835) was the local counterpart of the Great Reform Act. It swept away 178 old, self-elected, and usually Tory, corporations and replaced them with ratepayer-elected borough councils. This Act helped to acclimatise ratepayers to the need to register as voters. The local electorate expanded significantly in 1850 when the Small Tenements Rating Act permitted occupiers who paid rates only indirectly, through rent to a landlord, to vote.[18] It was these elected corporations which took the key decisions on water-supplies, paving, lighting and the rest, although borough councillors were as likely to be elected on the basis of their stance on national as on local issues.[19]

Reforms in the 1830s and 1840s covered a range of religious and 'social' issues, including a series of reforms in 1836–40 which strengthened the Church of England (see Chapter 22), a controversial Poor Law Amendment Act (see Chapter 28), factory, mines and public health legislation (see Chapter 26), state grants for, and the inspection and regulation of, education (see Chapter 29) and the extension to county level of professional policing broadly along the lines introduced by Peel in London in 1829. Many of these were informed, and supported by, legislative commissions of enquiry. After 1832, government began to identify, and get to grips with, what was increasingly called 'the social question'. All of this involved a much more extensive legislative programme, longer parliamentary sessions – and an increasingly professionalised government to manage that programme.

IV. Radicalism and Chartism

Given the intentions of the Whigs in passing reform, it is hardly surprising that the new political order which emerged after 1832 was challenged by those excluded from it. Within months of its passing, the radical journalist **Henry Hetherington** was railing against the Whigs' attempt to 'quell the rising spirit of democracy in England'. Henry Hunt used more lurid language. He talked of 'seven millions of men in the United Kingdom, who are rendered so many political outlaws . . . by the provisions of that [Reform] Act, they are to all intents and purposes so many political slaves.'[20]

Henry Hetherington, 1792–1849

Born in London, the son of a tailor, he was apprenticed to Luke Hansard, who printed a record of parliamentary debates. Hetherington is best known as the publisher of *Poor Man's Guardian*, one of a large number of 'unstamped' newspapers which attacked the Whig government in the 1830s. His writings led to prosecution on charges of seditious libel and to imprisonment. He helped to found the London Working Men's Association, which agitated for a democratic government. He was a prominent figure in the early years of the Chartist movement, touring the country as a Chartist lecturer and supporting the expansion of educational opportunities for working people. This emphasis on 'knowledge Chartism' brought him into conflict with Feargus O'Connor.

The radical press kept up the pressure on the Whigs during the early and mid-1830s by campaigning to repeal the stamp duties on newspapers. These duties took the price of a newspaper out of the range of ordinary citizens. Radicals attacked them as 'taxes on knowledge'. The campaign achieved its aim in 1836 when the duty was reduced from 4d to 1d.[21] Out of this campaign emerged the London Working Men's Association (LWMA). Its aim was to benefit the 'useful classes . . . politically, socially and morally'.[22] Until the later 1830s, relatively benign economic conditions and lower food prices inhibited mass support for further reform. However, a commercial downswing in 1837 and the return of higher prices, rising unemployment and, especially in the north of England, concerted opposition to the new Poor Law Amendment Act (see Chapter 28) concentrated attention on popular agitation once more.

The **'People's Charter'** was drawn up by the LWMA early in 1838, supported by the Birmingham Political Union. At a mass meeting held on Glasgow Green on 21 May 1838, and attended by about 150,000 people, Thomas Attwood told his audience that the Reform Act had changed nothing and therefore 'through the power of the people, it shall be cast into the fire'.[23] Copies of the People's Charter, 'to provide for a just representation of the people of Great Britain in the Commons House of Parliament', were in wide circulation a few days later.

The People's Charter

The word 'Charter' was intended to link in people's minds with Magna Carta (which translates as 'The Great Charter') of 1215, which identified the rights and liberties which the barons insisted that King John should respect. None of its famous six points was new. They had been widely debated in radical circles since the mid-1770s. However, the Charter became the focal point of the largest political movement in nineteenth-century Britain. The six points are:

1. Universal Manhood Suffrage
2. No property qualifications to become a member of parliament
3. Elections for parliament to be held every year
4. Equality of representation, by establishing electoral districts (constituencies) with the same number of electors
5. Members of parliament to receive payment for their work
6. Voting by secret ballot

Thus began the first of three brief periods during which the Chartist movement challenged the authorities. Elections were held for a working man's parliament, formally known as the National Convention of the Industrial Classes, which met in 1839 first in London and then in Birmingham. Almost two million people signed a petition to parliament calling for the implementation of the Six Points. Precisely 46 MPs voted for it and 235 against; 377 did not think it worth the bother of attending to vote down such an outlandish proposition. Rejection was followed first by a series of strikes and then by an abortive attempt at revolution in Newport (Monmouth) in November.

In 1840, the Chartists responded to their reverses by establishing a National Charter Association, to provide a secure organisation from which to launch further campaigns and the election of Chartist-supporting town councillors. It has been called 'the first working class political party'[24] but the most prominent Chartist leader, **Feargus O'Connor**, was concerned that the NCA might make Chartism more bureaucratic and less militant. The darkening economic scene averted this threat. Chartism gathered large number of supporters during 1841–42, which witnessed one of the sharpest economic slumps of the nineteenth century. It led to the presentation of a second petition, rejected again by a huge Commons majority. A general strike followed as did industrial sabotage in the so-called Plug Plot.

Feargus O'Connor, 1794–1855

Born in County Cork, he was the son of a wealthy Protestant landlord. He entered parliament for an Irish seat in 1832 as a supporter of Daniel O'Connell (see Chapter 14) but quarrelled with him over his support for the new poor law and other matters. He associated with London radicals and, by 1835, was touring the industrial north as a political 'missionary' calling for universal manhood suffrage. He was a powerful speaker who became the most prominent, as well as the most divisive, of the Chartist leaders. He established the journal *Northern Star* in 1837 and used both it and his own speeches to urge northern working men to support the People's Charter. He maintained his popularity with rank-and-file Chartists but his personality made him a difficult colleague. In 1845, he founded the Chartist Co-operative Land Society and launched his 'Land Plan'. It aimed to settle working men on rural smallholdings. Only five Chartist communities were established and O'Connor was criticised for his plan to put working people back on the land when the needs of the industrial working class should take priority. In 1847, he was elected to parliament, becoming Chartism's only MP.

Chartism's final phase as a mass movement occurred in 1847–48. It reached a climax on 10 April when the authorities prevented a large gathering assembled on Kennington Common (London) from marching to parliament to deliver another reform petition. As before, the authorities were well prepared to meet force with force. The Chartist failure was rapidly branded 'a fiasco' by the loyalist press. Still, police and troops had been out in force to defend the capital. Both the numbers summoned and the hasty departure of Queen Victoria and Prince Albert for Osborne House, their newly refurbished residence on the Isle of Wight, indicated a high level of concern. In Bradford, which had a large community of economically depressed woolcombers, some of them Irish immigrants, considerable public disturbances occurred in May. Preparations for armed rising to break out on both sides of the Pennines in August were easily forestalled, intercepted by the usual array of informers.[25] In London the next month, the Home Office ordered the police to break up Chartist meetings. The London police were neither popular nor trusted and considerable street violence ensued. Chartist leaders lacked the means to sustain their activities after a specially convened 'National Assembly' broke up.[26] Chartism lingered on into the 1850s. Its end was protracted and messy, but after 1848 it posed no further threats to the authorities.

Once its threat was over Chartism's detractors dismissed it as a sporadically threatening, but doomed, movement. Its rank-and-file supporters were characterised as hungry, desperate people misled and manipulated by preening, self-important and quarrelsome leaders. Recent historiography has revised this assessment. It has emphasised Chartism's seriousness of purpose, the influence and commercial success of its newspapers, the extraordinarily effective organisation of Chartist meetings and lectures and its role in increasing educational opportunities available to the working classes.[27] It also confirms Chartism as a truly national movement, rather than a series of interlocking local 'episodes', although Chartist activities were frequently an expression of community awareness. Chartism had lasting cultural resonance.

A large number of Chartist sermons were published, reminding us of the centrality of the religious context. Teetotal Chartist social gatherings further nourished the movement's nonconformist roots. Chartist-sponsored libraries and Chartist sports societies were also frequently encountered. For many working people in the 1840s, Chartism, and its associated support mechanisms, became an important part of their identity and 'social place'. For them, Chartism was not just, or even primarily, about presenting petitions to parliament and assembling *en masse* to hear tub-thumping pro-democracy speeches when times were hard.

And yet, this engaged collective of rehabilitation has probably gone too far. Chartism did have weaknesses. The movement frightened the authorities, but only at times of economic dislocation. It is unlikely that Chartism would have made the impact – or engendered the historiography – it did if Britain had not experienced a decade of unusual economic turbulence in the late 1830s and early 1840s. The long Victorian boom killed off any prospect of reviving the so-called 'mass platform', leaving the NCA a rump in which **George Julian Harney** was prominent. Harney attempted – with mixed success – to preserve Chartism via alliances with skilled workers, the co-operative movement and Christian socialism.

George Julian Harney, 1817–1897

Born into a poor family in London, he worked as a ship's cabin boy before becoming involved in radical politics through his association with Henry Hetherington. He helped to found the London Democratic Association in 1838. It had genuinely revolutionary objectives, in direct contrast to the London Working Men's Association, which, Harney believed, had become too close to the middle-class radicals. He was recognised as a 'physical-force' Chartist in the 1840s, although he did not believe that a British revolution could succeed. He increasingly associated with Friedrich Engels and became increasingly interested in socialist ideas about improving conditions for working people.

Excessive concentration on the vitality of the Chartist movement also underplays the significance of internal divisions, of which contemporaries were well aware. Many of these involve Feargus O'Connor. O'Connor was a powerful figure who worked with immense energy to present Chartism as a unified national movement. He never understood the extent to which his own self-absorptions militated against this objective. His split with **William Lovett** was damaging. He also later broke with George Julian Harney. He was, as Malcolm Chase puts it, 'suspicious of anything that lay beyond his capacity to control'.[28] His suspicions included London, which he said 'ever has been, and ever will be, rotten'. His reluctance to use his formidable energies to sustain effective communication and mutual support between radicals in the capital and the industrial north was also damaging.

William Lovett, 1800–1877

Born in Cornwall, the son of a ship's captain, he arrived in London in 1821 to pursue a career as a cabinet maker. He was self-taught and retained his passion for knowledge and self-improvement. He helped to form the National Union of the Working Classes in 1831 and was also a founder of the London Working Men's Association in 1836. His main objective as a Chartist was to improve working people's levels of education. He advocated the establishment of a National Education system, including lecture halls, schools and libraries to be paid for by small subscriptions from working men. Lovett's close associations with the middle classes drew the anger of O'Connor and he increasingly withdrew to pursue schemes of self-improvement. He helped to draft the constitution of Joseph Sturge's Complete Suffrage Union, founded in 1842. This organisation incorporated all six points of the Charter but was roundly attacked by O'Connor and the National Charter Association for working too closely with the middle classes.

The Chartists had no realistic prospect of achieving their six points. No landowners' parliament would experience a Damascene conversion over democracy. Likewise, as almost all realistic Chartists themselves conceded, ideas about a British revolution in the 1840s were a romantic delusion. In facing down mass meetings and street protests, the British state was by then both experienced and unprecedentedly strong.[29] We can acknowledge both the immense cultural significance of Chartism and also the richly impressive legacy it handed down to later Victorian radicals. We should not, however, as some sympathetic historians have done, romanticise the movement or play down its deficiencies. In particular, and like most early nineteenth-century radical movements, it had its fair share of leaders whose rhetoric substantially outdistanced their sense of reality. In particular, the rehabilitation of the fractious Feargus O'Connor has gone several notches too far.

22

. . . .

The age of Peel? Policies and parties, 1832–1846

I. From Grey to Melbourne

The period 1832–46 is often called 'the Age of Peel'.[1] At first sight, this seems paradoxical. Peel was in power for only a third of a period which began with **Earl Grey** passing a reform bill and ended with Peel losing office and breaking up his party. The Whigs were also in government for much longer than Peel's Tories: nine of the fourteen years. **Viscount Melbourne**'s tenure as Prime Minister was also longer, at six years and ten months, than Peel's, at five years and one month.

Charles Grey, second Earl Grey, 1764–1845

Born in Northumberland, the son of a senior army officer from a landed family, he was educated at Eton and Cambridge University. He became an MP in 1786 and his subsequent career as a Foxite Whig politician was influenced by his affair with Georgeana, Duchess of Devonshire, an important figure in the party. He founded the Society of the Friends of the People in 1792, an impetuous move because he had not consulted Fox about this initiative and was anyway no revolutionary sympathiser. He also presented two reform bills in the Commons in 1793 and 1797. Since the Whigs were so rarely in office, his ministerial career before 1830 was limited to short stints as First Lord of the Admiralty and Foreign Secretary in 1806–7. He inherited his earldom, and a seat in the Lords, on his father's death in 1807. Although the post of leader of the opposition did not exist, he was generally acknowledged as the principal Whig figure by about 1810. This was a thankless role, since Liverpool had a clear majority in parliament and Grey was neither liked nor trusted by the Prince Regent (George IV). His long-delayed return to office in 1830, at the age of 66, was unexpected (see Chapter 21), but his political energies, frequently diverted elsewhere during his career, were focused entirely on parliamentary reform. Such commitment proved critical in the face of stern opposition in the Lords. Although his ministry passed other reform measures, Grey's vigour waned after 1832. When his Cabinet split over Irish policy in 1834, he resigned and did not hold office again.

William Lamb, second Viscount Melbourne, 1779–1848

Born in London, the son of a substantial Midlands landowner and MP, he was educated at Eton and Cambridge University and trained as a lawyer. He associated with high Whig society from an early age and it was through this connection that he entered parliament in 1806. He was an able man with a wide range of intellectual interests but his early Whig enthusiasms dimmed and he became linked to the political grouping led by George Canning. He became Chief Secretary for Ireland in 1827 and served in that post for a year, resigning with Huskisson from Wellington's government in 1828. As Home Secretary in Grey's coalition government, he acted as a restraint on some of the more radical Whigs during the reform crisis. He had no strong opinions about the Reform Act, but accepted that it was necessary to restore the confidence of propertied opinion about governments. After his early years, he was never attracted by theories of government or speculative opinions, but, along with the aura of both cynical detachment and laziness which he liked to affect, he could act promptly, efficiently and sensibly during a crisis, as he did to calm the alarm felt by many landowners during the Swing Riots (1830–31). He succeeded Grey as Prime Minister in 1834, but was dismissed by William IV a few months later, returning to office in 1835 when Peel was unable to win a majority in the Commons. His ministry passed a number of significant reforms (see Chapter 21) but he was often reluctant to get into the drearier details either of administration or of party management. He did, however, play an important role in keeping a Cabinet of self-important, fractious and ambitious individuals together under his leadership. From 1837 he acted as unofficial tutor in the political arts to the young and impressionable Queen Victoria, who was dazzled both by his insights and by his languid manner. He offered only limited opposition to Peel's government from 1841 and his political career was ended by the cerebral haemorrhage which he suffered in 1842.

Perhaps less controversially, this period has also been called 'the age of Reform'. The Whig/Liberal–Tory coalition which passed the Reform Act had a broader reform agenda. It moved first to tackle slavery. The newly elected parliament of 1832 contained far more pro-abolitionist MPs, especially from larger urban constituencies. The Anti-Slavery Society, founded in 1823, had rained petitions down on parliament in 1831 and lobbied candidates at the general election of 1832 to pledge support for abolition.[2] For Foxite Whigs in Grey's coalition this was pushing at an open door. Opposition both to the slave trade and to slavery in the colonies was already a central part of their libertarian platform. An Act abolishing slavery in the British Empire (but specifically not in India, where 'British' territories remained the property of the East India Company – see Chapter 19) was passed in 1833 and came into effect in August 1834. Slave owners got compensation for their loss of property. This cost £20m in about 40,000 separate grants.[3] The Canningite Tory **Edward Stanley** introduced the bill and saw to it that the compensation terms were generous enough to prevent a landowner revolt in the West Indies.

Edward George Stanley, fourteenth Earl of Derby, 1799–1869

Born at Knowsley Hall (the ancestral home of the Earls of Derby), the son of the thirteenth Earl, he was educated at Eton and Oxford University. The main political influences on him in the 1820s were the Whig Marquess of Lansdowne and George Canning. He entered the House of Commons in 1822, first supporting the Whigs and then the liberal wing of the Tory party. He favoured the main 'liberal' causes in religion and also trade liberalisation. His first ministerial appointment was as Chief Secretary for Ireland in Grey's government in 1830 and he entered the Cabinet a year later. As Chief Secretary, he frequently clashed with Daniel O'Connell and introduced coercive measures to quell violence in Ireland. He became Secretary for War and the Colonies in 1833, but left the government in 1834 on the issue of 'appropriation'. The remainder of his career was spent in the Tory party. He sat with Peel on the opposition benches from 1835. He served as Colonial Secretary in the Peel government of 1841–45 but resigned from the Cabinet over repeal of the Corn Laws. He became leader of the Conservatives after the party split of 1846, a post he held until 1868, serving as Prime Minister of minority governments in 1852, 1858–59 and 1866–68. Throughout this long period, he suffered from the fact that most of the able Conservatives left the party with Peel in 1846 and few returned. He became a member of the House of Lords as Lord Stanley of Bickerstaff in 1844 and succeeded to the Earldom of Derby on his father's death in 1851. He remained committed to moderate reform and introduced a further parliamentary reform bill in 1859, which narrowly failed. A well-read, quick-minded man and an able debater, his long tenure of the Conservative leadership ensured that the party did not default to narrow reaction. He could, however, be aloof and arrogant in his judgments and he made few close friendships.

Ireland was quite another matter. Attempts to resolve both violence and festering resentment there caused the resignation of Grey, a split in the governing coalition and, arguably, precipitated the emergence of a new 'Liberal party'. Catholic Emancipation had not brought peace to Ireland. Rather it had emboldened those, particularly O'Connell, who wished to end the Union then and there. The government's response to the challenge revealed how little unity Grey's Cabinet possessed. As more than one historian has noticed, it was 'full of prima donnas'. It was also led by a Prime Minister prone to bouts of gloom who, with parliamentary reform now in the bag, wanted an excuse to get out of the heat of the kitchen. Grey was too fastidious for the daily grind of political leadership and complained impotently of constant harassment by 'wrong-headed [political] friends'.[4] He blanched at the prospect of continuous attacks by the forty or so O'Connellite MPs now sitting in the Commons.

The government's plans for extending educational opportunities for Catholic children and for extensive public works were not enough for them. On one side of a Cabinet division were those who urged a constructive response, involving conciliation of increasingly politicised Catholic priests and the **appropriation** of church funds.

On the other were those who saw no alternative to firmness and force. Sir James Graham put it bluntly: 'Until that unhappy and insane people be re-conquered there will be no peace.'[5] An Irish Church Temporalities Bill proposing Church reform passed in 1833 but only after an appropriation clause had been removed. Pressure from radical MPs forced the introduction of another appropriation bill. In June 1834, this precipitated the co-ordinated resignation of Stanley, Graham, the Earl of Ripon, and the high Tory Duke of Richmond. A month later, Grey retired to his estates in the North-East, genuinely to spend more time with his family. He nevertheless kept a watchful, and increasingly reproachful, eye on his successor.

Appropriation

The word used in the 1830s to describe the policy of diverting some of the large income (about £800,000 yearly) enjoyed by the established Church of Ireland, which represented only 10 per cent of Ireland's population, to other, mostly non-religious, purposes. This policy was designed to reduce poverty, support charitable causes and improve the educational prospects of Catholic children. Its ultimate objective was to end violence and persuade the Catholic majority of the benefits of Union with Britain.

That successor was Viscount Melbourne, who headed a government which William IV thought bereft of stabilising influences, particularly after Viscount Althorp, an able leader of the government in the Commons, became Earl Spencer on his father's death. He moved to the Lords and, in effect, retirement from full-time politics. The King dismissed Melbourne in November. Peel took over as head of a minority Tory government in December. The King eagerly agreed to dissolve parliament, and the general election in January 1835 returned about a hundred more Tory MPs than before. This was a significant morale boost after the disaster of 1832 but it fell short of a majority. Peel resigned in April and the King was resentfully required to have Melbourne back. This little episode confirmed a dramatic decline in the powers of the monarch. No monarch would again dismiss a ministry. Royal will was not enough to sustain a government. On most matters, ministers could ignore it, albeit with tact and at least some show of deference.

Peel launched his election appeal in December 1834 with his 'Tamworth Manifesto'. This was the first direct national appeal for support from the party leader on the basis of stated policies.[6] Peel was increasingly describing his party as 'Conservative' rather than 'Tory'. He hoped that the new label would connote a party freed from the reactionary shackles of 'high' or 'Ultra' Toryism and not afraid to present sensible, and sometimes reformist, policies to the electorate. The aim was to 'conserve' the essentials: defence of the nation; financial stability; government in the hands of, and elected by, property owners; an established Church.

II. Whigs into Liberals? 1835–1841

Melbourne's ministry was significantly different from that of Grey. Whereas Grey led a coalition government, Melbourne's was indisputably Whig. It made accommodations with radical MPs, Dissenters and, increasingly as his majorities declined, with Irish MPs. The purpose of the so-called Lichfield House Compact of March 1835 between the Whigs and disparate anti-Tory elements was to ensure only that Peel's government was turned out. It did not presage a new coalition. For many voters, especially in the shires, Melbourne's willingness to consort with radicals and Irishmen was sufficient evidence of unfitness to govern. This was a factor in his declining majorities of 1835 and 1837 as well as in Peel's victory of 1841. Melbourne's government, however, was dominated by Foxite Whigs. Lansdowne remained Lord President of the Council, Lord John Russell was promoted to Home Secretary and Palmerston remained as Foreign Secretary. New ministers, including Thomas Spring Rice, the Marquis of Normanby and Viscount Howick, now held important positions.

The dominant figure in the Commons was Russell, a Bedford, one of the bluest-blooded of all the aristocratic Whig families. True to Whig traditions, Russell believed in reforms which secured the liberties of the people and conduced to their well-being. He co-operated with Dissenters and introduced important educational initiatives in both England and Ireland. These would have included a rates-supported national system of state education but, influenced by the furious lobbying of the numerous religious societies, Melbourne blocked the idea. Not for the last time sectarian priorities determined the direction of education. Russell had to settle for the establishment in 1839 of a Privy Council Committee to administer state grants and inspect the schools thus supported.[7] Russell also supported appropriation as a means of creating a better-educated Irish population, with Catholics educated alongside Protestants. Although Russell was heavily criticised for permitting Daniel O'Connell to dictate terms, by the 1840s, almost 400,000 children were being educated in more than 3,000 schools via what amounted to an Irish national education system.[8]

Newspapers increasingly described Melbourne's party as the 'Liberals' (see Chapter 21). Thomas Spring Rice, who stated that he gloried in the legacy of Whig politics, argued in 1840 in the *Edinburgh Review* that the key attributes of a Liberal were toleration of diverse opinions and support for freedom of enquiry. Only if such attributes were to the fore could 'the sum of human virtue, happiness and freedom' be increased.[9] These were principles to which most eighteenth-century Whigs would happily have subscribed – however self-deludingly. Liberalism grew out of Whig attitudes and policies adapted to changed political circumstances.

Close relations with the Dissenters proved entirely compatible with the government's approval of reform proposals devised by senior bishops of the Church of England. Whigs were at one with Tories in believing that a strong Established

Church remained a stabilising force in a nation undergoing a process of rapid change. Thus, the Established Church Act (1836) standardised episcopal stipends at £4,000 a year, except for the five most senior bishoprics. Although the influence of the government of the day remained an important element in promoting clerics to bishoprics, a much larger number of bishops after 1840 began their careers near the bottom of the ecclesiastical ladder as parish priests, gaining on-the-ground experience before they moved up.[10] A Pluralities Act (1838) prohibited clergymen from holding two church 'livings' simultaneously if they were more than 10 miles apart and also restricted the clergy from engaging in trade or farming without specific episcopal permission. The Ecclesiastical Duties and Revenues Act (1840) abolished many non-resident cathedral appointments. The money saved augmented livings with low stipends and helped create new parishes. Only from the 1830s did a substantial church-building programme in the towns enable Anglicanism to compete with nonconformity. In the words of the Archbishop of Canterbury, it also placed the 'Church Establishment . . . in a condition to resist the attacks of its enemies'.[11] Between 1832 and 1851, more than 2,000 Anglican churches were built.[12] Perhaps of most practical value to English landowners, however, was the Tithe Commutation Act of 1836. This abolished payment of tithes in kind (see Chapter 7), substituting compulsory 'rent charges' which gave farmers and landowners much more incentive to invest in improvements. This Act removed one of rural society's festering sores.[13]

The promotion of reform increasingly became the responsibility of central government rather than, as before, backbenchers. From the 1830s, the increasing use of Royal Commissions 'as a characteristic forum for the shaping of social policy radically diminished the role of the back-bench reformer, thus signalling a significant decline in the influence of the Commons in the development of social legislation'.[14] This was the great decade of evidence collection. Those wishing to influence legislation needed to turn themselves into fact-grubbers. A welter of statistical societies sprang up to help them in their task.[15]

Melbourne's government passed many substantial and significant reforms. Its Achilles heel, however, was fiscal policy and here Peel excelled. Benign Whig inaction sufficed in the mid-1830s when trade boomed and the government accumulated budget surpluses in excess of £1m a year. The situation changed radically from 1837 when a severe depression hit the manufacturing districts. Increased unemployment, and Chartism, followed (see Chapter 21). Compensation costs to West Indian plantation owners increased the deficit while unrest in Canada necessitated increased defence expenditure. The new Chancellor of the Exchequer, Sir Francis Baring, came from a banking family with strong links to the East India Company but he had little idea how to cope with the crisis. He noted wryly in 1839, 'We have everything except a revenue and a majority.'[16] He attempted to rectify the former by raising loans but was told by Melbourne and Russell that increased taxes were necessary. Little could be done about the latter, since the government had been dependent for its survival on radical or Irish votes since the 1837 election.

Till 1839, Peel had condescended to support Whig governments on measures he approved. As the government got into ever hotter water, and he glimpsed a return to office, that support became rarer. The budget of 1841 was critical. A parliamentary Select Committee investigating import duties recommended, and Baring consequently proposed, lower duties to promote export-led economic growth. He also included a proposal greatly to reduce tariff advantages enjoyed by colonial over foreign sugar traders. The Whigs also proposed, by revising the Corn Law, to reduce the level of protection for British farmers. Although many industrial towns welcomed this initiative since it promised cheap bread and growing prosperity, it was predictably hated in the shires. Baring's budget, savaged by Peel, was defeated and the government lost a subsequent confidence motion by one vote.

III. Peel as Prime Minister

The general election of 1841 was a triumph for the Conservatives. The mechanics of victory are more than usually significant since they help to explain Peel's travails towards the end of his ministry. Party allegiance, though hardening, was still far from precise, so the following figures are approximates. Still, their overall message is clear. Peel had an overall majority of more than seventy seats. This stretched to over a hundred in England and Wales (302 Tory; 198 Whig–Liberal) but his party was in a minority in both Ireland (43; 62) and Scotland (22; 31). Whig representation in the English counties almost disappeared (124; 20) but the party preserved its majority in the English boroughs (157; 170). In the largest boroughs, those with more than 2,000 electors, the Whigs won almost three times as many seats as the Tories (15; 43).[17]

These figures convey two important messages. First, the Tory victory was based on English county seats, where the Whigs reaped a bitter harvest from enfranchising tenants-at-will (see Chapter 21), who voted overwhelmingly for candidates of their landlords' choice.[18] Secondly, the Tories did best in boroughs where the electorates were smallest and least changed by the Reform Act. However, they also did well in some of the largest ports, especially London, Liverpool and Hull, where the views of overseas traders were strong and generally favoured continued protection. The conclusion is clear. Peel had won the election because economic circumstances were unfavourable and the Whig government's economic policies uncertain. Behind this bland conclusion, however, lies a brutal reality. The Tories won because voters believed that Peel was the safer bet to maintain agricultural and other forms of trade protection. Unsurprisingly, the majority of his parliamentary colleagues were also fiercely protectionist.

Peel was not. His political views had matured under Liverpool and the so-called liberal Tories in the 1820s (see Chapter 17). His view was that ministers should provide strong government in the national interest, recognising that they were discharging duties and responsibilities given to them by their Sovereign. Government should also be efficient and 'clean'. Effective public service entailed earning and retaining public trust. Like Pitt and Liverpool before him, he believed that those who sought government appointments should be actuated by disinterested motives. He was concerned that most applicants for government posts made 'unreasonable demands' and 'exaggerated pretensions for office'.[19] If he were finally to scotch accusations of waste and 'Old Corruption' such as those still being made by the Chartists in the early 1840s, it was necessary to demonstrate that the government was effective, efficient and, above all, fair.

In essence, Peel governed in the 'liberal Tory' tradition of the 1820s, but this was no easy task. His government lacked experienced talent. Leading liberal Tories, notably Canning and Huskisson, were dead. Others, like Lansdowne and Palmerston, having left Peel and Wellington in 1827–28 to join the Whigs (see Chapter 17), never returned. Others again, notably the Earl of Ripon, were in decline. Peel had to appoint and nurture his own new 'men of business', mostly from the junior ranks. Stanley was able and experienced, but he was Colonial Secretary. Since Jamaica and Canada remained disturbed, his was a full-time job and not at the core of domestic policy-making.[20] In any case, Peel never quite trusted Stanley's independence of mind. Sir James Graham, promoted Home Secretary by Peel, was loyal and immensely efficient, although insensitive to the fall-out from attacking local magistrates for not dealing sternly enough with Chartist disturbances in 1842 (see Chapter 21). Graham shared his leader's distaste for the immutably reactionary attitudes of so many of the party's backbenchers. The future 'Peelites' – Gladstone and Aberdeen among them – were able and ambitious, but they could not yet punch their full weight within the Conservative party.

It was also clear that the majority of the party was ill-disposed towards liberal Toryism anyway. Most backbenchers retained their strong 'Ultra' Tory links, renewed by frequent engagement with equally reactionary constituents. They believed that the land was the property which mattered most and, mattering most, needed constant nurture and unwavering Protection.

The inherent tensions between Peel and his backbenchers were initially assuaged by the soothing balm of election victory. Peel used what was to prove a short honeymoon by initiating measures to improve public finances. By the beginning of 1842, the government's overall financial deficit stood at £7.5m, with the annual deficit accumulating at an unsustainable £2.4m. The government's 1842 budget – nominally the responsibility of Henry Goulburn as Chancellor of the Exchequer but in practice the work of Peel – cut duties on imported raw materials and on manufactured goods even more. While the 1828 sliding scale of duties on corn imports was retained, the level of duty was rather more than halved. All of this represented both a continuation of Huskissonite policies (see Chapter 17) and a substantial lurch in the direction of free trade. Peel also succeeded where Liverpool had failed in 1816 (see Chapter 16) by imposing the first income tax in time of peace. Tight control was maintained over all Treasury expenditure, and Peel reaped the benefits of the return of commercial prosperity in 1843. The first government surplus for almost a decade was achieved in 1844 and Peel used its psychological impact to produce a radical budget in 1845. This removed all export duties on British manufactured goods, and from more than four hundred imported articles, including all raw materials. Income tax, presented in 1842 as a temporary expedient to reduce the deficit, was extended for three more years, even though the government was in surplus.

Economic recovery was to be secured by what Peel, who vividly recalled both his role in returning the currency to the gold standard in 1819 and the banking disasters of 1825–26 (see Chapter 17), considered long-delayed reforms to the banking system. The answer was a strict monetarist policy. In introducing the Bank Charter Act in 1844, he referred to his part in 're-establishing the ancient standard of value' in 1819 and the 'great personal satisfaction' he would take in carrying the present measure into law a quarter of a century later. It would guarantee the permanence, stability and practicality of a system grounded in strict monetary discipline.[21] The Act limited the note-issuing powers of the Bank of England to the value of its bullion reserves and other securities. The right of some four hundred joint-stock and country banks to issue their own **promissory notes** was severely curtailed before being phased out. Newly established banks were not allowed to issue them at all. Over time, the Bank of England gained a monopoly over note issues. The government retained the power to suspend operation of the Act at times of financial crisis. It was used as early as 1847, when 'railway mania' drained the Bank of cash and Lord John Russell authorised it to increase note issues beyond the agreed limit. The Act was suspended again during the crises of 1857 and 1866.

Promissory banknotes

Bank of England notes include the phrase, albeit in minuscule print, 'I promise to pay the bearer on demand the sum of . . .'. This means that the owner of the note has the right to demand the value of the note from the Bank. Peel was attempting in 1844 to stop the practice of banks issuing notes which, collectively, exceeded the value of the bullion (precious metals, usually gold and silver) they kept in their vaults.

IV. Catholics, free trade, and the fall of Peel

Financial rehabilitation was one thing, and Peel managed it brilliantly. His successes in trade liberalisation, which had lasting effects, represent the strongest case for seeing this as 'the age of Peel'. Free trade, though, split his party. Tariff reductions in 1842 lost Peel his only 'high Tory' Cabinet member, the Duke of Buckingham. Peel, having nodded cursorily in the direction of coalition government in 1841, nodded its main symbol farewell with no regret. The Bank Charter Act of 1844 caused unease among Tory-supporting London financiers but the backbenchers generally approved of policies aimed at 'sound money'. Much more serious was the backbench rebellion in support of Lord Ashley's motion in 1844 for a maximum ten-hour working day (see Chapter 26), which Peel opposed. In the same year, more than sixty Conservatives opposed the government reduction of import duties on sugar produced in non-slave colonies. Backbenchers saw this as another assault on the colonies. In both cases, Peel got his way not by persuasion but by threatening to resign. In truth, he felt little but contempt for that majority of his parliamentary party – 'superficial and irresponsible observers' he called them – which had not been trained in the arts of government and who lacked the 'more extensive information and deeper insight' reserved to himself and his acolytes.[22]

Worse was to follow in 1845. In response to renewed disturbances in Ireland, Peel continued to woo the Irish middle classes to support for the Union. He tripled the grant to the Catholic seminary at Maynooth and made it a permanent charge on the Exchequer. This split the Conservative benches almost equally. One of the rising stars of the Cabinet, William Gladstone, also resigned. The High Tory Sir Robert Inglis objected, with characteristically self-righteous volubility, to endowing the Church of Rome with cash taken from the pockets of God-fearing Anglican taxpayers. Even the ultra-loyal Graham felt constrained to tell Peel that 'our party is shivered and angry and we had lost the slight hold we ever possessed over the hearts and kind feelings of our followers'.[23] Peel, secure in the knowledge that the Liberals would certainly vote for the measure, pressed ahead. This was the clearest signal yet that, when push came to shove, he favoured his version of principle over party interest.

The proposal to repeal the Corn Laws in 1845–46 provided the most mightily Wagnerian of shoves. This peculiarly Conservative *Götterdämmerung* brought its recently completed Valhalla of majority government crashing down, with more than a hundred collective Brünnhildes flinging themselves loyally onto Peel's funeral pyre. Among them was the returning Gladstone, who supported trade liberalisation as fervently as he was suspicious of Catholics. The Ring of Free Trade was indeed preserved, but it was returned to the care of Lord John Russell, the Marquess of Lansdowne and Viscount Palmerston, an unlikely trio of Rhinemaidens heading a new Liberal government (see Chapter 30).

Peel favoured repeal because he believed that free trade was the appropriate policy for an executive government bent on aiming to increase the prosperity of the British people. This had been his view since at least 1843. Perhaps he delayed Corn Law repeal, hoping that returning prosperity would appease his backbench critics. More likely he waited until some of the steam had gone from that most effective of extra-parliamentary pressure groups, the Anti-Corn Law League (see Chapter 26).[24] In either event, party considerations assumed secondary importance. Having lost Stanley to resignation at the end of 1845, and knowing that the Liberals were securely in the free-trade camp, he attempted to persuade his political opponents to take office and secure repeal. When Lord John Russell, foreseeing the public immolation which awaited his opponents, unsurprisingly declined the offer, Peel proved 'more than ready to relish a second dose of martyrdom'[25] (see Chapter 20). He felt himself now 'liberated politically . . . from the trammels of party'[26] and ploughed on. He braved both the withering and cynical sarcasm of Benjamin Disraeli, that new scorpion of the Tory backbenches, who denounced 'the huckstering tyranny of the Treasury bench',[27] and the more heartfelt contempt of Lord George Bentinck, son of the fourth Duke of Portland and fanatic of the Turf, who, in April 1846, dragged himself away from the horses long enough to take up the cudgels for the Protectionist backbenchers and drive the final nails into Peel's coffin. Several commentators felt that it should not have come to this. Charles Arbuthnot, close friend of the Duke of Wellington, thought that 'had Sir Robert been more conciliatory to his supporters & more confidential to them, none of the evil would have occurred'.[28]

The crucial Commons vote in May 1846 produced a pro-Repeal majority of 98. Of course, for Peel's political future, most of his supporters were on the wrong side of the political fence. Liberals and other radicals supported Peel by 235 votes to 10; his own side voted against him by 241 votes to 114. The next month, defeated on a Coercion Bill for Ireland, he resigned immediately. He would not return to office again.

Section 4

A Mature Industrial Society, *c*1850–1914

Children in their first year of formal education at Walton Lane School, Liverpool, *c*1910

Source: thislife pictures/Alamy

This photograph shows small children sitting in a classroom. Notice the neat clothing which most of the children are wearing and the fact that they are sitting in rows. Some of the children are smiling but the picture conveys an overall impression of order and discipline. Thousands of children who had experienced no formal education before 1870 were now being taught in schoolrooms like this. State involvement in the provision of education grew significantly in the second half of the nineteenth century, particularly though the building of so-called 'Board Schools' (Chapter 29). The education provided was mostly basic and it did depend upon 'rote-learning' in usually large classes. The development of state education does, however, indicate that in the second half of the nineteenth century, the state acknowledged a responsibility to fund basic services such as education and poverty relief. In both of these areas, provision was limited and, especially in the case of poverty, available only on terms which most of the recipients found humiliating. The Victorians drew a stricter line than the tangled and complex evidence warranted between the 'deserving' and the 'undeserving' poor (Chapter 28) and maintained the distinction with considerable severity. The state was nevertheless spending much more on what might be called 'social provision' in 1900 than in 1850. Central government expenditure on education, for example, rose from £0.75m in 1870 to £7m in 1895. As the experience of other societies which industrialised later also indicates, such expenditure was characteristic of states as they entered into a more mature industrial phase.

The phrase 'mature industrial society' implies an economy with a wide range of industrial activity and a growing financial sector to fund investment and stimulate economic expansion. In Britain, the most immediately recognisable feature of Britain's economy is the rapid expansion of metals-based industrial production and the further development of a mining industry to provide the fuel, not least for railway construction. Chapter 23 evaluates the success of the British economy during the so-called 'Great Victorian Boom', while Chapter 24 explains the social changes which took place during a period of rapid economic expansion. Chapter 25 examines what it meant to be a British citizen in the mid-Victorian period and how aspirations, not least for women, needed adjustment in the bigger, more complex and generally more prosperous society which was being created in industrial Britain. Chapter 27 offers a judgment on how far contemporaries were correct to judge that, after 1880, Britain was entering a period of relative decline in the face of industrial and other forms of competition from Germany and the United States.

Despite increased social provision, state expenditure in this period fell as a proportion of Britain's Gross National Product. One reason for this was the dominance in mid-Victorian Britain of the doctrine of *laissez-faire*, which implied greater freedom from state intervention for manufacturers, traders and bankers. Chapter 26 explains how this dominance was achieved and examines the extent to which British prosperity was dependent upon policies of free trade rather than protection in the form of tariffs and other trading restrictions. This chapter also examines the changing role of the state, while education and poverty relief are treated in Chapters 28 and 29 as case studies which help to exemplify the nature of this change.

23

A 'Second Industrial Revolution'?:
British economic performance,
*c*1850–*c*1880

I. A stable economy

The story of British economic performance during the nineteenth century used to be simple. The first half of the century was characterised by revolutionary growth, fuelled by rapid increases in output, particularly in the textile industry, but punctuated also by significant slumps. These were often accompanied by popular protest, including riots. From 1850, Britain entered a period of smoother, though still substantial, growth. Employment was more secure and living standards rose. Popular protest was much less frequent in consequence. This was the 'Great Victorian Boom' and it lasted until 1873. Thereafter, growth rates fell; Britain felt the ever keener winds of foreign competition and lost its industrial lead. Worse, important sectors of the economy, particularly agriculture, endured a slump. The so-called 'Agricultural Depression' lasted until 1896.

Revisionism has radically altered this picture, just as it has produced a more nuanced picture of the first wave of industrial growth (see Chapter 5). We should use the phrase 'Victorian Boom' to describe economic performance in the 1850s and 1860s with care. The balance of statistics suggests consolidation rather than massive expansion. Indeed, annual growth rates were beginning to slacken by the 1850s. The changing balance of employment between agriculture and the manufacturing industries had begun much earlier. During the 1850s and 1860s, stability characterised the nature of Britain's exports. In 1830, 91 per cent of British exports were of manufacturing goods; the proportion was identical in 1870. Only the composition of the manufactures showed significant change. Whereas textiles had comprised 67 per cent of manufactured exports in 1830 and metals and engineering products only 11 per cent, the proportions were 56 per cent and 21 per cent respectively by 1870. Also, it was the mining, construction and metals industries which were expanding much more during the so-called 'Boom' than were manufacturing industries. The career of **Thomas Cubitt** pointed the way towards new forms of organisation and higher standards in the construction industry. The numbers employed in mining industries increased by 34 per cent in the period 1851–71, those in construction by 44 per cent and those in metals by 60 per cent. By contrast, the numbers in textiles grew by only 1 per cent.[1]

Thomas Cubitt, 1788–1855

Born near Norwich, the son of a carpenter, he became one of the most celebrated builders of the age. After training as a carpenter, he set up a building business in London in 1810. His main innovation lay in the direct employment of large numbers of craftsmen rather than, as had been the practice, negotiating with craftsmen to do short-term specific tasks. The Cubitts controlled the entire process. Cubitt employed architects, surveyors and lawyers, and his good relations with bankers enabled him to borrow at premium rates. He made his name on prestige building projects in fashionable London: for the Duke of Bedford in Bloomsbury in the 1820s and for Earl Grosvenor, Marquess of Westminster, in Belgrave and Eaton Squares. In the 1840s, he worked with Prince Albert on the reconstruction of Osborne House, on the Isle of Wight, which became a favoured royal residence. He was also involved in environmental improvement schemes, especially London's sewerage system, and in advocating better building practice in dwellings built for the poor.

The mean size of firms in Britain grew only slowly during the second half of the nineteenth century. The average number of employees in each cotton mill hardly rose at all between 1850 and 1880; engineering firms also remained predominantly small scale. The hundred largest manufacturing firms produced 10 per cent of total manufacturing output in 1800, a proportion which had risen only to 16 per cent by 1909. The application of steam power also proceeded slowly. More than half of the output of steam power was still being used in textile factories as late as 1870.[2] Likewise, the population of Victorian towns and cities grew very fast (see Chapter 24) but most Victorian towns were not dominated by huge commercial enterprises, or even by 'big government'. As Martin Daunton has put it, 'The economy of Victorian cities was dominated by small-scale units, owned by families or partnerships, whose success depended on the creation of trustworthiness and a reputation for probity in order to secure credit.'[3] This was why social networking via church, chapel and membership of a wide range of clubs and societies was so important.

II. The service sector

Perhaps the most dramatic change in the 1850s and 1860s concerned the **service sector** of the economy. Services represent the leading sector of what we might call the second industrial revolution. The service sector is very diverse. It includes railway engine drivers and domestic servants, surgeons and museum curators, policemen and bankers, civil servants and music hall entertainers. What all these occupations have in common, apart from inclusion within a necessarily abstract definition, is that demand for the services they provide tends to grow alongside the increasing wealth, diversity and complexity of a given society. As the United Kingdom became a wealthier, and arguably more unequal, society during the first half of the nineteenth century, its overall demand for services increased. Technological developments obviously played a part. By 1900, the service sector included typists, telephonists and car salesmen. However, the growth of service occupations during the second half of the century was a direct reflection of overall growth in the first half. On one set of calculations at least, the service sector is also considerably more efficient than either the agricultural or the manufacturing sectors. In 1851, it was more than twice as productive as either agriculture or manufacturing. By the end of the nineteenth century, it was still 40 per cent more productive than manufacturing and 60 per cent more than agriculture.[4]

Service sector

That part of the economy related to the provision of services rather than the production of manufactured goods. The term covers work in education, health, utilities such as gas and water, in the retail trades and also in administration and management. It is sometimes known as the 'tertiary sector' to distinguish it both from a 'primary sector' covering agriculture, mining and fishing and a 'secondary sector' which is involved in manufactures.

The service sector made an immense contribution to the expansion of the job market in the middle of the nineteenth century. Much the largest single occupation was that of domestic service. About 853,000 men and women were so described in the 1851 census. By 1871, the number had grown to 1,341,000, an increase of 57 per cent. Reflecting an already well-established middle-class passion for shopping, the retail sector also grew rapidly. Almost a million were employed in it in 1871, an increase of 47 per cent in twenty years. Most shops were small and independently owned, but some, such as the drapery firm of Shoolbred and Company who traded in London's Tottenham Court Road, had an annual turnover of about £1m and employed 500 workers.[5]

The numbers working in transport and communication sectors increased from 356,000 in 1851 to 556,000 in 1871, an increase of 56 per cent. The iconic transport workers were, of course, the railway labourers, the so-called 'navvies' who did back-breaking work at high speed to create the world's first railway network. During the railway boom of the 1840s, about 180,000 navvies were employed in the construction of the new 'iron roads'.[6]

Too much economic quantification relates to products bought and sold and to profits made. Not enough attention has been paid to the, admittedly more complex, issue of the contribution made by the service sector to the economy as a whole. If the service sector is given appropriate weight, then part of the difficulty involved in determining whether or not there was a 'mid-Victorian boom' disappears. In reductively quantitative terms, however, the extent to which textile production and exports weight the overall index does matter. As Hoppen notes, 'It was the comparatively slow growth rates in the textile, iron and coal industries during the half century after 1850, not much faster rates in, for example, land and sea transport, which dominated economic performance generally.'[7]

Smaller increases were recorded for those working in education, mostly, of course, teachers. Their numbers increased from 90,000 to 127,000 (41 per cent) between 1851 and 1871. The County and Borough Police Act of 1856 required the establishment of professional police forces in both counties and boroughs for the first time. It is, therefore, unsurprising that the number of policemen went up from 107,000 in 1851 to 172,000 in 1871, an increase of 61 per cent.[8]

III. Imports and exports

British economic performance in the middle years of the nineteenth century should be assessed against the enormous growth of worldwide international trade. It is an interesting paradox that the value of UK exports during the first period of factory-based production was not particularly high. Their average annual value (calculated over five-year cycles) was never less than £35.9m (in 1826–30) or more than £42.9m (in 1811–15). Price inflation affects these figures, and helps to explain the odd maximum value during the period of Napoleon's economic blockade (see Chapter 13). However, it does not explain away the significant growth in trade values after the mid-1830s. The value of exports increased to £49.8m by 1840 and continued to rise dramatically. During the 'boom' of the 1850s and 1860s, export values increased by 111 per cent, more than at any other period. The biggest change in the export portfolio was the export of iron and steel goods. In the 1830s, about 180m tons were exported. By 1870, this had leapt to 1,781m tons. The five-year average of export values stood at £239.5m in the early 1870s, after which there was further stagnation until the early twentieth century. Not surprisingly, the relative importance of foreign trade grew *vis-à-vis* national income from about 10 per cent in the 1830s to 27 per cent in the 1860s.[9]

The value of imports, largely of raw materials, always exceeded that of exports. In the 1850s, 1860s and 1870s, the average deficit on exports was £60.6m. In 1855, almost a quarter of all the goods and food consumed in Britain was imported.[10] The size of that deficit had reached £124.5m by the late 1870s. Never again before the First World War would the deficit stand at less than £100m. Part of the explanation lies in Britain's growing wealth and its increasing desire, and ability, to consume the exotic and the luxurious. On a more mundane level, Britain's population was continuing to increase, although at a rather slower rate than during the first half of the century, and British agriculture was rarely productive enough or, from the 1870s onwards, competitive enough to feed its own.

Overseas trade contributed to Britain's prosperity not because of the movement of goods in and out but because of 'invisibles': shipping credits, the insurance of goods, banking charges and the like. Thanks to the efficiency, and in some cases audacity, of Britain's insurance and banking systems, the invisibles were always in credit. They more than wiped out adverse trade balances. British banks adopted a generally conservative approach to funding entrepreneurial investment. Less than 20 per cent of money raised in the City of London between 1865 and 1914 for investment in Britain went to entrepreneurs. In the wake of four significant bank crashes in 1847, 1857, 1866 and 1878, banks became increasingly risk-averse. The 1878 crash, precipitated by the failure of the City of Glasgow Bank, had repercussions across Britain. Two banks in the south-west of England failed within months; others reduced their liabilities and the Bank of England was called upon as lender of last resort.[11] Banking amalgamations were common. More than four hundred banks in the mid-1850s had been reduced to seventy by 1914. Since most British businesses were relatively small-scale, their owners tended to be every bit as risk-averse as the banks, particularly if applying for large investment loans involved loss of the independence of family-owned firms.[12]

IV. The impact of railways

The most dramatic structural development of this period was the creation of a railway network. The first lines were constructed in the late 1820s and the first line between major towns was from Liverpool to Manchester, opened to traffic in September 1830. The first 'railway mania', involving huge levels of speculative investment, occurred in 1839–40. It was followed by others in 1847 and 1865–66. On occasion, railway construction absorbed almost 5 per cent of national income. Demand for investment was so great that provincial stock exchanges were set up in Liverpool, Manchester, Leeds, Glasgow and Edinburgh in the 1830s and 1840s. Railway manias substantially increased the number of middle-class shareholders in mid-nineteenth-century Britain.

By 1850, with more than 6,000 miles of track laid down, the mainline network was already virtually complete and 67m passenger journeys a year were being made. Passenger numbers continued to grow at nearly 7 per cent a year as the track extended to link rural areas and smaller market towns. Passenger journeys increased almost fivefold between 1850 and 1870 and track miles totalled 13,500.[13] This was a formidable engineering achievement both in terms of administration and the technical expertise required to construct bridges, cuttings and tunnels. Railway engineers such as **I. K. Brunel** were widely feted and the success of railway construction seemed perfectly to epitomise the early Victorian ideal of progress.

Isambard Kingdom Brunel, 1806–1859

Born at Portsea near Portsmouth, the son of the engineer Marc Isambard Brunel, he was an apprentice under his father, who was working on Rotherhithe, the first tunnel under the Thames, which eventually became a part of the London underground system. He became engineer to the Great Western Railway in 1833, developing the 'broad gauge' system. He also designed, but did not build, the Clifton Suspension Bridge in Bristol. From 1836, his main interest lay in ships. He pioneered the *Great Western* steamship, which could carry a full load of coals across the Atlantic. He also designed the 'screw propeller' to replace paddle-ship design for the *Great Britain*, the first large iron ship, which was launched in 1843. He designed the *Great Eastern* for voyages to India and the Far East under steam propulsion. It was launched in 1858 and became the largest ship of the age but it was never a commercial success. He was the most fertile, and high-profile, engineer of the Victorian era and was engaged on a range of other projects, including the Great Exhibition of 1851 and work on both gun technology and hospital construction.

Railway construction stimulated other industries, most notably iron. In 1848, about 40 per cent of domestic iron production was used in railway construction.[14] Railways created entire new towns. Crewe emerged from the village of Monks Coppenhall to service the London and North Western Railway. Its population grew from 4,000 to 18,000 in the twenty years 1851–71. Swindon had a similar relationship with the Great Western and its population grew sixfold in the period 1841–71.[15]

The railway phenomenon was by no means casualty-free. Wholly dependent on private capital, railway companies were vulnerable to competition, to trade downswings and to fraud. Accidents to railway construction workers were distressingly frequent. Competition killed railway companies which proved less efficient than others operating on similar routes. Amalgamations were frequent. By 1871, twenty-eight companies controlled 80 per cent of the track.[16] Some railway entrepreneurs sailed very close to the wind – none more so than the so-called 'railway king', George Hudson (1800–71). He used an inherited fortune to invest in railway development from the early 1830s. By the mid-1840s, he owned roughly half of the track in Britain, with a virtual monopoly over railway transport in the Midlands and North-East. He was not scrupulous in his reporting to shareholders, however, and fraudulently traded the shares of companies he controlled. By 1849, most of his fortune was gone. *The Times* newspaper bemoaned the consequences of unbridled capitalist activity: 'a system without rule, without order, without even a definite morality'.[17]

Transport developments provided a huge stimulus for both iron and mining industries. Engineering and machine-tool companies began to proliferate in larger cities from the 1840s. The inventions of **James Nasmyth** facilitated the construction of ever larger ships. Between 1840 and 1870, the tonnage of British-built ships increased by more than 180 per cent. The Crimean War (see Chapter 34) boosted the armaments industry. Specialist metal towns developed more quickly from the

1840s onwards. The combination of iron, coal and water in effect created Middlesbrough in England's North-East. The extension of the pioneer Stockton–Darlington railway to Middlesbrough in 1833 encouraged dock construction to transport coking coals from the pit villages of nearby County Durham. Iron ores were discovered in the Eston Hills, just south of Middlesbrough, in 1850 and pig-iron production in the town began almost immediately when an iron foundry was established by the partnership of Henry Bolckow and John Vaughan. Bell Brothers, mineowners who established ironstone mines locally, became the largest employers in the town. Middlesbrough, a town of 6,000 people in 1841, had expanded to 40,000 by 1871 and 70,000 by 1891. By 1871, the town was producing almost a third of Britain's pig iron.[18]

James Nasmyth, 1808–1890

Born in Edinburgh, the son of a portrait artist, much training for his subsequent career as a mechanical engineer came unofficially from observing work in an iron foundry. He went to London in 1829 and worked as an assistant to the engineering toolmaker Henry Maudslay. He established an iron foundry at Patricroft, near Manchester, in 1836. His best-known invention was the steam hammer, which he made in response to a request from Brunel in 1839 for a huge paddle-shaft to fit into his steamship *Great Britain*. He made his hammer self-acting, which proved a commercially important refinement to the process. The hammer made Nasmyth's fortune. He retired in 1856 and pursued hobbies in astronomy and photography.

Steel had been produced in low quantities in small furnaces before the 1850s. Production technology was revolutionised, first by **Henry Bessemer**'s converter (1856) and then by William Siemens's open-hearth furnace in the mid-1860s. These inventions enabled the mass production of steel to begin. Steel is a stronger, less brittle and more malleable metal than iron. Because of this, railway companies increasingly converted to using steel rails and mild steel plates were incorporated into ship-building. Between 1870 and 1890 the production of steel quadrupled.

Henry Bessemer, 1813–1898

Born in Hertfordshire, the son of an engineer and engraver who had fled to England from the French Revolution, Henry's education incorporated much practical experience in his father's workshop. He was responsible for two important innovations, the use of perforated, and timed, date-stamps in 1833 and the so-called 'Bessemer Converter'. This converter blew air through molten pig iron to produce a metal called 'mild steel' which proved superior to iron and much cheaper than tool steel. Its widespread use as a building material for railways, ships, bridges and other forms of engineering from 1860 transformed the construction industry. It enabled Sheffield, where Bessemer established his own company, to become the steel capital of the world. After further technological refinements, Bessemer steel production reached 1m tons a year by 1880 and 2m by 1890.

V. Agriculture and high farming

Did agriculture experience a 'great Victorian boom'? Most landowners had fiercely opposed the repeal of the Corn Laws (see Chapter 22). Those doughty reactionary Dukes, and erstwhile Cabinet members, Richmond and Buckingham placed themselves at the head of a Central Agricultural Protection Society in February 1844 to counter anti-landlord propaganda from the Anti-Corn Law League. It was soon known as the 'Anti-League' and it did a fair job of uniting landowners and tenant farmers behind continued Protection. Throughout the shires, apocalyptic messages circulated, bemoaning the imminent destruction of the landed interest. Richmond told the Lords that repeal would 'shake the very foundations of the throne . . . cripple the Church . . . endanger our institutions, and convert our hitherto happy and contented people . . . into . . . misery and wretchedness'.[19] Backbench squires representing rural seats in the Commons, such as the romantic, patriotic Middlesex landowner Charles Newdegate (North Warwickshire) and William Miles (East Somerset), pressed home the so-called 'Anti-League' message and helped to solidify the Tory rural interest against Peel.

The Protectionists lost in 1846 but the heavens did not fall. Instead, British agriculture experienced a period of a quarter century or so generally known as '**high farming**'. Arable farming continued to prosper in the 1850s and 1860s because little surplus grain was waiting to flood into Britain from Europe. European populations were also increasing; supplying continental domestic markets was profitable enough for large granaries being developed in Germany and Russia. Also, the American Midwest was not yet fully developed or geared towards the mass export of grain. Wheat imports did increase, especially in the 1860s, but domestic production was two and a half times greater and, critically for British farmers, wheat prices remained stable.[20]

High farming

This phrase has been used to describe the period, from the later 1840s to the early 1870s, when British farming experienced good harvests, secure prices and investment in agricultural improvements. The main areas of improvement were: drainage; the addition of phosphate fertilisers; artificial feed for animals; and the increased use of farm machinery.

Perhaps the most important aspect of high farming was investment in drainage. As part of the package of measures linked to the repeal of the Corn Laws, Peel had introduced a loan scheme to finance the drainage of cold, stiff lands, which were plentiful, especially in the arable east of England. Land could be drained at an average cost of about £3 an acre and, for many farmers, this proved a wise investment indeed.[21] High farming also involved greater investment both in fertilisers and in the import of food for stock, enabling a larger number of animals to be kept per acre. This, in turn, generated more animal dung for use in increasing the fertility of arable soil.[22] As living standards improved for the lower middle classes and artisan-craftsmen, so their consumption of meat increased and diets became more varied, nutritious and appetising. Pastoral farming became more profitable as meat prices rose.[23] Market gardening also flourished as producers used railways to transport fruit and other perishable goods more quickly to urban markets.[24] Some economic historians have doubted whether the considerable investment which went into agriculture in the 1850s and 1860s reaped the anticipated rewards. Wheat yields failed to reach the peak yield of 30 bushels per acre achieved in the 1840s.[25] Against this, overall agricultural productivity did increase, although less in Ireland than in Britain. The trend towards pastoral farming was not only managed efficiently but proved vital for the agricultural sector as a whole during the so-called 'Great Depression' (see Chapter 27). Agricultural developments during the period of high farming were broadly successful.

The quantitative indicators suggest that the description 'a second industrial revolution' for developments in this period is overdone. The 1850s and 1860s were a period of consolidation rather than revolution, although they would hardly have seemed so to those caught up in the massive expansion of the metals and transport industries. From the perspective of contemporaries, also, this was welcome consolidation. The period confirmed Britain as the world's leading trading nation and it was now less disturbed by slumps and their attendant social dislocations. It may be better to leave angels-on-a-pinhead debates about what qualifies as a boom – or a slump – to econometricians. They now have access to formidable number-crunching techniques. We should nevertheless remember that the mid-nineteenth-century data available to them is much less complete and reliable than are the means for measuring it.

24

....

Social structure and social change in a maturing economy

I. Urban communities

Although historians are now much more cautious than once they were about arguing that the Industrial Revolution led to the emergence of mutually antagonistic relations between social classes (see Chapter 8), there is no doubt that major changes in production techniques and the distribution of wealth generated substantial social change. When these changes are analysed from the perspective of social function within the overall system of production, then attention tends to focus on defined groups: landowners; owners of substantial capital, both industrial and commercial; small proprietors with limited capital (such as shopkeepers); and those who were employed, and mostly worked for wages. Alternatively, the emphasis can also be placed on differences in status, which are grounded in perceptions of where individuals fit within a given social hierarchy.[1] Neither categorisation is watertight but the latter is probably a more fruitful way of capturing the dynamics of social change.

The most important social change related to place. In 1851, for the first time, more than half of the population lived in towns with populations exceeding 10,000. Urban consolidation continued. The total urban population of England and Wales, just short of 10m in 1851, had grown to more than 25m by 1900.[2] Not surprisingly, town sizes increased. By 1901, almost a third of England and Wales's population lived in cities of more than 100,000 people and nearly 15 per cent lived in London. A similar concentration was observable in Scotland, 20 per cent of whose population lived in Glasgow.[3] By 1900, the largest cities were, in effect, conurbations whose commercial influence extended well beyond their borders. Distinctive civic pride apart, Salford, Bolton and Rochdale operated as satellite towns for Manchester. West Bromwich, Walsall and Dudley, in the heart of Staffordshire's Black Country, had a similar relationship with Birmingham. Such smaller communities tended to be more purely manufacturing communities. Many were based on a single industry – cotton manufacturing in Bolton, say, or iron working in Dudley. The biggest towns assumed the function, if never the title, of regional capitals incorporating a range of functions: commercial; centres for a range of social and intellectual activities; transport nodes.

The phrase 'urban dweller' needs greater clarification. Another key aspect of change in the second half of the nineteenth century was social stratification. The rapidity of urban growth from the 1820s precluded the kind of careful town planning which underpinned the development of eighteenth-century Bath, the redevelopment of

Edinburgh's 'new town' or even the layout of some of the new seaside towns. Birmingham housed 71,000 people in 1801 and 630,000 in 1901, by which time it was the second city of the United Kingdom. The pressure on urban space became intense, particularly with the rapid construction of tenements and other properties for occupation by working people, usually close to the place of work. The quality of construction in some places, like Ancoats in Manchester or Nechells in Birmingham, was so low that they qualified almost as purpose-built slums. Overcrowding, poor drainage and inadequate sewerage systems all combined to provide environmental degradation on a massive scale, generating exceptionally high death rates (see Chapter 28).

Such areas were occupied by those who could afford nothing better. Skilled craftsmen and other 'aristocrats' of labour could afford better, since they usually had stability of employment with wages and working conditions protected by small but effective craft unions. Employers could easily replace unskilled workers; they needed to keep hold of those with specialist skills. Workers had to pay higher rents to live in better-built properties with reliable access to a proper water supply. These were usually located a little further from the city centre. During the second half of the century, workers in regular employment enjoyed a modest improvement in housing standards as speculative builders kept pace with a somewhat slower rate of population increase. Improvements were generally less marked in the poorer areas of London and much of urban Scotland.[4] More occupiers were able for the first time to enjoy the luxury of rooms with specific purposes as bedrooms or kitchens.

A small minority did much better, thanks to the benevolence of paternalist employers. Titus Salt, the Congregationalist, built a model village community at Saltaire, near Shipley in West Yorkshire, from 1853 to provide superior accommodation for his workers to that available in nearby Bradford. At the end of the century, Cadbury, the Quaker chocolate manufacturers, created a model village at Bournville, four miles south-west of Birmingham. Their community stressed health and fitness for the workforce. Space for parks and recreation was a priority. In 1900, an independent Bournville village trust was established to develop the project by providing schools and a hospital.

Perhaps the most extensive experiment in factory paternalism was begun in 1888 by the soap manufacturer William Hesketh Lever. He created a model community for his employees at Port Sunlight, near Birkenhead on the Wirral peninsula, which included allotments and a cottage hospital. Though the new buildings were modern and well-equipped, Lever's stated aim was almost romantically old-fashioned. He stated that he 'wanted to socialize and Christianise business relations and get back to that close family brotherhood that existed in the good old days of hand labour'. Lever's Christianising mission was only a partial success but his factory community did provide a healthy working environment and, during a time of labour unrest nationally (see Chapter 40), a strike-free one. A dewy-eyed journalist in 1913 contrasted the dirt and grime of the typical northern factory town with Port Sunlight, where 'bright-faced girls in blue aprons and caps . . . make and pack soap in large airy rooms, dine for a few coppers in a great hall hung with beautiful pictures and after their day's work have the clubs, the gymnasium, the swimming bath, the halls, the museum, and the garden spaces . . . for their pleasure and their rest'.[5]

II. Landowners and middle classes

In the 1850s and 1860s the aristocracy was represented by not more than 2,000 titled families. They remained at the apex of society, their status still reflected at the highest political levels and their social influence unchallengeable, especially in England's broad acres. Whig aristocrats still played a leading role in Gladstone's reforming Liberal government of 1868–74 (see Chapter 31). It was not until the parliament elected in 1885 that the business and professional classes were in a majority. Even then, Lord Salisbury's third government, formed as late as 1895, was dominated by peers of the realm.

The ownership of land conferred greater status than any other property. Challenges to the hereditary principle were confined a small number of Liberal radicals and an even smaller number of socialists. Successful businessmen still sank significant chunks of their profits in purchasing landed estates (see Chapter 3). Not until the 1870s, when the agricultural depression began to eat into landed fortunes (see Chapter 27), were significant changes discernible. The value of arable land went down by more than 60 per cent between 1875 and 1910 and the value of arable output declined from £24m to £6m.[6] Even then the old social, and indeed school, ties retained their resonance. The aristocracy proved adept at diversifying beyond its agricultural portfolio, using social influence to maintain profitable connections with the City of London and make even more profitable marital links with eligible American heiresses.[7]

The aristocracy retained substantial economic interests in urban Britain, not least as developers, although increasingly they maintained a significant physical presence only in the fashionable quarters of London and then for just part of the year. A distinctive elite urban culture developed rapidly in the second half of the nineteenth century as business leaders and professional men associated in clubs, literary and philosophical societies and, with their wives, attended music clubs and concerts increasingly given by professional symphony orchestras. Local landowners could make a contribution to urban life. At the turn of the twentieth century, some were elected as mayors of major cities such as Liverpool and Preston.[8] Such men did not challenge urban culture; rather by their investments and their patronage they bought recognition from it.

Demographic urban dominance played a part in redefining the essence of a 'gentleman'. Landed values were grounded in inherited wealth, codes of honour and available leisure time. Leisure might be used purposefully, in high-level social networking and matchmaking at balls and weekend shooting parties where codes of 'polite' behaviour were observed and social obligations acknowledged. By the later nineteenth century, the criteria used to recognise a 'gentleman' had shifted to robust, and perhaps more puritanical, virtues: hard work, self-reliance and achievement. Victorian businessmen and higher professionals were expected to have lively, absorbent minds, and to put them to use outside the narrow frame of their trade or calling. Literary, Philosophical and Statistical Societies encouraged debate and reflection. They also facilitated the assimilation of, and selection from, those ever greater piles of knowledge which diligent research was making available to the curious mind. The Victorian ethic, of course, took it as read that wealth-creation benefited society as a whole since it increased job opportunities and advanced national prosperity.[9]

In the middle years of the nineteenth century, the proportion of the population considering itself 'middle class', or 'bourgeois' (see Chapter 4) increased substantially. This change reflected both the diversity of industrial and commercial activity in urban Britain and the ever-growing need for specialised financial, legal and educational services in a more wealthy and complex society. One calculation made on the basis of income in the late 1860s indicated that roughly 20 per cent of the population could be considered upper or middle class and 80 per cent 'working class'. Census evidence from 1911 suggested similar proportions. Both of these indicators understate women's involvement in the workforce. Many worked part-time in unskilled or semi-skilled occupations. They were frequently not recorded as 'employed' in census returns (see Chapter 25).[10] Had they been, then the proportion of the 'working class' indicated by these estimates would have been higher.

About four in five of the middle classes identified in the 1911 census worked in commerce and industry. Direct comparisons are not possible, but 'higher' or 'lower' professionals are likely to have been lower in numbers half a century earlier when employment opportunities in administration were more limited (see Chapter 26). From the 1830s, however, many professional organisations were established. Accountancy, engineering and surveying were particularly prominent. Such professional organisations defined and maintained standards and also regulated entry. The fastest growing profession in the later nineteenth century, and also the least socially exclusive, was school-teaching, reflecting both the growing involvement of the state in popular education and also the expansion of the so-called public schools (see Chapter 29). The number of schoolteachers identified in the census grew by 32 per cent in the 1850s and continued to increase significantly thereafter. The other rapidly increasing profession was dentists. Their numbers went up by 34 per cent in the 1850s, albeit from a very low base, and by 63 per cent in the 1900s.[11] Such increases are unusual. Although there was some acceleration after 1880, the numbers of the professionally qualified barely kept pace with the population as a whole.

The lower middle classes (or 'petit bourgeoisie') grew in numbers in the second half of the nineteenth century because of the growth of the service sector in the economy. Although clerks in legal and other professional firms were often in secure employment, albeit earning low wages, many in the lower middle classes were economically insecure. This was particularly true of small shopkeepers. The clientele of the proprietor of a 'corner shop' in urban Britain were usually the working classes. Corner shopkeepers usually calculated that they needed to offer credit, rather than requiring cash payment, when workers were on strike or vulnerable to dismissal during trade depressions. Small proprietors had little or no protection against bad debts. The risk of bankruptcy was high. The lower middle classes often adopted different lifestyles from the working classes, with whom they generally lived cheek-by-jowl. It is important to avoid crude stereotypes, since what follows is subject to numerous exceptions and the evidence is remarkably scanty anyway. Still, it is probably true that more petit bourgeois sought respectability through prudent habits and careful financial planning. They also emphasised the need to give their children a 'decent start' in life through 'a good education'. For many, leisure activities were more reflective, less boisterous and depended heavily on family participation.[12]

Not surprisingly, income inequalities within the middle classes are particularly striking. The survey from 1867 calculated 'large earnings' as £1,000 or more. This translates to £590,000 in early twenty-first-century earnings and included only about 5 per cent of the middle class. At this level, the income of the most successful bankers, overseas traders and factory owners overlapped that of the richest landowners. Indeed, many, like the MP James Morrison, proprietor of Morrison, Dillon and Co., whose immense fortune derived from haberdashery, bought land with their profits. On his death in 1857, he left about £5m – and a priceless collection of paintings. Richard Thornton, the son of a very modest yeoman farmer in Burton-in-Lonsdale, near the Yorkshire–Lancashire border, became one of the most successful insurance brokers of the age. His extensive international connections, especially via the Baltic Exchange with Russia, contributed to probate on his death in 1865 valued at £2.8m.[13]

The earnings of the great majority of the middle classes fell at the other end of the spectrum. About half of the middle classes earned less than £100 a year and did not qualify to pay income tax. Just over 40 per cent earned between £300 and £1,000 a year and did. These incomes are subject to considerable regional variation. In one-industry factory towns in the 1860s the proportion of male income taxpayers was usually less than 10 per cent. In provincial 'capitals' such as Manchester or Leeds, it was between 10 and 20 per cent, while in more prosperous environments, with a wealthy leisured class and a need for a variety of services, such as Brighton or Cambridge, it was over 20 per cent. Unsurprisingly, London had by far the highest proportion. About a third of its adult males were income tax payers.[14]

III. Bourgeois culture

The political influence of the upper bourgeoisie increased over the period. In most towns after the Municipal Corporations Act of 1835, its role in local affairs was decisive. Parliamentary representation also increased. In Lancashire, the textile capital of the world, only four Lancashire cotton employers had become MPs in the period

1800–31. In the years 1832–52, they provided twenty-four of the county's eighty-nine MPs, one more than the previously dominant landowners. Most of the remainder came from the professions or from commerce.[15]

Many successful self-made businessmen were dominant in the life of nineteenth-century towns, especially those in which one industry predominated. In the factory towns of Lancashire, the dominance of richer mill owners enabled them to act almost in the manner of country squires and lords of the manor.[16] They provided treats for their workers; they supported charities and enhanced their towns with legacies and bequests in the form of parks, statues, drinking fountains and other urban amenities. In return, they expected to have their own way on the big decisions.

The nineteenth-century bourgeoisie both cherished and enhanced the public face of their towns. They placed particular emphasis on display. Urban Britain competed fiercely throughout the nineteenth century to build the most architecturally distinguished and durable civic buildings. Perhaps the most eye-catching of all was the St George's Hall in Liverpool, almost twenty years in the planning. A public subscription list was opened in 1836 to fund a new concert hall for the town's triennial music festival and also to provide accommodation for large public meetings. It raised the equivalent of £1.75m in barely a year. The London architect Harvey Elmes designed the building, which also accommodated Liverpool's assize courts. The Hall was opened in 1854, to the approval – among others – of Queen Victoria, who opined that it was 'worthy of ancient Athens'. Birmingham's contribution to civic glory, its Town Hall, opened in 1834, was also classical, in the style of a Greek temple. Bolton's contributions, including its lion-guarded Town Hall (1873) and its solidly Gothic Fire Station (1899), were distinctive. Manchester's third, and most extravagant, Royal Exchange opened in St Ann's Square in 1874. It became the largest trading room in England but was soon vying for attention with the city's lavish Town Hall in Albert Square, designed by Alfred Waterhouse in thirteenth-century Gothic style (1887). Both buildings were considered appropriate adornments to Manchester's achievement of city status in 1854, the first non-cathedral town to be so honoured. A sense of civic pride, seemingly alien to the early twenty-first-century mind, demanded substantial investment.

Culture was also brought to Britain's great cities, partly as a means of making money, partly at the behest of a bourgeoisie keen to add lustre to their town's reputation. A group of city worthies came together to establish the Liverpool Philharmonic Society in 1840, from which grew the Royal Liverpool Philharmonic Orchestra, the oldest surviving symphony orchestra in Britain. Not to be outdone, the German-born conductor Charles Hallé formed what became Britain's first fully professional symphony orchestra in Manchester in 1857. Subscription to the Hallé concert series in the Free Trade Hall cost £1.[17] By the 1870s, London had five functioning symphony orchestras.

Libraries and art galleries reflected a similar culture of improvement. One case study indicates the interplay between wealthy citizens, the town council and parliament in passing 'enabling legislation' to support a major civic project. Liverpool's main art gallery began from the collection of paintings which a local businessman, William

Roscoe, was forced to sell when his business failed in the early nineteenth century. A purpose-built art gallery was erected in 1843 and seven years later a group of prominent citizens planned a combined museum, art gallery and library. An Act of Parliament sanctioned the project in 1852 and the benefaction of a successful local merchant, William Brown, encouraged the town council to bring the plans to fruition.[18]

IV. Working classes

About 80 per cent of adult males earned a living in the second half of the nineteenth century by manual labour. A smaller proportion worked in factories than might be thought, given the emphasis on mechanisation and other forms of technological change in standard accounts of the Industrial Revolution. Those employed in tailoring, shoe and umbrella manufacturing overwhelmingly worked by hand rather than by machine and in small workshops rather than factories. In 1851, they slightly outnumbered male workers in the textile industries. By 1891, tailors still outnumbered men working in the woollen trade.[19] At the same time, the average workshop was employing about thirty workers. British industry remained surprisingly small in scale.

Factory work in the textile industry was predominantly a female preserve, although the most skilled, and highly paid, jobs went overwhelmingly to men. More women were employed in tailoring and dressmaking than in cottons or woollens in 1851, though this conceals substantial regional variation. Most of the former were working in the south of England in small workshops, or at home. Most of the textile factory workers lived in the north, particularly in south and east Lancashire, the West Riding of Yorkshire and central Scotland.

Even in a rapidly expanding economy, women's work was being increasingly squeezed. Most of the new jobs in the second half of the nineteenth century were in metals, mines and transport (see Chapter 23). They generally required hard physical labour for which women were not suited. The most rapidly growing occupation for women was domestic service, especially in London. It has been estimated that more than 250,000 domestic servants worked in the capital in 1861. Five-sixths of them were women, mostly single, young and recent migrants.[20] Census evidence undoubtedly underestimates the extent of female participation in the workforce since many census enumerators were encouraged to disregard both part-time work and work done by women in the home (see Chapter 25).

Female participation in the workforce was predominantly supportive. Women workers earned less than men, and they were encouraged to think that their status as full-time workers would end on marriage or, at least, on the birth of the first child, which event usually occurred within, often substantially within, a year of marriage. There was, therefore, little incentive, and perhaps less opportunity, for women to acquire higher-order skills.

During this period, patterns of employment in the United Kingdom showed a decline in agriculture and textiles and a significant increase in heavy industry, transport and service industries. In Scotland, 25 per cent of employees were working in agriculture in 1851 but only 11 per cent in 1911. The change in textiles was from 20 per cent to 8. The proportion in the heavy industries rose from 8 per cent to 17 and in transport and other service industries from 20 per cent to 35.[21]

Skilled workers enjoyed a double advantage in the workforce over the unskilled or semi-skilled. In England and Wales in 1867, the net average earnings for skilled workers varied between £1 3s 0d (£1.15) and £1 8s 0d (£1.40) a week. For those with lesser skill, earnings varied between 17s 3d (£0.88) and week and £1.[22] Skilled workers were also much more likely to keep their jobs when trade was slack or depressed. Most were members of powerful craft unions and the wider culture militated against recent migrants being able to break into a heavily protected jobs market. In mining and textiles, where formal apprenticeships were rare, unions were usually able to maintain skill differentials by an effective form of 'succession planning'. They recruited younger and less skilled workers who would work alongside older, skilled men, learn their trade and replace them when the older men retired.[23] Skill differentials were effectively maintained down to the First World War.

Finally, did workers' living standards rise during the thirty or so years from the late 1840s to the early 1880s – a period during which overt and threatening social protest declined? Much more ink has been spilled on this question in respect of the first half of the nineteenth century (see Chapter 8). Even from 1850, the question will remain an open one because of data deficiencies. We cannot reliably compute the extent, and therefore the impact, of unemployment nationally, though unemployment levels varied from region to region as well as year to year. It has similarly proved difficult to judge whether, or by how much, employees worked longer hours in the nineteenth century than in the eighteenth. Perhaps hours of work were slightly fewer in the 1850s and 1860s than in the 1830s and 1840s. Workers in powerful trade unions, mostly the skilled, seem to have won some concessions from employers during the generally calmer economic waters of the 1850s and early 1860s. The most sophisticated computation of real wages, which includes an adjustment for unemployment, suggests a significant improvement in the period 1848–52 over that for 1843–47.[24] The improvement is sustained during the remainder of the 1850s and 1860s. However, it is noticeable that the most rapid rises in the index relate to the 1870s and early 1880s. This suggests that unambiguous improvements in living standards for the largest number of working people occur not when money wages go up but when, as happened for much of the 1870s and 1880s, prices – particularly of foodstuffs – drop significantly. Even then, more work on unemployment is necessary before we can confidently assert that, if we wait long enough (as those who lived through the period could not), the Industrial Revolution brought significant and long-term improvements both to the living standards and to the quality of life of most working people. As Professor Feinstein puts it: 'For the majority of the working class the historical reality was that they had to endure almost a century of hard toil with little or no advance from a low base before they really began to share in any of the benefits of the economic transformation they had helped to create.'[25]

25

Identities, aspirations and gender

I. Welsh identity

What, in the second half of the nineteenth century, did it mean to be British? On one level, it is an impossible question to answer, since every individual is likely to have a different answer. At the national level, where generalities may be less problematic, Britain comprises three nations with distinctive cultural identities (see Chapter 1). The Union with Ireland in 1801 has spawned no adjective. We do not speak of United Kingdom-ish traits and cultures. Quite apart from intrinsic linguistic awkwardness, it is appropriate that no such adjective exists. First, the Union between England and Ireland was never easy and usually fraught (see below and Chapters 14 and 40). Far more Irishmen spent the nineteenth century wishing to see the back of the Union than wished to see it work. Secondly, unlike England, Scotland and Wales, Ireland was predominantly Catholic and religious allegiance was a key component of identity.

One influential, if over-stated, interpretation holds that the Protestant religion forged a British nation during the frequent struggles against the 'Catholic other' – nearly always France[1] – in the eighteenth and early nineteenth centuries. The argument has plausibility but Britain had no unifying Protestant religion. The dominant Church was Anglican, England's Established Church. The Church of England was a political construct of the sixteenth century, its doctrinal flabbiness and internal inconsistencies the product of compromises fashioned in the reign of Elizabeth I. It had no purchase in Scotland, whose Episcopalian Church had bishops with broadly similar functions to those in England but which was not part of the Church of England. By the second half of the nineteenth century, religion was more a divisive than a uniting factor in the United Kingdom.

The Established Church's presence in Wales was limited, despite the presence of poorly financed and under-regarded bishoprics in St Asaph, St David's and Llandaff. Wales was a strongly nonconformist country. By the middle of the nineteenth century, it was predominantly Baptist and Methodist, although the Church of England remained the 'state Church' until a clearly overdue Disestablishment in 1920. During the second half of the nineteenth century, nationalist pressure built, with religion and language the main drivers for separation. When the Liberal Henry Richard was elected MP for Merthyr Tydfil in 1868, he asserted that 'the Nonconformists of Wales are the People of Wales'.[2] Welsh-language newspapers flourished and the chapel became an integral part of Welsh culture.

Language was also a divisive issue. English was the dominant language of the British Empire and Britain's cultural and political elite thought it anomalous, if not demeaning, that so many people in a nation forming part of the United Kingdom should not speak it. Perhaps three-quarters of the population of Wales in 1850 spoke Welsh as their dominant language. In rural Wales and the north the proportion was nearer to 90 per cent; many of these spoke no English. The elite responded by associating the Welsh language with 'backwardness'. A parliamentary commission on the state of education considered the Welsh language to be 'peculiar', isolating 'the mass from the upper portion of society'. The Welsh speaker 'is left in an under-world of his own, and the march of society goes so completely over his head that he is never heard of, except when the strange and abnormal features of a [religious] Revival, or a . . . Chartist outbreak, call attention to a phase of society . . . so contrary to all we experience elsewhere'.[3]

A reaction to this linguistic imperialism was inevitable. *Eisteddfodau* increased in number during the nineteenth century and cultural revival was rooted in the Welsh language. A Welsh Manuscripts Society, established in 1836, led to pressure for a university in Wales. The first University College opened at Aberystwyth in 1872 and the University of Wales, a federation of university colleges including both Cardiff and Bangor, received its royal charter in 1893.

Eisteddfod

A festival celebrating Welsh language, music and culture. After a long period in eclipse, the first attempt at revival occurred in 1792 when Edward Williams established a meeting of the 'Bards of Britain', held, perhaps incongruously, in Primrose Hill in London. A National Eisteddfod has been held at different Welsh venues every year, except 1914, since the gathering at Aberdare in 1861 established the modern pattern.

How much such cultural revivals were distinctively Welsh is open to doubt. Their impact was, at best, double edged. As one historian put it, the revival of Welsh may have excluded 'dangerous thoughts which English transmitted', but it was 'an English and largely middle-class-cum-populist-culture translated and transmuted . . . It locked Welsh up in a particular world which was rapidly becoming marginal.'[4] Friedrich Engels would have agreed. He argued that the English tolerated, and even celebrated, distinctive national characteristics in greater Britain because they 'know how to reconcile people of the most diverse races with their rule; the Welsh, who fought tenaciously for their language and culture, have become entirely reconciled with the British Empire'.[5]

The revival of Welsh identity, however Anglicised, changed the nature of political allegiance. The campaign to disestablish the Church of England in Wales won increasing support, to the benefit of the Liberal party, out of whose deep nonconformist roots sprouted fiery political eloquence. The Church of England, after all, was dubbed 'the Tory party at prayer'. Conservatives usually held a majority in Welsh seats until the later 1850s. The general election of 1868, when the Liberals won two-thirds of the seats, proved to be the breakthrough. In 1885, they won thirty of Wales's thirty-four seats. In the so-called 'Khaki election' of 1900, a triumph for the Conservatives in Britain as a whole, the Liberal conscience rebelled over the Boer War (see Chapter 36) and Wales did not return a single Conservative to Westminster.[6]

II. The Scottish dimension

In Scotland, language had a much more tenuous hold on national allegiance. By the end of the nineteenth century, only about 250,000 Scots (6 per cent) spoke Gaelic, almost all of them Highlanders.[7] In general, and despite the extraordinary expansion of the mining and iron industries in South Wales, it remained the more prosperous and self-confident nation. Scotland had contributed significantly to the eighteenth-century European Enlightenment and it still prided itself – perhaps too much – on the quality and the widespread availability of its educational provision (see Chapter 1).

Many Scots also did well out of the Union of 1707. Scottish merchants gained new opportunities in Britain's expanding trading empire and used them well. There was also a growing national convergence between lowland Scots and the English, a development enhanced by intermarriage, particularly among upper mercantile and aristocratic families. Economically and socially, this example of a greater Britain worked. The difficulty, however, was that it was too easy to characterise Scotland as two nations: the more prosperous Lowlands and the poorer, backward Highlands. The distinction is painted too crudely but it existed and, for those aiming to create an integrated Scottish identity, the problem needed addressing. The confected solution was 'Heritage Scotland' – a romanticised nation conjured into existence by the novelist Sir Walter Scott, his friends and acolytes. It incorporated study of ancient literature and a version of Scottish history in which Highland and Lowland did not occupy separate universes.

George IV played a part in this grandiose myth-making. In the summer of 1822, he made the first monarchical visit to Scotland since Charles I's in 1633. Charles had come because he needed money, but at least he was a genuine Scot. George IV needed to make a favourable impression. Up to that point, the Hanoverian dynasty's most decisive intervention had been the destruction of the ragtag Highland army of the 'Young Pretender' at the Battle of Culloden in 1746 (see Chapter 1). The Hanoverian army was commanded by the Duke of Cumberland, George II's son. That was followed by brutality. The clan system was outlawed, as was the wearing of the kilt. Many Highlanders were butchered. George IV enjoyed dressing up and the Scottish, though London-based, artist David Wilkie was commissioned to produce a portrait of a Scottish king, rehabilitated kilt and all. The result is an odious mixture of pure kitsch and gross insensitivity.

The stage-managed royal visit, a series of choreographed pageants and parades, aimed at presenting a King as much Jacobite as Hanoverian and thus healing Scotland's internal wounds. It was also hoped that George's visit would trump any threat from radicals in Scotland. Activists calling for a 'Provisional Government' had organised a series of strikes, aggressive protests and demands for political reform less than two years earlier in what became known as the 'Scottish Insurrection'.

The consequence was ribaldry rather than respect. The girth of the self-indulgent monarch, and his all too evident difficulty in mounting a horse, were widely lampooned as a contrivance to show 'our fat friend' in the most favourable light. Still, humour did deflect entrenched anti-Hanoverian feelings. The royalist cause in Scotland was far from lost. Queen Victoria, the last Hanoverian monarch, bought Balmoral, a Highland estate in Perthshire, in 1848. She and Prince Albert rebuilt and extended its genuine medieval castle and the Queen visited almost annually. Her commitment to Balmoral – 'my paradise in the Highlands' she called it – was a public relations masterstroke. Her 'long career of Highlandolatry' personally re-connected Scotland to monarchy and more Scots to a manipulative, selective, but oddly powerful, misrepresentation of their country.[8]

Of the three smaller nations within the United Kingdom, Scotland experienced the least upsurge in nationalist feeling and probably the least anti-Englishness too. A National Association for the Vindication of Scottish Rights was established in 1883 and a more coherent Scottish Home Rule Association followed in 1886, but neither made significant headway. The important divisions were those *within* Scotland, rather than those between Scotland and England. It was a Presbyterian Church – or 'Kirk' – which split in the so-called Disruption of 1843, leaving a separate Church of Scotland and a rival 'Free Church'.[9] The most important division, however, remained that between Highland (or, as it was sometimes termed, 'Celtic') Scotland – much less extensively populated and far less economically developed – and Lowland Scotland (more 'Teutonic' with pronounced Germanic origins), with its richer, more productive agricultural land, its great commercial centres and a flourishing industrial sector. In 1889, the Prime Minister, the Marquess of Salisbury, offered an English perception: 'the Highlands of Scotland are more unlike the Lowlands of Scotland . . . than the Lowlands are unlike the North of England . . . Linguistically, ethnologically, in the character of the people . . . I boldly state that the line of division is not between England and Scotland, but some line to be drawn far north of that.'[10]

Salisbury was tapping into a vigorous strain of cultural debate which emphasised racial differences. Historians, journalists and informed commentators mused on the differences, and potential conflicts, between Celts and Teutons in Scotland. On this analysis, Teutons, or Anglo-Saxons, were disciplined and hard-working, having imbided the Protestant work ethic. Their achievements were celebrated both in industrial advance and in their substantial contribution to the development of the

British Empire. Even supporters of Home Rule for Scotland in the 1880s agreed that emphasis on Celtic influences was unhelpful. W. Scott Dalgleish stated that the 'distinctive nationality of Scotland is not Celtic but Teutonic'. The MP George Clark, speaking in favour of Scottish Home Rule in the House of Commons, expressed the desire that a successful outcome for the bill would 'preserve intact the great Anglo-Saxon Union that has done so much for civilisation'. The Scottish lawyer William Burns tried, with only limited success, to prevent the racialist chariot driven by the Scottish intelligentsia from scything down all who came into its path. He feared that the 'Anglo-Saxon theory' would 'pluck out from the history of Scotland its very heart and soul'.[11]

III. The impact of the Irish Famine

As a leading economic historian has said, the Irish Famine was 'the main event in modern Irish history, as important to Ireland as, say, the French Revolution in France or the first Industrial Revolution to England'.[12] During the Famine and its immediate aftermath, from 1845 to 1851, Ireland experienced about a million more deaths than would normally have occurred over the period. Hunger and cholera were responsible for most of the additional fatalities when supplies of safe drinking water dwindled later on. Ireland's population did not recover. By 1911, at 4.4m, it was barely more than half the number immediately before the Famine.

Immigration from Ireland to the rest of the United Kingdom had been significant before the Famine as first young adults and then whole families attempted to escape the consequences of rapid population growth in a predominantly rural economy. The agricultural depression after 1815 precipitated extensive emigration. Ireland experienced one of the highest emigration rates in Europe in the generation before the Famine.[13] This increased sharply from the later 1840s. In 1851, the Scottish census revealed that more than 200,000 (7 per cent) of Scotland's total population of 2.89m had been born in Ireland. The proportion was still above 6 per cent twenty years later. Roughly three times as many Irish migrants settled in England and Wales but, because of the larger indigenous population, overall proportions were smaller. The peak of 3 per cent Irish-born in 1861 declined to 2.2 per cent in 1881.[14]

Overall proportions were not alarming but Irish immigrants concentrated where large numbers of unskilled jobs were on offer and newcomers more readily absorbed within the general population. That meant the large towns, particularly ports and commercial centres. Liverpool, where the proportion of Irish-born stood at 22 per cent in 1851, and Glasgow, at 18 per cent, had the highest concentrations, as the nearest large towns to Ireland.

The predominant view among the elite was that substantial Irish immigration would taint Saxon blood. The Registrar-General for Scotland put the matter brutally in 1871. The recent arrival of so many from the 'Irish Celtic race' would precipitate overall

This 1788 painting by the Spanish artist Goya shows an aristocratic family at play. The family is Spanish but this picture admirably captures how European aristocrats, including the British, liked to portray themselves: lovers of the countryside and thus out of doors, carefree, at play and, of course, in expensive, fashionable clothing.

Source: Prado, Madrid, Spain/The Bridgeman Art Library

A late eighteenth-century engraving of the area around the London Stock Exchange.

Source: DEA/A. DAGLI ORTI/Getty Images

A CONSULTATION.

'The Doctor's Consultation', a cartoon by Thomas Rowlandson (1756–1827). Rowlandson's faith in the medical profession was limited and this cartoon gives the impression of collective perplexity rather than of calm, informed and professional deliberation.

"My little friend Grildrig, you have made a most admirable "panegyric upon, Yourself and Country, but from what I can "gather from your own relation & the answers I have with "much pains wringed & extorted from you; I cannot but con- -clude you to be, one of the most pernicious, little odious- -reptiles, that nature ever suffer'd to crawl upon the surface of the Earth."

The KING of BROBDINGNAG, and GULLIVER.

—Vide Swift's Gulliver: Voyage to Brobdingnag

Pub.d June 26 1803. by H.Humphrey 27 St James's Street

This propaganda cartoon by James Gillray (1757–1815) takes its inspiration from Jonathan Swift's *Gulliver's Travels*. It shows George III as the giant king of Brobdingnag with a minute Napoleon (Gulliver) in the palm of his hand. The King tells Bonaparte: 'I cannot but conclude you to be one the most pernicious little odious reptiles that nature ever suffered to crawl upon the surface of the earth'. For the next five years, the 'reptile' proceeded to trample triumphantly over most of western Europe.

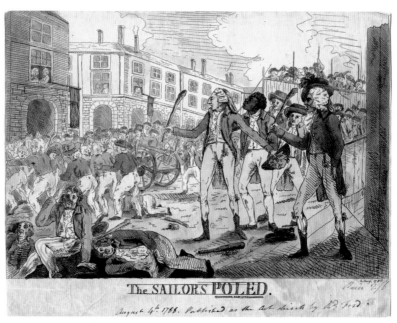

Entitled 'An Election Riot in Covent Garden', this anonymous print from 1788 depicts what we might call 'rough canvassing'. The well-dressed men are wearing the blue and buff colours of the Whig party and have been using cudgels to beat up ordinary voters in Westminster, including three sailors. One of the assailants bears a striking resemblance to George Hanger, later Baron Coleraine, a dissolute friend of the Prince of Wales and Charles James Fox.

This engraving dates from 1819. It shows an imposing three-storey building which was designed by an architect working with the Bengal Engineers who used Kedleston Hall (Derbyshire) as his model. Government House was built from 1799 to 1803 while Marquess Wellesley was Governor-General of India. It symbolises wealth, opulence and power.

One of the most opulent of all civic buildings in Victorian Britain, St George's Hall, Liverpool, was opened in 1854. Its huge space incorporates both a public concert hall and two law courts. The Hall's decorated floor, shown here, comprises 30,000 tiles made by Thomas Minton & Sons, a ceramics firm from Stoke-of-Trent.

Source: Pete Carr

A portrait painted by David Wilkie in 1829 of George IV on his propaganda visit to Scotland seven years earlier. The artist took good care to paint the King in as flattering a manner as possible. The lighting is artfully contrived and it had been many years since George had been as slender as he is pictured here.

A photograph of Queen Victoria's procession through the City of London on Diamond Jubilee Day, 22 June 1897. The focus of the celebrations was on the Queen as head of the British Empire. Eleven prime ministers from the Colonies attended and the procession included troops from all over the Empire.

Source: © Hulton-Deutsch Collection/Corbis

As part of their militant campaign, the Suffragettes attacked a number of high-profile properties. This photograph from March 1912 shows broken windows at the front of the fashionable Department Store, Swan and Edgar, in Piccadilly Circus, London, after one of these attacks.

Source: © Hulton-Deutsch Collection/Corbis

Indian troops arrived in France little more
than a month after the First World War
began. This photograph of September
1914 shows them guarding ammunition
at Orleans, south of Paris.

Source: © Mirrorpix

This recruiting poster was commissioned
by the United Kingdom's Parliamentary
Recruiting Committee in 1915 from
the English painter Arthur Wardle
(1860–1949). Wardle was especially
well known for his pictures of animals
and here the old British lion roars out
his request for help from the Dominions.
The 'young lions' – Australia, Canada,
India and New Zealand – answer the call.

Source: © Swim Ink 2, LLC/Corbis

racial degeneration: 'It is painful to contemplate what may be the ultimate effect of this Irish immigration on the morals and habits of the people, and of the future prospects of the country.'[15] Similar comments were made south of the border. Liverpool's Medical Officer of Health noted in 1859 that the Irish were 'not only the most destitute but the most improvident' element in the city's population. He made what was to him the obvious conclusion that the highest death rates would always be found where the concentration of Irish-born was densest.[16]

In some areas substantial Irish immigration brought conflict with the established population. Street brawls were a common occurrence in Liverpool even before the Famine. The Lancashire towns of Ashton-under-Lyne, Oldham, Preston, Blackburn and Wigan all experienced anti-Catholic riots in the years 1852–54. Popular anti-Catholicism precipitated a Conservative party revival in Lancashire in the 1850s and 1860s. Not all Irish emigrants were Catholics, but the Protestant Orangemen who arrived in the North-West were even more fervently pro-Conservative. Protestant patriotism defined identity as citizens of the United Kingdom.[17]

By no means all Irish immigrants were unskilled rural workers prone as much to drunkenness as fecklessness. Anti-Irish hostility concentrated where unskilled immigrants were most numerous and the threat to jobs was greatest. In London, an area of extensive migration where many Irish joined the service sector, hostility to the Irish either as Catholic or as an ethnic group was muted. Social betterment was also possible. In Liverpool, Hull and York, among other towns, about 40 per cent of Irish-born residents were in professional or skilled working-class occupations by the 1880s.[18] Anti-Irish hostility in Britain was also considerably reduced as assimilation and intermarriage did their work.

IV. Britishness

Declining hostility between different ethnic groups might suggest that a distinctive British identity emerged towards the end of the nineteenth century. Attempts to encapsulate 'Englishness' had been made long before. In the eighteenth century, European observers saw a nation whose citizens enjoyed relative liberty and greater general levels of wealth. Representative government and a population able to afford meat as well as bread and cheese were distinctive features in an era of absolute rule. That observers exaggerated the extent both of Englishmen's liberties and the dispersal of growing national wealth is a relatively minor blemish. The English were seen as different and, for writers influenced by Enlightenment ideas, in some inchoate sense, 'better'.[19] Enlightenment thinkers emphasised the liberal, the optimistic and the progressive in their quest to improve the condition of mankind. They found in England the closest European approximation to their ideal.

English writers were, in general, less expansive. When nationalist movements gathered pace in Europe in the first half of the nineteenth century, they generally avoided appreciation of national sentiments. They saw nationalism as an indication of progress by peoples seeking to cast off oppressive rule and embrace liberty. That was the way in which civilisation should go. No nation had a monopoly of wisdom and any distinctive national traits should be seen as subordinate to the wider ambition of civilising mankind.[20] This civilisation, however, was imbued with deep Christian conviction. Protestant thinkers, especially those arguing for the consolidation of existing social forms, were obsessed with the idea of sin. Christian gentlemen should identify and advocate virtuous activity and urge sinners to 'atone'. This interpretation of civilisation reflected **Evangelical values**. If Christians atoned for their sins, then both spiritual renewal and material success would result.[21]

Evangelicalism

A movement for Church reform based on spiritual renewal. Evangelicals stressed the importance of the Bible as the literal word of God, of awareness of sinfulness and the need for conversion to 'real' Christianity, as opposed to mere formal religious observance. It is most associated in England with reform of the Church of England and the advance of Methodism in the later eighteenth and early nineteenth centuries. Recent research has stressed its influence on political, as well as religious, life, particularly from the 1790s to the 1840s. See also Chapter 15.

A clearer articulation of 'Britishness' had begun to emerge by the middle of the nineteenth century. In 1848, Britain, for the second time in half a century, escaped the revolutionary disruption which afflicted continental Europe. British institutions had been tested, and not found wanting. Why had this happened? A providential explanation was readily to hand. God had marked 'improving' Britain out for special favour. While other European nations reeled, Britain grew ever richer and more self-confident. The **Great Exhibition** of 1851 was an enormous success. Two years later, Absalom Watkin, a Methodist factory owner and a Vice-President of the Anti-Corn Law League, enthused: 'never . . . have I seen clearer evidence of general well-being. Our country is, no doubt, in a most happy and prosperous state. Free trade, peace, and freedom.'[22]

Great Exhibition, 1851

This was a trade exhibition, held in London's Hyde Park. It comprised over 100,000 exhibits from all over the world, although the emphasis was on inventions, machinery and manufactured goods, at which Britain excelled. The idea for the Exhibition came from Prince Albert and its purpose was to celebrate progress – particularly the industrial progress made by Britain over the previous century. It remained open for six months during which time about six million people attended. Many travelled by railway excursion trains on their first journey to the capital.

More writers began to talk about the 'English character'. The novelist and Christian socialist Charles Kingsley stressed the providential perspective: '. . . as surely as there is an English view of everything, so surely God intends us to develop its peculiarities . . . so each nation by learning to understand itself, may also learn to understand, and therefore to profit, by its neighbour'.[23] **John Stuart Mill** reflected on the processes underpinning national development. His ideas stimulated a generation of historians, some of whom placed particular stress on the Anglo-Saxon heritage. One of them, E. A. Freeman, offered a quasi-racist interpretation stressing ancient Teutonic virtues of right and justice in explaining how distinctive English attributes had developed. By the 1870s, a Liberal consensus had been reached. The English had a 'predilection for liberty and free-thought, a capacity for self-government, Protestant piety, enterprise, expansion'.[24]

John Stuart Mill, 1806–1873

Born in London, the son of the philosopher James Mill, he was educated at Edinburgh University and trained for the law before transferring to the government's India Office, where he worked for thirty-five years. He was a disciple of the utilitarian philosopher Jeremy Bentham in his youth. He believed in *laissez-faire* but argued that excessive reliance on the market often produced inefficient outcomes. He reappraised Bentham in his *Utilitarianism* (1861). His *On Liberty* (1859), which became a cornerstone of Liberal political thought, considered the nature of liberty and defended liberty on the basis of utilitarian values rather than the natural rights which were at the root of much Enlightenment philosophy. He was MP for Westminster from 1865 to 1868, where he advocated giving women the vote on the same terms as men.

The adjectives 'English' and 'British' were used interchangeably. Victorians stressed national attributes deriving from Protestantism, liberty and belief in the superiority of representative government. There were, of course, differences between the nations which comprised Britain just as there were between different regions within England. Citizens also recognised their multiple identities, manifested at work, within the family, in sporting allegiance and much else. However, no confusion existed over which nation negotiated with others, which ruled the seas and which governed an unprecedentedly large land mass. Few spoke of the 'English Empire'. It was the values of British civilisation and British forms of Christianity which were so assiduously disseminated across that Empire (see Chapter 36). Despite some complaints about details of specific representation within the United Kingdom parliament, few challenged the supremacy of Britain. Only the predominantly Catholic, famine-ravaged and under-developed Irish failed to accept an assimilationist model – unless, of course, they lived as Protestants in Ulster (see Chapter 40), in which case their enthusiasm for the Union knew no bounds. By the late 1880s, few disagreed with the assertion of the Liberal MP James Bryce that the Scots and

Welsh treasured 'a distinct national feeling, though happily not incompatible with attachment to the greater nationality of the United Kingdom'. By contrast, the Englishman has 'but one patriotism, because England and the United Kingdom are to him practically the same thing'.[25]

V. Women in a man's world

Gender bias cut across the virtues and values trumpeted as distinctively 'British' or 'English': independence, self-reliance, a belief in progress through commerce and free trade. The unspoken assumption was that these belonged to an overwhelmingly male public domain, through politics, industry and the professions. Victorians tended not only to stereotype women's roles and virtues. They also implied that these were universal, lacking distinctive national characteristics.

Legally, women in 1850 remained second-class citizens. The 1832 Reform Act had confirmed that they could not vote in parliamentary elections. On marriage, a woman's property became her husband's to dispose of as he wished, unless a bride's family rights were protected by a trust, a device available only to the wealthy. Divorce was not possible without an Act of Parliament. Even after the Matrimonial Causes Act was passed in 1857, it remained much easier for men to divorce their wives than vice versa. Women could be divorced on the grounds of a single act of adultery; family law did not admit male adultery as an offence.

It was also expected that women would marry – and so enter upon a state of subordination. Not to marry carried a stigma at least until the outbreak of the First World War. In consequence, marriage rates were very high. The percentage of women who had been married was never less than 60 per cent in the period 1871–1911. For those who had reached their late forties, it was well above 80 per cent.[26] The minority of women who never married – an inevitable state for many, given the birth of more males than females – were dismissed as being 'on the shelf'.

Over this period, and not without considerable struggle, women's property rights were redefined. The Married Woman's Property Act of 1870 permitted married women to retain their own earnings from employment. From 1882 they could keep property acquired before marriage separate from that of their husbands. How much this legislation mattered in practice remains a matter of debate. Clearly, it gave protection against gross exploitation but most husbands were not grossly exploitative. Then, as now, definitive evidence about how marriages actually worked is hard to come by, but it is unwise to assume that Victorian women as a whole felt confined and belittled by the institution of marriage. If some found it stifling and wrote volubly about their experiences, many others seem 'to have invested their domestic-orientated lives with a plethora of political, religious, imperial and social meanings' in a relationship with a husband which was both accommodating and supportive.[27]

Much discussion of women's identity focuses on the so-called 'separate spheres' in which men and women were supposed to move – the public for men, the private for women. On this reading, men worked and provided for the family's material needs; women occupied the domestic sphere, acting, in the words of glutinous religiosity framed by the librarian and second-rate poet, Coventry Patmore, as the 'angel in the house'.[28] The reality was more complex. The education of middle-class women was usually more limited than that of their husbands but many developed complementary domestic 'accomplishments', such as reading and performing music, embroidery or watercolour painting, to a high and satisfying level. Formal educational opportunities for middle-class women increased significantly from the 1860s onwards (see Chapter 29). Many middle- and upper-class women involved themselves in philanthropic work, which they found both beneficial and satisfying (see Chapter 28). Some stretched the definition of 'philanthropy' to campaign for improved rights for working-class women. Unions for women were recognised by the Trades Union Congress from 1875 onwards, although at the end of the century only 150,000 women were in unions, about 3 per cent of the total.[29] The Women's Protective and Provident League, founded in 1874, encouraged women to organise in trade unions.

Although there are important exceptions, it seems that work became for most women a less important element in their identity. The Industrial Revolution had created work for them, especially in the textile industries, where rather more than half of the workforce was female and where wages were relatively high.[30] However, it was difficult to remain in the factory labour force after marriage, since long hours and the inflexibility of working arrangements presented problems which had not existed when home was the workplace and women could juggle family and working responsibilities. Female participation declined during the second half of the nineteenth century. The reasons seem clear. Living standards were rising at least from the 1870s and a male breadwinner could increasingly earn enough to feed and clothe his family. Trade union members increasingly embraced the 'male-only breadwinner' model of family life. Notions of respectability depended on married women playing a full-time family role. By 1911, only about 10 per cent of married women were still in paid employment.[31] Except in areas such as textile Lancashire and in Dundee, where women worked in the jute industry, waged work had become a temporary and transient phase in women's lives. In mining areas such as the Rhondda in South Wales, it was not even that. Only the disproportionate involvement of young, unmarried women explains a work participation rate of between 30 and 35 per cent in the years 1851 to 1911.[32]

So much attention has been given to the suffrage movement (see Chapter 39), which gained impetus from the 1880s, that women's earlier political involvement has been neglected until recently. If gender boundaries did exist, many women refused to be confined to the domestic sphere and became active political participants. The call for a female franchise, however, was relatively muted until the 1870s. Women's political activity often related directly to their domestic role. They had campaigned against George IV's attempt to divorce his wife in 1820 (see Chapter 16). They also supported humanitarian causes, including Elizabeth Fry's Society for 'Promoting the Reformation of Female Prisoners' in the later 1820s. They sustained boycotts of slave-grown sugar as part of the anti-slavery campaign which finally succeeded in 1833.

In the later 1830s and 1840s, thousands of women supported the Chartist move-ment (see Chapter 21); about one hundred and fifty female Chartist associations were formed. Few of these, however, agitated for female suffrage. Some felt that the political elite would consider 'votes for women' an outlandish cause which would weaken the case for manhood suffrage. Others thought that support for Chartism would enhance the family unit by strengthening the hand of the male breadwinner. As one historian has concluded, 'Most Chartist women defined themselves as wives and mothers, auxiliaries to their husbands and fathers.' Such women also accepted that, at times of high unemployment, women should not compete for jobs with men.[33]

Although women were proscribed from participating directly in politics both at the national and, until 1869, municipal levels, they were frequently influential. When the Municipal Franchise Act gave female ratepayers in England and Wales the vote in 1869, direct influence increased. Women could also be elected onto School Boards from 1870 (see Chapter 39), become Poor Law Guardians by 1875 and join parish and district councils from 1894.[34] By the end of the 1880s, the two main poli-tical parties had responded to the enthusiasm particularly of middle-class women for involvement. Although much support was given 'behind-the-scenes', the role of women both in the Conservative Primrose League, founded in 1883, and in The Women's Liberal Federation, established in 1887, was substantial.[35] Women contributed substantially to the professionalisation of party political organisation.

26

Free trade, *laissez-faire* and state regulation, *c*1830–*c*1880

I. The era of free trade

Britain's so-called 'Fiscal-Military State' was dismantled in the thirty years after 1815 as governments embraced both free trade to increase national wealth and a low taxation regime. The latter provided incentives for entrepreneurs and other wealth creators but it also aimed to release the lower orders from the burden of direct taxation altogether (Chapters 16, 17 and 22). As Robert Peel put it at the beginning of 1846, his government's policy had been to encourage 'the idea amongst the great body of the people, that we, the rich and powerful, are willing to take a more than ordinary share of the public burdens, and to remove those burdens from the people as far as possible'.[1] When Peel first introduced a peacetime income tax in 1842, the threshold for payment was deliberately set at a level – £150 per year (the equivalent of £116,000 in early twenty-first-century values) – which would exempt the lower orders. He could justifiably claim that this redistributive move represented 'a juster principle of taxation'.[2]

Free trade had established itself as the dominant economic ideology of Britain by the early 1860s but how this came about has been the subject of fierce debate. The traditional view stresses the influence of the Anti-Corn Law League, founded by northern businessmen and industrialists in Manchester in March 1839, and from 1841 led by **Richard Cobden**. The League was to be an exceptionally effective propaganda organisation which 'transformed free trade into a national political issue',[3] creating in the process a more extensive audience for radical politics. The League was far more than a businessman's self-interested pressure group. Its influence spread beyond its heartland of northern industrialists and exporters, though they provided the bulk of the funding. Anti-Corn Law League propaganda presented the free-trade case as part of a campaign against aristocratic waste and in support of cheaper and more effective government. One campaigner predicted in 1846 that corn-law repeal would bring 'new light and strength to us all' and that the methods used by the Leaguers would then be applied elsewhere, to 'poor laws, taxation, education, sanitary reform, ecclesiastical reform, and organic political reform'.[4] Peel's famous personal tribute to Cobden when reform passed is also cited as testimony to the League's influence. It is therefore ironic that protection for corn operated as a significant constraint only in the first years after the implementation of the new Corn Law in 1815. Especially after 1828, prohibitive levels of protection were rare and the import of corn was encouraged at low levels of duty. Well before the establishment of the Anti-Corn Law League, trade in corn was an integral element in the Huskissonian move towards trade liberalisation more generally (see Chapter 19).[5]

Richard Cobden, 1804–1865

Born into a modest farming family in Sussex, he was largely self-educated and always retained a passion for reading and the accumulation of knowledge. He was first a commercial traveller seeking orders for muslin and calico before setting up his own business in London. He moved to Manchester in 1832, where he oversaw a successful calico-printing business located near Burnley. He campaigned for Lancashire boroughs to take advantage of the Municipal Corporations Act (see Chapter 21), publishing a pamphlet on the subject – *Incorporate Your Borough* – in 1837. It led him to contact with radical thinkers across the country. He was a prominent member of the Anti-Corn Law League and argued that Protection held back consumption and thus economic growth. He was elected MP for Stockport in 1841 and for the West Riding of Yorkshire in 1847. After corn-law repeal was passed, he remained a Liberal MP and supported the National Schools movement. His commitment to *laissez-faire* was absolute. He argued for retrenchment and reform and supported policies of peace to secure prosperity. He naturally opposed the Crimean War and viewed Palmerston with great suspicion. Towards the end of his career he largely withdrew from domestic politics but was the British representative at the trade talks which produced the Cobden–Chevalier Treaty of 1860 which abolished most tariffs on exports from France to Britain.

Interpretations which stress the centrality of the Anti-Corn Law League also emphasise the importance of class divisions, seeing the League as a movement by the industrial middle classes against a wasteful aristocracy. League propaganda, not least in the mouth of **John Bright**, emphasised the class divide. It is not surprising that Karl Marx should echo League sentiments when he called the free traders 'the official representatives of modern English society' who would effect 'the complete annihilation of Old England as an aristocratic country'.[6]

John Bright, 1811–1889

Born in Rochdale, the son of a Quaker bookkeeper in a local cotton firm who later established his own successful business, Bright attended a number of schools in the north of England. He was a prominent figure in the Anti-Corn Law League, acting as a lecturer on free-trade 'missionary' tours. He enhanced nonconformist support for the League and also believed that the aristocracy was a wasteful drain on society. He became one of a small number of nonconformists sitting in the House of Commons when he was elected in 1843. After the repeal of the Corn Laws, Bright supported a wide range of radical causes, including further parliamentary reform, Irish land and Church reform, the abolition of compulsory rates paid to the Church of England and a state educational system. He was also a powerful supporter of the Empire both as an economic resource and as a medium by which to transmit civilised values. He was President of the Board of Trade from 1868 to 1870 and Chancellor of the Duchy of Lancaster from 1880 to 1882 but a combination of illness and lack of flair for administration made him a less effective government minister than an orator and advocate of causes. He opposed Gladstone on Home Rule for Ireland in 1886.

But the aristocratic country had far more staying power than Marx understood. The alternative explanation for the triumph of free trade stresses a revised government ethic. The war over economic policy which raged from 1815 to the 1840s touched all political groups. The key battles, however, were waged in parliament between existing interest groups – landowners, bankers and the commercial interest – rather than between the classes. Peel's trade liberalisation policies followed the lead of Liverpool and Huskisson. He was trying to reduce the influence of such vested interests, be they landowners who believed that land, as the key property, must be protected at all costs, overseas traders with commercial interests in sugar or cotton plantations worked by slaves, or bankers who too readily responded to **liquidity problems** by heedless printing of additional bank notes. At the cost of his own career (see Chapter 22), Peel won the battle. The governing consensus, adopted seamlessly by the Whig–Liberal administration which succeeded Peel's (see Chapter 30), was that free trade policies, pursued in tandem with stringency in public expenditure, were almost the moral duty in a modern state. As William Gladstone put it, with uncharacteristic pithiness, 'Public economy is part of public virtue.'[7]

Liquidity problems

Since economists define 'liquidity' as a measure of a firm's, or an individual's, ability quickly to acquire cash to meet financial obligations which fall due, 'liquidity problems' refer to difficulties in being able to meet these obligations.

On this definition, mid-century governments were hell-bent on virtue. The landed interest was forced to accept free trade. The long-resented, and increasingly anachronistic, privileges of the East India Company (see Chapter 19) were removed. In 1848–49, protective Navigation Laws were finally repealed. This, along with corn-law repeal, led to unprecedentedly high corn imports. In the early 1840s, imported corn accounted for only a twelfth of British consumption; by 1870, it was almost a half.[8] In his 1860 budget, Gladstone announced the removal of tariffs from a huge array of goods, including the abolition of duties on newspapers. He accompanied his proposals, during a speech which lasted four hours, with a homily on the virtues of trade liberalisation, efficiency and cheap government. As Eric Hobsbawm has said, the cumulative effect was that 'government policy in Britain came as near laissez-faire as has ever been practicable in a modern state'.[9] The contribution to government revenue made by customs duties plummeted. It stood at 32 per cent in the early 1840s but fell to 11 per cent in the early 1860s and a mere 5 per cent by the end of the century.[10]

II. A smaller state?

Laissez-faire is often used rather more loosely than 'free trade', identifying a prevalent attitude towards the role of government. However, the terms are two sides of the same coin. It is true that mid-Victorian governments intervened with reluctance in commercial activities and tried, in particular, to avoid being seen as the ultimate regulator of business or commercial ventures. The absence of regulation was not always an option, however. The Medical Act of 1858 established a Medical Register upon which those qualified to practise should be placed. Unregistered practice was not declared illegal but responsibility for determining who should appear on the Register was delegated to the General Medical Council, which had no truck with free trade in medical practice. The borderline between qualification and non-qualification was anyway very difficult to enforce. Before the end of the nineteenth century, a high court judge described it as 'a state of utter fog'.[11]

Laissez-faire

A French phrase which literally means 'leave to do'. In economic terms, however, it means non-interference by government. Associated with the ideas of Adam Smith and Jeremy Bentham, a *laissez-faire* policy leaves agriculture, industry and commerce to operate in a climate of free competition. It also holds that individuals should be free to control their own lives, make their own decisions and operate in a free market unconfined by tariffs, tolls or other restrictions. The role of the state should be reduced to bare essentials – defence of the nation and the provision of a framework within which the liberty of law-abiding citizens is guaranteed. When the state does little, it can keep taxes – especially direct taxes on income and wealth – low.

Railway development was another hard case for free traders. Uniquely among European nations, British railways developed wholly under private enterprise. Yet concerns about financial probity, safety and even about excess of competition working against the public interest all compelled the government to regulate and prescribe. As early as 1836, parliament issued regulations governing the subscription of capital to a railway company and a company's powers of borrowing. As early as the 1840s, government acknowledged a responsibility to ensure that railways ran safely. From 1844, every passenger train company was required to provide third-class fares at fixed rates to enable the poor to travel. As one transport historian says, by 1870 railway companies were among the largest businesses operating in mid-Victorian Britain, but they did so 'under a considerable measure of state control'.[12] Control was extended further in 1873 when Gladstone's government appointed a Board of Railway Commissioners to supervise railway working and, if necessary, to arbitrate in disputes between the companies.

In the years 1830–60, central government spending, as a proportion of national income, declined significantly and it is tempting to see this as a period of *laissez-faire* government. However, it was also a period of significant government intervention as the state began to come to terms with the range of social problems thrown up by massive economic expansion, especially in the towns. Was this inconsistent? Two answers suggest themselves. The first relates to the reasons for intervention. Industrialisation created its own imperatives in the form of overly rapid growth, environmental degradation and sky-high death rates in the cities. Some degree of state intervention was unavoidable to prevent political disorder, perhaps even revolution, and social catastrophe. Labelling this period 'an age of *laissez-faire*' is permissible if both the reasons for intervention and the means used to intervene are understood. State intervention happened because the government decided that non-intervention would encourage greater dangers. *Laissez-faire* governments continued to argue that state control would deter individual initiatives and might lead to collective deterioration. As **Samuel Smiles** put it, 'The spirit of self-help is the root of all genuine growth in the individual; and, exhibited in the lives of the many, it constitutes the true source of national vigour and strength.'[13] While government intervention might do little positive good it could prevent greater harm.[14]

Samuel Smiles, 1812–1904

Born near Edinburgh, the son of a merchant, he trained as a doctor and briefly practised medicine until he left for England, becoming editor of the *Leeds Times* in 1838. He was first a supporter of radical causes, but physical-force Chartism tempered his radicalism. He was increasingly associated with Liberal politics and wrote much about forms of self-improvement. From the 1840s to the 1860s he was a railway administrator. He is best known, however, as a writer and, particularly, as the author of brief biographies of individuals, like the engineer James Watt and the entrepreneur Matthew Boulton, who had used their own talents to improve themselves. His most famous work, *Self-Help, with Illustrations of Character and Conduct*, was published in 1859. It had sold 75,000 copies by the time of his death.

The second response concerns how governments intervened. They had no desire to challenge the primacy of local interests. Wherever possible, they worked through municipal borough councils, improvement commissioners, highway authorities, or poor law unions or other local agencies. Governments believed that local issues were best addressed by people with the appropriate local knowledge. Centralisation was too often both blunt and ineffective. Also, as one cynical MP put it in 1850, 'it is evidently wise to put as little on the Government whose overthrow causes a revolution as you can and to have as much as you can on the local bodies which may be overthrown a dozen times and nobody be the worse'.[15] It is not surprising that the annual increase in expenditure by local government in the years 1850–1900 was almost twice as great as that by central government.[16]

Most government intervention until the 1880s involved advising local agencies what they might do rather than telling them what they must. Central administrators might find this irksome. As one senior civil servant put in the 1850s, 'in the general working of central departments, charged with duties which bring them into contact with local authorities, the tendency is rather to over-timidity than to excessive dictation'.[17] However, governments were striving to find an appropriate balance between conflicting interests. The era of Protectionism was, in effect, over by 1850. Support for Protection, previously strong among the shipping, imperial and merchant banking interests in the City of London, dwindled after a major banking crisis brought a number of bankruptcies in 1847. Elsewhere, monopolies were being broken up as free trade was increasingly 'propagated as a value to which all Victorians subscribed'.[18] Government policy on poverty after the passage of the Poor Law Amendment Act in 1834 was to encourage people to be more self-reliant (see Chapter 28). However, self-reliance was not an option for some citizens – orphan children, for example, or the elderly who had no family support. In practice, therefore, government acknowledged the need for regulation, albeit as a last resort. It did so increasingly in respect of child labour. The Factory Act of 1833 set a maximum of eight hours of work for children of 9 to 13 years employed in textile factories. Children below 9 years were prohibited from factory work. Crucially, four inspectors were appointed whose remit was to ensure that factory owners complied. Factory legislation was supported on humanitarian grounds, and Richard Oastler's famous assertion that thousands of factory children were 'sacrificed at the shrine of avarice' in 'Yorkshire slavery' elicited widespread public sympathy.[19] However, the government's rationale for the legislation was that, unlike adult workers, children were not free agents who could bargain with their employers over wages and working conditions. In a civilised country, therefore, intervention was inescapable.

However minimally governments intended to intervene, most 'social' legislation developed a momentum of its own. Government inspectors' reports identified gaps and deficiencies in existing legislation and suggested appropriate remedies – which often required amending legislation. What one historian has called 'a pattern of government growth' resulted.[20] Legislation covering work is a good example. The so-called Mines Act of 1842 forbade women and children from working underground. In 1844, the working hours of children in textile factories were reduced. After a long campaign by humanitarian reformers and trade unionists, an important Act passed in 1847 prescribed a maximum of ten hours in a working day for women and children.

The so-called 'Ten Hours Act' was itself amended in both 1850 and 1853, after which, because of the way factory work was organised, a maximum ten-hour day became, in practice, a universal norm. Almost without realising it, therefore, the government found itself protecting all factory textile workers, irrespective of whether they were free agents or not. Further legislation extended the provisions of textile factory legislation to most factories and workshops in 1867. In the same year the employment of young children in agricultural labour was prohibited. Finally, in 1878, all factory and workshop employees were protected by the provisions in existing Factory Acts.

Government intervention on social questions grew significantly in the years to 1870 but social legislation remained permissive and its administration remarkably low-cost. As Horace Mann, registrar of the civil service commission, reported in 1869, the cost of the civil service establishment had increased from £3.7m in 1848 to £15.2m in 1868. However, only 2.1 per cent of the government's gross expenditure of £75.5m in 1869 was spent on civil servants' salaries and on the running of public departments. Despite recent expansion, the annual cost of the public health department was only £13,000 and that of the factory inspectorate £12,500. Much larger proportions were being spent in the late 1860s on servicing the National Debt (38 per cent) and on the armed forces (36 per cent) than on civil administration as a whole (16 per cent).[21]

III. The drift towards compulsion

Most social legislation remained permissive after 1870, even if government 'nudging' of local authorities became somewhat more persistent. It was adept at issuing what might nowadays be called 'best practice guidelines' in many areas, including effective drainage systems, appropriate width for roads and housing standards[22] and it had a range of experts on whom it relied for authoritative information. Permissive legislation was often ignored at local level. Many authorities were unwilling to alarm the ratepayers with new, but expensive, schemes for fear of being rejected at the next elections.

In housing, for example, despite abundant evidence of the relationship between poor-quality housing provision and high levels of mortality, the government responded only by widening the range of options available to local authorities. An Artisans' and Labourers' Dwellings Act, passed in 1868, empowered local authorities to compel owners of insanitary houses either to demolish or to repair them. A further Act of 1875 gave local authorities the power compulsorily to purchase areas in which dwellings had inadequate sanitation and sewerage, so that they could be rebuilt and re-let by the authorities. Some authorities took up the challenge. The face of central Birmingham was significantly changed as a result. However, the majority did little or nothing, calculating that ratepayers would not tolerate stumping up for the compensation payable to owners of slum properties. The 1890 Housing of the

Working Classes Act empowered local authorities to acquire land, if necessary with government loans, for the purpose of building or improving dwelling houses for the poor. Again, the results were limited, and especially so in the rural areas, where almost nothing was done.[23]

The pendulum was, however, swinging towards compulsion. A decisive breakthrough was made in the field of public health. Pressure from local doctors and persistent administrators, of whom none was more persistent than **Edwin Chadwick**, had led to the establishment of a Health of Towns Commission in 1844. In 1848 the first national Public Health Act was passed. A Board of Health was established and local authorities were required to adopt sanitary measures if the death rate in their area exceeded the national average of twenty-three per thousand. The Board's remit was mostly advisory, however. In the 1860s, pressure increased for introduction of more thoroughgoing measures. Dr John Simon, London's first Medical Officer of Health, was appointed Chief Medical Officer reporting to the Privy Council in 1858. His view both on the diversity of practice and the effectiveness of sanitary provision in different towns led him by 1865 to conclude 'that the time has arrived when it ought not to be discretional in a place whether that place shall be kept filthy or not'.[24] The fact that thirty years of pressure and legislation in the years 1842–72 had seen hardly any movement in the national death rate strengthened his hand. During Gladstone's first government (see Chapter 32), Poor Law Guardians were required to appoint a salaried vaccination officer. From 1871 to 1898, Britain became a country of compulsory vaccination, with the result that smallpox was almost eliminated. Gladstone's Public Health Act of 1872 required for the first time that every sanitary authority must appoint a Medical Officer of Health.

Edwin Chadwick, 1800–1890

Born in Manchester, the son of a journalist, he was educated locally before the family moved to London when he was 10. As a young man, he trained for the law and also wrote articles on important social questions, including public health and the need for a professional police force. Influenced by Jeremy Bentham, for whom he served as private secretary, he worked on the Royal Commission enquiring into the operation of the poor laws. With Nassau Senior, he wrote most of the Report. He then served as Secretary to the Poor Law Commission (see Chapter 28) from 1834. He used his position to investigate other social questions, particularly public health. His *Report on the Sanitary Condition of the Labouring Poor* (1842) proved influential in confirming direct links between dirt and disease. During the 1840s, he also worked on schemes for private enterprise to address sanitary questions. He persuaded the Whig government to establish a General Board of Health in 1848 and served as Commissioner on that Board. His arrogance, intolerance of criticism and tendency to exceed his remit limited his effectiveness and was a major cause of his removal as Commissioner in 1854. The Board of Health was wound up when a new Local Government and Public Health Act was passed in 1858.

The Tory MP C. D. Newdegate protested that this Health Bill would 'break up the system of local government, and substitute for it a system of centralization'. He also objected to having the administration of the new system in the hands of 'permanent officials' who were unaccountable to parliament.[25] Three years later, Disraeli could still plausibly claim that 'permissive legislation is the characteristic of a free people',[26] although the case for compulsion was being made with increasing insistence, especially by Liberal radical politicians arguing that the state could be a powerful agency for civilising the people. Joseph Chamberlain was mayor of Birmingham from 1873 to 1876 and used local powers to take first gas and then water supplies out of private hands for administration by the town council.[27] Within ten years, the price of gas in Birmingham was 30 per cent lower than it had been when in private hands.

Although Chamberlain continued to believe that local authorities could do more good for the people than could Westminster, the principles of what became known as 'gas and water socialism' took root within the Liberal party. Local government structures remained intact but the relationship with the central authority was changing. By 1880, Westminster was prepared, in exceptional cases supported by detailed expert evidence, to identify and then compel uniform minimum provision. Developments after 1880 (see Chapters 38 and 41) would demonstrate how a state which had been committed to principles of *laissez-faire* would embrace what the political philosopher **J. A. Hobson** would call 'a positive progressive policy which involves a new conception of the functions of the state'.[28]

J. A. Hobson, 1858–1940

Born in Derby, the son of a newspaper proprietor who was also mayor of the town, he developed as one of the leading theorists of Liberalism in the late nineteenth and early twentieth centuries. He was educated at Oxford University and trained in economics. He was a leading proponent of the theory of 'under-consumption', which held that the wealthiest in society retained income which they could not consume, thereby leading to under-investment and crises of capitalism. Comparing the workings of society to those of a biological organism, he argued that wealth was distributed inefficiently. To address this, the state should develop taxation and welfare policies to raise living standards so that the poor could consume more. His work converted many liberals in the late nineteenth and early twentieth centuries from *laissez-faire* to interventionism. His study of *Imperialism* (1902) was also influential in arguing that European nations competed to acquire colonies in order to get hold of scarce mineral and other resources and to deal with growing economic problems associated with under-consumption.

27

....

Supremacy under threat? Economy and society, 1880–1914

I. Britain's reality check?

In 1896, the author E. E. Williams published a series of articles in *The Times* in which he argued that Britain's competitiveness in world markets was being eroded, particularly by Germany. Williams turned his articles into a book, *Made in Germany*, which enjoyed great commercial success. Like so much well-targeted propaganda, it simplified and personalised what was a hugely complex, and would later become a hugely controversial, topic. 'Roam the house over', he advised his middle-class readers, and 'the fateful mark ["Made in Germany"] will greet you at every turn, from the piano in your drawing room to the mug on your kitchen dresser.'[1]

Williams's book was so successful precisely because it played on collective unease. Despite stock-market volatility, price slumps, banking crises and the like, Britain had grown used to the idea not only that it was the world's most powerful nation but also that its economic organisation, social structure and dominant ideology of *laissez-faire* (see Chapter 26) provided a secure basis for continued enjoyment of that supremacy. Contemporaries agonised over Williams's message. Economic and social historians since have engaged in furious controversy about whether Britain was indeed underperforming in the years before 1914 or whether, in the words of one leading contributor to the debate, the British economy was 'growing as rapidly as permitted by the growth of its resources and the effective exploitation of the available technology'.[2]

On the face of it, this case seems difficult to argue. Britain's growth rates were slackening off. An economy which grew on average at 2.4 per cent a year between 1831 and 1873 was growing at only 1.9 per cent in the years 1873–1913.[3] Straightforward comparisons of market share enjoyed by the leading manufacturing producers also sound a pessimistic note. Britain's share of world manufacturing output peaked at just short of 23 per cent in 1881, when the United States had a 14.7 per cent share and Germany 8.9 per cent. By 1913, the United States had a 32 per cent share, Germany 14.8 per cent and the United Kingdom 13.6 per cent. The turnaround seemed dramatic, especially since the UK's annual percentage growth rate in the period immediately before the First World War was 2.1, compared with the USA's 5.4 per cent and Germany's 4.4. All three countries, however, were experiencing lower growth rates than in the 1870s and 1880s. The major power whose growth rate was significantly higher in 1900–13 than in any previous period was France.[4] One simple explanation, therefore, relates to the timing of industrial revolution. Of these four powers, the UK was first to industrialise and France last.

Britain's share of export markets for manufactured goods remained buoyant, at least during the earlier period of the so-called 'Great Depression'. In the early 1880s, Britain accounted for almost 44 per cent of the world's exports of manufactured goods. Increased competition from Germany and the United States reduced market share during the later 1880s and 1890s. At the turn of the century, Britain held on to less than 35 per cent,[5] still very substantial given the country's size and population but no longer dominant. Contemporary commentators stressed decline from what had been a virtual mid-century monopoly rather than the continued resilience of so much of Britain's manufacturing sector. They noticed that the United States and Germany were now dominant in armaments, machine tools and transport, markets which had previously been dominated by the British. The following gloomy assessment from 1880 is typical:

> It may be interesting to know that the production of steel is being developed in America at a much more rapid rate than in England . . . In the United States the production of Bessemer ingots was eighteen times as great as it was in 1870 . . . whilst in Britain the production had not become four times as great as it was nine years ago.[6]

There was no mention of the obvious point which any statistician would make. The apparently hugely superior performance of the United States is in significant part explained by the later launch of its iron industry. Percentage increases usually look more spectacular when calculated from a low base.

Contemporaries also worried that Britain's declining share of world trade was being sustained by increasing exports of minerals, particularly coal, which were not a renewable resource.[7] The coal industry expanded rapidly in the half century from 1860. Britain produced 83m tons of coal in 1860 and 287m in 1913, by which time coal was contributing about 7 per cent of the Gross National Product.[8] Contemporaries paid little heed to indicators suggesting both that the British workforce was becoming more productive and also that by the 1880s and 1890s British workers were consuming considerably more than before. Many also bemoaned the actions of workers who, during difficult times, took strike action. The strikes launched in London in 1888–89 by the match girls at Bryant & Mays, by the Gas Workers in support of an eight-hour day and the Dockers to achieve an extra 6d (2½p) a week were widely condemned by employers. British economic performance was being jeopardised just as the economy was beginning to recover[9] (see Chapter 41). Contemporaries also concentrated on the performance of the established industries – textiles, metals and arable farming – rather than the exploitation of new opportunities in commerce and the provision of services.

The finance industry was particularly important. In the last thirty years of the nineteenth century, huge quantities of capital were exported from Britain in the form of investments to fund colonial and foreign enterprises. Most went through the City of London, which confirmed its position as the world's financial capital, brokering international trade deals and payments. The editor of *The Economist* magazine rhapsodised in 1907:

> [The City] is the greatest shop, the greatest store, the freest market for commodities, gold and securities, the greatest disposer of capital, the greatest disposer of credit, but above and beyond . . . by reason of all these marks of financial and commercial supremacy, it is the world's clearing house.

As its historian has argued, the years 1890–1914 represented the golden age of the City of London. The numbers employed in the City increased by more than a quarter in the years 1881–1901. By the early twentieth century, more than 330,000 people worked there. A 'commercial culture' held sway, grounded in acknowledged rules and practices, a hierarchical dress code and the working lunch with clients.[10] The City thought in ever more grandiose terms. The editor of *Financial News* asserted in 1912 that 'financial and economic forces have become the predominant factors in our twentieth-century life, while the political elements have receded into the second place . . . This is a distinct gain for humanity as a whole . . . political forces are capable of being distorted, minimized, outwitted, while economic power is the absolute and inexorable auxiliary effort to advance the prosperity of the world.'[11]

Conventional accounts of Britain's economic and social transformation in the nineteenth century tend to concentrate on machine-led production, but manufactured goods do not of themselves a balanced economy make. One historian sees Britain 'even at the height of the industrial revolution, essentially [as] a commercial, financial and service-based economy whose comparative advantage always lay with commerce and finance'. What contemporaries considered to be the country's industrial decline in the late nineteenth century was 'a transfer of resources and entrepreneurial energies into other forms of business life . . . in moving from industry to commerce, Britain's entrepreneurs were responding intelligently to perceived opportunities'.[12]

Even if this position is accepted, it still raises the question of whether the massive outflows of capital from Britain restricted investment in research and development of newer industries, thus compounding the country's structural problems. Economic historians have found little evidence that new enterprises were starved of capital to start up or to expand businesses. Both established and newer industries invested strongly in new machinery and steam power in the last thirty years of the nineteenth century. Indeed, Britain mechanised faster during this period than before. Steam engines were providing British industry with approximately ten times as much horsepower in 1907 as in 1870.[13] Newer industries, particularly chemicals and electrical goods, established themselves. It is true that some of the newer enterprises made less dramatic headway in Britain than in Germany or the United States. The motor-car industry stands out. However, Britain's main competitor, the USA, had greater natural resources and a more abundant workforce reinforced by large numbers of recent immigrants.

Britain, alone among the major powers, retained free trade during the economic depressions of the later 1870s, the mid-1880s and the early 1890s. Germany imposed tariffs in 1879 and France in 1881. The United States became the most heavily protected nation of all after the imposition of a 48.4 per cent tax on imports from 1891 in order to protect domestic manufactures. Duties were further increased, by nearly 60 per cent in some cases, by the Dingley Tariff of 1897. Britain's free trade policy brought the country cheaper food but also more foreign manufactured goods, thereby apparently strengthening the case made by E. E. Williams.

It is, though, difficult to condemn the overall quality of British entrepreneurship in this period. Britain was outgunned by bigger, wealthier competitors, but they were successful competitors because they had industrialised and, in the process, learned lessons from Britain as the first industrialising nation. In particular, the view that British business suffered from 'gentrification', as second- and third-generation owners evinced a less lean, mean competitive edge than the factory pioneers has received short shrift in recent years.[14] Businessmen had bought land and set themselves up as country gentlemen long before the Industrial Revolution, and the links between land, industry and urban development were generally stronger in Britain than in other European countries. The British aristocracy was used to taking risks, whether on the turf or in property, stocks and shares. 'Gentrification' did not imply either that the social elite was anti-business or that it had, by 1900, somehow 'gone soft'. It is not logically inconsistent for a manufacturing economy, at a particular time, both to be performing as well as could reasonably be expected while also being outpaced by more powerful competitors. That was Britain's case in the last quarter of the nineteenth century.

II. Late nineteenth-century agriculture

If Britain as a whole did not endure a 'Great Depression', perhaps the agricultural sector did. On the face of it, British agriculture was substantially depressed in the last quarter of the nineteenth century. From the mid-1870s, the downside of free trade for a small nation with limited resources was uncomfortably experienced by Britain's arable farmers. Britain was swamped with imported foreign wheat, particularly from the United States. Just as the tide of imports reached its flood in the later 1870s, long spells of bad weather took hold, bringing poor growing seasons and a succession of bad harvests. The combination proved devastating. Over the last quarter of the century, more than 5m acres of arable land fell out of cultivation. A fair proportion of it was converted to pasture and rough grazing, although some became reserved for game birds. As one observer told the novelist Rider Haggard in the 1890s, only half his tongue in cheek, Suffolk landowners would do best to give their tenants notice to quit, develop the breeding of partridges and lease the resultant shooting rights to South African gold and diamond millionaires on holiday in Britain.[15]

As arable food prices plummeted, so did the price of agricultural land, if hard-pressed landowners could find buyers at all. Rents on arable land were at least 25 per cent lower in 1913 than in 1875. Not surprisingly, farmers laid off their labourers. The proportion of those employed in farming in England and Wales declined by more than 30 per cent during this period. As domestic wheat production fell by 44 per cent, imports crowded in to fill the gap. Imports of 28m hundredweight a year in the early 1860s had grown to 70m in the period 1901–5. Britain had rarely been self-sufficient in food during the industrial period but the need for imports now grew alarmingly. By 1914, Britain was importing more than 75 per cent of its cereals and about 40 per cent of its meat.[16]

Yet one leading social and agrarian historian has asserted that there was 'no general or chronic depression in English agriculture' at this time.[17] This apparently perverse judgment derives from a consideration of agriculture as a whole. Across the sector, output and productivity continued to increase, albeit modestly. Emphasis is usually placed on wheat production, for two main reasons. Britain's staple food was wheaten bread. Also, the main arable estates were owned by the politically powerful, who used their influence to considerable effect. Great landowners presented a crisis on arable farms as a crisis for agriculture as a whole and a crisis for agriculture as a disaster for the nation. The evidence on which the case for a great agricultural depression was based derives in significant part from the Royal Commission on the Depressed State of the Agricultural Interest, which sat from 1879–1882 under the chairmanship of the Duke of Richmond. Richmond led the Conservative party in the Lords and had family estates in Sussex. The evidence it heard was detailed, gloomy and heavily skewed. Three times as many witnesses were called to give evidence from the leading wheat-growing counties than from those where dairying predominated.[18]

It was not that the dairying sector enjoyed a period of unprecedented boom. The number of cattle did increase significantly over this period but one of the key indicators of health in the agricultural sector, demand for farming tenancies linked to rising rents, was noticeably absent. Rents fell in the North-West by 12 per cent from the mid-1870s to the mid-1890s. This, though, compared favourably with a decline of 41 per cent in the South-East. Also, although it got under way a little later than in the arable sector, pasture farmers faced growing overseas competition, particularly once refrigerated ships capable of carrying beef and mutton from Australia, New Zealand and the Americas arrived at British ports.[19]

The key point, however, was that dairy farmers could withstand such competition better than their arable colleagues because market demand for their produce was more buoyant. Also, plummeting oat and barley prices reduced feed costs for pastoral farmers. Market gardening was also developing strongly. Both the lower middle classes and those in secure, well-paid, working-class employment could afford a more varied diet. London had led by generating a mass market for fruit and vegetables grown in Surrey, Kent and Essex in the eighteenth century. Now transport improvements and the growth of provincial towns opened up ever more profitable opportunities for market gardeners. By the 1870s, the railway network was almost complete, linking larger towns with their rural hinterland and enabling more perishable products to be brought to town markets.

Output figures also confirm the divergent experience of arable and pastoral farmers. Wheat output in 1901 was only a quarter of that achieved in 1871. Hay, however, was 50 per cent greater while fruit production comfortably more than doubled.[20] The route to salvation for some farmers was diversification, to which growing markets in the towns contributed, but this was not an option for many debt-burdened arable producers. At the depths of the depression in the early 1890s, farming bankruptcies were running at more than five hundred a year.[21]

Even arable agriculture did not experience one long, uniform agricultural depression. It is more accurate to identify two sharp depressions in the late 1870s and early 1880s and again in the early 1890s. In between, and then particularly from 1894 to 1914, able, hard-working and fortunate agriculturalists could rebuild. The depression also stimulated more rational use of farming land, especially in the two decades from 1895 to 1914. If the term 'Great Depression' is used at all, then it should cover the experience of the less flexible or less fortunate landowners and farmers working in arable England.

The scale of depression in much of the English Midlands and South-East should not be under-estimated. The depression here finally destroyed the primacy of the landed interest while confirming that Britain had become overwhelmingly an urban nation. Detailed regional studies offer more fine-grained contrasts. They indicate, for example, how the rural North-West of England was able to escape significant depression. While the gross value of landed output in such arable counties as Oxfordshire and Berkshire declined by about 20 per cent between 1873 and 1894, that of Lancashire and Cheshire increased by 12 per cent and 11 per cent respectively.[22] Against the general aristocratic trend, furthermore, the sixteenth Earl of Derby enhanced the fortunes of the Stanley family. The family's extensive Lancashire estates, in which the Duke took direct interest, were mostly pastoral, and he retained a wide portfolio of urban investments, especially in Liverpool and Preston. It is no accident that he became the first mayor of the newly expanded borough of Liverpool in 1895 and also the first Chancellor of the city's university when it received its Royal Charter in 1903.[23]

III. Aristocracy, finance and ennoblement

In an attempt to mitigate the effects of depression, many great landowners sought to diversify their sources of income. Some obtained an instant injection of funds by marrying into money. The ninth Duke of Marlborough, head of the Churchill family, married the American heiress Consuelo Vanderbilt in 1895. Between 1870 and 1914, 10 per cent of peers and sons of peers married into well-connected and wealthy American families.[24] The Earl of Rosebery, a future Prime Minister, had set both the acquisitive tone and also a fair few anti-Semitic aristocratic hares running when he married Hannah Rothschild of the pre-eminent banking family in 1878. Four years earlier, on her father's death, Hannah had become the richest commoner in Britain.

The landed interest also developed a more systematic, even symbiotic, engagement with the City of London. Not only was the City thriving in the 1880s and 1890s, with many new companies floated on the stock exchange, but landowners and City gents had a common interest: gambling. One of the great passions of the aristocracy was horse-racing, whose only rationale is what might politely be termed 'speculation' on the outcome. Likewise, the great City fortunes were grounded in risk-taking. 'Playing the stock market' is, at root, gambling, although London brokers usually enjoyed the luxury of gambling with other people's money. This mutuality of cultural interest saved many a landowning family in the late nineteenth and early twentieth centuries. Large landowners sought new sources of wealth in the City; leading City figures were happy to accommodate them, especially if they gained in return. As one commentator noted in 1881, a 'Noble Lord's character' – unless his gambling debts were grotesquely high – was marketable: 'he may command good terms for letting his name be put on a [company] prospectus. His patronage means success.'[25] The aristocracy needed no second invitation. By the mid-1890s, about a quarter of their number were company directors. Some proved shrewd players of the City game; more were content to benefit almost as sleeping partners, knowing that their social contact books opened profitable doors for many a **joint stock company**.

> **Joint stock company**
>
> A company whose capital is provided by investors who buy 'shares' in the company. Investors share the profits but also acknowledge their joint liability, limited to the combined value of the 'stock', or shares, which they own.

The great City financiers gained reciprocal benefit also. Gladstone elevated the merchant banker Nathaniel Rothschild to the aristocracy in 1885. His father, Lionel Rothschild, had become the first Jew to be elected an MP in 1850. He was elected as member for the City of London four more times until Russell's Oaths Act of 1858 enabled him to take an oath which would not compromise his religious faith and thus allowed him finally to take his seat. Now his son became the first Jewish peer. He stressed his religious allegiance by retaining the family's Jewish surname as Baron Rothschild of Tring. In the same year, Edward Baring, grandson of the founder of the bank which bore his name, was ennobled as Baron Revelstoke.[26] These two headed banks which led the charge to confirm London as the world's financial capital and also, in the eyes of critics, to accelerate the flight of British capital to profitable investment overseas.

These ennoblements were part of a much wider inflation of honours. The numbers were startling. The Conservatives granted 146 peerages while they were in office from 1885 to 1892 and 1895 to 1905. The Liberals were only in office for nine years during the same period, but still managed to create more than a hundred.[27] Lower honours – baronetcies, knighthoods, the Royal Victorian Order and the like – were bestowed in profusion from the 1870s. Relatively few were offered to the established landed class. Most went to successful professionals, including members of the armed forces, and commercial figures. Mere entertainers were also included, though it seems demeaning thus to describe Britain's greatest composer, Edward Elgar, knighted in 1904. W. S. Gilbert and Arthur Sullivan, brilliant providers of classy, satirical operetta to the middle classes of the 1870s and 1880s, were both honoured, although the librettist Gilbert (knighted by the raffish Edward VII in 1907) was made to wait. Queen Victoria considered him altogether too subversive for serious recognition. Sullivan, who the Queen thought – wrongly – had it in him to be a great serious composer, was fast-tracked to a knighthood in 1883 at the early age of 41.

The inflation and, as many hereditary peers considered it, dilution of honours accurately reflected the waning influence of the landed interest. Not until the last quarter of the nineteenth century did the middle classes outnumber the landed interest in the House of Commons. From the 1880s, however, the process accelerated. Honours could, of course, accommodate the aspirations and the vanity of long-serving members of parliament. A significant number of senior politicians first elected in the 1880s and 1890s were granted titles on retirement. Almost three-quarters of the MPs elected at the general election of 1918 became peers and baronets or were knighted.[28] David Lloyd George, Prime Minister at the time and never the most morally scrupulous of politicians, was heavily complicit. He sustained his long-held contempt for titles by, in effect, personally selling them to the vain and the wealthy. Lloyd George would heartily have endorsed the sentiments of W. S. Gilbert in *The Gondoliers* (1889): 'When everyone is somebody, then no one's anybody.'

IV. Rising living standards

For most of Britain's labouring population, price falls of up to 40 per cent (see above) were good news. It is one of the ironies of nineteenth-century social history that a period which most middle- and upper-class contemporaries considered to be one of depression, decline, falling profits and, for many, bankruptcy witnessed the most sustained period of rising living standards. Boom conditions tend to be accompanied by rising prices and even faster increasing profits. The consequence is that, although working people may experience modest rises in living standards, the gap between rich and poor widens. During depressions, the trend is in the opposite direction. Wages fall but prices fall faster. Consequently, **real wages** increase. The only exception to this optimistic picture concerns the casualties of business failure: those who lose their jobs and remain unemployed over a long period.

Real wages

This is the term used to describe the purchasing power of wages. It takes into account price movements. In its more sophisticated forms, calculations of real wages include analysis of prices of a 'basket of goods' which it is reasonable to assume working people would need to buy. During the so-called Great Depression, property rents tended to fall and food prices fell faster.

Real wages increased by about a third in the last quarter of the nineteenth century. This had significant consequences. Many working-class families included meat as part of their regular diet for the first time, while plummeting prices of both tea and sugar made the famous 'cuppa' a staple for entertaining, fortifying or consoling family members and guests. Mass-consumed tea, now hygienically wrapped and supplied by local **Co-operative** stores, was usually taken with at least two teaspoonfuls of sugar. Consumption of sugar more than doubled between the 1860s and the early twentieth century.[29] The combination of greater purchasing power and shorter hours of work enabled families to find time to eat together. Among the middle classes and better-off workers, time was set aside either for a family 'Sunday roast' or, particularly in the northern counties, 'high tea' with fish or meat. A more varied diet linked to improved nutrition gave beleaguered arable farmers even more problems, since consumption of wheaten bread began to decline. It is highly likely that the rising energy intakes which were part of this nutritional revolution helped to explain declining death rates later in the nineteenth century. More people now had greater physical strength to fight off infectious diseases which had killed their parents and grandparents. Calcium levels, however, remained low since regular consumption of fresh milk, and other dairy products, remained outside the range of many working-class families until after the First World War.

Co-operative Societies

These emerged from the ideas of the factory owner and philanthropist Robert Owen (1771–1858), who wanted his workers to be able to purchase the necessities of life at low prices and without the intervention of profit-taking middle men. His visionary schemes based on workers and owners co-operating for their mutual benefit came to little, but co-operative trading survived. The Rochdale Pioneer Society was founded in 1844 on the basis of subscriptions from working men which set up a fund for the purchase of essential items. The so-called Co-operative Wholesale Society (CWS) was established in Manchester in 1863 and expanded rapidly, with close links to trade unions.

It is important not to exaggerate working-class gains. Despite improvements in gas supply and more widespread provision of water closets, the overall quality of housing before 1914 remained low. A combination of poor levels of education and local custom often precluded optimal use of improved dietary and other opportunities. Better diets were enjoyed disproportionately by the male breadwinner, with the mother most usually sacrificing her own health by 'going short'. Many women still considered proprietary milk for babies superior to breast milk despite substantially higher risks of infection.[30] Commenting on still high levels of infant mortality, County Durham Medical Officers of Health in 1906 bemoaned 'the vitiating taste for stimulating rather than nutritious foods' and noted that 'much further improvement' was contingent on 'healthy mothers rearing breast-fed children'.[31]

Despite such continuing problems, which a socially aware professional class was documenting with both increased assiduity and concern in the first decade of the twentieth century, the tide was turning. By 1914, more of the working classes were at last beginning to experience the benefits, as well as the all too apparent disadvantages, of industrial expansion.

28

....

The state, charity and the poor, *c*1830–*c*1900

I. The coming of a new poor law

Industrialism created great fortunes but even greater social divisions. Ever the fluent, if sometimes facile, phrase maker, Benjamin Disraeli talked of

> Two Nations between whom there is no intercourse and no sympathy; who are ignorant of each other's habits, thoughts and feelings, as if they were inhabitants of different planets . . . and are not governed by the same laws – THE RICH AND THE POOR.[1]

But the poor did not inhabit a different planet. As ratepayers up and down the land could have told the future Prime Minister, through 'poor rates' they were paying through the nose for their upkeep in their own parishes. In the early nineteenth century, poor law costs formed the largest part of local expenditure. The old system had come under severe criticism from political economists and others, on grounds of inefficiency, the alleged disincentive to independent labour and, above all, cost. Poor law expenditure virtually quadrupled between 1783 and 1818, when its average yearly cost per head of the population was 12 shillings (60p: the equivalent, on the basis of average earnings then and now, of £439 in early twenty-first-century values).[2]

Pressure for poor law reform had been building for years. **Jeremy Bentham** and his acolytes were developing strategies for radical change, while David Ricardo had argued in 1817 that one of the most comprehensive structures in Europe for helping the poor was counterproductive: 'the clear and direct tendency of the poor law . . . is not, as the legislature benevolently intended, to amend the condition of the poor, but to deteriorate the condition of both poor and rich'.[3] He urged its abolition. However, it was the Whig government's recognition that the old, locally based system was not securing the social order against riot and radical discontent, and especially the Swing Riots (see Chapter 7), which precipitated change. Landowning MPs were used to popular disturbances in the towns, and most lived well away from their consequences. Agricultural labourers they thought they understood and could control. The Swing Riots persuaded them differently. In 1832, the government established a Royal Commission to investigate the operation of the unreformed poor law. Heavily influenced by Benthamites, particularly Edwin Chadwick (see Chapter 26) and Nassau Senior, Professor of Political Economy at Oxford University, the Commission's conclusions were predictable. The Commission stated that, in parishes up and down the land, unnecessarily large amounts were being spent on poor relief. Waste was endemic, administration chaotic, controls non-existent. Lavish hand-outs were turning agricultural labourers into idlers – 'benefit scroungers' in derogatory modern parlance.

Jeremy Bentham, 1748–1832

Born the son of a lawyer in London, he was taught by his father, who wanted him to be a lawyer, before he became an undergraduate at Oxford at the age of 12. He was strongly influenced by the ideas of the European Enlightenment. He wrote works which aimed at simplifying and codifying the English law on rational lines but is best known for developing the system of thought known as 'Utilitarianism'. This judged political and other systems according to their usefulness. He aimed to deter the able-bodied from applying for poor law relief. He suggested the creation of 'industry houses' in which the idle and provident would be placed in order to learn habits of frugality and industry.

This was a heavily slanted analysis. The Commissioners highlighted evidence supporting their presuppositions and sidelined the rest. They ignored the extent to which parishes had already cut back on poor law relief during the agricultural depressions of the 1820s (see Chapter 7). The country gentry were abandoning support for an inclusive, paternalist solution to the problem of poverty in favour of harsher policies, which included the building of parish workhouses.[4] Unsurprisingly, overall expenditure on poor relief was 37 per cent lower in 1824 than it had been in 1818 and, although it increased in the early 1830s, it was still 20 per cent lower when the Poor Law Amendment Act was passed in 1834.[5] The Commissioners were also far less interested in the administration of the poor law in the towns than in the countryside because the problem was misleadingly assumed to derive from long-term rural under-employment rather than from the shorter, but much sharper, effects of a trade depression in, say, Bolton or Huddersfield.

The main purposes of the Act were to produce a more rational, uniform and national system and, particularly, to save ratepayers money. The Bishop of Oxford's assessment that the 'new Bill is the result of much patient and diligent investigation [by] . . . persons who have the comfort and happiness of the lower orders at heart'[6] was wildly wide of the mark. The Act's key principle was that those unable or unwilling to work should not be better off than those in work. Applying for poor relief was to be made demeaning rather than commonplace – 'less eligible' as contemporaries termed it – and the relief given more stringent. It set up a central Poor Law Commission to develop general principles governing relief and to oversee the new arrangements. It also provided for locally elected Poor Law Guardians who replaced the discredited 'overseers of the poor'. Ratepayers, it was calculated, would know their own interests and would not vote for spendthrift Guardians. The Royal Commission had also recommended that poor relief should in future be available only in closely regulated workhouses, thus ending so-called 'outdoor relief' altogether. The government was not prepared to go so far, although it did expect rigorous administration by assistant commissioners as they set up the new Poor Law Unions.

II. The new poor law in operation

The Poor Law Amendment Act had a profound, and long-lasting, deterrent effect. The spectre of the workhouse was a constant presence in the households of the poor, the ultimate signifier of the chasm which Victorians saw between the respectability of the independent wage earner and the degradation of the 'pauper'. In the words of one historian, 'To apply for relief was a cause of self-reproach and private humiliation; to enter the workhouse was a public admission of personal and moral failure.'[7]

Workhouses were built to resemble prisons. The architecture was stark and forbidding. Provision was made to isolate troublesome paupers. No workhouse was under-provided with locks. The design facilitated close supervision, depriving inmates of privacy.[8] The anti-poor law campaigner Richard Oastler stated that the new Act laid 'the axe to the root of the social compact: it must break up society and make England a wilderness'.[9] Oastler was wrong. Society was not broken up, but it increasingly functioned on a market, rather than a paternalist, basis. 'Social cohesion and economic growth were now seen as functions of a "natural order" based on individual self-reliance and market forces.'[10] Individuals were encouraged to migrate from countryside to town, where the labour market was usually much more buoyant. Not surprisingly, the new poor law cost less than the old. Despite rising population, poor law expenditure declined. It did not exceed its 1834 level until the impact of the American Civil War made its impact on the textile trade in 1863.

The government's response to rising unemployment in 1863 was the Public Works (Manufacturing Districts) Act. Local authorities were offered loans at preferential rates to encourage them to create employment opportunities in road building, minor works on canal towpaths, pavement improvements and the like. The Chancellor of the Exchequer, William Gladstone, did not wish to jeopardise social harmony by forcing into the dreaded workhouse respectable workers fallen upon hard times.[11] The line between the 'worthy' and the 'unworthy' poor – such as drunks hanging around Liverpool dockyards, or the 'outcasts' who troubling the metropolitan police force in London's East End – remained sharply in the Victorian mind.

The overall effectiveness of the new poor law is easily overstated. It was designed to deal with the two main problems. The first related to the able-bodied, immobile, adult male rural labourer living in the countryside for whom there were insufficient incentives, as the auditor of the Poor Law Union established in Uckfield (Sussex) put it in 1837, 'to look out' for work.[12] The second was an expensive, ramshackle, diverse and poorly supervised structure of relief. The Poor Law Commission had considerable success in addressing both problems in the rural south and east of England. However, its powers were limited. It could not force the new Unions to put all their paupers into workhouses. The Commission's Outdoor Relief Prohibitory Order, passed in 1844, still gave Unions the latitude to continue with outdoor relief. In 1847, the Commission was replaced by a Poor Law Board, with a government minister as its President. The Board was directly accountable to parliament. Its attempt to end outdoor relief – the 'Outdoor Relief Regulation Order' of 1852 – was still evaded by Unions, which argued that, in most cases, outdoor relief was both cheaper and more flexible. By the mid-1850s, however, fewer and fewer able-bodied men were given relief outside the workhouse.[13]

The scope of the problem, however, was much broader. Women and children were more likely to fall into poverty than were adult males. Most women's work was part-time and casual, although crucial to the family economy (see Chapter 25). A married woman's assessment by Poor Law Guardians depended entirely on her husband's status. The position of a widow was often worse. Under regulations regarding '**settlement**', she could be removed to her husband's place of birth, where she might have no connections whatsoever. Resettlement was very common; 40,000 paupers were forcibly moved in 1840 alone.[14] Women with illegitimate children generally had to go into the workhouse. Women mostly lived longer than men and might need more longer-term support. The cost of their relief was substantial.

Poor law settlement

'Settlement' related to the place which had responsibility for providing poor relief to an individual. It was usually either the place of birth or where an individual had lived independently for a set period. From 1662, settlement had been a key feature of the old poor law. Settlement laws were not repealed in 1834, although they often acted as a considerable disincentive to labour mobility.

Legislation framed to address a rural problem was bound to be unwelcome in many urban areas. Implementation in the industrial towns began later and proceeded at a slower pace. The return of economic depression in the later 1830s demonstrated the impracticability of a workhouse test for able-bodied urban males. Mass unemployment could not be relieved in a workhouse. Political protest was already under way in a number of northern towns, organised by Anti-Poor Law Associations. In many parts of the north, opposition to the new law led directly into support for Chartism (see Chapter 21). In Bradford, Dewsbury and Todmorden, when poor law assistant commissioners arrived to begin the process of establishing a Poor Law Union, they found that their meetings were forcibly broken up. In 1838, the Poor Law Commission was forced to instruct its assistant commissioners not to press for workhouse construction in Lancashire or the West Riding of Yorkshire. In effect, and if only for a few years, poor law arrangements in the industrial north continued as if the Poor Law Amendment Act had not been passed. The old arrangements nevertheless proved quite inadequate to meet the textile unemployment crisis of 1841–42. When trade conditions improved in the 1850s, a programme of rapid workhouse construction was put in train.

Given the many different guises in which poverty presented itself and the limited direct powers available to the Poor Law Commission, it is not surprising that many pre-1834 practices continued in the new regime. Forms of relief continued to be diverse. Similar applicants could receive quite different treatment at the hands of the local Guardians. Some Poor Law Unions continued to offer wage supplements to women whose part-time wages were inadequate; others did not. Some Unions were much better funded by their ratepayers than others. Some could honourably provide less relief because established local charities functioned effectively and relations between the Guardians and the charities were constructive. The one clear conclusion which can be drawn is that, for all the concentration on the workhouse, a substantial majority of all paupers received 'outdoor' relief rather than in a workhouse. In the 1850s, only 12–14 per cent of all paupers were in workhouses.

This proportion increased in the 1870s. A new Local Government Board (LGB) was established in 1871. It absorbed the work not only of the Poor Law Board but also a range of locally administered functions, including public health and the registration of births, marriages and deaths. The first annual report emphasised the Board's priorities: 'out-door relief is in many cases granted by the Guardians too readily and without sufficient enquiry . . . in numerous instances it would be more judicious to apply the workhouse test . . . in numerous instances the Guardians disregard the advantages which result from the offer of in-door in preference to out-door relief'.[15]

The LGB operated with characteristic Gladstonian efficiency. It treated the poor, as has been wryly noted, 'according to the most scientifically approved and parsimonious standards of the day'.[16] The standards in question were usually those of the self-confident, unforgiving and judgmental Charity Organisation Society (see below). Its members believed that 'pauperism' was associated with inveterate idleness and depravity of character and that nothing less than the harsh regime of the workhouse would provide corrective therapy. In 1872, the proportion of applicants relieved in the workhouse had risen to more than 15 per cent. By the end of a decade, this 'crusade against out-relief' had increased the proportion to 22 per cent. Poor Law Guardians were now encouraged to deny out-relief to women as well as men.[17] It is true that the response to the ever more stringent LGB circulars on the dangers of 'indiscriminate relief' was patchy. Some Boards of Guardians continued to act independently, believing that they understood the nature and causes of poverty in their area better than could pen-pushing bureaucrats in London. In the 1870s and 1880s, however, the general trend in the larger cities was towards greater use of the workhouse and reductions in poor law expenditure.

The later 1870s and 1880s also saw an economic downturn (see Chapter 27) and increasing concern about Britain's inability to fight off commercial competition from Germany and the United States. An atmosphere of national introspection ensued, to which the problem of the poor contributed. In 1883, Andrew Mearns (1837–1925), Secretary of the nonconformist London Congregational Union, produced a short pamphlet entitled *The Bitter Cry of Outcast London: An Inquiry into the Condition of the Abject Poor*. It drew attention to the 'pestilential human rookeries' which engendered so much 'child-misery'. He argued that only substantial 'State interference' could help the condition of 'this pitiable outcast population'.[18] The concern generated by Mearns's pamphlet helped the much larger project undertaken by **Charles Booth** to get off the ground from the mid-1880s. Booth's *Life and Labour of the People of London* had substantial methodological flaws[19] but its findings, however strongly contested, strengthened the position of those who argued that *laissez-faire* policies linked to stern lessons in self-improvement administered by the comfortably off would not improve a desperate situation. Booth had concluded that more than 30 per cent of Londoners were living in poverty. The majority of these were not idlers who 'work when they like and play when they like' but folk who had intermittent or 'small regular' earnings insufficient to keep them out of poverty. **Seebohm Rowntree**'s researches in York, published in 1901, were more sophisticated. Rowntree concluded that a very similar proportion of York's population was living in poverty. He included a commentary on a 'life cycle' which drew large numbers of honest, independent workers into poverty at certain times of their lives. He also recognised that many families lived in what he called 'primary poverty', where income was insufficient to maintain health and well-being however efficient the domestic management. Rowntree's work also challenged the idea that London was the exception to every rule. It provided powerful support for using the power of the state to address the worst effects of poverty (see Chapter 41).

Charles Booth, 1840–1916

Born into a prosperous Liverpool family, his father – a corn merchant – and mother were both nonconformists. He was educated in Liverpool, where he took an early interest in science and philosophy. Booth weakened his faith in orthodox religion. His desire to produce a genuinely scientific analysis of poverty in London was stimulated by the economic and social crises besetting Britain in the 1880s. He worked with a small army of investigators, committed to quantitative analysis. His study began in the London borough of Tower Hamlets in 1887 and was not published in its seventeen-volume final form as *Life and Labour of the People in London* until 1902. His study divided London's population into eight categories and calculated that, at any one time, about a third of the population was living in poverty. His findings added to growing concern about the validity of *laissez-faire* as a guiding principle for social action.

Seebohm Rowntree, 1871–1954

Born in York to Joseph Rowntree, the Quaker founder of the cocoa and chocolate business, he joined the family concern in 1889. The Rowntrees were enlightened employers, seeing their employees as virtual partners in the business. In 1895, a visit to the slums in Newcastle upon Tyne awakened Seebohm Rowntree's interest in researching the causes, and possible alleviation, of poverty. He began working on York in 1897, using similar methods to those of Charles Booth. His conclusions, published in 1901 as *Poverty: A Study in Town Life*, were similar to those of Booth, thereby suggesting that London was not a unique case and that the causes of poverty were similar in otherwise very different urban communities. Rowntree updated his study in the 1930s and 1940s and also served in the welfare department of Lloyd George's wartime Cabinet.

In the 1880s, however, politicians were not wrestling with the need for an ideological conversion but with the more immediate problem of making the poor law work in exceptional circumstances. In 1886 unemployment exceeded 10 per cent of the working population. On 8 February, protest marches organised by the London United Working Men's Committee and the Social Democratic Federation led to violence and attacks on property in Pall Mall and Oxford Street. These were the first serious public disturbances in the capital for twenty years. Joseph Chamberlain, the new President of the Local Government Board, wrote a 'Circular Letter' to Poor Law Guardians, urging them to consider implementing job-creation schemes. Chamberlain wished to preserve the 'spirit of independence which leads so many of the working classes to make great personal sacrifices rather than incur the stigma of pauperism'.[20] Many Guardians responded enthusiastically. Like Chamberlain, they believed in the clear distinction between the worthiness of the respectable working man and the dangerous 'residuum' from whom society needed protection. The validity of this distinction, however, was coming under serious challenge.

III. Charity – with strings?

Though less studied by historians, charitable activity made at least as great a monetary contribution to the alleviation of poverty as did the poor law. It has been estimated that in 1870, more six hundred charities were operating in London alone, raising between £5 and £7½m. In the same year £7m was spent nationally on poor relief.[21]

Charitable giving was widely considered to be the duty of a Christian gentleman. It played an important role in the lives of many middle-class families, especially women. Local newspapers frequently referred to the contributions made by local businessmen and professionals. In towns, subscriptions to charity represented a calling card of 'worthiness' for the prosperous middle classes. Charity was part of their engagement with the wider local community. It assumed a similar social role as regular attendance at church or chapel. A survey of middle-class households taken in 1890 calculated that, on average, they spent a larger share of their income on charity than on any other single item, except food. Placed in a wider cultural context, this is a less surprising finding than it at first seems.[22]

There was no shortage of individuals willing to help the poor. However, they wanted to help the poor to be more like them: God-fearing, hard-working, disciplined and, above all, committed to self-improvement. From the early nineteenth century, Evangelicalism (see Chapter 11) played an important role. It taught that the charitable impulse not only helped those less fortunate than the giver, it also saved souls. Churches established a large number of their own charities but the influence of Christian zeal was apparent everywhere. Nowhere was it more evident than in the district-visiting societies and 'home-missionary' work which sprang up in the larger cities from the 1820s. These were staffed by volunteers, predominantly middle-class women who were culturally debarred from seeking paid employment and who, with most domestic work done by servants, had time on their hands. They channelled their energies into 'good works'. A Metropolitan Visiting and Relief Association was established in 1843 to collect funds centrally for organised distribution to the poor during domestic visits.[23] Well-intentioned though much of this work was, it was done by folk who could not comprehend the difficulties of living a self-disciplined and 'improving' life in a slum on inadequate, irregular incomes in a family whose main breadwinner drowned his sorrows in beer on payday.

Voluntary societies and associations also straddled the middle classes and regularly employed working men. They concentrated on thrift and the accumulation of small sums as 'rainy-day' money. Nonconformists, in particular, were attracted by the **temperance movement**. Insurance and other benefit clubs and societies were also common. In working-class communities, the ability to show respect for the dead was integral to 'respectable' behaviour. With death, and particularly infant mortality, rates so high, it was a frequent duty. The Victorians saw death all around them and communities wished to ensure that the dead received a properly respectful 'send-off'.

Temperance movement

The aims of this movement were to reduce the consumption of alcohol and to encourage individuals to abandon alcohol ('sign the pledge'), thus becoming 'teetotal'. It began in the 1820s and expanded rapidly in the mid-Victorian period. A number of separate organisations, such as the British Association for the Promotion of Temperance (founded in 1835), the Band of Hope (1847) and the United Kingdom Alliance (1853), were established. The movement developed as an effective pressure group on the radical wing of the Liberal party. Temperance societies also developed social functions, arranging trips to beauty spots and the countryside, as well as regular meetings in the larger towns.

Voluntary associations paid particular attention to children in the hope of encouraging them to grow up imbued with 'respectable habits'. The first so-called 'ragged schools' were established in Aberdeen in the early 1840s and their numbers expanded rapidly. **Anthony Ashley Cooper**, later Earl of Shaftesbury, became President of the 'Ragged School Union' in 1844 and held the post for almost forty years. The Schools provided a decent, if basic, free education to orphans and children born into poverty. By the time the Elementary Education Act was passed in 1870, more than 350 were in existence.

Anthony Ashley Cooper, seventh Earl of Shaftesbury, 1801–1885

Born in London, the son of the sixth Duke, he was educated at Harrow and Oxford University. He became an MP in 1826 and remained in the House of Commons almost without a break until he succeeded to the earldom on his father's death in 1851. He had always been serious-minded but was increasingly influenced by Evangelicalism in the 1830s. This governed much of his philanthropic and political activity for the rest of his life. It also confirmed his anti-Catholicism. He supported Factory Acts to reduce working hours, supported legislation in 1840 to protect child chimney-sweeps and sponsored the first Mines Act in 1842. He was also prominent in the British and Foreign Bible Society, the Lord's Day Observance Society and the Society for Improving the Condition of the Labouring Classes. He was a paternalistic Tory who believed that the wealthy should support the poor. In their turn, the poor should show deference to, and follow the example of, their betters.

Charities were extensive in number and diverse in character. The superior tone of many must have grated on the recipients of cash weighed down, as they were, by moralistic messages. An extreme example was the work of the Edinburgh Society for the Suppression of Beggars, established in 1812. Its members were effective in getting 'roughs' off the streets, because they had an interest in ensuring that beggars did not lower the tone of Scotland's capital city or intimidate its visitors. So they asked the local police to prosecute those found begging in the streets if they had rejected, or even avoided taking, the Society's help.[24]

No overall regulatory mechanism applied to charities. Their activities duplicated one another and few adopted an introspective or self-critical view of their effectiveness. At worst, giving could be self-defeating. Some charities 'raised money from those who could not afford it only to pass it on to those who did not need it'.[25] The best-organised charities linked their benevolence to evidence of 'worthiness' in the recipients. The best-known of all, the Charity Organisation Society (COS), founded in 1869, actively promoted an ethic of improvement. It made a vital distinction between 'poverty' and 'pauperism'. The former state, properly handled, was temporary and the Society was anxious to aid worthy folk in temporary difficulty, for example, during a trade depression or when an employer went bankrupt. 'Pauperism', on the other hand, was permanent. The non-respectable or 'residuum' had drifted into it because of their own failings.[26] The COS put substantial effort into helping other charities distinguish between 'deserving' and 'undeserving' cases. The latter needed charity less than they needed discipline and hard labour. One of the Society's most prominent members, **Octavia Hill**, made tenancies of the extensively improved properties she rented out contingent on evidence of 'respectable' habits and good behaviour.

Octavia Hill, 1838–1912

Born in Wisbech, Cambridgeshire, the daughter of a corn merchant who became bankrupt and the granddaughter of the public health expert Thomas Southwood Smith, she was brought up by her mother. She moved to London in 1852, where she was much influenced by the writings of John Ruskin, which awakened her interest in women's rights. In 1864, Ruskin used part of a legacy to invest in Hill's scheme to improve the housing of the poor in London. She bought properties in Marylebone, improved them and installed tenants who were mostly casual or seasonal labourers, not respectable artisans. Tenants were expected to be regular and sober in their habits. Hill believed that good-quality accommodation and moral improvement went hand in hand. She did not tolerate either disruptive behaviour or habitual falling behind with the rent. As more investment came in, she improved the social environment, making playgrounds for children and erecting halls for meetings and social activities. She was a member of the Charity Organisation Society and believed that support for the poor should be conditional on good behaviour and commitment to 'improvement'.

The Bishop of London summed up the dominant ethos of charitable giving when he addressed the annual meeting of the COS in 1886:

> . . . a very large number of people consider that they are fulfilling the commands of charity by simply giving such assistance as they can easily afford to the most importunate applicants they come across. In doing this, they do no real good to the receiver, but simply find a relief for their own feelings . . . The Charity Organisation Society aims at helping . . . in such a way as to make the benefit permanent. It always endeavours . . . to give a man such help as will enable him to be afterwards independent of charity altogether.[27]

As this passage suggests, charitable giving in Victorian Britain was extensive but rarely informed by empathetic understanding.

29

Education, leisure and society

I. Education and social division

Educational provision was socially stratified and highly gendered. So far as the poor were concerned, it was also little concerned with 'education' in the original Latin sense. Its intention was not to 'lead its recipients out' by opening their minds. Popular education was about socialisation. It would keep children off the streets where they learned bad habits. It would address the ignorance which led to vice, dirt and disease by inculcating regular and frugal habits. It would teach children to know and respect the Bible. Above all, it fitted people better to accept the social station into which they were born.

After their earliest years in the hands of nannies, governesses and sometimes private tutors, sons of the aristocracy were sent away to be educated in one of a small number of long-established fee-paying 'public schools', such as Eton (founded in 1440) or Winchester (1382). The curriculum was governed by classical languages, grammar and civilisation – and leavened by a little mathematics. Their educational standards in the early nineteenth century were not high and discipline was often lax. Under the influence of reformers such as **Thomas Arnold**, they revived in the middle years of the century. The emphasis shifted to giving pupils the skills needed to exercise leadership in public life, whether in the United Kingdom or the colonies. Following the recommendations of the Clarendon Royal Commission (1861–64), the Public Schools Act of 1868 established independent boards of governors for the nine leading establishments, freeing them from Church or government interference but demanding that they institute proper financial controls and robust administration.

Thomas Arnold, 1795–1842

Born on the Isle of Wight, the son of a customs collector, he was educated first at Warminster (Wiltshire) and Winchester before going to Oxford. From an early age, he developed an interest in history and the classics. He part-owned a school at Laleham (Middlesex) before being appointed Headmaster of Rugby in 1827. His reforms there, adopted by most of the other public schools in the middle years of the century, raised the status of housemasters, who had a pastoral as well as an educational role, and assistant masters. Although classical languages and civilisation remained at the core of the curriculum, more emphasis was placed on modern languages and science. He also raised standards of discipline and his school's 'moral tone'. The overall aim was to educate young gentlemen to accept responsibility and to develop leadership skills linked to a sense of duty and Christian mission.

By the 1860s a number of new public schools were being established. These catered mostly for the sons of the upper middle classes and the gentry. Most had religious sponsorship. Radley College, near Abingdon, for example, was established in 1847 by supporters of the **Oxford Movement** and was organised along the lines of an Oxford college. Rossall School, near Fleetwood (Lancashire), was founded three years earlier as an Anglican boarding school 'with the object of giving to the sons of clergymen and others an education similar to that of the great public schools, but without the great cost of Eton and Harrow'. Rossall's choice of location, as for many nineteenth-century foundations, was significant. Its then draughty and gaunt buildings were situated on a promontory exposed to storms and gales from the north and west. The next generation of the nation's leaders were expected to exercise regularly and to endure physical discomfort away from the distractions of town life. To use a Latin phrase well known to privileged children in Victorian England, the objective was *mens sana in corpore sano*: 'a healthy mind in a healthy body'.

Oxford Movement

This developed in the 1830s in reaction to the Whig government's policies towards the Established Church both in England and Ireland. It got its name from a sermon preached by John Keble in Oxford in 1833. It wanted to move the Church closer to Catholicism both in doctrine and in the use of ritual and was termed a 'High Church' movement in contrast to 'Low Church' Evangelicalism (see Chapter 25). Some members, following the example of one of its leading figures, John Henry Newman in 1845, converted to Roman Catholicism. An alternative name is the 'Tractarian Movement', following the publication of a series of 'Tracts for the Times' in defence of High Church doctrine.

The definition 'middle class' encompassed an enormous social and income range (see Chapter 4) and an almost equally wide variety of schools catered to its educational needs. The wealthiest urban families, many of them nonconformists, sent their children to be educated in Scottish academies, predominantly in Glasgow and Edinburgh, in view of Anglican domination of education south of the border. The other problem was that English schools were extremely variable in quality. The largest urban centres, Leeds, Birmingham and the like, possessed high-quality grammar schools to which the commercial elite and the higher professionals could confidently send their sons.[1] Many, like the King Edward VI Schools, had been founded during the Reformation of the sixteenth century from money released when Catholic chantries or religious guilds were dissolved. As the Taunton Commission reported in 1868, however, two-thirds of English towns had no schools which provided any education beyond the basic or 'elementary'. The Commission also confirmed the variability of those which did exist. The Endowed Schools Act of 1869 set up a new framework to support the development of more consistently effective secondary schools.[2]

In the first half of the nineteenth century, most daughters of aristocratic families were taught at home, usually by a governess. Education might incorporate language tuition, perhaps useful for a titled hostess in later life; overall it was practical. Young ladies acquired the social skills befitting their status: interesting conversation for use at formal dinners when receiving visitors, artistic accomplishments, domestic management. Their primary value to the family name lay in their ability to 'marry well'.[3]

Opportunities for girls from comfortable middle-class families improved after 1850. The North London Collegiate School, which grew out of a private school established in 1845, pioneered education for middle-class girls, under the sternly unbending leadership of **Frances Buss**, its headmistress. Cheltenham Ladies' College was founded in 1854. Thereafter, increasing numbers of endowed girls' proprietary and grammar schools emerged. By the 1890s, they numbered more than two hundred, though still of varying quality.[4] The curricula of many schools continued to reinforce 'domesticated' stereotypes. Parents were complicit in this since few were anxious to see supposedly 'feminine traits' submerged beneath a welter of 'book learning'.[5] Book learning which continued to university level brought significant rewards for a small minority. Women could attend Cambridge University, via Girton College, from 1873 and Oxford, via Lady Margaret Hall and Somerville, from 1879. Neither university, however, would grant them full degrees until well into the twentieth century. Women could obtain a degree at London University from 1878 and from all of the provincial universities established in the decade or so before the First World War.

Frances Buss, 1827–1894

Born in London, the daughter of a painter, she was educated at a private school before teaching at a school set up by her mother. It was renamed North London Collegiate School for Ladies in 1850 with Frances as Headmistress, a post she held for forty years. The School aimed to educate girls from lower-middle-class families – tradesmen, clerks and the like. Buss insisted that educating the girls of such families was as important as it was for the boys. By the 1860s, she was acknowledged as a leading authority on female education. She aimed to increase the status of teaching from that of a 'mere trade' into a respected profession. She advocated competitive examinations for girls on the same basis as for boys and also urged women to take up the new opportunities opening up from the 1870s for political involvement on school boards and in local government.

Some able and determined women at least were prising ajar the doors to a satisfying professional career. Elizabeth Garrett-Anderson (1836–1917) could not graduate in medicine from any British university but, bearing a degree from the University of Paris awarded in 1870, become the first female member of the British Medical Association three years later. By 1900, however, scarcely more than four hundred women were on the medical register and thus able to practise medicine.[6] Only 6 per cent of doctors and lawyers were women in 1900.[7] By contrast, they comprised about 70 per cent of the teaching profession at the turn of the century, but teaching lacked the status, and the salary, of a 'higher' profession.

II. Education and the state

Very few people in England and Wales received formal, sustained education before the reign of Queen Victoria. One estimate suggests that about 4 per cent of the population of England and Wales attended day school in 1750, a proportion which rose marginally to 6 per cent in 1818. In Scotland, proportions were up to three times higher.[8] Sunday Schools, promoted both by Anglican pioneers like the Gloucester newspaper proprietor Robert Raikes (1736–1811) and as offshoots of nonconformist chapels, made some impact. So did the National Society for Promoting the Poor in the Principles of the Established Church (1811) and the **non-denominational** British and Foreign Schools Society (1814), founded by the Quaker Joseph Lancaster. Such organisations taught poor children to read Bible stories, which could provide a route to wider literacy. Marriage data suggest that, by 1840, just under half of women and about a third of married men could not sign the marriage register. This is an uncertain guide to levels of literacy, since people who had learned to sign their names, perhaps just for this special occasion, might not be able to write anything else.

Non-denominational

An organisation which is neither controlled nor influenced by one of the Christian Churches. Much nineteenth-century educational provision depended on support from the Churches, but Anglicans and nonconformists frequently clashed. Non-denominational organisations tried to operate across, rather than within, religious divides.

On the other hand, more folk could read than write. Many young men apprenticed to a trade in the eighteenth and early nineteenth centuries acquired decent levels of literacy from the skilled workers responsible for their training. Add to this the frequency with which newspaper articles were read out in beer shops, meeting rooms and other public places and it is clear that, for men (who disproportionately congregated in such spaces) at least, lack of formal education did not necessarily mean a lack of literacy.[9]

Before the 1830s, the state claimed no direct involvement in education. When it did, the main concerns were for public order in the towns and the instruction of the lower orders in habits of regularity and discipline. In 1833, the radical MP J. A. Roebuck proposed a national system of compulsory education for all children between 6 and 12. He asserted that 'the education of the people is a matter of national concern' and that only via education would the poor gain 'a thorough understanding on their part of the circumstances on which their happiness depended . . . They would learn what a government could, and . . . could not do to relieve their distresses . . . [and] what depended on themselves.'[10] Most MPs believed that the Churches, not the state, should provide the poor with all the education they needed and Roebuck's proposal failed. However, a thinly attended House of Commons voted to approve state grants of £20,000 in support of church or chapel education for the poor.

Six years later, the Whig government established an inspectorate to monitor, and report on, the quality of education provided in grant-aided schools (see Chapter 22). Under the leadership of **James Kay-Shuttleworth**, the Committee of the Privy Council on Education developed standards for assessing the quality of education. The Committee's bureaucracy ensured that, however much politicians supporting Church education might resent it, government involvement in supporting the education of the poor was growing. A pupil-teacher training scheme was introduced in 1846, while the number of school inspectors grew rapidly. In 1847, the government grant had risen to £100,000 a year, the equivalent of almost £7m in early twenty-first-century values. The growth of an educational bureaucracy is also an excellent early example of increasing government intervention, during a period generally associated with *laissez-faire* (see Chapter 26).[11]

James Kay-Shuttleworth, 1804–1877

Born as James Kay into a devout Congregational family in Rochdale, his father was a successful cotton merchant. He took the name Kay-Shuttleworth in 1842 when he married Janet Shuttleworth, the daughter of a baronet and heiress to Gawthorpe Hall in Padiham near Burnley. He was educated at a grammar school in Salford and studied medicine at Edinburgh University. He worked as a doctor in Manchester during the cholera epidemic of 1832, serving on the local Board of Health. His pamphlet *The Moral and Physical Condition of the Working Classes Employed in the Cotton Manufacture in Manchester*, published in 1832, was influential in suggesting a link between environmental conditions and high levels of both dissipation and disease. He became increasingly interested in the education of the poor, believing that mass education would help to civilise society. He published a *Report on the Training of Pauper Children* in 1838 and began training teachers in south London in the same year. He was appointed Assistant Secretary – in effect senior administrator – of the Committee of the Privy Council on Education in 1839. While in office, he established a teacher-training college in Battersea (1840) and argued that the state, not the Churches, should take the lead in the development of education policy.

Policy on elementary education from the 1830s onwards was bedevilled by conflict between religious sects. Peel's Factory Bill of 1843, proposing that all education for factory children be provided by Anglican clergymen, confirmed nonconformist fears that state involvement would disadvantage them. The successful campaign against the bill, which the Leeds journalist Edward Baines Jnr called a 'war against all Nonconformists', provided powerful evidence of growing nonconformist influence in urban Britain.[12] Noncomformists favoured '**voluntarism**'.

Voluntarism

The belief that the state should not involve itself in elementary education. Education should be the responsibility of 'voluntary' effort by various religious sects. Most 'voluntaryists' either were, or were sympathetic to, the nonconformists who believed that state involvement in education resulted in a strong bias towards the Church of England, the 'state Church'.

As early as 1850, a Royal Commission on Elementary Education was calling for local government involvement in funding education. Squabbling between nonconformists and Anglicans put paid to that but the Commission's proposal that payment should be on the basis of results was taken up.[13] A further Royal Commission, chaired by the Duke of Newcastle, sat from 1858 to 1861 and endorsed the idea. Palmerston's government eagerly seized the opportunity to cut back on expenditure, which, by 1861, exceeded £800,000 a year. The so-called Revised Code of 1862 resulted. The size of grant provided to a school became dependent both on pupils' regular attendance and on test results in reading, writing and arithmetic. This was widely criticised. Shuttleworth saw pupil teachers as the 'raw recruits of an army suddenly raised' who had nevertheless become 'the pioneers of civilisation'. Payment by results would give 'the people a worse education from motives of short-sighted economy'.[14]

The response of **Robert Lowe**, Vice-President of Council, was predictable. The House of Commons wished to avoid 'extravagance' in expenditure on a system whose intention was to 'fix a minimum of education' which it would pay for, not a maximum. The state's role was not that of social engineer. 'It must never be forgotten that those for whom this system is designed are the children of persons who are not able to pay for the teaching. We do not profess to give those children an education that will raise them above their station and business in life . . . but to give them an education that may fit them for that business'.[15]

Robert Lowe, 1811–1892

Born in Nottinghamshire, the son of an Anglican clergyman, he was educated at Winchester College and Oxford University. He trained as a lawyer before spending eight years in Australia, where he was a member of the New South Wales Legislative Council. On his return, he was elected as a Liberal MP in 1852. He was Vice-President of the Board of Trade from 1855 to 1858, piloting legislation for the establishment of limited liability public companies. From 1859 to 1864, he was in charge of Privy Council Committees on both Health and Education. In the latter role, with the senior civil servant R. R. W. Lingen, he developed the Revised Code, which attracted widespread criticism, especially from those who resented what they saw as increased government interference. He opposed parliamentary reform in 1866–67 and his role as leader of the 'Adullamites'

▶

led to the resignation of Russell's government (see Chapter 31). He was Chancellor of the Exchequer from 1868 to 1873 and Home Secretary in 1873–74. Gladstone did not invite him back into the Cabinet after his election victory in 1880 and he was ennobled as Viscount Sherbooke. He opposed Gladstone on Home Rule in 1885–86 and became a Liberal Unionist (see Chapter 38).

This limited ambition did indeed prove economical. Between 1862 and 1865, the level of the educational grant fell by 22 per cent.[16] Efficiently and economically administered, the principle of state aid now received overwhelming acceptance in parliament. The key task now was to address the often grotesque inequalities in provision. Both sides of the sectarian divide voiced grievances. Nonconformists resented the fact that most of the state grant supported Anglican schools. They formed the National Education League in 1869 to press for a system of rate-supported schools to provide non-sectarian education.[17] They also lobbied for more expenditure in the towns, where only about 20 per cent of children attended school. A survey of Manchester in the late 1860s revealed that there were considerably fewer school places available than had been supposed.[18]

The Church of England calculated that only 58 per cent of its day schools were receiving any state aid in the late 1860s because insufficient staffing levels and inadequate local income rendered them ineligible. Poor parishes often supported poor schools. As one clergyman noted, 'rich localities who are able to pay certificated masters get all, the poorer who are not able get none'.[19]

Whether in parts of the teeming towns or in sleepy, under-populated areas, therefore, the existing system left big gaps. It was to deal with these, and also to broker a politically driven compromise between Anglican and nonconformist positions, that Gladstone's first government passed the Education Act of 1870. Contrary to widely held belief, it made elementary education neither compulsory nor free. It did, however, generate an unstoppable momentum which would bring about the former in 1880 and the latter in 1891 (see Chapters 37 and 38).

Scotland, moving faster towards compulsory attendance with a separate Act passed in 1872, transferred responsibility for its burgh (urban) schools from town councils to new School Boards. The most academic schools were classified as 'higher class'; these had a specific remit to develop secondary education. By the early twentieth century, Scotland had almost sixty endowed, higher-class schools, while in almost two hundred others, some secondary work was extending the basic framework of elementary education. School attendance in Scotland was running at almost 100 per cent by 1891, against less than 70 per cent in England and Wales.[20]

As with much earlier 'social legislation' (see Chapter 26), the 1870 Act devolved operative responsibility to the localities, telling authorities what they could do, not what they must. New School Boards were locally elected by ratepayers. The Boards created and ran 'public elementary schools', to fill up the gaps in existing provision. The new 'elementary schools' would be fee-paying but School Boards could provide free places to the needy if they chose. Boards could also make attendance compulsory for children between 5 and 10 years of age. As a major concession to its nonconformist constituency, the Liberal government stated that no specifically denominational education would be provided in board schools.

Most School Boards took up their new responsibilities with enthusiasm. By the 1890s, they had opened more than two thousand schools in England and Wales, against fourteen thousand existing voluntary schools.[21] Teaching was mostly formal; rote-learning and repetition in class were the favoured strategies. Inspectors remarked particularly on standards of spelling, grammar, arithmetic and, in girls' classes, 'domestic economy'. They also commented on standards of discipline.[22] Educational opportunities for the children of poor parents grew substantially but unequally. Some board schools offered high-quality education which went beyond 'elementary' level; others struggled to meet the criteria for a state grant. Meanwhile, the Church of England fretted that many of its voluntary schools needed to charge higher fees, while anyway being outflanked by rate-supported board schools. In 1890 *The Times* expressed concern that free education would put unsupportable pressure on many voluntary schools which 'although their efficiency occasionally leaves something to be desired' remained 'immensely valuable as auxiliaries to our State schools'.[23] This observation reflected still unresolved tensions between nonconformists and Anglicans. These fed into party politics and are considered in that context (see Chapters 32, 33, 37 and 38).

Above all, elementary education after 1870 was designed to be functional and perhaps also dreary. Most pupils continued to be taught only what fitted their station and business in life. The writer and satirist W. S. Gilbert expressed it pithily in the operetta *Iolanthe* (1882). His glamorous shepherdess Phyllis tells members of the House of Lords, all of whom – implausibly – wanted to marry her: 'I can spell all the words that I use and my grammar's as good as my neighbours'.' Her sentence construction spot on and her apostrophes correctly located, she could have been the product of a well-ordered elementary school.

III. Leisure: improving and entertaining

Improved living standards and lowered working hours (see Chapter 27) made for more leisure time. For the high-minded, this meant more time for education and 'improvement'. One observer of the Co-operative Movement noted in the early 1860s that 'Rochdale Pioneers' had built a library and a newsroom 'well-supplied with newspapers and periodicals . . . free to all members' as a means of 'social and intellectual advancement'.[24] The Liberal MP William Ewart sponsored a Free Libraries Act in 1850. This gave larger towns the opportunity to levy a rate to set up public libraries. More towns took up the opportunity once the Education Act had been passed.

Blackpool, in 1879, became one of the earlier seaside resorts to establish a public library, believing that it would attract 'better-class' visitors and address the town's growing image problem as a place to visit for 'mere' entertainment, insobriety and debauchery. Councillors themselves did little to counteract this. In 1908, when offered substantial funds by the Carnegie Foundation to extend library provision, they objected that libraries had proved themselves mere 'machines to grind away the public money'.[25]

Many trade unionists subscribed to the idea that leisure should be devoted to improvement projects. As part of their campaign for an extension of the franchise in the 1860s, they argued that they deserved the vote as educated and informed citizens. Libraries and other forms of 'rational' recreation showed their betters that they were their equals in knowledge, understanding and powers of reasoning. Many union leaders were nonconformists and their ideas of improvement reflected the wider Evangelical agenda (see Chapters 11 and 15), especially in its 'worthiness'. The nonconformist conscience viewed time as a resource to be 'spent' – and spent profitably.[26] As fewer people worked from home and the organisation of work became more regularised and disciplined, previously blurred distinctions between work and leisure became much sharper.

The legislature acknowledged this division when it defined and protected leisure time. In 1871, the banker and Liberal MP Sir John Lubbock (1834–1913) introduced the first Bank Holidays Act. Good Friday and Christmas Day were already widely observed as holidays and the state recognised four additional public holidays for England and five (with the addition of New Year's Day) for Scotland. Lubbock, a disciple of Charles Darwin's ideas on evolution, was a 'rational improver'. He made himself into a noted anthropologist, publishing on how 'primitive' societies evolved into 'civilised' ones. His initiative met with a mixed response from the improving artisans he was trying to help. Some objected to missing a day's paid labour. The new August Bank Holiday Monday did, however, quickly establish itself as a focal point for family day trips to the seaside, especially in the south of England. Further north, customary 'wakes weeks' were still observed as factory and workshop holidays.[27]

Union pressure led to the adoption by agreement of a nine-hour day across much of manufacturing industry. A Factory Act in 1874 restricted textile workers to a weekly maximum of $56\frac{1}{2}$ hours. Over the next forty years, the division between working time and non-working time became sharper. Celebration of 'Saint Monday' (see Chapter 6) dwindled but defined working hours became a little shorter. By the outbreak of the First World War, few were working more than an eight-hour day.

The variety of leisure pursuits increased significantly. In many northern towns, particularly those in which a small number of factory owners dominated, leisure became almost an extension of work. Brass bands and male-voice choirs were recruited, often with active owner involvement and sponsorship, from the ranks of the workers. Here and in South Wales formal competition between different works bands developed and rivalry was keen.[28] Other activities particularly associated with working men were pigeon 'fancying' and tending allotments – small patches of land let out for both recreational and economic gardening and vegetable cultivation.[29] Allotment production supplemented labourers' incomes while it provided urban workers with a link to the land. The Dukes of Richmond and Newcastle were leasing allotment land as early as the 1840s. The Church of England and local authorities followed suit. The Allotments and Cottage Gardens Act of 1887 obliged local authorities to provide allotments if local demand could be shown. By 1914, more than half a million allotments were being worked.

The transport revolution opened up new horizons. In the 1850s and 1860s, the middle classes led the way with railway trips to the seaside. By the 1870s, many working-class families could afford day trips and some took longer holidays. The railway consummated the love affair between the urban masses, sea and sand. As seaside resorts grew, so did residential zoning. The idea was to segregate those who had come to Brighton, or Scarborough, for more refined pleasures, such as recuperation, sea air and Strauss waltzes played by professional musicians, well away from those who craved excitement, fun-fairs, drink and gambling. Seaside resorts learned that turning a profit depended upon status-awareness. Even Blackpool, usually considered the most showy, even vulgar, of seaside resorts, had a North Shore considerably more 'select' than its South Shore. Four miles further south, Lytham St Anne's developed as a commuter and retirement town, particularly favoured by well-heeled Manchester businessmen and lawyers. Successful resorts grew quickly in the 1880s and 1890s. Blackpool's population, already a substantial 14,000 in 1881, had more than tripled to 47,000 by 1901. Visitor numbers, day trippers and holiday makers, were into the millions by 1913. Demand was particularly heavy from textile workers in nearby industrial Lancashire, but Blackpool had a national presence as the country's most brashly successful resort.[30]

Professional sport, especially association football, flourished as working-class incomes stretched a little further. 'Fans' could now support their team; some could afford trips to watch away games. Professional football clubs were initially concentrated in the industrial and commercial centres of the North and Midlands. They competed in a Football League, which began in 1888. Many, including Aston Villa, the most successful pre-First World War club since it had won both the League Championship and the F. A. Cup five times by 1914, had strong initial religious affiliations. Villa originated from the sporting interests of young men attending a Wesleyan Chapel in north Birmingham. Others, like Manchester United, grew out of works teams. United's original, if unsnappy, name was Newton Heath Lancashire and Yorkshire Railway Football Club. Further south, and away from industrial cities, professional sport was considered vulgar. This explains the paucity of southern teams in the early years of the Football League.

Growing leisure opportunities advantaged men more than women, especially among the working classes. It was men's disposable income which was used to buy tickets for football matches and predominantly men who worked on allotments. The public house, probably the most established leisure activity of all, was a male preserve, except of course for the presence of female barmaids, whose sexual allure doubtless often enhanced the prospect of a convivial evening with workmates and friends.[31] Cheap day trips and holidays – a not insignificant exception – apart, few working-class women participated directly in the world of commercialised leisure. They could, however, enrich free time with social intercourse at the corner shop, in the street or in each other's houses.[32] Gossip sounds trivial, but opportunities for regular contact were part of the intricate network of support on which working-class women struggling to bring up families so often depended. A further constraint on women's leisure time was the virtual absence of mechanised aids to cleaning and mending. Looking after a home and large family was a full-time job, if housewifely duties were taken seriously.

It is tempting to see leisure opportunities as part of a process of social control from above. Much emphasis has been placed on bourgeois attempts to 'civilise' towns and cities during a time of rapid expansion and volatility, to which high levels of inward migration contributed. The new police forces spent much time attempting to mitigate threats of disorder and violence, especially from those the Victorians called 'roughs': the casual poor, whose intemperate habits, boorish ways and culture of petty thievery was inimical to 'respectable' urban society. To this end, the emphasis in the second half of the century was on 'preventive' policing, using the physical presence of the police 'on the beat' to deter crime.[33] However, just as the 'respectable' encompassed both the middle and the working classes, so no clear line of demarcation existed between the leisure activities of the middle classes and those of manual workers. Many in both groups embraced that culture of improvement so often preached both from the pulpit and by political theorists and social commentators.

Likewise, the bourgeoisie and the working classes both patronised music halls, especially in the 1880s and 1890s, when large numbers of new theatres were built. The 'halls' provided much popular and undemanding entertainment in the form of song, dance, conjuring and the like, but they could also present biting social comment and satire. Established stars such as Marie Lloyd (1870–1922) and the male impersonator Vesta Tilley (1864–1952) took comedy to a new level. Marie Lloyd's use of *double entendre* and other forms of sexual suggestiveness regularly brought her to the attention of the authorities. Immense popularity was her only defence: 'They don't pay their sixpences and shillings at a music hall to hear the Salvation Army. If I was to try to sing highly moral songs, they would fire ginger beer bottles and beer mugs at me.'[34] Recreation in late Victorian Britain was by no means always 'rational' but neither was it always successfully manipulated or controlled.

Section 5

Party, Policy and Diplomacy: 1846–1880

A photograph of William Gladstone, aged approximately sixty, as Prime Minister at the beginning of his first ministry

Source: © Michael Nicholson/corbis

William Gladstone was the dominant figure in British politics in the second half of the twentieth century. Not only was he Prime Minister on four occasions but also Chancellor of the Exchequer four times. In a political journey lasting more than sixty years, he made both a significant contribution to the development of the Conservative party as a young minister under Peel and was at, or near, the centre of affairs as the Liberal party emerged from its Whig background to become the dominant political force. His involvement with the biggest issues of the age – free trade, cheap government, administrative efficiency, direct engagement with a mass electorate and the future of Ireland – made him highly controversial. It is possible to argue equally plausibly either that Gladstone made the Liberal party into the political force it became during the second half of the century or that, by the force of his intellect and driven personality, he led it in directions which contributed substantially to its later downfall. Either way, no historian can dispute that he made the political weather. His significance within the Liberal party is specifically considered in Chapter 32 but his wider influence pervades almost every chapter in this Section.

The Conservative party split in 1846 complicated party politics, although Chapter 30 argues that the minority and coalition governments of the 1850s are better seen as a continuation of earlier nineteenth-century party political activity than as breaking up a two-party system. A recognisably modern two-party system was not established until the 1860s at the earliest. Nevertheless, it is difficult to deny that, for most of the period covered by this Section, the Conservatives were in the minority. Their election victory of 1874 was their first for more than thirty years. Chapters 31 and 33 examine Conservative principles and policies during this period and assess how the leadership of Derby and Disraeli contributed to the revival of the party's fortunes.

Chapter 31 discusses how, and why, parliamentary reform resurfaced as a major issue, examines the extent of the changes brought about by the Reform Acts of 1867–68 and assesses the organisational and policy initiatives employed by the two parties to manage an electorate which almost doubled in size. The chapter also considers the extent to which parliamentary reform contributed to the modernisation of the political system and encouraged politicians to take their arguments directly to the people.

The main objectives of British foreign policy in this period were to secure Britain's trade routes, sustain its commercial dominance and protect its Empire. These objectives led to growing suspicion of Russian objectives, to war with China in the Far East and to threatened war with France over competing interests in the Middle East. Chapter 34 assesses the success of foreign policy in a period dominated by Viscount Palmerston and discusses the weaknesses in both strategy and in military operations which the Crimean War revealed. It discusses the extent to which giving priority to objectives outside Europe led to diplomatic failures and setbacks in Europe itself. It also assesses whether Britain was slow in reacting to the growing power of Germany. Chapter 35 explains why the Eastern Question dominated diplomatic activity in the 1870s and assesses whether the settlement made by Disraeli and Salisbury at the Congress of Berlin in 1878 did, as claimed, bring Britain 'peace with honour'. Overall, did British overseas influence decline in this period?

30

Party politics confounded, 1846–1859

I. The Whigs in office, 1846–1852

On the face of it, Peel's resignation in 1846 and the secession from the Conservative party of a hundred or so 'Peelites' threw politics into confusion. However, we should be wary of considering this as a period of an aberrant party indiscipline which rudely interrupted the steady progress towards a two-party political system under first Peel and then **Palmerston**. Even in the later 1840s, when, compared to the succeeding decade, Westminster politics seemed relatively straight-forward, party allegiance was not strong. It was the close approximation to two-party politics from 1841 to 1846 which was the aberration. Peel's Conservative party had developed in the 1830s from an anti-reform Tory core to which 'liberal Tories', returning after 1834, had added diversity and leadership (see Chapter 22). Grey's government of 1830–34 was a coalition between Whigs and liberal Tories, while Liverpool's Tory government of 1812–27 had grown out of the Pitt–Portland coalition of 1794 (see Chapter 12), reinforced by the defection of the Grenville Whigs after 1818 (see Chapters 16 and 17).[1] Defections, side-switching and a general uncertainty of party loyalties predominated before 1846. Often it was aristocratic family, rather than party, allegiance which mattered most.

Henry Temple, third Viscount Palmerston, 1784–1865

Born in London, the eldest son of the second Viscount, he was educated at Edinburgh University. Because he was an Irish peer, he sat in the Commons rather than the Lords. He became an MP in 1807, thus beginning an extraordinary parliamentary career lasting without a break until his death. For forty-eight of his fifty-eight years in parliament, he was a minister. He was Secretary at War from 1809–1828, Foreign Secretary three times between 1830 and 1851, Home Secretary 1852–55 and Prime Minister 1855–58 and 1859–65. He first took office as a Pittite Tory and established a reputation for efficient administration at the War Office. As a supporter of Catholic Emancipation, he left Wellington's government with Huskisson in 1828 and never returned to the Tories. He became Foreign Secretary in Grey's administration. In his belief that the British should be sensitive to principles of liberty, he was following the foreign policy principles of George Canning. Like him, he saw the value of informing, and then courting, public opinion. This made him unpopular with Queen Victoria, who thought he was a showman, and led to his dismissal from Russell's government in 1851 when he congratulated Louis Napoleon of France on his *coup d'état* without consulting the Prime Minister or the Queen.

▶

Like most foreign secretaries, he tried to sustain a balance of power in Europe, which often involved support for the Turks against Russia's attempts to increase its influence in south-east Europe. He was out of office when the Crimean War began. This worked to his advantage and helped him become Prime Minister in 1855. As Prime Minister from 1859, and with the support of Gladstone, he helped to shape the modern Liberal party. His interests were usually more focused on foreign than on domestic policy. In domestic matters, he was a reluctant reformer, believing that governments were too willing to clutter up the statute book with unnecessary legislation.

From 1846 to 1852, **Lord John Russell** headed a Whig–Liberal administration which governed with the tacit, and sometimes active, support of the Peelites. Russell, remembering how Grey had acted in 1830 (see Chapter 20), attempted to form a Liberal–Peelite coalition but the three Peelites to whom offers were made – Dalhousie, Herbert and Lincoln – refused, as did Sir James Graham in 1849.[2] Peel was gratified at such expressions of continued personal loyalty. The general election of 1847 produced a Liberal majority of more than a hundred over the Conservatives but, with more than ninety Peelites returning to the Commons, Russell's overall majority was small and unreliable.

Lord John Russell, 1792–1878

Born prematurely, the son of Lord John Russell (who became sixth Duke of Bedford in 1802), he was educated at Westminster and Edinburgh University. Small of stature, he frequently endured periods of ill-health. He became an MP – for the closed Bedford family borough of Tavistock – in 1813 and remained a loyal aristocratic Whig all his life. He was one of the most committed supporters of parliamentary reform, arguing in 1822, that 'the House of Commons does not possess the esteem and reverence of the people'. His list of Cabinet offices was long. He was Paymaster-General of the Forces under Grey (1831–34), Home Secretary and Secretary for War and the Colonies under Melbourne (1835–39 and 1839–41), Prime Minister (1846–52 and 1865–66), Foreign Secretary under Aberdeen and Palmerston (1852–53 and 1859–65), Lord President of the Council under Aberdeen (1854–55) and Secretary for the Colonies under Palmerston (1855). He helped to draft the Reform Bill in 1831, believed that the Whigs had a historic role to guide the people in the ways of reform and enlightenment. He resented what he saw as the pretension of extra-parliamentary radicals in seeking to usurp the Whigs' responsibility to effect 'safe' reforms. He was an able, intellectually curious man, with a wide range of civilised and artistic contacts. He was frequently ill at ease socially, and rather quarrelsome. His rivalry with Palmerston was intense and long-lasting, although their policies had much in common, not least support for nationalist movements in Europe. By contrast, Russell's relationship with Gladstone was usually warm. He was created Earl Russell in 1861. After his government was defeated over parliamentary reform in 1866, his last twelve years were spent out of office, although in 1868 he refused a place in Gladstone's first Cabinet.

Russell's notional supporters included a number of radicals and nonconformists from Scottish and northern urban constituencies who resented the fact that Britain was still governed by landed aristocrats and who put support for industry and commerce well above allegiance to a Whig-led Liberal party. John Bright (see Chapter 26) would become the most prominent of these. The Scottish MP and prison reformer, Joseph Hume, one of the earliest supporters of abolition of the death penalty, and J. A. Roebuck, pioneer supporter of state support for education (see Chapter 26), who had lost his seat in 1847 but was returned for Sheffield at a by-election in 1849, were good examples of high-minded urban radical independence. In 1848, about fifty radicals declared themselves an 'independent party', broadly supporting Chartist aims. Their household suffrage bill was heavily defeated in the Commons and, since independence meant more to the radicals than did party allegiance, the initiative foundered both quickly and predictably.[3]

Nevertheless, what was often called a 'reform party' of about a hundred MPs continued to operate. Its loyalty to Russell scarcely stretched further than their preference for him as Prime Minister over the Earl of Derby and a Conservative government. On a wide range of issues, including further franchise reforms, taxation and foreign policy, however, a significant minority of the reform party regularly voted against the government.[4]

Radicals and 'the reform party' were not one and the same, although there was much overlap. Some radicals elected for urban seats were genuinely 'one-issue' politicians but a broader fault line could be discerned. On the one hand, alongside Cobden and Bright, stood free-traders, supporters of religious toleration, cheap government and advocates of internationalism. On the other were 'humanitarians' and believers in a strong, reformed executive government. These included J. A. Roebuck and the archaeologist and administrative reformer A. H. Layard, who became an MP in 1852. Although a disparate group, they were generally less concerned with the size of tax bills and favoured both more state regulation and extensions of the franchise. Increasingly, and in stark contrast to Cobden and Bright, they aligned themselves behind Palmerston, rather than Russell, as likely to prove a more amenable Liberal leader.

Had the radicals been less fractious, they might have influenced policy more. Russell headed what has been called 'the last truly Whig cabinet in British history'.[5] Eleven of its initial members were either peers or, in the case of Viscount Morpeth, the son of an earl who would succeed to the title in 1848. After Whig losses in the 1847 election to nonconformists and business candidates, especially in the larger urban seats, Russell's government stood at an increasingly large social distance from the bulk of its parliamentary party.

This did not, however, offer much of an obstacle to its survival. True to its Whig heritage, the government was reformist. It increased the education grant in 1847 (see Chapter 29), did not attempt to block Fielden's Ten Hours Bill protecting factory workers and extended free trade by repealing the Navigation Laws in 1849 (Chapter 26). It increased government involvement in the social question by creating a new Poor Law Board in 1847 and passed a Public Health Act in 1848, also with a new Board directly responsible to parliament (see Chapter 28).

Despite difficulties with his own party, Russell's hand was strengthened both by Conservative weakness and Peelite compliance. The Corn Law crisis had left the Tories shorn of talent and overly dependent on Stanley, now in the House of Lords as Earl of Derby. In the Commons, Benjamin Disraeli was clever but capricious. He was not trusted by a party which voted viscerally against most forms of religious toleration. Lord George Bentinck, the other Protectionist champion from 1845–1846, also lost credit with backbenchers because he supported both religious toleration and the decidedly 'non-English' Disraeli. In any case, he died prematurely in 1848. The Conservatives, who most reluctantly accepted Disraeli as their Commons leader in 1851, were rudderless.

Russell also knew both that the Peelites were free traders and that Peel himself harboured no further ambitions for office. He declared in September 1846: 'I intend to keep aloof from party combinations'[6] and kept to his word – to the frustration of many of his colleagues. William Gladstone, in particular, believed that the Peelites could decisively influence Russell's government if they acted like a party, which they had the numbers to do. He disagreed with Peel both on the unconditional repeal of the Navigation Laws and on policy to deal with agricultural depression in 1849–50. Gladstone told the Earl of Aberdeen in October 1849 that he considered the position of Peel and his most loyal henchman Sir James Graham 'false and . . . almost immoral . . . in every critical vote [they] are governed by the intention to keep the ministers in office & sacrifice every thing to that intention'.[7]

The fall of Russell's government, unlike that of Peel, was not caused by basic disagreement over one heroic issue but by misjudgments on a series of relatively small ones. The agricultural distress of the late 1840s was poorly handled. It gave Disraeli the opportunity for rousing speeches aimed at winning over Conservative backbenchers. It also confirmed that, when major difficulties arose, the Chancellor of the Exchequer, Charles Wood, who had been all at sea in dealing with the economic fall-out from the Irish famine (see Chapter 40), was not up to the job. The death of Peel in July 1850 also liberated some of the Peelites. Herbert and Gladstone, in particular, were much more openly critical of Russell's ministry thereafter.

The farrago over the Ecclesiastical Titles Act demonstrated that aristocrats should not play at populism. When Pope Pius IX decided to restore all the Roman Catholic bishoprics in Ireland, which had been in abeyance since the 1580s, he launched a stream of anti-Catholic hostility. Knowing the strong feelings of his nonconformist supporters, and wishing to take control of a deteriorating situation in Ireland, Russell pushed through the Ecclesiastical Titles Act in 1851. This forbade Roman Catholic bishops from attaching any United Kingdom place names to the titles of their bishoprics. The Act was largely ignored by the Catholic hierarchy and it also split nonconformist opinion. John Bright attacked it as intolerant, peevish and unworthy. Among the so-called 'Irish brigade' of pro-Catholic MPs, it earned Russell permanent suspicion, if not outright hostility.

Russell's other attempt to assert himself in 1851–52, a modest Parliamentary Reform Bill, also fell flat. It would have given votes to more small property owners in both the counties and the boroughs. It was deemed too modest by the radicals and unnecessary by ministers increasingly disenchanted with their leader. It also gave Palmerston – whose foreign policy, though popular nationally (see Chapter 34), had led to his dismissal on grounds of insubordination – an opportunity to rally support and defeat Russell in February 1852 on a minor Militia Bill. Russell resigned immediately, much to most ministers' relief.

There had always been moans about Russell's lack of order and his inefficiency in handling government business. These mattered less while the ministry could point to significant achievements and reasonably secure Commons majorities. When things were going wrong, however, the meetings Russell had missed, the letters he had mislaid and the pervasive feeling of general sloppiness at the top all caused increasing resentment. The Duke of Bedford cut through all the oblique references when he told his brother bluntly, 'The complaint is that you were not sufficiently prime minister.'[8]

II. Conservative and coalition governments, 1852–1855

Russell's increasingly beleaguered government survived for nearly six years. Palmerston's second ministry, established in 1859, would end only with his death almost six years later. In between, four other ministries were formed. None lasted longer than three years and a bit. Because of internal divisions among the Liberals, the Conservatives usually formed the largest coherent political group in the Commons. Their support increased after 1850 partly because a number of Peelites returned after their leader's death and partly because the party gained support in the general election of 1852. Anti-Catholic prejudice, especially the furore roused by Ecclesiastical Titles, was at the root of this. The Peelite Edward Cardwell was defeated by old-school 'Protestant' Tories in Liverpool, the city most dramatically affected by Catholic immigration after the Famine. The Conservatives won just short of three hundred seats. Meanwhile, the Peelite complement was declining rapidly. Only about forty were returned to parliament in 1852.

After Russell's government fell, Derby formed a minority administration lasting only ten months.[9] It was pulled in divergent directions. The bulk of Derby's party remained firmly Protectionist (see Chapter 22), but maintaining any kind of Conservative majority depended on support from free-trade Peelites. This was grudgingly given on condition that a fresh election be held, with new budget proposals thereafter. Derby's government was also inexperienced. In addition to Derby, only J. C. Herries and the second Earl of Lonsdale had previously held government office, neither with any distinction. Despite protesting ignorance of financial affairs, Disraeli became Chancellor of the Exchequer. It was the rejection of his technically flawed budget which led to Derby's resignation at the end of 1852. Gladstone, although he privately considered Disraeli's speech in defence of an incoherent financial plan 'as a whole grand . . . the most powerful I ever heard from him', did not hesitate to demolish its arguments and, with it, the government.[10]

This brief Conservative interlude was nevertheless significant. The leadership was convinced that Protectionism was no longer tenable. Disraeli had also refused to end payment of the educational grant to the College at Maynooth (see Chapter 22). Both of the policies on which Peel's destruction in 1845–46 was plotted were, therefore, abandoned within six years. Derby also knew that any permanent Conservative revival must require a broadening of the electoral base beyond its narrow, reactionary base in the English counties. More seats were needed in the towns and in Scotland.

A minority Conservative government was succeeded by a Peelite–Liberal coalition headed by the Peelite **Earl of Aberdeen**. Parliamentary arithmetic suggested potential for permanence. No one could doubt the new government's collective ability and experience. It included the brightest Peelites, crucially Gladstone at the Exchequer and **Sir James Graham**, the Duke of Newcastle and Sidney Herbert too. From the Whig side, Palmerston, as Home Secretary, and Russell, Foreign Secretary, returned along with Earl Granville, an able young politician who had replaced Palmerston when Russell forced his resignation in 1851. A confection of ability often conduces to internal rivalry, however. Palmerston and Russell jockeyed noisily for supremacy. Newcastle would rather have stitched together a coalition of the highly born, with himself at its head. The 'reform party' within the Liberal party resented being marginalised. Only Sir William Molesworth represented its interests and he, having been refused the post of Colonial Secretary for which past experience amply fitted him, chafed in the minor Cabinet post of Commissioner for the Board of Works. He opened Kew Gardens to the public on Sundays but this was hardly likely to protect him from Cobden's charges of apostasy when he vigorously defended the coalition's policy of war in the Crimea (see Chapter 34).[11] The Earl of Derby's view was that it was 'difficult to imagine how a government can go on formed of such discordant materials as . . . Aberdeen has brought together'.[12]

George Hamilton Gordon, fourth Earl of Aberdeen, 1784–1860

Born in Edinburgh, the son of a peer, he moved to England as a child after his father's early death. He was educated at Harrow and Cambridge University and his early political career was spent under the influence of the Younger Pitt. He entered parliament in 1806, elected as one of the sixteen 'Scottish representative peers' entitled to sit there under the terms of the Act of Union (see Chapter 1). He was ambassador to the Austrian Emperor in Vienna in 1813 and, after some early embarrassments, developed into a respected diplomat. Much of his political career turned on diplomacy. He was Foreign Secretary under both Wellington (1828–30) and Peel (1841–46). He was instrumental in bringing the Opium War with China to a successful conclusion in 1842 and he helped to negotiate agreed boundaries between the USA and Canada in the same year. He was a firm supporter of Peel and left office with him in 1846. He became Prime Minister in the Peelite–Liberal coalition in 1852. After its collapse in 1855, he did not hold office again. His overall reputation was unfairly maligned by problems in the Crimea. He was an able, scholarly man, highly respected by fellow Conservatives and Peelites, including Wellington, Peel and Gladstone. He was also an enlightened, reforming landlord.

Sir James Graham, 1792–1861

Born in Cumberland, the son of a landowner and baronet, he was educated at Westminster School and Oxford University. He spent much time and money improving the family's landed estate, which he inherited in 1824, and this experience helped to focus his political views. He became MP for Carlisle in 1826 and supported reduced government expenditure and lower taxes to help the landed interest. He joined Grey's Cabinet in 1830 as First Lord of the Admiralty but resigned with Stanley in 1834 over the appropriation of church revenues (see Chapter 22). Like Stanley, he also joined the Conservatives and proved a highly efficient Home Secretary in Peel's government of 1841–46. His priorities in government remained the creation of a strong executive, efficiency and the elimination of waste. He left government with Peel in 1846 and became the first senior Peelite to join the Liberals. After his election for Carlisle in 1852, he helped to shape the direction of the Liberal party. He became First Lord of the Admiralty in the Aberdeen coalition, which he had helped to establish, and played an important role in Crimean war strategy. Though he never liked or trusted Palmerston, Graham briefly joined his government in 1855, but resigned almost immediately.

Go on, however, it did, for a little over three years, and with some notable achievements. Gladstone's 1853 budget reduced yet more duties while extending income tax, an impost he promised to repeal by 1860. The budget held out the tantalising Peelite prospect of permanently pegged public expenditure. Some Conservatives began to support a coalition which they believed would secure and enhance Britain's prosperity. What neither Gladstone nor Aberdeen could do, however, was budget for war, and little of the grand fiscal design survived the imbroglio in the Crimea.

The coalition also accepted the recommendations of the Northcote-Trevelyan report that a competitive 'system of examination' would increase 'the supply of the public service with a thoroughly efficient class of men'. Aberdeen agreed that too many of 'the unambitious, and the indolent and incapable' were currently recruited into the civil service.[13]

Internal tensions also ate away at the credibility of the coalition. In eerie anticipation of a similar early twenty-first-century spat over the succession, Lord John Russell believed that Aberdeen had promised an early resignation upon which he would be reinstated as Prime Minister. Disappointed in his expectation, Russell returned to pick at the old sore of parliamentary reform with predictably divisive results. His 1854 bill proposed to extend the vote to £10 householders in the counties and £6 householders in the boroughs as well as disfranchising more than sixty smaller boroughs, transferring most of their seats to the counties. The bill was withdrawn when the Crimean War broke out but it had already done considerable damage, not least since principle conflicted with party interest. With the Conservatives already dominant in the counties, many Liberals thought it madness to gift them yet more seats.

Unsurprisingly, however, allegations of waste and incompetence in the Crimea did the most damage. Thanks to vivid newspaper reporting and the invention of the telegraph bringing news of fresh disasters much more quickly to the breakfast tables of the nation, the public were both better, and more damagingly, informed about this war than any before. This increased the pressure on Aberdeen. When, in late January 1855, the patriotic reformer J. A. Roebuck overwhelmingly carried a motion for an enquiry into the conduct of the war, Aberdeen resigned almost immediately.

III. Palmerston ascendant

Palmerston was the fortunate, and not entirely deserving, beneficiary of the coalition's collapse. With the exception of a couple of weeks, he had been a senior minister throughout the coalition. In that capacity, he had argued for resistance to Russian demands in 1853–54 and his plan for war included the grandiose, and almost certainly unattainable, objective of a partial partition of Russia.[14] However, as Home Secretary, he was shielded from the direct criticism which came the way of Aberdeen and Russell. He also maintained that more robust diplomacy would have prevented war in the first place. Above all, his existing reputation as a statesman who would stand up for Britain's interests (see Chapter 34) vindicated him in the court of public opinion. He responded with disdain to invitations from both Russell and Derby to become a minister under them. He could also ignore Queen Victoria's severe reservations about his bombast and his populist ways. In February 1855, the 35-year-old Queen had no option but to appoint as Prime Minister a man twice her age though, as she saw it, with less than half of her integrity and common sense.

Palmerston's ministry began as a Whig–Peelite coalition but did not remain so for long. Aberdeen, Newcastle and Russell were not included in the new Cabinet, but within a fortnight the leading Peelites, Gladstone, Herbert and Graham, had resigned over Palmerston's agreement to press on with Roebuck's enquiry into the conduct of the Crimean War. The Peelites' reasoning was typically high-minded. Gladstone stated that the new government should have the 'right to believe that Parlt wd not inflict this Committee on a Govt which had its confidence', since 'the Committee was itself a Censure on the Govt.'[15] The consequences were significant. The Crimean War was turning in Britain's favour, enabling Palmerston to see off criticism from within the Liberal 'Reform Party'. Meanwhile, the Peelites were divided. Argyll, Canning and Harrowby remained with Palmerston in minor office. Since the big Peelite guns stayed out, Palmerston was, in effect, presiding 'over the destruction of Peelism as a separate political entity'.[16]

Palmerston's political style was distinctive. Like his political tutor, George Canning, he believed in talking directly to the people. He put the most favourable possible gloss on his ministry's achievements, especially in the Crimea. A well-publicised visit to Manchester in 1856 increased his popularity in the industrial north. Westminster, meanwhile, was sceptical going on hostile. Palmerston's style was denounced as vulgar, histrionic and populist. Disraeli, ever the man for a waspish put-down, called him 'an old painted Pantaloon' while acknowledging that 'he is a name which the country resolves to associate with energy, wisdom and eloquence'.[17] In short, style worked. It also helped to refashion the Liberal party.

Palmerston was the dominant figure but his choice of ministerial subordinates indicated what kind of liberalism he favoured. He could make tub-thumping speeches on foreign affairs but his domestic policies were cautious. Like his Home Secretary, Sir George Grey, and his Chancellor, Cornewall Lewis, he believed in the continued importance of rule by property owners, in reform sufficient to demonstrate competence, in fairness and a determination to attack abuses of power. He also let his ministers get on with their jobs, freeing him to fashion wittily effective debating points and make grand gestures – usually about British patriotism and the national interest (see Chapter 34). Lewis likewise believed that a good 'liberal system of government' should be in the hands of 'the old whig party of England', which should govern economically while being willing to address issues in an open and reformist spirit.[18] A number of such problems were tackled. The ministry passed an important law on divorce (see Chapter 25), helped to make the civil service more efficient and introduced **limited liability** to company legislation. In 1856, the County and Borough Police Act required every county to establish its own police force. In 1857, Lewis's budget lowered the fixed rate of income tax to 7d in the pound, Peel's level fifteen years earlier. In doing so, Lewis faced down that unusual spectacle: a combined assault by Gladstone and Disraeli. Both argued that reductions in state borrowing should have priority over lower taxation.

Limited liability

The principle that the liability of someone who invests in a company should be formally limited, usually to the amount of capital invested. If a limited liability company failed, then creditors were only entitled to claim their share from the assets of the company and not from any additional wealth a shareholder or the company owner might have. The Limited Liability Act of 1855 established this principle, which was then incorporated into the Joint Stock Companies Act of 1856. This allowed a joint stock company to claim limited liability status if it had as few as seven shareholders. Limited liability was supported as a means of reducing personal risk and thus offering an attractive incentive to industrial or commercial investment.

Palmerston won an increased majority in a general election which he decided to hold in 1857 after Cobden had passed a motion of censure on the government for unwarranted aggression towards China (see Chapter 34). Although not the plebiscite on Palmerstonian government which some historians suggest, the election saw the Liberals making modest gains in the counties while many of Palmerston's liberal reformist opponents were defeated in the boroughs. These defeats did not usually result from their opposition to the Prime Minister, sincere though that was, but because many reformers failed to connect with the priorities of their constituents. Voters tended to be less impressed by moral arguments about international diplomacy and the need for a parliament free from excessive 'executive influence' than they were about effective representation of ratepayers' interests.[19]

His election victory did not secure Palmerston's hold over the Commons. Continued anti-Palmerstonian malice from Russell combined with the surprising, if temporary, unity of opposition Peelites, radicals and Conservatives to produce a resolution criticising the Prime Minister for caving in to French pressure for action after the Emperor Napoleon III had narrowly survived an assassination attempt plotted in Britain. When it was carried, after about ninety Liberals voted with Russell against Palmerston, the Prime Minister decided to resign immediately. He thus invited the ironic observation that an overly aggressive patriot had been forced to resign on grounds of servility towards the French.

Derby replaced Palmerston as Prime Minister. Predictably failing to lure either Gladstone or Newcastle back into the Tory fold, he formed his second minority Conservative government in February 1858. It lasted for sixteen months. The mere fact of office after almost thirteen years spent in the political wilderness revived Conservative morale. A fresh election in May 1859 increased the party's seats by forty but this was still more than forty seats short of a majority. The new ministry was not short of legislative achievement either. Derby had assured parliament on taking office that a Conservative ministry would not be a 'stationary Ministry' and would respond to the needs of 'an age of constant progress'.[20] With help from assorted and diverse radicals, it abolished the property qualification for MPs, the first of the Chartist six points to be achieved. It accepted the case for admitting Jews to parliament and, at long last, it ended the direct involvement of the East India Company in the government of India. It was not enough. An administration comprising much the same ministers as in 1852 had similar strengths and, particularly, weaknesses. By early 1859, however, it was faced by a Liberal party with fewer loose cannons and a greater sense of common purpose (see Chapter 32). Crucially, it also had more votes in the House of Commons and these were used to pass a vote of no confidence in the government in June 1859. The frustration of Derby and Disraeli would last a while longer yet.

31

Parliamentary reform, 1850–1880: intention and impact

I. The reform question revived

The 1832 Reform Act (see Chapter 21) did not lack for critics both inside and outside parliament. Since those most dissatisfied with the Act were the most assiduous in analysing its impact, it is not surprising that the conclusions were unfavourable. The radicals George Grote, MP for London, and Sir Henry Ward, MP for Sheffield, vainly attempted to secure a secret ballot in the late 1830s and early 1840s and thus rectify what they considered a major deficiency of 1832.[1] Grote got 200 MPs to vote his way in 1838, more than four times as many as those who voted to receive Chartist petitions. In 1849, the Liverpool corn merchant and MP for Bolton, Joshua Walmsley, became the first President of the National Parliamentary and Financial Reform Association, which called for equal electoral districts. A doughty minority of liberal radicals kept parliamentary reform alive through the 1840s and 1850s.

One historian has called such efforts 'sporadic bouts of ill-co-ordinated activity' while 'the cause of franchise reform . . . came at times to resemble nothing so much as a corpse on the dissecting table'.[2] This is too harsh. Pressure for further parliamentary reform was an important element in the radical campaign to secure the sovereignty of parliament over a landed-dominated executive. If rotten boroughs, constituencies of unequal size and landowner pressure on voters remained, then parliament would remain under the control of hereditary landowners. Larger electorates were essential if the aristocracy were not to dominate an increasingly urban nation in perpetuity. Lord John Russell's Cabinet in 1850 was almost as aristocratic as the Younger Pitt's had been. As the *Liverpool Mercury* argued in 1849, 'Boroughs *will* be bought so long as boroughs *can* be bought. The sole guarantee for the incorruptibility of a constituency is that it shall be so large as to render its purchase an impossibility.' The answer was more votes for working men – and bridge-building by the business classes to reconnect with the bruised working class. As the *Manchester Examiner* pleaded in March 1848, 'Let us not commit the folly of separating classes, of arraying shopkeepers . . . against *all* who subsist by weekly wages.'[3] Enough urban radicals heeded this message to keep parliamentary reform on the political agenda, despite disagreements with the liberal radicals who believed in the primacy of property and feared that male democracy was too high a price to pay for an urban middle class dominant over landowners.

From the other side of the fence, the physical-force Chartist, George Julian Harney, writing as Chartism was on the wane and the European revolutions of 1848 crumbled to dust, spoke of 'the old rulers of the world' having been 'trained to the exercise of force and fraud. They understand thoroughly the full use of these weapons.' He did, however, perceive movement: 'Inch by inch the ground has been forced from the oligarchy; every advantage thus slowly won has been as sturdily retained, and with each successive advance the power of the people grows stronger.'[4]

Demographic and social change also pointed to further reform. A combination of increased rental values, patchy increases in prosperity and more efficient registration procedures produced an increase of more than 60 per cent in the number of enfranchised adult males in England and Wales between the first and second Reform Acts. This increase, however, did little more than keep pace with population growth. The quickening pace of emigration from the countryside and consequential rural depopulation also changed the social composition of many constituencies. By the mid-1860s, a third of the voters in notionally rural south Hampshire were actually resident in Portsmouth and Southampton. It is not surprising that an objective of reform bills introduced in the 1850s was the limitation of urban influence in county seats.[5]

Senior politicians used parliamentary reform as a political football. Russell, of course, had form, having introduced a bill to disfranchise small parliamentary boroughs as far back as 1822. His commitment to reform, as part of the implicit Whig pact with 'the people', remained strong. By 1848, he had conceded that the 1832 Act was no 'final' solution. In addition to the Irish Franchise Act (see Chapter 40), he introduced three reform bills, in 1852, when he was Prime Minister, in 1854 as a member of the Aberdeen coalition and in 1860 as Palmerston's Foreign Secretary. All would have increased the size of the electorate by reducing the householder rating threshold; none got as far as a formal parliamentary vote. The 1860 initiative, in particular, had a tactical element to it. Russell insisted on introducing a reform bill as a symbol of his continued authority, knowing that Palmerston was, at best, a very lukewarm reformer. The year before, Derby and Disraeli hoped for increased support, especially in the urban north, by sponsoring a reform bill proposing a uniform borough and county franchise. It was defeated by 39 votes.

II. Dropping the ball: the Liberals and reform

Fierce debate about the nature and extent of the reform required precluded speedy resolution. Those debates explain why the Liberal party skewered itself over reform in 1865–66. Virtually all were agreed on one point, however. It would not be safe to enfranchise the 'residuum': those casual labourers, unemployed and marginal folk eking out meagre and vulnerable livings on both sides of the law. Support for universal manhood suffrage was no stronger in the 1860s than it had been in the 1840s.

The language in which support for a franchise extension was couched did, however, change. It now emphasised moral and constitutional factors. In introducing his 1860 bill, Russell wished to recognise 'that large number of the working classes who, by their knowledge, their character and their qualifications, are fitted to exercise the franchise freely and independently'.[6] Gladstone had hitherto been a most reluctant reformer. He had voted for the Conservatives' Reform Bill in 1859 only because it preserved a number of the smallest boroughs which he saw as a necessary nursery for well-connected young men wishing to enter parliament, as he had done in 1832, in their early twenties. In the early 1860s, he witnessed the stoical refusal of Lancashire cotton workers to support the slave-owning South during the American Civil War, despite the threat to their jobs from much reduced raw cotton imports. Such moral fibre made at least a qualified convert of Gladstone. In addressing the Commons in 1864, he listed 'the qualities which fit a man for the exercise of a privilege such as the franchise': 'Self-command, self-control, respect for order, patience under suffering, confidence in the law, regard for superiors'. In case honourable members still failed to get the message, he reassured them that 'I am speaking only of a limited portion of the working class'.[7]

The largely middle-class National Reform Union, founded in Manchester in 1864, was less cautious than Gladstone. It proposed both a household suffrage and equal electoral districts. The Union's political orientation was strongly pro-Liberal and many of its prominent members had also been members of the Anti-Corn Law League (see Chapter 22). The following year, a Reform League was founded in London, by the prominent lawyer-radical Edmond Beales. It sought full manhood suffrage and a secret ballot. A number of old Chartists joined the League but its leadership came from the 'new model' trade unions. George Howell and Robert Applegarth happily collaborated with the Reform Union 'without animosity'.[8]

Some manufacturers were happy to offer reciprocal endorsement. John Platt, a wealthy cotton manufacturer, engineering innovator and first mayor of Oldham, 'had no fear whatever' of the working class. He believed that parliament 'would place more responsibility on the workmen by giving them votes and teaching them political economy'. Some manufacturers even provided financial support for the Reform League. Peter Taylor, of the Courtaulds textile firm, was atypical. He embraced a very wide range of radical causes in the 1860s and 1870s, including votes for women. Both T. B. Potter, Manchester's first mayor and successor in 1865 to Cobden as MP for Rochdale, and the London hosiery manufacturer Samuel Morley had close relations with working men which persuaded them of the value of franchise extension.[9]

John Bright explicitly linked the franchise with economic and moral improvement. He told the working classes that their efforts had built the railways and the cities, thus mightily contributing to national prosperity. He linked respect for manual labour with an equal respect for 'our ancient Constitution' since it 'afforded support for freedom'.[10] Gladstone's approach was similar. He told a public meeting in Chester in 1865 that the education of working men had been 'infinitely extended' since 1832, while their loyalty to the existing order had glowed 'more fervently than ever'. Their character had been tested 'in the fire of affliction' during the Cotton Famine of the early 1860s. The conclusion was obvious: working men should comprise 'a sensible fraction' of the electors in borough constituencies so that their feelings would be more warmly enlisted in the interest and welfare of our common country'.[11]

Palmerston's death in October 1865 seemed to remove the last obstacle to the passage of a Liberal reform bill, not least since his successor was Earl Russell. In the general election three months earlier – the first since 1841 with no Peelite candidates – the Liberals increased their majority over the generally anti-reform Conservatives to almost a hundred. As always with questions of representation, however, it was much easier to agree the general principle than the particular details. Gladstone presented the Russell government's reform bill to the Commons in March 1866. It proposed giving votes to those who paid rent of at least £14 in the counties and £7 in the boroughs, together with other apparently 'safe' folk such as lodgers of relatively extensive property and those who had at least £50 in a savings bank. The numbers enfranchised would have been modest – fewer than half a million. The intended beneficiaries were skilled working men in the towns and business people who had bought domestic property in an adjacent county seat. Gladstone ran into a volley of criticism, most of it from his own side. The government had failed to make sufficient allowance for two facts. First, more than a quarter of borough voters were already working men. Secondly, the counties were palpably under-represented. The 334 English and Welsh boroughs on average represented 26,000 people, the 162 county seats an average of 70,000. These were killer facts for many Liberal MPs, not all of them landowning Palmerstonians. The first fact suggested that working men had sufficient representation already and the second that the government should give priority to the redistribution of seats over endlessly fiddly numerical projections. It did not help that no one discoursed about fiddly numbers at such wearisome and sententious length as Gladstone. A group of malcontents, headed by Lord Elcho and Robert Lowe, opposed the bill with vituperation. They became known collectively as 'the **Adullamites**'.

Adullamites

The name given to Liberal MPs who opposed parliamentary reform in 1866. It was coined by John Bright, using a metaphor taken from the Old Testament of the Bible. In the first book of Samuel, David, who had been expelled from the court of King Saul, took refuge in the Cave of Adullam, where he gathered together 'every one that was in distress, and every one that was in debt, and every one that was discontented'. A ready sense of humour was not Bright's strongest point and this was a strained metaphor for aristocrats like Lansdowne, who was also a powerful businessman as chairman of the Great Western Railway, or Hugh Grosvenor, later first Duke of Westminster. Grosvenor was not opposed to an extension of the franchise but wanted to see it linked to a substantial redistribution of seats. Nevertheless, the description stuck, although the term 'the Cave' was sometimes used as an alternative.

Lowe argued offensively that the bill would enfranchise large numbers of people who were venal, frequently drunken and who, as a class, tended to the 'impulsive, unreflecting and violent'.[12] The railway administrator and author Samuel Laing fretted about premature enfranchisement of honest working men lacking the education and political maturity to make rational judgments on complex social questions.[13] On the other side, many radicals considered Russell's proposals inadequate. Despite its hasty introduction of a bill to effect a modest redistribution of seats, it was clear that the government had lost control of the Commons. When it was defeated on an obscure amendment by nine votes in June 1866, Russell had had enough. He redundantly told Gladstone, 'I am afraid . . . there is a great amount of antipathy to our Reform Bill.'[14] Against the advice of Gladstone, who preferred a dissolution of parliament and a direct appeal to the voters, Russell resigned. Queen Victoria summoned Derby to form his third, and final, minority Conservative government.[15]

III. Touching down: a Conservative Reform Act

Benjamin Disraeli had little or no principled interest in the franchise but he was not averse to trophy-hunting. Both he and Derby considered a Reform Act passed by a minority government the biggest prize on offer and opinion outside parliament put wind into their sails. The failure of Russell's bill precipitated substantial but peaceful street demonstrations in Birmingham, Bristol and Norwich. In late July 1866, a mass meeting in London's Hyde Park led to skirmishes with the police. When parliament reassembled in early 1867, further pro-reform meetings were held in Trafalgar Square at which trade union leaders called for a Grand National Holiday (or strike). Chartist tactics employed almost thirty years earlier (see Chapter 21) remained part of the extra-parliamentary political culture. In May, a further Hyde Park demonstration involving a crowd of 150,000, which the authorities tried, but failed, to prevent, provoked the resignation of the Home Secretary, Spencer Walpole.[16]

Despite these incidents, violence – still less any threat of revolution – played little part in explaining why a second Reform Act was passed in 1867.[17] Credit for passing the Act usually goes to Disraeli for his mastery of parliamentary tactics or his unscrupulous manoeuvring, according to political choice. However, it was Derby who put reform firmly back on the legislative agenda, when Disraeli was reluctant. As the Prime Minister said, '[I] did not intend for a third time to be made a mere stop-gap . . . I determined that I would convert . . . an existing minority into a practical majority . . . carrying a measure . . . the agitation for which was standing in the way of every measure . . . of practical legislation.'[18] Given the parliamentary arithmetic, his best hope was to win popular support by showing that a minority Tory government could be 'responsive, enlightened, and capable of reform'.[19] The Earl of Shaftesbury agreed with Derby (see Chapter 28) that 'a measure of reform is indispensible'. In saying that he looked to the Prime Minister to fashion one which would be 'extensive, safe and satisfactory', he expressed what by October 1866 was becoming an increasingly common view. Like almost all Conservatives, he was anxious to 'stem the tide of democracy'. Though certainly 'extensive', he would not have considered what ensued either 'safe' or 'satisfactory'.[20]

Derby's 'safe' starting point was a household suffrage. However, so many changes were made to the original bill between Disraeli's presentation to the Commons in mid-February 1867 and the royal assent to the Second Reform Act six months later that it is of limited value to track them. During that period Derby's policy was appropriated by Disraeli. Derby was ill and anyway as a peer unable to exercise much influence in the Commons. Behind Disraeli's ducking, weaving and general fleet-footedness lay two sticking points. First, whatever emerged must be a measure for which the Conservatives could claim sole credit. Secondly, any reform settlement must be sufficiently extensive to demonstrate that a Conservative government did not fear 'the people'. In pursuance of the first principle, Disraeli refused to accept any amendments from the Liberal front bench, while giving open-minded consideration to those from other quarters. Achieving the second necessitated the stripping away of safeguard after safeguard to gain a Commons majority for a minority government.

There were casualties. Three Cabinet ministers – Viscount Cranborne (later both Marquess of Salisbury and Conservative Prime Minister), the Earl of Carnarvon, the Colonial Secretary, and General Jonathan Peel, the Secretary for War – resigned in March 1867. All considered the idea of a working-class majority in any constituency both dangerous and distasteful. All found Disraeli's tactics unprincipled. Disraeli was undeterred. Since he aimed to drive a wedge between the Liberal hierarchy and its radical backbenchers, most of the amendments he accepted increased the number of potential voters. The famous Hodgkinson amendment, enabling '**compounders**' to vote in borough constituencies, put half a million borough-dwellers onto the electoral roll at a stroke. Most were poorer working men. Over the period 1866–71, the borough electorate increased from half a million to one million and a quarter.

Compounders

This term was used for those who did not pay their rates separately but made an arrangement with their landlord. The landlord paid directly to the rating authority and adjusted the level of rent accordingly. The Hodgkinson amendment simply, and briefly, abolished the distinction between personal payment of rates and compounding.

The Second Reform Act produced a modest redistribution of seats (27 in all) from the boroughs to counties and gave an extra parliamentary seat to the four largest provincial English towns: Birmingham, Leeds, Liverpool and Manchester. Adult male owners and occupiers of dwelling houses, if resident for at least twelve months, could now vote, as could lodgers occupying rooms with a rental value of at least £10 a year. As a result, the number of voters in the boroughs in England and Wales increased by 138 per cent. In county seats, tenant farmers occupying land with a rateable value of £12 a year were enfranchised. The county franchise in England and Wales went up by about 46 per cent. Overall, the numbers entitled to vote in England and Wales increased by about 90 per cent to just short of 2m (36 per cent of the total adult male population). A separate Scottish Reform Act was passed in 1868. This increased the number of voters to about 230,000, rather more than a quarter of the adult male population. The 1868 Reform Act in Ireland raised the number of urban voters by about 50 per cent. Ireland's electorate now comprised about 20 per cent of the adult male population.[21]

IV. Collecting, guiding and controlling: the Second Reform Act in operation

The Earl of Derby famously, if derivatively (he was appropriating a phrase used by Palmerston in respect of Russell's much less radical proposals of 1854), called the 1867 Reform Act a 'leap in the dark'.[22] The Liberal Chief Whip, George Glyn, used the same metaphor in conversation with Gladstone: 'all is new and changed and large and I must say in some respects *dark*'.[23] It was 'dark' particularly since so few politicians were prepared for it. After almost twenty years of circumspect and largely futile initiatives, Disraeli and Derby had turned existing assumptions upside-down within the space of six months. Reform in 1867–68, besides enfranchising far more people than had the 1832 Act, produced working-class majorities in a number of large towns for the first time. This implied a challenge to the basic principle that government should be in the hands of men of property.

In truth, any challenge was likely to be pretty weak. No Labour party was formed in the 1870s to advance the interests of working people. Much more modest changes in the county franchise restricted the rural vote to those with property. Less than a quarter of adult males could vote in county constituencies after 1867. Also about eighty borough seats were still controlled by great landowners in the 1870s.[24] The House of Commons remained dominated by landowners throughout the 1870s, although the numbers from the professional middle classes were growing. When two working men, both trade unionists and both staunch Gladstonian Liberals, were elected to the Commons in 1874, it seemed like tokenism. Sober analysis suggests plenty of method in Disraeli's apparent madness.

Nevertheless, many believed that their political world had been turned upside-down. Robert Lowe was one of many who railed against hasty, politically driven change. He discoursed on 'the shame, the rage, the scorn, the indignation and the despair with which this measure is viewed by every cultivated Englishman'. For him, it represented the triumph of the 'principle of numbers as against wealth and intellect'.[25] Walter Bagehot, the anti-democratic political journalist and constitutional expert, fretted about concessions made to what he called the 'ignorant multitude'.[26]

Unsurprisingly, John Bright took entirely the opposite view. He welcomed the fact that the Reform Act would require a change of approach. Sovereignty might pass from the 'wealth and intellect' arrayed in parliament into the hands of the electorate. As he told an Edinburgh audience in 1868: 'We now have to appeal to you.'[27] Bright was at least partly right. Both the circulation and the wider role of newspapers expanded as the spread of elementary schools increased general levels of literacy (see Chapter 29). Newspapers could operate both as reflectors of public opinion and as mouthpieces for party policy. As we shall see (Chapters 32 and 33), political parties found many novel ways by which to engage with the electorate.

The changes brought about by 1867 are much more nuanced than they at first appear. Voter numbers increased hugely in some urban constituencies. Merthyr Tydfil had ten times more voters in 1868 than in 1866. The electorates in Stoke-on-Trent, Halifax, South Shields and Blackburn all increased by at least five times. In some places – Plymouth and Swansea stand out – the number of new voters registered in the 1870s and early 1880s massively outstripped population increase. In others, such as Leeds, Leicester and Nottingham, voter numbers increased by less than did population growth. Although the proportion of adult males who could vote in England's larger boroughs increased across the board, wide variations remained. In 1871, 97 per cent of Gloucester's and 89 per cent of Northampton's adult males could vote, while in Portsmouth only 39 per cent and in Bath only 44 per cent could do so.[28]

The size of urban constituencies differed substantially but few were very large. In the period 1867–85, 40 per cent of English borough MPs represented towns with populations of less than 20,000.[29] In such seats, the majority of the electorate remained middle class; new voters were disproportionately 'respectable', unionised and strongly Gladstonian Liberal (see Chapter 32). However, by no means all the new urban voters after 1867 were artisans, or otherwise 'respectable'. As one historian has pointed out, by the turn of the twentieth century some towns had a sizeable 'slum vote'.[30] The degree of variability is largely explained by the administrative complexities involved. Hodgkinson's notorious 'amendment' proved unworkable and 'compounding' returned through the back door, via an amending Act passed in 1869 which was mainly concerned with poor law administration. Confusion and inconsistency between constituencies continued until Charles Dilke's Parliamentary and Municipal Registration Act of 1878 finally clarified that an adult male renting one room for separate occupation within a larger house could register for a vote.[31]

The other important disequilibrium in the value of votes concerned the under-representation of large towns. Birmingham had 63,000 voters in 1880 and returned three MPs to the Commons – 21,000 votes per MP. The small Devon town of Totnes had an electorate of 1,300 but was still returning two MPs, at 650 votes each. This and similar grotesque anomalies were not addressed until the Redistribution Act of 1885. Even then a number of smaller inconsistencies remained into the twentieth century.[32]

The need to identify and then to collect voters in the boroughs increased the need for professional party organisations. Organisations had existed since the 1830s but both activity and effectiveness had been patchy. The Liberals had established a Registration Association in 1861 to co-ordinate activities. In response to the Liberals' continued electoral successes and also to maximise opportunities provided by a larger electorate, a National Union of Conservative and Constitutional Associations (NUCCA) was established in 1867. Its chairman was **John Eldon Gorst**. In 1870, a Conservative Central Office was founded, with Gorst as its Principal Agent. Central Office organised visits to each constituency 'to meet the most influential local Conservatives at each place, and to persuade them to form a com- mittee for the purpose of propagating Conservative principles and arranging about a local candidate'.[33] While these new arrangements strengthened the Conservative presence in many constituencies in the 1870s and played a modest role in the party's election victory of 1874 (see Chapter 33), they were not widely welcomed. In most county seats, local arrangements for selecting candidates were well established. The work of a national organisation was therefore likely to be considered intrusive.[34]

Similar reservations were harboured on the other side of the political fence after Joseph Chamberlain established the National Liberal Federation (NLF) in 1877. Its aim was partly to rebuild the party's support in constituencies lost to the Tories in 1874 and partly to encourage constructive engagement with Liberal policy at local level. Chamberlain provocatively called the NLF 'a really Liberal Parliament . . . elected by universal suffrage'.[35] Like its Conservative counterpart, local organisations often sponsored social and recreational activities, aimed particularly at working men. Like its counterpart also, the NLF was controversial. Chamberlain's political ambitions (see Chapters 32 and 38) were deeply suspect to many Liberals and his organisational methods to corral the Liberal vote in his native Birmingham were considered both intrusive in method and hectoring in tone.

John Eldon Gorst, 1835–1916

Born in Preston, he was educated at the local grammar school and Cambridge University before going to New Zealand as a missionary and as an inspector of schools. On return- ing to Britain, he became MP for Cambridge in 1866 but lost his seat in the general election of 1868. He was appointed Central Agent for the Conservative Party in 1870. Claiming that he was a true 'Tory democrat', he built up Conservative strength in the boroughs, frequently clashing with the Whips and local party managers who wished to maintain existing organisational structures. Disraeli did not give him government office. He combined his political career with a successful London law practice. Salisbury appointed him Solicitor-General in 1885. Gorst refused reappointment in 1886 but served in a number of minor posts, including Financial Secretary to the Treasury from 1891 to 1894. He became increasingly interested in social reform in the 1890s and served both on an enquiry into poor law schools and as Vice-President of the Committee of Council in 1895. He abandoned his Conservative allegiance in 1903, sitting as an independent MP, in which capacity he attacked Balfour's government for its timid social policy.

Some constituencies were indignant that what they called a 'caucus' should seek to impose a national perspective without adequate knowledge of, or sympathy for, local circumstances. The new organisations lacked both the means and the support to steam-roller their way through the urban constituencies, determining the choice of candidates, changing local procedures and generally 'professionalising' politics as they went. By 1884, fewer than ninety English boroughs were affiliated to the NLF.[36] Many experienced liberal radicals, such as Joseph Cowen, MP for Newcastle upon Tyne from 1873 and proprietor and editor of the *Newcastle Chronicle*, was firm in his view that the relationship between an individual candidate and his constituents should retain priority over the party machine.[37] He supported working-class Liberal parliamentary candidates in the 1880s, partly as a means of challenging 'caucus politics' which strengthened middle-class influence. Although new political organisations did appear and although more direct national appeals to electors were made, the overall influence of party professionalism in the 1870s is easily exaggerated.

32

....

Gladstone and the Liberal party, 1859–1880

I. Gladstone and his new party

William Gladstone was the dominant political figure of mid- and late-Victorian Britain. His massive presence irritated at least as much as it inspired and his increasingly non-negotiable position on key issues often made it seem as if Liberal politics revolved around the whims of Mr Gladstone. Yet Gladstone did not become a Liberal until 1859 and did not become a Liberal Prime Minister until the end of 1868. We also need to note the important developments which had taken place in the Liberal party before Gladstone joined it.

William Gladstone, 1809–1898

Born in Liverpool into a wealthy and Evangelical commercial family, he was educated at Eton and Oxford University. He entered parliament as a high Tory in 1832. He served continuously as an MP until 1895. He gained his first Cabinet post under Peel as President of the Board of Trade from 1843 to 1845. He was then Secretary for War and the Colonies in 1845–46. Along with nearly all of Peel's close colleagues, he went into opposition as a Peelite. In that capacity he was Chancellor of the Exchequer in the Aberdeen government. He joined the Liberal party in 1859 and was Chancellor under Palmerston and Russell from 1859 to 1866. He led the Liberal party from 1867 but resigned in 1875 after his government's defeat by the Conservatives. He became leader of the party again in 1880, a position he retained until 1894. He was Prime Minister four times: 1868–74, 1880–85, 1886 and 1892–94. He was a strong advocate of free trade and low taxation but his relationships with colleagues in the Liberal party were often difficult. He was by temperament a believer in 'aristocratic government', in the sense of rule by the best, and he was always a strong supporter of the Church of England. However, he led a party with a strong nonconformist base supported by disparate groups and he never truly understood the interests and priorities of many on the radical wing of the Liberal party. His relations with Joseph Chamberlain in the 1870s and 1880s were frosty. His leadership style was to take big issues – free trade, low taxation in his first government; a solution to the problems of Ireland in later administrations – and use these as guiding principles for leadership. His conversion to Home Rule for Ireland in 1885–86 split the Liberals. Like Peel, he put big issues of policy before the interests of his party and would not tolerate debate on the issues he considered to be vital. He was a man of ferocious intellectual energy who epitomised Victorian values of earnestness, religious fervour and high moral purpose. These values did not make him an easy colleague and many in his party greatly regretted that his final retirement was delayed into the mid-1890s.

The social composition of the parliamentary Liberal party changed significantly over this period. When Gladstone threw in his lot with Palmerston in 1859, almost two-thirds of Liberal MPs in the Commons were landowners and policy making remained very largely in the hands of the great Whig proprietors. By 1874 the proportion of landowning Liberal MPs had declined to 46 per cent and slid to barely a third by 1886. Lawyers remained as an influential, if relatively small, minority – holding between 11 and 16 per cent of Liberal seats. The most significant difference was the rise of the business classes, many of them (see Chapter 30) nonconformists. Businessmen comprised 16 per cent of the parliamentary party in 1859 but almost 32 per cent by 1874. Most were merchants or manufacturers; bankers were overwhelmingly Conservatives.[1] Even before the great Liberal split over Ireland, therefore, the party had transformed itself into one increasingly rooted in business and professional backgrounds. The Whigs remained important, not least for their financial support, but their grip on the party was loosening by 1880.

Nonconformist links with liberalism remained strong, not least since the Tories put much energy into maintaining the symbolically critical link between the state and its Established Church. The Liberal 'reform party' (see Chapter 30) had a strong nonconformist core which pressed for the abolition of the remaining advantages Anglicans enjoyed, particularly in respect of education and the financing of the Church of England. 'Voluntarism' (see Chapter 29) and nonconformity worked hand in hand.[2] Also, it was hardly surprising that the Liberals' record on religious toleration should attract voters in Scotland, Wales and Ireland. In the four general elections held between 1865 and 1880, the Liberals won a majority of the seats in these countries. The dominance was particularly marked in the boroughs, where, in 1880, the Liberals won 66 seats to the Conservatives' 16. Even when, at the 1874 general election, the Conservatives won a strong overall majority they won only 19 non-English borough seats to the Liberals' 63. In the five elections held between 1859 and 1880, the Liberals won a total of 640 Scottish, Welsh and Irish seats to the Conservatives' 315 – a ratio of more than two to one. No wonder Gladstone exulted in 1868 that 'our three *corps d'armée* . . . have been Scotch Presbyterians, English and Welsh nonconformity and Irish Roman catholics'.[3]

II. Liberals ascendant and divided, 1859–1868

As we have seen (see Chapter 30), the Liberals had been divided on a number of issues in the 1850s. The personal rivalry between Russell and Palmerston is well known but was not the most important factor. The key divisions among Liberal backbenchers were two. First, should foreign policy be framed to secure continuous peace and prosperity? This question had obvious implications for the size and the management of government budgets for defence and diplomacy. The second division concerned the role of parliament itself. Many radical MPs believed that the main benefit of the 1832

Reform Act (see Chapter 21) was that it increased parliament's opportunities to hold ministers to account and to check the natural propensity of the executive towards spending other people's – usually taxpayers' – money. For this reason, many backbenchers continued to reject party labels, believing that political parties would become mere agencies of the executive – too readily appropriated by ministers for their own purposes, infringing freedom of political action as a result. In that, as the history of political parties over the hundred and fifty years since 1860 amply demonstrates, they were absolutely correct. In the late 1850s, however, as Miles Taylor has shown, liberal radicals were on the losing side of this argument.[4] Parliamentary sovereignty was increasingly, and eventually fatally, compromised by the emergence of disciplined party politics.

In the short term, however, the radicals' defeat enabled the guiding principles of parliamentary liberalism to emerge more clearly. Most Liberals could agree on the importance of free trade, **retrenchment** linked to government efficiency and reforms with a 'moral' purpose, such as increased educational opportunity. These were prominent aspects of Sir Robert Peel's agenda (see Chapter 22). The Peelite legacy was an important factor in persuading Gladstone to quit his semi-independence in June 1859 and become Chancellor of the Exchequer under Palmerston. There were others: personal ambition, the sense that his already demonstrable abilities as a minister were going to waste, and an almost alarming personal detestation of Disraeli on the Tory side. His close friend and fellow Peelite Sidney Herbert became Secretary for War. The Duke of Newcastle became Colonial Secretary, while also chairing the Royal Commission on the education of the children of the working classes.

Retrenchment

This word literally means the act of 'cutting' or curtailing. In the context of nineteenth-century politics, it describes a policy of economy by government, cutting back on plans for expenditure and reducing taxes to the lowest feasible level.

Most historians see the famous meeting of 280 Liberal, Peelite, Radical and Reformist MPs at Willis's Rooms in London on 6 June 1859, which Gladstone incidentally did not attend, as marking the emergence of the modern Liberal party.[5] Russell and Palmerston made a public declaration of reconciliation after years of squabbling and the meeting decided on a strategy both for ending Derby's minority Tory government and for articulating the principles on which its Liberal successor might appeal to the nation. In both personnel and policy, the Peelites bequeathed a powerful legacy to mid-Victorian liberalism. The key decision – who should lead the new government – was determined by Queen Victoria since, despite their rapproachement, neither Palmerston nor Russell would willingly defer to the other. Victoria, as so often, was decisive in her judgment, if deficient in her evidence. Of her 'two terrible old men', she found Russell the greater of two evils – 'ever ready to *make* mischief and to do his country harm'.[6] Palmerston it was, but Russell held out for the Foreign Office, where, the Queen might have reflected, he was best placed to do his country yet more harm (see Chapter 34).

Gladstone's period as Chancellor of the Exchequer confirmed and consolidated the primacy of free trade as national policy. In contrast to his Liberal predecessors, Sir Charles Wood and Cornewall Lewis (see Chapter 30), he regarded annual budgets, saving money and the promotion of international trade as essential for strong government. He increased income tax first to 9d in 1859 and then to 10d (4p) in the pound in 1859. This reduced a government deficit which had ballooned during the Crimean War and also paid for the defence costs Palmerston insisted on at a time of national uncertainty (see Chapter 34). Gladstone's 1860 Budget removed virtually all the protective tariffs, substantially reducing levels of indirect taxation. In 1861, after one of many jousts with Palmerston, he succeeded in removing the Paper Duty, the final 'tax of knowledge' (see Chapter 21), thus reducing the price of newspapers and giving the working classes greater access to 'useful knowledge'. The free market in knowledge responded accordingly. The number of London newspapers in circulation increased by 70 per cent in the period 1856–71, while provincial newspapers increased by 127 per cent.[7] Gladstone's Post Office Savings Banks opened in 1861 for 'the encouragement of the working classes in provident habits',[8] although only workers in full-time, regular employment were able to take full advantage.

Gladstone also established a Committee of Public Accounts in 1864 to subject government expenditure to close scrutiny. As in so much else, he was continuing and extending the policies of Peel (see Chapter 22). He persuaded both the income-tax paying minority of British citizens and the majority who paid indirect taxes through their purchases that their money was being carefully and watchfully – even (to use Gladstone's own phrase) 'cheese-paringly' – spent. Between 1860 and 1865, government expenditure declined from £70m to £67m, at which point it represented 8 per cent of Gross National Product. Gladstone would have liked more savings, and blamed Palmerston for blocking them.[9] He was, however, able to reduce income tax to 4d (1½p) in the pound by the end of 1865.

Palmerston's death in October 1865 seemed like the passing of an age. Though a controversial minister, he had run his departments efficiently. He was a natural, hard-working administrator able to stir public opinion to bursts of constructive patriotism. He was a shrewd, experienced and, when necessary, cynical politician who knew how to handle men. He even made a decent fist of managing that force of nature which was William Gladstone. He was not snobbish. Many liberal radicals who resented Russell's affectedly superior demeanour found Palmerston more congenial. He did much to forge bonds between the Whigs and the various urban groupings. He was also capable of charming audiences on his provincial tours in the 1860s. In his last years, he became a popular public figure. In direct contrast to Gladstone, he was not a great believer in legislation, believing that governments were inclined to pass too much of it and, in doing so, expose their parties to divisive debate. He had dominated political life and so, in the words of one historian, 'Palmerston's passing opened up the Pandora's box of Liberal aspirations'.[10]

The problem, of course, was that these aspirations remained contradictory. Queen Victoria sent for Russell, who, in terms of age, experience and long service to the party, was the only plausible choice. Given Russell's continued preoccupation with parliamentary reform, it was one which gave maximum opportunity for different 'aspirations' within the party to be divisively aired. The results were a terminal defeat for Russell and, by June 1866, a third minority Conservative government under the Earl of Derby (see Chapter 31). Since Russell had been sitting in the House of Lords since 1861, the Liberals needed a leader in the Commons and Gladstone was now the obvious choice, despite the reservations expressed by some MPs.

Gladstone used the time well, shifting his party from its recent reluctant focus on parliamentary reform to religious matters, where the potential for united action was much greater. While still in opposition, albeit with a theoretical majority in the Commons, Gladstone shepherded the abolition of compulsory **church rates** through parliament in 1868 and began the process of disestablishing the Anglican Church in Ireland (see Chapter 40). Since Russell had announced at the end of 1867 that he was withdrawing from public office, the way lay clear for the Liberals to accept Gladstone as their new leader. His successes in restoring and rebalancing the party during the minority administrations first of Derby and then Disraeli almost made the party's decision for it.

Church rates

In effect, church rates were taxes. They were liable to be levied in every Church of England parish, providing a fund to cover church expenses, including the costs of church upkeep and payment of salaries to church clerks and other parish officers. In some large towns, rectors and vicars had not required payment of church rates for many years. However, the rate remained controversial because, where the law was enforced, non-members of the Church of England were required to pay it – and saw no reason to. After a long campaign orchestrated by leading nonconformists, Gladstone's first government passed the Compulsory Church Rates Abolition Act of 1868.

When Disraeli finally called an election at the end of 1868, the Liberals won it comfortably, with an overall majority of about 110, a small advance on the outcome in 1865. Clouds were apparent on the Liberal horizon, however. Against the national trend, the party did badly in Lancashire. They had won 15 of the 27 seats there in 1865 but were reduced to 11 of the 33 refashioned seats in 1868. Gladstone famously lost his seat in South-West Lancashire and had to retreat to the borough of Greenwich, which had been reserved for him in case of emergency. Every other

Lancashire county constituency was also lost, largely to a strong anti-Catholic feeling which the Conservatives were able to exploit. The results from urban constituencies also suggested that enfranchised working men were prepared to vote Conservative. In Blackburn, where the electorate was increased more than fourfold, working men voted predominantly for the Conservative candidates, William Henry Hornby, a paternalist Tory, the town's first mayor and a member of its leading mill-owning family, and Joseph Feilden.[11] Tory successes in greater London were also a portent of things to come (see Chapter 37).

III. Ireland, efficiency and the moral high ground, 1868–1880

Gladstone's leadership of the Liberal party was, to say the least of it, distinctive. It was driven by three guiding principles. First, Peel's lessons in the diligent preparation of every legislative case, in sound administration and sounder money still resonated. Intellectually, Gladstone always remained a Peelite. Secondly, he needed to finesse continuing divisions within the Liberal party. Since he believed that it was the responsibility of government to do good by maintaining stable conditions within which citizens could make the best of themselves, and also that no good would come out of any administration led by Benjamin Disraeli, he sought to articulate policies in the form of what he called 'big bills'. These were those he considered would have the best chance of uniting the Liberal party while giving Disraeli least opportunity to demonstrate his mastery of parliamentary tactics, as he had done to such devastating effect in 1845–46 (see Chapter 22) and in 1866–67 (see Chapter 31). The third principle linked directly with the second. Gladstone had a driven, evangelical belief in the responsibility of government ministers to do God's work on earth. This helps to explain the moral dimension with which Gladstone invested all his policies, whether secular, as with free trade and cheap government, or religious, as with Irish Church reform and the abolition of religious tests for applicants to Oxford and Cambridge.

His opponents, both outside the Liberal party and within it, thought this pure humbug. Gladstone was finding a moral or religious rationale for political actions intended to work to his own advantage. The maverick Liberal radical Henry Labouchere famously stated: 'I don't object to Gladstone always having the ace of trumps up his sleeve, but merely to his belief that the Almighty put it there.'[12] Disraeli summed up his rival's tendency to sanctimony in an ironic sentence: 'He has not a single redeeming defect.'[13] Gladstone's supporters were frequently exasperated not only by his determination to take the lead on every big issue but to determine, with minimal debate, what the big issues should be. Nevertheless, they accepted that their Prime Minister was a man of exceptional talent who was attempting to provide both high-minded and, to use a seventeenth-century phrase, 'godly' government. Mid-Victorian politics cannot be understood without appreciating that most of its practitioners believed unreservedly both in providence and in divine intervention. Most emphatically, they 'did God', none more so than William Gladstone.

Gladstone had two dominant concerns during his first ministry: Ireland and more efficient government. Gladstone's Irish policy is considered elsewhere (see Chapter 40). The government's administrative reforms followed a broadly Peelite 'efficiency' path, moderated by Gladstone's brand of evangelical Anglican fervour and frequently compromised to minimise the effect of party division. Thus, Forster's proposed Elementary Education Act, passed in 1870 (see Chapter 29), also included increased funding for Anglican 'voluntary schools' at Gladstone's behest. After long Cabinet debate, it was agreed that the bill should include a clause prohibiting denominational religious instruction in board schools. The schools which wished to evade this requirement, however, found few obstacles in their path.

Much rationalisation of local government also took place under the financial expert George Joachim Goschen. A Local Government Board was established in 1871 (see Chapter 28) to superintend a wide range of functions, including the poor law and public health. The Chief Commissioner of the Poor Law Board argued that 'This Bill, instead of destroying, would give new force to the principle of local government in this country'.[14] The 1872 Public Health Act set a new threshold provision by requiring each local authority to appoint a Medical Officer of Health. Local authorities now worked to a clearer specification and gained greater financial autonomy. Some larger boroughs responded with a spurt of municipal activism which significantly increased public health provision. The number of urban districts providing a water supply increased from 250 to 413 during the 1870s. Joseph Chamberlain's Birmingham radically improved the city's sanitation and sewerage systems.[15]

Edward Cardwell's army reforms of 1869–71 aimed to address the inefficiencies revealed during the Crimean War (see Chapter 34) and to professionalise the service. The War Office was reorganised and the army divided into sixty-six territorial districts to enhance soldiers' sense of identity, thus, it was hoped, boosting recruitment. The most contentious measure was the abolition of the practice of purchasing army commissions. Cardwell was more concerned to reduce the size of payments than, as his numerous opponents in the House of Lords believed, to effect a social revolution by imposing a rigid system of promotion by merit.[16] Cardwell's changes, however, brought little benefit and less change to the social composition of the officer corps.

Nonconformists, many of whom were closely linked to the United Kingdom Alliance, the dominant temperance association, were anxious to control an unregulated beer trade. When the Home Secretary, H. A. Bruce, presented a bill giving local magistrates power to introduce strict licensing controls and much reduced drinking hours, there was a furore. The influential drinks trade lobbied furiously against it, to which Bruce responded with a weaker bill which became law in 1872. His Licensing Act established compulsory drinking hours and increased penalties for drunkenness which police forces in many areas prosecuted with vigour. The number of prosecutions for drunkenness doubled in the five years after the passing of the Act.

The Criminal Law Amendment Act of 1871 confirmed the legal status of trade unions and protected their funds. The courts, however, ruled against the attempt to legalise peaceful picketing. The Ballot Act of 1872 ensured that voters would exercise their choice secretly. It pleased the constitutional reformers in the party, particularly John Bright, and it ticked off another of the Chartists' six points but it roused little or no popular interest or enthusiasm.

By 1872, Gladstone's efforts to keep the Liberals anchored to a broad programme of reform were running into the sand. Palmerstonians considered that too much had been done in a rush while many urban radicals thought that an insufficient number of nettles had been grasped. Gladstone was increasingly fretful. Disraeli's charge that the ministry resembled a range of exhausted volcanoes contained more than a grain of truth, though nothing, it seems, was capable of exhausting Gladstone himself.

Nevertheless, he was aware that the end was nigh. The Liberals lost twenty-three seats in by-elections held in 1871–73.[17] Disraeli denounced the government's excessive, controversial and harassing legislation (see Chapter 33). Gladstone was unhappy with the performance of Robert Lowe as Chancellor of the Exchequer, being 'wretchedly deficient' – Gladstone's words – in making savings. The Prime Minister's decision in 1873 to become his own Chancellor suggested both arrogance and over-reach. Economic conditions were also much less favourable in 1873 than they had been in 1868–69. Gladstone's own analysis, in a long letter to Lansdowne written in January 1874, was acute: 'The state of markets, and course of prices . . . were so terribly against us last year . . . The signs of weakness multiply, and for some time have multiplied, upon the Government . . . [it] is approaching . . . the condition, in which it will have ceased to possess that amount of power, which is necessary for the dignity of the Crown and the welfare of the country . . . the nation appears to think that it has had enough of us, that our lease is out.'[18] He was right. Many Liberals from a Palmerston background deserted the government, mostly over the government's education policy, which was thought to be anti-Church of England. Some radical nonconformists, annoyed either by the Education Act or the Licensing Act, or both, put up candidates who split the Liberal vote in the boroughs. Importantly, after the formation of the Home Rule League in Ireland (see Chapter 40), the Liberals lost their usual majorities there. The 1874 election produced an overall Conservative majority of nearly sixty.

Gladstone, the executive politician *par excellence*, had no taste for opposition. In 1875, he resigned the leadership, which passed to the **Marquess of Hartington** in the Commons and **Earl Granville** in the Lords. This aristocratic duo quietened things down, at least on the domestic front. Disraeli's government, however, was dominated by foreign affairs (see Chapter 35) and here Gladstone would not be silenced. His furious invective against the Turks began in 1876 and set up his famous Midlothian Campaign of 1879–80.

Spencer Compton Cavendish, Marquess of Hartington and eighth Duke of Devonshire, 1833–1908

Born in North Lancashire, the son of the later seventh Duke, he was educated first at home by his father and then at Cambridge University. He took the honorary title of Marquess of Hartington when his father became Duke of Devonshire in 1858. He entered parliament in 1857 as a supporter of Palmerston. He sat in the Commons, with one brief break, continuously until he inherited the Dukedom in 1891 and moved to the Lords. A shrewd, amiable man who never abandoned his Whig background and principles, he was Secretary for War under Russell (1866) and Gladstone (1882–85). He led the Liberal party in the Commons from 1875 to 1880 before becoming Secretary for India. He served Gladstone loyally and piloted the Ballot Act through the Commons in 1872. He broke with Gladstone over Home Rule, forming a Unionist party with Joseph Chamberlain. Both men soon joined with the Conservatives. He refused Salisbury's suggestion that he become Prime Minister of a formal Liberal–Unionist coalition in 1886. He was Lord President of the Council under Salisbury from 1895 to 1903, where he supported local authorities who wished to provide secondary education for the lower orders.

Granville George Leveson-Gower, second Earl Granville, 1815–1891

Born in London, the son of the first Earl and connected to most of the leading aristocratic families, he was educated at Eton and Oxford University. He was elected to parliament for a closed borough in 1837. He served in Russell's government of 1846–52, entering the Cabinet for the first time in 1851. He was Lord President of the Council and Whig leader in the Lords during Palmerston's government of 1855–58, returning as Lord President from 1859 to 1866. Under Gladstone, he was Colonial Secretary (1868–70) and Foreign Secretary (1870–74 and 1880–85). During the 1880s, he struggled to keep up with the pace of change, especially in Africa (see Chapters 36 and 42). After the Liberal split over Home Rule, he remained loyal to Gladstone, acting as Liberal leader in the House of Lords.

Superficially, this was about Gladstone's attempt to win the Scottish seat of Midlothian at the general election of 1880. In reality, it was about re-energising the Liberal party, confirming Gladstone's central place in it and practising a new kind of politics. Gladstone's intention, in speaking directly to a small electorate, was to have his words read in the newspapers at breakfast the following morning, thus making a national impact. Such an approach had never been sustained before throughout an election campaign. In addition to his excoriation of Disraeli's foreign policy, Gladstone preached a moral message. Recent material advances, he told the students of Glasgow University, had created a class of property owners who gloried in wealth for its own sake. 'Among them, the pursuit of material enjoyment, and of wealth as the means of it, has made a progress wholly out of proportion to any advancement they may have effected.' He referred to the presence of a 'new class' united only by the 'bond of gain' and without a moral anchorage.[19] Gladstone offered the Liberal party as the organisation to right this disordered world and establish a partnership with an active, aware citizenry.

As has been said, the Midlothian speeches 'offered a remarkable solution to the problem of marrying a representative system to a large-scale franchise'.[20] Many moderate Liberals thought that Gladstone was merely playing to the gallery and that such direct communication with the voters coarsened politics. A similar fault line runs through historians' assessments not just about the Midlothian campaign but about Gladstone's overall motivation. Some argue that he created a new 'liberal consensus' based on free trade and expanding political participation.[21] Others see him as an unreconstructed Peelite who used religion, ideology and party alike as a cloak to cover boundless personal ambition.[22] There is no doubting the effectiveness of his Scottish speeches and the warm reception they received. Gladstone had aroused public passions, put the Liberals back centre-stage and made a significant contribution to the party's substantial victory at the general election of 1880.

33

Disraeli and the Conservative party, 1860–1880

I. Derby and the value of change

In these years, the Conservative party at last recovered from the disaster of 1845–46 and laid down at least some of the foundations for its long period of political dominance from the late nineteenth century to the late twentieth. Just as Gladstone came to dominate the Liberal party at this time, so **Benjamin Disraeli** exerted similar primacy over the Conservatives. Since their careers contrast so starkly in terms of priorities, style and attitude, it is worth identifying two aspects of similarity. Both were outsiders to their parties. Gladstone transferred to the Liberals at the age of 49 after a successful career as a Tory-Peelite. Disraeli was an ethnic and cultural outsider: the son of a Jewish intellectual with literary pretensions in a party dominated by English landowners innately suspicious of 'foreigners'. The careers of both also owed more than is generally acknowledged to their predecessors. Gladstone's debt to Peel is well enough known, although its abiding importance even forty years after his mentor's death remains insufficiently stressed. Disraeli owed much to the patient spadework of recovery undertaken by the Earl of Derby.

Benjamin Disraeli, Earl of Beaconsfield, 1804–1881

Born in London, the son of a Jewish writer and grandson of an Italian immigrant who had moved to Britain in 1748, he was educated at home and in various London schools. He was baptised into the Christian faith in 1817, soon after his grandfather's death. Disraeli's grandfather had been an orthodox Jew but his father, a rationalist sceptic, saw more opportunities opening up for his son as a member of the Established Church. Without aristocratic connections, getting into parliament was a struggle. He was first elected for Maidstone in 1837 and became one of the leaders of the romantic Tory Young England movement which upheld rural values and attacked Peel's leadership of the Conservative party. Early in his career, he also wrote some successful novels. *Coningsby* (1844) and *Sybil* (1845) made a particular impact, especially in their discussion of political and social conditions. He came to national political prominence through his attacks on Peel for repealing the Corn Laws. His career opportunities were enhanced when the Conservatives split in 1846. The early death of Lord George Bentinck made him, under Derby, in practice the leader of the party in the Commons from 1849. He was Chancellor of the Exchequer in each of Derby's minority governments (1852–55, 1858–59 and 1866–68),

▶

though his economic analysis proved no match for Gladstone's detailed knowledge. He became Prime Minister of another minority government on Derby's resignation in 1868, although many on the Conservative backbenches resented his exotic flamboyance and his Jewish origins. They would have preferred a more obviously 'English' leader. Nevertheless, he successfully continued the rehabilitation of the Conservatives begun under Derby. He attacked Gladstone's first government with gusto and developed active foreign and imperial policies. After he won the general election of 1874, his interest was overwhelmingly in matters overseas. His diplomacy over the Eastern Question (see Chapter 35) won widespread praise. He left many of the details of domestic policy and social reform to other ministers, some of whom were disappointed by his apparent lack of interest. He died a year after the Conservative defeat in the general election of 1880. His contribution to the revival of the Conservative party and to its emergence as the 'natural party of government' from the 1880s is undeniably considerable, although some historians have considered him much stronger on image – 'One Nation' Toryism, Imperial grandeur, Patriotism – than on substance.

Derby had led the Conservative party since 1846 and remained in post until ill health forced his resignation in February 1868. Both his skill as a leader and his patience in waiting for opportunities during the long period of Liberal dominance have been underestimated. He led a party of reactionaries, many of whom would have undone the industrial revolution if they could. As he told members of the House of Lords in 1858, however, a Conservative government in an age of radical change could never be a 'stationary ministry'. It was Derby, not Disraeli, who taught the Tories the need for change[1] and Derby who first recognised the inherent instabilities of Liberalism with which Gladstone was to wrestle in his characteristically muscular way for almost forty years.

Derby's last years were politically frustrating. He had left office in the summer of 1859 convinced that Palmerston's new government – almost a new ministry of all the talents, except his own and Disraeli's – was insufficiently coherent to survive long. He told his party that he would follow a policy of 'masterly inactivity' until Palmerston's baggy coalition fell apart.[2] He underestimated both Palmerston's political wiliness and his sheer longevity. By the time he died in 1865, a more or less united Liberal party was in control and William Gladstone had been reassured to find that he could pursue Peelite economic policies inside a Liberal government (see Chapter 31). Disraeli, meanwhile, built bridges with the hierarchy of the Church of England, seeing it as the most reliable support for the Conservative party. He opposed the yearly bills which came forward to abolish church rates, knowing that this was one of the few chinks which Palmerston had left open to attack since the Liberal party contained fervent defenders of the Church alongside militant nonconformists.[3] Derby meanwhile reiterated his message: 'Our game must be purely defensive.'[4] This did not console Disraeli. The general election of 1865 (see Chapter 32) demonstrated the lack of Conservative progress. Meanwhile, Disraeli was ageing – he was 61 in 1865 – apparently no nearer power and frequently absent from Commons debates.[5]

The wisdom of Derby's defensive strategy took time to reveal itself, but it paid handsome dividends in 1866–67 when Lowe and the Adullamites broke with the Liberal leadership over parliamentary reform (see Chapter 32). Derby returned as Prime Minister in June 1866, declaring that he intended to hold on to office as long as he could. He could present his party as moderately reformist and, whatever some of his backbenchers might say, its Protectionist days were over (see Chapters 22 and 30). Derby's very narrow defeat over parliamentary reform in 1859 suggested that the Conservatives might have a better chance of passing parliamentary reform than did the Liberals. The 1867 Reform Act, though divisive within the party (see Chapter 31), was a massive tactical triumph. The government also passed measures of social reform. There was a further regulation of factory hours. A Sanitary Act (1866) also widened the scope of public health legislation by requiring local authorities to tackle bad drainage and other 'nuisances' in private dwellings as well as in factories and workplaces.[6] Derby's last minority government achieved much and promised more.

II. A voice for the mass electorate: Disraeli in opposition, 1868–1874

Derby left his successor a legacy on which to build. Indeed, Disraeli was assembling the building blocks even before Derby resigned. Two months after the 1867 Reform Act received the royal assent, he stated that 'the Tory party is the party of England . . . formed of all classes from the highest to the most homely' and that his intention was to 'educate our party' to understand that 'the interests of the labouring classes [were] . . . essentially the most conservative interests of the country'.[7] He achieved little during the nine months in 1868 when he headed yet another Conservative minority government before the Liberal election victory swept him from office (see Chapter 31). That it was Disraeli's government, however, was significant. Despite his credentials and experience, many in the party had wanted to prevent the succession of a Prime Minister of Jewish origin. Since other names, including those of Derby's own son, Lord Edward Stanley, were put forward, the **Queen's** influence may have been decisive in preventing a protracted struggle over the succession.

Victoria, 1819–1901

She was the only legitimate child of Edward, Duke of Kent, fourth son of George III, and Princess Victoria of Saxe-Coburg-Gotha. Her father died when she was less than one year old. Because none of George III's elder sons had any legitimate children, Victoria succeeded to the throne at the age of 18 on the death of her uncle, William IV, in June

1837. Her early political life was dominated by two men, Viscount Melbourne, who acted as her political tutor while Prime Minister, and her husband, Prince Albert, whom she married in 1840 and with whom she produced nine children between 1841 and 1857. Reasonably intelligent and well-read, she was also wilful and opinionated, although usually happy to take advice from Albert. They worked together on public business. It was Albert who persuaded the Queen to respect the abilities of Sir Robert Peel, against whom she had taken a strong dislike before her marriage. Albert's death in 1861 was a blow from which she never recovered during a widowhood which lasted for almost forty years. She withdrew from public life for much of the 1860s, drawing much adverse comment in political circles and strengthening the republican movement in Britain. She was coaxed back into public life in the later 1860s, particularly by Disraeli, who flattered her shamelessly and manipulatively. She became devoted to him, considering him 'full of poetry, romance and chivalry'. She was devastated when he lost power at the 1880 general election. She had developed a strong dislike for Gladstone, who, she famously alleged, addressed her as if she were a public meeting. She tried to prevent his appointment as Prime Minister. From the 1870s onwards, her preference for Conservative governments was barely concealed. Her reputation was fashioned much more in the second half of her reign than in the first. Through her children's marriages, she became matriarch to most of the royal houses of Europe. Disraeli engineered for her the title of Empress of India in 1876, which she adored; the title 'Queen-Empress' was regularly used. The golden (1887) and diamond (1897) jubilees of her accession to the throne occasioned huge celebrations, both in the United Kingdom and in the wider Empire. She developed a strong sense of imperial identity. Her age and experience helped to settle the late Victorian image of Britain as the most powerful nation in the world ruled over by a gracious and wise monarch. This carefully massaged image was a distortion. Victoria symbolised many of the virtues of the improving middle classes. Her long period of mourning apart, she was a conscientious monarch who worked hard at her public duties, and her successful marriage was used to symbolise the Victorian family ideal. She was not, however, especially fond of most of her children or her grandchildren. Her political partisanship and frequent attempts to influence the policies of her ministers, especially on foreign or imperial matters, were the cause of much comment and some alarm among ministers. She too easily persuaded herself that her own views automatically represented the national interest.

Disraeli's stint as leader of the opposition lasted more than five years and the first three were little short of disastrous. He was working on another novel, *Lothair*, published in 1870 and this took priority over his parliamentary duties. His wife, Mary Anne, twelve years older than him, was seriously ill; she died at the end of 1872. In all, Disraeli's eclipse in these years seemed almost as pronounced as Queen Victoria's had been after the death of her beloved Albert. In January 1872, senior Conservatives held a private meeting to discuss who might replace their lacklustre leader. Disraeli had made influential enemies in the party over parliamentary reform (see Chapter 31); Lord Salisbury (Viscount Cranborne until he succeeded to the peerage in 1868), in particular, was a potent enemy. He was particularly suspicious of what he called 'Dizzyism', by which he meant 'playing fast and loose' with principles.[8] There were thoughts of replacing Disraeli with the new Earl of Derby (previously Lord Stanley) and a more decisive man might have dislodged him.

Disraeli survived for three reasons. The Conservatives lacked alternatives anywhere near as able or ambitious. The Liberals' reform policies were more effective at exposing party divisions than building electoral support (see Chapter 22). Most famously, Disraeli made two influential speeches, in Manchester's Free Trade Hall in March 1872 and to the National Union of Conservative Associations in London's Crystal Palace two months later. They were well-publicised, greeted with much acclaim and finally killed off thoughts of a leadership challenge.

These speeches are often presented as characteristically well-timed tactical Disraelian master-strokes articulating a new and inclusive philosophy of Conservatism. In fact, the timing of the Manchester speech had little to do with Disraeli. A visit to Lancashire, where the Conservatives had done well in the 1868 general election (see Chapter 31), had been two years in the planning and was the idea of John Eldon Gorst, who hoped to plant seeds of working-class Conservatism in what had seemed like particularly fertile soil. Disraeli – whose true métier was the House of Commons, not large public meetings – was hesitant about travelling north and speaking even to a predominantly Conservative audience when even one 'ill-considered phrase' might prove disastrous.[9] The speeches presented effective attacks on Gladstone's government but were less successful in articulating a coherent Conservative philosophy. In any case, Disraeli's statements of Conservative belief were not new; he had expressed them, in one form or another, many times before. As so often in politics, it was the timing, rather than the ideas, which mattered.

In Manchester, Disraeli treated his audience to a long disquisition about the Constitution before attacking Liberal education policies which, he said, had seduced nonconformists into partisanship on secular education rather than encouraging them to work with the Church to expand opportunities for the poor. This led on to a more general attack on the Liberal party for failing to curb its extremists' insistent and noisy pressure to overthrow of the Church of England, the House of Lords and the monarchy. He ended by flattering a sympathetic audience with the assertion that all the distinctive institutions which had made Britain a prosperous and civilised nation would be safe in Conservative hands.

Though much of the speech attacked the weakness of Liberal foreign policy (see Chapter 35), Disraeli included a passage asserting that 'the first consideration of a Minister should be the health of the people'. At Crystal Palace, he developed this theme, indicating that a Conservative government would pay attention to 'the state of the dwellings of the people'. It needed also to regulate factory conditions, hours of work and to protect working people against food adulteration.[10] Again, these themes had been rehearsed before; some dated back to Disraeli's flirtation with romantic Young England radicalism in the 1840s.

At Crystal Palace, Disraeli stressed that the Conservatives were pledged 'to uphold the Empire of England', whereas the Liberals desired 'to effect . . . [its] disintegration'.

The Empire was critical both to Britain's economic prosperity and to its standing in the nations of the world. Its support was a patriotic duty and he was sure that the working classes would know how to make their choice between 'national' [i.e. Conservative] and 'cosmopolitan' [i.e. Liberal] principles.[11]

It is possible to distil an ethic of Conservatism from these two speeches. The Conservatives presented themselves as a genuinely national party, drawing support from all classes and addressing the needs and aspirations of all classes. It would uphold the established institutions of the nation, of which the Empire was seen as an integral part. It identified Britain's national interests abroad and would defend these as vigorously as may be. These were not intended to represent precise policy statements but they were coherent, easy to grasp and afforded scope for development. In order to gain power, however, as Disraeli well knew, it was more important to attack Liberal failings and divisions. He gave a by-election candidate an indication of how this might be done a few months before the general election was held: 'For nearly five years the present ministers have harassed every trade, worried every profession, and assailed or menaced every class, institution and property in the country . . . and this they call a policy.'[12] This approach was criticised by more fastidious Conservatives, including the Earl of Derby, but it did offer an early intimation of the general lore of elections: negative messages are usually the most persuasive.

III. Atop the greasy pole: Disraeli and the Conservatives, 1874–1880

The size of the Conservative victory in 1874 surprised everyone, especially the Conservatives, inured as they were to defeat at every general election since Russell's Liberal government was confirmed in power in 1847 (see Chapter 30). Yet they won an overall majority of more than fifty, forty-seven more than a pre-election estimate by John Eldon Gorst which many Tories thought optimistic. In England, they held an overall majority comfortably in excess of a hundred and won 145 county seats to only 27 by the Liberals. Montagu Corry, Disraeli's increasingly influential private secretary and general factotum, reported triumphantly that at Brooks's Club, the Liberal headquarters, 'There is a panic . . . for all is now bitterness and despair . . . Gladstone is prostrate and astounded.'[13] The Whig element in the party blamed the excessive influence of strident nonconformity and of Irish Catholics both of which the fervently Anglican Gladstone should have done more to restrain.[14]

How effectively did Disraeli use the power his secure parliamentary majority bestowed? The impact of foreign and imperial policy is considered elsewhere (Chapter 35) but his Cabinet appointments give a clear indication of the relative importance he gave to foreign and domestic policy. The Cabinet, like Gladstone's in 1868, was dominated by large landowners. It included a Marquess, three Earls and a Duke. The most senior Tories, the Earl of Derby, the Marquess of Salisbury and the

Earl of Carnarvon, got the plum posts of Foreign, Indian and Colonial Secretary, respectively. Salisbury, however, was anything but reconciled to Disraeli's leadership (see Chapter 31). As he wrote to his wife, 'the prospect of having to serve with this man again is like a nightmare'.[15] The Chancellor of the Exchequer was **Sir Stafford Northcote** and the Home Secretary, appointed on the advice of Derby, was a fellow Lancastrian, **R. A. Cross**.

Stafford Northcote, first Earl of Iddesleigh, 1818–1887

Born into a long-established family of Devon landowners, he was educated at Eton and Oxford University before training for the law. He was private secretary to Gladstone from 1842 to 1850. He was co-author of the Northcote-Trevelyan Report of 1853 on civil service reform and entered parliament at a by-election in 1855 on Gladstone's recommendation before becoming financial secretary to the Treasury under Disraeli in 1858–59. He became a Cabinet minister in 1866, working first at the Board of Trade and then the India Office. As Chancellor of the Exchequer from 1874 to 1880, he was capable and orthodox, introducing a new sinking fund (see Chapter 10) to service the National Debt and reduce other debts. From 1876, he was faced with growing government deficits, caused by commercial depression and colonial wars. He was leader of the Conservatives in the Commons from 1880 to 1885, when Gladstone frequently outmanoeuvred him. Conservatives criticised him for his lack of partisan fervour. In 1885, he took a peerage and was, from 1886 to 1887, Foreign Secretary before losing office when Salisbury included Liberal Unionists in his government.

Richard Assheton Cross, first Viscount Cross, 1823–1914

Born near Preston into a comfortable middle-class family of lawyers, he was educated at Rugby and Cambridge University and for a time also practised law. He entered the Commons as Conservative MP for Preston in 1857 but left parliament in 1862 to pursue a second, highly successful, career as a banker. He became chairman of the pioneer Limited Liability Parr's Bank (see Chapter 30) in 1870. By then, he had returned to parliament, defeating Gladstone in the famous South-West Lancashire election of 1868. He became Home Secretary in 1874, having held no previous government post, but was the architect of most of the social legislation passed by Disraeli's administration. Disraeli thought him one of his most successful appointments. He was Home Secretary again briefly in 1885–86 and then Secretary for India from 1886 to 1892, having been raised to the peerage when he took up this new post. Although he did not retire from parliament until 1902, his political influence in his last decade there was slight.

Disraeli, 69 years of age when his second government was formed, asthmatic and frequently ill, knew that real power had come to him too late. He felt the need to concentrate only on matters which interested him most and usually left domestic business to the initiative of the relevant ministers. Years later, Cross expressed surprise and disappointment that, in view of his statements about the working man before becoming Prime Minister, Disraeli had thought so little about social legislation.[16] What he had said was either general or turned into a criticism of the Liberals, although he had promised to 'propose or support all measures calculated to improve the condition of the people of this Kingdom' while denying that 'this great end . . . [could be] advanced by incessant and harassing legislation'.[17]

Cross did indeed present a range of measures. The 1874 Factory Act reduced the maximum number of hours which women and children could work in textile factories to 56½ a week. The Factory and Workshops Act of 1878 consolidated the entire corpus of factory legislation, which now became universally applicable across all trades. It confirmed that all children under the age of 10 should receive compulsory education. Cross's Employers and Workmen Act and the Conspiracy and Protection of Property Act of 1875 stated that labour disputes were civil matters and should not give rise to any criminal action. Peaceful picketing by workers in support of a labour dispute was specifically permitted, a fence which Liberal legislation in 1871 had failed to jump. Some of Cross's Cabinet colleagues considered that this shifted the balance between capital and labour too far, and Disraeli claimed the credit for supporting him and ensuring that his legislation was pushed through.[18] The Liberal trade union leader, George Howell, considered it 'a political *coup* which astounded the trade union world' and the Trades Union Congress in 1875 passed a vote of thanks to Cross for his 'great boon to the industrial classes'.[19] The Artisans' Dwellings Act (1875) was enthusiastically taken up by a small number of local authorities (see Chapter 26) but, like the Public Health Act (1875) and Sale of Food and Drugs Act (1876) sponsored by George Sclater-Booth, President of the Local Government Board, this was permissive rather than compulsory legislation.

Northcote and Cross also combined on a new Friendly Societies Act (1875). This modestly increased the confidence which working people might have that their limited funds invested in personal insurance schemes would be secure against failure or fraud. Northcote stressed that no state guarantees were on offer. The Merchant Shipping Acts of 1875–76 likewise gave sailors only limited protection against overloading by profit-hungry ship-owners, though they did require foreign-bound vessels to paint a so-called **Plimsoll Line** on their ships.

Plimsoll Line

The marking, or 'loading line', on a ship's side which indicates the legal limit for the ship's immersion in water when fully laden with cargo. It was named after the Liberal MP Samuel Plimsoll (1824–98), who campaigned for protection for sailors against what he believed was a conspiracy of insurers with ship-owners to send out unseaworthy vessels, many of which sank.

Disraeli's rhetoric about the government's commitment to the health of the people was taken, like 'Tory democracy', at face value for many years. Recent historical assessments have been less kind.[20] The key points made relate first to Disraeli's limited engagement with his own government's initiatives, secondly to the opportunistic nature of much legislation and thirdly to its place along a continuum of social initiatives in the 1860s and 1870s which relied on local authority initiative rather than any 'collectivising' spirit. On this reading, Disraeli's legislation did little more than dot 'i's and cross 't's on a blueprint laid down by Gladstone. There is some truth in all of this. Disraeli had no master plan to help the lower orders. Also, neither Northcote nor Cross believed in excessive state intervention or regulation. Northcote stated that his purpose was only to 'assist' the working classes 'to work out their own improvement for themselves'.[21]

It may be, however, that the pendulum has swung too far. Under Gladstone's much tighter control of government business and given his ideological fixity of purpose, the administrative initiatives of 1868–74, though they were more professionally drafted and more tightly scrutinised, often fell short, giving opportunities for the Conservatives to exploit, as they emphatically did with their own trade union legislation in 1875. Also, the sheer range of activity in the space of only three or four years is impressive. Finally, Northcote, Cross and Sclater-Booth knew that Disraeli had sanctioned a general direction of travel. Free from the kind of 'supportive interference' in which Gladstone specialised, they were able to plot generally effective routes. By 1880, the idea that the Conservative party had no interest in 'the condition of the people' was no longer sustainable.

None of this offered any assurances that a grateful electorate would confirm the Conservatives in power. From 1878, the government faced economic depression, an agricultural crisis (see Chapter 27), falling prices, declining profits, growing deficits and colonial wars. The most severe effects of the depression were felt in the rural areas which had been a Conservative fortress in the election of 1874. In 1879, a Farmers' Alliance was formed to put pressure on the government to implement agricultural protection. Disraeli, the Protectionists' friend in 1845–46, was now as doctrinaire a free-trader as Gladstone. He would not budge and paid a severe electoral price. Additionally, Ireland was disturbed and Irish Home Rule MPs were disrupting parliamentary proceedings. The government had no response either to Irish disruption or to Gladstone's mighty Midlothian orations (see Chapter 32). The general election of April 1880 was almost a mirror image of that held in 1874. The Liberals gained more than a hundred seats, the Conservatives lost more than a hundred and ten, twenty-nine of them in the English counties. The Conservatives also lost heavily in the medium-sized and larger boroughs. They won only two seats in Wales and six in Scotland.[22] Disraeli complained about the discontent produced by a run of six bad harvests and wished that he had asked the Queen to dissolve parliament sooner.

Against such a combination of malign forces, timing would have made little difference, especially since Disraeli himself, now 75 years of age, had lost all his impish sparkle. It is too tempting to read off lessons from history in the knowledge of what came next. The simple fact in the spring of 1880 was that the Liberals were back in power with a majority even larger than that of 1868. The natural order of Liberal dominance, in place since 1846, seemed to have been reasserted. As he entered what was to be his last year of life, Disraeli must have wondered what his political career had been for. He did not live to see what a huge and, as it transpired, permanent boost to his stricken party Mr Gladstone would shortly deliver (see Chapter 38).

34

·················

Diplomacy and war: the *Pax Britannica* challenged, *c*1830–1865

I. Palmerston's foreign policy objectives

Viscount Palmerston dominated British foreign policy in this period. He was Foreign Secretary for fifteen of the twenty-five years from 1830 until he became Prime Minister in 1855. As Prime Minister for almost ten years – with only a sixteen-month gap filled by Derby's minority government in 1858–59 – until his death in 1865 he was still the dominant force in British diplomacy. It is not for longevity that he is remembered, however, but for style. As a Liberal-Tory near the beginning of his political career, he had learned many political lessons from George Canning (see Chapters 17 and 18), including the value of publicity to explain his policies directly to the electorate, either in speeches or via newspapers. Like Canning, Palmerston stressed the importance of maintaining British interests, especially in Europe where the aftershocks from the Napoleonic Wars still produced disturbing eruptions. His methods were controversial. He was accused of making diplomacy, traditionally a closed, secretive affair carried on between small numbers of national leaders and senior officials, into a matter for dangerously open public debate.

Palmerston's methods irritated the other powers and annoyed both Queen Victoria and **Prince Albert**. They considered his methods bombastic, his policies dangerously 'liberal' and likely to lead to war. In the late 1840s, they urged Lord John Russell, the Prime Minister, to dismiss him. Palmerston had largely abandoned the practice, on which William IV had insisted, of showing all diplomatic correspondence to the monarch before it was transmitted to embassies and foreign powers. Victoria expected Palmerston to keep her fully informed so that she 'may know . . . to what she has given her royal sanction'.[1] Albert, who wished to see existing European boundaries maintained, was especially scathing. His concerns were moral as well as political. In 1850, recalling an incident ten years earlier, he asked Russell how the Queen could 'consent to take a man as her chief adviser and confidential counsellor who . . . as her Secretary of State, and while under her roof in Windsor Castle, had . . . at night and by stealth . . . committed a brutal attack upon one of her ladies.[2] Palmerston's extra-curricular social arrangements with the opposite sex attracted excitable gossip throughout his life.

Prince Albert, 1819–1861

Born in the German state of Saxe-Coburg-Saarfeld to its ruler, Duke Ernest, and his wife, Princess Louise of Saxe-Coburg-Altenberg, he was educated privately. Albert first visited England in 1836 and met Princess Victoria a year before she succeeded to the throne. Their marriage was arranged in October 1839 and took place in February 1840. Although not technically titled 'Prince Consort' to the Queen until 1857, Albert so strongly supported Victoria's work that what amounted to a 'dual monarchy' developed in the 1840s and 1850s. Intellectually abler and much more self-disciplined than Victoria, Albert reorganised the court and grew close to a number of leading political figures, particularly Sir Robert Peel and the Duke of Wellington. In his capacity as President of the Royal Society of Arts, he took a leading role in organising the Great Exhibition of 1851. In the late 1840s and early 1850s, Victoria and Albert became increasingly frustrated at what they considered to be the tactless and bellicose foreign policy of Palmerston. During the Crimean War, however, Albert was very active in military preparations, and recommended the establishment of a new army training camp at Aldershot. Albert's health was rarely robust and both his devotion to hard work and the frustration caused by seeing his eldest son (the later Edward VII) growing up as an idle pleasure-seeker eventually outran his physical resources. His health deteriorated during 1861 and an infection, which may have been typhoid, could not be fought off. He died in December.

Palmerston's foreign policy objectives were orthodox enough. Like all his recent predecessors, he aimed at sustaining a balance of power in Europe. France must be kept in check and Russian expansionism, especially in the eastern Mediterranean and on routes to India, curbed. While these objectives retained wide cross-party support for most of the period, they provoked division within the Liberal party. Richard Cobden spoke for many in the 'peace grouping' in 1864 when he contested 'a policy founded on what is called "the balance of power" – a thing I could never understand . . . a figment [of the imagination] that was supposed to have grown out of what is termed the great settlement of Vienna [in 1814–15], but which I term the great unsettlement of Vienna'.[3]

Palmerston's second priority was to support the emergence of more 'constitutional' regimes struggling for autonomy from autocratic, and generally imperial, regimes, while trying to avoid direct involvement on the continent of Europe. As he told the Commons in 1832: 'Constitutional States I consider to be the natural Allies of this country . . . I am persuaded that no English Ministry will perform its duty if it be inattentive to the interests of such States.'[4] This assertion was widely supported in Britain, especially by educated middle-class opinion. Representative governments usually ruled over nations containing an increasingly prosperous middle-class, and Britain, which liked to see itself as the most advanced representative and commercial state on earth, felt that it could do profitable business with such regimes.

Thirdly, Palmerston aimed to protect and extend opportunities for British traders overseas and to consolidate Britain's more recent status as the world's pre-eminent power. This had significant implications for defence policy. Priority was generally given to naval over army expenditure. There were at least two risks here. First, as Britain's so-called 'empire of free trade' continued to expand, with naval expenditure geared to protecting it, by means of '**Gunboat diplomacy**', if need be, so the dangers of geographical over-extension grew. Secondly, European diplomats knew that Britain was spending less on its defence. If the army was starved of funds, then the risk of British military involvement designed to threaten any of the great powers was 'low'. Military expenditure was indeed savagely cut. The army and ordnance budget was more than six times lower in 1845 than in 1815 and the navy's budget four times lower.[5] Overall, Britain's defence budget did not match the nation's great-power status. Palmerston's always formidable bark was likely to prove much worse than his bite. By the early 1860s, Britain's bluff was increasingly being called.

Gunboat diplomacy

A term used to indicate the use of superior power to extract concessions, usually from a weaker power. Gunboats were light, manoeuvrable vessels carrying medium-sized guns. The term was applied particularly to Palmerston's diplomacy, particularly when China was forcibly opened up to European trade during the so-called Opium Wars of 1839–42 and 1856–60 and during the 'Don Pacifico' incident of 1850 when the property of David Pacifico, a Portuguese Jewish trader and the Portuguese consul in Athens, was attacked by Greeks and the Greek government would not pay compensation. Pacifico had been born in Gibraltar, a British possession, and was thus technically a British subject. Palmerston, as Foreign Secretary, sent a squadron into the Aegean Sea and blockaded the port of Piraeus. The Greek government was forced to pay compensation. However, since Greece was under the joint protection of Britain, France and Russia, Palmerston's unilateral action caused a major diplomatic row. In defending his policy to the House of Commons in June 1850, Palmerston argued that any wronged British citizen was entitled to seek redress from the British government. Such a citizen 'shall feel confident that the watchful eye and the strong arm of England will protect him from injustice and wrong'.

II. Uncertainty in Europe and the Middle East, 1830–1841

Despite considerable turbulence, Europe avoided major wars during the 1830s. 1830 was a year of revolutions, particularly affecting France, the Low Countries, Poland and the Italian states. Palmerston considered the revolutions to be 'decisive of the ascendancy of Liberal Principles throughout Europe'[6] but they threatened the balance of power. The issue of most concern to Britain, because the Low Countries represented a substantial land buffer against French expansionism (see Chapter 18), was the successful revolt of the southern Netherlands against the Dutch to their north. Stability was threatened, since France supported the creation of a new Belgian state while Austria and Prussia supported the Dutch to preserve the status quo of 1815.

At a Conference in London in 1830, Palmerston persuaded the powers to recognise Belgian independence. The boundaries of the new state were not yet fixed, however, and William I, the Dutch monarch, launched a successful invasion of Belgium the following year. This provoked the French, under their new ruler Louis-Philippe, to move troops in support of the predominantly Catholic Belgium, while Britain despatched a naval squadron to compel Dutch withdrawal. Palmerston also threatened war with France unless its large army was withdrawn. Agreement between the great powers was reached in the autumn of 1831 but the boundaries of Belgium were not confirmed until 1839. Though the process of Belgian independence was inordinately protracted, Palmerston could claim that his policy of diplomacy spiced by occasional threat had secured an outcome in Britain's interest. He claimed in 1832 that 'There never was a period when England was more respected than at present in her foreign relations, in consequence of her good faith, moderation and firmness'.[7]

Despite Palmerston's confidence, British diplomacy was less successful elsewhere. The Russians put down a Polish revolution in 1831; Poland became, in effect, an extension of the Russian empire. Nationalist rebellions against Austrian rule in Italy were snuffed out. French troops arrived in Italy to prevent Austrian dominance of the entire peninsula. Britain could influence neither of these developments, which threatened the integrity of the Vienna Settlement of 1814–15 (see Chapter 18).

Weaknesses in the Ottoman Empire affected Britain more since they threatened British trade routes in the Middle East. In 1831, the Pasha (military commander) of Egypt, Mehemet Ali, renounced his allegiance to the Turks, captured Syria and threatened to march on Constantinople. The British Prime Minister, Earl Grey, refused the Ottoman Empire's appeal for assistance, much to Palmerston's annoyance. Russia, seeing the opportunity for increased influence in the Middle East, responded more favourably. They supported Turkish resistance to Mehemet Ali and concluded a favourable Treaty (Unkiar Skelessi) with the Ottomans in 1833. This was followed by agreement with the Austrian Emperor – the so-called Convention of Munchengrätz. Palmerston feared that the 'eventual partition of Turkey between Austria and Russia' was on the agenda, since this Convention seemed to mirror the aims of Alexander I's Holy Alliance of 1815 (see Chapter 15).[8] He hastily brokered a Quadruple Alliance comprising Britain, France, Spain and Portugal. Its stated purpose was to support the rights of Queen Isabella of Spain and Queen Maria II of Portugal against absolutist male claimants to their thrones but the wider objective was to establish 'a quadruple alliance among the constitutional states of the West which will serve as a powerful counterpoise to the Holy Alliance of the East'.[9]

Although Congress Diplomacy had failed in the 1820s, international accord had been preserved over independence for both Greece and Belgium. Old rivalries between Britain and France soon threatened the stability of their 'liberal' alliance, however. It reached the point of rupture over a fresh crisis in the Near East in 1839–40. France had recently increased its influence in North Africa and calculated that its presence there would be further enhanced if it supported Mehemet Ali in his renewed struggle with notional Turkish masters. Palmerston aimed to secure continued British influence in the Mediterranean and also to humiliate a man he privately considered 'an ignorant barbarian' who was 'as great a tyrant and oppressor as ever made a people wretched'.[10] With the Ottoman Empire on the verge of collapse in 1839, Palmerston worked with Austria and Russia to preserve Turkish autonomy and clip Mehemet Ali's wings. A heavy British naval bombardment of Acre forced Mehemet Ali to give up Syria, restricting his direct power to Egypt alone. France felt betrayed by Britain and Palmerston twisted the knife further by refusing France any influence over a settlement dictated by the other great powers. Only when the terms for resolving the crisis were agreed was France permitted to be a signatory to the so-called Straits Convention of 1841. This guaranteed Ottoman independence and closed the Dardanelles and the Bosphorus to all warships during time of peace. Palmerston was gratified to note also that Russian advantages, negotiated at Unkiar Skelessi eight years before, were negated by this new Convention. British interests in the Mediterranean seemed secure.

III. Asia, 1830–1842

Further east, Britain's rocky relations with China were driven by the opium trade. China had forbidden the import of opium as far back as 1729 but its government was unable to enforce its will. The East India Company had derived considerable profits from opium in the late eighteenth century, which it usually exchanged for China tea. After the Company's monopoly was ended in 1833, pressure grew to develop the China market further. Chinese resistance was grounded in profound cultural differences which British merchants characterised as the product of a backward mentality. Once China began seizing consignments of opium from both smugglers and legitimate traders in 1836, relations with Britain deteriorated rapidly. Hoping to persuade China to negotiate, Palmerston sent a small naval detachment to the Chinese coast. The Chinese regarded this as an affront. Leading merchants were either imprisoned or expelled. Britain declared a war which proved highly controversial. Gladstone called it 'unjust and iniquitous' and attacked Palmerston for defending the 'infamous contraband traffic' in opium.[11] The Whigs survived a censure motion in the House of Commons by only nine votes. The First Opium War, lasting from 1839 to 1842, resulted in complete victory. At the resultant peace treaty of Nanking the Chinese ceded the strategically important port of Hong Kong to Britain and also granted unrestricted access to four further Chinese ports. The Chinese government was also forced to pay compensation both for the opium it had confiscated and the costs of the war.

This victory led to a rapid increase in British commercial and religious activity in the Far East. Missionaries had considerable success in converting uneducated Chinese peasants, but much less in persuading British governments to halt the damaging, but immensely profitable, opium trade. Full diplomatic relations with the Chinese government were impossible to achieve. In a climate of mutual hostility, and against a background of increased commercial activity, much of which was unlicensed and piratical, further conflict was inevitable. It began in 1856 after the Chinese boarded a small trading boat, the *Arrow*, and arrested its crew. The Governor of Hong Kong, Sir John Bowring, ordered a retaliatory bombardment of Canton. Palmerston, now Prime Minister (see Chapter 30), worked on public opinion. The predominant view, though the facts of the case hardly supported it, was that the *Arrow* affair represented a calculated insult to the British flag, to which war as the only appropriate response. A further British victory resulted, this time with French support since France was anxious to increase its own trading presence in the Far East. The Treaty of Peking (1860) extended British trading rights and confirmed the legality of the opium trade, to the chagrin of Cobden and other liberal radicals.

Palmerston had been one of the earliest British statesmen to appreciate Russia's growing threat to British interests in the East and especially to its commercial dominance in India. By 1835, he was advising Charles Ellis, Britain's ambassador to Persia, that 'the interest and policy of Russia, as regards Persia, are in almost all things not only different, but opposite to those of Great Britain'.[12] India lacked natural, defensible frontiers on its northern and western sides. A number of small states, which bordered Persia, were open to influence from Russia, whose ambitions beyond its southern borders became ever more apparent. Palmerston feared a Russian invasion of India, possibly through Afghanistan. The decision of Lord Auckland, Governor-General of India, to install a new pro-British ruler in Afghanistan to forestall Russian aggression led to war. Had the 20,000 British and India troops which invaded Afghanistan in 1839 been successful, it is likely that Afghanistan would have been annexed to become part of Britain's Empire. However, early successes, including the capture of Kandahar, were not consolidated. Afghan tribesmen resented the imposition of a British 'puppet' ruler and mounted a successful insurgency which ended with the massacre of British and Indian troops in 1842. Although the Afghan capital, Kabul, was eventually re-taken, the new Tory government ended the war. Afghanistan had been pacified but at considerable cost. Russia, meanwhile, continued to consolidate its position in central Asia. The threat to India remained.[13]

IV. British diplomacy in the 1840s

The Earl of Aberdeen was Foreign Secretary throughout the Peel government of 1841–46. He was a civilised, emollient character. Smooth diplomatic language, with its attendant evasions and intentional ambiguities, came much more naturally to him than it did to Palmerston. Characteristically, Palmerston thought him an 'appeaser', likely to compromise British interests, especially in the Americas, where Palmerston saw the United States as an ever more powerful commercial rival. Aberdeen inherited a geographically wide range of problems, some created or exacerbated by Palmerston's aggressive approach. His intention was to improve diplomatic relations, especially with the United States and France. The essential objectives of British foreign policy, however, remained largely unchanged.

Improved relations with the United States were necessary partly because of border disputes, especially with Canada after the constitutional settlement there in 1840 (see Chapter 19), and partly because of the threat of an aggressive US alliance with France. The alliance of 1778 during the US war for independence was frequently recalled. Palmerston had recently soured relations by attempting to check US westward expansion and opposing the incorporation of Texas into the USA after it broke away from Mexico in 1836. Britain, which had abolished slavery in 1833, also supported claims for freedom from slaves escaping from the southern states of the USA, where slave labour remained dominant, when they pitched up in the West Indies.

Careful diplomacy and, in the eyes of some, excessive concessions combined to avert the threat of war. The Webster-Ashburton Treaty of 1842 fixed the US–Canadian border and resolved a specific disagreement over the border between Maine and New Brunswick, in Canada. In 1845 Texas was annexed by the United States after Britain refused to support Texas's right to continued independence. In 1846, the western border of Canada was finally settled, again by compromise and further north than Aberdeen had wanted, although Vancouver Island remained wholly British. A seventy-year boil had finally been lanced. Britain was to remain on generally amicable terms with the United States thereafter. The short-term commercial benefits were substantial. The value of British exports to the US trebled almost immediately.[14]

Russell replaced Peel in 1846 at the head of a Whig/Liberal administration. To the frustration of Victoria and Albert, who much preferred Aberdeen, the abrasive Palmerston returned as Foreign Secretary. A diplomatic blunder ensued almost immediately over the long-lasting issue of the marriages of the Queen of Spain and her sister, the Infanta, in 1846. Palmerston annoyed the Spanish court, which was a significant factor in the decision to choose pro-French marriages. Indeed, the Infanta's marriage to the youngest son of King Louis-Philippe opened up the prospect of a joint monarchy. Palmerston asserted that this development 'betokens a revival of those ambitious designs of France over Spain which disturbed the peace of Europe in the beginning of the last century'.[15]

This diplomatic reverse was more embarrassing than costly, since the revolutions of 1847–49 were to sweep away Louis-Philippe's regime in France, threaten most of the other established monarchies and empires and throw central and western Europe into confusion. Out of this, Palmerston, a social conservative, gained a reputation as an advanced liberal, largely because of initiatives in Italy designed to promote reform in some of the states and to curtail French influence in the north. Palmerston was, at best, a limited and hesitant advocate of Italian Unification.

V. Conflict in the Crimea

Palmerston was not Foreign Secretary when the crisis which led to war in the Crimea blew up. Russell dismissed him in December 1851 and the Whig ministry itself fell a couple of months later (see Chapter 30). When he returned to office, it was as Home Secretary in Aberdeen's coalition government. Primary responsibility for foreign affairs lay with Russell, until 1853, and thereafter with the Earl of Clarendon until the coalition fell in 1855.

None of the eventual combatants wanted a war in the Crimea. The context had hardly changed since the early 1840s: the Ottoman Empire remained weak and Russia was believed to be exploiting this to increase its influence in south-east Europe. The threat to British commerce was obvious. Quite apart from trade routes to India, British trade with Turkey had increased eightfold in the previous twenty years. However, the new Tsar, Nicholas I, had no plans to precipitate the dismemberment of the Turkish empire and anyway wished to avoid conflict with Britain. He did, however, consider that the Turkish Empire was approaching utter collapse, which Britain did not. He further believed that the French, under their new ruler Napoleon III, were exploiting the situation by negotiating fresh undertakings from the Sultan to protect Roman Catholic privileges in the so-called Holy Places of Palestine. These had been threatened not by the Turks but by Greek Orthodox monks whom Russia supported. Knowing Anglo-French relations still to be delicate, the Tsar misinterpreted a remark by Russell as meaning that Britain was content for Russia to provide protection for Christian subjects anywhere in the Ottoman Empire.

This was a double misinterpretation and it led to war. First, Russell was not giving the assurances which Nicholas assumed. Secondly, he was not speaking for the British government as a whole. Aberdeen believed that he could use his experience as a negotiator to prevent a conflict; Clarendon took the same view. Palmerston and Russell, in one of the very rare occasions on which they saw eye to eye, joined with other 'hawks' in the Cabinet to argue that only stern warnings to Russia about the consequences of aggression would suffice. A further factor came into play. Newspapers, learning quickly that a chauvinistic line usually sells copies, had become by 1853 strongly anti-Russian. The predominant line was that Britain's interests depended on checking Russia by offering protection to Turkey.

On the basis of an assumed agreement with Britain, the Tsar attempted to extract a concession from the Sultan about protection for Christians in the Ottoman Empire. When the Sultan refused, the Tsar moved troops into Turkish provinces bounded by the River Danube in July 1853. This shattered Russian hopes of an agreement with Britain; it also brought France and Britain into alignment. The Turks declared war on Russia in October. The destruction of the Turkish fleet near Sinope in November fuelled anti-Russian hysteria in Britain. In January 1854, Britain and France moved fleets into the Black Sea. Two months later, they concluded an alliance to support Turkey and, on 28 March, declared war on Russia.

British ministers anticipated a rapid victory. From the Home Office, Palmerston even sketched out grandiose plans for a punitive peace at the expense of Russia, including the restoration of an independent Poland and the destruction of the Black Sea fleet.[16] Easy victories failed to materialise; rather the effects on the army of underfunding and stagnation since 1815 were embarrassingly revealed. Disorganisation, inefficiency and inadequacy of supply characterised the British war effort. Cholera and dysentery wreaked havoc among the troops; the army suffered far more casualties from disease than from warfare. Inadequate medical services resulted in far more troops dying from wounds which need not have been fatal. Only 2,000 of the 18,000 British casualties were killed outright in battle. Reorganisation of the army began during 1854, after the war was under way, not in preparation for it. Newspaper accounts of the war turned public opinion against Aberdeen's coalition and led to its replacement by a government led by Palmerston in 1855, just in time for 'Pam' to reap unwarranted benefits from tighter military organisation.

Victories, such as the Battle of the Alma in September 1854, were not followed up. Also, a spectacular own goal was registered at the Battle of Balaclava when the misunderstanding of an order by the commanding officer, Lord Raglan, led to the amazingly courageous charge of the Light Brigade. Alfred, Lord Tennyson's poem captured the imagination of the nation, but the Charge was into the wrong valley and was a total waste of time and life. It took almost a year from landing in the Crimea for the key objective, the fall of the port of Sebastopol, to be attained. Although the allies eventually won, the peace settlement signed in Paris in March 1856 did not begin to match up to Palmerston's hopes. The combatants agreed to respect the independence of the Ottoman Empire and the declaration that the Black Sea was to be neutral reduced the immediate threat from Russia. The peace was no knock-out blow, however. The Eastern Question would be posed time and again, in ever more threatening forms, before 1914 (see Chapters 35, 42 and 43).

VI. The *Pax Britannica* challenged

In the years after 1856, the idea that economic power could dictate a favourable diplomatic outcome – the so-called *Pax Britannica* – came under increasing challenge. The Unification of Italy, mostly complete after 1861, came upon Britain unawares. It posed no threat to British interests but Unification was achieved with substantial French help and at the expense of Austria. The balance of power had shifted. The Cobden-Chevalier trade treaty of 1860 (see Chapter 26) took some of the acrimony out of Anglo-French relations but the powers rarely co-operated. A suggestion from Napoleon III that they offer joint mediation to the Americans involved in their civil war was rebuffed.

With some difficulty, Britain remained neutral during the American Civil War. Gladstone overstepped the mark in 1862 when, in a speech in Newcastle, he celebrated Southern Confederate success at building up an army and a navy: 'they have made what is more than either, they have made a nation'.[17] Palmerston, more experienced and more cynical, preferred not to declare his hand, at least until the outcome became clear. Even so, the interception in November 1861 of a British ship, *The Trent*, by a Northern vessel almost led to war since *The Trent* was carrying two Confederate spies to England. The North considered this an act of treachery.

Britain's lack of influence on the continent of Europe was revealed by two important developments in the early 1860s. In 1863, a further revolt in Poland was put down
by Russian and Prussian forces. Napoleon III asked Britain to join in a formal
alliance to condemn Russia for what Lord Robert Cecil called 'a great violation of
public law'.[18] Palmerston refused, knowing that Britain had neither the resources nor
the motivation to send troops in support of Poland and that any such action would
almost certainly fail. During the American Civil War, furthermore, a large proportion of Britain's forces were engaged in defending Canada's borders against possible
incursion.[19]

If events in Poland indicated British impotence in continental Europe, its actions
during the so-called Schleswig-Holstein crisis of 1863–64 invited ridicule. The question of who should rule these two duchies was one of famous complexity. The King
of Denmark, Christian VIII, had tried to incorporate them into Denmark in 1846,
but both the law of succession and a strong German-speaking presence in the
duchies worked against him. The great powers had made an agreement with
Denmark at a Convention held in London in 1852 but Denmark worked to undermine it. One final attempt, in 1863, provoked an unprecedentedly strong response
from Prussia. Palmerston attempted to broker a compromise, although he unwisely
stated that 'the independence, the integrity and the rights of Denmark' must be respected
and threatened British intervention if they were not.[20] Napoleon III, used by now to
British rebuffs, turned the tables and refused to support Britain. Late in the year,
Prussian troops took over Holstein and a combined Prussian and Austrian army entered
the more northerly Schleswig a little later. After a further international conference
early in 1864 failed, a brief war ensued at the end of which the Danish King revoked
his rights to both duchies.

Russell, as Foreign Secretary, came in for the sharpest public criticism for a
policy which the Earl of Derby called 'meddle and muddle'.[21] Discontent, however,
went deeper than the alleged failings of one ageing minister. The Cabinet gave no
strong lead and Queen Victoria, whose eldest child was married to Prince Frederick
William, second in line to the Prussian throne, was, as usual, stridently pro-
German. Her allegiance was not swayed by the fact that the Prince of Wales had recently
married Alexandra, the daughter of the new King of Denmark. British public opinion, generally pro-Danish, was critical of pusillanimous political leadership. Perhaps
the most important consequence of the affair, however, concerned the reactions
in Europe. Britain seemed now to lack both the willpower and the resources to influence
power politics on the continent. Palmerston, still anachronistically concerned with
watching France, had certainly been slow to recognise how quickly and how
substantially the power of Prussia had increased. The Prussian Chief of Staff Helmut
von Moltke offered this devastating verdict in 1865: 'England is as powerless on the
Continent as she is presuming.'[22]

35

Diplomacy and the Eastern Question, 1865–1880

I. Britain and the rise of Prussia, 1865–1874

At his state funeral, the Dean of Westminster asserted that Viscount Palmerston had 'an unfailing trust in the greatness of England'. Despite the setbacks of the early 1860s, his European adversaries respected him. A German newspaper forecast that 'from one generation of Englishmen to another, the saying will be handed down: We are all proud of him'. This opinion was not universally shared. John Bright spoke for the many nonconformists and moralists in the Liberal party when he said in 1886 that Palmerston's administration at the Foreign Office was 'one long crime'.[1] Palmerston, whose faults did not include self-delusion, would have been gratified at the widespread respect in which he was held while almost certainly acknowledging that his international reputation would have stood higher if he had died in 1860 rather than 1865 (see Chapter 34).

In continental Europe, **Lord Stanley**, Foreign Secretary in 1866, considered Britain 'simply a spectator of events'.[2] He came back to office while the so-called Seven Weeks' War between Austria and Prussia was in progress. It ended in crushing defeat for Austria and the universal acknowledgment that Prussia was now the major German-speaking power. Fears that France or Russia, rather than Britain, might intervene persuaded the Prussian Chancellor Otto von Bismarck to press for a speedy peace. Britain did intervene to secure the independence of Luxemburg and to reaffirm its commitment to an independent Belgium (see Chapter 34) but it did so tentatively. Like many of his countrymen, Stanley considered the rise of Prussia unthreatening. The Queen remained staunchly pro-German, while many in the middle classes valued cultural links with a 'central European tradition', especially in music, where the German Beethoven was revered much more than the French Hector Berlioz. Stanley suggested to Victoria that 'There never was a time when the English public was more thoroughly bent on incurring no fresh responsibilities for Continental objects'.[3] Disraeli put a favourable gloss on Britain's non-interventionism as 'the consequence, not of her decline of power, but of her increased worldwide strength. England is no longer a mere European power; she is the metropolis of a great maritime empire, extending to the boundaries of the farthest ocean.' He acknowledged that Britain had 'almost systematically' declined to interfere in continental

Europe. Elsewhere, however, 'There is no Power . . . that interferes more than England. She interferes in Asia, because she is really more an Asiatic Power than a European. She interferes in Australia, in Africa, and New Zealand.'[4]

Edward Henry Stanley, fifteenth Earl of Derby, 1826–1893

Born at the family home, Knowsley Hall (Lancashire), the son of the fourteenth Earl, he was educated at Eton and Cambridge University. He became an MP in 1848 and remained in the Commons until inheriting his peerage on the death of his father in 1869. He gained early Cabinet experience as Colonial Secretary and President of the Indian Board of Control in his father's second minority government (1858–59) and he worked with Disraeli, with whom relations were close, on the Tory Reform Bill of 1859. He was Foreign Secretary in his father's third minority government (1866–68) and remained in post under Disraeli until the Conservatives lost the election. He returned as Foreign Secretary under Disraeli in 1874, but resigned early in 1878 over what he considered his chief's overly aggressive policy towards Russia. The split with Disraeli and Salisbury was the main reason for his move to the Liberal party. He became Gladstone's Colonial Secretary in 1882, where he attempted to moderate the effects of growing pressure for the partition of Africa (see Chapter 36). In particular, he argued against the annexation of Egypt. He left Gladstone over Ireland and became a Unionist in 1886, although opposing formal coalition with the Conservatives. He led the Unionist party in the House of Lords until 1891.

Gladstone would not have appreciated overblown Disraelian rhetoric but his own government abided by the philosophy. In the run-up to the Franco-Prussian war of 1870–71, Gladstone wished publicly both to censure Bismarck for unnecessary aggression and to urge Napoleon III to draw back from conflict. The Cabinet would not support Gladstone's suggestion. Lord Granville, **Clarendon**'s replacement as Foreign Secretary on the latter's death in 1870, needed all his tact to dissuade Gladstone from directing the full force of his stentorian moralism across the North Sea in the direction of Prussia. Granville believed that Palmerston's policy of bragging without back-up had reduced Britain's influence (see Chapter 34) during the early 1860s. He feared the consequences of 'laying down general principles when nobody will attend to them'.[5] War duly broke out in July 1870. France was crushed within a year, and in January 1871 Bismarck announced that the process of **German unification** was complete. Germany had hardly risen without trace but both its power and its potential for further aggrandisement dawned on most British statesmen too late. Gladstone, noting the implications of Germany's annexation of Alsace and much of Lorraine from France in 1871, was one of the first to sound an alarm. A newly independent greater Germany was a threat to the balance of power in Europe which had been maintained, albeit precariously, since the Vienna settlement of 1815.

George Villiers, fourth Earl of Clarendon, 1800–1870

Born in London, the grandson of the first Earl, he was educated at Christ's Hospital, London and Cambridge University. He came to the notice of Palmerston in the early 1830s and acted as **Minister Plenipotentiary** to Spain from 1833 to 1839. Here he supported Palmerston's policy and worked to save Spain's liberal regime from defeat during a civil war lasting from 1833 to 1840. He dissented from Palmerston's policy in the Middle East in the 1830s and early 1840s (see Chapter 34), which he thought forged too close an alliance with absolutist rulers. He inherited his title on his uncle's death in 1838. He joined Melbourne's Cabinet in 1840 and was President of the Board of Trade under Russell in 1846 before becoming Viceroy of Ireland (1847–52) during a very troubled period. He was Foreign Secretary both in the Aberdeen coalition (1852–55) and under Palmerston (1855–58). He remained on the sidelines in the early 1860s but resumed as Foreign Secretary under Russell (1865–66) and Gladstone (1868–70). He was extremely well connected, with close political friends in the Conservative as well as the Liberal party. He became less liberal in his views as he grew older and he annoyed Queen Victoria in the 1860s by uncomplimentary references to German princes. As Foreign Secretary, he was shrewd. Good personal relations came naturally to him but he was reluctant to take policies forward on his own initiative.

Minister Plenipotentiary

A minister who is given full authority to execute policy, as envoy or ambassador to a foreign power. A minister plenipotentiary is normally expected to act within the framework of policy set down by the government he is representing but has day-to-day powers within that framework. Such a minister is also expected to report regularly to the government or monarch being represented.

German unification

Germany became a unified Empire (or 'Reich') in 1871. A loose grouping of thirty-nine states had been formed into a Confederation in 1815, but each one remained a separate nation. The Austrian Empire and the Kingdom of Prussia had dominated the Confederation. After the Austro-Prussian war of 1866, a North German Confederation was created. Dominated by Prussia, it acted as a unified, but federal, state. After the Franco-Prussian war, the remaining states of southern Germany, plus Alsace and Lorraine – captured from France – joined the Northern Confederation to create a German Empire. King Wilhelm of Prussia became German Emperor. Meanwhile, Hungary was formally united with Austria by a compromise settlement (*Ausgleich*) signed in 1867. This gave Hungary greater autonomy within the 'dual monarchy' ruled by the Habsburg emperor. Austria-Hungary therefore remained outside the Reich. Habsburg interests increasingly focused on south-eastern Europe, especially the Balkan lands.

The foreign policy of Gladstone's first government (1868–74) followed the general pattern of the 1860s. Conflict, especially in continental Europe, was avoided and compromises sought. The Earl of Clarendon sounded warnings about imperial 'over-stretch' when he asserted in 1869 that 'It is the unfriendly state of our relations with America that to a great extent paralyses our action in Europe'.[6] The spectre of joint Franco-American action was also invoked: 'There is not the slightest doubt that if we were engaged in a Continental quarrel we should immediately find ourselves at war with the United States.'

Relations with the United States were 'unfriendly' because of the legacy of its Civil War. The victorious North felt that British sympathies had always lain with the South and pursued compensation claims when the war ended. The *cause célèbre* concerned the activities of the privateer vessel *Alabama*, which had been built in Britain but became part of the Confederate fleet. The US argued that Britain had violated its status as a neutral nation and, by equipping southern forces, had helped to prolong the war. Its compensation claim in 1869 called for Britain to cede Canada to the United States. While rejecting what he considered a grossly impudent claim, Gladstone agreed to refer the wider compensation issue to international arbitration. The Treaty of Washington settled the matter in 1871. The British paid the US $15m, while the US paid $7.5m to the new 'Dominion' of Canada (see Chapter 34) in compensation for losses sustained during the Civil War.

In retrospect, this outcome appears both fair and civilised, setting a precedent for the settlement of many later international disputes. It also enabled the demilitarisation of the border between the United States and Canada. After 1871, relations between the US and the British Empire were much more commonly convergent than divergent. In the hurly-burly of contemporary British politics, however, agreement to arbitration could be presented as an act of weakness. It seemed to signify that Britain lacked the resources to challenge United States domination of the American continent. Considered alongside the lack of British response either to the Franco-Prussian war or to the declaration by the Russian Tsar in 1870 that he no longer felt bound by clauses in the Treaty of Paris respecting the neutrality of the Black Sea (see Chapter 34), it left the Gladstone government open to charges of drift, weakness and uncertainty in foreign affairs.

Disraeli did not miss open targets. At the opening of parliament in 1871, he asserted that 'Not a single principle in the management of our foreign affairs, accepted by all statesmen for guidance up to six months ago, any longer exists . . . We used to have discussions in this House about the balance of power . . . But what has really come to pass? The balance of power has been entirely destroyed, and the country which suffers most, and feels the effects of this great change most, is England.'[7] When the election reckoning came in early 1874, Gladstone famously considered that his government had been 'swept away, literally, by a torrent of beer and gin'.[8] This was an oversimplification. An excess of interventionist domestic policies played an important part (see Chapter 32). However, what was widely seen as foreign policy mismanagement probably helped to explain why the Liberal defeat was so decisive.

II. Disraeli and the question of the East, 1874–1880

Foreign policy during the Disraeli government of 1874–80 was dominated by events in south-east Europe. The creation of a united Germany under the diplomatic control of Bismarck decisively shifted the balance of power, if not to Britain's immediate disadvantage, then at least without its intervention. The new German Reich soon negotiated an agreement with Russia that each power would help the other if attacked. When Austria also agreed to involve Russia in discussions in case of any threat, a 'League of Three Emperors' – in effect an alliance of conservative powers – emerged in 1873. It sounded awkward echoes of the Holy Alliance in 1815 (see Chapter 18) and it left Britain isolated among the European great powers.

Disraeli, however, was able to make the most of the bankruptcy of the Khedive (the Ottoman equivalent of Viceroy) of Egypt by purchasing his shares in the Suez Canal for £4m. The Canal, opened in 1869, connected the Mediterranean with the Red Sea. It provided water-borne access from Europe into Asia without navigation around Africa. Disraeli's purchase did not give Britain control of the Canal but it did prevent French control at a time when its interest in North Africa was growing. In a Commons debate on the sale, Disraeli stressed that the purchase was 'a political transaction . . . which . . . is calculated to strengthen the Empire'. The 'country', he asserted, had accepted that Britain was 'obtaining a great hold and interest in this important portion of Africa . . . [which] secures to us a highway to our Indian Empire and our other dependencies'.[9] Both Disraeli's most potent appeal to the electorate and his imperial legacy to the Conservative party were thus advanced (see Chapters 34 and 36).

In the summer of 1875, nationalist uprisings against the enfeebled Turks occurred in Herzegovina and Bosnia.[10] Russia, Germany and Austria responded by issuing the so-called 'Andrassy Note', urging the Ottoman Empire to institute reforms and to protect its Christian citizens. Britain was asked to associate itself with this concerted action. Disraeli agreed, though he resented the fact that the Three Emperors had not sought his involvement and approval at an earlier stage.

The **Marquess of Salisbury**, as clear-eyed and unsentimental as any politician in Britain at the time, believed that the country was relatively weak and also friendless. Following France's humiliating defeat in 1871, the contours of world power had been redrawn. Salisbury had reached the startling conclusion that only three great powers now existed – and Great Britain was not one of them. Germany, Russia and the United States all had greater resources, including much larger armies. Britain's was only 100,000 strong; Russia and Germany could each readily assemble more than a million soldiers, which the North had done during the American Civil War. Neither the Royal Navy nor conscription – culturally out of the question for a nation inured to enjoyment of civil liberties and low taxation – could compensate. Salisbury calculated that Britain needed closer relations with Germany, the European power apparently least interested in challenging Britain's commercial and imperial influence in south-east Europe.[11]

Robert Gascoyne-Cecil, Marquess of Cranborne and third Marquess of Salisbury, 1830–1903

Born at Hatfield House, Hertfordshire, the family estate, the son of the second Marquess of Salisbury, he was educated at Eton and Oxford University. He was known as Lord Robert Cecil until 1865, and then Viscount Cranborne when his brother died and he became heir to his father's title. He entered the Commons as a Conservative MP in 1853 and remained there, never having to fight an election, until he became Marquess on his father's death in 1868. Thereafter he sat in the House of Lords. He first entered the Cabinet in 1866 and was thereafter a powerful figure in the Conservative party, despite a deep personal dislike for, and distrust of, Disraeli. His main offices were Secretary of State for India (1866–67 and 1874–76), Foreign Secretary (1878–80, 1887–92 and 1895–1900), Leader of the Conservative Party (1881–1902) and Prime Minister (1885–86, 1886–92 and 1895–1902). As India Secretary, he appreciated the importance of winning the confidence of the indigenous population. His main interests lay in foreign affairs, where he opposed continued Turkish control over the Balkans, while also resisting Russian advances in the area. His cool brain produced careful analysis of foreign policy options and he was, in general, a highly successful Foreign Secretary, maintaining British interests and avoiding war. He acted as his own Foreign Secretary for much of the time that he was Prime Minister and often delegated oversight of domestic policy to others. His main contributions to the development of the Conservative party at the end of the nineteenth century included: offering a welcome to Liberal opponents of Home Rule, which led to the development of Liberal Unionism linked to the Conservative party; a strong determination to sustain the British Empire, including Ireland, as a civilising force and focus for popular patriotism; cautious reform of local government and the development of effective power bases for Conservatives at constituency level.

In the spring of 1876, the Bulgarians also tried to throw off the Ottoman yoke. Their revolt was put down with particular brutality and ferocity. The British government was in a dilemma. Old fears of Russian expansionism, which had precipitated the Crimean War (see Chapter 34), resurfaced but supporting the Turks was problematic. First, it might not work. Most European powers believed that the Ottoman Empire was on the point of implosion. Secondly, the mounting evidence of Turkish 'atrocities' appalled many British citizens. Newspapers competed to outdo each other with graphic, lurid but not always strongly supported reports of Muslim mistreatment of Christians in a foreign land.

Those seeking reprisals against the Turks found a formidable champion in William Gladstone. Gladstone did not discover his new 'cause' unaided. He was alerted to it by the Irishman James Lewis Farley, who had worked successfully as a senior banker in Constantinople for many years and had reluctantly concluded that the Ottoman Empire was incapable of reforming itself. In 1876, Farley would publish *Turks and Christians: A Solution of the Eastern Question*, which proposed giving Christian subjects of the Ottoman Empire self-government while maintaining the rule of the Sultan. His most significant intervention, however, had come a year earlier in a pamphlet entitled *The Decline of Turkey Financially and Politically*. On the back of that, he implored Gladstone for assistance: 'You, Sir, have before raised your voice on behalf of freedom . . . Will you not . . . say a word on behalf of the Christians of European Turkey who are now fighting for their religion and their homes?'[12]

Even withdrawn as he had recently been from the political fray (see Chapter 32), Gladstone was congenitally incapable of saying 'a word'. He was genetically programmed for torrents. These now gushed forth both in print and in speeches. Energised in August 1876 by news of a rally of working men gathering in Hyde Park to condemn Turkish actions in Bulgaria, he dashed off his pamphlet *Bulgarian Horrors and the Question of the East*, which appeared at the beginning of September. It was a thoroughgoing condemnation of what Gladstone considered Turkish barbarity, and included the famous exhortation for the Ottomans to 'clear out . . . bag and baggage . . . from the province they have desolated and profaned'.[13] The newspapers gave it great publicity and the pamphlet sold almost a quarter of a million copies within a month. By the end of October, almost five hundred demonstrations had been held protesting against the government's pro-Turkish policy. Gladstone had discovered an effective means of connecting with his public. In the process, however, he had split the Liberal party. What went down a storm with nonconformists and many 'peace' radicals was considered overly emotional, rabble-rousing and downright embarrassing in the polite, London-bound, Whiggish society inhabited by Granville and Hartington. They realised, as most of Gladstone's supporters did not, that his famous 'bag and baggage' sentence referred to ending what Gladstone, in deliberately foggy language, called the Turks' 'administrative action' in the Christian provinces, not to the wholesale expulsion of the Ottomans from Europe. Gladstone's intervention did nothing to affect British foreign policy but much to advance 'popular politics' in an age of mass electorates (see Chapter 30). Nor was it coincidental that it did much to advance the last, and most populist, phase of Gladstone's political career (see Chapters 32 and 38).

Disraeli's handling of the crisis was less secure than its eventually successful conclusion might suggest. By August 1876, he had clarified that his pre-eminent consideration was the preservation of the British Empire. Russian ambitions in the Balkans must be checked. Russians must neither gain control of the Bosphorus nor occupy Constantinople.[14] This meant preventing the Ottoman Empire from collapse. Disraeli rode out an anti-Turkish political storm in the second half of 1876. Gladstone found it difficult to sustain the intensity of his campaign, particularly in the face of opposition from the Liberal leadership. In May 1877, his strongly worded resolutions censuring the government were voted down by large majorities in the Commons. Gladstone's timing was unfortunate. A month earlier, Russia, gaining no concessions from the Turks, unilaterally declared war and marched purposefully towards Constantinople. Public opinion in Britain, following Disraeli's exhortations, became ever more belligerent in the winter of 1877–78 as news arrived of further Russian advances. Russia ended the war on its own terms in March 1878 when the Treaty of San Stefano created a new state of Bulgaria, ostensibly independent but in practice under Russian control.

Disraeli obtained Cabinet support for calling up reserve troops and moving Indian troops into the Mediterranean. He was prepared to go to war unless Russia backed down. Not all of his colleagues were prepared to go so far. After much havering, both Derby and Carnarvon, Foreign and Colonial Secretaries respectively, resigned. Disraeli was able to withstand their departure, partly because of strong national anti-Russian sentiment, and partly because he had, in Salisbury and Michael Hicks-Beach, more than adequate replacements. The rapprochement with Salisbury (see Chapter 31) was particularly striking because Salisbury's dislike of the Prime Minister was both of long standing and went well beyond political disagreement. It was Salisbury who in June 1878 accompanied Disraeli to Berlin to attend a Congress, summoned by Bismarck, in an attempt to prevent general European war. It was also Salisbury who mastered the complex geographical Balkan details. This left a patently ailing Disraeli free to make the grand gestures about patriotism and the British national interest in one final theatrical performance on an ideal stage: one provided by Bismarck.

The Congress prevented war. Russia agreed to the division of Bulgaria mapped out at San Stefano, while Serbia and Romania also gained independence from Turkey. Austria meanwhile occupied Bosnia-Herzegovina. Britain obtained Cyprus from the Turks, which it hoped would be a powerful civil and military base to support its presence in the eastern Mediterranean. The Ottoman Empire, though significantly reduced in scale and, as ever, resentful at having to make any concessions, nevertheless survived.

Ever the showman, Disraeli kept up his performance on returning to Britain in July. He stated that 'Lord Salisbury and myself have brought you back peace – and a peace I hope with honour which may satisfy our sovereign and tend to the welfare of our country'. Satisfying Queen Victoria was an easy matter where Disraeli, practised by now in all the arts of royal flattery, was concerned. She offered him a Dukedom, which he politely declined, while accepting the title of Knight of the Garter.[15] The prospect of peace was lavishly welcomed and it had been 'honourably' achieved without duplicity. However, Disraeli's 'peace with honour' was built on sand. The lines which had been drawn on a map of the Balkans owed little or nothing to knowledge of the social and cultural realities of the region. The newly created states were politically unstable from the outset. Meanwhile, Turkey and Russia were both resentful, though for opposing reasons, and were quickly looking to destabilise the Berlin settlement. If war had been averted in 1878, it seemed ever more likely not only that conflicts in the Balkans would recur but also that they might explode into something much larger. Events since 1870 had confirmed that the Congress System of 1815, to which Palmerston and Gladstone were, in their different ways, so attached had finally hit the buffers. It was being replaced by alliance systems (see Chapter 42) grounded more in competition and coercion than in co-operation and conciliation. With, or without, 'honour', for how long could 'peace' be preserved?

Section 6

······························

Empire, Democracy and the Road to War, 1880–1914

A photograph of Lord Curzon, Viceroy of India, 1899–1905, leading a tiger-shooting party with his wife in 1903

In the last quarter of the nineteenth century, the British were encouraged to recognise and celebrate their Empire as never before. There was particular focus on the ageing Queen as the benign symbol of imperial authority and on India as the jewel in the Queen-Empress's crown. The symbolic and practical importance of Empire was presented to British people in two masterpieces of symbolic manipulation, the Queen's Golden Jubilee of 1887 and the Diamond Jubilee of 1897. Chapter 36 explains why its Empire was seen as such a critical part of Britain's national identity, discusses Britain's role in the so-called 'Scramble for Africa' and attempts to separate pro-imperial propaganda from reality.

This period also witnessed substantial fluctuations in the balance of power between the political parties. Gladstone's increasing obsession with Ireland split his party in 1886 and gave opportunities for his Conservative counterpart, the Marquess of Salisbury, to exploit. Chapter 37 argues that Salisbury deserves at least as much credit for the success of the Conservative party as Disraeli. It investigates how he exploited the opportunities presented by Liberal difficulties and also by an increased and re-organised franchise in 1884–85 to produce a virtual monopoly of power at Westminster from 1886 to 1905. Chapter 38 examines the consequences of Gladstone's political longevity and argues that his reasons for remaining Liberal leader worked against the interests of the party. His valiant, but frustrated, obsession with producing a viable solution to the 'problem' of Ireland (Chapter 40) was not electorally popular. His usually distant relations with Liberal radicals, many of whom wished to preserve the Union with Ireland, made Salisbury's task in forging a successful 'Conservative and Unionist' party considerably easier. Chapter 40 also analyses the factors which brought Irish Home Rule back to the centre of political controversy, despite apparent settlement of the Land Question. The chapter also focuses on the reasons why opposition to Home Rule in the north of Ireland was both so implacable and so influential and indicates how close to Home Rule Ireland had come by the time the First World War broke out.

Chapters 37 and 38 also explain why there was such a reversal of political fortunes in the first decade of the twentieth century. The reasons for Conservative decline after Salisbury's retirement are considered as are those explaining how, and why, the Liberals seized their opportunities so successfully. They also investigate the significance of Joseph Chamberlain's conversion away from free trade to a policy of imperial pref-erence and explain why this had such serious consequences for the Conservatives. The progressive social policies followed by the Liberals under Campbell-Bannerman and Asquith are considered in Chapter 41. Some have seen the so-called 'Liberal wel-fare reforms' as harbingers of the Welfare State which the Labour party established in the later 1940s. The significance of these earlier reforms are considered, as also is the role of David Lloyd George, perhaps the most able, and one of the most devious, politicians of the age. This chapter also considers why the decade before the First World War produced so much political and constitutional conflict, includ-ing a battle between the Commons and the Lords and the concentrated flexing of industrial muscle by what was now a much larger and more forceful trade union move-ment. The rise of the movement for women's suffrage is also explained (Chapter 39), including a discussion of the impact of the militant tactics employed by the so-called 'suffragettes' from 1903. Did these tactics advance, or delay, the cause of women's suffrage?

36

'This vast Empire on which the sun never sets': imperial expansion and cultural icon

I. An imperial ethic

The quotation above was widely, indeed both persistently and adoringly, used to describe the British Empire in its heyday: the thirty years or so before the outbreak of the First World War. It comes as a surprise, therefore, to learn that it was coined more than a century earlier by the Irish peer and diplomat, Lord George Macartney. Macartney was a great advocate of imperial government and served in both India and southern Africa, but he was celebrating the much more modest imperial acquisitions which followed Britain's successes in the Seven Years War (1756–63).[1] The ending of Macartney's sentence – 'whose bounds nature has not yet ascertained' – is much less often quoted. However, those 'bounds', when computed in the early years of the twentieth century, were enormous. On George V's accession as King in 1910, the British Empire covered more than 11m square miles, and was a presence in every continent of the globe. Only 11 per cent of the Empire's total population of 400m lived in the United Kingdom itself.

But it was neither the spatial nor the demographic dimensions which mattered. For many British citizens at the turn of the twentieth century, the Empire's importance was not quantitative. The Empire symbolised British power and its assumed ascendancy over competitor nations. It also symbolised that civilising influence which many in the British propertied classes assumed to be an essential element of their imperial mission. On this construction, the Empire was about commercial expansion and was widely seen as a means of enrichment. Imperialism was not generally seen as greedy, grasping or as a posh name for extensive land-grabbing. The British, they believed, brought benign power along with them as they traversed the globe. They brought the example of representative government in action and used power in the service of instruction, enlightenment and improvement. The colonised would themselves be the beneficiaries if they were taught to understand British attitudes and values.

The British, and more particularly the Scots, who provided disproportionately large numbers of missionaries, traders and administrators, also brought Christianity with them.[2] The same people who considered the British version of **Imperialism** particularly advanced and enlightened believed implicitly in the uniquely beneficent message of Christianity. As **Lord Curzon** put it in 1894, the British Empire was, under God, 'the greatest empire for good that the world has seen'.[3] **Cecil Rhodes**, perhaps the largest personal beneficiary of the imperialism which transformed Africa in the 1880s and 1890s, was even more bullish. The British, he asserted, 'are the first race in the world, and the more of the world we inhabit, the better it is for the human race'.[4] The sentiment was echoed by the Earl of Rosebery, who marvelled that the Empire had been built 'not by saints and angels but by the work of men's hands . . . Human, and not yet wholly human, for the most heedless and cynical must see the finger of the divine'.[5]

Imperialism

Imperialism derives from the process of acquiring an empire, through the takeover of territories as a political and/or economic resource to increase the power of the state. Although Britain had acquired many territories before the late nineteenth century, largely for strategic and commercial reasons, the term 'British Imperialism' is most frequently used in respect of the rapid takeover of land in Africa – the so-called 'Scramble for Africa' in the 1880s and 1890s.

George Nathaniel Curzon, Marquess Curzon of Kedleston, 1859–1925

Born at the family home of Kedleston in Derbyshire, the son of Baron Scarsdale, he was educated at Eton and Oxford University. Burningly ambitious, he became an explorer, administrator and Conservative politician. In his youth, he travelled widely through Asia. He became an MP in 1886, where he spoke eloquently against Gladstone's Home Rule policy. He served in Lord Salisbury's governments in 1891–92 and 1895–98. An ardent supporter of imperialism, his first major post was as Viceroy of India (1898–1905) and he later served in wartime governments, eventually becoming Foreign Secretary (1919–24).

Cecil Rhodes, 1853–1902

Born in Hertfordshire, the son of an Anglican vicar, he was educated at Bishop Stortford Grammar School. He was a hyper-active achiever who made his fortune in diamond mining. He founded the de Beers mining corporation, diversifying into gold in the 1880s. With financial backing from the Rothschild banking family, who supported most of his ventures, he founded the British South Africa Company in 1887 in territory which later became known as Rhodesia after his Company defeated the Matabele tribe at the Battle of Shangani River in 1893. Rhodes was a businessman of genius but his dealings, especially with the indigenous leaders of Africa, were controversial and unscrupulous. His arrogant dismissal of the Matabele as 'savages' gives a fair indication of his attitude towards indigenous peoples.

For Rhodes and Curzon, imperialism and the acquisition of ever more territory owned by Britain were two sides of the same coin. Rhodes planned to build a railway stretching the entire length of Africa, from Cape Town in the south-west to Cairo in the north, a distance of some 7,500 miles. His aim was for Britain to dominate the entire continent. Until the 1880s, however, territorial acquisition was more often an incidental, and often an unintended, by-product of the British imperial mission. Britain, while recognising the need to protect its traders and commercial adventurers from attack, practised what has been famously called an 'informal empire of free trade'.[6] Until the late nineteenth century, the nation was much more interested in negotiating, or coercing, dominant trading rights than in acquiring territory. Free trade, as the British rapidly found in the late eighteenth and early nineteenth centuries, benefits already powerful, well-organised and technologically advanced countries much more than it does those with fewer goods to sell at necessarily higher prices.

II. Expansion and conflict

In the early 1780s, the only substantial land masses outside the British Isles which Britain directly ruled were in the Americas. Canada had been ceded to Britain by France at the end of the Seven Years War in 1763. The thirteen eastern seaboard states of what would become the United States of America broke away from their British governors in 1783. The remaining territories were concentrated in the Caribbean and, through the agency of the East India Company (see Chapter 19), in coastal India, especially Bombay, Madras and Bengal. By the middle of the nineteenth century, Britain had taken over recently discovered Australia and New Zealand and, from the initial establishment of Cape Colony in 1795, had extended its influence north-eastwards in what would become South Africa. Meanwhile, strategically important places in the East Indies, Penang (1786), Singapore (1819), Burma (1826) and Hong Kong (1842) had been acquired. [See Map 6, p. xxvii.]

Meanwhile, India was coming ever more extensively under British control. England's East India Company had first been given rights to trade in India by the Mughal Emperor Jehangir in 1617.[7] The Company rapidly established trading monopolies and proved politically adept at exploiting local Indian disputes and growing weaknesses in the Mughal empire. After French defeats during the Seven Years War, Britain established itself as the dominant trading nation in the subcontinent, although the wings of the East India Company were clipped. The Younger Pitt established a Board of Control for India, which was accountable to parliament. The government of Lord Liverpool ended the Company's monopoly in 1813 and its power of independent action was severely circumscribed.

The decisive turning point on the complicated route by which India became an integral part of the British empire was what the British call the Indian Mutiny and what Indian authorities call 'The First War of Independence' of 1857–58.[8] It began with a specific mutiny of Indian soldiers (sepoys) stationed at Meerut against their British officers. From there, it spread rapidly. The Mutiny's causes ranged from the relatively mundane (pay, conditions and the limited opportunities for the promotion of indigenous soldiers) to the more profound (more oppressive rule from Britain, attacks on traditional Hindu customs, different and – so many Indians felt – disadvantageous, interpretations of land laws, the vigorous work of Christian missionaries, often interpreted as a plan to Christianise the entire subcontinent). Although the rising was concentrated in the north of India, especially Bengal, and left much of the subcontinent untouched, its consequences were significant. It took almost a year to quell the rising, during which time both newspaper reports and letters from British soldiers contained reports of Indian soldiers running amok, killing every European, soldier or civilian, they could find and raping their women. Although the rising was brutally suppressed by thousands of Indian sepoys as well as by British officers, the impression given was of unbridled and primitive native savagery unleashed against blameless and well-intentioned Christians.

The Government of India Act (1858) formally ended the role of the East India Company, but it had been increasingly a dead letter anyway. A new Legislative Council was established, and the role of Viceroy (literally someone who exercised powers on behalf of the monarch), signifying Britain's more direct engagement with the process of Indian rule. In effect, India became a formal part of the Empire, although about a third of the subcontinent remained owned by almost six hundred quasi-autonomous Indian princes. Behind the scenes, however, loyal Indian princes were rewarded with honours. The vigorous modernising policies favoured by Governor-General **Dalhousie**, and widely interpreted after the Mutiny as insensitively 'Westernising', were slackened somewhat, although the proportion of British troops serving in the Indian army was significantly increased.[9]

James Andrew Ramsay, first Marquess of Dalhousie, 1812–1860

He was born in Midlothian (Scotland), the son of the ninth Earl of Dalhousie. He was educated at Harrow and Oxford University. He came to prominence when he replaced Gladstone as Vice-President of the Board of Trade in 1843 in the Peel government of 1841–46. He became an MP in 1837 but succeeded to a peerage on his father's death in the following year. He became Governor-General of India in 1848 and pursued policies of 'modernisation' there, also seeking to expand British interest in India to the subcontinent's natural boundaries. To this end, as opportunity arose, the Punjab was annexed in 1849 and Oudh in 1856. His administrative reforms were also part of the policy to consolidate British power.

Now that it was a fully integrated colony, the process of celebrating India's distinctive importance could begin. Few were thinking of the Mutiny when Disraeli persuaded Queen Victoria to accept the confected title of Empress of India in 1876. She replaced the defunct Mughal emperor and became 'an eastern potentate as well as a western sovereign'.[10] The British could now reflect comfortably on the extent and value of India's natural resources – cotton, wheat, diamonds and the rest – on its strategic importance and, increasingly, on the value of loyal Indian princes, whose children were often educated in British public schools, and of honourable, well-educated British civil servants. Thus was created the image of imperial India as 'the Jewel in the Crown'.

It might have been convenient to emphasise the image of the British Empire as both informal and focused on trade. Like all empires, however, its development required bloodshed, and commercial concerns readily defaulted to strategic considerations. Britain may have been involved in only one European war – the Crimean – during the nineteenth century, but colonial and commercial conflicts elsewhere were common enough. The spoils of victory in the two wars fought with China included Hong Kong, ready access to many more Chinese ports and the legalisation of the opium trade (see Chapter 34).

Britain lost the first of two wars in Afghanistan (1839–42) and was forced to withdraw from the country. After increasing Russian encroachments in central Asia and with evidence of clear Afghan hostility towards Britain, a second invasion of the country was attempted in 1878. This was more successful, and peace was restored on the basis of British rule over parts of Afghanistan and control of Afghan foreign policy, which could be used to block further Russian advances.

In South Africa, tensions between the Boers, descendants of the original Dutch settlers, and the British were endemic. The Boers resented the use of English as the dominant language. The British were affronted by Dutch use of slave labour on many Boer settlements. Territorial disputes were also frequent and increased in intensity after the discovery of diamonds in 1867 and a consequentially large influx of new settlers looking to make their fortunes. Britain's action in annexing the Boer province of Transvaal in 1877 precipitated a Boer rebellion and the outbreak of the first of the two Boer wars in 1880. The British lost three important battles and, when peace was signed at the Convention of Pretoria in 1881, Transvaal became, in effect, an internally self-governing colony, albeit with some checks against Boer reversion to the use of Africans as slaves.

III. Scrambling for Africa

Britain's 'informal empire' was being 'formalised' in the years 1830–80, and often at considerable cost. Until the 1880s, however, there was no systematic policy of territorial acquisition. Why did the policy of 'nibbling at Africa' change, with European powers suddenly seizing 'huge chunks of the continent'?[11]

Sir John Scott Keltie had a straightforward explanation for what he briskly called the parcelling out of 'the bulk of one barbarous continent . . . among the most civilized powers of Europe': competition among the great powers for industrial markets.[12] Only the great powers mattered. On this analysis, the role of even the most significant of indigenous potentates was a merely reactive one. They were there to be persuaded or cowed by the superior force of the Maxim gun into accepting whatever arrangements best suited European interests. In Sir John Keltie's unfortunate words, even the best of them was 'but a barbarous potentate, living in a big hut, surrounded by a large **kraal**'.[13]

Kraal

An Afrikaans word, originally of Portuguese origin, meaning either a village made up of huts surrounded by a fence or an enclosure for cattle or sheep. Its use was mostly restricted to southern Africa.

Of course, 'European interests' were not uniform. Historians have to explain why adventurers like Rhodes in southern Africa and **George Goldie** in west Africa were able to secure so much more government support for territorial expansion in the 1880s and 1890s than earlier trading adventurers had done. Most early interpretations stressed changing economic factors in Europe. European countries, needing to sustain economic growth, were increasingly persuaded that they needed new markets for investment since domestic returns in the last quarter of the nineteenth century were falling. Alternatively, perhaps the problem was not so much returns on investment as growing competition between the leading European states. This period saw many nations introducing new tariffs, not least Germany, by the 1880s Britain's leading competitor. The challenge to the domination of *laissez-faire* (see Chapter 26) and 'informal empire' over the previous half-century might well have provoked radical new responses grounded in territorial acquisition. It was also the case that most

George Goldie, 1846–1925

Born on the Isle of Man, the son of an army officer, he was educated at the Royal Military Academy, Woolwich. After a brief career in the Royal Engineers and using a legacy from a relative, he took over a small trading company on the River Niger in West Africa in 1875. He expanded it and, after amalgamating other companies, formed the United African Company in 1879. He formed the New African Company in 1882 and proposed that it took over the whole of the lower and middle Niger under a Royal Charter. In 1866 this was granted to Goldie's Royal Niger Company, which operated both effectively and profitably as a monopoly.

of the raw materials needed to establish industrial growth in Europe were widely available in Africa. As industrial expansion entered a more mature phase, so the need for raw materials such as rubber, copper and vegetable oils grew rapidly. Africa was known to have substantial, but as yet under-prospected, reserves both of key raw materials and, in southern Africa, gold.

Explanations grounded in European economic exploitation are not by themselves particularly convincing. Less European investment was made in Africa than in any other inhabited continent, even after the territorial carve-up. It was also difficult to see where mass markets for manufactured goods might be developed in an overwhelmingly rural continent with low population densities and no ready-made consumer base. Also, raw materials had been profitably extracted from Africa long before the 1880s.

It is not surprising, therefore, that emphases began to shift towards more politically grounded explanations. Germany and Italy had become fully integrated nation states only in the early 1870s. Both were anxious to flex their muscles and to demonstrate that they were worthy to be considered great European powers. France was also seeking to recover prestige lost during the Franco-Prussian war of 1870–71 (see Chapter 35) and was an active coloniser, especially in north and west Africa. Tensions were building in the late 1870s and early 1880s, especially over Egypt, which Britain, in effect, took over in 1882 (see Chapter 42). Entrenched British preferences for 'informal' empire were clearly being challenged at this time by changes in European spheres of influence. Powerful and successful colonists in Africa, such as Rhodes, Goldie and **Frederick Lugard**, were also political animals. Their personal attitudes were expansionist and their sometimes highly risky activities put pressure on Westminster-based governments to respond in support. European expansion may owe as much to such dominant, and domineering, supporters of colonialism as to great-power rivalry.

Frederick Lugard, 1858–1945

Lugard is best known as Governor-General of Nigeria from 1912 to 1918. Born in Madras into a military family, he was educated at Rossall School and the Royal Military College, Sandhurst. He travelled widely, holding down various military and trading posts in Asia and East, West and Southern Africa in the 1880s and 1890s. In 1897, Joseph Chamberlain appointed him Her Majesty's Commissioner for the Nigerian hinterland and commandant of a new West African Frontier Force. He quickly established control over Nigeria before becoming Governor-General of Hong Kong in 1907. He served there until being appointed Governor-General of the newly created single territory of Nigeria.

Until recently, African perspectives on Partition have been conspicuous by their absence. Recent research has shed considerable new light on the role of African rulers. Clearly, although abilities and opportunities varied considerably, they were far from the 'barbarians' or 'savages' so heedlessly portrayed by the likes of J. S. Keltie. Some quickly appreciated the new opportunities presented to them by rival European traders and commercial interests. Several struck highly profitable deals via concessions granted to traders and adventurers. Some looked first for protection, often in the form of European armaments, against rivals.[14] Work on the African dimension has successfully refuted simplistic arguments about Africa as Europe's plaything. By the 1880s, however, military might and modern technology would be the predominant factors determining the continent's future – and with these, African chieftains, however cunning or able, could not compete.[15]

For this reason, it is difficult to sustain the proposition that African rulers had much to do with the timing of what by September 1884 *The Times* was calling 'The Scramble for Africa'. It commented: 'Within the last year annexations and "protections" have been announced with such bewildering rapidity that we hardly know where we are; no map maker can keep pace.'[16] Within a couple of months, Bismarck, the German Chancellor, was hosting a Conference at Berlin which one historian has called 'a true thieves' compact: a charter for the partition of Africa into "spheres of influence" based on nothing more than their "effective occupation"' by the great European powers.[17]

The timing of the 'Scramble' thus resulted from a range of factors, relating to changing situations and priorities both in Europe and in Africa, which built up the pressure for territorial acquisition. Although the key decisions, at Berlin and elsewhere in the 1880s, were political, economic factors – perhaps particularly the potential value of raw materials, diamonds and gold to European markets – also played an important role.

IV. Propaganda and Empire

Taking on the burden of additional territorial responsibility was, of course, expensive, and criticism of Britain's over-stretched commitments was heard from contemporaries as well as from later historians.[18] How, then, was the British Empire in its 'New Imperial' phase sold to its citizens and with how much success?

The **public schools** played an important role. They expanded in numbers in the second half of the nineteenth century, and the key messages they inculcated – duty, responsibility, Christian morality, self-sacrifice and vigorous, manly 'team-playing' – were uniform and almost precisely translatable to the needs of colonial rule. As J. A. Mangan puts it, 'Public-school staff were persuasive and persistent propagators of imperialism.'[19] Many of their most able alumni became colonial administrators and adventurers. It also suited Benjamin Disraeli's political purpose to advocate Empire as a noble and patriotic cause around which the nation could coalesce. His political antennae were always acute and, although he did not live to see it, the hegemony of the Conservatives in the last two decades of the nineteenth century owed much to their effective deployment of patriotic messages as a means of asserting the importance of national unity against enemies – real or pretended (see Chapter 37). In this sense, the imperial policies of Disraeli and Joseph Chamberlain were travelling further along the same populist road marked out by Palmerston in the 1850s (see Chapter 34).

Public school

This term, as used in England, can easily mislead. It refers, not to schools freely open to the public, but to schools which charge fees and which are not in receipt of central or local government financial support. They mostly educate pupils from the age of 11 or 13 to 18. The number of such schools expanded greatly in the nineteenth century. The overwhelming majority were single-sex boys' schools. Some pupils from very modest backgrounds could attend because they were awarded scholarships (usually for demonstrating a particular accomplishment or strong academic ability) or were in receipt of money from a named charity. Most pupils at public school were from comfortable or privileged backgrounds.

The emergent popular press also did much to spread the imperial word. The most commercially successful daily newspapers, the *Daily Express*, founded in 1896, and the *Daily Mail*, publishing from 1900, devoted much space to the Empire and particularly to the reporting of war. The *Mail* had the greatest resources at its disposal. It paid substantial fees to its front-line reporters, who provided vivid and usually strongly pro-British 'copy'. It established an editorial office in Cape Town and used news cables to get stories back to Britain at maximum speed.[20]

Patriotic policies work best when they have a sharp, and preferably a personal, focus. Late Victorian Britain had the perfect candidate in its eponymous Queen. It was Disraeli who brought the frumpy, and increasingly dumpy, Victoria out of the reclusive, careworn shadows of widowhood and dressed her up as the supreme imperial symbol. The 'Empress of India' kick-started the process of selling the British Empire. Mere longevity, allied to deft image-manufacture, sustained and enhanced it. The Queen's Golden (1887) and Diamond (1897) Jubilees were occasions for imperial, rather than national, celebrations. *The Times* proudly published information about events in European capitals to commemorate the Golden Jubilee. It quoted approvingly from an article which had first appeared in a French magazine: 'History will certainly place Queen Victoria in the ranks of the great sovereigns . . . In a few days, her children and grandchildren, coming from all parts of Europe and from India, even the vassal potentates of Asia and Africa, her whole people, united in a common sentiment of love and respect, will celebrate the jubilee of her reign.'[21] The celebrations also afforded opportunities for crumbs to fall from the imperial table, frequently in the form of well-publicised treats for the children of the poor. In June 1887, for example, the London Drapers' Company provided 'amusements and refreshments' for 'virtually the whole of the children in the public elementary schools of the Tower Hamlets and Hackney'.[22]

The increasing popularity of the music halls from 1870 also had an impact. Patriotic songs in the 1880s frequently portrayed Britain as in need of popular support to defend its empire against growing threats from avaricious competitors, particularly Germany, France and Belgium. The message was remorselessly upbeat. Audiences were told that all would be well, however, since 'Willing hands, loyal hearts, the noblest and the best' were staunchly in the imperial camp: 'There's little fear for England, with brave Colonial sons, Ready at the hour of need.'[23] J. A. Hobson argued that the music halls were 'a more potent educator' of the working classes than 'the church, the school, the political meeting, or even the press'.[24] John Mackenzie draws attention also to a growing 'British imperial cult' nourished by the 'new traditions of Christian militarism, militarist athleticism in the public schools and a recreated and perverted "medieval" chivalry' which involved playing the game according to the rules.[25]

The messages supporters of imperialism wanted to put across were pretty clear. Evidence from the churches, through the popularity of pro-Empire music hall songs, in the sales figures of adventure stories with a strongly patriotic slant and from the enthusiastic flag-waving captured in grainy photographs on festival or celebration days, all suggest that the messages got through. As one observer concluded as the second Boer War began in 1899, 'the instincts of the British public are those of an imperial race'.[26] Many of that public voted pro-imperial with their own, and their families', feet. Emigration from Britain quickened after 1870, just as the national birth rate began to reduce. It has been estimated that more than seven million left the British Isles in the years 1870–1900. The 1890s saw the highest emigration rate. About three-quarters of emigrants were empire-bound.[27]

Some caution is necessary, however. We know much more about the thoughts of the upper and middle than of the working classes. Imperialist propaganda blasts echoing through school textbooks were much more likely to be read by the children of those who could pay for their schooling than by those receiving free education. Elementary school syllabuses available to the poor after 1870 were mostly penny-plain, concentrating on basic literacy and numeracy. Scope for flights of imperial fancy was strictly limited, although some teachers, having absorbed the imperial message, put it across vividly to their pupils.[28] Imperialism also had many critics, not least among the ranks of trade unionists and the radical middle classes, who thought the Empire a drain on resources, and considered many imperialist messages narrowly xenophobic and thus likely to increase national rivalries rather than to create international peace and harmony.[29]

V. A tainted image: the impact of the second Boer War, 1899–1902

The warm imperial glow created by the old Queen's Diamond Jubilee was soon doused by the bloody reality of another imperial war. The second Boer War, which broke out in 1899, had its origins in substantial migration into South Africa from Europe, and particularly Britain. The lure was gold, discovered in the Transvaal in 1886.[30] The next decade witnessed a growing number of conflicts between established Boer settlers and recent migrant 'Uitlanders', climaxing in the **Jameson Raid** at the end of 1895.

Jameson Raid, 29 December 1895

An attempt by Leander Starr Jameson (1853–1917), a colonial administrator in southern Rhodesia, to overthrow Kruger's government by launching a raid designed to stimulate a Uitlander (British migrant) rebellion. It failed miserably within days, embarrassing both the British government and Cecil Rhodes.

Continued Boer fears about the loss of their independence combined with British desire to assert Uitlander rights boiled over in September 1899 when Paul Kruger, head of the Boer government, issued an ultimatum to the British to withdraw all their troops from Transvaal. The war which followed lasted until 1902 and was a source of much embarrassment to the British. The early months of the war saw a number of Boer victories followed by sieges of British forces in the towns of Ladysmith and Mafeking before the arrival of British reinforcements and a change of command. Field Marshal Frederick Roberts took over from the ineffective Redvers Buller in December 1899. Aided by his Chief of Staff and Deputy Baron Kitchener and with the support of troops with morale boosted by victories, the tide rapidly turned. Kimberley was relieved in February 1900 and Mafeking in May.[31]

When the British formally took over Transvaal in October 1900 and Orange Free State in May 1901, the war appeared to be over, but victories brought no lustre to the imperial image. The Boers were able to sustain a long guerrilla campaign on territory they knew well. Kitchener responded with 'scorched earth' tactics, destroying Boer crops and homesteads and poisoning their wells. Boer families, mostly women and children, were herded into crowded and insanitary refugee or 'concentration' camps. It has been estimated that more than 25,000 died in them.

The Boers were, in effect, starved into submission. The terms of the Treaty of Vereeniging, signed in May 1902, were reasonable. The Boers were promised limited internal self-government, which they achieved within five years. The continued use of their Afrikaans language was also protected. The British could present themselves as magnanimous victors, though this was not how many commentators saw it. It is true that the relief of Ladysmith and Mafeking had been received with joy throughout the Empire. *The Times* reported that Wellington, New Zealand, was preparing extensive celebrations to mark the relief of Mafeking, while the announcement had 'been received with intense enthusiasm' in Montreal and 'with great excitement' in Sydney. Back in the Mother Country, the risibly inadequate Poet Laureate Alfred Austin penned some off-the-cuff doggerel:

Once again, banners fly!
Clang again, bells, on high,
Sounding to sea and sky,
Longer and louder,
Mafeking's glory with Kimberley, Ladysmith,
Of our unconquered kith Prouder and prouder.[32]

Broader perspectives on the second Boer War tended to be much more sober. The conflict revealed important military weaknesses and it damaged the British imperial 'brand'. At the beginning of the war, the might of the British army, which eventually – albeit after overcoming considerable recruitment difficulties – totalled half a million combatants, had been embarrassed by a much weaker foe. It was then held up for almost three years before victory, of a sort, was achieved. Although deaths in combat, at 7,500, were relatively modest, almost twice as many soldiers died from disease. This suggested that lessons of the Crimea about proper troop support had still not been absorbed (see Chapter 34). Worse, Kitchener's war strategy in 1900–1, though undeniably effective, attracted huge criticism on humanitarian grounds. It was Britain, rather than Germany, which pioneered the concentration camp. At home, the Liberal leader Henry Campbell-Bannerman (see Chapter 38) denounced the war as having been fought with 'methods of barbarism'. To its main rivals, Britain no longer seemed impregnable. This perception would influence both how alliances were made and the development of the arms race in the years which preceded the First World War (see Chapter 43).

37

Conservatism in the era of Salisbury, 1880–1914

I. The reputation of Disraeli

Benjamin Disraeli, now Earl of Beaconsfield, lived for just over a year after his election defeat in March 1880. He spent it as the Conservative leader in opposition. There was symmetry in this since he had first reached the Conservative party's front bench in 1847 as an opposition spokesman. In the intervening thirty-three years, he had spent just under eleven years in office, only the final six with a majority. The result of the 1880 general election (see Chapter 33) almost exactly reversed the outcome of Disraeli's triumph in 1874. Worse, it seemed to confirm semi-permanent minority status for the Conservatives. Judged purely on election outcomes, Disraeli's time at the centre of Conservative politics must be judged a substantial failure.

Yet Disraeli is almost certain to be judged by almost any subsequent Tory politician as one of the two or three most successful Conservative Prime Ministers.[1] By contrast, Salisbury, who dominated the political life of the 1880s and 1890s and who arguably established the Conservatives as the natural party of government, is much less frequently placed in the pantheon.

There was, of course, more to Disraeli than the winning of elections, although historians are divided about his contribution to the party. Those who value attention to detail and legislative achievement rank him lowly. He depended on the spadework of others. The recent rehabilitation of the fourteenth Earl of Derby has been largely at Disraeli's expense.[2] Derby was the leader who sustained a depressed party during long years of opposition and who retained a sense of direction. Disraeli followed in his wake. Others have noted that Disraeli's financial and economic policies, once Protection had served its turn in advancing his career, were orthodox and much closer to Gladstone's than either man would have liked to admit.[3] Perhaps Disraeli's main value to his party lay in his exoticism and his 'difference'. His origins were Jewish and his background literary. His quick-wittedness and shrewd assessments of character were honed via his secondary career as a novelist. Such qualities alienated 'traditional', landowning Tories – not least Salisbury, at least until 1878 (see Chapter 35) – while making him more attractive to new voters in a mass electorate. Disraeli understood that most citizens are not much interested in the detail of politics but do respond to clear messages and powerful images. Disraeli gave them a sense of self-worth as English patriots and as supporters of the British Empire as a force for good and for improvement. He also believed, though he was disinclined to master the requisite details, in 'improving the condition of the people'. Disraeli in the 1870s also shaped the Conservatives as a national party in which political differences could be submerged in support for a greater, if simplistically articulated, good. Only rarely could Disraeli capitalise on Liberal weakness and internal dissension; hence the Conservatives' limited electoral success until the 1880s. But he did leave behind a potent legacy on which others could build.

II. Leadership consolidated: Salisbury and the Conservatives, 1881–1886

Salisbury was Disraeli's obvious successor, although the party decided initially to divide the leadership. Salisbury led in the Lords and Sir Stafford Northcote (see Chapter 33) in the Commons. The latter remained dutiful and well-prepared but dull. He did little to energise the opposition benches. In his early years as leader, Salisbury was a much more effective advocate on foreign affairs than he was in articulating coherent domestic policies. Frustrated at the lack of progress, a so-called 'Fourth Party' emerged from within the Conservative ranks. It was led by **Lord Randolph Churchill** and also comprised the Conservative party organiser John Eldon Gorst (see Chapter 33), the diplomat Sir Henry Wolff and, if only as a bit-part player, **Arthur Balfour**, Salisbury's nephew. Its main function was to wake the opposition up, but for Churchill, the most buoyant and able of the quartet, it was also about striking popular attitudes and career-building. The Earl of Derby, now a Liberal minister, considered Churchill extremely clever but 'thoroughly untrustworthy'.[4] Lord Randolph was difficult to miss in a crowd and he angled to put himself into a position of influence if the Liberals faltered. The prominence of the Fourth Party in the Commons also confirmed the suspicions of many Conservative MPs in the Commons that Northcote was not up to the job of opposing Gladstone. Soon, in practice if not in theory until 1885, Salisbury was acting as the sole leader of the party.

Lord Randolph Churchill, 1849–1895

Born the son of the seventh Duke of Marlborough, he was educated at Eton and Oxford University. His family's wealth was depleted and he became one of the first to replenish an aristocratic fortune when, in 1874, he married the daughter of a wealthy financier from New York. Their elder son was Winston Churchill. He became an MP in 1874 but made little impression in the Commons until Gladstone returned as Prime Minister in 1880. He then developed debating skills to attack both the Liberal government and also his own party's leaders for lack of bite. He became known for his defence of 'Tory democracy' but he was little interested in extension of the franchise, wishing rather to rally support for defence of the monarchy, House of Lords and the Church of England. Salisbury rewarded his contribution to defeating the Gladstone government in 1885 by making him Secretary of State for India. In the next Conservative government in 1886, he became Leader of the House of Commons and Chancellor of the Exchequer. His relationship with Salisbury was always uneasy, although the two men's political views were similar. When, hoping to consolidate his position in the Conservative hierarchy by demonstrating his importance to the government, he offered his resignation in December 1886, Salisbury accepted it. Despite remaining within the party, and supporting its Irish policy in the late 1880s (see Chapter 40), he never took office again.

Arthur Balfour, 1848–1930

He was born in East Lothian, the son of a prosperous Scottish landowner and his wife, the daughter of the second Marquess of Salisbury. Balfour's uncle was Robert Cecil, the third Marquess and Conservative Prime Minister. Balfour was educated at Eton and Cambridge University and retained intellectual interests, particularly in the study of philosophy, all his life. He became a Conservative MP in 1874 but took some time to make his mark. Salisbury appointed him President of the Local Government Board in 1886 and he became Chief Secretary for Ireland in 1887. He remained in that post until 1891, employing coercive tactics to quell unrest while also passing two measures of land reform (see Chapter 40). He became Leader of the House of Commons in 1891 and retained that post – except during the brief Liberal governments of 1892–95 – until his uncle resigned as Prime Minister in 1902 and Balfour succeeded him. Many contemporaries felt him a weak Prime Minister, being both overly cerebral (never an attribute which sits happily with Conservative leaders) and associated with increasingly anachronistic aristocratic rule. He fared little better as leader of the opposition from 1905. He encouraged the House of Lords to reject much Liberal legislation. This led to the constitutional crisis of 1909–11. After the Conservatives failed to block House of Lords reform, he resigned as party leader. He returned to office as Foreign Secretary in the Lloyd George coalition government (1916–19) and also served in Stanley Baldwin's Conservative government (1926–29).

The Fourth Party was never as important as it thought it was, although Churchill and Wolff could claim to have founded the Primrose League. Launched in 1883 to support 'Tory principles – the maintenance of religion, of the estates of the realm, and of the Imperial Ascendancy of Great Britain',[5] it was named after what was supposed to be Disraeli's favourite flower, and intended to anchor his memory within a framework of effective political organisation. The League attracted significant numbers of middle-class women into local work for the National Union of Conservative organisations. By 1900, the Primrose League had more than 2,000 branches and well over 1m members.[6] It also performed the extremely important function of integrating urban middle-class Conservatives into an established landed milieu. This helped to address the damaging perception that the Tories remained a party of aristocrats and rural squires operating anachronistically in a nation which was, by 1900, 80 per cent urban.[7]

It was Salisbury who most effectively exploited the new opportunities which further electoral reform afforded from the mid-1880s. Although he had been a leading opponent of Disraeli over parliamentary reform in 1867, he came to see that increasing the size of the electorate did not threaten the Conservative party. He no longer opposed further franchise extensions. He was, however, anxious to ensure that any new system worked in the Conservative interest. He persuaded a reluctant Gladstone to link the growing demand for an equal franchise in county and borough seats to a radical redistribution of seats. The 1884 Reform Act increased the electorate by about 72 per cent. This gave about 60 per cent of adult males the vote and incidentally strengthened the case for male democracy which Joseph Chamberlain and many Liberal radical MPs were making.[8] Salisbury was more interested in the attendant Redistribution Act which reached the statute book in the following year. This was the first Act to make a significant assault in the direction of the Chartists' 'equal electoral districts'. Politically neutral boundary commissioners were appointed to create parliamentary constituencies comprising approximately 50,000 voters each. A number of anomalies remained, including the right of many property owners to vote in a number of different constituencies. Still, a much greater degree of consistency and rationality was achieved.

Salisbury's negotiating skills, in working with the Liberal Charles Dilke on the details of redistribution, worked to the Conservatives' advantage. 132 small boroughs were disfranchised, the majority of them won by the Liberals at the 1880 election. These were transferred both to the counties and to newly suburban boroughs, especially on the outskirts of London. Conservatives had traditionally done well in the counties, while in the new suburbs indications suggested that lower-middle-class voters were, at least potentially, Tory (see Chapter 31). In the 1885 general election, although the Conservatives won about eighty seats fewer than the Liberals, they made striking gains in the suburbs of London and in Lancashire. In the first general election at which the number of uncontested seats fell below fifty, it became easier to detect where the political parties' specific geographical strength lay.[9] Although many individual variations – local issues, the strength and durability of particular candidates, and the relative effectiveness of local organisations – clouded the national picture, Salisbury's Conservatives had established a particularly strong bridgehead in the South-East. They also did better than expected in the English counties, where agricultural labourers could vote for the first time. Many were now in trade unions (see Chapter 41), nonconformist in religion and therefore expected to be predominantly Liberal.

By the time of this election, Salisbury was Prime Minister. Gladstone's government had resigned in June 1885 when a Conservative amendment to the budget was narrowly carried in the Commons.[10] Salisbury was an uncontroversial choice to head the minority government which followed. Parliamentary arithmetic would grant his first ministry only a seven-month lease but it sufficed for him to reset the

Conservative compass. In Newport (Monmouthshire) he delivered a speech as pregnant with potential as it was teasing in its opacity. He pondered on ways to lance the Irish boil (see Chapter 40) through a more constructive relationship between Britain and Ireland. In foreign policy, he committed his party to nothing more specific than a policy aimed to secure European peace (see Chapter 42). On domestic matters, he indicated that the Conservatives would seek reforms in local government, housing for the masses and popular education. Lest these might seem unduly 'liberal' to his own supporters, he identified clear water separating Conservatives from Liberals on religion. With many Liberals clamouring for the disestablishment of the Church of England, Salisbury asserted that its established status would be sacrosanct for a Conservative government. He recalled the implacably high Tory stance which Gladstone adopted in his youth. Like many other of Gladstone's principles, Salisbury asserted that it had been 'sacrificed upon the altar of party'.[11]

III. Salisbury and the Liberal Unionists

Salisbury's government fell in January 1886, when the Liberals carried an amendment to the Queen's Speech at the opening of parliament. The story of the intervening six months, which set the course of British politics for a decade and more, is followed elsewhere (see Chapter 38). It ended with the collapse of the Liberal government over Home Rule, which triggered a further general election in July. This gave the Conservatives an overall majority of more than a hundred and fifty, thanks to support from 'Liberal Unionists', who left their party over Home Rule. Salisbury returned to No. 10 Downing Street in August 1886.

He was to remain there, with a three-year break from 1892 to 1895 (see Chapter 38), for thirteen years and his party would stay in government for almost sixteen. Over the next century, the Conservatives became the natural party of government. They were in office, either alone or as the dominant force in coalitions, for seventy-five of the years from Disraeli's election victory of 1874 to the massive defeat of John Major's government in 1997. How did the Conservatives in the 1880s and 1890s effect such a transformation in fortunes which would have amazed Disraeli as much as it would have delighted him?

The simplest answer to this question is also the most persuasive. They did so because the Liberals let them (see Chapter 38). With memories of 1846 and the 'wilderness years' which followed still sharp, none knew better than the Conservatives that parties which split do not win general elections and that recovery and rehabilitation takes time. The travails of the Liberals, however, only offer a partial explanation. Two other factors deserve consideration. The first is the leadership of Salisbury and the second the cohesiveness of the Liberal Unionists.

An intelligent, cynical aristocrat with some strong reactionary prejudices and a private contempt for many with less education and acuity than himself, Salisbury proved more effective than Disraeli at directing his party onto the path of cautious, calculated reform while reasserting established Conservative principles: governance in the hands of property owners, respect for authority, implicit belief in – and support for – an Established Church and, perhaps above all, Britain's imperial mission.[12]

The Liberal Unionists deserve more sympathetic consideration than they have generally been given. As Ian Cawood has noted, they were a disparate group comprising landed aristocrats, who generally followed Hartington's lead, wealthy businessmen and erstwhile radical Liberals, many of whom shared Joseph Chamberlain's views about the need for increased state intervention to improve conditions and life chances for working people. Some Unionist radicals concentrated on specific issues, such as free, non-sectarian education for the children of the poor. Others evinced a 'manly' integrity, holding fast to their beliefs without compromising to satisfy the preferences of a local party caucus or to curry favour with the national leadership.[13] Although their commitment to the Union with Ireland was implacable, they were far more than a one-issue group. They operated as a distinct grouping in the Commons and were resistant to the idea of mere assimilation within the Conservative party. Salisbury did not push either for Liberal Unionists to enter the Cabinet or for assimilation with the Conservatives, for fear of seeing many scurry back to Gladstone. Chamberlain, the most senior Unionist, maintained some distance from the Conservatives and continued to pursue radical social policies.[14] Even so, it is probable that the Unionists would have returned to the Liberal party had Gladstone resigned the leadership in the late 1880s. Salisbury managed the long period of Unionist acclimatisation with skill. It was not until 1895 that four Liberal Unionists – the Duke of Devonshire (as Hartington had now become), Chamberlain, Lansdowne and Henry James – joined a Salisbury government. There was no formal merger until 1912, when the Conservatives became known as the Unionist party.

IV. Salisbury and the policy of cautious reform

Salisbury pursued a more active domestic policy than is often recognised. His experience as a member of the 1884 Royal Commission on Housing influenced subsequent legislation. The Housing of the Working Classes Act, passed during the minority government of 1885, gave the Local Government Board power to force local authorities to shut down unhealthy houses and to take action against landlords who let out insanitary properties. In 1890 local authorities were given additional powers to buy up and demolish insanitary dwellings and to re-house tenants. Like other housing legislation before the First World War, however, the lack of Treasury funding discouraged substantial local authority initiatives in this area. An Allotments Act of 1887 and a Smallholdings Act of 1892 also gave local authorities the power to purchase land to let out at economic rents.

Salisbury had always believed that powers in the hands of local authorities provided a necessary break on 'centralism'. This was a practical, as well as an ideological, position to take since far more citizens' lives were affected by the work of local agencies in popular education, street paving, support for the poor and the like than they were by happenings at Westminster. As part of Salisbury's conversion, if not to democracy, then at least to the development of representative structures, the government passed a Local Government Act in 1888. This created fifty county councils in England, elected on a franchise similar to that used for parliamentary elections. However, 'aldermen' were elected by, and from within, the elected councillors. While providing elements of continuity, stability and experience, aldermen might also prevent hasty policy changes when local elections changed the political balance of a council. In most cases, neither the selection of candidates nor the choice of the electorate justified alarmist Tory fears that the new system of local government would challenge the influence of the propertied classes.

The 1888 Act also established a London County Council and so-called 'county boroughs' for the towns and cities with a population of 50,000 or more. While these county boroughs were self-governing, the new county councils worked alongside the Municipal Corporations which had been in existence since the 1830s (see Chapter 21). In 1894, the Liberal Local Government Act required all rural parishes with populations of at least 300 to set up directly elected parish councils. These operated under the authority of new Rural District Councils. This legislation completed the lengthy process whereby all representative authorities derived their authority from an electorate.

In 1897, Joseph Chamberlain, for once freed from the mounting burdens of the Colonial Office (see Chapter 36), managed to pilot a Workmen's Compensation Act through parliament. This provided government-funded compensation for workers who incurred accidents at work on the railways and in mining and quarrying, factories and laundries. Its scope was narrower than Chamberlain intended since Conservatives in the Lords lobbied hard to identify a number of exceptions. Chamberlain compromised to get his legislation through. The effect was a significant reduction in eligibility for compensation.[15]

Much the most controversial, as well as radical, Conservative domestic legislation in this period concerned education. The Fee Grant Act of 1891, by providing government grants to schools, made free schooling almost universally available. A ten-shilling (50p) grant was payable yearly to each public elementary school, based on attendance, and fees could be remitted entirely. Many schools continued to charge, however, arguing that parents were more likely to ensure that their children were attending when they were paying for the privilege. The main purpose of the Act, though, was political. Conservatives had feared for some time that Anglican 'voluntary' schools, which educated about a third of all English children in the 1890s, were being squeezed by board schools which, ratepayer-financed, had more resources. Salisbury confirmed that 'The gift of free or assisted education must be so conducted as not to diminish in the slightest degree the guarantee that we now possess for religious liberty as expressed by the voluntary schools'.[16] Liberals complained that state money was being used to finance sectarian education for the benefit of the Established Church.

The 1902 Education Act, though much more radical in scope, had a similarly defensive intention. That legislation was needed was beyond doubt. The School Board structure established in 1870 (see Chapter 32) had developed at different speeds and in unpredicted ways across the country. Some offered courses which took education well beyond the 'elementary' level in so-called 'Higher Grade Schools'. The mainly Anglican education provided in Church schools could only limp along in its wake. Arthur Balfour, who became Prime Minister as his Education Bill was proceeding through parliament, said that 'the existing educational system is chaotic, is ineffectual, is utterly beyond the age [and] makes us the laughing stock of every advanced nation in Europe and America'.[17] Under guidance from R. L. Morant, a senior official in the Education Department, the government rationalised educational provision. School Boards were abolished and their responsibilities transferred to more than three hundred new Local Education Authorities (LEAs). These took responsibility for elementary, secondary and technical education.

Administratively, the new education authorities worked well. Elementary education became better organised and opportunities for secondary education markedly increased, although in most areas take-up was dominated by the middle classes. By 1914, more than a thousand secondary schools were in operation. Unprecedentedly sharp controversy ensued, which galvanised the Liberal party. Nonconformists bitterly resented that, not only were Church schools incorporated within the new LEAs, they were on life-support provided at the ratepayer's expense. Worse, voluntary schools retained control over the appointment of their teachers. The young David Lloyd George (see Chapter 38) first came to national attention by urging local authorities to ignore the new Act. A National Passive Resistance Committee was established in England, and almost two hundred men went to prison for refusing to pay 'school taxes'. The Women's Local Government Society opposed the Act because women had played an important role in School Boards but could not be elected to serve on the county and county borough councils which administered the new education authority.[18]

V. The balloon bursts: Balfour, division and defeat

The long period of Conservative domination came to an abrupt halt in the Edwardian period. At the 1906 general election, the party won only 157 seats to the Liberals' 396. It did mount a significant recovery at the two elections of 1910 (see Chapter 38) when in January the party trailed Liberals and Labour by 42 seats and in December came within a single seat of the Liberals alone.[19] However, more than a hundred solidly anti-Tory seats won by the Irish parliamentary and the Labour parties condemned the Conservatives to a further period in opposition.

The party's misfortunes began soon after the election victory in 1900. It took much flak from its maladministration of the Boer War (see Chapter 36). After the war ended, revelations that Chinese labourers working in South African gold mines (usually referred to as 'coolies') were being treated almost as slave labour were damaging. The 1902 Education Act significantly reduced Liberal Unionist support for the government. Greatest damage, however, was done by the split over **Tariff Reform** in 1903. This issue caused the resignation of Balfour's ablest minister, Joseph Chamberlain, and it challenged Free Trade, an economic orthodoxy which British people had been told for more than half a century was the foundation of their prosperity. The Liberals considered Chamberlain's conversion to imperial preference as manna from heaven (see Chapter 38). British businessmen, anxious to exploit growing American markets, feared that imperial preference would provoke a trade war with the United States which they would lose. No wonder many bemused contemporaries believed that the Conservative party was, in the words of one historian, indulging in 'an act of self-immolation'.[20]

Tariff Reform and Imperial Preference

A policy which challenged the long-established orthodoxy of Free Trade as an economic policy. Pressure for tariff reform developed at the end of the nineteenth century in response to the imposition of import duties by most of Britain's main industrial competitors. To counter the effects on British manufacturing industry, Joseph Chamberlain gave a speech in Birmingham in May 1903 calling for a policy of 'Imperial Preference', which would bring the states of the British Empire closer together as an economic unit. The plan was that Britain would impose duties only on food imported from outside the Empire, while British colonies would not levy import duties on goods manufactured in Britain. In September 1903, Chamberlain resigned from the government in order to campaign for imperial preference. His policy was unsuccessful partly because some of the wealthier colonies themselves opposed it. In particular Canada, now manufacturing its own goods and seeking world markets for them, believed it would work against its economic interests. The policy also split the Conservative party. Imperial preference did not become official British economic policy until 1932, eighteen years after Chamberlain's death.

From July 1902 to November 1911 the Conservative leader was Arthur Balfour. Since this period is one of almost unrelieved gloom for the Conservatives, it is hardly surprising that his leadership met with considerable criticism. Salisbury, for all his contempt for those more lowly born and less able than he was, had been a consummately professional politician who used his considerable abilities to secure and then hold on to power for as long as possible. His nephew was equally aristocratic but much less committed to the dirty work to which effective politicians often have to stoop. His languid style, literary affectations and preference for philosophical argument over the crude hurly-burly of political debate did not endear him to his backbenchers. In recent years, attempts have been made to rescue Balfour's reputation. Geoffrey Searle calls him 'an unlucky Prime Minister' who inherited a tired Cabinet from his uncle and a growing crisis over Tariff Reform.[21] E. H. H. Green pointed out that Balfour faced a united and increasingly confident Liberal party, which, after 1886, Salisbury never had to do.

Tariff Reform was not some whim of Joseph Chamberlain's but a logical, if controversial, response to perceptions of British decline (see Chapter 27). It created a crisis of identity for the party, cutting across the established fault line between 'Conservative' and 'Unionist' with damaging results.[22] Both Tariff Reform and Irish Home Rule (see Chapter 40) placed substantial strains on a party which, thanks to Disraeli and Salisbury, was no longer completely landowner-dominated and which offered policies stretching beyond defence of established institutions and support for the British Empire. By the early twentieth century, it had considerable support both in the suburbs and among the working classes. A number of successful Conservative working men's clubs had been established and working-class Conservatism was especially strong in areas of substantial Irish immigration. Much more diverse than it had been, the Conservative party had become more difficult to lead.

That said, Balfour's replacement, **Bonar Law**, was much more to Tory backbenchers' taste. He took the fight to the Liberals. He warned the Prime Minister in 1912: 'I shall have to show myself very vicious, Mr Asquith, this session. I hope you will understand.'[23] Selectively vicious to the Liberals he may have been, but he was no healer of deep party divisions. His strong support both for Tariff Reform and Ulster Protestants widened the splits and prolonged its identity crisis. On the outbreak of the First World War, the Conservatives seemed no nearer office than they had after their shuddering defeat in the 1906 election.

Andrew Bonar Law, 1858–1923

Born in New Brunswick, Canada, the son of a Presbyterian minister whose family came from Ulster, his mother, who was related to the Scottish banking firm of Kidston, died when he was 2 and he emigrated to Scotland at the age of 12. He was educated at Glasgow High School before entering the Kidston banking firm. He later joined the iron merchants Jacks and Company, where he established himself as a successful businessman. He became a Conservative MP in 1900. He supported Tariff Reform and his reputation for effective advocacy was grounded in a series of powerful speeches supporting the policy. When Balfour resigned as Conservative party leader, Law was unanimously elected to succeed him. In the years before the First World War, however, Bonar Law faced strident opposition within his party both for sustaining Tariff Reform and for supporting Ulster's right to reject Home Rule (see Chapter 40). He was a Cabinet member in the wartime coalitions of Asquith and Lloyd George and was briefly Prime Minister in 1922–23 before inoperable throat cancer was diagnosed. He resigned shortly before his death.

38

The Liberal party, 1880–1914: sundered and saved?

I. Gladstone's return

The political and personal duel between Gladstone and Disraeli was ended by the latter's death in 1881 (see Chapter 37). Gladstone, however, stayed – and stayed. The effects of his political longevity would not have been so serious had he not promised to retire so often, especially in the early 1880s.[1] Though most colleagues wanted him to remain in office, at least until 1886, portents of impending departure had a destabilising effect on the Liberal party. He would remain its leader for another fourteen years, finally resigning at the age of 83. He formed three more governments, none of them successful, and his Irish policies (see Chapter 40) all but destroyed his party. It is said that colleagues shed copious tears as Gladstone, with characteristic impassivity, chaired his last Cabinet meeting on 1 March 1894.[2] Many must have been of the crocodile variety as senior Liberal politicians reflected on the disastrous events of the previous ten years. Many, perhaps most, political leaders outstay their welcome. Few manage it on such a grand, destabilising scale as William Gladstone.

What has been called 'the last of the old-style Liberal ministries'[3] began promisingly enough. The 1880 general election had a decisive outcome and, as the Marquess of Hartington (see Chapter 32) told Queen Victoria when she asked him to form a government, it had been Gladstone's Midlothian-charged victory (see Chapter 32). Victoria had to re-appoint as Prime Minister a man she had called '*a half-mad fire-brand* who would soon ruin everything, and be a *Dictator*'.[4] Hartington's advice contained a strong element of self-preservation. He could surmise what trouble Gladstone would cause if deprived of the premiership.

The nature of the Liberal victory in 1880 smoothed Gladstone's preference for a Cabinet stuffed full of titled Whigs. Its fifteen initial members included six earls or dukes. The number increased to seven when Selborne, the Lord Chancellor, was granted an earldom in 1881. When the Earl of Derby joined the Cabinet as Colonial Secretary at the end of 1882, he noted, to his evident satisfaction, that it was 'as little democratic as any we have had in the present century'.[5]

The Liberals did particularly well in the counties, boosting the complement of Liberal landowners. Almost seventy of the Liberal MPs returned to the Commons were the heirs, or other close relatives, of peers or baronets. With more than seventy non-titled large landowners also elected, more than 40 per cent of Liberal MPs represented the landed interest.[6] The Cabinet reflected this emphasis. Most had held office under Gladstone before. Despite popular reputation as 'the People's William', Gladstone never wavered in his belief in 'government by the best', with a pronounced predilection for the best-born. The radicals were marginalised. **Joseph Chamberlain**, whom Gladstone never trusted and whose populism he grew to abhor,[7] became President of the Board of Trade. John Bright, as Chancellor of the Duchy of Lancaster, occupied the most junior and least onerous Cabinet post. He was appointed, it seems, to keep up the appearance of a Prime Minister at ease with radical colleagues. In any case, radicals did not come any more respectable than Bright.

Joseph Chamberlain, 1836–1914

Born in Camberwell (Surrey), the son of a nonconformist metals manufacturer, he was educated at University College School, London, before being apprenticed to his father's business. In 1854, his father sent him to Birmingham to help develop the screw-manufacturing business in which he had invested with his brother-in-law. The business thrived and made Chamberlain rich. He pursued enlightened policies in the family business, including the introduction of a maximum nine-hour working day. He first came to national attention in the National Education League (see Chapter 29). He was elected Lord Mayor of Birmingham in 1873 and was responsible for initiating a number of civic reforms commonly called 'Gas and Water Socialism'. He became MP for Birmingham in 1876 and founded the Birmingham Liberal Association, which became the model for the National Federation of Liberal Associations in 1877. His organisational work was instrumental in securing a Liberal majority at the election of 1880. Gladstone appointed him President of the Board of Trade (1880–85), where his achievements were limited. He split with Gladstone over Irish Home Rule; his own preference was for more limited devolution. He supported Salisbury's government from 1886 but did not return to government until becoming Colonial Secretary in 1895. He was a strong imperialist, believing that Tariff Reform and imperial preference (see Chapter 38) would revive British competitiveness. Tariff Reform split the Conservative party and played a major part in its election defeat of 1906 – the year in which a stroke ended Chamberlain's political career.

In a government which would be dominated by Ireland and by foreign and imperial policy (see Chapters 40 and 42), the supercharged septuagenarian led from the front. He acted as his own Chancellor of the Exchequer until the end of 1882. A number of measures designed to stabilise the economy resulted, although the government needed tax increases to pay for an active foreign and imperial policy. Important land reforms were passed. The 1882 Settled Land Act gave agricultural tenants-for-life greater freedom to improve, lease or even to sell their estates, thus enhancing their freedom to invest as they considered best. The Agricultural Holdings Act (1883) gave tenants compensation for their investment in land improvements.

II. Division and defeat

The news that Gladstone proposed to support Home Rule for Ireland emerged in December 1885 via newspaper reports on the authority of his son Herbert. Known as the 'Hawarden Kite', after the name of Gladstone's country residence in Flintshire, it transformed the political situation. Although Gladstone had not formally committed the Liberals to Home Rule when, in February 1886, he became Prime Minister for the third time, the Marquess of Hartington believed the message of the 'Kite'. He refused to serve in Gladstone's government. Gladstone also had refusals from Derby and Selborne. Chamberlain became President of the Local Government Board but resigned theatrically a month later when he walked out of the Cabinet Room.[8] He immediately began campaigning against Home Rule. On 8 June, after pledges to vote against Home Rule from many radicals and most Whigs in the parliamentary party, Gladstone's Government of Ireland Bill was defeated in the Commons by thirty votes. At the consequent general election, Gladstonian Liberals and the so-called 'Liberal Unionists' campaigned as separate parties. Chamberlain mused that Gladstone's public rebuff on Home Rule would force his resignation, which he believed would be followed by the selection of a more accommodating leader and a quick healing of Liberal wounds. Chamberlain was wrong, and his own standing in the party was damaged since many thought his reflections on the leadership a stratagem to strengthen his own position in any contest.

Divisions within the Liberal party are discernible from the 1850s or even earlier. In an era of mass politics, to which the parliamentary reforms of 1883–85 substantially contributed (see Chapter 37), the different power bases of great Whig landowners and urban radicals seemed to be pulling the party in opposite directions. The former were concerned to preserve the established order and especially the rights of property; many of the latter urged state intervention to address great social questions such as public health and education. On this analysis, a party split was inevitable sooner or later. Gladstone's Home Rule proposals were merely a catalyst for schism. Such an analysis, however, is flawed. The Whigs, though cautious, were no reactionaries; they had supported a number of land reforms during the government of 1880–85. Also, their long, slow decline in the face of industrialism and urbanisation was far from inevitable. Gladstone apart, they had been the dominant force in the recent government.

Like most radicals most of the time, the so-called 'Liberal radicals' found it very difficult to agree on which issues to be radical about. They were a disunited, self-important, often self-deluding and generally disagreeable bunch who bickered about one another while pursuing mutually inconsistent objectives. Even Joseph Chamberlain, the most senior radical in the party, could not count on more than twenty to twenty-five personal supporters. He was responsible for Liberal radicalism's highest profile initiative, the 'Radical (or 'Unauthorised') Programme' of 1885. This aimed to make a national policy of the 'municipal socialism' he had developed in Birmingham. It advocated free education, the disestablishment of the Church of England and a graduated taxation system. Its venom was directed at rent-gobbling landlords – 'those who toil not, neither do they spin'.[9] Chamberlain called the Liberal party 'the great agency of progress and reform' while noting that he had been 'solemnly excommunicated by some of the great authorities who claim a monopoly of the orthodox Liberal faith'.[10] The Programme annoyed both Gladstone and the Whigs. It gained only limited support from Liberal radicals and was also treated suspiciously by working-class leaders. It had limited purchase. Until 1885, the Liberal party was not headed for schism. It was driven there by the force of Gladstone's personality on probably the only issue which could have torn it apart. It is difficult to dissent from Jonathan Parry's withering assessment: 'Gladstone's behaviour [in 1885–86] turned the Liberal party from a great party of government into a gaggle of outsiders.'[11]

Although the Liberals were in opposition from 1886 to 1892, the party, shorn of Whig Unionists and many troublesome radicals, could boast greater coherence than before. Gladstone found the party easier to lead as he continued to pursue his prime objective: 'the speedy concession to Ireland of what she most desires'.[12] A Round Table Conference aimed at reuniting the Liberal party was held in 1887 but achieved almost nothing since Gladstone refused any compromise on Irish Home Rule.

It has been argued that the split did relatively little damage to Liberalism, especially at grass-roots level. With most of the Whigs departed – a process which had begun before 1886 – party organisation was easier to manage, usually through a network of nonconformist groups. Also, Home Rule had established 'a simple test of orthodoxy' for a party which had hitherto been extraordinarily heterodox.[13] Some radical Unionists who had voted against Gladstone in 1886 returned to the Liberals in the late 1880s and early 1890s. With their return, and once Gladstone had retired, the now reduced Liberal party might concentrate on policies of 'positive social welfare'.[14]

However, this argument should not be pushed too far. Liberal cohesion in the early 1890s is easily exaggerated. The aristocratic Whigs who remained loyal were rewarded with important Cabinet posts when Gladstone formed his fourth ministry in 1892. **Rosebery** went to the Foreign Office, Earl Spencer was First Lord of the Admiralty and the Earl of Kimberley was appointed Secretary for India. As ever, Gladstone found working with aristocrats much more congenial than the tortuous business of finding common ground with nonconformists. Gladstone's obsession with his version of Home Rule fitted his own conception of politics as the working out of a higher moral code. It did, however, commit his party to backing a horse nobbled at the starting-gate. The bill which Gladstone presented to the Commons in 1893 was less ambitious than that of 1886; it was passed there with a comfortable majority in September, though success was dependent on the Irish nationalist bloc vote. The next week the Lords, arguing that there was no 'British' mandate for Home Rule', provided a humiliating rejection by 419 votes to 41. The fixated Gladstone was all for carrying on the vain struggle the following year. Only then did his Cabinet summon up the courage to tell him that both a new horse and a fresh jockey would be needed – for a race to be run much later on. Thanks to Gladstone, the Liberals wasted a huge amount of time on a contest they were bound to lose.

Archibald Primrose, fifth Earl of Rosebery, 1847–1929

Born in London into a Scottish aristocratic family, he was the son of Lord Dalmeny, a Whig MP who died when he was 4 years old. He succeeded to the peerage on his grand-father's death in 1868. He was educated at Eton and Oxford University. His marriage to the daughter of the international banker Baron Mayer de Rothschild in 1878 made him exceptionally wealthy. Highly intelligent and well-read, yet besotted by horse-racing both as gambler and breeder, he twice refused junior office under Gladstone before becoming Lord Privy Seal in 1885 and Foreign Secretary (1886 and 1892–94). He championed the Empire and visited Australia, New Zealand and India during the 1880s. He became the first President of the Imperial Federation League in 1884 and advocated close co-operation between largely self-governing white colonies. Unlike most Whigs, he admired Gladstone's leadership, supporting him through the Home Rule crisis. He became the first Chairman of the London County Council in 1889. As Prime Minister, he struggled to keep the Liberals united. His brief tenure of the post, which he did not enjoy, revealed the problems of having two strong-minded senior ministers – himself and Harcourt – in different Houses of Parliament. In 1895 he was damaged by accusations of a homo-sexual relationship with the Marquess of Queensbury's son. He resigned as Prime Minister in June 1895 and as leader of the opposition in 1896. Though he remained active in the House of Lords, he did not hold office again. In later life he wrote a num-ber of political biographies.

Some of that time could profitably have been spent in the late 1880s cementing links with trade unionists and ensuring that the 'rise of Labour' took place within the Liberal party (see Chapter 41). Few trade unionists were socialists; most were staunchly Gladstonian. When Keir Hardie fought a by-election in Mid-Lanark in 1888, he campaigned on the slogan 'a vote for Hardie is a vote for Gladstone'.[15] Gladstone did little to reciprocate such trade union loyalty. He made half-hearted gestures towards proposals for the payment of MPs, which would have encouraged more working-class men to stand for parliament. The idea found its way into **the Newcastle Programme** of 1891, a rag-bag of vaguely radical proposals, but Gladstone's mind was elsewhere. He hardly noticed that local Liberal party organisations were regularly turning down working-class applicants for parliamentary candidature in favour of solicitors, journalists and other members of the professional middle class. Working men wished to make their own distinctive contribution to a developing **progressivist** political agenda. The rise of a separate Labour party owes much to the Liberals' mar-ginalisation of the politically aware working man.

The Newcastle Programme

A collection of radical policies endorsed at the annual conference of the National Liberal Federation in 1891 and used as the basis for a Liberal manifesto in the general election of 1892. It reiterated Liberal support for Irish Home Rule, and also included: further land reform; direct elections for local government; recognition that employers should bear liability for accidents at work; the disestablishment of the Church in Scotland and Wales. It was a radical, but incoherent, programme, endorsed only half-heartedly by Gladstone. It dissuaded Liberal Unionists from any further attempt to re-unite with Gladstonian Liberalism.

Progressivism

Dating from the 1890s, progressivism relates to policies designed to facilitate social or political progress. Progressives supported franchise extensions, equal opportunities and votes for women. Progressive social policies were designed to improve standards of living for working people, by providing better education, sanitary improvements and less basic housing. Progressives often supported redistributive taxation to reduce the gap in wealth and opportunity between rich and poor. In late nineteenth-century Britain, there is a clear, but by no means straightforward or uniform, link between progressive policies and radical Liberalism. Progressives within the Liberal party were often called 'New Liberals'.

The Liberal ministries of 1892–95, though not without achievement, were generally unsuccessful. Gladstone's last ministry was dominated by a further titanic, unavailing effort to achieve Home Rule, while potentially valuable 'social' measures such as a compulsory eight-hour maximum working day went on the back burner. The Grand Old Man was finally prised from office in early 1894 when Earl Spencer presented estimates for expenditure of more than £30m on the navy over the next five years (see Chapter 42) and the Cabinet supported the First Lord of the Admiralty over Gladstone. While his Cabinet mused on darkening diplomatic skies, the Grand Old Man babbled of balanced budgets and pared-down defence expenditure.

Gladstone's successor was Rosebery, highly strung and unsure that he was fitted to be a Prime Minister, a job he had privately called 'a dunghill'.[16] His main rival had been the Chancellor of the Exchequer, Sir William Harcourt. Choleric and abrasive though he was, Harcourt would have been the sounder choice. He was more popular with the radicals, very experienced, more ambitious and a feisty, accomplished Commons debater. Although the Rosebery government passed important legislation on local government (see Chapter 37), his brief ministry was dominated by his rivalry with Harcourt. This was partly driven by personal animosity and envy but, more importantly, especially in the light of future events, by ideological differences. Harcourt headed a group of Liberal radicals favouring interventionist social policy.

He was particularly keen on the so-called 'Local Option', which would have given individual local authorities power to prevent the sale of alcohol in the areas under their control. This was popular with nonconformists, many of whom were teetotal. Understandably, it faced fierce opposition from brewers and landlords. It also represented a useful indicator of the division between 'interventionist' and 'libertarian' Liberalism. Rosebery was firmly in the latter camp.

The two men clashed over Harcourt's 1894 Budget, which, in addition to raising the rate of income tax to pay for increased naval expenditure, also introduced death duties to be paid on all property, real estate and personal. Against Rosebery's advice, the Cabinet supported a measure which infuriated the owners of great estates. They opposed redistributive taxation on principle but particularly resented this new imposition at a time when many landed estates were under pressure (see Chapter 27). The Budget was passed while Rosebery fretted about its impact on all substantial property owners.

He was right to do so. A riven, demoralised government, headed by a depressed Prime Minister, resigned in June 1895. Salisbury formed a new administration and called an immediate general election. With their Unionist allies, the Conservatives won more than four hundred seats and an overall majority in excess of a hundred and fifty. High levels of unemployment in industrial areas and low agricultural prices did not incline voters to reward the outgoing Liberal government anyway, but the degree of punishment they exacted was unexpected. As so often before, the electorate was disinclined to trust a government which was divided against itself. The Liberals won only seventeen of the hundred and fourteen contests in the largest metropolitan areas. The Liberal Unionists, overwhelmingly rural in their support since 1886, now won significant victories in the towns.[17] Harcourt lost his seat at Derby.

III. Revival and conflict

Further drift, division and low morale characterised the Liberals' performance in opposition. After 1895, they contrived a further high-profile issue on which to disagree: the Empire. Harcourt criticised what he considered Salisbury and Chamberlain's over-energetic and aggressive imperial policies; Rosebery, when he could stir himself so far, offered elegant and lucid assessments of the economic and cultural importance of the Empire (see Chapter 26). After Rosebery resigned the leadership, Harcourt became *de facto* leader but resigned in December 1898, complaining that the party was so divided that effective leadership was virtually impossible. In February 1899, the parliamentary Liberal party elected **Sir Henry Campbell-Bannerman** as leader. He was unable to prevent the strong patriotic and pro-Conservative tide which carried Salisbury to a further large election victory in 1900. The Conservatives and Unionists amassed between them more than four hundred seats; the Liberals barely exceeded a hundred and eighty. Although a Liberal victory was not feasible, the scale of defeat says much about Liberal difficulties, including an alarming lack of funds. In fielding only 402 candidates, it left too many seats uncontested. A revived and reinvigorated party would fight 528 in 1906.

Henry Campbell-Bannerman, 1836–1908

Born in Glasgow, the son of a successful tradesman, he was educated at Glasgow High School and at the universities of Glasgow and Cambridge. He was elected MP for Stirling Boroughs in 1868 and held the seat continuously until his death. He served a long apprenticeship on the back benches until appointed Chief Secretary for Ireland in 1884. He first entered the Cabinet, albeit briefly, as Secretary of State for War, an office to which he returned in the Liberal governments of 1892–95. As Liberal leader, his conciliatory talents proved valuable in healing party divisions. However, his criticism of the Salisbury government's conduct of the Boer War in 1901 caused a temporary rift with the Liberal Imperialists. His effective campaign against Tariff Reform from 1903 (see Chapter 37) helped to re-unite the Liberals. He maintained good relations with most Irish Nationalist leaders and in 1905 promised them Home Rule, albeit 'step by step'. He succeeded Balfour as Prime Minister in December 1905. The Liberals' comprehensive victory at the general election of 1906 confirmed Campbell-Bannerman's control over his party. As Prime Minister, he presided over a number of important social and welfare reforms while also preparing the way for South African self-government. His political position was immensely strong when he suffered the first of a number of heart attacks in 1906. He resigned on grounds of ill-health in April 1908 and died three weeks later.

Campbell-Bannerman was undervalued when he took over. However, shrewdness, moderated by stubbornness, calm refusal to be derailed by the fractious statements of more 'glamorous' Liberals – particularly the ever-troublesome Rosebery – won the party over. His effective speeches at political meetings outside Westminster consolidated his reputation. He proved the ideal leader to capitalise on the weakness and divisions of the Unionists under Balfour.

In 1906, like 1900 in reverse, it is necessary to explain not why the Liberals won, but why their majority was so large. The Liberals had experienced nothing like it for more than a quarter of a century. The so-called Lib–Lab pact (see Chapter 41) helped, especially in places, such as the industrial North-West, where the Conservatives had previously been successful. In 1906, the Tories lost all six Manchester and Salford seats.[18] Growing Conservative difficulties are discussed elsewhere (see Chapter 37), but how important was the Liberal shibboleth of Free Trade to its electoral success? First, of course, it split the Conservatives. Liberals argued that free trade had secured low prices and cheap imports, thus contributing to rising prosperity and a considerable recent growth in consumer expenditure. Free Traders also argued that Chamberlain's policy of imperial preference (see Chapter 37) was impractical. It had divided rather than united the Empire. Also, taxes on food were **regressive**, harming the poor much more than the rich. Tariff Reform posed a powerful threat to working people's living standards. Free Traders also argued that new social and welfare policies (see Chapter 41) should be supported by direct taxation, such as income taxes levied at different rates and taxes on the value of land.[19]

Regressive taxation

Taxation which is levied at a uniform rate, irrespective of income, resources or ability to pay. Examples in our own day include Value Added Tax and taxes on fuel. They are called 'regressive' because they bear harder on people with lower incomes. Most indirect taxes are regressive.

The Liberal governments of Campbell-Bannerman and **Asquith** which lasted from the end of 1905 to the spring of 1915 were among the most crowded, constructive and controversial of the nineteenth or twentieth centuries. Britain's diplomatic entanglements would lead Britain into war in 1914 (see Chapter 43). At home, the Liberals pioneered social policies which some have suggested marked the true origins of Britain's welfare state (see Chapter 41). Irish Home Rule continued to loom large (see Chapter 40), and both Prime Ministers also had to deal with the issues presented by an insistent and imaginative campaign to secure votes for women (see Chapter 39). An unprecedentedly powerful trade union movement flexed its muscles to considerable effect in the decade before the First World War (see Chapter 41).

Herbert, Asquith, 1852–1928

Born in Morley (Yorkshire), the son of a small woollen manufacturer, he was brought up as a nonconformist. After his father died in 1860, he moved to London and was educated at the City of London School and Oxford University. He trained for the law and became a barrister in 1876. He became a Liberal MP in 1886 and made his mark speedily as a powerful advocate for Home Rule. He was Home Secretary from 1892 to 1895. Though not an out-and-out Liberal Imperialist, he supported the government's policy over the Boer War. Much more interested in domestic affairs, he mounted powerful attacks on Chamberlain's arguments for tariff reform. He became Chancellor of the Exchequer in Campbell-Bannerman's government of 1905–8, where he reduced taxes and lowered expenditure on the navy. He also drafted legislation on the payment of Old Age Pensions which passed into law when he was Prime Minister. As Prime Minister (1908–16), he encouraged his ministers to formulate radical social reforms and supported Lloyd George's Budget of 1909. His elegant articulation of issues and his political skills helped to prevent party divisions over industrial policy and Irish Home Rule. He formed a coalition government in 1915 but was ousted as Prime Minister by Lloyd George in December 1916. He remained leader of the Liberal party until 1926, and was the last Prime Minister to head a Liberal administration.

Liberal social and economic policies brought the Commons into a conflict with the House of Lords which led to constitutional crisis. In mid-Victorian Britain, the Lords had an inbuilt Conservative majority of between sixty and seventy. From the mid-1880s, this increased substantially since Liberal Unionist peers generally voted with the Conservatives. From the 1890s, the Lords' veto on unpalatable legislation coming from the Liberal majority in the Commons was used more tactically. No parliamentary bill could pass into law until approved by both houses of parliament and the monarch. Victoria, much given to pro-Tory interference behind the scenes, had advisers who warned her of possibly terminal damage which would be done to the monarchy if the royal veto were ever to be used. No such restraint applied in the Lords. Frustrated Liberals were not slow to point out that, with MPs in the Commons now much more representative of public opinion, a Lords' veto seemed more anomalous or even constitutionally improper. They also noted that the Lords hardly ever rejected Conservative legislation.

David Lloyd George, 1863–1945

Born in Manchester, the son of a Welsh schoolmaster, he moved as an infant to live in North Wales on the death of his father. Brought up by his uncle, a strong Liberal supporter, he imbibed political culture early in life. He worked in a solicitor's firm, passing the Law Society's examinations in 1884. He set himself up as a solicitor in North Wales. He became a Liberal MP at a by-election for Caernarfon Boroughs (North Wales) in 1890, a seat he then held continuously until, incongruously as a staunch opponent of the aristocracy, he accepted an earldom two months before his death. He spoke fluently in the Commons in favour of land reform, temperance and the disestablishment of the Church in Wales. His egalitarian radicalism earned him enemies within the party, especially among the Liberal Imperialists. His speeches contributed to the Liberal revival in the early years of the new century and he was rewarded by Campbell-Bannerman with a Cabinet post – his first ministerial job – as President of the Board of Trade (1905–8). Here he promoted legislation protecting British commerce and learned how to negotiate with trade unions. He was one of the most radical Chancellors of the Exchequer of the twentieth century. He pioneered the 'People's Budget' through parliament, calling it 'a war budget' against 'poverty and squalidness'. He also played the leading role in the development of National Insurance legislation, which began the process of loosening the poor law's grip on the destitute. He was a controversial politician and his political style was heavily personalised. He was often accused of duplicity and of gaining unfair advantage over adversaries, but his achievements, both in peace and war, were enormous. He was an outstanding orator and he used immense personal charm to devastating political and sexual effect. His reputation was sullied by accusations of corruption over the Marconi Scandal in 1913 and the sale of peerages at the end of the First World War. His career reached its peak during the First World War when he was Minister for Munitions (1915–16), Secretary for War (1916) and then, after a brutal coup against Asquith, Prime Minister (1916–22). The bitter and unresolved split between Asquith and Lloyd George had devastating consequences for the Liberal party.

The Lords frequently thwarted the Campbell-Bannerman government, using a Unionist majority which, by 1908, was more than four to one.[20] Ever anxious to support the Established Church, peers rejected Liberal Education Bills in 1906 and 1908 which would have strengthened public control over Church schools and abolished religious tests. In 1907, Campbell-Bannerman passed Resolutions through the Commons which stated that the Lords had no right to tamper with any Commons bill on finance and that any Lords veto should be 'suspensory' rather than permanent and thus fall if the same measure were passed through the Commons in three successive parliamentary sessions. The Resolution also proposed a maximum length of five years, rather than seven, for parliament. The Lords ploughed on. The government's Licensing Bill, another measure favoured by its teetotal and nonconformist support, was vetoed in 1908. Land-reform proposals were also stymied. In all, the Lords rejected ten Liberal bills in the years 1906–9 and radically revised more than forty more.

Lloyd George's Budget of 1909, which Campbell-Bannerman's successor Asquith endorsed, was partially motivated by the need to get round Lords' opposition to almost any kind of land reform. It included four new land taxes, including a 20 per cent tax on any improvement in land values, the so-called 'unearned increment' which got under so many Liberal skins. The budget was also redistributive. It included both a higher rate of income tax and a 'supertax' on incomes of more than £5,000 a year (almost £400,000 in early twenty-first-century values). Death duties were also raised.[21] The Lords rejected the Budget in November, precipitating a constitutional crisis. This high-risk strategy was the product of genuine outrage both at what was seen as punitive taxation of the landed interest and at the principle of redistributive taxation, which many peers considered a form of socialism.

The general election of 1910, which the government called having lost a finance bill, delivered an equivocal verdict on four years of frenetic Liberal activity. The party lost more than a hundred seats and thus its overall majority. The Conservative recovery was strongest in London and the rural south of England. The Liberals remained dependent on Labour and Irish votes until the outbreak of the First World War. They re-presented the Budget in April 1910, which the Lords passed, largely on the grounds that the Liberals now had a fresh mandate from the electorate, if an exiguous one. Asquith now introduced a Parliament Bill containing changes to the powers of the Lords very similar to those in the Campbell-Bannerman Resolutions three years earlier. In May, Edward VII died and was succeeded by his son George V. Rather than expose an inexperienced monarch to the possibility of direct intervention on an important constitutional issue, both major parties agreed to set up a Constitutional Conference in the hope of securing a compromise, possibly via a coalition government. The Conference ground on over the summer. It gave Lloyd George opportunity for that baroque plotting and dissimulation in which he excelled, though on this occasion fruitlessly. When the Conference collapsed in the autumn, Asquith called a further general election, having privately secured the King's reluctant agreement to create enough Liberal peers for a Lords majority if the party won the election and the Lords refused to pass the Parliament Bill.

The second 1910 election produced an outcome almost identical to the first. Asquith remained Prime Minister and his Parliament Bill, noisily debated, was passed by the Commons in May 1911. The Lords immediately tabled a number of amendments which would have wrecked the Bill. The government rejected them and in mid-August, after heated internal disagreements and in the knowledge that sufficient Liberal peers would be created anyway, most Conservative peers abstained on the crucial vote. The government only got its majority without new peers because thirty Conservatives, immediately labelled 'the Judas Group', voted with the government rather than see the Upper House 'diluted' by the unworthy and ill-bred. The Parliament Act, ending the crisis, finally became law in the autumn. It almost exactly followed the Campbell-Bannerman Resolutions. A hard-pressed minority Liberal government was now free to turn its attention, with a profound lack of enthusiasm in many cases, to the workaday issues being pressed by the Irish, the suffragettes and an increasingly unionised working class.

39

'Votes for Women'

I. The development of the suffrage campaign

Many women in the nineteenth century were politicised.[1] The attention of historians has always concentrated on their enfranchisement campaign but this was not the focal point of most women's concerns, at least before the 1870s. For women with property, there were more urgent battles to fight – over rights within marriage, access to appropriate educational opportunities, qualification for, and entry to, the professions (see Chapter 25). Although many working-class women were active in support of campaigns for political rights and in the nurturing of a distinctive and supportive community culture (see Chapter 21), they also had battles to fight over job opportunities, wages and working conditions. While relatively few men had the vote anyway, there was no particular reason to concentrate on franchise issues.

That situation changed when a mass electorate began to emerge after 1867. John Stuart Mill did, of course, make his famous case for a female suffrage during debates on the Conservative Reform Bill in 1867. While parliament was debating precisely where franchise thresholds for men should be set, honourable members were excluding all women almost without a second thought. Was there, Mill rhetorically asked, 'any adequate justification for continuing to exclude an entire half of the community, not only from admission, but from the capability of ever being admitted within the pale of the Constitution, though they may fulfil all the conditions legally and constitutionally sufficient in every case but theirs . . . There is no other example of an exclusion which is absolute.'[2] Mill's intervention had modest success. Seventy-three MPs voted for the principle of a female suffrage, substantially more than was ever achieved in debates on the Chartist petitions.[3]

The pioneer organisation for Women's Suffrage appears to have been the Manchester Women's Suffrage Committee, founded in January 1867. It was quickly joined by similar organisations in London, Birmingham and Bristol. The London society, in which **Millicent Fawcett** was prominent, provided a degree of national co-ordination.[4] However, members of the various local organisations saw no particular need to concentrate their efforts on developing a mass membership. Many readily diverted their activities, as opportunity arose, into pressure for other changes of benefit to women, such as new educational opportunities or the repeal of the grotesquely discriminatory **Contagious Diseases Act**. It is unwise to infer from this, however, that in 'fighting for enfranchisement, suffragists sought no less than the total transformation of the lives of women'.[5] This was undoubtedly true for some, particularly well-heeled middle-class Liberals who bought into one of the various radical packages on offer. It was not true for most, as the asymmetry between the proportion of feminists supporting suffrage reform (89 per cent on one calculation) and the campaign led by **Josephine Butler** against the Contagious Diseases Act (13 per cent) suggests.[6] Nor were late nineteenth-century feminists as implacably hostile to men as might be supposed. They co-operated with them on a number of political campaigns. Most were also happily married and considered marriage a healthy state if entered into without coercion.

Millicent Fawcett, 1847–1929

Born Millicent Garrett at Aldeburgh (Suffolk), the daughter of a merchant and ship-owner, her elder sister was the pioneer physician Elizabeth Garrett Anderson. Like her husband, Henry Fawcett, whom she married in 1867, she was strongly influenced by John Stuart Mill. She embraced a range of radical causes and helped to found Newnham Hall (later College) in 1875 and supported a range of educational developments. After her husband's death in 1884, she devoted more time to writing on contemporary political topics. She was also active in attempting to improve the welfare of working-class women. She supported compulsory education for children but opposed moves to make it free, believing that parents should pay fees since this would encourage them to place higher value on education. She was a prominent Liberal Unionist and her refusal to work with organisations supporting Home Rule split the National Society for Women's Suffrage. She became President of the National Union of Women's Suffrage Societies (NUWSS) in 1897. When mass support for the suffrage campaign was secured during the Edwardian period, she continued to advocate constitutional methods and opposed the militant tactics of the Pankhursts. After the failure of the Conciliation Bill in 1910, she advocated full adult suffrage and increasingly favoured Labour as the only party likely to press for it. During the First World War, she encouraged NUWSS to support the war effort to the utmost.

Contagious Diseases Act

This highly controversial measure, passed in 1864, gave police the power to arrest prostitutes working in ports and army towns and to have them tested for venereal disease. If infected, they were confined in secure hospitals until cured. Women's campaigners were incensed about the double standard involved in this attempt to curb venereal disease. Prostitutes' clients were not subjected to similar treatment. Josephine Butler led the 'Ladies Association against the Contagious Diseases Act' which secured repeal in 1886.

Josephine Butler, 1828–1906

Born in Northumberland, the daughter of John Grey, a prosperous land agent who was the cousin of the third Earl Grey, she was educated at home. She married George Butler, an Anglican clergyman, in 1852. She worked in Liverpool to improve the lives of the poor and campaigned to improve the rights of women. While she was a suffragist, her main interests lay elsewhere. She wrote pamphlets on social questions and campaigned to increase women's opportunities for higher education and professional advancement. She publicised evidence of the traffic of women for sexual purposes and of child prostitution. She was an influential member of a network of women with a feminist perspective on a range of social questions. Her language could be extreme. In 1871, in a speech to the Ladies' National Association, she said that she regarded 'all men (however pure their own conduct) as depravers of society, who hold the loathsome and deadly doctrine that God has made man for unchastity and woman for his degraded slave'.

Women argued for the vote on a number of grounds. It was possible to deploy the argument grounded in equality of rights – adult men and women were all citizens and deserved to be treated equally. In the 1870s and 1880s, however, suffragists such as Millicent Fawcett began to argue that women should be enfranchised because they were different from men. This line of attack was intended to stymie a central anti-suffragist argument, which was that women were emotional creatures whose proper, and honoured, place was in the home. As Fawcett argued, 'womanliness', love of children, 'self-control' and 'obedience to conscience and duty' were distinctive characteristics and 'all these things are terribly wanted in politics'.[7]

Meanwhile, male supporters of female suffrage ensured that bills on the subject were presented to parliament almost every year. The impact on parliament was greater than is often realised. The leading campaigners were Hugh Mason (1817–86), MP for Ashton-under-Lyne from 1880 to 1885, and William Woodall (1832–1901), MP for Stoke-on-Trent and Hanley from 1880 to 1900. The latter was chairman of the Central Committee for Women's Suffrage. When Gladstone presented his parliamentary reform bill in 1884, Woodall proposed an amendment on behalf of more than a hundred MPs requiring that 'words having reference to the right of voting at parliamentary elections, importing the masculine gender, include women'.[8] Gladstone, who never evinced much interest in, or enthusiasm for, female suffrage believed that its insertion would risk the entire reform bill.[9] In any case, having been outmanoeuvred on a franchise bill in 1866 (see Chapter 31), he was unwilling to risk a second franchise rebuff.

Salisbury was no enthusiast either but he could see the inconsistencies implicit in merely extending the existing male franchise: 'When I am told that my ploughmen are capable citizens, it seems to me ridiculous to say that educated women are not just as capable.' In an aside which would have infuriated the suffrage campaigners, he envisaged women as a force for solid conservative values in the turbulent times which he believed lay ahead. 'A good deal of the political battle of the future will be a conflict between religion and unbelief & the women will in that controversy be on the right side.'[10]

One hundred and thirty-five members voted for Woodall's amendment; a hundred or so were constrained by Gladstone's strong Liberal **party whip**. It seems likely that a majority in the Commons wished to enfranchise women as early as the 1880s, albeit only the economically independent: freeholders and householders qualifying in their own right rather than through marriage. Even had Woodall's amendment been carried in the Commons, however, a woman's franchise would have been over-whelmingly rejected in the Lords.

Party whip

A device used by the leadership of a political party to keep discipline and to ensure that official policy is followed. The Chief Whip (the term comes from fox hunting where the 'whipper in' keeps the dog pack together when hunting the fox) issues a list of motions for debate and indicates how party members are expected to vote. Refusal may result in demotion or other damage to a member's career prospects. The whipping system became more important in the second half of the nineteenth century as party discipline tightened.

The franchise campaign did not experience a strong or consistent upward trajec-tory in the last thirty years of the nineteenth century. The number of signatures on suffrage petitions fell off, as did funding for many of the pro-suffrage societies.[11] A number of these, such as the Manchester National Society for Women's Suffrage, sustained an overwhelmingly local focus. They co-operated only in a limited fashion and often for different overall objectives. Some wanted full adult suffrage, others agi-tated for a female franchise on the same basis as men. Others again linked suffrage with other demands relating to the status or economic position of women. Some women's organisations saw the vote as ancillary to the main purpose. The Women's Liberal Federation, established in 1887, was active in educational initiatives, supported Irish Home Rule and during the Second Boer War (see Chapter 36) took a strongly Liberal-Imperialist stance.[12] From 1870 to 1890, the *Women's Suffrage Journal*, edited by the Manchester activist Lydia Becker (1827–90), provided both a central refer-ence point about local suffrage activities and more general support for the women's cause.[13] However, it ceased publication on her death.

The effective contributions made by mainly propertied women on School Boards or as Poor Law Guardians did influence members of parliament. Support for female suffrage was no longer confined to the usual Liberal-Radical suspects. Two Conservatives, the London MP Sir Albert Rollit and Ferdinand Faithfull Begg, representing Glasgow, introduced franchise bills in the Commons in 1892 and 1897. The first failed narrowly, but Begg's motion was passed by seventy-one votes; all parties except the Liberal Unionists gave it majority support.[14] Although many MPs made only general statements of support rather than demanding immediate priority for women's suffrage, this vote represented a breakthrough. The Commons would consistently express support for the principle during the Edwardian age. The establishment of central organisation through the National Union of Women's Suffrage Societies (NUWSS), also in 1897, was an indication of revived morale. Active campaigning for the vote began in earnest.[15]

II. Direct action

Millicent Fawcett thought women would get the vote when broader political and social changes were in place: 'women's suffrage will not come . . . as an isolated phenomenon, it will come as a necessary corollary of other changes which have been gradually and steadily modifying . . . the social history of our country.'[16]

Her assessment proved correct. By the early twentieth century, however, many suffragists had had quite enough of 'gradually and steadily'. **Emmeline Pankhurst** and her daughter **Christabel** founded the Women's Social and Political Union (WSPU) in Manchester in 1903 as a breakaway group from the North of England Society, an affiliated group of the NUWSS. It was closely linked to the Independent Labour Party (see Chapter 41) and worked with a number of local trade unions and trade councils. In its early years, the WSPU actively sought – as many suffrage groups did not – the support of working-class women, many of whom were already politicised as members of textile trade unions. Christabel Pankhurst and Annie Kenney (1879–1953), a textile worker from Oldham, launched the militant phase of the suffrage movement. At an election meeting in Manchester Free Trade Hall in October 1905, they demanded that the future Foreign Secretary, Sir Edward Grey, and the Liberal candidate for Oldham, the young Winston Churchill, state the party's position on female suffrage. When they got no answer, they unfurled a suffrage banner and Pankhurst spat at a police officer. Both women were arrested, charged with obstruction and, refusing to defend themselves or pay a fine, were briefly imprisoned.

Emmeline Pankhurst, 1858–1928

Born in Hulme, near Manchester, the daughter of Robert Goulden, a calico manufacturer, she was educated at a local girls' school and later in Paris. She married the radical lawyer Dr Richard Pankhurst in 1879. In 1880, she became a member of the executive of the Manchester National Society for Women's Suffrage. She resigned from the Women's Liberal Association to join the new Independent Labour Party in 1893. In 1903, she founded the Women's Social and Political Union (WSPU) in Manchester. It campaigned for women to gain the vote on the same qualifications as men. The Union's early activities were peaceful but direct action began at the end of 1905. The WSPU, not without opposition from within the Pankhurst family as well as more widely, resigned from the Independent Labour Party and declared itself independent of party support. The pace of militancy picked up from 1908, involving her in periods of imprisonment. When war broke out in 1914, she called a temporary halt to militant protest and urged the Union to support the war effort. After the war, she travelled widely, giving lectures on social hygiene. Her health began to fail in 1924 and she died of septicaemia four years later.

Christabel Pankhurst, 1880–1958

Born in Manchester, the daughter of Richard and Emmeline Pankhurst, she was educated in High Schools in Southport and Manchester, though her main education was political and provided at home. She obtained a law degree from Manchester University. An able administrator and organiser, she increasingly took over the direction of the WSPU, though her autocratic style was resented by many members and led to splits in the movement. She did, however, identify the forms of direct action likely to attract maximum publicity for the suffrage cause. She was the editor of the WSPU newspaper *The Suffragette*, published from October 1912. After the war, and with female suffrage achieved, she travelled to the Americas where she preached evangelical Christianity as a 'Second Adventist'. She also published a number of books on religion and the suffrage movement.

Militant action accelerated after the Pankhursts moved to London in 1906. The WSPU's aim was to co-ordinate attention-grabbing activity in the capital city not only to influence MPs but also to alert journalists working on the increasingly influential popular newspapers. Some such activities – mass meetings, angry speeches asserting the strength of support and threats of violence if reform was blocked – had been the staple diet of radical groups for almost a century (see Chapters 20, 21 and 31). Thus, a march on, and mass meeting in, Hyde Park in February 1907 involved about forty suffrage societies. A quarter of a million women converged on Hyde Park in June 1908. Perhaps the largest mass meeting ever held in London assembled to test the assertion of the new Prime Minister, Herbert Asquith, that he would abandon his opposition to a female suffrage if women could demonstrate the extent of support for the vote. The WSPU also organised a mass march through 'beautiful, haughty, dignified, stern Edinburgh' in the autumn of 1909.

Other suffragette methods were either new or were given distinctive twists. In January 1908, two WSPU members chained themselves to the railings of No. 10 Downing Street; in June others bombarded its windows with stones. The intention was to invite arrest – and thereby more publicity in the popular press. By the middle of 1909, some imprisoned suffrage campaigners were on hunger strike. The Home Secretary, Herbert Gladstone, required them to be force-fed by male doctors. Women turned this into a propaganda triumph, claiming that men were using force to violate the female body. An outcry against 'brutal outrages upon defenceless women' ensued.[17]

The WSPU's militant tactics, orchestrated by Christabel Pankhurst, were highly controversial. Christabel's younger sisters Sylvia and Adela were socialist sympathisers and resented the emphasis on middle-class support. They moved to work in London's East End, where, with the support of the Labour MP George Lansbury, they founded the separate East London Federation of Suffragettes in 1913. Christabel's self-confident assurance was often interpreted as arrogance, not least since she rarely consulted others on tactics and was notoriously sensitive to criticism. Teresa Billington-Greig (1876–1964), admittedly no consensualist herself, was particularly scathing. She condemned 'the small pettiness . . . the playing for effects and not for results – in short, the exploitation of revolutionary forces and enthusiastic women for the purposes of advertisement'.[18] She was one of about seventy members of the WSPU who left the organisation in 1907 to found the Women's Freedom League, a militant organisation which frequently transgressed the law but which condemned both personal violence and attacks on property. Billington-Greig, however, resigned in 1910. As a journalist and speaker, she now advocated only passive resistance.[19]

The WSPU may have grabbed the lion's share of attention, but the National Union of Women's Suffrage Societies was always much larger. Its numerical dominance increased in the years immediately before the War. It had more branches than the WSPU even in London and more than seven times as many elsewhere in England. Overall, NUWSS paid-up membership had reached about 50,000 by 1914, more than ten times greater than that of the WSPU.[20] The NUWSS was not non-militant in principle. Many of its members were highly critical of the Pankhursts but their leaders recognised the contribution which militant actions had made. Millicent Fawcett may have had no patience with 'idiots who go out smashing windows and bashing ministers' but she acknowledged in 1909 that the courage shown by women prepared to face imprisonment for their beliefs had 'touched the imagination of the country in a manner which quieter methods did not succeed in doing'.[21] The success of WSPU marches also encouraged the NUWSS to give more attention to mass demonstrations.

III. Parliamentary focus, 1910–1914

The WSPU halted its campaigns after the first general election of 1910 when a majority of MPs confirmed that they supported votes for women. An all-party 'Conciliation Committee' recommended that women should be able to vote in parliamentary elections on the same basis as for municipal elections (see Chapter 37). This received a Commons majority of more than a hundred, but Asquith called a general election in November and the bill could not proceed. The WSPU sent three hundred women to march on parliament in protest but, in what became known as

'Black Friday', they were repulsed by a large police contingent using what a parliamentary committee later condemned as excessive violence.

A second Conciliation Bill early in 1911 gained a majority of almost two hundred. However, many Liberals were concerned that a 'municipal franchise' would add large numbers of property-owning Conservative women to the voting register. Asquith's ingenious compromise solution was to propose a revision of the electoral roll, which would give votes to most of the men still without it, present a government bill on that basis, and leaving supporters of votes for women to move amendments which he would not block. While the NUWSS accepted the plan, the WSPU rejected it. The militant campaign was not only revived but extended. Private property of anti-suffragists was targeted for the first time. In March 1912, alienated by what they considered unwarranted suffragette violence, many MPs abandoned support for a female franchise. The third Conciliation Bill was defeated by a majority of fourteen. Asquith's Liberal Franchise and Registration Bill finally came before the Commons in January 1913. However, the Speaker ruled that encouraging amendments for women's suffrage fundamentally changed the purpose and the substance of the bill. He refused to accept them, leaving women no further forward.

Encouraged by rebuffs such as this, which most WSPU members believed had resulted from a backstairs deal between Speaker and Prime Minister, militancy continued until 1914. Violence accompanied Lloyd George's opening of a new village institute in his Welsh home of Llanystumdwy in September 1912. Pictures of women being attacked appeared in the next day's newspapers. The WSPU activist Emily Davidson planted a bomb in Lloyd George's new home in 1913, causing substantial damage. Shortly afterwards, she threw herself under King George V's horse at the Derby, becoming the highest-profile martyr of the campaign. A few weeks before the War brought a truce, Mary Richardson took a meat cleaver to Velázquez's portrait, the *Rokeby Venus*, which was hanging in the National Gallery and which many women considered salacious and titillating.

It is difficult to see what, beyond publicity, the prolongation of the WSPU campaign of violence achieved. One historian has called it 'counter-productive' and overall suffragette tactics 'simply inept'.[22] Its impact on politicians after 1911 seems to have been wholly adverse. They were more irritated than intimidated. Votes for women could only be agreed by a parliament of men, and shock tactics, even carefully orchestrated suicides, were a wasting asset. Even before 1910, unity of pro-suffrage purpose had shown itself to be a fissile and combustible commodity. From 1911, it weakened the bargaining power of the NUWSS, the dominant organisation with which the politicians expected to do business.

Outside parliament, militancy polarised views and, again, not to the advantage of the suffragettes. Some trotted out the old arguments. The WSPU's antics merely confirmed what they had known all along: women were far too emotional to be trusted with the vote. Policemen, at the sharp end of the more imaginative forms of direct action, were among the most censorious. The memoirs of an officer working in

Special Branch, published just before the Second World War, neatly capture the sense of irritation and outrage that women should 'betray' their gender:

> The 'Votes for Women' Movement was at its hysterical worst about this time [1911–12]. The 'Wild Women' were behaving like demented idiots in order to prove to the nation that they were fit and proper persons to have a hand in government affairs. The most insane deeds of sabotage were being carried out by the fanatics of the movement, and women who a short while before had been courteous and charming specimens of English femininity were prancing and howling in the streets, chaining themselves to railings outside Number 10 Downing Street, slashing the nation's art treasures to pieces and setting fire to the residences of politicians, statesmen, and national leaders.[23]

IV. The party-political dimension

The women's movement posed tactical problems for all four political parties. The Conservatives had the largest number of backwoodsmen who just 'knew' that giving women the vote was not right. It offended those mutually respected 'separate spheres' and disrupted the even tenor of domestic arrangements. However, their leaders, particularly Balfour, were not opposed in principle. They calculated, like Lloyd George, that women property owners were more naturally Conservative than Liberal. The Liberals, as the governing party, had the responsibility to frame legislation but they had other priorities. After 1911, Ireland and the darkening diplomatic situation were given much more parliamentary time. Asquith was anyway among the least enthusiastic feminists in the Cabinet. Under Lloyd George or Herbert Gladstone, more decisive initiatives might have been expected. By 1914, the governing party was probably paying a price for its dilatoriness. The Women's Liberal Federation, a considerable organisational strength during general elections, was haemorrhaging members and closing branches. Meanwhile, politically active women were transferring their allegiance to Labour.

The parliamentary Labour party mostly favoured franchise reform. Even after increasing its parliamentary complement in the 1910 elections, however, it was still in a small minority and feared the consequences of antagonising the Liberals. Like the Conservatives, it had some strongly anti-feminist grass-roots members. Coal miners, the most extensively unionised group of workers, operated within a strongly accentuated male culture. In many constituency parties, the emphasis was on achieving a full adult male franchise. The issue for Irish nationalists was simple. Everything beyond Home Rule was a side-show. They well understood the tactical advantages of having a Liberal government without an overall majority. Nationalists had greater leverage. On the other hand, a minority government is always vulnerable to the vicissitudes of political fortune and the Conservative alternative was vastly less palatable (see Chapter 41). Irish Nationalists wanted the Liberal government to survive. A female franchise was not only an unwanted distraction; it was also potentially dangerous.

It is difficult to escape the conclusion that, after years of frustration, it was the War which unlocked the door. The abandonment of militancy in 1914 and the powerful contribution made by women during the First World War made it much easier for previously sceptical or antagonistic male politicians to support the women's case. The North-Eastern businessman and Liberal MP Cecil Cochrane expressed a typical view in 1917. He praised the 'conspicuous services that women have rendered to the nation during the War' and expressed relief at the ending of 'those militant methods which . . . did far more damage to their cause than their strongest opponents ever realised'. For these reasons, 'the case for the extension of the franchise to women has been enormously strengthened during the last three years'.[24] When it finally arrived in 1918, even confirmed anti-suffragists could not deny that female suffrage had been hard-earned by patriotic endeavour.

Ireland and British politics, *c*1845–1914

I. The political impact of the Famine

Conflict over Ireland reconfigured the political landscape of the United Kingdom during the 1880s and brought the UK close to civil conflict at the outbreak of the First World War. From the Famine of the mid-1840s onwards, affairs in Ireland had been casting a very long, and very dark, shadow (see Chapters 25 and 38). The natural reaction of both survivors in, and emigrants from, Ireland was to blame Britain for the conditions which brought the Famine about and for its partial and inefficient response. A fierce debate has raged about alleged British 'betrayal'.[1] Though Russell's Liberal government was swamped by the scale of the problem, it did attempt to mitigate hardship and also suspended the Navigation Laws. Corn and other grain – much of it from India – was imported and taken to the west of Ireland. By 1847, five times as much grain was being imported to Ireland for domestic consumption as was being exported.[2] The government also established soup kitchens and expanded poor law provision.

In an attempt to re-stabilise landed society, the government passed the Encumbered Estates Act in 1849. This made land sales, including those of bankrupt estates, easier while encouraging investment in land. It helped to stabilise the land market and also had the effect of increasing the proportion of Catholic landowners.[3] The structure of landed society changed dramatically, mainly because the Famine had hit small peasant proprietors so hard. The proportion of farms of one to five acres declined from about 45 per cent of total Irish land in 1831 to 15 per cent in 1851. The decline continued during the second half of the nineteenth century, while the proportion of those of between fifteen and thirty acres increased from about 50 to 57 per cent. The proportion of large Irish estates increased substantially during the Famine but much more modestly thereafter. By 1891 about 17 per cent of estates were in excess of fifty acres. Tenant farming remained dominant; three-quarters of all Ireland's land was under tenancy.[4] Tenancy arrangements were at the heart of growing pressure for Home Rule from the 1870s onwards. Tenants lacked security of tenure and often received inadequate landowner compensation for the improvements they made. Relations between landlords and tenants in the two decades after the Famine, however, were relatively harmonious. A Tenant Right League, representing the interests of Protestants as well as Catholics across the whole of Ireland, was established in 1850 but achieved little.

The Franchise Act of 1850 was much more significant. The Famine had reduced the Irish electorate by more than a half. The new Act changed the system of registration and introduced a qualification in both borough and county seats based on occupation – a rateable value of £12 a year in the counties and £8 a year in the boroughs. This increased the total Irish electorate to over 160,000, more than 80 per cent of whom voted in the counties. The numerical beneficiaries were the tenant farmers who would form the bedrock of support for Home Rule in the 1870s and 1880s.[5] In the shorter term, however, rising prices for pastoral goods strengthened the political influence of the landlords. In social origin, Irish MPs in 1850s and 1860s were barely distinguishable from their British counterparts. The majority were substantial landowners. Sixty-seven of the eighty-seven elected in 1859 owned estates in excess of 2,000 acres. Political allegiance, too, was conformist. Successful candidates, although not exactly disciplined supporters of one party or the other, happily accepted Tory or Liberal labels when seeking election.[6] Only in one sense were the Irish MPs distinctive. Thirty-two Roman Catholics were elected to the 1859 parliament; thirty-one of them represented Irish constituencies. In the 1850s and 1860s, about a third of the Irish MPs were Catholic.

The only significant revolutionary organisation active in the 1850s and 1860s was the secret Irish Republic Brotherhood (or Fenians). It grew out of an earlier Young Ireland movement, organised by John O'Mahony (1816–77) and James Stephens (1825–1901). Its aim was to overthrow British rule in Ireland by violent revolution. Under-funded and lacking coherent leadership, it achieved little, although its best known exploit – the rescue of nationalists from a prison van in Manchester in 1867 – resulted in the arrest and execution of three Fenians, thus providing the cause with useful martyrs.

II. Gladstone and Land reform, 1868–1874

For a quarter of a century, relations between Ireland and Britain revolved around the conscience, the indefatigable energy and the sheer stubbornness of William Gladstone. Famously, on becoming Prime Minister in 1868, he declared that his mission was to 'pacify Ireland'. Ireland was not at that time particularly 'un-pacified', so why was Gladstone concerned? He was an extraordinary man and, in many respects, extra-ordinarily odd. He did, however, have a coherent vision for Ireland. It was Peelite. Like Peel (see Chapter 22), he wished to give the Catholic middle classes good reason to value the Union. Peel's voice can almost be heard through Gladstone's when he introduced his bill to disestablish the Church of Ireland, that 'token and symbol of [Protestant] ascendancy'.[7] Gladstone also believed that politicians should see government both as a trust and as an opportunity to identify and nurture 'great moral causes'. The great battles over free trade, *laissez-faire* and low levels of taxation having been won (see Chapter 26), Gladstone identified Ireland as the 'great moral cause' to sustain the latter part of his career.

Peel's struggle over the repeal of the Corn Laws and its grave consequences for the Conservative party (see Chapter 22) had taught Gladstone that great causes are not to be sacrificed on the rackety wheel of party politics. If Ireland helped to sustain unity in a divided Liberal party in the 1870s, so much the better, but that was not the main point. Gladstone's self-appointed mission was to settle great questions and he considered the Irish question the greatest of all. On this reading of Gladstone's complex psychological make-up, what happened to his party in 1886 exactly mirrored what had happened to Peel's forty years earlier – and for much the same reasons.

It was entirely typical of Gladstone that he trusted no one but himself to draft the details of an extremely complex Disestablishment Bill. Its scope extended beyond Disestablishment to the much trickier area of disendowment. All state grants to religious bodies were to be terminated and Church of Ireland funds, after existing obligations had been met, used for various poor relief schemes. The essence of his bill survived tussles in the House of Lords and, after some compromises, the Disestablishment Act was passed in 1869.

The Land Act of 1870 enjoyed less success because it mattered more. As one historian elegantly put it, with only limited exaggeration, 'Disestablishment . . . had all the advantages of symbolic importance and practical insignificance.'[8] By total contrast, land reform was critical for the majority of Irish tenant farmers. Tenants wanted to become landowners. It was an element in the '**3 Fs**' package. Tenants resented that Protestant 'incomers' still owned most Irish land. It was irrelevant that many of the Protestants had 'come in' in the late sixteenth or early seventeenth centuries, or that, from the mid-nineteenth century, ever more land was coming into Catholic ownership. Landownership remained at the root of the 'Irish problem' that Gladstone had set himself to solve.

'3 Fs'

These were the three objectives of Irish tenant farmers. They demanded: free sale of land (by which a predominantly Catholic proprietorship could emerge); fair rents (a constant complaint was that landowners often increased rents substantially and without warning); fixity of tenure (smaller tenants, in particular, were likely to be evicted by their landlords, usually without compensation).

Gladstone's Act was designed to give Irish tenants greater protection against both eviction and sudden rent rises. The so-called **Ulster Custom** was given formal legal recognition. Tenants were to be compensated for any improvements made if they were subsequently evicted. Those evicted for any other reason than non-payment of rent were to receive compensation. Limited though it was, the Act alienated many British, as well as Irish, landowners, who thought it a blatant attack on property. In any case, it did not work. Many landowners responded by raising rents to a sufficient level to facilitate eviction and by requiring tenants to take up restrictive leases putting them outside the protection of the new law.[9] Also, the tenants most able, and likely, to make land improvements were the tenants landowners least wished to evict.

Ulster Custom

Ulster tenants received greater security of tenure than elsewhere in Ireland if they kept up with their rental payments. They were also entitled to sell the occupancy of their land-holding to the highest bidder. Since summary eviction was a basic grievance of tenants elsewhere, pressure grew from Tenant Protection Societies for the implementation of 'Ulster Custom' throughout Ireland. The Custom, which had limited legal basis, also applied in some places outside Ulster.

Gladstone's Irish Universities Bill of 1873 added fuel to Irish fires. Its aim was to secure mixed education for Protestants and Catholics in a new federal university. It divided his own party and was roundly condemned by the Conservatives. Catholic bishops wanted more influence over higher education; radical Liberals, favouring secular education, wanted them to have none. The main consequence was a closer alignment between the Roman Catholic Church and nationalism. Its defeat marked the beginning of the end for Gladstone's first government.

III. Land reform and the growth of nationalism, 1873–1886

By the 1870s, Ireland had a nationwide movement calling for major constitutional change. **Isaac Butt**'s Home Government Association was launched in Dublin in September 1870 and called for **federal self-government**. Butt asserted that federalism would give the country 'independence without breaking up the Empire, interfering with the monarchy or endangering the rights or liberties of any class of Irishman'.[10] The Catholic Archbishop of Dublin, Cardinal Paul Cullen, was wary, since its leaders were 'Professors . . . who have never heretofore manifested any good feeling towards the people of Ireland, and Orangemen who are still worse'.[11]

Isaac Butt, 1813–1879

Born the son of a Church of Ireland rector in County Donegal, he was educated in Cork and at the University of Dublin. He trained as a lawyer and was appointed to a professorship in Political Economy in Dublin in 1836. As an Alderman of the Dublin corporation, he opposed O'Connell's proposals to repeal the Union in 1843. He became a UK MP in 1852. He supported Fenian activists in the late 1860s and became leader of the Irish Tenant League in 1869. In the Home Government Association formed in 1870, he argued for a federal Ireland. Somewhat reluctantly, he was persuaded to make the Association into a popular movement, known as the Home Rule Association from 1873. Though a powerful speaker, Butt was not effective on popular platforms and his strategy of 'parliamentarianism' – working through the UK parliament for economic and social reforms while planning for eventual Home Rule – was considered too moderate by both Fenians and other nationalists. He was increasingly outmanoeuvred by Parnell, who advocated disrupting parliamentary business and a more activist campaign. Butt's influence had declined substantially by the time of his death.

Federal government

This form of government is headed by a sovereign nation state with individual states or regions enjoying self-government, usually over some, or all, domestic matters. The United States of America and Australia are examples of contemporary federal states.

Butt remained nominal leader of the Home Rule League from 1873 but his leadership lacked sparkle and he failed to exploit the presence of an increasing number of nationalist sympathisers at Westminster. The Ballot Act of 1872 reduced the political influence of landowners over Irish tenants at election time. On the increased, if still restricted, ratepayer franchise created in Ireland from 1868, sixty Home Rulers were elected in 1874 and sixty-three in 1880.

Ireland's profile at Westminster was enhanced because of an agricultural depression which began in 1874 and because the charismatic **Charles Stewart Parnell** was becoming increasingly influential.[12] Falling agricultural prices reduced tenants' incomes and thus their ability to pay their rents. That precipitated first widespread evictions and then a full-blown 'land war' between tenants and landowners which lasted from 1879 to 1882. Tenants refused to pay rent or to take over estates vacated by forcible evictions. The Land War's moving force was Michael Davitt (1846–1906), an active Fenian, a supporter of land nationalisation and a socialist. He became Secretary of the Irish National Land League, founded in 1879. Parnell, who feared the impact of violence on the credibility of the campaign, was elected the League's President. In the years 1879–82, he successfully co-ordinated the nationalist aspirations of Fenians with the campaigns by impoverished tenants, while also acting as leader of the Irish MPs in Westminster. Given the divergent interests this involved, it was a political *tour de force*.

Charles Stewart Parnell, 1846–1891

Born in County Wicklow into a family of prosperous Anglo-Irish landowners settled in Ireland since the seventeenth century, he left Ireland as a child when his parents separated. He was educated at schools in Somerset and at Cambridge University. He was the first member of his family to support Home Rule and was rapidly adopted by the Home Rule League, becoming an MP in 1875. He obstructed parliamentary business to draw attention to the Home Rule case. He became President of the Irish National Land League, in support of tenants' rights, in 1879 and led the Home Rule party from 1880. As leader, he had to find a balance between supporting the violence to achieve Home Rule which his radical followers demanded and using his influence to gain concessions from British political leaders. He was never converted to the need for violence and, Home Rule apart, had conservative views on most political questions. He developed close relations with several progressive Liberal MPs. After the Home Rule Bill of 1886 failed, he was attacked by many in his party for being too close to an alliance to the Liberals. Some felt that he spent insufficient time in Ireland. His career was ruined in 1889–90 when he was exposed as the lover of Kittie O'Shea when her husband sued for divorce. This led to bitter criticism from Catholic nationalists.

Gladstone's objective after the Liberals returned to office in 1880 was to break the Land League. He knew that, behind the specific short-term objective of establishing effective tenants' rights, its leaders' real objective was to achieve peasant proprietorship and thus to destroy the established, and predominantly Protestant, landowning class in Ireland. Gladstone had a strong bias towards landlords. As Professor Matthew has said, 'he saw the occupation of property as a God-given privilege . . . The landowner . . . was the executor of "a kind of sacred trust".'[13] Even if he considered Irish landowners a broken reed, Gladstone's Land Act of 1881 left them, technically at least, as owners of their land. The Act seemed to grant all of the '3 Fs'. It provided a Land Commission to determine fair rents, which were generally reduced by about 20 per cent. It also confirmed that tenants had security of tenure. Freedom of sale could be inferred but the Act gave tenants no incentive to buy their land. Only some seven hundred of Ireland's tenants made use of the Act's 'freedom of sale' provisions.[14] As Gladstone intended, peasant proprietorship remained some way off. The Act was welcomed much more by the wealthier tenants, especially in Ulster, than it was by the smaller men. Landless labourers were, of course, outside its remit. Spokesmen for the Land League bickered over the appropriate reaction, again as Gladstone had wanted. A proposed rent strike in the autumn of 1881 fell hopelessly flat.

This second Land Act did little to encourage economic growth. Its concern with legalities also missed the point that the events of the past decade had engendered a greater sense of Irish cultural identity, fostered, for better or worse, by the Catholic clergy. It did, however, break up the Land League. It was replaced by a new 'National League'. This was dominated by Irish MPs and manipulated by Parnell to his own political advantage.[15]

As always when political disturbances affected Ireland, British governments were prepared to use their considerable powers of coercion. Gladstone's Cabinet agreed in October 1881 to arrest a number of Land League officials; Habeas Corpus was suspended and almost a thousand League supporters were detained without trial. Parnell found himself in Dublin's Kilmainham gaol for six months, glad both of a breathing space and also of the increased support which the display of Britain's iron fist produced in Ireland. He emerged to resume his political role at Westminster. This he much preferred to 'platform speeches' addressed to the great unwashed. The **Kilmainham compromise** of March 1882 was a coup for Parnell, who feared that land protests were running out of steam. While it brought Parnell and Gladstone closer together, it further alienated the Whigs, who thought that, yet again, Gladstone had conceded too much. The Chief Secretary for Ireland, W. E. Forster, no Whig, also resigned in protest. In May 1882, Lord Frederick Cavendish, the new Chief Secretary, and his Under-Secretary were murdered in Phoenix Park, Dublin by 'the Invincibles', a terrorist offshoot of the Irish Republican Brotherhood. Parnell condemned the action, which took place four days after his release from prison, but it substantially increased tensions. Parnell found himself under pressure from Irish Catholics as well as Unionists.

Kilmainham Treaty, 1882

This was not a formal treaty but an agreement between Gladstone and Parnell. By it, the terms of the Irish Land Act 1881 were revised to provide more security for Irish tenants. Most of those who were in arrears with their rents had their debts written off. Gladstone made the agreement to prevent further violence. As a condition of the agreement, Parnell, who had been imprisoned in Dublin's Kilmainham Gaol, was released.

The 1884 Reform Act more than trebled the Irish electorate; after it, more than 60 per cent of adult males were entitled to vote. Modest tenant farmers appeared on the electoral roll for the first time. The redistribution of parliamentary seats in 1885 transferred twenty-two Irish borough seats to the counties, which made Ireland more representative of its predominantly rural social structure.[16] Indeed, because the Irish population had declined since the 1840s with no downward adjustment to the number of overall seats, Ireland was significantly over-represented at Westminster. By the early twentieth century, Ireland elected one MP for every 44,000 people; England's proportion was one for every 67,000.[17] The Home Rule cause benefited from both developments. Parnell's Irish Parliamentary party won eighty-six seats in the November 1885 general election, taking every seat in Ireland outside Protestant Ulster and Dublin University. It also held the balance of power at Westminster. After 1885, Irish Nationalist MPs never won fewer than seventy Westminster seats and they quickly learned how best to exploit the substantial political influence which these numbers afforded. In 1892, the Liberals returned to government – and to another Home Rule Bill the following year – only because of Nationalist support. The social composition of the Irish Parliamentary party was also changing. Landowner dominance was increasingly challenged by the election of more lawyers, small businessmen and tenant farmers.[18]

IV. Home Rule and its opponents, 1886–1905

The story of the Hawarden Kite is told elsewhere (see Chapter 38). What was Gladstone's objective in launching a Home Rule Bill in 1886? The simple answer, of course, was that he sought an acceptable solution to a fearsomely complex Irish conundrum. The prize was substantial. Successful Home Rule for Ireland would put an end to disruption and violence, while also keeping Ireland as a key element of the British Empire.

With Gladstone, however, simple answers never suffice. He was prepared to sacrifice his party to settle the Irish question. Being Gladstone, he had done formidable preliminary work. He visited Ireland only once, for a month in the autumn of 1877 when he ventured only into Dublin and adjacent County Wicklow, 'the least

Irish part of Ireland' as he later called it.[19] He did, however, talk to ordinary Irish folk. Back at his home in Hawarden, he steeped himself in Ireland's history and mulled over the political issues involved. His studies convinced him that a stable Ireland was dependent on large numbers of Catholic peasants owning their land. A satisfied, so-called 'peasant proprietary' therefore became a key objective. He also accepted the self-justifying argument of the nationalist politicians: Ireland was indeed a nation. Gladstone asserted that Ireland possessed a 'collective or corporate individuality, tested by reason, and sufficiently confirmed by history'.[20] Finally, he convinced himself that the question now required urgent attention. As he wrote to the journalist Frank Hill in December 1886: 'The public are slowly opening their eyes to . . . the bigness, and the urgency, of the question of Irish government.'[21]

Neither of Gladstone's two Home Rule Bills would have produced independence for Ireland. The 1886 bill proposed the creation of an Irish parliament with two houses. Matters concerning the Crown, the armed forces, diplomacy, war and peace and the United Kingdom coinage were reserved to the Westminster parliament, from which Irish representation would be withdrawn. The 1893 bill was similar, although eighty Irish MPs would have kept seats at Westminster. In a logical and practical refinement, which lesser politicians failed to use as an analogy in the cases of Scottish and Welsh devolution at the end of the twentieth century, Irish MPs would have been prohibited from voting on issues which related exclusively to Great Britain rather than to the United Kingdom.

The failure of both of Gladstone's bills (see Chapter 38) afforded some kind of breathing space during which the protagonists could take stock. Irish nationalism took a major knock with the departure of Parnell, much the most gifted leader Ireland produced in the second half of the nineteenth century. The Nationalists split, the majority working closely with the Catholic Church in Ireland and the Liberals at Westminster. The minority, no less attached to Home Rule, wished to retain greater freedom of political action. After Parnell's death, Irish nationalism was 'catholicised'. The denominational divide in Ireland became both more pronounced and more political. Ireland was overwhelmingly Catholic outside the six north-eastern counties of Ulster, parts of Dublin and, to a lesser extent, Cork in the far south. North-Eastern Ulster was much the most economically developed and industrialised region in Ireland. By the early twentieth century, its population was two-thirds Protestant.[22] Support for the Union came from two bases: a predominantly industrial working class in Antrim, Armagh, Down and Londonderry, and generally wealthy Protestant landowners, many of them in Ulster but with a pronounced concentration also in Leinster.

Competing with the Roman Catholic Church for the 'soul' of Ireland was a Gaelic revival. Its aim was to cleanse Ireland of debilitating Saxon influences and reassert the primacy of Gaelic culture. A Gaelic League was founded in 1892. One of its leaders, Patrick Pearse, stated that 'To preserve and spread the [Gaelic] language . . . is the single idea . . . When the position of Ireland's language as her greatest heritage is once fixed, all other matters will insensibly adjust themselves.'[23] A Gaelic Athletic Association helped to popularise Gaelic sports, particularly hurling.[24]

When he took over as Chief Secretary for Ireland from his brother Arthur in 1895, Gerald Balfour told a meeting of his Leeds constituents that 'The government would, of course, be very glad if they were able by kindness to kill Home Rule'. The phrase stuck, although Conservative policy in the 1890s and 1900s was rather more tactical, and rather less charitable, than Gerald Balfour implied. Like his predecessors, Arthur Balfour, on becoming Chief Secretary in 1887, used coercion to suppress disorder. Vigorous police action in suppressing an illegal nationalist demonstration at Michelstown led to fatalities and earned the new man the sobriquet 'Bloody Balfour'.[25] Nevertheless, the Conservatives threw a fair amount of money at Ireland. Balfour's 1891 Land Act provided generous loans to encourage further land sales. In the absence of compulsion, however, the scheme had fewer takers than the government hoped for. Wyndham's Act of 1903 was more successful. Originating in discussions between tenants and sympathetic landlords, it offered sufficiently substantial large bonuses to encouraged landowners to sell up to their tenants. It finally killed the land question as a nationalist grievance. By 1906, about 85,000 land purchase agreements had been made under the Wyndham Act.[26] Overall, Land Acts facilitated the transfer of more than 11 million acres of Irish land, at a cost of about £100m.[27]

The Conservatives also extended Ireland's railway network, enabling remote rural communities to be connected to the larger centres of population. Roughly seven hundred extra miles of track were laid down in the period 1886–1905,[28] which stimulated the dairy industry, market-gardening and the breeding of chickens for meat and eggs. Subsidies also supported local craft industries such as hand-knitting. This was 'constructive Unionism' in action. The most far-reaching development was the Local Government Act of 1898. This replaced the old 'Grand Juries', dominated by Protestant landlords and their relatives, with County, Urban and Rural District Councils elected on the recent English model (see Chapter 39). Catholic Irish Nationalists won most of the seats on a representative franchise. Centuries of upper-class Protestant domination of local government in Catholic Ireland came to an end.

IV. 'Ulster will fight'

Home Rule, if not killed by kindness, seemed by the turn of the century to have been pretty strongly anaesthetised. Virtually everything that the nationalists had wanted for Ireland, short of Home Rule itself, had been conceded. Any hope a returning Liberal government at the end of 1905 (see Chapter 38) would bring some latter-day Gladstone to the fore, trailing clouds of moral energy, were soon dashed. As the senior Conservative and Unionist politician Austen Chamberlain said in November 1906, 'just now, for an Englishman, at any rate, a speech on Home Rule is like flogging a dead horse'.[29] Campbell-Bannerman's government would support an Irish Councils Bill, giving the Irish greater responsibilities in local government, but the Nationalist leader, **John Redmond**, rejected his proposal out of hand. He felt betrayed, believing that he had been promised a much greater degree of devolution.

John Redmond, 1856–1918

Born in County Wexford into a well-established Catholic gentry family, he was educated by Jesuits in County Kildare. He was a follower of Parnell and became an MP in 1881. He was the leader of the small number of Nationalists remaining loyal to Parnell's policies and, in the 1890s, urged co-operation with non-Nationalists. When the Nationalists reunited in 1900, Redmond was chairman of the party. He discussed limited devolution proposals in 1907 when the Liberals would not support Home Rule. When the Nationalists held the balance of power in parliament from 1910, he pushed the Liberals to introduce a new Home Rule Bill, which ran into difficulties over intractable opposition from Ulster Unionists. He made an agreement with Asquith for Nationalists to support the war effort in return for the Liberals' passage of a Home Rule Bill. He did not take part in the Easter Rising (1916) and his influence had waned by the time of his death. He was a conciliator and a democrat ill-equipped to deal with those who adopted a violent course in pursuit of an independent Ireland.

Opposition to conventional Nationalist strategies was growing in Ireland. The journalist Arthur Griffith founded the Sinn Fein League in 1905. This advocated withdrawal from the UK parliament and cultural separation from Britain: 'ourselves alone' in the literal translation of the League's Gaelic name. Sinn Fein made some early impact on which it was unable to build before 1914. By contrast, the determination and discipline of Ulster Unionists in their opposition to any form of Home Rule grew apace. Orange and Ulster Unionist associations were by 1910 launching a powerful propaganda campaign. Battle lines were being drawn.

The Home Rule issue reached crisis point in the wake of the Liberals' attempt to pass the People's Budget (see Chapter 38) in 1909–10. The general elections of 1910 (see Chapter 38) increased Nationalist leverage over Asquith's government. The price of Nationalist support for passing the Parliament Bill was Liberal support for a new Home Rule Bill.

The Irish Unionists at Westminster, led by the persuasive **Edward Carson** with vigorous, streetwise support from the East Down MP James Craig (1871–1940), became seriously alarmed. Redmond was alerted, probably for the first time, to the extent of Ulster's hostility to rule from Dublin, with (as Ulstermen believed) Roman Catholic priests pulling the strings. Asquith's Home Bill was presented to parliament in April 1912. It proposed giving Ireland what amounted to internal self-government within the United Kingdom. A two-chamber Irish parliament would sit in Dublin and forty-two MPs, elected for Irish constituencies, would sit in the UK parliament in Westminster. Although the Lords rejected it twice, in 1912 and 1913, by huge majorities, Asquith used the terms of the recently passed Parliament Act [see Chapter 38] to override the House of Lords. The bill was ready to pass into law in 1914.

Sir Edward Carson, 1854–1935

Born in Dublin into a successful Protestant professional family, he was educated at Trinity College Dublin and trained as a lawyer. He was appointed Solicitor-General for Ireland in 1892, becoming an MP in the same year. He was appointed Solicitor-General for England, with a knighthood, in 1900. He was the 'celebrity lawyer' of his day, whose cross-examination destroyed Oscar Wilde in his legal battle with the Marquess of Queensbury. He became leader of the Irish Unionist MPs in 1910. He hoped that his lucid, and increasingly threatening, defences of Ulster's opposition to Home Rule would derail the Liberals' Home Rule Bill. By 1914, he was concentrating on excluding the six predominantly Protestant counties of Ulster from Home Rule. During the First World War, he served briefly as Attorney-General in Asquith's coalition government and as First Lord of the Admiralty and member of the War Cabinet in the Lloyd George coalition which followed it.

Meanwhile, Craig was selling the Ulster case with considerable skill, both to Unionist MPs and on the ground. On 28 September the Ulster Unionists pledged themselves to the terms of a 'Solemn League and Covenant', condemning Home Rule as 'disastrous to the material well-being of Ulster as well as the whole of Ireland, subversive of our civil and religious freedom, destructive of our citizenship, and perilous to the unity of the Empire'. To maintain 'our cherished position of equal citizenship in the United Kingdom', Ulster Unionists would use all means necessary to defeat the present conspiracy to set up a Home Rule Parliament in Ireland'. About half a million people signed the Covenant. 'Ulster Day' was to remain an icon of effective Protestant resistance throughout the twentieth century and beyond.[30] Intentionally, the Unionists used the same title that the Scots had devised in 1641 during the civil wars. Although, privately, neither Carson nor Craig wanted violence, which they thought would be counter-productive, the Westminster parliament was to understand that its Home Rule plans could lead to civil war.

By the beginning of 1914, many Unionist supporters had joined an Ulster Volunteer Force while supporters of Home Rule in Ireland had formed the Irish Volunteers. Both were well armed. The Government moved army detachments into Ireland to defend key strategic points and installations. In March 1914, most of the officers on duty at the Curragh Army Camp threatened resignation rather than accepting orders to enforce Home Rule on loyal Ulster Unionists. Plans were hastily, though tardily, assembled to remove Protestant Ulster from the terms of the Home Rule Bill. These, of course, risked flat rejection by the Catholic majority. Asquith, whose leadership during these dangerous months is perhaps most charitably described as 'masterly inactivity', was given a lifeline almost a month after the First World War broke out. The Unionists agreed to suspend Home Rule hostilities and to support the war effort if the government would postpone Home Rule legislation. Asquith responded by putting the Home Rule Bill onto the statute book in September but delaying its implementation either for six months or until the war ended. Civil war in Ireland, it seems, had been avoided by the skin of the teeth. Asquith anticipated a return to normality which never came for him, for his political party, for Ireland or for the United Kingdom. Much blood would be shed in Ireland, both during the War and afterwards, before a political settlement, removing Protestant Ulster from arrangements for an 'Irish Free State', could be agreed.

....

Labour, welfare and social conflict, 1900–1914

I. The health of the nation

The new century revealed new problems and brought old problems to a head. Sepia-tinted images of sun-drenched Edwardian summers providing an appropriately effulgent backdrop against which a relaxed and self-confident bourgeois society went about its prosperous business are frequently summoned to nostalgic effect. Unfortunately they are wide of the mark. The Edwardian age was one of uncertainty and growing domestic conflict.

In 1903, Major-General Sir Frederick Maurice wrote an article on 'National Health'. It turned on an alarming statistic about military recruitment for the Boer War: 'out of every five men who wish to enlist . . . you will find that by the end of two years' service there are only two men remaining in the Army as effective soldiers'. He drew a soldierly conclusion: 'I think it is safe to say that no nation was ever yet for any long time great and free when the army it put into the field no longer represented its own virility and manhood.'[1] These and many similar reflections led to a campaign to secure greater national efficiency[2] in order to withstand both challenges from abroad (see Chapter 27) and alleged 'physical deterioration' at home. The Unionist government established an inter-departmental government committee to examine the question. It reported in 1904, rejecting the idea that British people were experiencing 'general progressive physical deterioration'. Rather, 'very abundant signs of physical defect' were caused by 'neglect, poverty and ignorance'. The committee believed that there was 'every reason to anticipate RAPID amelioration of physique so soon as improvement occurs in external conditions, particularly as regards food, clothing, overcrowding, cleanliness, drunkenness, and the spread of common practical knowledge of home management'.[3]

Others were not convinced by this analysis. An increasing emphasis was being placed on what the scientist Sir Francis Galton termed 'eugenics', which he defined as 'the study of the agencies under social control that may improve or impair the racial qualities of future generations either physically or mentally'.[4] A Eugenic Education Society was founded in 1907. By 1909, it was producing its own journal, the *Eugenics Review*. Eugenicists argued that social policies, albeit with the best of intentions, were counterproductive. It was 'penalizing the fit for the sake of the unfit'. One contemporary suggested that 'preventive medicine and civilisation between them have already deteriorated in marked degree the healthy vigour of our race . . . the effect is already discernible – race decay'.[5] The remedy was selective breeding. It was argued that, while the prudent, educated middle classes were already using rational means of birth control, the 'unfit' were conceiving large numbers of children whom they could not properly maintain and care for and, in simple terms, degenerating the national gene-pool. Meanwhile, ever higher rates and taxes were being demanded of the prudent in order to support the 'unfit'. The existing trend needed to be reversed.

Such arguments had currency among a number of scientists, doctors and intellectuals. They also persuaded many who believed welfare policies to be wrong-headed, and counterproductive. An extreme expression from this camp came from the distinguished legal expert A. V. Dicey. He was deeply sceptical of the Liberal policy in favour of free school meals for the needy. To him, such a need bespoke parental fecklessness. 'Why a man who first neglects his duty as a father and then defrauds the State should retain his full political rights is a question easier to ask than to answer.'[6] The general currency of eugenics ideas was limited. However, when Home Secretary, **Winston Churchill** was briefly a convert, favouring compulsory sterilisation of the mentally unfit.[7] Rather, the lessons taken from the Boer War were those recommended by the Inter-Departmental Committee. Edwardian Britain saw something of a blitz on social policy, particularly after the Liberal government came to power at the end of 1905. The work of the Local Government Board, established in 1870 (see Chapters 28 and 32), had already contributed to improved social conditions in many urban areas but Edwardian Britain still experienced huge variations in provision, depending on the resources available to different local authorities. Concerned about stubbornly high levels of infant mortality, local authorities began to direct particular attention to the education of inexperienced and prospective mothers. Maternity and child welfare clinics were established and mothers were advised to breast-feed rather than risk infecting their infant with contaminated liquid milk. George Newman (1870–1948), who became chief medical adviser to the Board of Education, wrote *The Health of the State*, which he considered 'a missionary handbook, sent forth as a reminder that the physical health and fitness of the people is the primary asset of the British Empire'.[8]

Winston Churchill, 1874–1965

He is perhaps the most famous of all British Prime Ministers; he held that post from 1940–45 and 1951–55. This note deals with his career only to 1914. Born at Blenheim Palace (Oxfordshire), the son of Lord Randolph Churchill, who was the third son of the seventh Duke of Marlborough, Winston was educated at Harrow and Sandhurst. His father did not think him clever enough to go to university. He served as a cavalry officer from 1895 to 1899 and educated himself by voracious reading while serving in India. He saw action at the Battle of Omdurman in the Sudan. He reported on the Boer War for the *Morning Post*. Already well-known as a war correspondent, he became an MP as a Unionist in 1900. He left the party in opposition to Tariff Reform in 1904, becoming a Liberal MP in 1905. He became President of the Board of Trade under Asquith in 1908. He was responsible for introducing statutory minimum wage legislation and state-run Labour Exchanges. With Lloyd George, he led the Liberals' attack on the Lords' rejection of the Budget in 1909. He was regarded as a leading progressive reformer, although his radicalism is easily over-stated. He was primarily interested in power and in making things happen. He was irritated by suffragette activities and a staunch upholder of law and order. As Home Secretary in 1910–11, he was heavily criticised for his forceful handling of labour unrest. Asquith moved him to First Lord of the Admiralty, where he was an active moderniser and reformer of the navy who often fell out with the naval establishment.

The advent of compulsory education was also turned to good effect. In response to the recommendations of an Inter-Departmental Committee on Medical Inspection and Feeding of Children attending Public Elementary Schools (1905), a Labour MP, William Wilson (1855–1921), sponsored the Education (Provision of Meals) Act in 1906. This permitted local authorities to provide meals for children attending elementary schools. As usual with permissive legislation which required local authorities to find funding, take-up outside the county boroughs was slow. The government decided in 1914 that provision of school meals should be compulsory and provided some limited funding to ease the transition.[9] School medical inspections had become compulsory in 1907. George Newman and Robert Morant (1863–1920), senior civil servant at the Board of Education, established a school medical service. It quickly revealed how many children needed treatment for a wide variety of ailments from the trivial, though embarrassing – such as nits – to the more serious, including tuberculosis.

By 1914, about 260 school clinics were in operation to support medical inspections. Although no direct causal connection can be proved, the fact that, after a long period in which little changed, both infant and child mortality rates almost halved in the twenty years from 1891 to 1911 is indicative of the significance of state intervention. The infant mortality rate fell particularly sharply – from 140 per thousand to 108 in the first decade of the twentieth century.[10] Substantial regional variations, however, remained. Two Medical Officers of Health working in the North-East reported infant mortality rates declining but still around one hundred and forty per thousand in 1908. Unfit mothers, inappropriate use of patent medicines and 'the indifference of the community in general to the science of Eugenics' were all factors cited to explain the statistics.[11] The 1908 Children's Act set up an inspection regime to ensure that local authority provision was adequate, and parental neglect identified and, as far as possible, rectified.[12]

II. The poor law challenged

By the late nineteenth century, the work of Charles Booth and other social reformers (see Chapter 28) had helped to change attitudes towards the poor law. As living standards increased, Poor Law Guardians were able to trim provision of outdoor relief. Indoor relief, however, remained problematic. An increasing number of urban Guardians – not least those the working classes elected after property qualifications were abolished by the Local Government Act of 1894 – argued that it would be both cheaper and more humane to pay old age pensions than 'relieve' the elderly in the workhouse. As medical provision in workhouses was extended, so costs rose and rates went up. The depression of the early twentieth century put further burdens on the poor law. Pauper numbers increased by almost 100,000 in the years 1900–5 and expenditure on poor relief went up by more than 20 per cent.[13] Wishing to streamline the system and save costs, Balfour's Conservative government established a Royal Commission in 1905 to investigate the poor law.

The Commission was high-powered and its members debated citizenship, poverty and opportunity in 'perhaps [a] unique episode in the history of the relationship between British society and the various administrative organs of the state'.[14] The Commission produced two famously divergent reports. The Majority Report recommended retaining the poor law but giving more emphasis to work with philanthropic and charitable societies in order to 'rescue' people from poverty by example and incentives. It reflected the continuing influence of Charity Organisation Society ideology (see Chapter 28), which was well represented by the ideas of **Helen Bosanquet**. It asserted that 'Great Britain is the home of voluntary effort, and its triumphs and successes constitute in themselves much of the history of the country'. All that was needed was greater discipline and leadership.[15]

Helen Bosanquet, 1860–1925

Born in Manchester, the daughter of a nonconformist minister, she became a leading social theorist and writer. She was educated at Newnham College, Cambridge, where she studied moral sciences. After graduating she moved to London, becoming district secretary of the Shoreditch branch of the Charity Organisation Society. She disagreed with Rowntree's analysis of 'primary poverty' and laid stress on the importance of family life and its wider role in shaping society. She was a member of the Royal Commission on the Poor Laws (1905–9) and drafted much of the Majority Report, which clashed with the views of Beatrice Webb. She believed in the importance of case work and proper training in charity work. Charity should be targeted at helping recipients become more efficient, both as economic producers and in their family lives.

The Minority Report identified much 'overlapping, confusion and waste' resulting from the involvement of numerous local authorities with frequently overlapping voluntary agencies. It recommended winding up the poor law altogether and closing the hated workhouses. Specialist agencies of County and County Borough Councils should be established to meet the various categories of need. It also proposed that support for the non-able bodied should be entirely separate from that provided for the able-bodied, both unemployed and vagrants.[16]

The Minority Report was much influenced by Sidney and **Beatrice Webb** and **Fabian Socialism**. Despite their anxiety to pursue policies which conduced to National Efficiency, both Lloyd George and Churchill baulked at the idea of embracing any 'socialistic' remedies. The Minority Report's recommendation for the establishment of Labour Exchanges was cherry-picked but the poor law stayed.

Beatrice Webb, 1858–1943

Born as Beatrice Potter in Gloucestershire, the daughter of a successful businessman and railway director, she worked with Charles Booth on his study of the London poor (see Chapter 28). Her diagnosis of social problems distanced her from the charitable, case-work approach undertaken by many middle-class women. She worked in Bacup (Lancashire) in the mid-1880s, where she became a firm supporter of the Co-operative movement, before moving back to London as an urban 'missionary' working in the East London district of Whitechapel. These experiences made her a reluctant convert to suffragism. At least until her declaration of support for 'Votes for Women' in 1906, she believed that practical policies to improve women's lives should have higher priority. She married Sidney Webb in 1892 and they worked together on a variety of social programmes. Both were central figures in the Fabian Society. Together, they founded the London School of Economics in 1895 and were both members of the Royal Commission on the Poor Laws, drafting the famous Minority Report which called for the 'final suppression of the Poor Law Authority'.

Fabian Society

An intellectual organisation founded in 1884 whose objective was to advance socialism – particularly the common ownership of the means of production, distribution and exchange – by gradual and reformist methods rather than by the revolutionary action which had been advocated by Karl Marx and Friedrich Engels. It attracted a large number of left-wing thinkers, writers and politicians, including George Bernard Shaw, H. G. Wells, Leonard and Virginia Woolf, Ramsay MacDonald and Emmeline Pankhurst.

III. Liberal welfare legislation

Old age pensions and national insurance are the social policy initiatives for which the Liberals are best remembered. They are associated with the 'Progressive' wing of Liberalism and its belief that the state should acknowledge a responsibility for the wellbeing of its citizens (see Chapter 26). Progressive Liberalism became dominant in Edwardian Britain but it was frequently challenged not only by Conservatives but by Liberals who believed that state support should be limited, on the grounds of disincentive to individual effort and independence. This was a difficult line to take with pensions, however, since the scheme which Asquith prepared before he became Prime Minister was so limited to start with. The Old Age Pensions Act (1908) gave a weekly pension of five shillings (about £20 in early twenty-first-century values) to men and women aged 70 and over, who were not recipients of poor relief, except medical aid, and whose income was less than eight shillings (40p) a week. Just short of half a million people qualified to collect their first state pensions on New Year's Day in 1909. Most were women, reflecting differential life expectancies, but the overall number of beneficiaries was small. Pensions were payable to people with limited incomes; most would have done manual work when they were younger. Few would have had any earning capacity by the time they reached 70 and most would not have survived to collect a pension at all. Life expectancy at the beginning of the twentieth century was 45 years for men and 49 for women.[17] Even after some loosening of the criteria by 1911, only 40 per cent of the relevant age-group qualified for a state pension.[18]

Old age pensions were funded by the taxpayer. The more extensive national insurance schemes shared the burden between taxpayer, employer and employee. The National Insurance Bill was presented to parliament in two parts. The first, the responsibility of Lloyd George, concerned health insurance and covered all workers between the ages of 16 and 70 who earned £160 a year or less. Men contributed 4d a week into the scheme and women 3d. The employer's contribution was 3d a week and the state's 2d. When sick, insured men received a weekly benefit of ten shillings (50p) and women seven shillings and sixpence ($37\frac{1}{2}$p) for the first three months and five shillings for the next three. The second part of the bill, relating to unemployment, was introduced by Winston Churchill as Home Secretary. Employees in the trades most affected by seasonal unemployment paid a weekly contribution of $2\frac{1}{2}$d, again with further contributions by employer and state. Unemployment benefit was payable at seven shillings a week (35p) for five weeks, after an initial week without benefit. Trade unions helped to administer the scheme, and Labour Exchanges, which had been set up in 1909, checked whether an applicant was genuinely out of work.

National insurance was a fertile initiative. Its scope was regularly expanded between the wars and compulsory insurance formed the basis of the Welfare State which the Labour government established in the later 1940s. In 1911, the scheme was highly controversial. The principle of compulsory contributions both from employer and employee was widely disliked. Applying the principle to domestic servants attracted particular criticism. One newspaper complained that the new scheme meddled 'in every home' and that Lloyd George required of the employer 'three new and separate taxes, two of them levied in the most disagreeable way'. The Secretary of the National Association of Domestic Servants wrote to Lloyd George to explain why the scheme 'will do us serious injury'. The benefits were said to be 'of small use' while 'the regulations are likely to destroy the friendly relationship that I am glad to say still prevails between Mistress and Maid . . .'.[19]

IV. The emergence of the Labour party

The Labour party did not emerge smoothly, still less inevitably, from the growth of an integrated working class in the late nineteenth and early twentieth centuries. Divisions abounded. Skilled workers often looked down on the less skilled, believing that the army of casual labourers lacked both self-discipline and integrity. Divisions along religious and gender lines also ran deep and the nature of work in different parts of the country often produced quite separate working cultures.[20] As has been said, 'The early Labour party, once held up as the epitome of modern, national class-based politics, is now seen to have been rooted in specifically local political cultures.' Its political philosophy was more communitarian than class-based.[21]

This disunited working class tended to be sceptical of collectivism. Much the largest organisations for working people were Friendly Societies, with about six million members in the 1890s. Friendly society members mostly considered state aid intrusive. They preferred to support trade union objectives since higher wages and improved working conditions afforded greater security and dignity than did state pensions or other handouts. The Independent Labour Party, established in 1893 under the initiative of **Keir Hardie** as an avowedly socialist body with considerable support from the professional middle class, warned against excessive emphasis on social reform. The prescription of those who were called 'advanced liberals' was directed not to real improvement but at producing 'a contented race of wage slaves'.[22]

James Keir Hardie, 1856–1915

Born in Lanarkshire, the illegitimate son of a farm worker and a local miner, he had no formal education and as a young man worked as a miner. He became Secretary of the Ayrshire Miners' Union in 1886 and Secretary of the newly formed Scottish Labour party in 1888. He was elected as a Liberal MP for the London constituency of West Ham South in 1892 but his views became increasingly socialist. He lost his seat in 1895. His leadership and work to link socialist societies with the trade union movement were central to the establishment of the Labour Representation Committee in 1900. He became Labour MP for Merthyr Tydfil in the same year and elected Chairman of the parliamentary Labour party in 1906, in which role he continued to encourage alliances between trade unions and socialists. He was not an effective political operator but was very successful in representing the parliamentary Labour party to its grass-roots support. He retained many of the values associated with Liberal radicalism, supporting education as a means of improvement, and temperance reform as a means of keeping families sober, solvent and together.

Trade unions were growing in size and changing in nature. For most of the nineteenth century, they had been organisations of relatively secure, well-paid craft workers. Most had small numbers and were local in their activities. Successful strikes, such as that of gas workers organised by Will Thorne in 1889, initiated so-called 'New

Unionism', in which the emphasis was on unskilled workers and putting pressure on an employer by weight of numbers. Trade unionism grew spectacularly in the thirty years before the First World War. In 1870, its total membership was 250,000. This had risen to 700,000 by 1890, to 1.5m in 1895, to 2m in 1900 and 2.5m in 1910. In less than five years thereafter, and thanks in no small measure to the number of successful strikes during the period, membership increased by a further 60 per cent.

Trade unionism had been transformed. Its campaigns against legal restraints radicalised the leadership. A previously anti-socialist movement now had a number of socialist leaders. Links with the Independent Labour Party, founded in 1893, were substantial. Employers responded to meet the threat. The Shipping Federation was established in 1890; an Employers' Federation of Engineering Associations followed in 1897. Employers also used the law to curb union threats. The Lyons v Wilkins case in 1896 prevented leather workers from picketing Lyons' premises. In 1901, the Taff Vale case in South Wales also produced an injunction preventing peaceful picketing. More importantly, the judgment permitted union funds to be sequestered as payment for damages incurred by the Taff Vale Railway Company during its dispute with the Amalgamated Society of Railway Servants. The so-called 'Osborne Judgment' by the House of Lords in December 1909 was the most damaging of all. It ruled that subscriptions and other financial donations to a political party could not be considered a legitimate use of trade union funds. All these adverse rulings were eventually reversed. The Liberal party, however, waited almost four years before passing a Trade Union Act (1913) which righted what most unionists considered an egregious wrong. It allowed unions to create a 'political fund' to which members would contribute for use by the political party of the Union's choice – nearly always the Labour Party. Individual trade unionists had an explicit right to contract out of the fund.

This Act was passed during a period of unprecedentedly bitter and extensive industrial conflict. This coincided with a trade revival, enabling unions to maximise the impact of strikes. Although there were some high-profile defeats, most strikes had at least some success. Striking workers often enjoyed substantial local support. South Wales miners were on strike for ten months in 1910. Dockers, railway workers and seamen all struck in 1911. The Miners' Federation of Great Britain called a national strike in support of a minimum wage rate of five shillings per shift in 1912. In both 1908 and 1910, more than 10m working days were lost to strikes. In 1912, the loss totalled almost 41m days, much the most disruptive period of labour relations to date.[23] The state also became involved to keep order, although reading the Riot Act, as happened in Liverpool in August 1911, only strengthened local support for the strikers. More than two thousand troops were stationed in Liverpool by the end of the year. Concern mounted that the nation was coming close to civil war.[24]

These disputes involved the new Labour Party, established as the 'Labour Representation Committee' (LRC) in 1900. This grew out of agreement between the Independent Labour Party, the Fabian Society and the Social Democratic Federation. Its initial base was predominantly middle-class. Trade unions only joined in numbers after the Taff Vale judgment, which was followed by powerful lobbying from the party's Secretary, **Ramsay MacDonald**. More than a hundred unions, most of them small, had affiliated to the LRC by 1903. The party used its informal links with Liberals, especially in London, to set up secret negotiations between MacDonald and W. E. Gladstone's son, Herbert. By the resulting electoral pact of 1903, the Liberals agreed not to stand against Labour at the next general election in thirty seats.

James Ramsay MacDonald, 1866–1937

Born in Morayshire (north-east Scotland), the illegitimate son of a farm servant and a ploughman, he worked as a pupil teacher in the local parish school. He came to London in 1886 and spent much time looking for work. He associated with a number of Liberal and socialist organisations. He worked to support a progressive alliance between Liberal radicals and socialists and, having been rejected as a Liberal parliamentary candidate, he joined the Independent Labour party in 1893. As Secretary of the Labour Representation Committee from 1900, he was an architect of the Lib–Lab pact and also worked to increase trade union support for the party. He first became an MP in 1906 when, under the terms of the pact, he was unopposed by a Liberal candidate at Leicester. He became leader of the party in 1911. The labour unrest of 1911–13 widened splits within Labour, which entered the First World War still deeply divided. MacDonald resigned the leadership in 1914 when he found himself much more lukewarm in support for the war than most of his party. He became leader again from 1922 to 1931 and was twice Prime Minister: in 1924 and from 1929 to 1935.

The MacDonald–Gladstone pact proved to be a turning point. It gave the LRC a bridgehead in parliament, with twenty-nine of its candidates elected in 1906. By the end of 1910, the Labour party (as it was known from 1906) had forty-two MPs. Although still a small minority party, with only half the strength of the Irish Nationalists, it now became a visible presence. Its support helped Lloyd George to push through National Insurance against considerable opposition from within his own party. It might almost be said that a progressive Lib–Lab alliance was driving government policy in the years 1910–14. In return for Labour support, the Liberals conceded payment of MPs, which enabled more working men to become parliamentary candidates.

With the benefit of hindsight, the MacDonald–Gladstone pact looks to have been a tactical disaster for the Liberals. In a first-past-the-post system, minority parties almost always win a smaller proportion of seats than votes. The Liberals' decision not to contest thirty critical seats enabled Labour to win twenty-nine seats in all, an outcome almost exactly in proportion to the party's overall share (4.3 per cent) of the vote. It achieved similar proportional equipoise in the two elections of 1910. On deeper investigation, Gladstone's decision is defensible and might even have been the best option. The parties were already co-operating informally, so the arrangement was hardly contrived. Also, the Liberals had been out of office for fourteen of the previous seventeen years. They were likely to support any option which improved their chances at the next election. The Tory implosion over Tariff Reform (see Chapter 39) had hardly yet begun. The Conservatives looked much more likely winners in 1903 than they did in 1906. It is true that the Lib–Lab alliance was under considerable strain by 1914. It had broken down totally in local government in some areas. Nationally, Lloyd George was sufficiently concerned about a Conservative revival to offer MacDonald a new pact based on an agreed programme of progressive reform and seats in what would have become a coalition Cabinet. It took a complex range of circumstances, which none foresaw, to have Labour replace the Liberals first as the main opposition party (1918) and then as a minority government (1924). In 1914, as in 1903, the Labour party remained very much the junior partner in progressive politics. Though its advances in the interim were significant, Labour still had little mass support at the national level.

Recent research has emphasised how little Labour's progress before the First World War relied on class politics. There was no direct transfer from the massive expansion of trade union membership of 1910–14 into Labour successes in either local or Westminster elections. Labour's advance in local government resulted from a concentration of resources in winnable seats, when many others were not contested. Thus, Liberals could hang on comfortably in some working-class seats. In the predominantly working-class West Riding of Yorkshire, for example, Labour made some spectacular gains, but nearly all were in the adjacent cities of Bradford and Leeds. Elsewhere in the county progressive Liberal candidates were doing as well in 1914 as they had in 1906,[25] when Liberals had also won twenty of the twenty-three parliamentary seats. We should also note that by-election losses reduced the number of Labour seats from 42 in November 1910 to 37 on the outbreak of war. Had the anticipated general election of 1915 taken place, it is very likely that Labour would have lost more. It is difficult to contest the argument that it was the war, and not any surge of working-class enthusiasm for the Labour party before 1914, which changed the nature of the political game.

42

A greater need for security: diplomacy and alliance systems, 1880–1902

I. Gladstonian foreign policy, 1880–1885: principles and pragmatism

In 1880, as part of his Midlothian Campaign (see Chapter 32), Gladstone articulated what he called six 'right principles of foreign policy': fostering the strength of the Empire to secure wealth and contentment and using that wealth 'for great and worthy occasions abroad'; preserving peace; 'to keep the Powers of Europe in union together'; the avoidance of 'needless and entangling engagements' overseas; to 'acknowledge the equal rights of all nations'; and 'the foreign policy of England should always be inspired by the love of freedom'.[1] These principles represented what might now be called an 'ethical' foreign policy. Within two years, Gladstone had the opportunity to show whether Britain's foreign policy would sustain and develop these 'right principles' through choppy diplomatic waters or whether their main purpose was party-political advantage: an opportunity to damn 'Beaconsfieldism' and to dismiss it, to coin a phrase, 'bag and baggage'. The evidence was to show that Gladstone's 'right principles' could be no more than that. They could not act as chapter headings for a practical manual on diplomacy in a rapidly changing world. The rest of the world was unlikely to prioritise policy in order to accord with the conscience of Mr Gladstone.

Despite his frequent pronouncements on them, foreign affairs were not Gladstone's métier. He was a master of detail but the bigger picture often eluded him. In any case, and as his Midlothian Speeches abundantly demonstrate, he was happier in the worlds of sweeping moral pronouncements and financial calculations than of *realpolitik*. During his second ministry (1880–85), he laboured under two disadvantages. The German Chancellor, Otto von Bismarck, was a master tactician. His key foreign-policy objectives were to protect and advance the interests of the new German Empire and also to rein in the excessive economic and imperial power of the United Kingdom. Also, Gladstone's Foreign Secretary throughout this ministry was Earl Granville (see Chapter 32), who did nothing to compensate for the Prime Minister's deficiencies. As Sir Evelyn Baring said of him, 'His power of eluding the main point at issue was extraordinary.'[2] Granville gave every appearance of aristocratic assurance but he was lazy and disinclined to take decisions. He was, however, well aware that, from the late 1870s, Bismarck had been dealt a strong diplomatic hand which he played with considerable skill. When Gladstone complained to his

Foreign Secretary in 1884, 'I think we are all too much afraid of Bismarck', Granville understood why extreme caution was necessary, though he was all too prone to mistake extreme caution for stasis.[3] Had Gladstone been more sympathetic to the radical wing of his party, he would surely have used the opportunity to promote Joseph Chamberlain in Granville's stead.

Realpolitik

This word of German origin roughly translates as 'practical politics'. It is usually employed to describe an attitude to foreign affairs characterised by calculations about specific national interests and advantages rather than by matters of principle or moral scruple.

Gladstone's stated desire to 'keep the powers of Europe in union together' was unrealistic. There was no 'union' to maintain. The best that could be hoped for was the resolution of divergent interests by peaceful means. By 1880, nationalism had destabilised a Europe previously dominated by established great powers. Italian unification contributed significantly to the territorial losses and consequent relative decline of the Austrian empire. Central Europe was dominated by imperial Germany, whose growing economic strength was challenging Britain's industrial dominance (see Chapter 27).[4] Gladstone regarded Austria as an unworthy and inappropriate counterbalance either to growing German strength or, which was of more immediate importance, Russian expansionism in south-east Europe and Asia (see Chapters 34 and 35). His observation that 'Austria has ever been the unflinching foe of freedom in every country of Europe'[5] was tendentious and anyway anachronistic when diplomatic relations were being increasingly determined by alliance systems.

France's defeat by Germany and the subsequent emergence of republican government in the early 1870s (see Chapter 35) had temporarily improved relations with Britain. Old antagonisms were easily aroused, however, as events in North Africa demonstrated in the early 1880s. France considered North Africa a natural territory for its imperial expansion but Gladstone made plain his opposition to France's occupation of Tunis in 1881. This caused much resentment in Paris.[6] Worse damage was done by the failure of joint attempts to resolve growing problems in Egypt in 1881–82. Egypt was part of the Ottoman Empire but its Khedives (local rulers) increasingly acted as if the region were entirely independent and had entered into various arrangements with European bankers and businessmen. The overthrow of Khedive Ismael in 1879 led to a period of instability during which an army officer, Colonel Arabi, led a military coup aimed at establishing Egypt as an independent Muslim state resistant to any further Western influences. This alarmed the British government since 80 per cent of Egyptian exports came to Britain and about a third of the country's debt was secured by British bond-holders. During further disturbances in May 1882, both the French and the British sent navies to Alexandria but only

Britain followed this up with a full-scale expeditionary force. General Garnet Wolseley routed nationalist resistance at the Battle of Tel-el-Kebir in September. By the end of the year, in blatant disregard of the 'Midlothian Principles', Gladstone's government had in effect annexed Egypt. The diplomatic fall-out was substantial and long-lasting. France bitterly resented Britain's independent initiative, and the imperial gains which it promised. In an atmosphere of mutual distrust, rapprochement between the two nations came to a shuddering halt.

Relations were not to be repaired for twenty years, much to the frustration of Salisbury, who initially opposed the occupation, considering Egypt an expensive, and apparently interminable, commitment. The work of Evelyn Baring (1841–1917; from 1892 Baron Cromer and from 1901 Earl of Cromer), however, transformed the situation. In his role as Consul-General working under the Khedive but, in reality, directing operations, Baring drew on his family's banking experience and contacts first to reduce Egypt's financial deficit and then to modernise and Westernise the region. In consequence, by the mid-1890s, Egypt was too important to give up. Together with Britain's control of the Suez Canal and its growing interests further south in the Nile Valley, control of Egypt enabled Britain to dominate the eastern Mediterranean. None of this was foreseeable in 1882 when Gladstone claimed credit for Britain's victory in a 'Christian war' at the cost of dousing the few lingering hopes of maintaining his treasured, but anachronistic, 'Concert of Europe'.

Liberal radicals like **Charles Dilke** apart, the government's Egyptian policy was broadly popular at home. A little further south, however, in the vast territory of Sudan the consequences of another uprising had a different outcome. The insurgency was led by Mohammed Ahmad, otherwise known as the Mahdi. His revolt against the Khedive, in which Islamic ideology was as potent a factor as nationalism, began in 1881 and rapidly gathered strength. In November 1883, the Mahdi won a decisive victory at El Obeid, in which William Hicks Pasha, the British commander of an Egyptian force, was killed. Gladstone, who had no desire permanently to colonise Egypt, let alone Sudan, ordered the Khedive to evacuate the remaining garrisons. **Major-General Charles Gordon** was despatched to organise the evacuation. The expedition proved a disaster. Gordon exceeded his authority, got into difficulty and a relief force was sent out to rescue him. It arrived in the Sudanese capital, Khartoum, two days after its defences had fallen to the Mahdi and Gordon had been killed.

Charles Dilke, 1843–1911

Born in London, the son of a successful patron of the arts and a commissioner for the Great Exhibition, he was brought up in a cultivated family and educated at Cambridge University. He became an MP in 1868 and took up a number of radical causes, including support for women to vote in municipal elections and, much less successfully, republicanism. The Queen's return to more prominent public life in the early 1870s and Prince

▶

Edward's recovery from typhoid hugely increased the popularity of the monarchy. His republicanism made him many enemies and hindered his political career. He worked closely with Joseph Chamberlain in the later 1870s and became an effective advocate for radical Liberalism. He became a junior minister in 1880 and a Cabinet minister in 1882. He was a key figure in framing the Third Reform Act (1884) and the redistribution of parliamentary seats which followed in 1885. His career stalled following a divorce scandal in 1886. He returned to parliament in 1892 and continued to champion radical causes, including trade union rights, until his death.

Major-General Charles Gordon, 1833–1885

Born in Woolwich (London), the son of a senior army officer, he was educated privately and at a school in Taunton before entering the Royal Military Academy. He served both in the Crimea and in China in the 1850s. He served under the Khedive of Egypt as Governor of a small province in Sudan from 1874 to 1877 before becoming Sudan's Governor-General in 1877, where he served for two years, with a self-appointed mission to suppress slavery. When despatched to Sudan again in 1883, rather than concentrating on evacuating British troops out of danger, he instead attempted to reconstruct the Sudanese government. He established himself in Khartoum, where his forces were besieged by the Mahdi. He was killed in January 1885, two days before a relief force reached Khartoum. Gordon was widely admired as a dedicated, heroic soldier with a strong moral sense but he was often obstinate and even insubordinate. He was a complex individual, driven from the early 1860s by profound religious belief. The Earl of Derby called him 'A fanatic of the Puritan type', difficult to control, still less command. Gladstone's secretary was even less complimentary. He believed Gordon to be 'a half-cracked fatalist'.

News of Gordon's death was greeted with horror from Queen Victoria down through all levels of society. Gladstone took most of the blame. He was execrated as 'M.O.G.' – Murderer of Gordon – in a neat inversion of the unofficial title used by Gladstone's admirers, 'G.O.M.', Grand Old Man. Salisbury, as leader of the opposition, proposed a vote of censure on the government in which he criticised its wholly inadequate response to the crisis. The 'terrible responsibility and blame rests upon the government' because, although warned in March 1884 that Gordon was in danger, 'they delayed . . . right down to 15 August before they took a single measure to relieve him'.[7]

Tales of Gordon's heroism and self-sacrifice were legion, though widely embellished. Visual representations of his death – the precise details of which are unknown – were produced which exactly fitted the image of duty and self-sacrifice widely believed to have underpinned the creation of the British Empire (see Chapter 36). The journalist W. H. Stead, in an appraisal made shortly before Gordon's death, called him 'one of the ablest men of the century', a 'unique figure' who has 'fascinated the imagination of the English people'. He acknowledged that many considered him impulsive, changeable and almost 'mad' but 'he is one of those madmen whose madness is of the nature of inspiration'.[8]

A further crisis in Afghanistan began in the last months of Gladstone's government and was concluded during the brief Salisbury Conservative minority government which followed (see Chapter 37). Stability had been secured in Afghanistan's mountainous territories north of the Punjab after British intervention in 1878 (see Chapter 36). However, the threat to British India from Russia remained real. When Russian incursions led to a military victory at Penjedh in 1885 and they established themselves on the strategically vital pass of Zulficar, the road to northern India lay open. Gladstone reluctantly prepared for war. When Salisbury took over, he sent his private secretary on a mission to Germany, asking 'Prince Bismarck to mediate between the 2 countries' and prevent 'a rupture . . . which would lead to hostilities, not only in Central Asia, but in every part of the world where England could deal a blow at her antagonist'.[9] Salisbury anyway wanted to make early contact with Germany but war was averted because Russia backed away from a direct confrontation. Britain accepted Russian control of the less strategically important Penjedh and Russia withdrew from the Zulficar Pass, thus leaving the strategically important town of Herat, in north-western Afghanistan, secure. Thereafter, Anglo-Russian relations retreated from crisis point. Foreign Office suspicions about Russia continued but, in contrast to the Palmerston period (see Chapter 34), they were rarely dominant factors in British diplomacy after 1885.

II. The personal fiefdom: Salisbury and foreign policy, 1885–1892

On becoming Prime Minister in June 1885, Salisbury drenched in irony his predecessor's record in foreign policy. Gladstone and his ministers had 'at least achieved their long-desired "Concert of Europe". They have succeeded in uniting the continent of Europe – against us.'[10] This was standard political knockabout, and Salisbury was good at it, but his assessment did contain more than a grain of truth. In the mid-1880s, Britain had no powerful allies, was not widely trusted and had begun to doubt the extent of its own power (see Chapter 27). Europe had no 'Concert' as Gladstone understood the term. Any like-mindedness between nations rested on the increasingly common view that diplomacy was about the practice of self-interest. Nations sought allies, not because they had common interests in preserving peace, but to make themselves more powerful or more difficult to attack. The idea that to pursue peace as an end in itself was to work on a higher moral plane was becoming less fashionable. Late nineteenth-century diplomacy suited the mindset of Bismarck much more than it did that of Gladstone.

As the new Prime Minister demonstrated, it suited him also. Salisbury's foreign policy objectives were not significantly different from Gladstone's. Both men accepted that the Empire and British trading routes took priority. Like Gladstone, he believed that Russia posed the greatest threat. The protection of India from Russian advances in Asia always had high priority. Salisbury also accepted the fact of French hostility, though in 1885–86 he did not believe it posed a direct threat. Like Gladstone also, he recognised that stability in central Europe depended upon Germany. Unlike Gladstone, though, he had the respect of Bismarck. He did, however, express the private, wholly undiplomatic, but heartfelt view that 'Mr Gladstone knew nothing of foreign affairs and was impossible to do business with'.[11]

The note presented to Bismarck by Salisbury's private secretary in August 1885 (see above) suggested a possible later alliance:

> the English people . . . have the strongest leaning towards their Protestant ally . . . A close union between the greatest military power and the greatest naval power could produce a combination that would not only secure the peace of the world, but would also be in the highest degree advantageous to the interests of the two Countries.

Bismarck, knowing that at least as much divided the two nations as linked them and suspecting that Salisbury was as wily an operator as himself, did not take the bait.

Salisbury conducted foreign policy almost as a personal fiefdom. After the ineffective Earl of Iddesleigh's (see Stafford Northcote, Chapter 33) resignation was accepted at the beginning of 1887, Salisbury acted as his own Foreign Secretary until his last two years in office. It was a considerable burden for the most part lightly borne. Salisbury's cynical, untrusting personality was well suited to the job of decoding diplomatic messages for real meaning beneath the practised *politesse*. For him, diplomacy was about calculating percentages. In his early interchanges with Bismarck, he seemed to be offering an alliance between states with complementary strengths. He did not believe that a firm alliance with Germany would be beneficial and he calculated, first, that Bismarck would know this and, secondly, that, since a Anglo-German alliance would threaten Germany's relationship with Russia, he would not take up the offer, considering that friendly relations with a powerful neighbour on Germany's eastern border had higher priority. Through the smoke and mirrors, Salisbury's intention was to send Bismarck two messages. First, Britain wished Germany no harm. Secondly, occasions might arise on which the two states might work together to achieve a specific objective. Shrewd, calm and knowledgeable, the third Marquess of Salisbury would have made an excellent poker player.

For advice and support, Salisbury looked not to Cabinet colleagues but to his officials. Civil servants in the Foreign Office were exempted from the general requirement that entry depended on success in competitive examinations. They did, however, need to be rich and well connected. Britain's foreign policy was conducted by old Etonians and aristocrats whose families were well known to the Prime Minister and not infrequently related to his own.[12] Liberal radicals resented this anachronistic arrangement but were ignored. Salisbury saw nothing wrong with nepotism and could argue that diplomacy across most of Europe was conducted by men from similar privileged landed backgrounds. Between such folk, shared assumptions were expressed and understood in the raising of an eyebrow. Conversely, a strong case presented by an 'outsider' in the wrong tone could be counter-productive. It was, of course, important to pick the right privileged men but Salisbury trusted to his judgment on that.

It is probable that Queen Victoria knew more about Salisbury's diplomatic manoeuvres than did most of his Cabinet, let alone parliament as a whole. Monarchs generally take a strong interest in foreign affairs. Victoria, who had been on the throne for almost fifty years when Salisbury first became Prime Minister, was not only knowledgeable and opinionated; she was related to most of the crowned heads of Europe. From 1888, the German Kaiser was Wilhelm II, her grandson, and all but one of her nine children had married into royal or princely families, five of them German. Salisbury judged it a wise precaution, as well as a constitutional duty, to keep the Queen abreast of events.

III. The Eastern Question and Empire

For most of the late 1880s and 1890s, Britain's foreign policy was dictated by imperial considerations (see Chapter 36) and by problems created by Russian expansionism, especially in the Balkans. Bismarck had created the so-called 'Triple Alliance' of Germany, Austria-Hungary and Italy in 1882 primarily to provide the central European powers with safeguards against aggression. This might come either from France against German or Italian borders or from Russia through the Black Sea and into the Balkans. Salisbury handled the Russian threat to Britain differently. Such close alliances risked committing Britain to actions – not excluding full-scale war – on issues marginal to its central concerns. However, an understanding with the central powers might be valuable. In his words, 'we wish to lean to the Triple Alliance without belonging to it'.[13] Though the phrase 'splendid isolation' was coined at the end of the nineteenth century to describe Salisbury's relationship with the other great powers, it fails to capture the subtlety of the Prime Minister's position. Salisbury was no isolationist. The Foreign Office always kept in close diplomatic touch with the other great powers. He also understood how claims for territory in Africa during the 'Scramble' affected great-power relationships in Europe and the Near East.[14] The key objective, however, was to avoid over-commitment.

'Leaning' towards the Triple Alliance generated some important initiatives. Two 'Mediterreanean Agreements' were signed with Austria-Hungary and Italy in 1887. They confirmed the status quo in the Mediterreanean, which was much to Britain's advantage. While giving Italy security against French attacks in North Africa, they also secured Britain's main trade route to the East, shoring up the Ottoman regime and checking renewed Russian ambitions in the Balkans after the Tsar's frustrated attempt to establish a pro-Russian autocracy in Bulgaria. A Cabinet Memorandum to the Queen explained the need for agreement in terms of the potential danger. If 'England was left out in isolation . . . though England could defend herself, it would be at fearful risk, and cost'.[15] These agreements strengthened Britain's position in the Mediterreanean, particularly since Salisbury was able to extract from Bismarck a commitment to support Britain in any future conflict with Russia.[16]

These agreements also influenced the government's defence priorities. Salisbury had become increasingly concerned about the inefficiency and under-manning of the navy. By the late 1880s, some doubted whether the fleet was sufficiently well organised even to meet an invasion threat. The response was the Naval Defence Act of 1889. This committed Britain to the maintenance of a navy which, in the words of the First Lord of the Admiralty, would be 'on such a scale that it should at least be the equal to the naval strength of any two other countries'.[17] Over the next eight years, expenditure on the navy increased by 65 per cent. Britain thus played an important role in accelerating the naval armaments race and the militarisation of the great powers during the first decade of the twentieth century (see Chapter 43).

In 1890, Salisbury negotiated a bilateral agreement by which Germany agreed to give up its claims to territory in East Africa in exchange for Heligoland, an island about thirty miles west of the German coast, which Britain had captured from the Danes in 1807. The islanders complained, considering themselves British, and the Queen was not amused to lose some subjects. However, Salisbury calculated that a small concession in the North Sea was justified by a now smoother expansion of British interests in eastern Africa and Zanzibar.[18] Salisbury, though no enthusiastic imperialist, was sensitive to growing domestic enthusiasm about Empire, recently stimulated by the Golden Jubilee celebrations of 1887 (see Chapter 36).

British foreign policy aims altered little until the end of the 1890s. The change from a Conservative to a Liberal government in 1892 brought first Rosebery and then the Earl of Kimberley to the Foreign Office. Rosebery had been a discreet admirer of Salisbury's diplomacy but he was a much more ardent imperialist and encouraged further colonial expansion in Africa. While he was in office, Uganda became a British protectorate. Rosebery was no more inclined than Salisbury to risk initiatives which threatened the existing balance of European power. Salisbury needlessly fretted that Rosebery might commit Britain to closer links with Russia. A specific arrangement with Russia on an agreed frontier between Afghanistan and India did remove one source of tension. Rosebery went no further. Temperamentally, he was considerably more pro-German than pro-Russian. Kimberley, already highly experienced in colonial affairs and bringing with him a reputation for hard work and competence, adopted Rosebery's view that party politics should inform decisions concerning foreign policy. He too followed the same broad objectives.

Salisbury, therefore, returned to office in 1895 to a recognisably familiar diplomatic landscape. During his last years as Prime Minister, the emphasis overseas was largely on the colonies, although colonial developments had a significant impact on relations with the European powers. The most significant clash before the Second Boer War (see Chapter 36) occurred with France over Britain's determination to consolidate influence over the entire Nile region. This decision was influenced by the powers' failure to renew the Mediterranean Agreements in 1896, a development which marked the end of Salisbury's long, but never consummated, flirtation with the Triple Alliance. Since the western Mediterranean was now less secure, the strategic importance of Egypt and Sudan increased. The French had never accepted Sudan as a British sphere of influence and sent an expeditionary force to Fashoda on the Upper Nile as a warning presence. Meanwhile, Britain had despatched General Kitchener to secure Sudan, which, since the death of Gordon thirteen years earlier, had been in the hands of the dervishes. In September 1898, Kitchener defeated them at the Battle of Omdurman and entered Khartoum. These developments were accompanied by maximum brutality. In addition to the Khalifa – the dervish Chief – more than 10,000 of his troops were massacred. Kitchener had made a reality of what Salisbury had a year earlier called 'our desire to extirpate from the earth one of the vilest despotisms ... ever seen'.[19] Omdurman was widely criticised in the British press and also widened splits between imperialists and anti-imperialists in the Liberal party (see Chapter 38).

Meanwhile, the French had reached Fashoda on the Upper Nile, where, a fortnight after Omdurman, they encountered Kitchener's much larger force. A stand-off ensued while British and French governments considered their respective positions and popular newspapers called for war, bloodshed and imperial glory. The French foreign minister, Théophile Delcassé, knew which nation would be the more blooded. As he ruefully remarked, 'we have nothing but arguments, and they have got troops'.[20] The French wisely withdrew. In March 1899, an Anglo-French Convention was signed, identifying the powers' respective spheres of influence. The French conceded British domination of the Upper Nile. Within months, conflict broke out in South Africa between Britain and the Boers (see Chapter 36).

Events in both the north and the south of Africa in the late 1890s revealed significant divisions within Salisbury's government. These were accentuated by a public opinion increasingly influenced by the sensationalism of the popular press. Joseph Chamberlain, Salisbury's Colonial Secretary, developed a so-called 'New Imperialism'. This saw the Empire as a vital economic resource and as Britain's main claim to be considered the world's leading power. Vigorous colonialism was the answer to increasing concern about Britain's relative decline (see Chapter 27). Germany was seen as the main threat. To meet it, new imperialists called for exactly the kind of close defensive alliance which Salisbury had spent his career trying to avoid. Salisbury's followers still wished to avoid such entanglements and saw Russian ambitions as the main threat, although the French humiliation at Fashoda made any improvement in Anglo-French relations most unlikely.

Salisbury was ageing; he resigned as Foreign Secretary in October 1900. The Boer War was far from over and, among the other great powers, a consensus was growing that it had gravely damaged Britain's prestige. The war also provoked much introspection, shaking many imperialists' belief that Britain's Empire would suffice to maintain its international standing. To the end of his life, Salisbury believed that, with an efficient, expanded navy to protect its Empire, Britain would be ill served by close alliance with any European power. It is significant that Lansdowne, his successor as Foreign Secretary, took a much more pessimistic view of Britain's standing in Europe. He initiated a new policy, grounded first in rapprochements with France and Russia, on which he hoped to build closer alliances. With Salisbury gone, Britain entered upon a new diplomatic era in a world which, as would shortly be revealed, was growing ever more dangerous.

43

An accidental catastrophe? The origins
of the First World War

I. The creation of the *Ententes*

At the beginning of the twentieth century, the Foreign Office still fretted about
Russia. Worries about its long-standing ambitions in Asia, and particularly
their implications for Britain's control over India, lay behind Britain's unusual
initiative for an alliance with Japan, which was signed in January 1902. The Foreign
Secretary, the **Marquess of Lansdowne**, believed that Britain's naval presence in the
Far East needed strengthening if existing imperial and commercial links were to be
secured. Although expenditure on the navy increased by 80 per cent in the years
1897–1904, the Russian threat in Asia was still judged stronger than Britain could
meet alone. By the Anglo-Japanese alliance, of five years' duration in the first instance,
both nations agreed to remain neutral if one of the signatories went to war with only
one other power but to intervene if more than one were involved. Parliament was
startled by an agreement which some MPs considered exotic. Lansdowne confirmed
that its purpose was essentially defensive. He hoped to develop a range of limited
regional agreements which did not threaten the overall status quo and indicated that
Britain had no offensive designs in the relevant area.

Henry Petty-Fitzmaurice, fifth Marquess of Lansdowne, 1845–1927

Born in London into one of the most senior aristocratic families in Britain, he was the
son of the fourth Marquess, the grandson of the important Whig politician who became
the third Marquess (see Chapter 20) and the great-grandson of Lord Shelburne, Prime
Minister in 1782–83 (see Chapter 1). He was educated at Eton and Oxford University.
He became Marquess on his father's death in 1866, when he sat in the House of Lords
as a Liberal peer. He disagreed with Gladstone over Irish policy in 1880 – well before
the Home Rule crisis. His imperial experience was extensive. He was Governor-General
of Canada from 1883 to 1888 and Viceroy of India from 1888 to 1894. His political
career was heavily influenced by the Marquess of Salisbury, who made him Secretary for
War in his Unionist government of 1895. He succeeded Salisbury as Foreign Secretary
in 1900 and remained in that office under Balfour until the government resigned in 1905.

▶

As Foreign Secretary, he helped negotiate the 1904 *Entente* with France. He was leader of the Unionists in the House of Lords from 1903 and, as such, organised the opposition to the Lloyd George Budget. He was in the eye of the constitutional storm which followed but his indecisive leadership led to a split in the Unionist peers between 'die-hards', who opposed the Parliament Bill to the end, and 'hedgers', who were prepared to let it pass. He was a minister in Asquith's War Coalition of May 1915 but left government when Lloyd George became Prime Minister at the end of 1916. During 1917, he argued for a negotiated peace with Germany.

Japanese success against Russia in a brief war between the two nations in 1904–5 eased Britain's worries over India. Pressure on the navy was reduced since Japan had comprehensively routed the Russian fleet.[1] Furthermore, the result of post-war Russian introspection was greater receptivity towards overtures from Britain for an accommodation over outstanding matters of disagreement.

Meanwhile, the United States had established itself as overwhelmingly the most powerful nation to the west of the Atlantic Ocean. The so-called Hay-Pauncefote Treaty of 1901 was 'an open recognition by Great Britain that she must now concede naval, as well as military, supremacy to the United States'.[2] Its terms read almost as an act of homage to an established feudal lord. Britain's objective was to secure the neutral benevolence of the US if conflicts with other powers developed in the western Atlantic. Reduced military and naval presence in the Americas enabled Britain to concentrate on defending on home waters. The United States had a further incentive to invest in the construction of a canal which would link the Pacific and Atlantic Oceans. Construction began in 1904 and the Panama Canal was opened to traffic in August 1914 – a week after the British Expeditionary Force embarked for France on the outbreak of the First World War.

Although far from crisis-point, Britain's relations with Germany in the early years of the century remained uneasy. Joseph Chamberlain's two initiatives in 1898 and 1899 led nowhere and German criticism of Britain's conduct during the Boer War exacerbated tensions. Lansdowne had no more success. Russia remained the sticking point (see Chapter 42). Although Germany and Britain had agreed in 1900 not to threaten any of China's territories, Russia, which had recently extracted concessions from China, had sent 100,000 troops into Manchuria and was refusing to withdraw them. Britain's request for German co-operation in exerting diplomatic pressure on Russia was brusquely refused. Germany's view was that Britain was more interested in checking Russia than in achieving a meaningful Anglo-German accord.

Britain now saw a new stumbling block. Germany's two Naval Laws of 1899 and 1900 were designed to convert the country into a major sea power. The aim was to create a navy as powerful as Britain's as quickly as possible, thus challenging the so-called '**Two-Power Standard**', which was the objective of Britain's Naval Defence

Act (see Chapter 42). By 1902, the First Lord of the Admiralty, the Earl of Selborne, was seriously alarmed. Why was Germany, a predominantly landlocked nation, launching a naval competition against the British Isles? British intelligence in Berlin reported, 'the German Navy is professedly aimed at that of the greatest sea power – us'.[3] He told the Cabinet, 'I am convinced that the great new Germany navy is being carefully built up from the point of view of a war with us.'[4] While some of his colleagues still saw an Anglo-German accord as the most 'natural' European relationship, Germany's challenge to Britain's naval strength, the foundation of its defence and security, changed perceptions. The build-up of anti-German hostility, to which the popular press would contribute much, had begun.

Two-Power Standard

This shorthand phrase describes the objective of the British Naval Defence Act of 1889. Britain attempted to maintain a fleet of battleships which were the same size as the world's second and third largest fleets combined. Unsurprisingly, other powers, especially Germany, resented this as inappropriate and arrogant.

Lansdowne's search for an accommodation with a major European power achieved success via an ***Entente*** with France in April 1904. This seems a more radical foreign-policy departure in retrospect than it did at the time. France, like Britain, was concerned about Germany. It too was also a substantial naval power. Britain's interest in a closer arrangement, however, reflected growing concern about the protection of its sprawling overseas commercial and imperial interests. Mutual goodwill visits in 1903 to Paris by the new King, **Edward VII**, and by the French President to London received extensive and favourable publicity, though they were a side-show. The *Entente*, wildly applauded by many in Britain as a diplomatic triumph, was not a binding alliance but a series of practical agreements over colonial issues. Remembering its reverse of 1882 (see Chapter 42), France swallowed hard before agreeing to acknowledge Britain's dominant position in Egypt. In return, Britain accepted French control over Morocco, which it considered an essential element of its North African empire. France also gave up fishing rights in Newfoundland in return for some favourable border adjustments in West Africa.

Entente

A French term meaning a 'friendly understanding', usually between nations rather than individuals. It is often presented as '*Entente Cordiale*', which implies a greater degree of friendliness, although the two forms are often used interchangeably.

Edward VII, 1841–1910

Born in London, the first son and second child of Queen Victoria and Prince Albert, he was something of a problem to his parents. He resisted his father's strict educational routine and, from the late 1850s, rumours circulated of a lavish lifestyle and sexual excess. Later, he became increasingly frustrated with his role as heir to the throne since Victoria did not trust him to read official papers or allow him much opportunity to act in her stead at ceremonial occasions. He did, however, visit India in his official capacity in 1875–76, as part of the ceremonial associated with the creation of the Queen as Empress of India. He took an increasing interest in international relations and expressed concern in the 1890s about what he saw as Britain's increasing isolation from other great powers. He was sociable and affable, but his relations with his nephew Wilhelm II of Germany, whom he considered authoritarian and unpredictable, were poor. He got on much better with Nicholas II, Tsar of Russia. As King from 1901 to 1910, he reorganised the royal court, which became much more lively than under his widowed mother. He placed considerable emphasis on ceremonial, and returned to the old practice of opening each session of parliament personally. Like his eighteenth-century monarchical ancestors, he took army and defence matters very seriously. He played some role in foreign affairs, where he supported his governments' attempts to make alliances through high-profile meetings with foreign dignitaries. His visit to Paris in 1903 was successful and helped to dissipate long-harboured, and mutual, Anglo-French antagonisms.

The *Entente* was tested in the following year. In 1905, Germany, alarmed by an agreement it had not anticipated, challenged France's rights and claimed that the Sultan of Morocco should be able to exercise complete independence. Germany also calculated that, when under pressure, Britain would not give unequivocal support to France. Germany's hope, of course, was the *Entente* would break up. Lansdowne believed that the purpose of Germany's initiative was 'to make mischief'.[5] An international conference to settle the issue was held in the Spanish port of Algeciras from January to April 1906 and attended by thirteen nations. It was soon clear that Germany had miscalculated. A new Liberal government was now in office (see Chapter 38) and its Foreign Secretary, **Sir Edward Grey**, was more suspicious of German aggressive intent than Lansdowne had been. He sustained his predecessor's policy but with more of an eye to the wider European ramifications. The *Entente* held. With the solitary exception of its Triple Alliance partner, Austria-Hungary, Germany found itself isolated at Algeciras. The port it gained on the Moroccan coast was little more than a face-saving gesture. France retained control over policy and finance in Morocco, while the *Entente* powers began to talk about a military alliance. As the Foreign Office official Eyre Crowe put it in a famous Memorandum to Grey in 1907, the Anglo-French *Entente*, which had begun as 'a friendly settlement of particular outstanding differences', had moved on: 'there had emerged an element of common resistance to outside dictation and aggression . . . tending to develop into active co-operation against a third power'.[6]

Sir Edward Grey, Viscount Grey of Fallodon, 1862–1923

Born in London, the son of an army colonel, he came from one of the most established aristocratic families in the north of England. It produced the third Earl Grey (see Chapter 22). His grandfather, Sir George Grey, was Home Secretary under both Russell and Palmerston. The young Edward was educated at Winchester College and Oxford University, though he did little work there. He became an MP in 1885, remaining loyal to Gladstone over Irish Home Rule the following year. He was a junior minister in the Foreign Office from 1892–95. He supported the government's position on the Boer War and, with Asquith and Haldane, operated as a 'Liberal Imperialist'. He frequently criticised his party leader, Campbell-Bannerman, who nevertheless appointed him Foreign Secretary in 1905. He remained in that post for more than eleven years. He was a competent Foreign Secretary but, like most of his predecessors, believed that the details of diplomacy were private. Even the decision to go to war in August 1914 was not formally brought to Cabinet for discussion. Though no warmonger, Grey's policies tied Britain into an increasingly military Triple *Entente* from which retreat with honour was, by the summer of 1914, not possible. He was ennobled as Viscount Grey in the summer of 1916 but resigned from government when Lloyd George overthrew Asquith at the end of the year. He never held office again, though he remained active, not least in trying to establish legally protected bird sanctuaries. Bird-watching had always been a passion.

By the end of 1907, Russia had joined what became a 'Triple *Entente*'. As with France, the accord between Britain and Russia in August was not a military alliance. It settled outstanding differences in Asia, very much along the lines Lansdowne had devised a few years earlier. Both powers acknowledged 'a special interest in the maintenance of peace and order' in and around Persia and were 'desirous of avoiding all cause of conflict between their respective interests'.[7] Specifically, Russia agreed to respect China's control of Tibet while Britain agreed not to pursue its own claims there. The northern half of Persia was agreed to be an area of Russian influence and the southern half a British one. The powers agreed to 'confer' over any outstanding differences concerning Afghanistan. The whole package promised greater stability both in Asia and, crucially, security for India's impossibly extended northern land frontier. The new *Entente* was vigorously criticised, not least within India. Lord Curzon, returning from a stint as Viceroy, was particularly choleric. Russia, he was certain, could never be trusted. Many Liberal Radicals also opposed the new *Entente*, on the usual grounds that it tied Britain to a brutal, backward-looking and authoritarian regime.

But the Triple *Entente* held, even if Britain did not wish to acknowledge that it had entered into an alliance system. As late as the beginning of 1914, Grey was still maintaining in public that the agreements with France and Russia dealt with specific areas of previous difficulty: 'alliances, especially Continental alliances, [are] not in accordance with our traditions'.[8] This was no longer the whole truth. Grey knew how threatening Germany considered these arrangements to be. Grey himself believed that they secured a balance of power against the continuing Triple Alliance of Germany, Austria-Hungary and Italy. He also knew that an increasing number of MPs were now seeing the *Entente* in this way.

II. Anglo-German naval rivalry

In any case, the European balance of power was not static. Grey might prefer to negotiate limited agreements with Germany on matters of specific contention, as had happened with both France and Russia. Such negotiations were taking place almost until the outbreak of war. However, they were never likely to reach resolution because Germany was determined to be considered at least Britain's equal. Its growing power was, in itself, a cause of European destabilisation. The German foreign minister, and later Chancellor, Bernhard von Bülow, had famously asserted in 1897: 'we do not want to put anyone in our shadow, but we also demand our place in the sun'. It is not so commonly mentioned that he was talking specifically about imperial expansion, not the balance of power in Europe. Still, his statement resonated most within Europe.

In 1906, Britain's launch of HMS *Dreadnought*, the first of a new generation of fast, heavily armed British battleships, accelerated the naval race between Britain and Germany. By 1914, Britain had built 38 Dreadnought battleships and the faster, lighter Dreadnought battle cruisers; Germany had 24. This substantial advantage almost crippled Britain's defence budget, not least because its munitions expenditure had been cut in the years 1905–12. Both nations were preparing contingency war plans. In Britain, however, a culture of secrecy (which came naturally to the reclusive Grey) and rivalry between top brass in the navy and army led to almost diametrically competing strategies. One was based on an all-powerful navy exerting a vice-like grip on everything that moved in the North Sea; the more balanced alternative was dependent on a significant army presence in support of France and against Germany. In response to this 'land strategy', the head of the navy, Admiral John Fisher, waspishly remarked in 1908: 'The Army is too big for a little war, too little for a big war.'[9] Meanwhile, the Kaiser's frequent boastful references to the overwhelming size of his army stirred the pot.

France, having a contested common boundary with Germany, was even more alarmed about developments. While German population was growing and its economy increasingly productive, particularly in its main mining and industrial regions, the French population was static and its industrial revolution had barely begun. By 1910, Germany was out-producing France four times in steel and seven times in coal.[10] France's military preparations were hampered by its limited industrial productivity. Russia's problem was not shortage of manpower. Its population was about a third larger than that of Germany and France combined and, although its productivity was low, it had recently embarked on rapid industrial growth. Both the recent reverse in the Russo-Japanese war and evidence of growing internal opposition to the Tsar also suggested that Russia's massive population would not punch its weight in any future conflict. It is easy to understand why all three Triple *Entente* powers felt that they needed collective strength to maintain any semblance of a European balance of power.

In Britain, fear of Germany represented a significant cultural development in the first decade of the twentieth century. A good indicator of the fevered atmosphere was the enormous commercial success of William Le Queux's novel *The Invasion of 1910*. Originally appearing in serial form in Alfred Harmsworth's popular newspaper the *Daily Mail* in 1906, it told the story of a successful German invasion four years into the future which surprises Britain and leads to the occupation of London. The message was crystal clear: a German war, for which Britain was unprepared, was imminent. The book could also claim greater authenticity since its author, with a French father and an English mother, was widely travelled and well-known as a journalist as well as a novelist. *The Invasion* was translated into almost thirty languages and sold more than a million copies. Others profited from engendering and exploiting hostility to Germany. Erskine Childers's *The Riddle of the Sands* (1903), a spy novel whose plot turned on German invasion plans, was one example.

Such publications bred paranoia in an alarmed but under-informed population. Any nugget of evidence about German strength, guile or brutality was liable to huge exaggeration. The work of Lieutenant-General James Edmonds, head of counter-intelligence and profoundly anti-German, produced much more heat than enlightenment. He seems to have broken almost every rule of valid evidence-gathering and found spies, if not under every bed, then certainly operating as devious customers at local post offices. His lurid reports contributed much to the growing alarm.[11] Anyone who spoke with a foreign accent was liable to be suspected of spying for Germany. The Home Secretary, Winston Churchill, compiled a list of aliens living in Britain and demanded additional powers to open the correspondence of persons suspected of espionage activities.[12]

As Geoffrey Searle has pointed out, Germanophobia, although increasingly dominant, was only one side of the coin.[13] Particularly among the educated elite, there was both admiration for recent German achievements and the belief that ancient Anglo-Saxon bonds still mattered. Germany and Britain were progressive nations. Germany was praised for being 'highly civilised with a culture that has contributed greatly in the past to western civilisation, racially allied to ourselves and with moral ideals largely resembling our own'.[14] Culturally, Britain seemed much closer to Germany than to France. Concert-goers in general much preferred the music of Bach, Beethoven and Brahms to that of Couperin, Rameau or Berlioz, to say nothing of the irritating wash of wispy sound contrived by modernists such as Debussy and Ravel. Sir Edward Elgar was mortified at the thought of war with a nation whose cultural legacy had so influenced his own musical development.

III. The edge of the precipice, 1911–1914

Explaining why the great European powers went to war in the summer of 1914 is complex, generating a considerable number of conflicting interpretations. If one reason has to be isolated (and probably it should not be), it is currently fashionable to stress the effects of Germany's aggressive ambitions – and particularly to concentrate on the arrogant, politically insensitive, unsophisticated, glory-seeking and often unstable Kaiser Wilhelm II. The purpose here is not to analyse the general causes of the First World War but to explain why Britain entered the conflict in early August 1914.[15]

Few in the early summer of that year believed that war was near. If told that 1914 would see an armed conflict, then the smart money would have been placed on its location being Ireland rather than northern France (see Chapter 40). Though the international situation increasingly concerned the Foreign Office, it had been occupying less space in the newspapers, shoved aside by growing political, economic and imperial crises much nearer home (see Chapters 39 and 41). It was business as normal for the London financial markets. Fortunes were being made, particularly by investors in foreign stocks. On 22 June, the London Chamber of Commerce gave a lunch for more than a hundred members of the Association of Merchants and Manufacturers in Berlin. Afterwards, the President of the Association of Chambers of Commerce saw no cause for concern: 'the question of Anglo-German relations was not one for politicians but for the commercial men of the two countries'. Six days later, the heir to the Austro-Hungarian Empire was assassinated at Sarajevo in Serbia. Thirty-one days after the lunch, the government of Austria-Hungary sent an ultimatum to Serbia. Forty-three days after, Britain declared war on Germany. Anglo-German relations were indubitably now for the politicians and the generals. The merchant banker Gaspard Ferrer spluttered that 'The war came like a bolt from the blue and no one was prepared'.[16]

This was partly because the years 1908–13 had witnessed a number of local conflicts which had been resolved well short of European war. Most of the trouble had been in the Balkans. The 'Eastern Question' (see Chapter 35) was re-opened with a vengeance. In 1908, Austria-Hungary annexed the Balkan provinces of Bosnia and Herzegovina. Supported by Germany, it saw off protests both from Serbia and, of greater significance, Russia. British involvement was minimal. Grey attempted to set up an international conference to settle the question but Austria and Germany refused.

Britain had greater involvement in the second Morocco crisis which erupted in 1911. After a rebellion against the Sultan, the French sent troops to Morocco to re-establish their influence. Germany saw an opportunity to influence events and sent a gunboat, the *Panther*, with an eye to extending its influence in West Africa. Britain, concerned that Germany's prime intention was to establish a naval base at Agadir, on Morocco's western coast, to rival its own at Gibraltar, despatched a naval force. The Moroccan crisis ended in compromise. France retained control of much of north-west Africa. For Britain, the true significance of the crisis was that it supported France, even though its *Entente* partner had ignored British advice when it sent troops to Morocco. Lloyd George, the Chancellor of the Exchequer, raised the Moroccan crisis to an issue of national importance when he declared that British interests were 'vitally affected'.[17] The implications were clear: seeking to humiliate 'a great country like ours' would be to risk war. Such a war would pit Britain and France against

Germany. After 1911, it was undeniable that the *Entente* implied military co-operation and support.

In 1912–13, the Balkans were severely destabilised, first by the rebellion of the so-called 'Young Turks' against the Ottoman rulers and then by two wars. The first of these, in 1912, brought victory for a Christian 'Balkan League' of Bulgaria, Serbia, Greece and Montenegro against the Ottoman Empire. Russia hoped to profit by expelling the Turks from all the Balkan lands. Grey summoned an international conference in London which led to a peace treaty from which the Ottomans lost virtually all their territory in Europe, including Macedonia and Albania. Macedonian territory was to be divided between the triumphant Balkan League states. This outcome led within months to a second war in the summer of 1913 when the victors fell out over competing land claims. The war was short but decisive. By the Treaty of Bucharest, Bulgaria was forced to give up some of the territory it had taken the previous year. Serbia and Greece were the main beneficiaries.

All of the disputes of 1908–13 had been contained, largely because the great powers, while guarding their own interests carefully, did not fan the flames. The irony of the next Balkan crisis, which *did* provoke a general European war, was that it came against a background of somewhat improved Anglo-German relations. Only a fortnight before the assassination at Sarajevo, Britain had withdrawn its objections to the Berlin–Baghdad railway project and reached agreement with Germany over its territorial claims in the Middle East. Neither side believed in 1914 that local conflicts were likely to lead to great-power hostilities. Ministers representing the great powers, not least Sir Edward Grey, had managed increasingly complex and unpredictable squabbles in the Balkans since 1908 with considerable success.

Yet the assassination of Franz Ferdinand, heir to Emperor Franz Joseph of Austria, by a Serbian terrorist in the Bosnian capital of Sarajevo on 28 June 1914, lit the powder keg which exploded into full European war five weeks later. No one seems to have anticipated this outcome. For almost four of those five weeks, nothing much happened. Thereafter things happened at such breakneck speed that there was no time for the powers to draw breath or reflect on the implications of their initiatives. Austria's famously stern ultimatum to Serbia, aimed at curbing nationalist outbreaks and reinforcing its increasingly parlous position in the Balkans, was not issued until 23 July. Germany believed that Russia would not risk committing itself to defending Serbia but was prepared to support Austria in any case. On 24 July, Russia, knowing that it had gained very little from the collapse of the Ottoman Empire and wishing to confirm its continued influence in the Balkans, agreed to support Serbia. This led both Austria and Russia immediately to mobilise their armies. Two days later, and probably three days too late, Sir Edward Grey called for yet another international conference to settle matters, a proposal which Germany and Austria-Hungary immediately rejected.

Even then, war was not inevitable. Mobilisation does not mean that shots will be fired. Britain was further than most from making a decision about war. In the

Cabinet only a minority were in favour until the very last moment. The Liberal 'peace party' remained articulate, vocal and numerous. The City of London, fearing a massive slump in share prices, was also opposed, as was the Governor of the Bank of England. It was far from clear in late July that Grey had a mandate for war. Indeed, he was still trying to restrict conflict to the Balkans. Since this had happened with relatively little fuss in both 1912 and 1913, it seemed a realisable objective in 1914.

Amid the swirling mass of bluster, threat and uncertainty, though, only Germany had made definite plans to wage war beyond south-eastern Europe. This became the critical factor in creating a 'World War'. For Britain, it both raised points of principle and confirmed long-harboured prejudices. Germany's so-called Schlieffen Plan of war depended upon a pre-emptive strike against France by surprise invasion through Belgium. The points of principle concerned Britain's direct commitment (by the Treaty of London signed in 1839) to the defence of Belgium and its much more recent obligations to France. The prejudice was the Germanophobia long nurtured by many politicians, especially in the Conservative party, and increasingly by public opinion. Its origins lay partly in distaste for things German but mostly in fear of growing German power, aggressively asserted. As *The Times* put it: 'We dare not stand aside ... our strongest interest is the law of self-preservation'.[18] On 2 August, the Cabinet agreed that Britain must defend itself against German naval activity in the Channel and it also heard that the Conservatives would provide enough votes to pass a declaration of war through the Commons, should the government decide on this course of action.

So, when on 3 August Germany invaded Belgium *en route* for Paris, Britain responded with an ultimatum. The following day, Germany declared war on Belgium and Britain declared war on Germany. When the ultimate crisis came, the Triple *Entente* of Britain, France and Russia translated into a military commitment. Italy quit the Triple Alliance of central European powers, leaving Germany and Austria-Hungary to fight on two main fronts – against France and Britain in the west and Russia in the east.

Though Grey, in particular, was full of foreboding, the declaration of war was popular in the country. Men rushed to enlist. The first European war for half a century would give the British the opportunity to show that, though slow to anger, when roused they were very terrible. Moreover, so the assumption went, they would not need to be roused for long. A quick, cleansing war was the thing. Britain and its allies would rapidly establish a decisive advantage and peace would quickly follow: 'all over by Christmas', as the catchphrase had it. This was one of the most catastrophic misapprehensions of all time. Britain's involvement in war was to last for four years, three months and one week – as punishing, and for most of its space as pointless, a slog as could be imagined. When it ended, almost all of the old regimes and the political and cultural certainties which sustained them had collapsed. The post-war world was a different place, as was Britain's role and status in it.

44

....

Epilogue

I. The cost of war

In the early evening of 3 August 1914, Sir Edward Grey offered perhaps the most resonant reflection ever made by a British Foreign Secretary: 'The lights are going out all over Europe; we shall not see them lit again in our lifetime.'[1] As with so many famous quotations, its authenticity is not cast-iron. Grey used it in memoirs published later, where he notes that a friend present at the time told him he said it. If his original comments were rather more mundane, or not made at all, it hardly matters. Those eighteen words sum up the passing of an epic era in European history.

They were apposite precisely because the war lasted so long and cost so much. Easy talk in the summer of 1914 about the war being 'all over by Christmas' was soon exposed as hopelessly optimistic. Optimism did, however, characterise Britain's attitude to war in 1914. Given how wracked with political, social and constitutional conflict the country had been in the previous five years (see Chapters 39, 40 and 41) it is remarkable how quickly domestic squabbles were put aside to enable Britain to fight the enemy as a united nation. Even John Redmond, leader of the Irish Nationalist party, supported Lord Kitchener's campaign for troop recruitment. The suffragettes halted their activity almost immediately. Winston Churchill, no stranger to war by 1914, wrote about his enthusiasm for what he called 'this glorious delicious war'.[2] If expressed in less florid language, it seemed that the ordinary citizens of the United Kingdom felt much the same. Despite the best efforts of the propagandists, the 'evils' of the enemy were far less apparent than they would be on the outbreak of Hitler's war twenty-five years later. Yet the nation rallied with extraordinary unity of purpose to defend 'gallant little Belgium' against the 'invading Hun'.

From top to bottom, from landowner to casual labourer, the nation rallied to Kitchener's call for 100,000 volunteers to augment Britain's army of about half a million. By the end of the first month of the war, three times that number had volunteered. The recruiting strategy's emphasis on civic pride and local identity proved a master stroke. Cities and smaller towns competed with one another to recruit the largest proportion of men between 19 and 30 years of age. So-called 'Pals' brigades signed up, united by a common locality, a common trade – transport workers, for example – a common ethnic background, such as the Irishmen from Tyneside in the North-East or even a common sporting interest, as with the London 'footballers battalion'. What linked them was a strong sense of patriotism, almost certainly heightened by the emphasis on Britain's imperial heritage, but also a clear sense of belonging. Britain in the summer of 1914 presented the appearance of a series of interlocking social groups united in a common purpose as never before.

The enthusiasm of these volunteers found an echo within the Empire, which made a similarly substantial contribution. Of the forty-two million troops who fought on the allied side, nine million enlisted from the Dominions and other countries of the Empire.[3] Most of the imperial recruits, like those in Britain, went to war in 1914 loyally and willingly enough, if not always in the same spirit of unreflective patriotic enthusiasm found up and down the 'mother country' itself. Support was not universal. Reservations about joining an overwhelmingly European war were expressed in Australia, New Zealand and Canada. In particular, it rankled that so many young lives were being committed to a war thousands of miles away from home as representatives of countries which had inferior Dominion status.

Resentment grew as casualties mounted. Australia and New Zealand lost more than 10,000 men during the bloody and unsuccessful mission to the Dardanelles in 1915. Widespread colonial criticism was made of Britain's misbegotten war strategy and of the limited competence of its commanders. Meanwhile, and especially after the 'Easter Rising' of 1916, many Irish nationalists actively supported Germany rather than Britain, which they considered an oppressive imperial power. Nevertheless, in terms of separate national contributions, only Russia's twelve million combatants outnumbered troops recruited from across the British Empire.

The horrors of a bloody stalemate, which lasted more than four years and produced unprecedented carnage, permanently changed perspectives. Almost a million troops from the British Empire died during the war, about four-fifths of them British. The financial cost was astronomical. One estimate puts it at more than £768bn, another at £22,368,229,004 at early twentieth-century monetary values.[4] Neither was remotely affordable, and long-rehearsed arguments about imperial over-stretch (see Chapter 19) gained greater purchase when economies were depressed, as for much of the inter-war period they were. In any case, the imperial market for British manufactured industrial goods was much less secure than it used to be, not least because, by the 1920s and 1930s, many colonies had the capacity to produce their own. Much popular sentiment remained pro-imperial down to the Second World War and even beyond, when arguments about the benefits, or otherwise, of Britain's joining the European Common Market were often framed by continued concern for the interests of the British Commonwealth. Once the cultural and psychological benefits of maintaining a large Empire were clearly outweighed by the cost, however, then a shift in perception took place, to which the growth of independence movements in the colonies significantly contributed.

Post-war Britain was also to become less hierarchical. The 1918 Representation of the People Act gave votes to 8 million women and, less often remembered but almost as important, almost 6 million more men. Britain was almost a democracy.[5] The 1920s saw the first Labour governments, both headed by the illegitimate sons of two Scottish farm workers. British people were less inclined to accept that their social superiors always knew best. Many felt that they had been led to slaughter by high-born commanders who did not know what they were doing. Had they known – and most did not – that the casualty rate on the Western Front for Eton-educated officers was about four times higher than it was for the armed forces as a whole, it would have made no difference. Old certainties were challenged in a more egalitarian era. The novelist H. G. Wells summed it up as well as anyone: 'That England of the old Victorian men with its empire and its honours and its court and its precedences, it is all a dead body now.'[6]

Challenging the authority of the social elite did not mean that Britain was either enthusiastic about the emergence of more democratic politics or at ease with itself. It is easy to demonstrate that late Victorians and Edwardians did not live through a period of any special social cohesion, whatever pro-imperial propaganda might have claimed. However, the collective perplexity and gloom with which so much of British society was suffused was of a quite different order. The war produced profound psychological shock. Its aftermath was prolonged economic depression, leading to long-term unemployment for many, especially in Scotland, Wales and the North of England, who had barely survived their ordeal in the trenches. One newspaper in 1920 attempted to analyse what it called 'the deep causes of present discontents'. It identified a 'lack of collective confidence, apathy on matters of public concern' and a widespread belief that, despite a more democratic franchise, Britain's system of representative government no longer worked. 'Right and left equally share a lack of faith in the normal machinery of government. Our politics are unconvincing . . . the decline of parliamentary authority is a topic on every tongue. No national institution commands all it once did of the respect of the people to whom it belongs.'[7] From this perspective, the 'Great Britain' which went to war in 1914 seemed much diminished by the 1920s.

II. In retrospect: economy and society

We should end by looking back over the hundred and thirty or so years of British history which this book has attempted to cover. What are the key changes which took place and what was their longer-term significance? Britain in the nineteenth century was at its zenith. This, rather than the Elizabethan age of piracy and overseas exploration in the second half of the sixteenth century, was when Britain really 'ruled the waves'. Much of Britain's nineteenth-century greatness was based on maritime supremacy which protected both markets and territories. For all but the first twenty-five years of our period, British supremacy in both naval and mercantile shipping was not only unchallenged but unchallengeable. Recognising its importance, governments, anxious to pare back military expenditure after the end of the Napoleonic Wars in 1815, always gave priority to the navy. It proved a wise investment. Naval commanders were in no doubt that they represented Britain's 'senior service'.

Much has been made of the fact that Britain was the world's first industrial nation. This emphasis is perfectly understandable since industrialism gave access to apparently limitless potential for economic growth and the emergence of new, more prosperous societies. In recent years, perhaps too little attention has been paid to the sheer technical ingenuity displayed by British engineers who produced what has been dismissively referred to as the 'wave of gadgets' which helped transform the productive capacity of the nation. While it is true that the Patents Office, where new inventions were recorded, was stuffed full of bright ideas with limited, or no, practical utility, it is also the case that the increasingly commercial ethos in eighteenth-century Britain posed a series of challenges to inventors, innovators and builders. These were met by two or three generations of British mechanical engineers who can stand comparison with any in history. The field of Industrial Revolution studies was long dominated by number-crunchers anxious to quantify the extent of economic growth, changing productivity rates, demographic shifts and the rest. Their painstaking work, often with outrageously deficient data, has been of great importance, some of it revelatory. However, quantitative method can produce a one-eyed approach.

More attention needs to be paid to the human dimension. Here, historians have tended to concentrate on those who span or wove wool and cotton, tended machines, wrought the metals and carried the bales. It is surely time to revisit the contributions of those who designed the machines, the bridges and the rails, without whose prodigious ingenuity the Industrial Revolution would have been hamstrung. It is an odd reflection that, a handful of icons such as Stevenson and the Brunels apart, Britain's golden generation of engineers, whose influence was truly international, have received such limited attention in recent years.

The Industrial Revolution produced a radical shift in the geography of job creation and British wealth. There was a shift to the north. Textile production concentrated in the central valley of Scotland, in south and east Lancashire and in the West Riding of Yorkshire. The extraction of metals and ores was more broadly based but the larger and more profitable mines were concentrated in Yorkshire, Lancashire and Nottinghamshire rather than in Kent, Devon or Cornwall. The expansion of metal working transformed much of the industrial West Midlands, where large numbers of workshops, forges and and small factories were established for gun manufacture, nail and chain making and a host of other metal trades in Birmingham and the Black Country. Over the course of the nineteenth century, transport improvements generated a national economy rather than the series of interlocking local economies which characterised most commercial activity until the beginning of the nineteenth century. Only with the coming of the railways were producers optimally linked with suppliers and consumers. This facilitated more effective competition for the purchase of goods based on quality and price.

It is easy to sustain an image of nineteenth-century Britain dominated by huge factories employing hundreds, if not thousands, of employees. It was not. Most textile factories were relatively small in scale, employing fewer than two hundred operatives. While they grew in size over the century, factories as they developed in Germany and the United States in the second half of the nineteenth century tended on average to be larger, often offering greater opportunities for economies of scale. One among many reasons for the export of investment capital from Britain to other countries was that British firms often made relatively modest demands for improvement and expansion. In 1914, many were still run by private limited companies or small partnerships; many were also risk-averse and broadly conservative.[8] Although the conclusion is contentious, it is probable that the structure of textile firms in particular hampered an effective response to post-war foreign competition from countries which paid lower wages and, in some cases, used more modern technology.

Over the course of the nineteenth century, Britain became a nation of urban dwellers. By 1900, about 80 per cent of Britain's population was living in towns. These were not all great ports or industrial communities. We should note that alongside the conurbations which grew up around Manchester, Liverpool, Leeds or Newcastle, and which were predominantly factory, mining or port based, other types of town were also growing rapidly. Some, like Brighton, Scarborough and Blackpool, were predominantly seaside leisure resorts. Their nineteenth-century growth was remarkable. Other, much older, communities also expanded. Market towns, and centres for surrounding agricultural production such as Ipswich and Gainsborough, grew. So did towns whose earlier development had been largely dependent on the Church, such as Durham, Winchester or Worcester. They now experienced considerable commercial expansion.

London was the mighty exception to the changing, more northerly, demographic balance. As always, both its commercial importance and its role as the nation's capital sustained its economic and political status. Remarkably, it housed 10 per cent, or a little more, of Britain's population throughout our period. It was, of course, a temporary home for many, particularly the young who came to try their luck at finding new opportunities in an always buoyant labour market. Some succeeded, or at least survived, and stayed; others moved on or back to their homes. In his novels, Charles Dickens vividly brought to life the teeming transience of London, a city of great wealth and desperate, shiftless poverty.

III. In retrospect: politics and power

In some ways, the government of Britain changed relatively little over the period covered by this book. Central government remained in the hands of a landed elite at least until the 1880s, when the growing influence of the professional classes made itself felt, especially in the Liberal party. Nineteenth-century Reform Acts all significantly increased the number of voters, though women would not gain the vote until the First World War was over. In response to parliamentary reform, the political parties organised themselves more effectively at constituency level. Although much altered by divisions and splits, particularly in 1846 and 1886, the same two parties, albeit with different names – Conservative and Unionist for Tory, Liberal for Whig – were contesting power in 1914 as in the early nineteenth century. It is difficult to discern a direct link between increased number of voters and policy changes. Only in the years after 1900 do the parties tailor policies in direct appeal to the electorate. There is little evidence, however, that an electorate which after 1884 comprised more than 60 per cent of adult males was anxious to vote for parties which put up taxes in order to provide more services, in the form of pensions, national insurance and the like.

In 1914, as in 1780, Britain was still a 'limited monarchy'. How much the survival of the monarchy owed to good management, to strong personalities, to the fortunes of war (a victorious Napoleon would certainly have got rid of the Hanoverians) or to good luck is open to debate. In one encapsulation of limited monarchy, the monarch is a figurehead symbolic of the nation. None of the Hanoverian monarchs considered themselves figureheads. None of them was specially able. The most imaginative of the monarchs of this period was George IV (1820–30) but his aesthetic sensibilities could not disguise either a total lack of political judgment or a wantonly lubricious career. He was a very bad king, understandably the butt of ribald humour wherever he went. His father, George III (1760–1820), was dutiful and was made into a plausible symbol of national unity during the early stages of the French Wars before progressive mental instability overtook him. George IV's younger brother, William IV (1830–37), had not anticipated becoming King and made very little impression, beyond that of well-meaning inadequacy. Victoria's (1837–1901) reign dominates our period. Monarchs who reign for a long time learn a lot and those who are conscientious can use their acquired knowledge effectively. Victoria learned much from her first Prime Minister, Melbourne, and more from her husband, Prince Albert. The good lessons they imparted were mostly absorbed although she remained selfish, partial (she loved Disraeli and hated Gladstone) and, when not in seclusion after Albert's premature death, generally bossier than a constitutional monarch should be. In her later years, however, she was turned into perhaps the ideal symbol of Empire. The monarchy looked immeasurably stronger on Victoria's death than it had at her accession.

The major policy changes of the nineteenth century reflected changed external circumstances rather than internal electoral pressure. Governments after 1815 responded to the first prolonged period of peace since the early seventeenth century by dismantling what has been called the British 'Fiscal-Military State'. This meant spending far less on defence, reducing taxation and balancing budgets. Mid-Victorian Britain became an age of *laissez-faire*. Governments, and most informed commentators outside parliament, came to believe in free trade as an article of faith and minimal government interference as the best way for individuals to achieve sturdy independence. For those who could not, or would not, be independent enough to provide for themselves and their families, a combination of charity and the new poor law – that bleakest and most discriminatory of safety blankets – was available. Self-confident and self-righteous in their assessment that the causes of poverty lay with individual failings much more than external circumstances, the Victorians made rigid distinctions about those in poverty. The 'deserving' poor were characterised as well-meaning folk temporarily fallen on hard times. Charity, sometimes on a relatively lavish scale, was available to put them back on their feet. For the 'undeserving' – the disorganised, drunken, feckless and spineless – conditions were to be made as uncomfortable as possible. They must learn the hard way that sturdy independence was the only route to self-respect and self-improvement. Harsh and crude though the diagnosis of the causes of poverty was and even harsher though poor-relief policies could be, in stark contrast to Ireland during the Famine, few in Victorian Britain starved.

Only towards the end of the nineteenth century did dominant perspectives begin to change, not least because harsher economic conditions and potent external competition were driving home the message that low taxation and *laissez-faire* were not enough. More systematic analyses of the causes of poverty were made which amply confirmed the fallibility of the distinction between the 'deserving' and the 'undeserving'. More began to recognise that economic prosperity in the hey-day of *laissez-faire* was heavily dependent upon Britain's virtual monopoly status in the 1850s and 1860s when it was the only developed industrial nation and when its navy ruled the seas, protecting overseas trading ventures. The absence of tariff walls seemed an inadequate route to prosperity, not least when many of Britain's competitors were busy building them up again. Out of a surprising mood of national introspection in the 1880s and 1890s came modest social welfare proposals in the early twentieth century: free school meals and school medical inspections; old age pensions and national insurance provision against sickness and unemployment. Seen in a broader perspective, these were limited, even grudging, initiatives. However, they would have been unthinkable thirty years earlier and they were clearly the forerunner of what emerged as the Welfare State some forty years later.

For all the emphasis on continuity of personnel and policy, the government which Asquith led to war in 1914 would have been unrecognisable to Pitt when he had done the same in 1793. Also, as late Victorian commentators were never reluctant to point out, dramatic changes had been effected in Britain without recourse to those revolutions which had so scarred most of the other nations of Europe.

For most ordinary people in Victorian Britain, the most important services were provided not by central government but by local agencies, including the local government radically reorganised by the Whig government's Municipal Corporations Act in 1835. Local government thereafter generally reflected the preferences of the ratepayers who elected the borough councils. Aldermen and local councillors knew that their electors would not permit extravagance or waste but they did spend council money on a range of services. Some, such as a clean water and a proper gas supply, could be matters of life and death to the poor. Others, such as expenditure on public libraries or swimming baths, were characteristic of that 'rational recreation' designed to inform the mind and safeguard the body. In the second half of the nineteenth century, substantial sums were being spent on a range of municipal buildings, particularly town halls, which were erected as symbols of civic pride and local identity.

Such expressions were important in enhancing a sense of civic identity and even engagement. Without a range of facilities coming directly into the home, respectable Victorians joined things. They became members of a wide variety of groups and societies which fostered interest in hobbies. Church or chapel attendance was almost obligatory for the respectable middle and working classes. The pastoral role of the clergy remained important in what was a dutifully religious age. Sports clubs, literary and debating societies thrived. The power of oratory was celebrated, and attendance to hear a good speaker address a political meeting at election time was often an occasion to anticipate with relish. It is true that many of these associational opportunities were more attractive to the bourgeoisie than to the working classes but the distinction should not be over-drawn. Among the most assiduous and conscientious self-improvers were skilled working men, determined to make the most of opportunities which came their way and anxious to show that they could hold their own in political discussions with their 'betters'. In their perception of what constituted 'respectability' – honesty, hard work, thrift, concern for the family, a desire to 'get on' – there was little to separate a regularly employed skilled worker from the bourgeoisie. Lower down the social scale, too, 'good neighbourliness' was an important aspect of Victorian values. The biblical exhortation to do unto others as you would be done by was taken literally. What might nowadays be called 'neighbourhood support systems' might have been informal but they mattered, especially at times of need or bereavement. As their effective interaction suggests, the Victorians almost certainly had a stronger sense of social identity than operates in the early twenty-first century.

It is important not to romanticise. Much of Victorian Britain was dirty, unhealthy and dangerous. However, between 1780 and 1914 Britain's population grew faster, and became much more mobile, than any before it. Despite the very large number of social casualties, society as a whole grew richer within a polity which managed and absorbed rapid change without dislocation. The complex, though in general stable, society which Britain had become by 1900 has probably never been better governed than it was in the late nineteenth and twentieth centuries. As was suggested earlier, though its living standards were to rise and ever more startling examples of material prosperity would characterise most aspects of its society, Britain's standing in the world was never higher than in the Victorian period. Its history richly repays the study it should still receive.

Notes

Chapter 1. A 'Greater Britain' in 1780? (page 3)

1 *Leeds Intelligencer*, 18 Dec. 1781, quoted in J. Black, *British Foreign Policy in an Age of Revolutions, 1783–1793* (Cambridge University Press, 1994), p. 11.

2 E. J. Evans, *The Forging of the Modern State: Early Industrial Britain, 1783–1870*, 3rd edn (Longman, London, 2001), p. 512.

3 E. J. Evans, 'Ambivalences of English Identity in the Eighteenth Century', in C. Bjorn, A. Grant and K. J. Stringer (eds), *Nations, Nationalism and Patriotism in the European Past* (Academic Press, Copenhagen, 1994), pp. 145–60.

4 Julian Hoppit, *Land of Liberty: England 1689–1727* (Clarendon Press, Oxford, 2000), p. 243.

5 Useful studies of the history of Wales include J. Davies, *A History of Wales* (Allen Lane, London, 1993), Geraint Jenkins, *A Concise History of Wales* (Cambridge University Press, 2007) and G. A. Williams, *When Was Wales? A History of the Welsh* (Black Raven Press, London, 1985).

6 For detailed treatment of Whigs and Tories, see Chapters 9 and 10.

7 Entries on Mostyn and Wynn in *Oxford Dictionary of National Biography* (Oxford University Press, 2004), Nos 19416 and 30155 respectively.

8 John Ker, Earl of Roxburghe, was created a Duke in 1707 and the Duke of Queensberry was able to add the English dukedom of Dover, among other English titles, to his Scottish ones. For a fresh interpretation of the Act of Union which places less stress on a Union 'bought and sold for English gold', as the Scottish poet Robert Burns later had it, see Allan Macinnes, *Union and Empire: The Making of the United Kingdom in 1707* (Cambridge University Press, 2007).

9 T. M. Devine, 'Scotland', in R. Floud and P. Johnson (eds), *The Cambridge Economic History of Modern Britain. Vol. 1, 1700–1860* (Cambridge University Press, 2004), p. 399.

10 P. Langford, *A Polite and Commercial People: England 1727–1783* (Clarendon Press, Oxford, 1998), p. 328.

11 Entry on Henry Dundas, *Oxford Dictionary of National Biography*, No. 8250.

12 This is a central element in the rich argument of L. Colley, *Britons: Forging the Nation, 1707–1837*, 2nd edn (Yale University Press, 2005).

13 The literature on Scotland in the eighteenth century is substantial. The following recent publications are useful: T. C. Smout (ed.), *Anglo-Scottish Relations from 1603 to 1900* (Oxford University Press, 2005); T. C. Smout, *A History of the Scottish People, 1560–1830*, 2nd edn (Fontana, London, 1998); T. M. Devine, 'The Modern Economy: Scotland and the Act of Union', in T. M. Devine, C. H. Lee and G. C. Peden (eds), *The Transformation of Scotland: The Economy* (Edinburgh University Press, 2005); T. M. Devine, *Scotland's Empire, 1600–1815* (Allen Lane, London, 2003); R. A. Houston and I. D. Whyte (eds), *Scottish Society, 1500–1800* (Cambridge University Press, 1989).

14 C. Knick Harley, 'Trade: Discovery, Mercantilism and Technology', in Floud and Johnson (eds), *Cambridge Economic History of Modern Britain. Vol. 1*, pp. 176–86.

15 James Walvin, 'The Slave Trade, Abolition and Public Memory', *Transactions of the Royal Historical Society*, 6th series, Vol. 19 (2009), pp. 139–49. On the role of the slave trade more generally see Kenneth Morgan, *Slavery and the British Empire* (Oxford University Press, 2007).

16 M. Dresser, *Slavery Obscured: The Social History of the Slave Trade in an English Provincial Port* (Leicester University Press, 2001). See also J. Longmore, 'Civic Liverpool, 1680–1800', in J. Belchem (ed.), *Liverpool 800: Culture, Character and History* (Liverpool University Press, 2006), pp. 113–70.

17 Devine, 'Scotland', pp. 402–3.

18 Evans, *Forging of the Modern State*, p. 515.

19 E. A. Wrigley, 'British Population during the "Long" Eighteenth Century', in Floud and Johnson (eds), *Cambridge Economic History of Modern Britain. Vol. 1*, p. 88.

20 J. Uglow, *The Lunar Men: The Friends Who Made the Future* (Faber & Faber, London, 2002).

21 On urban development in the eighteenth century, see P. Borsay, *The English Urban Renaissance: Culture and Society in the Provincial Town* (Oxford University Press, 1989) and R. Sweet, *The English Town, 1680–1840: Government, Society and Culture* (Longman, London, 1999).

22 R. C. Allen, 'Agriculture during the Industrial Revolution, 1700–1850', in Floud and Johnson (eds), *Cambridge Economic History of Modern Britain. Vol. 1*, pp. 97–8.

Chapter 2. The demographic revolution in Britain and Ireland (page 13)

1 200 Years of the Census in Wales http://www.statistics.gov.uk/census2001/bicentenary/pdfs/wales.pdf

2 The literature generated by demographic history is very large and sometimes very complex. Two works by N. Tranter, *Population Since the Industrial Revolution: The Case of England and Wales* (Barnes & Noble, London, 1973) and *Population and Society, 1780–1940* (Longman, Harlow, 1985), remain useful introductions. More detailed, and giving access to much technical information, are E. A. Wrigley, 'British Population during the "Long" Eighteenth Century, 1680–1840', in R. Floud and P. Johnson (eds), *The Cambridge Economic History of Modern Britain. Vol. 1, 1700–1860* (Cambridge University Press, 2004), pp. 57–95, R. Schofield, 'British Population Change, 1700–1871', in R. Floud and D. McCloskey (eds), *The Economic History of Britain since 1700. Vol. 1, 1700–1860*, 2nd edn (Cambridge University Press, 1994), pp. 60–95, and D. Baines, 'Population, Migration and Regional Development, 1870–1939', ibid., *Vol. 2, 1860 to the 1970s* (Cambridge University Press, 1981), pp. 29–61.

3 Wrigley, 'British Population', pp. 57–8.

4 Valuable studies of Ireland include R. F. Foster, *Modern Ireland, 1600–1972* (Penguin, London, 1989) and L. M. Cullen, *The Emergence of Modern Ireland 1600–1900* (Batsford, London, 1981). M. J. Winstanley, *Ireland and the Land Question, 1800–1922* (Routledge, London, 1984) offers an accessible introduction. For a valuable summary which focuses on the eighteenth century, see S. J. Connolly 'Eighteenth-Century Ireland', in D. G. Boyce and A. O'Day (eds), *The Making of Modern Irish History: Revisionism and the Revisionist Controversy* (Routledge, London, 1996).

5 For a full discussion of the methodological difficulties, see S. Daltrey, D. Dickson and C. Ó Gráda, 'Eighteenth-Century Irish Population from Old Sources', *Journal of Economic History*, 41 (1981), pp. 601–28.

6 For a chart of UK population change, see E. J. Evans, *The Forging of the Modern State: Early Industrial Britain, 1783–1870*, 3rd edn (Longman, London, 2001), p. 512.

7 W. E. Vaughan and A. J. Fitzpatrick (eds), *Irish Historical Statistics: Population 1821–71* (Royal Irish Academy, 1978).

8 C. Ó Gráda, 'A Note on Nineteenth-Century Emigration Statistics', *Population* Studies, 29 (1975), pp. 143–9.

9 Ibid., p. 146. See also J. Mokyr, *Why Ireland Starved: A Quantitative and Analytical History of the Irish Economy, 1800–1850* (Allen & Unwin, London, 1983).

10 L. Kennedy, *An Economic History of Ulster, 1820–1939* (Manchester University Press, 1985), p. 139.

11 G. T. Griffith, *Population Problems of the Age of Malthus* (Cambridge University Press, 1926), p. 42.

12 This research has also been enhanced by sophisticated statistical analysis. The evidence which follows is indebted to the work of E. A. Wrigley and particularly to that summarised in 'British Population', pp. 64–81.

13 P. Langford, *A Polite and Commercial People: England, 1727–1783* (Clarendon Press, Oxford, 1998), pp. 134–43.

14 S. Szreter and A. Hardy, 'Urban Fertility and Mortality Patterns', in M. Daunton (ed.), *The Cambridge Urban History of Britain, 1840–1950* (Cambridge University Press, 2000).

Chapter 3. Aristocracy rampant? (page 20)

1 James Mill, *Essays on Government, Jurisprudence, the Liberty of the Press* . . . (Longman, London, 1828).

2 J. Cannon, *Aristocratic Century* (Cambridge University Press, 1984), pp. 24–6.

3 J. V. Beckett, *The Aristocracy in England, 1660–1914* (Blackwell, Oxford, 1986), p. 487.

4 F. M. L. Thompson, *English Landed Society in the Nineteenth Century* (Routledge, London, 1963) and Beckett, *Aristocracy in England*.

5 E. J. Evans, *The Forging of the Modern State: Early Industrial Britain, 1783–1870*, 3rd edn (Longman, London, 2001), p. 9.

6 For a very useful summary of a complex debate on the ownership of land in the eighteenth century, see J. V. Beckett, 'English Landownership in the Later Seventeenth and Eighteenth Centuries: The Debate and the Problems', *Economic History Review*, new series, vol. 30 (1977), pp. 567–81. See also H. J. Habbakuk, 'The Rise and Fall of English Landed Families', *Transactions of the Royal Historical Society*, 5th series, Vol. 29 (1979), pp. 187–207, Vol. 30 (1980), pp. 199–221, and Vol. 31 (1981), pp. 195–217.

7 Cannon, *Aristocratic Century*, p. 71.

8 For specific details, see *ibid.*, pp. 71–92.

9 E. Richards, *Leviathan of Wealth: The Sutherland Fortune in the Industrial Revolution* (Routledge, London, 1973). See also entry on George Granville Leveson-Gower, No. 16539, in *Oxford Dictionary of National Biography* (Oxford University Press, 2004).

10 *ibid.*, entry on William Cavendish, No. 58758.

11 *ibid.*, entry on the fifth Duke of Bedford, No. 24308.

12 *ibid.*, No. 24322.

13 W. H. Hoskins, *Devon* (Phillimore, Chichester, 2003), pp. 486–8.

14 For specific information on London's architecture in the later eighteenth century, see S. O'Connell, *London, 1753* (British Museum Trustees, London, 2003), esp. pp. 160–237.

15 R. S. Neale, 'Bath: Ideology and Utopia', in P. Borsay (ed.), *The Eighteenth-Century Town* (Longman, London, 1990), pp. 223–42.

16 T. H. S. Escott in 1885, quoted in R. Trainor, 'Peers on an Industrial Frontier: The Earls of Dartmouth and of Dudley in the Black Country, *c*1810–1914', in D. Cannadine (ed.), *Patricians, Power and Politics in Nineteenth-Century Towns* (Leicester University Press, 1982), pp. 70–132.

17 J. Davies, 'Aristocratic Town-Makers and the Coal Metropolis: The Marquesses of Bute and the Growth of Cardiff, 1776–1947', *ibid.*, pp. 18–67. For the second marquess, see No. 37322 in *Oxford Dictionary of National Biography*.

18 D. Hunt, *A History of Preston*, 2nd edn (Carnegie Publishing, Lancaster, 2009), pp. 155–6. See also J. K. Walton, *Lancashire: A Social History, 1558–1939* (Manchester University Press, 1987).

19 Cannon, *Aristocratic Century*, p. 113.

20 Figures quoted in Beckett, *Aristocracy in England*, p. 433.

21 M. W. McCahill, 'Peers, Patronage and the Industrial Revolution, 1760–1800', *Journal of British Studies*, 16 (1976), pp. 84–107, esp. pp. 88–90.

22 See, for example, D. Hay, P. Linebaugh and E. P. Thompson (eds), *Albion's Fatal Tree: Crime and Society in Eighteenth-Century England* (Allen Lane, London, 1975), J. M. Beattie, *Crime and the Courts in England, 1660–1800* (Oxford University Press, 1986), J. S. Cockburn (ed.), *Crime in England, 1550–1800* (Methuen, London, 1977) and J. Brewer and J. Styles (eds), *An Ungovernable People: The English and their Law in the Seventeenth and Eighteenth Centuries* (Hutchinson, London, 1980).

23 For a fully researched, engaged and, in places, tendentious account of the passage of the Act and of its significance for relations in the countryside, see E. P. Thompson, *Whigs and Hunters: The Origins of the Black Act* (Allen Lane, London, 1975).

24 See E. P. Thompson, *Customs in Common* (Merlin Press, London, 1991).

25 J. Hoppit, *A Land of Liberty: England 1689–1727* (Oxford University Press, 2000), pp. 471–91.

26 Cannadine (ed.), *Patricians, Power and Politics*, p. 9.

Chapter 4. The role and impact of the middle classes (page 31)

1 B. A. Holderness, 'The English Land Market in the Eighteenth Century: The Case of Lincolnshire', *Economic History Review*, 2nd series, Vol. 27 (1974), pp. 557–76.

2 Eric Richards, *Leviathan of Wealth* (Routledge, London, 1973) and *Oxford Dictionary of National Biography* (Oxford University Press, 2004), No. 16883.

3 See, for example, P. Langford, *A Polite and Commercial People: England, 1727–1783* (Clarendon Press, Oxford, 1998), pp. 62–3, and R. Sweet, *The English Town, 1680–1840: Government, Society and Culture* (Longman, Harlow, 1999), pp. 179–81.

4 See the analysis of the categorisations and calculations made by Patrick Colquhoun in 1801–3 in B. Hilton, *A Mad, Bad and Dangerous People? England 1783–1846* (Clarendon Press, Oxford, 2006), pp. 125–9.

5 *ibid.*, p. 129.

6 W. Rubinstein, *Men of Property: The Very Wealthy in Britain since the Industrial Revolution* (Croom Helm, Beckenham, 1981) and W. Rubinstein, *Who Were the Rich? 1809–39. Vol. 1, A Biographical Dictionary of British Wealth Holders* (Social Affairs Unit, London, 2009).

7 Most of the information which follows is taken from the *Oxford Dictionary of National Biography* No. 1382.

8 Hilton, *A Mad, Bad and Dangerous People?*, p. 155.

9 Figures taken from J. Gregory and J. Stevenson, *The Longman Companion to Britain in the Eighteenth Century* (Longman, London, 2000) and C. Cook, *The Longman Companion to Britain in the Nineteenth Century* (Longman, London, 1999).

10 For key contributions to the debate on 'the Fiscal-Military State' see J. Brewer, *The Sinews of Power: War, Money and the English State, 1688–1783* (Routledge, London, 1989) and P. Harling and P. Mandler, 'From "Fiscal-Military" State to Laissez-Faire State, 1760–1850', *Journal of British Studies*, 32 (1993), pp. 44–70.

11 Quoted in S. Brown, '"A Just and Profitable Commerce": Moral Economy and the Middle Classes in Eighteenth-Century London', *Journal of British Studies*, 32 (1993), pp. 305–32.

12 L. Davidoff, 'The Family in Britain', in F. M. L. Thompson (ed.), *The Cambridge Social History of Britain, 1750–1950. Vol. 2* (Cambridge University Press, 1990), pp. 71–130; F. M. L. Thompson, 'Town and City', *ibid.*, Vol. 1, pp. 1–86; and D. J. Rowe, 'The North-East', *ibid.*, Vol. 1, pp. 452–3.

13 N. McKendrick, J. Brewer and J. H. Plumb (eds), *The Birth of a Consumer Society: The Commercialisation of Eighteenth-Century England* (Harper Collins, London, 1984).

14 P. Borsay, 'The Culture of Improvement', in P. Langford (ed.), *The Eighteenth Century, 1688–1815* (Oxford University Press, 2002), p. 194.

15 Langford, *A Polite and Commercial People*, p. 83.

16 L. Davidoff, 'The Family in Britain', in Thompson (ed.), *Cambridge Social History of Britain, 1750–1950. Vol. 2*, pp. 78–81.

17 P. Hudson, 'Industrial Organisation and Structure', in R. Floud and P. Johnson (eds), *The Cambridge Economic History of Modern Britain. Vol. 1, 1700–1860* (Cambridge University Press, 2004), pp. 50–1.

18 Figures from E. J. Evans, *The Forging of the Modern State: Early Industrial Britain, 1783–1870*, 3rd edn (Longman, London, 2001), pp. 532–3.

19 The key elements are summarised in Sweet, *English Town*, p. 185. See also J. Innes, 'Politics and Morals: The Reformation of Manners Movement in Later Eighteenth-Century England', in E. Hellmuth (ed.), *The Transformation of Provincial Culture* (Oxford University Press, 1990), pp. 57–118.

20 H. Byerly Thomson, *The Choice of a Profession: A Concise Account and Comparative View of the English Professions* (London, 1857), quoted in P. Corfield, *Power and the Professions in England, 1700–1850* (Routledge, London, 1995), p. 200.

21 H. T. Dickinson, *Caricatures and the Constitution, 1760–1832* (Chadwyck Healey, Cambridge, 1986), F. G. Stephens and M. D. George (eds), *Catalogue of Personal and Political Satires*, 11 vols (British Museum Publications, 1978) and D. Alexander, *Richard Newton and English Caricature in the 1790s* (Whitworth Art Gallery, Manchester, 1998). On clerical magistrates, see E. J. Evans, 'Some Reasons for the Growth of English Rural Anti-Clericalism', *Past & Present*, 66 (1975), pp. 84–109.

22 P. Schlicke (ed.), *Oxford Reader's Companion to Dickens* (Oxford University Press, 1999).

23 Corfield, *Power and the Professions*, pp. 81, 91.

24 *ibid.*, p. 160. See also her wider treatment of the medical profession on pp. 137–73.

25 Hilton, *A Mad, Bad and Dangerous People?*, p. 160.

26 *ibid.*, pp. 145–52.

27 In a speech to the House of Commons in December 1819, quoted in Sweet, *English Town*, p. 179.

28 In an article in the journal *Westminster Review* in 1824. Quoted in D. Wahrman, *Imagining the Middle Class: The Political Representation of Class in Britain* (Cambridge University Press, 1995), p. 259.

29 Brown, ' "A Just and Profitable Commerce" ', p. 328.

30 D. R. Fisher (ed.), *The House of Commons, 1820–32. Vol. 1* (Cambridge University Press, 2009), pp. 247–8.

Chapter 5. Industrial revolution or industrial evolution? (page 42)

1 The historian was Arnold Toynbee and the phrase first came into common usage in his *Lectures on the Industrial Revolution in England* (London, 1884).

2 On road transport see W. Albert, *The Turnpike Road System in England, 1663–1840* (Cambridge University Press, 1972). For general studies of changes in transport, see P. Bagwell, *The Transport Revolution* (Routledge, London, 1988) and D. Aldcroft and M. Freeman (eds), *Transport in the Industrial Revolution* (Manchester University Press, 1983).

3 J. Gregory and J. Stevenson (eds), *Britain in the Eighteenth Century, 1688–1820* (Longman, London, 2000), p. 277.

4 M. J. Daunton, *Progress and Poverty: An Economic and Social History of Britain, 1700–1850* (Oxford University Press, 1995), p. 136.

(pp. 43–50)

5 H. J. Perkin, *The Origins of Modern English Society, 1780–1880* (Routledge, London, 1969), p. 3.

6 J. Mokyr (ed.), *The Economics of the Industrial Revolution* (Allen & Unwin, London, 1985), pp. 3–4.

7 S. Pollard, 'Industrialization and the European Economy', *ibid.*, p. 166. See also N. F. R. Crafts, 'Industrial Revolution in England and France', who argues that 'the question "Why was England first?" is misconceived' (*ibid.*, p. 124).

8 R. C. Allen, *The British Industrial Revolution in Global Perspective* (Cambridge University Press, 2009), ch. 4, esp. pp. 120–33.

9 Daunton, *Progress and Poverty*, p. 137. See also E. A. Wrigley, *People, Cities and Wealth: The Transformation of Traditional Society* (Wiley-Blackwell, Oxford, 1987), p. 179.

10 The title of the volume covering 1689–1727 by Julian Hoppit in the New Oxford History of England series. Significantly, Hoppit follows his main title with a question mark.

11 By the Bill of Rights of 1689 and the Act of Settlement of 1701.

12 Crafts, 'Industrial Revolution in England and France', p. 128.

13 In a book first published in 1948. For a modern revision, see T. S. Ashton, *The Industrial Revolution, 1760–1830* (1997 edn, with introduction by P. Hudson). The quotation appears on p. 48.

14 Figures of this order were calculated in P. Deane and W. A. Cole, *British Economic Growth, 1688–1959* (Cambridge University Press, 1967).

15 W. W. Rostow, 'The Take-Off into Self-Sustained Growth', *The Economic Journal*, 66 (1956), pp. 25–48. The selected quotation appears on p. 25.

16 The literature on this is considerable and much of it is highly technical. It can be followed in N. F. R. Crafts, 'English Economic Growth in the Eighteenth Century: A Re-Examination of Deane and Cole's Estimates', *Economic History Review*, 29 (1976), pp. 226–35, and *British Economic Growth During the Industrial Revolution* (Oxford University Press, 1985); C. K. Harley, 'Reassessing the Industrial Revolution', in J. Mokyr, *The British Industrial Revolution: An Economic Perspective*, 2nd edn (Westview Press, Boulder, Colo., 1999); C. K. Harley and N. F. R. Crafts, 'Simulating Two Views of the British Industrial Revolution', *Journal of Economic History*, 60 (2000), pp. 819–41.

17 Comparator figures are put together in Daunton, *Progress and Poverty*, p. 126.

18 N. F. R. Crafts and C. K. Harley, 'Output Growth and the British Industrial Revolution', *Economic History Review*, 45 (1992), p. 705.

19 D. McCloskey, 'The Industrial Revolution, 1780–1860: A Survey', in R. Floud and D. McCloskey (eds), *The Economic History of Britain since 1700. Vol. 1, 1700–1860* (Cambridge University Press, 1981), p. 109.

20 R. V. Jackson, 'Rates of Growth during the Industrial Revolution', *Economic History Review*, 45 (1992), pp. 1–23. The specific quotation cited is located on p. 21.

21 M. Berg and P. Hudson, 'Rehabilitating the Industrial Revolution', *Economic History Review*, 45 (1992), pp. 24–50. The cited quotations are on p. 39.

22 Daunton, *Progress and Poverty*, pp. 131–6.

23 Quoted in Berg and Hudson, 'Rehabilitating the Industrial Revolution', p. 26.

24 K. Morgan (ed.), *An American Quaker in the British Isles: The Travel Journals of Jabez Maud Fisher* (Oxford University Press, 1992), p. 265. See also K. Morgan, *The Birth of Industrial Britain* (Longman Seminar Studies, London, 1999), pp. 107–8.

25 W. Hardy, *The Origins of the Idea of the Industrial Revolution* (Trafford Publishing, Oxford, 2006).

26 P. K. O'Brien, 'The Industrial Revolution: A Historiographical Survey', quoted in Crafts and Harley, 'Output Growth', p. 704.

27 D. Landes, 'The Fable of the Dead Horse, or the Industrial Revolution Revisited', in Mokyr (ed.), *British Industrial Revolution*, pp. 132–70. For a discussion of this aspect of the revolution, see S. King and G. Timmins, *Making Sense of the Industrial Revolution* (Manchester University Press, 2001), pp. 10–32.

28 Crafts and Harley, 'Output Growth', p. 705.

Chapter 6. Urban growth, industrial development and regional diversity (page 51)

1 E. A. Wrigley, 'British Population during the "Long" Eighteenth Century, 1680–1840' in R. Floud and P. Johnson (eds), *The Cambridge Economic History of Modern Britain. Vol. 1, 1700–1860* (Cambridge University Press, 2004), p. 88.

2 F. M. L. Thompson 'Town and City', in F. M. L. Thompson (ed.), *The Cambridge Social History of Britain, 1750–1950. Vol. 2* (Cambridge University Press, 1990), p. 8.

3 *ibid.*, p. 15.

4 T. Devine, 'Scotland', in Floud and Johnson (eds), *Cambridge Economic History of Modern Britain. Vol. 1*, p. 403.

5 The statistics on which this section is based come from Wrigley, 'British Population'; P. Corfield, *The Impact of English Towns, 1700–1800* (Oxford University Press, 1982); J. Gregory and J. Stevenson, *The Longman Companion to Britain in the Eighteenth Century* (Longman, London, 1999); C. Cook, *The Longman Companion to Britain in the Nineteenth Century* (Longman, London, 1999); N. C. Fleming and A. O'Day, *The Longman Companion to Irish History since 1800* (Longman, London, 2005), pp. 489–502; and E. J. Evans, *The Forging of the Modern State: Early Industrial Britain, 1783–1870*, 3rd edn (Longman, London, 2001), pp. 512–20.

6 P. Brandon and B. Short, *The South-East from AD 1000* (Longman, London, 1990), p. 257.

7 J. R. Martin, *Report on the Sanitary Condition of Nottingham, Coventry [etc.]* (London, 1845), p. 250.

8 J. V. Beckett, *The East Midlands from AD 1000* (Longman, Harlow, 1988), p. 233.

9 R. Mitchison, 'Scotland, 1750–1850' in Thompson (ed.), *Cambridge Social History of Britain. Vol. 1*, p. 183.

10 C. B. Phillips and J. H. Smith, *Lancashire and Cheshire from AD 1540* (Longman, Harlow, 1994), pp. 139–40.

11 Figures from P. Hudson, *The Genesis of Industrial Capital: A Study of the West Riding Wool Textile Industry* (Cambridge University Press, 1986), cited in S. King and G. Timmins, *Making Sense of the Industrial Revolution: English Economy and Society, 1700–1850* (Manchester University Press, 2001), p. 51.

12 D. Hey, *Yorkshire from AD 1000* (Longman, Harlow, 1986), p. 237.

13 M. J. Daunton, *Progress and Poverty: An Economic and Social History of Britain, 1700–1850* (Oxford University Press, 1995), pp. 175–8.

14 Evans, *Forging of the Modern State*, p. 508.

15 M. W. Flinn, *The History of the British Coal Industry. Vol. 2, 1700–1830* (Clarendon Press, Oxford, 1982) and figures cited in Daunton, *Progress and Poverty*, p. 220.

16 M. Rowlands, *The West Midlands from AD 1000* (Longman, Harlow, 1987), pp. 236–7.

17 *ibid.*, pp. 243–5.

18 Daunton, *Progress and Poverty*, p. 232.

19 D. J. Rowe, 'The North-East', in Thompson (ed.), *Cambridge Social History of Britain. Vol. 1*, p. 424.

20 Phillips and Smith, *Lancashire and Cheshire from AD 1540*, p. 183.

21 Hey, *Yorkshire from AD 1000*, p. 278.

22 V. A. C. Gatrell, 'Labour, Power and the Size of Firms in Lancashire Cotton in the Second Quarter of the Nineteenth Century', *Economic History Review*, 2nd series, 30 (1977), p. 98.

23 P. Hudson, 'Industrial Organisation and Structure', in Floud and Johnson (eds), *Cambridge Economic History of Modern Britain. Vol. 1*, p. 37.

24 P. Borsay, 'Urban Life and Culture', in H. T. Dickinson (ed.), *A Companion to Eighteenth-Century Britain* (Blackwell, Oxford, 2002), p. 202.

25 Thompson, 'Town and City', p. 18; P. Langford, *A Polite and Commercial People: England, 1727–83* (Clarendon Press, Oxford, 1998), pp. 420–1.

26 As, for example, Shute Barrington, Bishop of Salisbury 1782–91 and later Bishop of Durham. Barrington's elder brother, William, who succeeded to a viscountcy on their father's early death in an accident, was in 1759 Secretary at War in the Duke of Newcastle's administration and used his position to secure Shute's early promotion within the Church. *Oxford Dictionary of National Biography* (Oxford University Press, 2004), No. 1534.

27 R. Sweet, *The English Town, 1680–1840: Government, Society and Culture* (Longman, London, 1999), p. 24.

Chapter 7. Agriculture in the early industrial age (page 62)

1 M. Overton, 'Land and Labour Productivity in English Agriculture, 1650–1850', in P. Mathias (ed.), *Agriculture and Industrialization from the Eighteenth Century to the Present Day* (Blackwell, Oxford, 1996), p. 18.

2 The classic study on Britain's supposed agricultural revolution is J. D. Chambers and G. E. Mingay, *The Agricultural Revolution, 1750–1880* (Batsford, London, 1966). For a discussion on the validity of the term, see J. V. Beckett, *The Agricultural Revolution* (Wiley-Blackwell, Oxford, 1990) and M. Overton, 'Re-Establishing the English Agricultural Revolution', *Agricultural History Review*, 43 (1996), pp. 1–20.

3 M. J. Daunton, *Progress and Poverty: An Economic and Social History of Britain, 1700–1850* (Oxford University Press, 1995), pp. 34–5. See also R. C. Allen, 'Agriculture during the Industrial Revolution', in R. Floud and P. Johnson (eds), *The Cambridge Economic History of Modern Britain. Vol. 1, 1700–1860* (Cambridge University Press, 2004), pp. 97–103, and R. C. Allen, *The British Industrial Revolution in Global Perspective* (Cambridge University Press, 2009).

4 G. E. Mingay (ed.), *The Agrarian History of England and Wales. Vol. 6, 1700–1850* (Cambridge University Press, 1989), p. 953.

5 The most detailed study of agriculture in this period is Mingay (ed.), *Agrarian History. Vol. 6.*

6 J. V. Beckett, 'Landownership and Estate Management', ibid., pp. 570–1.

7 A. Kussmaul, *Servants in Husbandry in Early Modern England* (Cambridge University Press, 1981) and W. A. Armstrong, 'The Countryside', in F. M. L. Thompson (ed.), *The Cambridge Social History of Britain, 1750–1950. Vol. 1* (Cambridge University Press, 1990), pp. 91–2.

8 E. L. Jones, 'The Agricultural Labour Market, 1793–1872', *Economic History Review*, 2nd series, 18 (1964–5), pp. 332–8.

9 Armstrong, 'The Countryside', pp. 101–2.

10 E. J. Evans, *The Forging of the Modern State: Early Industrial Britain, 1783–1870*, 3rd edn (Longman, London, 2001), p. 181.

11 Allen, 'Agriculture during the Industrial Revolution', p. 116.

12 *ibid.*, p. 115.

13 K. Honeyman, *Women, Gender and Industrialisation in England, 1700–1870* (Macmillan, Basingstoke, 2000), pp. 75–6.

14 A. Peacock, *Bread or Blood: The Agrarian Riots in East Anglia, 1816* (Gollancz, London, 1965).

15 E. J. Hobsbawm and G. Rudé, *Captain Swing* (Lawrence & Wishart, London, 1969); K. D. M. Snell, *Annals of the Labouring Poor: Social Change and Agrarian England* (Cambridge University Press, 1985), esp. pp. 220–9.

16 B. Hilton, *A Mad, Bad and Dangerous People? England, 1783–1846* (Clarendon Press, Oxford, 2006), p. 135.

17 Armstrong, 'The Countryside', p. 98.

18 G. E. Mingay, 'Agriculture and Rural Life', in H. T. Dickinson (ed.), *A Companion to Eighteenth-Century Britain* (Blackwell, Oxford, 2002), p. 141.

19 Daunton, *Progress and Poverty*, p. 324. The definitive history of brewing remains P. Mathias, *The Brewing Industry in England, 1700–1830* (Cambridge University Press, 1959).
20 For the relative production and beer stock figures of Barclay and Truman, see *ibid.*, p. 77.
21 *ibid.*, p. 176.
22 Armstrong, 'The Countryside', pp. 116–17, and Daunton, *Progress and Poverty*, p. 325.
23 I. Donnachie, *A History of the Brewing Industry in Scotland* (John Donald, Edinburgh, 1979), pp. 113–16 and 145–59.
24 A. Young, *General Report on Enclosures* (1808), quoted in Daunton, *Progress and Poverty*, p. 114.
25 E. J. Evans, *The Contentious Tithe: The Tithe Problem and English Agriculture, 1750–1850* (Routledge, London, 1976), pp. 94–114.
26 Chambers and Mingay, *Agricultural Revolution*, p. 84.
27 *ibid.*, p. 85.
28 M. E. Turner, *Parliamentary Enclosure: Its Historical Geography and Economic History* (Archon Books, Folkestone, 1980), p. 62.
29 For more detail on the enclosure movement, see Chambers and Mingay, *Agricultural Revolution*, pp. 77–105.
30 E. P. Thompson, *The Making of the English Working Class* (Penguin edn, London, 1968), p. 237.
31 The most developed arguments on the allegedly devastating effects of enclosure are found in J. Neeson, *Commoners: Common Rights, Enclosure and Social Change in England* (Cambridge University Press, 1993) and E. P. Thompson, *Customs in Common* (Penguin, London, 1993).
32 S. King and G. Timmins, *Making Sense of the Industrial Revolution: English Economy and Society 1700–1850* (Manchester University Press, 2001), pp. 185–9.
33 L. Shaw-Taylor, 'Labourers, Cows, Common Rights and Parliamentary Enclosure: The Evidence of Contemporary Comment, *c.*1760–1810', *Past & Present*, 171 (2001), pp. 95–126.
34 R. C. Allen, 'Tracking the Agricultural Revolution', *Economic History Review*, 52 (1999), pp. 209–35, and R. C. Allen, 'Agriculture during the Industrial Revolution', in Floud and Johnson (eds), *Cambridge Economic History of Modern Britain. Vol. 1*, pp. 96–116.

Chapter 8. Industrialism: impact and conflict (page 73)

1 L. Davidoff, 'The Family', in F. M. L. Thompson (ed.), *The Cambridge Social History of Britain, 1750–1950. Vol. 2* (Cambridge University Press, 1990), pp. 92–3.
2 J. Rule, *The Labouring Classes in Early Industrial England, 1750–1850* (Longman, London, 1986), p. 11.
3 P. Joyce, 'Work', in Thompson (ed.), *Cambridge Social History of Britain. Vol. 2*, pp. 148–51.
4 Henry Ashworth, *Letter to Lord Ashley on the Cotton Factory Question* (Manchester, 1833), pp. 13, 16–17.
5 Quoted in M. J. Daunton, *Progress and Poverty: An Economic and Social History of Britain, 1700–1850* (Oxford University Press, 1995), pp. 181–2.
6 *ibid.*, pp. 497–8. See also A. Randall, *Before the Luddites: Custom, Community and Machinery in the English Woollen Industry, 1776–1809* (Cambridge University Press, 1991).
7 Rule, *Labouring Classes*, p. 367.
8 The leading proponent of the view that a well-developed revolutionary underground was in place in Yorkshire and Lancashire is E. P. Thompson, *The Making of the English Working Class* (Penguin edn, London, 1963), pp. 569–659. The case for seeing Luddism as a primarily industrial movement throughout is developed in M. I. Thomis, *The Luddites: Machine Breaking in Regency England* (David & Charles, Newton Abbot, 1970) and M. I. Thomis, *Threats of Revolution in Britain* (Macmillan, Basingstoke, 1977).

9 A judicious selection of early contributions to the debate can be found in A. J. Taylor (ed.), *The Standard of Living Controversy in Britain in the Industrial Revolution* (Methuen, London, 1975).

10 P. Lindert and J. Williamson, 'English Workers' Living Standards during the Industrial Revolution: A New Look', *Economic History Review*, 36 (1983), pp. 1–25.

11 J. Mokyr, 'Is There Still Life in the Pessimist Case? Consumption during the Industrial Revolution, 1790–1850', *Journal of Economic History*, 481 (1988), pp. 69–92.

12 Perhaps the best brief discussion of this complex area is H.-J. Voth, 'Living Standards and the Urban Environment', in R. Floud and P. Johnson (eds), *The Cambridge Economic History of Modern Britain. Vol. 1, 1700–1860* (Cambridge University Press, 2004), pp. 268–94. See also Daunton, *Progress and Poverty*, pp. 420–46.

13 Thompson, *Making of the English Working Class* (Penguin edn, 1968), p. 366.

14 The pre-eminent Marxist analysis is that by Thompson, *Making of the English Working Class*, while H. J. Perkin, *The Origins of Modern English Society, 1780–1880* (Routledge, London, 1969) offers an innovative interpretation from a non-Marxist perspective and based on identification of separate 'aristocratic', 'middle-class' and 'working-class' ideals. For a more recent discussion of the debate, see D. Cannadine, *Class in Britain* (Yale University Press, London, 1999), pp. 57–105.

15 Edmund Burke, *Reflections on the Revolution in France* (London, 1790). The quotations from Burke are taken from *Works of Edmund Burke* (Rivington edn, London, 1826), Vol. 5. These are directly cited in J. G. A. Pocock, 'The Political Economy of Burke's Analysis of the French Revolution', *Historical Journal*, 25 (1982), pp. 331–49.

16 Cannadine, *Class in Britain*, pp. 71–2. See also D. Wahrman, *Imagining the Middle Class: The Political Representation of Class in Britain, c1780–1840* (Cambridge University Press, 1995).

17 As in Leeds: see R. J. Morris, *Class, Sect and Party: The Making of the British Middle Class, Leeds 1820–50* (Manchester University Press, 1990).

18 Thompson, *Making of the English Working Class*, p. 64; Perkin, *Origins of Modern English Society*, pp. 176–217.

19 G. Williams, *The Merthyr Rising* (Croom Helm, Beckenham, 1978), p. 225.

20 *Oxford Dictionary of National Biography* (Oxford University Press, 2004), entry on William Crawshay, No. 6656.

21 E. H. Hunt, *British Labour History, 1815–1914* (Weidenfeld & Nicolson, London, 1981).

22 E. J. Evans, *Chartism* (Longman, London, 2000), p. 19. For an excellent modern overview of Chartism, see M. Chase, *Chartism: A New History* (Manchester University Press, 2007).

Chapter 9. Government in crisis: the impact of the war for America (page 85)

1 For a study of Britain's eighteenth-century wars down to the loss of America, see B. Simms, *Three Victories and a Defeat: The Rise and Fall of the First British Empire, 1714–83* (Allen Lane, London, 2007).

2 H. M. Scott, *British Foreign Policy in the Age of the American Revolution* (Oxford University Press, 1990), pp. 339–40.

3 For reliable accounts of the politics of the period before 1780, see P. Langford, *A Polite and Commercial People: England 1727–1783* (Clarendon Press, Oxford, 1998) and G. Holmes and D. Szechi, *The Age of Oligarchy: Pre-Industrial Britain, 1727–83* (Longman, Harlow, 1993).

4 P. Jupp, *The Governing of Britain, 1688–1848* (Routledge, London, 2006), pp. 118–19.

5 I. R. Christie, 'Economical Reform and the "Influence of the Crown" 1780', *Cambridge Historical Journal*, 12 (1956), pp. 144–54. As Baron Ashburton, Dunning later served as Chancellor of the Duchy of Lancaster in the Shelburne administration.

6 *Oxford Dictionary of National Biography* (Oxford University Press, 2004), William Petty, No. 22070.

 7 Langford, *A Polite and Commercial People*, pp. 556–7.
 8 M. Duffy, *The Younger Pitt* (Longman Pearson, Harlow, 2000), p. 15.
 9 M. Turner, *Pitt the Younger: A Life* (Hambledon, London, 2003), pp. 46–7.
10 In a letter to the Duke of Rutland, 22 Nov. 1783, quoted *ibid.*, p. 16.
11 J. Ehrman, *The Younger Pitt. Vol. 1, The Years of Acclaim* (Constable, London, 1969), p. 127.
12 In the House of Commons, 17 Dec. 1783, quoted in *Oxford Dictionary of National Biography*, entry on Fox, No. 10024.
13 For more detail on this murky affair, see W. Hague, *William Pitt the Younger* (Harper Perennial edn, London, 2005), pp. 14–16.
14 Quoted in Duffy, *The Younger Pitt*, p. 166.
15 J. Williams, *British Commercial Policy and Trade Expansion, 1750–1850* (Clarendon Press, Oxford, 1972), p. 218.
16 L. Colley, *Captives: Britain, Empire and the World, 1600–1850* (Pantheon Books, New York, 2002).
17 Holmes and Szechi, *Age of Oligarchy*, p. 338.
18 C. Knick Harley, 'Trade: Discovery, Mercantilism and Technology', in R. Floud and P. Johnson (eds), *The Cambridge Economic History of Modern Britain. Vol. 1, 1700–1860* (Cambridge University Press, 2004), pp. 181–7.
19 House of Commons debate, 11 Apr. 1786, quoted in J. Ehrman, *The Younger Pitt. Vol. 1, The Years of Acclaim* (Constable, London, 1969), p. 338.
20 Williams, *British Commercial Policy*, p. 228.
21 Ehrman, *The Younger Pitt. Vol. 2*, pp. 512–16.
22 Williams, *British Commercial Policy*, p. 228. Calculations of British imports and exports are from R. Davis, *The Industrial Revolution and British Overseas Trade* (Cassell, London, 1979), pp. 94–109.
23 C. A. Bayly, *Imperial Meridian: The British Empire and the World* (Longman, Harlow, 1989), p. 98.

Chapter 10. National revival? Britain, 1783–1793 (page 95)

 1 J. Ehrman, *The Younger Pitt. Vol. 1, The Years of Acclaim* (Constable, London, 1969), p. 70.
 2 For specific details, see E. J. Evans, *The Forging of the Modern State: Early Industrial Britain, 1783–1870*, 3rd edn (Longman, London, 2001), p. 479.
 3 W. Hague, *William Pitt the Younger* (Harper Perennial edn, London, 2005), p. 154.
 4 M. J. Turner, *Pitt the Younger: A Life* (Hambledon, London, 2003), p. 57.
 5 B. Hilton, *A Mad, Bad and Dangerous People? England 1783–1846* (Clarendon Press, Oxford, 2006), p. 114.
 6 Quoted in Ehrman, *The Younger Pitt. Vol. 1*, p. 158.
 7 J. Torrance, 'Social Class and Bureaucratic Innovation: The Commissioners for Examining the Public Accounts', *Past & Present*, 78 (1978), pp. 56–81 and Hilton, *A Mad, Bad and Dangerous People?*, pp. 119–20.
 8 E. J. Evans, *William Pitt the Younger* (Routledge, London, 1999), p. 18.
 9 Hague, *William Pitt the Younger*, p. 181.
10 M. Duffy, *The Younger Pitt* (Longman Pearson, Harlow, 2000), pp. 81–2.
11 Entry on Horace Walpole, *Oxford Dictionary of National Biography* (Oxford, 2004), No. 28596.
12 Ehrman, *The Younger Pitt. Vol. 1*, pp. 288–91.
13 Charles Middleton, First Baron Barham *Oxford Dictionary of National Biography*, No. 18666.
14 J. Black, *British Foreign Policy in an Age of Revolutions, 1783–93* (Cambridge University Press, 1994), p. 13.
15 *ibid.*, pp. 43–4.
16 J. Holland Rose, *William Pitt and National Revival* (Bell, London, 1911), pp. 179–87.

474 Notes (pp. 104–16)

17 Duffy, *The Younger Pitt*, p. 279.
18 Hague, *William Pitt the Younger*, p. 585.
19 R. Davis, *The Industrial Revolution and British Overseas Trade* (Leicester University Press, 1979), pp. 94–109.
20 J. Mori, *William Pitt and the French Revolution* (Keele University Press, Edinburgh, 1997), p. 26.
21 Ehrman, *The Younger Pitt. Vol. 1*, p. 644.

Chapter 11. Britain in the 1790s: the impact of the French Revolution (page 107)

1 Lord John Russell, *Life and Times of Charles James Fox. Vol. 2* (London, 1859), p. 361.
2 For a discussion of the various meanings of 'reform', see J. Innes, ' "Reform" in English Public Life', in A. Burns and J. Innes (eds), *Rethinking the Age of Reform: Britain, 1780–1850* (Cambridge University Press, 2003), pp. 71–97.
3 T. Paine, *The Rights of Man* (Everyman edn, London, 1915), pp. 61–3.
4 Quoted in E. P. Thompson, *The Making of the English Working Class* (Penguin edn, London, 1968), p. 119.
5 H. T. Dickinson, *British Radicalism and the French Revolution* (Wiley-Blackwell, Oxford, 1985), and 'Popular Politics and Radical Ideas' in H. T. Dickinson (ed.), *A Companion to Eighteenth-Century Britain* (Blackwell, Oxford, 2002), pp. 97–111.
6 *Oxford Dictionary of National Biography* (Oxford, 2004), entries on Palmer (No. 21220) and Margarot (No. 63599).
7 B. Hilton, *A Mad, Bad and Dangerous People? England 1783–1846* (Clarendon Press, Oxford, 2006), p. 62.
8 L. G. Mitchell, *The Writings and Speeches of Edmund Burke. Vol. viii, The French Revolution, 1790–1794* (Clarendon Press, Oxford, 1989), p. 100.
9 L. Mitchell, *Charles James Fox* (Oxford University Press, 1992), p. 114.
10 *ibid.*, p. 127.
11 M. Turner, *Pitt the Younger: A Life* (Hambledon, London, 2003), p. 169.
12 E. V. Macleod, *A War of Ideas: British Attitudes to the Wars against Revolutionary France* (Ashgate, Aldershot, 1998).
13 For further details, see Thompson, *Making of the English Working Class*, pp. 521–8.
14 Plausible speculations on the extent of revolutionary activity in this period in the almost total absence of reliable evidence are offered by E. Royle, *Revolutionary Britannia: Reflections on the Threat of Revolution in Britain, 1789–1848* (Manchester University Press, 2000), pp. 26–35. See also E. V. Macleod, 'The Crisis of the French Revolution', in Dickinson (ed.), *Companion to Eighteenth-Century Britain*, pp. 118–24.
15 H. Dickinson, 'Popular Conservatism and Militant Loyalism', in H. Dickinson (ed.), *Britain and the French Revolution, 1789–1815* (Macmillan, Basingstoke, 1989), p. 114.
16 M. Philp, 'Vulgar Conservatism, 1792–3', *English Historical Review*, 110 (1995), pp. 42–69; O. Smith, *The Politics of Language, 1791–1819* (Oxford University Press, 1984), ch. 3 and esp. p. 76.
17 Macleod, *A War of Ideas*, p. 122; L. Colley, *Britons: Forging the Nation, 1714–1837* (Yale University Press, New Haven, 1992), p. 305.
18 *Oxford Dictionary of National Biography* (Oxford University Press, 2004), entry on George Canning, No. 4556.
19 Royle, *Revolutionary Britannia*, p. 166.
20 William Wilberforce, *A Practical View of the Prevailing Religious System of Professed Christians in the Higher and Middle Classes of this Country contrasted with Real Christianity* (London, 1797), quoted

in H. Perkin, *The Origins of Modern English Society, 1780–1880* (Routledge, London, 1969), pp. 280–6; William Hague, *William Wilberforce* (Harper Press, London, 2007). For the impact of Evangelicalism as a whole, see G. M. Ditchfield, *The Evangelical Revival* (Routledge, London, 1998) and D. W. Bebbington, *Evangelicalism in Modern Britain: A History from the 1730s to the 1980s* (Unwin Hyman, London, 1989).

Chapter 12. The French Revolutionary Wars, 1793–1801 (page 118)

1 Speech in the Commons, quoted in J. Ehrman, *The Younger Pitt. Vol. 2, The Reluctant Transition* (Constable, London, 1983), p. 47.
2 For details of the diplomatic events of 1792, see J. Mori, *William Pitt and the French Revolution, 1785–1795* (Keele University Press, Edinburgh, 1997), pp. 108–42, and J. Black, *British Foreign Policy in an Age of Revolutions* (Cambridge University Press, 1994), pp. 406–71.
3 In parliament on 1 Feb. 1793. Quoted in W. Hague, *William Pitt the Younger* (Harper Perennial edn, London, 2005), p. 329.
4 Mori, *William Pitt and the French Revolution*, p. 144.
5 Figures calculated by G. R. Porter, *The Progress of the Nation. Vol. 2* (London, 1838) and quoted in J. Gregory and J. Stevenson, *The Longman Companion to Britain in the Eighteenth Century, 1688–1820* (Pearson Education, Harlow, 2000), pp. 200–4.
6 Mori, *William Pitt and the French Revolution*, p. 222.
7 Statistics collected in Gregory and Stevenson, *Britain in the Eighteenth Century*, p. 199.
8 M. Duffy, 'World-Wide War, 1793–1815', in P. J. Marshall (ed.), *Oxford History of the British Empire. Vol. 2, The Eighteenth Century* (Oxford University Press, 1998), p. 189.
9 *ibid.*, pp. 189–91.
10 For a flavour of the interchanges, see D. Wahrman, 'Virtual Representation: Parliamentary Reporting and Languages of Class in the 1790s', *Past & Present*, 136 (1992), pp. 83–113.
11 Quoted in Hague, *William Pitt the Younger*, p. 495.
12 M. Turner, *Pitt the Younger: A Life* (Hambledon, London, 2003), pp. 198–9.

Chapter 13. The Napoleonic Wars, 1803–1815 (page 128)

1 C. Esdaile, *The French Wars, 1792–1815* (Routledge, London, 2001), pp. 27–9. For a detailed study, see C. Esdaile, *Napoleon's Wars: An International History, 1803–15* (Allen Lane, London, 2007).
2 J. E. Cookson, 'The English Volunteer Movement of the French Wars, 1793–1815: Some Contexts', *Historical Journal*, 32 (1989), p. 889.
3 For a useful account of Pitt's last months in office, see M. Turner, *Pitt the Younger: A Life* (Hambledon, London, 2003), pp. 249–73.
4 On the developing practice of memorialising heroes, see H. Hook, *Empires of the Imagination: Politics, War and the Arts in the British World, 1750–1850* (Profile Books, London, 2010), esp. pp. 186–7.
5 L. Mitchell, *Charles James Fox* (Oxford University Press, 1992), pp. 227–35.
6 L. Mitchell, *The Whig World* (Hambledon, London, 2005), p. 89.
7 For a detailed account of the origins of the Peninsular War, see R. Muir, *Britain and the Defeat of Napoleon, 1807–15* (Yale University Press, London, 1996), pp. 32–59.
8 For a detailed study of the war, see D. Gates, *The Spanish Ulcer: A History of the Peninsular War* (Pimlico, London, 2002).

9 In a letter written in April 1820 and quoted in *Oxford Dictionary of National Biography* (Oxford University Press, 2004), entry on Wellington, No. 29001.

10 Muir, *Britain and the Defeat of Napoleon*, pp. 198–9.

11 As reported by Thomas Creevey in *Creevey Papers* (London, 1903), p. 236.

12 Walter Scott, *Paul's Letters* (1816). The famous quotation is located in Letter 8.

13 Esdaile, *Napoleon's Wars*, pp. 3–5. Esdaile's is the most detailed modern treatment of the wars.

14 The whole issue of subsidies is discussed in detail in J. Sherwig, *Guineas and Gunpowder: British Foreign Aid in the Wars with France, 1783–1815* (Cambridge, Mass., 1969). See also B. Hilton, *A Mad, Bad and Dangerous People? England 1783–1846* (Clarendon Press, Oxford, 2006), pp. 223–4.

15 J. R. Ward 'The British West Indies, 1748–1815' in P. J. Marshall (ed.), *The Oxford History of the British Empire: The Eighteenth Century* (Oxford University Press, 1998), p. 427.

16 For a selection of recent writing on the French Wars as a whole, see T. C. W. Blanning, *The French Revolutionary Wars, 1787–1802* (Arnold, London, 1996); M. Broers, *Europe under Napoleon, 1799–1815* (Hodder Arnold, London, 1996); A. Forrest and P. G. Dwyer (eds), *Napoleon and his Empire: Europe 1804–14* (Palgrave, Basingstoke, 2007). For recent, clear-eyed perception of the French as they saw themselves, see A. Forrest, *The Legacy of the French Revolutionary Wars: The Nation-in-Arms in French Republican Memory* (Cambridge University Press, 2009).

Chapter 14. John Bull's other island: Ireland, conflict and Union, 1780–1815 (page 138)

1 G. Holmes and D. Szechi, *The Age of Oligarchy: Pre-Industrial Britain, 1722–83* (Longman, London, 1993), p. 227.

2 R. F. Foster, *Modern Ireland, 1600–1972* (Penguin, London, 1988), pp. 167–93.

3 Calculations from Holmes and Szechi, *Age of Oligarchy*, p. 380.

4 R. B. McDowell, 'Colonial Nationalism, 1760–82' in M.Vaughan (ed.), *A New History of Ireland* (Clarendon Press, Oxford, 1986), Vol. 4, p. 218.

5 Foster, *Modern Ireland*, p. 246.

6 McDowell, 'Colonial Nationalism', p. 225.

7 Quoted in Holmes and Szechi, *Age of Oligarchy*, p. 235.

8 McDowell, 'Colonial Nationalism', pp. 250–1.

9 V. T. Harlow and F. Madden, *British Colonial Developments, 1774–1834* (Clarendon Press, Oxford, 1953), p. 179.

10 B. Hilton, *A Mad, Bad and Dangerous People? England, 1783–1846* (Clarendon Press, Oxford, 2006), p. 52.

11 E. Curtis and R. B. McDowell (eds), *Irish Historical Documents, 1172–1922* (Methuen, London, 1943), pp. 198–202.

12 *Memoirs and Correspondence of Viscount Castlereagh*, 12 vols (1848–54), Vol. 1, p. 156.

13 *Oxford Dictionary of National Biography* (Oxford University Press, 2004), entry on Lake, No. 15900.

14 Foster, *Modern Ireland*, pp. 278–80. For more detail on the background both to rebellion and to French invasion projects, see M. Elliott, *Partners in Revolution: The United Irishmen and France* (Yale University Press edn, 1990).

15 Letter of 28 May 1798, quoted in J. Ehrman, *The Younger Pitt. Vol. 3, The Consuming Struggle* (Constable, London, 1996), p. 170. For a detailed modern study of the Union from an anti-Union Irish perspective, see P. M. Geoghegan, *The Irish Act of Union: A Study in High Politics, 1798–1801* (Gill & Macmillan, London, 2001). For a detailed analysis of the political developments, including

the specific roles of Pitt, Grenville and Dundas, see P. Jupp, 'Britain and the Union, 1797–1801', *Transactions of the Royal Historical Society*, 6th series, 10 (2000), pp. 197–219.

16 Speech of 23 January, quoted in Ehrman, *The Younger Pitt. Vol. 3*, pp. 181–2.

17 Foster, *Modern Ireland*, p. 282.

18 For details, see Ehrman, *The Younger Pitt. Vol. 3*, pp. 175–94, 508–10, 516–17; and W. Hague, *William Pitt the Younger* (Harper Perennial edn, London, 2005), pp. 470–7.

19 For more on the changing relationship between the King and Pitt, see Ehrman, *The Younger Pitt. Vol. 3*, pp. 518–25.

20 P. M. Geoghegan, 'The Catholics and the Union', *Transactions of the Royal Historical Society*, 6th series, 10 (2000), pp. 243–58.

21 S. Connolly, 'Reconsidering the Irish Act of Union', *Transactions of the Royal Historical Society*, 6th series, 10 (2000), pp. 399–408.

Chapter 15. Parties, politics and religion in early nineteenth-century Britain (page 149)

1 Calculations cited in P. Harling and P. Mandler, 'From "Fiscal-Military" State to Laissez-Faire State, 1760–1850', *Journal of British Studies*, 32 (1993), p. 48.

2 B. Hilton, *A Mad, Bad and Dangerous People? England 1783–1846* (Clarendon Press, Oxford, 2006), p. 191.

3 R. Harris, 'Government and the Economy', in R. Floud and P. Johnson (eds), *The Cambridge Economic History of Modern Britain. Vol. 1, 1700–1860* (Cambridge University Press, 2004), pp. 204–37.

4 Hilton, *A Mad, Bad and Dangerous People?*, p. 254.

5 N. Ferguson, *The House of Rothschild: Money's Prophets, 1798–1848* (Penguin, London, 1998), pp. 83–110, and N. Ferguson, *The Ascent of Money* (Allen Lane, London, 2008), pp. 80–4.

6 E. J. Evans, *The Forging of the Modern State: Early Industrial Britain, 1783–1870*, 3rd edn (Longman, London, 2001), p. 510.

7 E. P. Thompson, *The Making of the English Working Class* (Penguin edn, London, 1968), pp. 491–659.

8 W. A. Hay, *The Whig Revival, 1808–1830* (Palgrave Macmillan, Basingstoke, 2005), pp. 25–34.

9 Quoted in Hilton, *A Mad, Bad and Dangerous People?*, p. 254.

10 Letter from 'Amphictyon', *Liverpool Mercury*, 5 July 1811.

11 P. Spence, *The Birth of Romantic Radicalism: War, Popular Politics and English Radical Reformism* (Scolar Press, Aldershot, 1996).

12 On the key constitutional and party-political developments of this period, see P. Jupp, *The Governing of Britain, 1688–1848* (Routledge, London, 2006), pp. 105–44.

13 Hilton, *A Mad, Bad and Dangerous People?*, p. 101.

14 R. G. Thorne, *The History of Parliament: The House of Commons, 1790–1820* (Secker & Warburg, London, 1986), Vol. 1, p. 195.

15 One historian has, perhaps rashly, seen the period 1801–7 as critical in legitimising the idea of consistent, organised opposition as a valuable element in the political process: S. Lee, '"A New Language in Politicks": George Canning and the Idea of Opposition', *History*, 83 (1998), pp. 472–96.

16 On the role of the monarchy in this period, see Jupp, *The Governing of Britain*, pp. 110–23.

17 Hilton, *A Mad, Bad and Dangerous People?*, p. 196. See also pp. 195–209 for the most sophisticated brief discussion of what remains a complex area.

18 As, for example, that found in E. J. Evans, *The Forging of the Modern State: Early Industrial Britain, 1783–1870*, 3rd edn (Longman, London, 2001), pp. 484–7.

19 M. Watts, *The Dissenters. Vol. 2, The Expansion of Evangelical Nonconformity* (Clarendon Press, Oxford, 1995), p. 113.

20 *ibid.*, p. 28.

21 Quoted *ibid.*, p. 351.

22 For further development of this point, see D. Bebbington, *Religion and Political Culture in Britain and Ireland* (Cambridge University Press, 1996), pp. 25–48.

23 Watts, *The Dissenters*, pp. 438–40.

24 D. Hempton, *The Religion of the People: Methodism and Popular Religion, c1750–1900* (Routledge, London, 1996), pp. 163–5.

25 J. R. Ward, 'The British West Indies, 1748–1815', in P. J. Marshall (ed.), *The Oxford History of the British Empire* (Oxford University Press, 1998), pp. 426–8.

Chapter 16. The age of Lord Liverpool I: radicalism, reform and repression, 1815–1822 (page 163)

1 B. R. Mitchell and P. Deane, *Abstract of British Historical Statistics* (Cambridge University Press, 1962), pp. 488–9.

2 In a Memorandum to Liverpool, 4 Feb. 1819, quoted in B. Hilton, *A Mad, Bad and Dangerous People? England 1783–1846* (Oxford University Press, 2006), p. 259.

3 P. Harling and P. Mandler, 'From "Fiscal-Military" State to "Laissez-Faire" State, 1760–1850', *Journal of British Studies*, 32 (1993), pp. 44–70.

4 Hansard, 1st series, Vol. 30, col. 181, 15 Mar. 1815.

5 *Cobbett's Weekly Political Register*, 18 Mar. 1815.

6 As for example in *Cobbett's Weekly Political Register*, 25 Mar. 1815. See also E. J. Evans, *Britain Before the Reform Act: Politics and Society 1815–32*, 2nd edn (Pearson Education, London, 2008), pp. 17–18.

7 Quoted *ibid.*, p. 18.

8 On radicalism in this period see J. Belchem, *Popular Radicalism in Nineteenth-Century Britain* (Macmillan, London, 1996). For studies of Hunt and Cobbett, see J. Belchem, *Orator Hunt: Henry Hunt and English Working Class Radicalism* (Clarendon Press, Oxford, 1985) and D. Green, *Great Cobbett, the Noblest Agitator* (Oxford University Press, 1983). E. P. Thompson, *The Making of the English Working Class* (Penguin edn, London, 1968) remains a classic study: passionate, engaged and, some would say, both wonderfully well-written and lovingly over the top in its sympathy for its subjects. On revolutionary projects specifically, see E. Royle, *Revolutionary Britannia: Reflections on the Threat of Revolution in Britain, 1760–1848* (Harvester Press, Brighton, 2000).

9 Report of the Secret Committee into the Disturbed State of the Country, Hansard, 1st series, Vol. 35 (1817), col. 438.

10 P. Jupp, *Lord Grenville, 1759–1834* (Oxford University Press, 1985).

11 E. J. Evans, *The Forging of the Modern State: Early Industrial Britain, 1783–1870*, 3rd edn (Longman, London, 2001), p. 487.

12 Hilton, *A Mad, Bad and Dangerous People?*, p. 253.

13 A powerful case has been made for seeing this form of attack as increasingly outmoded. See P. Harling, *The Waning of 'Old Corruption', 1779–1846* (Clarendon Press, Oxford, 1996).

14 R. Poole, ' "By the Law or the Sword": Peterloo Revisited', *History*, 91 (2006), pp. 254–76.

15 For a discussion of the political role of visual culture, see M. Wood, *Radical Satire and Print Culture, 1790–1822* (Clarendon Press, Oxford, 1994).

16 Hilton, *A Mad, Bad and Dangerous People?*, p. 252.

17 See for example the analyses of the events of 1819 in Thompson, *Making of the English Working Class*, Poole, ' "By the Law or the Sword" ' and Belchem, *Orator Hunt*.

18 Details of the Conspiracy are located in *State Trials*, Vol. 33, especially cols 700–895.
19 Quote in J. Robins, *Rebel Queen: How the Trial of Caroline Brought England to the Brink of Revolution* (Simon & Schuster, London, 2006), p. 240.
20 The view of the anti-radical *Blackwood's Edinburgh Magazine* (Nov. 1820), p. 210 and quoted in J. Fulcher, 'The Loyalist Response to the Queen Caroline Agitations', *Journal of British Studies*, 34 (1995), pp. 481–502.
21 For more detail, see Evans, *Britain before the Reform Act*, pp. 29–33.
22 Hilton, *A Mad, Bad and Dangerous People?*, p. 269.
23 Fulcher, 'Loyalist Response', p. 500.

Chapter 17. The age of Lord Liverpool II: Liberal Toryism, 1822–1827 (page 173)

1 W. A. Hay, *The Whig Revival, 1808–30* (Palgrave Macmillan, Basingstoke, 2005), pp. 121–2.
2 *Oxford Dictionary of National Biography* (Oxford University Press, 2004), entries on Huskisson (No. 14264) and Vansittart (No. 28105).
3 In a speech delivered in Glasgow in 1837 and quoted in B. Hilton, *A Mad, Bad and Dangerous People? England 1783–1846* (Oxford University Press, 2006), p. 315. For a more detailed discussion on Liberal and High Toryism and their differences, see ibid., pp. 307–28.
4 For further argument on a contentious question, see B. Gordon, *Economic Doctrine and Tory Liberalism, 1824–30* (Macmillan, London, 1979), B. Hilton, *The Age of Atonement: The Influence of Evangelicalism on Social and Economic Thought, 1785–1865* (Oxford University Press, 1992) and S. M. Lee, *George Canning and Liberal Toryism, 1801–27* (Royal Historical Society, Boydell Press, Woodbridge, 2008).
5 *Annual Register*, Vol. 66 (1824), p. 5.
6 Quoted in Hilton, *A Mad, Bad and Dangerous People?*, p. 297.
7 *Oxford Dictionary of National Biography* (Oxford University Press, 2004), entry on Huskisson, No. 14264.
8 *Speeches of William Huskisson*, 3 vols (London, 1831), Vol. 2, pp. 344–6 and 25.
9 Statistics from C. Cook, *The Longman Companion to Britain in the Nineteenth Century* (Longman, London, 1999), pp. 201–3, and R. Floud and D. McCloskey (eds), *The Economic History of Britain since 1700, Vol. 1, 1700–1860*, 2nd edn (Cambridge University Press, 1994), p. 131.
10 Hilton, *A Mad, Bad and Dangerous People?*, pp. 300–5.
11 N. Gash, *Mr Secretary Peel: The Life of Sir Robert Peel to 1830*, 2nd edn (Longman, Harlow, 1985), p. 341.
12 *Oxford Dictionary of National Biography*, entry on Robert Peel, No. 21764.
13 Hilton, *A Mad, Bad and Dangerous People?*, p. 319.
14 C. Emsley, *Crime and Society in England, 1750–1900* (Longman, Harlow, 1987).
15 For two contrasting accounts of changes in labour law, see E. P. Thompson, *The Making of the English Working Class* (Penguin edn, London, 1968), pp. 561–9, and Hilton, *A Mad, Bad and Dangerous People?*, pp. 299–300.
16 Quoted in D. Hempton, *Religion and Political Culture in Britain and Ireland* (Cambridge University Press, 1996), p. 80.
17 Quoted in Lee, *George Canning*, p. 153.
18 Hilton, *A Mad, Bad and Dangerous People?*, p. 299.
19 D. R. Fisher, *The House of Commons, 1820–32* (History of Parliament, Cambridge University Press, 2009), Vol. 1, pp. 222–7.

Chapter 18. Congresses, commerce and conflicts: foreign policy, 1815–1830 (page 183)

1 Treaty of Paris, 30 May 1814, *British and Foreign State Papers. Vol. 1, 1812–14*, clause 5 and 'separate secret article' 3.

2 Quoted in H. Temperley and L. M. Penson (eds), *Foundations of British Foreign Policy from Pitt to Salisbury* (Cambridge University Press, 1938), pp. 147–8.

3 P. Schroeder, *The Transformation of European Politics, 1763–1848* (Clarendon Press, Oxford, 1994), pp. 305–15.

4 C. Esdaile, *Napoleon's War: An International History, 1803–15* (Allen Lane, London, 2007), p. 561.

5 Quoted in J. R. Davis, 'Britain and the European Balance of Power', in C. Williams (ed.), *A Companion to Nineteenth-Century Britain* (Blackwell, Oxford, 2004), p. 36.

6 Temperley and Penson, *Foundations of British Foreign Policy*, p. 61.

7 J. W. Derry, *Castlereagh* (Allen Lane, London, 1976), p. 208.

8 Marquess of Londonderry (ed.), *Correspondence, Letters and Despatches of Lord Castlereagh*, 12 vols (London, 1853), Vol. 12, pp. 56–7.

9 E. L. Woodward, *The Age of Reform, 1815–70*, 2nd edn (Clarendon Press, Oxford, 1962), p. 207.

10 Canning in the House of Commons, 14 Apr. 1823, quoted in M. E. Chamberlain, *Pax Britannica? British Foreign Policy, 1789–1914* (Longman, Harlow, 1988), p. 64.

11 Canning, House of Commons, 12 Dec. 1826, Hansard, 2nd series, Vol. 16, cols 367–9.

12 Quoted in W. Hinde, *George Canning* (Collins, London, 1973), p. 345.

13 In a letter to Lord Holland in March 1824. Quoted in P. Dixon, *Canning: Politician and Statesman* (Weidenfeld & Nicolson, London, 1976), p. 229.

14 Quoted in Chamberlain, *Pax Britannica?*, p. 81.

Chapter 19. Matters imperial, *c*1780–*c*1850 (page 193)

1 R. Hyam, *Britain's Imperial Century, 1815–1914: A Study of Empire and Expansion*, 3rd edn (Cambridge University Press, 2002). See also A. Porter (ed.), *The Oxford History of the British Empire. Vol. 3, The Nineteenth Century* (Oxford University Press, 1999), p. vii. For a recent perspective on Empire from the seventeenth century to the accession of Queen Victoria, which stresses both the economic and cultural benefits for Britain see P. K. Monod, *Imperial Island: A History of Britain and its Empire, 1660–1837* (Wiley-Blackwell, Oxford, 2009). R. Hyam, *Understanding the British Empire* (Cambridge University Press, 2010).

2 P. J. Marshall, 'Britain without America – A Second Empire?', in P. J. Marshall (ed.), *The Oxford History of the British Empire. Vol. 2, The Eighteenth Century* (Oxford University Press, 1998), p. 576.

3 V. T. Harlow, *The Founding of the Second British Empire, 1763–93*, 2 vols (Longmans, London, 1952, 1964).

4 Quoted in B. Hilton, *A Mad, Bad and Dangerous People? England 1783–1846* (Oxford University Press, 2006), p. 299.

5 *Memoir of Sir T. S. Raffles* by his widow, in V. T. Harlow and F. Madden (eds), *British Colonial Developments, 1774–1834* (Clarendon Press, Oxford, 1953), pp. 74–5.

6 P. J. Cain 'Economics: The Metropolitan Context' in Porter (ed.), *Oxford History of the British Empire. Vol. 3*, p. 39.

7 T. O. Lloyd, *The British Empire, 1558–1983* (Oxford University Press, 1984), pp. 120–3; P. Levine, *The British Empire: Sunrise to Sunset* (Pearson Education, Harlow, 2007), pp. 45–55.

8 A. Porter, 'Introduction', in Porter (ed.), *Oxford History of the British Empire. Vol. 3*, p. 5.

9   H. V. Bowen, 'India: The Metropolitan Context', ibid., p. 542.
10 A. Webster, *The Debate on the British Empire* (Manchester University Press, 2006), pp. 23–4.
11 J. Pebble, 'Resources and Techniques in the Second Maratha War', *Historical Journal*, 19 (1976), pp. 375–404.
12 *Oxford Dictionary of National Biography* (Oxford University Press, 2004), entry on Earl Cornwallis, No. 6338.
13 P. Brendon, *The Decline and Fall of the British Empire, 1781–1997* (Cape, London, 2007), pp. 52–3.
14 C. A. Bayly, *Imperial Meridian: The British Empire and the World, 1780–1830* (Longman, Harlow, 1989), p. 128; D. Washbrook, 'India, 1818–60: The Two Faces of Colonialism', in Porter (ed.), *Oxford History of the British Empire. Vol. 3*, pp. 399–421.
15 T. O. Lloyd, *The British Empire, 1558–1983* (Oxford University Press, 1984), p. 133.
16 For a detailed study of British involvement in Afghanistan, which precipitated the action in Sind, see M. E. Yapp, *Strategies of British India: Britain, Iran and Afghanistan, 1798–1850* (Clarendon Press, Oxford, 1980). See also Chapter 34 below.
17 *Oxford Dictionary of National Biography*, entry on Sir Charles Napier, No. 19748.
18 *Oxford Dictionary of National Biography*, entry on Lord William Henry Cavendish Bentinck, No. 2161.
19 In his *Political History of India from 1784 to 1823* and quoted in Washbrook, 'India', p. 403.
20 M. Harper 'British Migration and the Peopling of the Empire' in Porter (ed.), *Oxford History of the British Empire. Vol. 3*, p. 75.
21 J. Belich, *Replenishing the Earth: The Settler Revolution and the Rise of the Anglo-World, 1783–1939* (Oxford University Press, 2009).
22 *ibid.*, p. 78.
23 Phillip to Lord Grenville, 17 June 1790, quoted in Harlow and Madden (eds), *British Colonial Developments*, p. 439.
24 Bayly, *Imperial Meridian*, pp. 133–6.
25 J. Darwin, 'Imperialism and the Victorians', *English Historical Review*, 112 (1997), pp. 614–42.
26 Porter (ed.), *Oxford History of the British Empire. Vol. 3*, p. 4.
27 This argument is most extensively developed in L. Colley, *Captives: Britain, Empire and the World, 1600–1850* (Pimlico Press, London, 2003).

Chapter 20. The crisis of Toryism and the road to Reform, 1827–1832 (page 204)

1   We lack a modern, archivally researched, biography of Britain's third longest serving Prime Minister. In its absence N. Gash, *Lord Liverpool: The Life and Political Career of Robert Banks Jenkinson, Second Earl of Liverpool* (Weidenfeld & Nicolson, London, 1984), provides a useful assessment, though perhaps imbuing Liverpool with greater abilities than he possessed.
2   Wellington to Sir Colin Campbell, 16 Mar. 1828 (two months after becoming Prime Minister). Quoted in P. Jupp, *British Politics on the Eve of Reform: The Duke of Wellington's Administration, 1828–30* (Macmillan, Basingstoke, 1998), pp. 41–2.
3   Quoted *ibid.*, p. 57.
4   Quoted in D. R. Fisher, *The House of Commons, 1820–32* (History of Parliament, London, 2009), p. 335.
5   B. Hilton, *A Mad, Bad and Dangerous People? England 1783–1846* (Oxford University Press, 2006), p. 383.
6   Wellington originally preferred to put the Catholic Church in Ireland under state control, but changed his mind. See K. A. Noyce, 'The Duke of Wellington and the Catholic Question', in N. Gash (ed.), *Wellington: Studies in the Military and Political Career of the First Duke of Wellington* (Manchester University Press, 1990), pp. 139–58.

7 Hilton, *A Mad, Bad and Dangerous People?*, p. 408.

8 The literature on the route to parliamentary reform is vast. For a recent overall summary, see E. J. Evans, *Britain before the Reform Act: Politics and Society, 1815–1832*, 2nd edn (Pearson Education, Harlow, 2008), pp. 83–103. See also E. J. Evans, *Parliamentary Reform, c1770–1918* (Pearson Education, Harlow, 2000). The best detailed study remains M. Brock, *The Great Reform Act* (Hutchinson, London, 1973). J. A. Phillips, *The Great Reform Bill in the Boroughs: English Electoral Behaviour 1818–41* (Clarendon Press, Oxford, 1992).

9 Hilton, *A Mad, Bad and Dangerous People?*, p. 413.

10 Fisher, *House of Commons*, pp. 227–33.

11 Wellington in the House of Lords, 2 Nov. 1830, Hansard, 3rd series, Vol. 1, cols 52–3.

12 Quoted in Hilton, *A Mad, Bad and Dangerous People?*, p. 419.

13 *The Times*, 22 Nov. 1830.

14 *ibid.*, 1 Oct. 1831, quoted in E. P. Thompson, *The Making of the English Working Class* (Penguin edn, London, 1968), p. 890.

15 N. D. LoPatin, *Political Unions, Popular Politics and the Great Reform Act of 1832* (St Martin's, New York, 1999). On extra-parliamentary activity in the 1830s more generally, see Thompson, *Making of the English Working Class*, pp. 838–915; J. Belchem, *Popular Radicalism in Nineteenth-Century Britain* (Macmillan, Basingstoke, 1996); R. McWilliam, *Popular Politics in Nineteenth-Century England* (Routledge, London, 1998); and C. Flick, *The Birmingham Political Union, 1830–39* (Dawson, London, 1978).

16 J. V. Beckett, 'The Nottingham Reform Bill Riots of 1831', in C. Jones, P. Salmon and R. W. Davies (eds), *Partisan Politics, Principle and Reform in Parliament and the Constituencies, 1689–1880* (Edinburgh University Press, 2005), pp. 114–38.

17 E. A. Smith (ed.), *Reform or Revolution? A Diary of Reform in England, 1830–32* (Alan Sutton, Stroud, 1992), p. 29.

18 J. Stevenson, *Popular Disturbances in England, 1700–1870*.

Chapter 21. The reality of Reform: the new order and its critics (page 214)

1 *Correspondence of Earl Grey with William IV and Sir Herbert Taylor*, ed. H. Grey, 2 vols (London, 1867), Vol. 1, pp. 410–11.

2 Quoted in E. P. Thompson, *The Making of the English Working Class* (Penguin edn, London, 1968), p. 892.

3 For an accessible, brief introduction to the key issues see S. Farrell, 'A First Step towards Democracy', *History Today*, 60 (2010), pp. 10–17.

4 J. P. Parry, *The Rise and Fall of Liberal Government in Victorian Britain* (Yale University Press, 1993), p. 72.

5 Calculations derived from E. J. Evans, *The Forging of the Modern State: Early Industrial Britain, 1783–1870*, 3rd edn (Longman, London, 2001), pp. 473, 487. See also B. Hilton, *A Mad, Bad and Dangerous People? England 1783–1846* (Oxford University Press, 2006), p. 502. For an excellent explanation of Tory recovery in one largely rural county, see D. Eastwood, 'Toryism, Reform and Political Culture in Oxfordshire, 1826–37', *Parliamentary History*, 7 (1988), pp. 98–121.

6 J. R. M. Butler, *The Passing of the Great Reform Bill* (Longmans Green, London, 1914) p. vii; G. M. Trevelyan, *British History in the Nineteenth Century, 1782–1901* (Longman, London, 1922; 1966 edn), p. 241. See also G. S. Veitch, *The Genesis of Parliamentary Reform* (Constable, London, 1913).

7 From a large literature which has argued that the impact of 1832 has been exaggerated, see N. Gash, *Politics in the Age of Peel: A Study in the Technique of Parliamentary Representation, 1830–50*

(Longmans Green, London, 1953) and H. J. Hanham, *The Reformed Electoral System in Great Britain, 1832–1914* (Historical Association, London, 1969).

8   E. J. Evans, *Parliamentary Reform, c1770–1918* (Pearson Education, Harlow, 2000), pp. 27–8.

9   F. O'Gorman, *Voters, Patrons and Parties: The Unreformed Electorate of Hanoverian England 1714–1832* (Clarendon Press, Oxford, 1989), D. E. D. Beales, 'The Right to Vote and the Opportunity', *Parliamentary History*, 11 (1992), pp. 139–50 and the reply by F. O'Gorman, ibid., pp. 171–83.

10   J. Vernon, *Politics and the People: A Study in English Political Culture, 1815–67* (Cambridge University Press, 1993) argues that the Reform Act marked a move away from popular involvement in the political process.

11   Figures from J. Lawrence and M. Taylor (eds), *Party, State and Society: Electoral Behaviour in Britain since 1820* (Scolar Press, Aldershot, 1997), p. 57.

12   J. E. Thorold Rogers (ed.), *Public Addresses by John Bright* (Macmillan, London, 1879), p. 29.

13   In a letter of 1839 to the Tory political organiser Charles Arbuthnot, H. J. Hanham (ed.), *The Nineteenth Century Constitution* (Cambridge University Press, 1969), p. 263.

14   J. A. Phillips and C. Wetherell, 'The Great Reform Act of 1832 and the Political Modernization of England', *American Historical Review*, 100 (1995), pp. 419–22, 435.

15   I. Newbould, *Whiggery and Reform, 1830–41: The Politics of Government* (Stanford University Press, 1990), pp. 17–21.

16   M. S. Smith, 'Parliamentary Reform and the Electorate', in C. Williams (ed.), *The Companion to Nineteenth-Century Britain* (Blackwell, Oxford, 2004), p. 162.

17   M. Taylor, *The Decline of British Radicalism, 1847–60* (Clarendon Press, Oxford, 1995), pp. 27–9.

18   M. Roberts, *Political Movements in Urban England, 1832–1914* (Palgrave Macmillan, Basingstoke, 2009), p. 20.

19   Hilton, *A Mad, Bad and Dangerous People?*, p. 517.

20   *Poor Man's Guardian*, 27 Oct. 1832; J. Belchem, *Orator Hunt: Henry Hunt and English Working Class Politics* (Oxford University Press, 1985). The duty was removed entirely in 1861.

21   P. Hollis, *The Pauper Press: A Study of Working-Class Radicalism in the 1830s* (Oxford University Press, 1970).

22   E. Royle, *Chartism*, 3rd edn (Addison Wesley Longman, Harlow, 1996), p. 18.

23   M. Chase, *Chartism: A New History* (Manchester University Press, 2007), pp. 1–7. Chase's volume has established itself as the most detailed modern account of the movement.

24   J. Belchem, *Popular Radicalism in Nineteenth-Century Britain* (Macmillan, Basingstoke, 1996), p. 80.

25   E. Royle, *Revolutionary Britannia: Reflections on the Threat of Revolution in Britain* (Manchester University Press, 2000), pp. 128–35; D. Goodway, *London Chartism* (Cambridge University Press, 1982); J. Belchem, 'Nationalism, Republicanism and Exile: Irish Emigrants and the Revolutions of 1848', *Past & Present*, 146 (1995), pp. 101–35.

26   Chase, *Chartism*, pp. 318–26; Royle, *Chartism*, pp. 44–7.

27   Revisionist literature on Chartism is substantial. Among the most influential are D. Thompson, *The Chartists: Popular Politics in the Industrial Revolution* (Temple Smith, London, 1984); J. Epstein and D. Thompson (eds), *The Chartist Experience: Studies in Radicalism and Culture* (Macmillan, London, 1982); G. Stedman Jones, *Languages of Class: Studies in English Working-Class History, 1832–1932* (Cambridge University Press, 1983); J. Epstein, *The Lion of Freedom* (Croom Helm, London, 1982); M. Taylor, 'Rethinking the Chartists: Searching for Synthesis in the Historiography of Chartism', *Historical Journal*, 39 (1996), pp. 479–95; Chase, *Chartism*.

28   Chase, *Chartism*, p. 161. See also the assessment by a son of a Chartist handloom weaver that O'Connor was a 'man of unbounded conceit and egotism, extremely jealous of precedence, and regarding himself as a sort of uncrowned king of the working classes' (R. Balmforth, *Some Social and Political Pioneers of the Nineteenth Century* (London, 1900), quoted in Royle, *Chartism*, p. 130).

29   For further development of this theme, see J. Saville, *1848: The British State and the Chartist Movement* (Cambridge University Press, 1987).

Chapter 22. The Age of Peel? Policies and parties, 1832–1846 (page 225)

1 The phrase is widely used as a title for academic courses which cover this period. It was appropriated by Norman Gash, the most distinguished biographer of Peel, whose *Politics in the Age of Peel: A Study in the Technique of Parliamentary Representation, 1830–50* (Longmans Green, London, 1953) established the eponymous tone of these two decades.
2 J. Parry, *The Rise and Fall of Liberal Government in Victorian Britain* (Yale University Press, 1993), pp. 97–8.
3 J. Walvin, *Slaves and Slavery: The British Colonial Experience* (Manchester University Press, 1992), pp. 97–8. For wider debates on the reasons for abolition, see S. Engerman, *Slavery, Emancipation and Freedom: Comparative Perspectives* (Louisiana University Press, 2007) and J. Walvin, *Questioning Slavery* (Routledge, London, 1996).
4 B. Hilton, *A Mad, Bad and Dangerous People? England 1783–1846* (Oxford University Press, 2006), p. 493; Parry, *Rise and Fall*, p. 103.
5 Quoted in Hilton, *A Mad, Bad and Dangerous People?*, p. 495.
6 N. Gash, *Sir Robert Peel: The Life of Sir Robert Peel since 1830* (Longman, Harlow, 1986 edn), pp. 96–100; R. Stewart, *The Foundation of the Conservative Party, 1830–1867* (Longman, Harlow, 1978).
7 P. Mandler, *Aristocratic Government in the Age of Reform* (Clarendon Press, Oxford, 1990), p. 190.
8 Parry, *Rise and Fall*, p. 139.
9 Quoted *ibid.*, p. 131.
10 W. Gibson, 'The Professionalization of an Elite: The Nineteenth-Century Episcopate', *Albion*, 23 (1991), pp. 459–82.
11 Quoted in I. Newbould, *Whiggery and Reform, 1830–41: The Politics of Government* (Macmillan, Basingstoke, 1990), p. 271.
12 For a discussion of the Church of England's problems and its revival, see R. A. Soloway, *Prelates and People: Ecclesiastical Social Thought in England, 1783–1852* (Routledge, London, 1969) and P. Virgin, *The Church in an Age of Negligence: Ecclesiastical Structure and Problems of Church Reform, 1700–1840* (Cambridge University Press, 1989).
13 For more detail on tithe disputes and their resolution, see E. J. Evans, *The Contentious Tithe: The Tithe Question and English Agriculture, 1750–1850* (Routledge, London, 1976).
14 D. Eastwood, 'Men, Morals and the Machinery of Social Legislation, 1790–1840', *Parliamentary History*, 13 (1994), pp. 204–5.
15 L. M. Cullen, *The Statistical Movement in Early Victorian Britain: The Foundations of Empirical Social Research* (Harvester, Hassocks, 1975).
16 *Oxford Dictionary of National Biography* (Oxford University Press, 2004), entry on Francis Baring, No. 1383.
17 For further discussion of this election, see E. J. Evans, *Sir Robert Peel: Statesmanship, Power and Party*, 2nd edn (Routledge, London, 2006), pp. 48–52.
18 See the indicative case study by D. Eastwood, 'Toryism, Reform and Political Culture in Oxfordshire, 1826–1837', *Parliamentary History*, 7 (1988), pp. 98–121.
19 In a letter to T. W. Freshfield, 13 Sept. 1841, quoted in P. Harling, 'Rethinking "Old Corruption"', *Past & Present*, 147 (1995), p. 150.
20 On Peel's Cabinet-making, see Gash, *Sir Robert Peel*, pp. 273–88.
21 Quoted in R. A. Gaunt, *Sir Robert Peel: The Life and the Legacy* (I. B. Tauris, London, 2010), pp. 50–1.
22 From G. Peel (ed.), *Private Letters of Peel* (John Murray, London, 1920) and C. S. Parker, *Life and Letters of Sir James Graham* (London, 1907), quoted in Parry, *Rise and Fall*, p. 165.
23 R. Stewart, *Foundation of the Conservative Party*, p. 193.

24 For a modern interpretation of the work of the Anti-Corn Law League, see P. Pickering and A. Tyrell, *The People's Bread: A History of the Anti-Corn Law League* (Leicester University Press, London, 2000).

25 Hilton, *A Mad, Bad and Dangerous People?*, p. 509.

26 Gaunt, *Sir Robert Peel*, p. 127.

27 *ibid.*, p. 508.

28 Quoted *ibid.*, p. 128.

Chapter 23. A 'Second Industrial Revolution'? British economic performance, *c*1850–*c*1880 (page 239)

1 Calculations from statistics in P. Mathias, *The First Industrial Nation: The Economic History of Britain, 1700–1914*, 2nd edn (Routledge, London, 1983), pp. 223–4.

2 G. Magee, 'Manufacturing and Technological Change' in R. Floud and P. Johnson (eds), *The Cambridge Economic History of Modern Britain. Vol. 2, 1860–1939* (Cambridge University Press, 2004), p. 79; K. T. Hoppen, *The Mid-Victorian Generation, 1846–1886* (Clarendon Press, Oxford, 1998), p. 38.

3 M. Daunton, *State and Market in Victorian Britain: War, Welfare and Capitalism* (Boydell Press, Woodbridge, 2008), pp. 107–8.

4 M. Thomas, 'The Service Sector', in Floud and Johnson (eds), *Cambridge Economic History of Modern Britain. Vol. 2*, pp. 99–132.

5 D. Alexander, *Retailing in England during the Industrial Revolution* (Athlone Press, London, 1970), pp. 107–9.

6 T. R. Gourvish, *Railways and the British Economy, 1830–1914* (Studies in Economic and Social History, Macmillan, London, 1980), p. 20.

7 Hoppen, *Mid-Victorian Generation*, p. 284.

8 Percentage calculations made from data in M. Thomas, 'The Service Sector', in Floud and Johnson (eds), *Cambridge Economic History of Modern Britain. Vol. 2*, p. 100.

9 Mathias, *First Industrial Nation*, pp. 294 and 279.

10 R. Floud, *The People and the British Economy, 1830–1914* (Oxford University Press, 1997), p. 89.

11 M. Collins, 'The Banking Crisis of 1878', *Economic History Review*, 2nd series, 42 (1989), pp. 504–27; W. P. Kennedy, *Industrial Structure, Capital Markets and the Origins of British Economic Decline* (Cambridge University Press, 1987).

12 M. Collins, *Banks and Industrial Finance in Britain, 1800–1939* (Cambridge University Press, 1995); P. L. Cottrell, *Industrial Finance, 1830–1914: The Finance and Organisation of English Manufacturing Industry* (Routledge, London, 1980).

13 C. Cook, *The Longman Companion to Britain in the Nineteenth Century, 1815–1914* (Pearson Education, Harlow, 1999), p. 216.

14 T. Gourvish, 'Railways 1830–70: The Formative Years', in M. Freeman and D. H. Aldcroft (eds), *Transport in Victorian Britain* (Manchester University Press, 1988), p. 67.

15 E. J. Evans, *The Forging of the Modern State: Early Industrial Britain, 1783–1870*, 3rd edn (Longman, London, 2001), p. 517.

16 For useful introductions to railway development see H. J. Dyos and D. Aldcroft (eds), *British Transport* (Leicester University Press, London, 1969); H. J. Perkin, *The Age of the Railway* (Routledge, London, 1970); Gourvish, 'Railways 1830–70'; and P. J. Cain, 'Railways, 1870–1914: The Maturity of the Private System' in M. Freeman and D. H. Aldcroft (eds), *Transport in Victorian Britain* (Manchester University Press, 1988), pp. 57–133.

17 *The Times*, 10 Apr. 1849. Quoted in *Oxford Dictionary of National Biography* (Oxford, 2004), entry on Hudson, No. 14029.

18 D. J. Rowe, 'The North-East', in F. M. L. Thompson (ed.), *The Cambridge Social History of Britain, 1750–1950. Vol. 1* (Cambridge University Press, 1990), pp. 416–17, 428–9.

19 Hansard, 3rd series, Vol. 86, 25 May 1846, col. 1109; also quoted in *Oxford Dictionary of National Biography*, entry on fifth Duke of Richmond, No. 16453.

20 Calculation from statistics in M. Turner, 'Agriculture, 1860–1914', in Floud and Johnson (eds), *Cambridge Economic History of Modern Britain. Vol. 2*, p. 135.

21 A. D. M. Phillips, *The Underdraining of Farm Land in England during the Nineteenth Century* (Cambridge University Press, 1989).

22 P. Mathias, *The First Industrial Nation: The Economic History of Britain, 1700–1914*, 2nd edn (Methuen, London, 1983), pp. 312–14.

23 E. L. Jones, 'The Changing Basis of Agricultural Prosperity, 1853–73', *Agricultural History Review*, 10 (1962), pp. 102–19.

24 Evans, *Forging of the Modern State*, p. 174.

25 R. Perren, *Agriculture in Depression, 1870–1940* (Cambridge University Press, 1995), p. 4; Turner 'Agriculture, 1860–1914', pp. 139–40.

Chapter 24. Social structure and social change in a maturing economy (page 248)

1 This useful distinction frames the discussion in P. Thane, 'Social History, 1860–1914', in R. Floud and D. McCloskey (eds), *The Economic History of Britain since 1700. Vol. 2, 1860 to the 1970s* (Cambridge University Press, 1981), pp. 198–238.

2 F. M. L. Thompson, 'Town and City', in F. M. L. Thompson (ed.), *The Cambridge Social History of Britain. Vol. 1, 1750–1950* (Cambridge University Press, 1990), pp. 10–11.

3 Thane, 'Social History, 1860–1914', p. 199.

4 K. T. Hoppen, *The Mid-Victorian Generation, 1846–1886* (Clarendon Press, Oxford, 1998), p. 85.

5 D. Jeremy, 'The Enlightened Paternalist in Action: William Hesketh Lever at Port Sunlight before 1914', *Business History*, 33 (1991), pp. 58–91, esp. p. 72.

6 G. R. Searle, *A New England: Peace and War, 1886–1918* (Clarendon Press, Oxford, 2004), p. 179; M. Turner, 'Agriculture, 1860–1914', in R. Floud and P. Johnson (eds), *The Cambridge Economic History of Modern Britain. Vol. 2, Economic Maturity* (Cambridge University Press, 2004), pp. 133–60.

7 On aristocratic resilience and later collapse, see D. Cannadine, *The Decline and Fall of the British Aristocracy* (Yale University Press, London, 1990).

8 D. Cannadine, *Lords and Landlords: The Aristocracy and the Towns, 1774–1967* (Leicester University Press, London, 1967), pp. 46–52.

9 S. Collini, 'The Idea of "Character" in Victorian Political Thought', *Transactions of the Royal Historical Society*, 5th series, 35 (1985), pp. 29–50, and M. Daunton, '"Gentlemanly Capitalism" and British Industry', *Past & Present*, 122 (1989), p. 132.

10 The estimates were made by R. D. Baxter in *National Income*, published in 1868 and by G. Routh, *Occupation and Pay in Great Britain, 1906–60* (Cambridge University Press, 1965). See the analysis of both in P. Thane, 'Social History 1860–1914', in Floud and McCloskey (eds), *Economic History of Britain since 1700. Vol. 2*, pp. 203–6.

11 Figures quoted ibid., p. 224. For the growth of the professions, see W. Reader, *Professional Men: The Rise of the Professional Classes in Nineteenth-Century England* (Weidenfeld & Nicolson, London, 1966) and, for the later period, H. J. Perkin, *The Rise of Professional Society: England since 1880* (Routledge, London, 1990 edn).

12 A. Kidd and D. Nicholls (eds), *Gender, Civic Culture and Consumerism: Middle Class Identity in Britain, 1800–1940* (Manchester University Press, 1999); G. Crossick (ed.), *The Lower Middle Classes in*

Britain, 1870–1914 (Croom Helm, London, 1976); G. Anderson, *Victorian Clerks* (Manchester University Press, 1976); and C. Hosgood 'The "pigmies of commerce" and the Working Class Community: Small Shopkeepers in England, 1870–1914', *Journal of Social History*, 22 (1989), pp. 439–60.

13 *Oxford Dictionary of National Biography* (Oxford University Press, 2004), entries on James Morrison, No. 19326 and Richard Thornton, No. 38065. On the very wealthy, see W. D. Rubinstein, *Elites and the Wealthy in Modern British History* (Palgrave Macmillan, Basingstoke, 1987) and *Men of Property: The Very Wealthy in Britain since the Industrial Revolution*, 2nd edn (Social Affairs Unit, London, 2006).

14 W. D. Rubinstein, 'The Size and Distribution of the English Middle Classes in 1860', *Historical Research*, 61, pp. 65–89.

15 J. K. Walton, 'The North-West', in Thompson (ed.), *Cambridge Social History of Britain. Vol. 1*, p. 374.

16 J. Garrard, 'Urban Elites, 1850–1914: The Rule and Decline of a New Squirearchy', *Albion*, 27 (1995), pp. 583–621. On social and political leadership in urban England more generally, see E. P. Hennock, *Fit and Proper Persons: Ideal and Reality in Nineteenth-Century Urban Government* (Edward Arnold, London, 1973) and R. M. Trainor, *Black Country Elites: The Exercise of Authority in an Urban Area, 1830–1900* (Clarendon Press, Oxford, 1993).

17 S. Gunn, *The Public Culture of the Victorian Middle Class: Ritual and Authority in the English Industrial City, 1840–1914* (Manchester University Press, 2007), pp. 137–45.

18 National Museums Liverpool, History of the Walker Art Gallery: www.liverpoolmuseums.org.uk

19 Hoppen, *Mid-Victorian Generation*, p. 57.

20 P. L. Garside, 'London and the Home Counties', in Thompson (ed.), *Cambridge Social History of Britain. Vol. 1*, pp. 501–2. See also E. Higgs, 'Women, Occupations and Work in the Nineteenth-Century Censuses, *History Workshop Journal*, 23 (1987), pp. 59–80.

21 T. C. Smout, 'Scotland', in Thompson (ed.), *Cambridge Social History of Britain. Vol. 1*, p. 211.

22 Statistics from R. D. Baxter, *National Income: The United Kingdom* (London, 1868), quoted in Hoppen, *Mid-Victorian Generation*, p. 63.

23 D. E. Baines, 'The Labour Supply and Labour Market' in Floud and McCloskey (eds), *Economic History of Britain since 1700. Vol. 2*, p. 164.

24 C. Feinstein, 'Pessimism Perpetuated: Real Wages and the Standard of Living in Britain during and after the Industrial Revolution', *Journal of Economic History*, 58, pp. 625–58. The most useful and up-to-date brief survey is J. Humphries, 'Standard of Living, Quality of Life', in C. Williams (ed.), *The Companion to the Nineteenth Century* (Blackwell, Oxford, 2004), pp. 287–304. It is regrettable, however, that relatively little space is given to the period after 1850.

25 Feinstein, 'Pessimism Perpetuated', p. 652.

Chapter 25. Identities, aspirations and gender (page 256)

1 L. Colley, *Britons: Forging the Nation, 1714–1837* (Yale University Press, London, 1992).

2 D. Powell, *Nationhood and Identity: The British State since 1800* (I. B. Tauris, London, 2002), p. 62.

3 *ibid.*, p. 310.

4 G. A. Williams, *When was Wales? The History, People and Culture of an Ancient Country* (Penguin, London, 1985), p. 210.

5 P. Jenkins, *A History of Modern Wales, 1536–1990* (Longman, Harlow, 1992), p. 301.

6 Williams, *When was Wales?*, p. 226.

7 K. Robbins, *Nineteenth-Century Britain: Integration and Diversity* (Oxford University Press, 1988), pp. 39–41.

8 The phrase comes from K. T. Hoppen, *The Mid-Victorian Generation, 1846–1886* (Clarendon Press, Oxford, 1998), p. 541. For the reshaping of Scottish identity, see H. Trevor Roper, *The Invention of Scotland: Myth and History* (Yale University Press, London, 2008).

9 On Scotland, see M. Lynch, *Scotland: A New History*, 2nd edn (Pimlico, London, 1992) and I. Hutchinson, *A Political History of Scotland, 1832–1924* (John Donald, Edinburgh, 1986). The separate United Presbyterian congregation was formed in 1847 from a merger of the United Secession and the Relief Church. In turn, this congregation merged with the Free Church in 1900 to create the United Free Church of Scotland.

10 In a speech to the House of Lords, 9 Apr. 1889, quoted in C. Kidd, 'Race, Empire and the Limits of Scottish Nationhood', *Historical Journal*, 42 (2003), p. 875.

11 *ibid.*, pp. 888–9. The wider significance of racialism in Scottish politics is explored in this article, pp. 873–92.

12 C. Ó Gráda, *Ireland: A New Economic History, 1780–1939* (Oxford University Press, 1994), p. 173.

13 One revisionist interpretation has even gone so far as to say that the effects of this depression were greater than that of the Famine thirty years later: R. Foster, *Modern Ireland, 1600–1972* (Allen Lane, London, 1988), p. 318.

14 Hoppen, *Mid-Victorian Generation*, p. 440.

15 Kidd, 'Race, Empire', p. 884.

16 C. G. Pooley, 'Segregation or Integration? The Residential Experience of the Irish in Mid-Victorian Britain', in R. Swift and S. Gilley (eds), *The Irish in Britain* (Pinter, London, 1989), p. 60.

17 E. J. Evans, 'Englishness and Britishness *c*1790–*c*1870', in A. Grant and K. J. Stringer (eds), *Uniting the Kingdom: The Making of British History* (Routledge, London, 1995), pp. 238–9.

18 Pooley, 'Segregation or Integration?', p. 71.

19 The best, and most developed, discussion of Englishness in this earlier period is to be found in P. Langford, *Englishness Identified: Manners and Character* (Oxford University Press, 2000). See also E. J. Evans, 'National Consciousness? The Ambivalences of English Identity in the Eighteenth Century', in C. Bjorn, A. Grant and K. Stringer (eds), *Nations, Nationalism and Patriotism in the European Past* (Academic Press, Copenhagen, 1994), pp. 145–60.

20 For further development of this line of thought, see P. Mandler, *The English National Character* (Yale University Press, London, 2006), pp. 27–52.

21 B. Hilton, *The Age of Atonement. The Influence of Evangelicalism on Social and Economic Thought, 1785–1865* (Oxford University Press, 1988).

22 H. Perkin, *The Origins of Modern English Society, 1780–1880* (Routledge, London, 1969), p. 408.

23 Mandler, *English National Character*, p. 68.

24 P. Mandler, '"Race" and "Nation" in Mid-Victorian Thought', in S. Collini, R. Whatmore and B. Young (eds), *History, Religion and Culture: British Intellectual History, 1750–1950* (Cambridge University Press, 2000), p. 243.

25 Quoted in R. Colls and P. Dodd (eds), *Englishness: Politics and Culture, 1880–1920* (Croom Helm, Beckenham, 1986), p. 236.

26 J. Lewis, *Women in England, 1870–1950* (Wheatsheaf, Sussex, 1984), p. 3.

27 K. Gleadle, *British Women in the Nineteenth Century* (Palgrave, Basingstoke, 2001), p. 91.

28 S. D'Cruze, 'Women and the Family', in J. Purvis (ed.), *Women's History, Britain 1850–1914* (UCL Press, London, 1995), pp. 51–83.

29 J. Howarth, 'Gender, Domesticity and Sexual Politics', in C. Matthew (ed.), *The Nineteenth Century* (Oxford University Press, 2000), p. 178.

30 J. K. Walton, 'The North-West', in F. M. L. Thompson (ed.), *The Cambridge Social History of Britain, 1750–1950. Vol. 1* (Cambridge University Press, 1990), pp. 365–9.

31 Howarth, 'Gender', pp. 170–3, and R. Floud, *The People and the British Economy, 1830–1914* (Oxford University Press, 1997), p. 77. For detailed discussions of women in the labour force, see

S. Horrell and J. Humphries, 'Women's Labour Force Participation and the Transition to the Male-Breadwinner Family', *Economic History Review*, 48 (1995), pp. 89–117; M. Berg and P. Hudson, 'Rehabilitating the Industrial Revolution', *Economic History Review*, 45 (1992), pp. 24–50. For women and educational opportunity, see Chapter 29 below.

32 J. Humphries, 'Women and Paid Work', in Purvis (ed.), *Women's History*, pp. 92–4.

33 A. Clark, *The Struggle for the Breeches: Gender and the Making of the British Working Class* (University of California Press, London, 1995), p. 220. See also J. Schwartzkopf, *Women in the Chartist Movement* (Palgrave Macmillan, Basingstoke, 1991) and Howarth, 'Gender', p. 177.

34 P. Hollis, *Ladies Elect: Women in English Local Government, 1867–1914* (Clarendon Press, Oxford, 1989 edn). See also Gleadle, *British Women*, pp. 111–121, 154–71. Female Scottish and Irish ratepayers did not get a municipal vote until 1882 and 1898 respectively.

35 S. Richardson, 'Politics and Gender', in C. Williams (ed.), *A Companion to Nineteenth-Century Britain* (Blackwell, Oxford, 2007 edn), pp. 174–88. See also P. Jalland, *Women, Marriage and Politics, 1860–1914* (Oxford University Press, 1986) and P. Levine, *Feminist Lives in Victorian England: Private Roles and Public Commitment* (Blackwell, Oxford, 1990).

Chapter 26. Free trade, *laissez-faire* and state regulation, *c*1830–*c*1880 (page 267)

1 Speech in the House of Commons, 22 Jan. 1846. Quoted in P. Harling and P. Mandler, 'From "Fiscal-Military" State to "Laissez-Faire" State, 1760–1850', *Journal of British Studies*, 32 (1993), p. 70.

2 A. Howe, *Free Trade and Liberal England, 1846–1946* (Clarendon Press, Oxford, 1997), p. 20.

3 *ibid.*, p. 29. On the Anti-Corn Law League specifically, see N. McCord, *The Anti-Corn Law League* (Routledge, London, 1958 and e-edition, London, 2006); J. Prest, *Politics in the Age of Cobden* (Macmillan, London, 1977). On its wider significance for the formation of popular opinion and identity, see P. Pickering and A. Tyrell, *The People's Bread: A History of the Anti-Corn Law League* (Leicester University Press, London, 2000).

4 *Manchester Examiner*, 10 Jan. 1846, quoted *ibid.*, p. 248.

5 P. Sharp, '1846 and All That: The Rise and Fall of British Wheat Protection in the Nineteenth Century', *Agricultural History Review*, 58 (2010), pp. 76–94.

6 In an article 'The Chartists', published in 1852. Quoted in M. Daunton, '"Gentlemanly Capitalism" and British Industry, 1820–1914', *Past & Present*, 122 (1989), p. 119.

7 A. Howe, *Free Trade and Liberal England, 1846–1946* (Clarendon Press, Oxford, 1997), p. 19.

8 C. Ó Gráda, 'Agricultural Decline', in R. Floud and D. McCloskey (eds), *The Economic History of Britain since 1700. Vol. 2, 1860 to the 1970s* (Cambridge University Press, 1981), p. 195.

9 E. Hobsbawm, *Industry and Empire* (Penguin, London, 1968), p. 197.

10 M. Daunton 'Society and Economic Life', in H. G. C. Matthew (ed.), *The Nineteenth Century* (Oxford University Press, 2000), p. 48.

11 K. T. Hoppen, *The Mid-Victorian Generation, 1846–1886* (Clarendon Press, Oxford, 1998), p. 103; *British Medical Journal*, 6 June 1896.

12 T. Gourvish, 'Railways 1830–70: The Formative Years', in M. Freeman and D. H. Aldcroft (eds), *Transport in Victorian Britain* (Manchester University Press, 1988), p. 84.

13 Samuel Smiles, *Self-Help* (John Murray, London, 1859), pp. 1–3.

14 For further development, see E. J. Evans (ed.), *Social Policy, 1830–1914: Individualism, Collectivism and the Origins of the Welfare State* (Routledge, London, 1978).

15 M. Daunton, *State and Market in Victorian Britain: War, Welfare and Capitalism* (Boydell Press, Woodbridge, 2008). See also P. Waller, *Town, City and Nation: England 1850–1914* (Oxford

University Press, 1973) and J. Prest, *Liberty and Locality: Parliament, Permissive Legislation and Ratepayers' Democracies in the Mid-Nineteenth Century* (Clarendon Press, Oxford, 1990).

16 Daunton, *State and Market*, p. 82.

17 T. Taylor, 'On Central and Local Action in Relation to Town Improvement', *Transactions of the National Association for the Promotion of Social Science*, 1 (1857), pp. 476–7.

18 A. C. Howe, 'Free Trade and the City of London', *History*, 77 (1992), pp. 391–410. The quotation is found on p. 410.

19 Oastler's letter was published in the *Leeds Mercury* in October 1830, E. J. Evans, *The Forging of the Modern State: Early Industrial Britain, 1783–1870*, 3rd edn (Longman, Harlow, 2001), p. 287.

20 O. MacDonagh, *Early Victorian Government, 1830–70* (Weidenfeld & Nicolson, London, 1977). The cited phrase formed the title of an earlier book concerned with emigration policy.

21 H. Mann, 'On the Cost and Organisation of the Civil Service', *Journal of the Royal Statistical Society*, 32 (1869), p. 38; Evans, *Forging of the Modern State*, p. 496.

22 Hoppen, *Mid-Victorian Generation*, p. 339.

23 J. Burnett, *A Social History of Housing, 1815–1985*, 2nd edn (Methuen, London, 1986), esp. pp. 121–39.

24 E. J. Evans (ed.), *Social Policy, 1830–1914* (Routledge, London, 1978), p. 10.

25 Debate in the House of Commons, 1 Aug. 1872, quoted *ibid.*, p. 153.

26 House of Commons, 24 June 1875, Hansard, 3rd series, Vol. 225, col. 525.

27 P. Marsh, *Joseph Chamberlain: Entrepreneur in Politics* (Yale University Press, London, 1994).

28 J. A. Hobson, *The Crisis of Liberalism: New Issues of Democracy* (London, 1909), pp. xi–xii.

Chapter 27. Supremacy under threat? Economy and society, 1880–1914 (page 276)

1 E. E. Williams, *Made in Germany* (London, 1896), p. 11. Quoted in J. Tomlinson, *Government and the Enterprise since 1900: The Changing Problem of Efficiency* (Oxford University Press, 1994), p. 19.

2 D. McCloskey, 'Did Victorian Britain Fail?', *Economic History Review*, 2nd series, 23 (1970), pp. 446–59. This quotation appears on p. 451.

3 N. F. R. Crafts, 'Long Run Growth', in R. Floud and P. Johnson (eds), *The Cambridge Economic History of Modern Britain. Vol. 2, 1860–1939* (Cambridge University Press, 2004), p. 11.

4 Statistics taken from G. B. Magee, 'Manufacturing and Technological Change', *ibid.*, p. 81.

5 A. Howe, 'Britain and the World Economy', in C. Williams (ed.), *A Companion to Nineteenth-Century Britain* (Blackwell, Oxford, 2004), p. 26.

6 *The Economist*, 13 Mar. 1880.

7 P. J. Cain and A. G. Hopkins, *British Imperialism: Innovation and Expansion, 1688–1914* (Longman, Harlow, 1993), pp. 164–7.

8 L. G. Sandberg, 'The Entrepreneur and Technological Change' in R. Floud and D. McCloskey (eds), *The Economic History of Britain since 1700. Vol. 2, 1860 to the 1970s* (Cambridge University Press, 1981), pp. 99–120.

9 G. Searle, *A New England? Peace and War, 1886–1918* (Clarendon Press, Oxford, 2004), p. 185.

10 D. Kynaston, *The City of London. Vol. 2, 1890–1914* (Chatto & Windus, London, 1995), pp. 7, 242–58.

11 *ibid.*, p. 610.

12 W. D. Rubinstein, *Capitalism, Culture and Decline in Britain, 1750–1990* (Routledge, London, 1993), pp. 24–5.

13 A. E. Musson, *The Growth of British Industry* (Batsford, London, 1978), pp. 166–8.

14 The main exponent of this interpretation is M. J. Wiener, *English Culture and the Decline of the Industrial Spirit, 1850–1980* (Cambridge University Press, 1981). The most elegant summary of the opposite

case is found in F. M. L. Thompson, *Gentrification and the Enterprise Culture: Britain, 1780–1980* (Oxford University Press, 2001).

15 H. Rider Haggard, *Rural England* (London, 1902), quoted in Searle, *A New England*, p. 176.
16 Calculation from statistics in M. Turner, 'Agriculture 1860–1914', in Floud and Johnson (eds), *Cambridge Economic History of Modern Britain. Vol. 2*, p. 135. See also Searle, *A New England*, pp. 175–83.
17 F. M. L. Thompson, 'An Anatomy of English Agriculture, 1873–1896', in B. A. Holderness and M. E. Turner (eds), *Land, Labour and Agriculture, 1700–1920: Essays for Gordon Mingay* (Hambledon Press, London, 1991), pp. 211–41.
18 T. W. Fletcher, 'The Great Depression of English Agriculture, 1873–1896', in P. J. Perry, *British Agriculture, 1875–1914* (Routledge, London, 1973), pp. 44–5.
19 M. J. Winstanley, 'Agriculture and Rural Society', in C. Williams (ed.), *Companion to the Nineteenth Century* (Blackwell, Oxford, 2004), p. 209.
20 M. E. Turner, 'Agricultural Output, Income and Productivity', in G. E. Mingay (ed.), *The Agrarian History of England and Wales. Vol. 7* (Cambridge University Press, 2000), p. 263.
21 Searle, *A New England*, p. 178.
22 Turner, 'Agriculture 1860–1914', p. 152.
23 *Oxford Dictionary of National Biography* (Oxford, 2004), entry on sixteenth Earl of Derby, No. 36245.
24 Searle, *A New England*, p. 182.
25 E. C. Grenville Murray, *Side-Lights on English Society* (1881), quoted in D. Kynaston, *The City of London. Vol. 1, 1815–90* (Chatto & Windus, London, 1994), p. 381.
26 *ibid.*, p. 382.
27 D. Cannadine, *The Decline and Fall of the British Aristocracy* (Yale University Press, London, 1990), esp. pp. 297–387.
28 *ibid.*, pp. 305–6.
29 D. Oddy, 'Food, Drink and Nutrition' in F. M. L. Thompson, *The Cambridge Social History of Britain, 1750–1950. Vol. 2* (Cambridge University Press, 1990), pp. 269–71.
30 V. Berridge, 'Health and Medicine', ibid., *Vol. 3*, pp. 191–203.
31 Durham County Record Office, CC/H9, pp. 70–1, 108.

Chapter 28. The state, charity and the poor, *c*1830–*c*1900 (page 286)

1 In his novel *Sybil*, published in 1845.
2 E. J. Evans, *The Forging of the Modern State: Early Industrial Britain, 1783–1870*, 3rd edn (Longman, Harlow, 2001), p. 511.
3 D. Ricardo, *Principles of Political Economy and Taxation* (Penguin edn, 1971), p. 126.
4 P. Mandler, 'The Making of the New Poor Law Redivivus', *Past & Present*, 117 (1987), pp. 131–57.
5 Calculations from tables in A. Kidd, *State, Society and the Poor in Nineteenth-Century England* (Macmillan, Basingstoke, 1999), p. 168.
6 D. Eastwood, *Governing Rural England: Tradition and Transformation in Local Government, 1780–1840* (Oxford University Press, 1994), p. 184.
7 D. Englander, *Poverty and Poor Law Reform in Nineteenth-Century Britain, 1834–1914* (Addison Wesley Longman, Harlow, 1998), p. 44.
8 F. Driver, *Power and Pauperism: The Workhouse System, 1834–84* (Cambridge University Press, 1993); N. Longmate, *The Workhouse* (Temple Smith, London, 1974).
9 Quoted in J. T. Ward, *Popular Movements, 1830–50* (Macmillan, Basingstoke, 1970), p. 80.
10 Mandler, 'Making of the New Poor Law', p. 157.

11 M. Daunton, 'Society and Economic Life', in H. G. C. Matthew (ed.), *The Nineteenth Century, 1815–1901* (Oxford University Press, 2000), p. 72; Kidd, *State, Society and the Poor*, pp. 47–8.

12 E. Chadwick, *An Article on the Principles and Practice of the Poor Law Amendment Act* (London, 1837), p. 45.

13 K. Williams, *From Pauperism to Poverty* (Routledge, London, 1981). See particularly p. 220.

14 Englander, *Poverty*, p. 15.

15 First Annual Report of the Local Government Board, Appendix A 1871–2. Cited ibid., pp. 106–7.

16 K. T. Hoppen, *The Mid-Victorian Generation, 1846–1886* (Clarendon Press, Oxford, 1998), p. 344.

17 Calculations from Kidd, *State, Society and the Poor*, p. 169.

18 Quoted in E. J. Evans (ed.), *Social Policy, 1830–1914* (Routledge, London, 1978), p. 179.

19 For a summary of the deficiencies, see G. R. Searle, *A New England? Peace and War, 1886–1918* (Clarendon Press, Oxford, 2004), pp. 194–6.

20 Letter dated 15 Mar. 1886 in *Parliamentary Papers*, Vol. 36 (1886), pp. 179–181.

21 Kidd, *State, Society and the Poor*, p. 67; F. Prochaska 'Philanthropy', in F. M. L. Thompson (ed.), *The Cambridge Social History of Britain, 1750–1950. Vol. 3* (Cambridge University Press, 1990), pp. 357–98.

22 *ibid.*, p. 358.

23 Kidd, *State, Society and the Poor*, pp. 80–1.

24 R. J. Morris, 'Clubs, Societies and Associations', in Thompson (ed.), *Cambridge Social History of Britain, 1750–1950. Vol. 3*, p. 415.

25 Prochaska, 'Philanthropy', p. 387.

26 Searle, *A New England?*, pp. 192–3.

27 17th Annual Meeting of the Charity Organisation Society, 18 Jan. 1886, *Charity Organisation Review*, 2 (1886), pp. 52–60.

Chapter 29. Education, leisure and society (page 296)

1 S. Gunn, *The Public Culture of the Victorian Middle Class* (Manchester University Press, 2009), p. 19.

2 W. B. Stephens, *Education in Britain, 1750–1914* (Macmillan, Basingstoke, 1998), pp. 48, 98–105.

3 L. Davidoff, 'The Family', in F. M. L. Thompson (ed.), *The Cambridge Social History of Britain, 1750–1950, Vol. 2* (Cambridge University Press, 1990), pp. 80–5; L. Davidoff and C. Hall, *Family Fortunes: Men and Women of the English Middle Class, 1780–1850*, 2nd edn (Routledge, London, 2002).

4 Stephens, *Education*, pp. 109–10. See also C. Dyhouse, *Girls Growing Up in Late Victorian and Edwardian England* (Routledge, London, 1981).

5 F. Prochaska, *Women and Philanthropy in Nineteenth-Century England* (Oxford University Press, 1980), p. 3.

6 G. R. Searle, *A New England? Peace and War, 1886–1918* (Clarendon Press, Oxford, 2004), p. 61. On women's educational achievement and progress in the professions more generally, see J. Lewis, *Women in England, 1870–1950: Sexual Divisions and Social Change* (Prentice Hall, London, 1984).

7 *ibid.*, p. 194.

8 Stephens, *Education*, pp. 21–35.

9 G. Sutherland, 'Education', in Thompson (ed.), *Cambridge Social History of Britain, 1750–1950. Vol. 2*, pp. 122–6.

10 Hansard, 3rd series, Vol. 20, cols 733–5, 17 Aug. 1833.

11 See also O. MacDonagh, *A Pattern of Government Growth* (MacGibbon & Key, London, 1961) for a similar development in respect of government intervention to regulate policy on emigration.

12 T. A. Jenkins, *The Liberal Ascendancy, 1830–1886* (Macmillan, Basingstoke, 1994), p. 59; G. R. Searle, *Entrepreneurial Politics in Mid-Victorian Britain* (Oxford University Press, 1993), p. 241.

13 Sutherland, 'Education', p. 141.

14 J. Kay-Shuttleworth, *Four Periods of Public Education* (London, 1862), pp. 582–3.

15 Speech on 13 Feb. 1862, Hansard, 3rd series, Vol. 165, cols 206–7, 229–30, 237–8.

16 Calculation from Searle, *Entrepreneurial Politics*, pp. 251–2.

17 Stephens, *Education*, p. 78.

18 Searle, *Entrepreneurial Politics*, p. 236.

19 *ibid.*, p. 84.

20 R. D. Anderson, 'Secondary Schools and Scottish Society in the Nineteenth Century', *Past & Present*, 109 (1985), pp. 176–203, esp. pp. 192–3. See also Sutherland, 'Education', p. 146.

21 *ibid.*, p. 143.

22 For a typical example, see the inspection of Burley Road School, Leeds in December 1881. Leeds City Archives, Leeds School Board 14/1.

23 *The Times*, 31 Jan. 1890.

24 W. N. Molesworth, 'On the Extent and Results of Co-Operative Trading Associations at Rochdale', *Journal of the Royal Statistical Society*, 24 (1861), pp. 507–14.

25 J. K. Walton, 'The Holiday Industry in Blackpool', in J. K. Walton (ed.), *Leisure in Britain, 1780–1939* (Manchester University Press, 1983), p. 177.

26 P. Bailey, *Leisure and Class in Victorian England* (Routledge, London, 1978).

27 R. D. Storch, 'The Lancashire Wakes in the Nineteenth Century', in R. D. Storch (ed.), *Popular Culture and Custom in Nineteenth Century England* (Croom Helm, London, 1982), pp. 100–24.

28 H. Cunningham, 'Leisure and Culture' in Thompson (ed.), *Cambridge Social History of Britain, 1750–1950. Vol. 2*, pp. 305–6.

29 J. Burchardt, *The Allotment Movement in England, 1793–1873* (Royal Historical Society, London, 2002) and D. M. Moran, *The Allotment Movement in Britain* (P. Lang, New York, 1990).

30 J. K. Walton, *Blackpool* (Edinburgh University Press, 1998).

31 A. Croll, 'Popular Leisure and Sport', in C. Williams (ed.), *Companion to the Nineteenth Century* (Blackwell, Oxford, 2004), pp. 396–411.

32 M. Tebbutt, *Women's Talk? A Social History of 'Gossip' in Working-Class Neighbourhoods, 1880–1960* (Ashgate, Aldershot, 1997).

33 For police and policing, see C. Emsley, *The English Police: A Political and Social History* (Longman, Harlow, 1996) and D. Phillips and R. Storch, *Policing Provincial England, 1829–1856: The Politics of Reform* (Leicester University Press, London, 1999). For an argument about the suppression of 'traditional' customs and recreations, see R. W. Malcolmson, *Popular Recreations in English Society, 1700–1850* (Cambridge University Press, 1973).

34 For the role of music halls, see P. Bailey, 'Custom, Capital and Culture in the Victorian Music Hall', in Storch (ed.), *Popular Culture*, pp. 180–208.

Chapter 30. Party politics confounded, 1846–1859 (page 309)

1 For a useful summary of party developments and confusion in the early nineteenth century, see B. Hilton, *A Mad, Bad and Dangerous People? England 1783–1846* (Oxford University Press), pp. 195–209.

2 J. Prest, *Lord John Russell* (Macmillan, London, 1972), p. 223. For a more recent assessment of his career, see P. Scherer, *Lord John Russell: A Biography* (Associated University Presses, London, 1999).

3 T. A. Jenkins, *Parliament, Party and Politics in Victorian Britain* (Manchester University Press, 1996), p. 51; T. A. Jenkins, *The Liberal Ascendancy, 1830–86* (Macmillan, Basingstoke, 1994), p. 63.

4 M. Taylor, *The Decline of British Radicalism, 1847–1860* (Clarendon Press, Oxford, 1995), pp. 21–23, 347–9.

5 K. T. Hoppen, *The Mid-Victorian Generation, 1846–1886* (Clarendon Press, Oxford, 1998), p. 140.

6 Quoted in R. Stewart, *The Foundation of the Conservative Party, 1830–1867* (Longman, Harlow, 1978), p. 226.

7 E. J. Evans, '"The Strict Line of Political Succession?" Gladstone's Relationship with Peel', in D. Bebbington and R. Swift (eds), *Gladstone Centenary Essays* (Liverpool University Press, 2000), pp. 29–56.

8 In a note of September 1852, Prest, *Lord John Russell*, p. 345.

9 The most recent detailed reassessment of Derby is A. Hawkins, *The Forgotten Prime Minister: Ascent, 1799–1851* (Oxford University Press, 2007) and *The Forgotten Prime Minister: Achievement, 1852–1869* (Oxford University Press, 2008).

10 Quoted in I. Machin, *Disraeli* (Longman, Harlow, 1995), p. 80.

11 *Oxford Dictionary of National Biography* (Oxford University Press, 2004), entry on Molesworth, No. 189802.

12 In a private letter of 4 Jan. 1853, quoted in A. Hawkins, *British Party Politics, 1852–86* (Macmillan, Basingstoke, 1998), p. 53.

13 *Parliamentary Papers*, 1854, Vol. 26, pp. 1–3.

14 *Oxford Dictionary of National Biography*, entry on Palmerston, No. 27112.

15 M. Foot and H. G. C. Matthew (eds), *The Gladstone Diaries. Vol. 5, 1855–61* (Clarendon Press, Oxford, 1978), p. 27.

16 J. P. Parry, *The Rise and Fall of Liberal Government in Victorian Britain* (Yale University Press, London, 1993), p. 177.

17 R. Blake, *Disraeli* (Eyre & Spottiswoode, London, 1966), p. 363.

18 In the *Edinburgh Review* in January 1848. Quoted in Parry, *Rise and Fall*, p. 180.

19 For a detailed analysis of this election, see Taylor, *Decline*, pp. 269–84.

20 Hoppen, *Mid-Victorian Generation*, pp. 207–8.

Chapter 31. Parliamentary reform, 1850–1880: intention and impact (page 319)

1 *Oxford Dictionary of National Biography* (Oxford University Press, 2004), entry on George Grote, No. 11677; I. Machin, *The Rise of Democracy in Britain, 1830–1918* (Macmillan, Basingstoke, 2001), pp. 26–7.

2 K. T. Hoppen, *The Mid-Victorian Generation, 1846–1886* (Clarendon Press, Oxford, 1998), p. 237.

3 Quoted in G. R. Searle, *Entrepreneurial Politics in Mid-Victorian Britain* (Oxford University Press, 1993), p. 210.

4 Article by Harney in *Northern Star*, 17 Nov. 1849. Quoted in E. Royle, *Revolutionary Britannia: Reflections on the Threat of Revolution in Britain, 1789–1848* (Manchester University Press, 2000), pp. 192–3.

5 M. Taylor, 'Interests, Parties and the State: the Urban Electorate in England, *c*1820–72', in J. Lawrence and M. Taylor (eds), *Party, State and Society: Electoral Behaviour in Britain since 1820* (Scolar Press, Aldershot, 1997), p. 56.

6 Quoted in Hoppen, *Mid-Victorian Generation*, p. 239.

7 Hansard, 3rd series, Vol. 175, 11 May 1864, cols 324–7.

8 J. Belchem, *Popular Radicalism in Nineteenth-Century Britain* (Macmillan, Basingstoke, 1996), pp. 113–14.

9 Searle, *Entrepreneurial Politics*, pp. 221–2. See also *Oxford Dictionary of National Biography*, entries on Taylor, Potter and Morley, Nos. 27070, 22621 and 19291.

10 See the extracts from Bright's and Gladstone's speeches in the mid-1860s in P. Joyce, 'The Narrative Structure of Victorian Politics', in J. Vernon (ed.), *Re-reading the Constitution* (Cambridge University Press, 1996), pp. 188–94.

11 *The Times*, 2 June 1865.

12 In a speech to the House of Commons, Hansard, 3rd series, Vol. 182, 16 Apr. 1866, cols 147–8, quoted in Hoppen, *Mid-Victorian Generation*, p. 247.

13 Searle, *Entrepreneurial Politics*, pp. 217–19. See also *Oxford Dictionary of National Biography*, entry on Laing, No. 15892.

14 M. Foot and H. G. C. Matthew (eds), *The Gladstone Diaries. Vol. 6, 1861–69* (Clarendon Press, Oxford, 1978), p. 446.

15 On Gladstone's views, see R. T. Shannon, *Gladstone: Heroic Minister, 1865–1898* (Allen Lane, London, 1999), pp. 22–3.

16 Belchem, *Popular Radicalism*, pp. 117–18.

17 For a dissentient voice, see R. Harrison, *Before the Socialists* (Routledge, London, 1965).

18 F. B. Smith, *The Making of the Second Reform Bill* (Cambridge University Press, 1966), p. 134.

19 A. Hawkins, *British Party Politics, 1852–1886* (Macmillan, Basingstoke, 1998), p. 121.

20 M. Cowling, *1867: Disraeli, Gladstone and Revolution* (Cambridge University Press, 1967), p. 119. See also *Oxford Dictionary of National Biography*, entry on seventh Earl of Shaftesbury, No. 6210.

21 For further details, see E. J. Evans, *Parliamentary Reform, c1770–1918* (Pearson Education, Harlow, 2000), pp. 131–3.

22 Speaking in the House of Lords on 6 August 1867 and quoted in Hoppen, *Mid-Victorian Generation*, p. 253.

23 Quoted in R. Harrison, 'The British Working Class and the General Election of 1868', *International Review of Social History*, 5 (1960), pp. 424–55.

24 H. J. Hanham, *Elections and Party Management: Politics in the Time of Gladstone and Disraeli* (Longman, London, 1959), pp. 405–12.

25 Hansard, 3rd series, Vol. 188 (1867), cols 1528–50.

26 J. P. Parry, *The Rise and Fall of Liberal Government in Victorian Britain* (Yale University Press, London, 1993), p. 217; *Oxford Dictionary of National Biography*, entry on Bagehot, No. 1029.

27 Quoted in Hawkins, *British Party Politics*, p. 138.

28 Taylor, 'Interests', p. 57.

29 Hoppen, *Mid-Victorian Generation*, p. 255.

30 D. Tanner, *Political Change and the Labour Party, 1900–1918* (Cambridge University Press, 1990), pp. 111–23. See also J. Lawrence, 'The Dynamics of Urban Politics', in Lawrence and Taylor (eds), *Party, State and Society*, p. 88.

31 J. Davis and D. Tanner, 'The Borough Franchise after 1867', *Historical Research*, 69 (1996), pp. 306–27. See also Evans, *Parliamentary Reform*, pp. 55–64, 125–7.

32 Lawrence, 'Dynamics of Urban Politics', p. 83.

33 H. E. Gorst, *The Earl of Beaconsfield* (London, 1900), pp. 126–7.

34 M. Pugh, *The Making of Modern British Politics, 1867–1945*, 3rd edn (Blackwell, Oxford, 2002), pp. 48–50.

35 Parry, *Rise and Fall*, p. 275.

36 *ibid.*

37 *Oxford Dictionary of National Biography*, entry on Joseph Cowen Jnr, No. 6494.

Chapter 32. Gladstone and the Liberal party, 1859–1880 (page 329)

1 T. A. Jenkins, *The Liberal Ascendancy, 1830–1886* (Macmillan, Basingstoke, 1994), pp. 105, 127, 146, 198.
2 J. P. Parry, *The Rise and Fall of Liberal Government in Victorian Britain* (Yale University Press, London, 1993), pp. 200–3.
3 Electoral statistics calculated from data in C. Cook, *The Longman Companion to Britain in the Nineteenth Century* (Longman, London, 1999), pp. 79–83. K. T. Hoppen, *The Mid-Victorian Generation, 1846–1886* (Clarendon Press, Oxford, 1998), p. 260.
4 M. Taylor, *The Decline of British Radicalism, 1847–60* (Clarendon Press, Oxford, 1995), esp. pp. 308–46.
5 Hoppen, *Mid-Victorian Generation*, p. 209, and A. Hawkins, *Parliament, Party and the Art of Politics in Britain, 1855–1859* (Macmillan, 1987). For a different perspective, which sees the emergence of a modern Liberal party rather earlier, see J. P. Parry, *The Rise and Fall of Liberal Government in Victorian Britain* (Yale University Press, London, 2003).
6 A private view in a letter written to the Prince of Wales two months earlier: J. Prest, *Lord John Russell* (Macmillan, London, 1972), p. 383.
7 T. A. Jenkins, *Parliament, Party and Politics in Victorian Britain* (Manchester University Press, 1996), p. 21.
8 In the words of the Bank's first Comptroller, George Chetwynd, in a letter of 30 Nov. 1860. British Postal Museum and Archive, POST75/35.
9 Parry, *Rise and Fall*, pp. 184–6; A. Howe, *Free Trade and Liberal England, 1846–1886* (Clarendon Press, Oxford, 1997), pp. 93–5; *Oxford Dictionary of National Biography* (Oxford, 2004), entry on William Gladstone, No. 10787.
10 A. Hawkins, *British Party Politics, 1852–1886* (Macmillan Palgrave, Basingstoke, 1998), p. 107.
11 J. C. Lowe, 'The Tory Triumph of 1868 in Blackburn and Lancashire', *Historical Journal*, 16 (1973), pp. 733–48.
12 As quoted in Earl Curzon, *Modern Parliamentary Eloquence* (Rede Lecture to the University of Cambridge, Cambridge, 1913), p. 25.
13 As quoted in A. K. Adams, *The Home Book of Humorous Quotations* (Dodd, Mead & Co., New York, 1969).
14 J. Stansfeld, House of Commons, 20 July 1871, Hansard, 3rd series, Vol. 208, cols 78–81.
15 Parry, *Rise and Fall*, p. 239.
16 Hoppen, *Mid-Victorian Generation*, p. 604.
17 Parry, *Rise and Fall*, p. 272.
18 Gladstone's letter to Granville, 8 Jan. 1874, in A. Ramm (ed.), *The Gladstone–Granville Correspondence*, revised edn (Cambridge University Press, 1998), pp. 438–41.
19 Rectorial Address, 1879, in W. E. Gladstone, *Midlothian Speeches* (Leicester University Press edn, 1971), pp. 235–8.
20 H. C. G. Matthew, *Gladstone, 1875–1898* (Clarendon Press, Oxford, 1995), p. 60.
21 This is the general conclusion of E. Biagini, *Gladstone* (Palgrave Macmillan, Basingstoke, 2000).
22 R. T. Shannon, *Gladstone: Heroic Minister, 1865–1898* (Allen Lane, London, 1999).

Chapter 33. Disraeli and the Conservative party, 1860–1880 (page 339)

1 For a long-overdue reassessment of Derby, see A. Hawkins, *The Forgotten Prime Minister: The 14th Earl of Derby*, 2 vols (Oxford University Press, 2007, 2008). See also Chapter 30 above.

2 *Oxford Dictionary of National Biography* (Oxford, 2004), entry on fourteenth Earl of Derby, No. 26265.

3 I. Machin, *Disraeli* (Longman, Harlow, 1995), pp. 98–9.

4 *Oxford Dictionary of National Biography*, No. 26265.

5 In 1863, Disraeli voted in only 8 of 188 Commons divisions, in 1864 in 17 out of 156, A. Hawkins, *British Party Politics, 1852–1886* (Macmillan, Basingstoke, 1998), p. 179.

6 29 & 30 Vict c 90; E. J. Evans, *Social Policy, c1830–1914* (Routledge, London, 1978), pp. 72–3, 85–6.

7 In a speech in Edinburgh, quoted in E. Feuchtwanger, *Disraeli* (Hodder Headline, London, 2000), p. 141.

8 D. Steele, *Lord Salisbury: A Political Biography* (Routledge, London, 1999), p. 81.

9 Feuchtwanger, *Disraeli*, p. 159.

10 G. E. Buckle, *The Life of Benjamin Disraeli. Vol. 5, 1868–76* (John Murray, London, 1920), pp. 186–97.

11 Feuchtwanger, *Disraeli*, pp. 160–1, and Machin, *Disraeli*, pp. 120–1.

12 Feuchtwanger, *Disraeli*, p. 164.

13 Buckle, *Life*, p. 279.

14 J. Parry, *The Rise and Fall of Liberal Government in Victorian Britain* (Yale University Press, London, 1993), p. 272.

15 Quoted in K. T. Hoppen, *The Mid-Victorian Generation, 1846–1886* (Clarendon Press, Oxford, 1998), p. 613.

16 Feuchtwanger, *Disraeli*, p. 173.

17 Disraeli's Speech to the Electors of Buckinghamshire, *The Times*, 26 Jan. 1874.

18 *Oxford Dictionary of National Biography*, entry on Richard Cross, No. 32644.

19 R. T. Shannon, *The Age of Disraeli, 1868–81: The Rise of Tory Democracy* (Longman, Harlow, 1992), pp. 214–15 and Hawkins, *British Party Politics*, pp. 190–1.

20 The key revisionist assessments are P. Smith, *Disraelian Conservatism and Social Reform* (Routledge, London, 1967); B. Coleman, *Conservatism and the Conservative Party in the Nineteenth Century* (Hodder Arnold, London, 1988); and Shannon, *Age of Disraeli*.

21 Smith, *Disraelian Conservatism*, p. 205.

22 Hoppen, *Mid-Victorian Generation*, p. 635; Feuchtwanger, *Disraeli*, pp. 204–5.

Chapter 34. Diplomacy and war: the *Pax Britannica* challenged, *c*1830–1865 (page 349)

1 Letter from Victoria to Russell, 12 Aug. 1850, reproduced in M. E. Chamberlain, *British Foreign Policy in the Age of Palmerston* (Longman, Harlow, 1980), p. 126.

2 J. Ridley, *Lord Palmerston* (Constable, London, 1970), p. 394.

3 Chamberlain, *British Foreign Policy*, p. 97.

4 M. E. Chamberlain, *Lord Palmerston* (GPC Books, Cardiff, 1987), p. 49.

5 B. Hilton, *A Mad, Bad and Dangerous People? England 1783–1846* (Oxford University Press, 2006), p. 558.

6 K. Bourne, *The Foreign Policy of Victorian England* (Clarendon Press, Oxford, 1970), p. 29.

7 *ibid.*, p. 32.

8 *ibid.*, p. 221.

9 Chamberlain, *Lord Palmerston*, p. 51.

10 In a letter to Granville, the British ambassador to France, 10 June 1839. Quoted in Ridley, *Lord Palmerston*, p. 222.

11 P. Hayes, *The Nineteenth Century, 1814–80* (Black, London, 1975), pp. 272; Ridley, *Lord Palmerston*, pp. 255–7.

12 Hayes, *Nineteenth Century*, p. 286.

13 Bourne, *Foreign Policy*, pp. 34–7, 47–8.

14 Hilton, *A Mad, Bad and Dangerous People?*, p. 564.

15 Private letter from Palmerston to Victoria, 12 Sept. 1846, reprinted in Bourne, *Foreign Policy*, pp. 270–3.

16 Chamberlain, *Lord Palmerston*, pp. 94–5.

17 Quoted in K. T. Hoppen, *The Mid-Victorian Generation, 1846–1886* (Clarendon Press, Oxford, 1998), p. 230.

18 *ibid.*, p. 232.

19 J. R. Davis, 'Britain and the European Balance of Power', in C. Williams (ed.), *A Companion to Nineteenth-Century Britain* (Blackwell, Oxford, 2004), pp. 41–2.

20 Chamberlain, *Lord Palmerston*, p. 117.

21 During a speech in the House of Lords on 4 Feb. 1864, quoted in Hoppen, *Mid-Victorian Generation*, p. 233.

22 R. W. Seton-Watson, *Britain in Europe, 1789–1914* (Cambridge University Press, 1937), p. 395.

Chapter 35. Diplomacy and the Eastern Question, 1865–1880 (page 359)

1 Quotations from J. Ridley, *Lord Palmerston* (Constable, London, 1970), pp. 584, 591.

2 Diary entry of 30 July 1866, quoted in *Oxford Dictionary of National Biography* (Oxford University Press, 2004), entry on fifteenth Earl of Derby, No. 26266.

3 K. Bourne, *The Foreign Policy of Victorian England, 1830–1902* (Clarendon Press, 1970), p. 117.

4 Quoted in M. E. Chamberlain, *'Pax Britannica'? British Foreign Policy, 1789–1914* (Longman, London, 1988), p. 126.

5 Quoted in K. T. Hoppen, *The Mid-Victorian Generation, 1846–1886* (Clarendon Press, Oxford, 1998), pp. 603, 236.

6 Quoted in J. Lowe, *Britain and Foreign Affairs, 1815–1885* (Routledge, London, 1998), p. 71, and Bourne, *Foreign Policy*, p. 96.

7 G. E. Buckle, *The Life of Benjamin Disraeli. Vol. 5, 1868–1876* (John Murray, London, 1920), pp. 133–4.

8 From the Gladstone diary entry of 6 Feb. 1874, quoted in R. T. Shannon, *Gladstone, Heroic Minister, 1865–1898* (Allen Lane, London, 1999), p. 138.

9 Disraeli speech in the House of Commons, 21 Feb. 1876, Hansard, 3rd series, Vol. 227, cols 658–61.

10 The most authoritative and detailed analysis of the Balkan crisis is R. Millman, *Britain and the Eastern Question, 1875–1878* (Clarendon Press, Oxford, 1979).

11 D. Steele, *Lord Salisbury: A Political Biography* (Routledge, London, 2001 edn), pp. 106–7.

12 Quoted in Shannon, *Gladstone*, p. 159. See also *Oxford Dictionary of National Biography*, entry on Farley, No. 9164.

13 Quoted in Hoppen, *Mid-Victorian Generation*, p. 623.

14 On 12 August 1876, Disraeli took a peerage as Earl of Beaconsfield. Though technically incorrect from this point, his commoner name 'Disraeli' continues to be used to avoid confusion.

15 E. Feuchtwanger, *Disraeli* (Arnold, London, 2000), pp. 192–3.

Chapter 36. 'This vast Empire on which the sun never sets': imperial expansion and cultural icon (page 369)

1 In his *Account of Ireland in 1773* and quoted by Thomas Bartlett, 'Ireland, Empire and Union, 1690–1801', in K. Kenny (ed.), *Ireland and the British Empire*' (Oxford University Press, 2004), p. 72. See also Ronald Thorne, entry on Macartney, George, Earl Macartney, *Oxford Dictionary of National Biography* (Oxford University Press, 2004), No. 17341.
2 The Church of Scotland was prominent in missionary work within the Empire. It sent its first missionaries to India in 1829 and Nyasaland in 1876 (Church of Scotland Missionary Archive, National Library of Scotland).
3 George Curzon, *Problems of the Far East* (1894).
4 Quoted in Niall Ferguson, *Empire: How Britain Made the Modern World* (Allen Lane, London, 2003), p. 228.
5 Quoted in B. Porter, *The Lion's Share*, 4th edn (Longman Pearson, London), p. 138.
6 J. Gallagher and R. Robinson, 'The Imperialism of Free Trade', *Economic History Review*, 2nd series, vi (1953), pp. 1–15.
7 See, as a useful introduction to this phase of Indian history, C. A. Bayly, *Empire and Information* (Cambridge University Press, 1996); C. A. Bayly, *Indian Society and the Making of the British Empire* (Cambridge University Press, 1988); C. A. Bayly and D. H. A. Kolff (eds), *Two Colonial Empires* (Springer, New York, 1986).
8 G. Chakravarty, *The Indian Mutiny and the British Imagination* (Cambridge University Press, 2005); S. David, *The Indian Mutiny: 1857* (Penguin edn, 2002) and C. Hibbert, *The Great Mutiny: India 1857* (Penguin edn, 2002).
9 K. T. Hoppen, *The Mid-Victorian Generation, 1846–1886* (Clarendon Press, Oxford, 1998), p. 195.
10 D. Cannadine, *Ornamentalism: How the British Saw their Empire* (Allen Lane, London, 2001), p. 45.
11 J. M. MacKenzie, *The Scramble for Africa* (Routledge, London, 1983), p. 42.
12 J. S. Keltie, *The Partition of Africa* (London, 1895 edn), p. 1.
13 *ibid.*, p. 52, quoted in J. D. Hargreaves, 'Towards a History of the Partition of Africa', *The Journal of African History*, 1 (1960), pp. 97–109.
14 R. Hyam, *Understanding the British Empire* (Cambridge University Press, 2010), p. 107.
15 A good example of an approach which emphasises African perspectives is H. L. Wesseling, *Divide and Rule: The Partition of Africa* (Praeger, London, English trans., 1996).
16 *The Times*, 15 Sept. 1884.
17 Ferguson, *Empire*, p. 237.
18 A useful summary of the debate can be found in A. Offer, 'The British Empire, 1870–1914: A Waste of Money?', *Economic History Review*, 2nd series, 46 (1993), pp. 215–38.
19 J. A. Mangan 'The Grit of our Forefathers', in J. M. Mackenzie (ed.), *Imperialism and Popular Culture* (Manchester University Press, 1986), p. 118.
20 A. S. Thompson, *Imperial Britain: The Empire in British Politics, c1880–1932* (Pearson Education, Harlow, 2000), pp. 61–80.
21 *The Times*, 3 June 1887.
22 *The Times*, 11 June 1887.
23 From 'Britannia', a song of 1885, quoted by Penny Summerfield, 'Patriotism and Empire', in MacKenzie (ed.), *Imperialism and Popular Culture*, pp. 17–48.
24 In *The Psychology of Jingoism*, quoted in B. Porter, *The Absent-Minded Imperialists* (Manchester University Press, 2004), p. 196.
25 MacKenzie (ed.), *Imperialism*, p. 3.
26 The view of Edward Dicey, quoted in Porter, *Lion's Share*, p. 138.
27 *ibid.*, pp. 196–7.

28 For a discussion of how much the Empire influenced the thinking of working-class children see Porter, *Absent-Minded Imperialists*, pp. 194, 199–205.
29 The best introduction here remains B. Porter, *Critics of Empire* (Macmillan, London, 1968).
30 I. R. Smith, *The Origins of the South African War, 1899–1902* (Longman, London, 1996).
31 The most useful recent study of the war is D. Judd and K. Surridge, *The Boer War* (Palgrave, Macmillan, Basingstoke, 2003).
32 *The Times*, 19 and 21 May 1900.

Chapter 37. Conservatism in the era of Salisbury, 1880–1914 (page 381)

1 The other three conventionally in contention are Churchill, Thatcher and Peel. The claims of all three are problematic. Winston Churchill, who was a Liberal for much of his early career, was in the 1920s and 1930s both much disliked and deeply mistrusted by his Conservative colleagues. His reputation was rescued only by his leadership during the Second World War. Margaret Thatcher's radical economic policies, strongly reminiscent of mid-Victorian *laissez-faire*, made her perhaps the least 'conservative' Tory of all. Peel is the choice of many historically informed cognoscenti but the Conservative party broke up under his leadership in 1846.
2 See particularly A. Hawkins, *The Forgotten Prime Minister: The 14th Earl of Derby*, 2 vols (Oxford University Press, 2007, 2008).
3 P. Ghosh, 'Style and Substance in Disraelian Social Reform', in P. Waller (ed.), *Politics and Social Change c1860–1880* (Harvester, Brighton, 1987) and 'Disraelian Conservatism: A Financial Approach', *English Historical Review*, 99 (1984), pp. 268–96.
4 Quoted in D. Steele, *Lord Salisbury: A Political Biography* (Routledge, London, 2001 edn), p. 172.
5 Quoted in M. Pugh, *The Making of Modern British Politics, 1867–1945*, 3rd edn (Blackwell, Oxford, 2002), p. 52.
6 I. Machin, *The Rise of Democracy in Britain, 1830–1918* (Blackwell, Oxford, 2001), pp. 89–90.
7 E. H. H. Green, *The Crisis of Conservatism: The Politics, Economics and Ideology of the British Conservative Party, 1880–1914* (Routledge, London, 1995), p. 107.
8 E. J. Evans, *Parliamentary Reform, c1770–1918* (Pearson Education, Harlow, 2000), pp. 68–74, 133–5; G. R. Searle, *A New England? Peace and War 1886–1918* (Clarendon Press, Oxford, 2004), pp. 132–4.
9 For a detailed analysis, see H. Pelling, *The Social Geography of British Elections, 1885–1910* (Macmillan, London, 1967).
10 The standard work on the Conservative party in this period is R. T. Shannon, *The Age of Salisbury: Unionism and Empire, 1881–1902* (Longman, Harlow, 1996).
11 Steele, *Lord Salisbury*, p. 176.
12 For Salisbury's engagement with, and accommodation to, an increasingly urban world in which the aristocracy often felt itself on the defensive, see M. Bentley, *Lord Salisbury's World: Conservative Environments in Late-Victorian Britain* (Cambridge University Press, 2001).
13 I. J. Cawood, 'The Lost Party: Liberal Unionism, 1886–95', Ph.D. thesis, University of Leicester. This section has been considerably influenced by the results of Dr Cawood's researches, which are due to be published in 2011.
14 Searle, *A New England?*, p. 152.
15 *ibid.*, p. 219.
16 In a speech at Nottingham in Nov. 1889. Reported in *The Times*, 31 Jan. 1890.
17 Speech to Liberal Unionists at Manchester, 14 Oct. 1902. Reported in *The Times*, 15 Oct. 1902.

18 P. Hollis, *Ladies Elect: Women in English Local Government, 1865–1914* (Oxford University Press, 1987), pp. 125–33.
19 For details of voting proportions see C. Wrigley (ed.), *A Companion to Early Twentieth-Century Britain* (Blackwell, Oxford, 2003), p. 39. The standard account of the Conservative party in this period is J. Ramsden, *The Age of Balfour and Baldwin, 1902–1940* (Longman, London, 1978).
20 Green, *Crisis*, p. 2.
21 Searle, *A New England?*, pp. 311–12, 329–52.
22 Green, *Crisis*, esp. pp. 285–320. For a useful brief analysis of Conservative difficulties see P. Williamson, 'The Conservative Party, 1900–1939: From Crisis to Ascendancy', in Wrigley (ed.), *Companion*, pp. 3–22.
23 Quoted in Pugh, *Making of Modern British Politics*, p. 104.

Chapter 38. The Liberal party, 1880–1914: sundered and saved? (page 391)

1 H. G. C. Matthew, *Gladstone, 1875–1898* (Oxford University Press, 1995), pp. 99–105.
2 *Oxford Dictionary of National Biography* (Oxford University Press, 2004), entry on W. E. Gladstone, No. 10787.
3 J. Parry, *The Rise and Fall of Liberal Government in Victorian Britain* (Yale University Press, London, 1993), p. 278.
4 Quoted in K. T. Hoppen, *The Mid-Victorian Generation, 1846–1886* (Clarendon Press, Oxford, 1998), p. 636.
5 M. Swartz, *The Politics of British Foreign Policy in the Era of Disraeli and Gladstone* (Macmillan, Basingstoke, 1985), p. 145.
6 T. A. Jenkins, *Gladstone, Whiggery and the Liberal Party, 1874–1886* (Oxford University Press, 1988), p. 144.
7 For Gladstone's reaction to Chamberlain's 'Radical Programme' in 1885, see R. T. Shannon, *Gladstone: Heroic Minister, 1865–1898* (Allen Lane, London, 1999), p. 385.
8 A. Hawkins, *British Party Politics, 1852–1886* (Macmillan, Basingstoke, 1998), pp. 250–1.
9 J. Belchem, *Popular Radicalism in Nineteenth-Century Britain* (Macmillan, Basingstoke, 1996), pp. 137–40. Chamberlain first used the phrase in a speech in Birmingham in March 1883.
10 C. W. Boyd (ed.), *Mr Chamberlain's Speeches* (Constable, London, 1914), pp. 14–16, 166–70.
11 Parry, *Rise and Fall*, p. 306.
12 Matthew, *Gladstone*, p. 307.
13 M. Pugh, *The Making of Modern British Politics, 1867–1945*, 3rd edn (Blackwell, Oxford, 2002), pp. 36–9.
14 Matthew, *Gladstone*, p. 258.
15 Quoted *ibid.*, p. 319.
16 *Oxford Dictionary of National Biography* (Oxford, 2004), entry on fifth Earl of Rosebery, No. 35612.
17 G. R. Searle, *A New England? Peace and War 1886–1918* (Clarendon Press, Oxford, 2004), p. 214.
18 *ibid.*, pp. 358–9.
19 For further development of this argument, see A. Howe, *Free Trade and Liberal England, 1846–1946* (Clarendon Press, Oxford, 1997), pp. 246–52.
20 Searle, *A New England?*, p. 409.
21 Pugh, *Making of Modern British Politics*, p. 113. For a detailed account of the constitutional crisis which followed, see N. Blewett, *The Peers, the Parties and the People: The General Elections of 1910* (Macmillan, London, 1972) and R. Jenkins, *Mr Balfour's Poodle: Peers versus People* (Macmillan, London, 2001 edn).

Chapter 39. 'Votes for Women' (page 403)

1 A good brief introduction is S. Richardson, 'Politics and Gender', in C. Williams (ed.), *A Companion to Nineteenth-Century Britain* (Blackwell, Oxford, 2004), pp. 174–88. From a huge literature, J. Rendall (ed.), *Equal or Different? Women's Politics, 1800–1914* (Wiley-Blackwell, London, 1987); A. Vickery (ed.), *Women, Privilege and Power: British Politics, 1750 to the Present* (Stanford University Press, 2001); and J. Liddington and J. Norris, *One Hand Tied Behind Us: The Rise of the Women's Suffrage* 2nd edn (Rivers Oram Press, London 2001) provide a representative range.
2 John Stuart Mill, House of Commons, 20 May 1867, Hansard, 3rd series, Vol. 187, cols 817–28.
3 K. T. Hoppen, *The Mid-Victorian Generation, 1846–1886* (Clarendon Press, Oxford, 1998), p. 252.
4 S. Kent, *Sex and Suffrage in Britain, 1860–1914* (Princeton University Press, 1987), pp. 9–10.
5 *ibid.*, p. 3.
6 M. Pugh, *The March of the Women: A Revisionist Analysis of the Campaign for Women's Suffrage, 1886–1914* (Oxford University Press, 2000), pp. 28–30.
7 Quoted in G. R. Searle, *A New England? Peace and War, 1886–1918* (Clarendon Press, Oxford, 2004), p. 78.
8 *Oxford Dictionary of National Biography* (Oxford University Press, 2004), entry on Woodall, No. 37007.
9 H. G. C. Matthew, *Gladstone, 1875–98* (Clarendon Press, Oxford, 2005), pp. 324–6.
10 P. Smith (ed.), *Lord Salisbury on Politics: A Selection from his Articles in the Quarterly Review, 1860–83* (Cambridge University Press, 1972), p. 18.
11 B. Harrison, 'Women's Suffrage at Westminster, 1866–1928', in M. Bentley and J. Stevenson (eds), *High and Low Politics in Modern Britain* (Clarendon Press, Oxford, 1983), pp. 87–8.
12 Richardson, 'Politics and Gender', pp. 178–80.
13 Pugh, *March of the Women*, pp. 12–13.
14 *ibid.*, pp. 79–80.
15 For an assessment of the NUWSS, see L. Hume, *The National Union of Women's Suffrage Societies, 1897–1914* (Garland, New York, 1982).
16 From an article by Millicent Fawcett published in 1886 in the journal *Nineteenth Century*. Quoted in Pugh, *March of the Women*, p. 64.
17 Searle, *A New England?*, p. 458.
18 C. McPhee and A. Fitzgerald (eds), *The Non-Violent Militant: Selected Writings of Teresa Billington-Greig* (Routledge, London, 1987), p. 138.
19 *Oxford Dictionary of National Biography*, entry on Billington-Greig, No. 39074.
20 Pugh, *March of the Women*, p. 211.
21 Quoted, respectively, in Searle, *A New England?*, p. 463, and Pugh, *March of the Women*, p. 182.
22 Searle, *A New England?*, pp. 464, 468.
23 Harold Brust, *In Plain Clothes: Further Memoirs of a Political Police Officer* (Stanley Paul, London, 1937), p. 60, quoted in B. Porter, *Britannia's Burden: The Political Evolution of Modern Britain, 1851–1990* (Arnold, London, 1994), pp. 159–60.
24 Speech in the House of Commons, 22 May 1917, Hansard, 5th series, Vol. 93, cols 2207–8.

Chapter 40. Ireland and British politics, 1880–1914 (page 413)

1 For an introduction to the historiography, see C. Kinealey, 'Politics in Ireland', in C. Williams (ed.), *A Companion to the Nineteenth Century* (Blackwell, Oxford, 2004), pp. 473–88.
2 R. F. Foster, *Modern Ireland, 1600–1972* (Allen Lane, 1988), p. 325.
3 P. Bull, *Land, Politics and Nationalism: A Study of the Irish Land Question* (Gill & Macmillan, Dublin, 1996).

4 J. Mokyr, *Why Ireland Starved: A Quantitative and Analytical History of the Irish Economy, 1800–1850*
   (Routledge reprint edn, London, 2006); K. T. Hoppen, *Elections, Politics and Society in Ireland, 1832–1885*
   (Oxford University Press, 1984).
5 *ibid.*, pp. 17–33.
6 K. T. Hoppen, 'Tories, Catholics and the General Election of 1859', *Historical Journal*, 13 (1970),
   pp. 48–67.
7 R. T. Shannon, *Gladstone: Heroic Minister, 1865–1898* (Allen Lane, London, 1999), p. 65.
8 K. T. Hoppen, *The Mid-Victorian Generation, 1846–1886* (Clarendon Press, Oxford, 1998), p. 594.
9 Foster, *Modern Ireland*, p. 397.
10 *Oxford Dictionary of National Biography* (Oxford University Press, 2004), entry on Butt, No. 4222.
11 A. O'Day, *Irish Home Rule, 1867–1921* (Manchester University Press, 1998), p. 32.
12 For a good biography of Parnell, see P. Bew, *Charles Stewart Parnell*, 2nd edn (Gill and Macmillan,
   London, 1991).
13 H. G. C. Matthew, *Gladstone 1875–1898* (Oxford University Press, 1995), p. 193.
14 O'Day, *Irish Home Rule*, pp. 70–1.
15 P. Bull, 'Land and Politics', in D. G. Boyce (ed.), *The Revolution in Ireland, 1879–1923* (Macmillan,
   Basingstoke, 1988), p. 29.
16 For a detailed account of the political context, see K. T. Hoppen, *Elections, Politics and Society in
   Ireland, 1832–1885* (Oxford University Press, 1984). On the situation in 1885–86, see B. Walker,
   'The 1885 and 1886 General Elections in Ireland', *History Ireland*, 13 (2005), pp. 36–40. See also
   N. C. Fleming and A. O'Day, *The Longman Handbook of Modern Irish History since 1800* (Pearson
   Longman, Harlow, 2005), pp. 120, 315.
17 G. R. Searle, *A New England? Peace and War, 1886–1918* (Clarendon Press, Oxford, 2004), p. 120.
18 F. Campbell, *The Irish Establishment, 1879–1914* (Oxford University Press, 2009).
19 Matthew, *Gladstone*, p. 185.
20 Quoted in D. G. Boyce, *The Irish Question and British Politics, 1868–1996* (Macmillan, Basingstoke,
   1996), p. 33.
21 Quoted in Shannon, *Gladstone*, p. 393.
22 P. Jalland, *The Liberals and Ireland: The Ulster Question in British Politics to 1914* (Harvester,
   Brighton, 1980), pp. 50–1.
23 Patrick Pearse in *An Claidheamh Soluis*, 1903. Quoted in J. Smith, *Britain and Ireland: From Home
   Rule to Independence* (Longman, Harlow, 2000), p. 113.
24 J. Hutchinson, *The Dynamics of Cultural Nationalism: The Gaelic Revival and the Creation of the Irish
   Nation State* (Macmillan, Basingstoke, 1987).
25 Searle, *A New England?*, pp. 155–6.
26 D. G. Boyce, 'Ireland and British Politics, 1900–1939', in C. Wrigley (ed.), *A Companion to Early
   Twentieth-Century Britain* (Blackwell, Oxford, 2003), p. 103.
27 Boyce, *Irish Question*, p. 186.
28 Fleming and O'Day, *Longman Handbook of Modern Irish History*, p. 574.
29 Quoted in Boyce, *Irish Question*, p. 49.
30 A. Jackson, 'Unionist Myths, 1912–1985', *Past & Present*, 136 (1992), pp. 164–85.

Chapter 41. Labour, welfare and social conflict, 1900–1914 (page 425)

1 *Contemporary Review*, 83 (1903), pp. 41–56.
2 For a detailed account of an inchoate movement, see G. R. Searle, *The Quest for National Efficiency*
   (University of California Press, 1971).
3 Report of the Inter-Departmental Committee on Physical Deterioration, Cmd 2175, 1904, pp. 13–14.

4 Quoted in G. R. Searle, *A New England? Peace and War, 1886–1918* (Clarendon Press, Oxford, 2004), p. 376.
5 D. Porter, ' "Enemies of the Race": Biologism, Environmentalism and Public Health in Edwardian England', *Victorian Studies*, 34 (1991), pp. 159–78.
6 Quoted in M. Pugh, *State and Society: A Social and Political History of Britain, 1870–1997*, 2nd edn (Arnold, London, 1999), p. 128.
7 *Oxford Dictionary of National Biography* (Oxford University Press, 2004), entry on Winston Churchill, No. 32413.
8 Searle, *A New England?*, pp. 378–9, and J. Harris, *Private Lives, Public Spirit: Britain, 1870–1914* (Penguin, London, 1993), p. 60.
9 L. Andrews, 'The School Meals Service', *British Journal of Educational Studies*, 20 (1972), pp. 70–5; J. S. Hurt, *Elementary Schooling and the Working Classes, 1860–1918* (Routledge, London, 1979), p. 105.
10 Searle, *A New England?*, pp. 378–9; *A Century of Change: Trends in UK Statistics since 1900* (House of Commons Research Paper 99/111, Dec. 1999); D. Baines and R. Woods, 'Population and Regional Development', in R. Floud and P. Johnson (eds), *The Cambridge Economic History of Modern Britain. Vol. 2, 1860–1939* (Cambridge University Press, 2004), pp. 31–4.
11 Durham County Record Office, CC/H9, pp. 70–1 and 108, cited in E. J. Evans, *Social Policy, 1830–1914* (Routledge, London, 1978), p. 266.
12 'The Children Act – What it is and Does', *Liberal Monthly*, 4 (1909), p. 5.
13 G. R. Boyer, 'Living Standards, 1860–1939', in Floud and Johnson (eds), *Cambridge Economic History of Modern Britain. Vol. 2*, pp. 296–305; E. J. Evans, *Social Policy, c1830–1914* (Routledge, London, 1978) p. 259.
14 Harris, *Private Lives*, p. 206.
15 Parliamentary Papers, 1909, Vol. 37, pp. 643–4.
16 Ibid., pp. 248, 325–8, 516–17, 598–9.
17 Office for National Statistics, *Pension Trends*, ch. 1, p. 3. See also J. Macnicol, *The Politics of Retirement in Britain, 1878–1948* (Cambridge University Press, 1998) and M. Pelling and R. M. Smith (eds), *Life, Death and the Elderly: Historical Perspectives* (Routledge, London, 1991).
18 Searle, *A New England?*, p. 367.
19 *Daily Mail*, 4 Nov. 1911; National Archives, T 172/49.
20 For recent histories of the Labour party which avoid crude class stereotypes, see K. Laybourn, *A Century of Labour: A History of the Labour Party, 1900–2000* (Sutton, Stroud, 2000); D. Tanner, *Political Change and the Labour Party* (Cambridge University Press, 1987); A. Thorpe, *A History of the British Labour Party*, 3rd edn (Palgrave Macmillan, Basingstoke, 2008); and M. Pugh, *Speak for Britain! A New History of the Labour Party* (Bodley Head, London, 2010).
21 J. Lawrence, 'The Dynamics of Urban Politics', in J. Lawrence and M. Taylor (eds), *Party, State and Society: Electoral Behaviour in Britain since 1820* (Scolar Press, Aldershot, 1997), p. 97.
22 P. Thane, 'The Working Class and State "Welfare" in Britain, 1880–1914', *Historical Journal*, 27 (1984), pp. 877–900. The quotation is on p. 891.
23 C. Cook (ed.), *The Longman Companion to Britain in the Nineteenth Century, 1815–1914* (Longman, Harlow, 1999), p. 164.
24 Searle, *A New England?*, pp. 438–55.
25 For the most detailed analysis of the issue, see D. Tanner, 'Elections, Statistics and the Rise of the Labour Party, 1906–1931', *Historical Journal*, 33 (1991) pp. 893–908. A useful recent summary of the situation is provided by M. Roberts, *Political Movements in Urban England, 1832–1914* (Palgrave Macmillan, Basingstoke, 2009), pp. 128–60.

Chapter 42. A greater need for security: diplomacy and alliance systems, 1880–1902 (page 435)

1 Speech at West Calder, 27 Nov. 1879. Quoted in R. T. Shannon, *Gladstone: Heroic Minister, 1865–1898* (Allen Lane, London, 1999), pp. 238–9.
2 P. Hayes, *Modern British Foreign Policy: The Twentieth Century, 1880–1939* (Black, London, 1978), p. 20.
3 M. Swartz, *The Politics of British Foreign Policy in the Era of Disraeli and Gladstone* (Macmillan, Basingstoke, 1985), p. 152.
4 P. Kennedy, *The Rise of Anglo-German Antagonism, 1860–1914* (Ashfield, London, 1987).
5 A remark from March 1880, quoted in K. T. Hoppen, *The Mid-Victorian Generation, 1846–1886* (Clarendon Press, Oxford, 1998), pp. 656–7.
6 K. Bourne, *The Foreign Policy of Victorian England, 1830–1902* (Clarendon Press, Oxford, 1970), p. 139.
7 Salisbury, House of Lords, 26 Feb. 1885. Extract in W. D. Handcock (ed.), *English Historical Documents*, Vol. 12, Part 2 (Eyre & Spottiswoode, London, 1977), pp. 368–76.
8 W. H. Stead, 'Chinese Gordon', *The Century*, 28 (Aug. 1884).
9 Extract from a Paper presented by Sir Phillip Currie, Salisbury's private secretary, in Berlin, Aug. 1885. Published in Bourne, *Foreign Policy*, pp. 423–5.
10 Quoted in M. E. Chamberlain, *'Pax Britannica'? British Foreign Policy, 1789–1914* (Longman, London, 1988), p. 148.
11 *ibid.*, p. 154.
12 G. R. Searle, *A New England? Peace and War, 1886–1918* (Clarendon Press, Oxford, 2004), pp. 260–2.
13 Quoted in D. Steele, *Lord Salisbury: A Political Biography* (Routledge, London, 2001 edn), p. 318.
14 This aspect of Salisbury's diplomacy is treated in some depth in J. Charmley, *Splendid Isolation? Britain and the Balance of Power, 1874–1914* (Hodder & Stoughton, London, 1999).
15 Cabinet Report of 10 Feb. 1887, reproduced in Bourne, *Foreign Policy*, p. 426. See also C. L. Smith, *The Embassy of Sir William White at Constantinople, 1886–1891* (Oxford University Press, 1957).
16 F. H. Hinsley, 'Bismarck, Salisbury and the Mediterranean Agreements of 1887', *Historical Journal*, 1 (1958), pp. 76–81.
17 Quoted in Searle, *A New England?*, p. 245.
18 Kennedy, *Rise of Anglo-German Antagonism*, pp. 205–9.
19 Steele, *Lord Salisbury*, p. 345.
20 Searle, *A New England?*, p. 268.

Chapter 43. An accidental catastrophe? The origins of the First World War (page 445)

1 For a detailed account of relations between Britain and Russia, see K. Neilson, *Britain and the Last Tsar: British Policy and Russia, 1894–1917* (Clarendon Press, Oxford, 1995).
2 K. Bourne, *The Foreign Policy of Victorian England, 1830–1902* (Clarendon Press, Oxford, 1970), p. 175; G. R. Searle, *A New England? Peace and War, 1886–1918* (Clarendon Press, Oxford, 2004), pp. 320–1.
3 P. Kennedy, *The Rise of Anglo-German Antagonism, 1860–1914* (Humanity Books edn, New York, 1980), p. 252.
4 Quoted in Searle, *A New England?*, p. 323.
5 P. Hayes, *Modern British Foreign Policy: The Twentieth Century, 1880–1939* (A&C Black, London, 1978), p. 124.

6 Eyre Crowe, 'Memorandum on the Present State of British Relations with France and Germany', 1 Jan. 1907. See also E. T. Corp, 'Sir Eyre Crowe and the Administration of the Foreign Office, 1906–14', *Historical Journal*, 22 (1979), pp. 443–54, and G. P. Gooch and H. V. Temperley (eds), *British Documents on the Origins of the War* (HMSO, London, 1926–36), Vol. 3, pp. 397–431.

7 Parliamentary Papers (HMSO, London, 1908), Vol. 125, Cmd. 3750.

8 K. M. Wilson, *The Politics of the Entente: Essays on the Determination of British Foreign Policy* (Cambridge University Press, 1985), p. 42.

9 Quoted in Searle, *A New England?*, p. 492.

10 R. B. Henig, *The Origins of the First World War*, 3rd edn (Routledge, London, 2002), pp. 8–10.

11 D. French, 'Spy Fever in Britain, 1900–15', *Historical Journal*, 21 (1978), pp. 355–70.

12 B. Porter, *Plots and Paranoia: A History of Political Espionage in Britain, 1790–1988* (Routledge, London, 1992), pp. 120–50.

13 Searle, *A New England?*, pp. 517–20.

14 Norman Angel's views expressed through the 'Neutrality League' in 1914, Kennedy, *Rise of Anglo-German Antagonism*, p. 459.

15 An excellent, brief analysis of the problem as a whole is provided in Henig, *Origins of the First World War*.

16 D. Kynaston, *The City of London. Vol. 2, Golden Years, 1890–1914* (Chatto & Windus, London, 1995), pp. 593 and 610.

17 Quoted in M. E. Chamberlain, *Pax Britannica? British Foreign Policy, 1789–1914* (Longman, Harlow, 1988), p. 172.

18 Quoted in Kennedy, *Rise of Anglo-German Antagonism*, p. 459.

Chapter 44. Epilogue (page 455)

1 Viscount Grey of Fallodon, *Twenty Five Years, 1892–1916*, 4th edn (F. A. Stokes, New York, 1925), p. 20.

2 In a letter to Margot Asquith and quoted in G. R. Searle, *A New England? Peace and War, 1886–1918* (Clarendon Press, Oxford, 2004), p. 663.

3 BBC Series, *This Sceptred Isle: Empire*, Vol. 82: Broadcast 6 June 2006.

4 From calculations in *Daily Mail*, 29 Sept. 2010.

5 For details, see E. J. Evans, *Parliamentary Reform, c1770–1918* (Pearson Education, Harlow, 2000), pp. 87–95, 135.

6 Quoted in R. Pearce, *Contemporary Britain, 1914–1979* (Addison Wesley Longman, Halrow, 1996), p. 31.

7 Editorial in *The Observer*, 24 Oct. 1920.

8 For a full discussion of issues related to the financing of companies, see P. Cottrell, 'Domestic Finance, 1860–1914', in R. Floud and P. Johnson (eds), *The Cambridge Economic History of Modern Britain. Vol. 2, 1860–1939* (Cambridge University Press, 2004), pp. 252–79.

Select bibliography

Unsurprisingly, the relevant literature on Britain in this period is vast. The list below is arranged thematically, with separate sections covering Ireland, Scotland and Wales for those who wish to concentrate on the histories of those countries. What follows is inevitably selective though not, the author hopes, unrepresentative. Many of the books cited below have extensive bibliographies which will arm those wishing to go more deeply into any topic with the appropriate equipment.

General introduction

The most valuable series of detailed histories of Britain is 'The New Oxford History of England'. Readers should be aware that these are indeed histories of 'England', rather than 'Britain', although the relationship between England and the other constituent elements of the United Kingdom figures prominently in each of the volumes. In the later modern period, each weighty volume covers 60 years or fewer with commensurate opportunity for study in depth. The Series has won widespread, and entirely justified, plaudits. Each of the volumes is strong and each comes with a detailed critical bibliography. The strengths of each are distinctive but all recognise that political change derives from complex social, cultural and economic changes. The volumes covering the chronology of this book are:

P. Langford, *A Polite and Commercial People: England, 1727–1783* (Clarendon Press, Oxford, 1989)

A. B. Hilton, *A Mad, Bad and Dangerous People? England 1783–1846* (Clarendon Press, Oxford, 2006)

T. K. Hoppen, *The Mid-Victorian Generation: 1846–1886* (Clarendon Press, Oxford, 1998)

G. R. Searle, *A New England? Peace and War, 1886–1918* (Clarendon Press, Oxford, 2004)

Almost all subject experts now hold that this Series has superseded the 'Oxford History of England' partly, of course, because only volumes published in the late twentieth or early twenty-first centuries can adequately reflect the overall direction and emphasis of recent research. Also, the themes emphasised in earlier series derived unashamedly from the belief that high politics and diplomacy are what really mattered. Within that framework, however, the earlier volumes still have much to commend them. The relevant volumes are:

J. S. Watson, *The Reign of George III, 1760–1815* (Clarendon Press, Oxford, 1960)

E. L. Woodward, *The Age of Reform, 1815–1870*, 2nd edn (Clarendon Press, Oxford, 1962)

R. C. K. Ensor, *England, 1870–1914* (Clarendon Press, Oxford, 1936)

Useful statistical information will be found in the following works:

C. Cook, *The Routledge Companion to Britain in the Nineteenth Century* (Routledge, London, 2005)

J. Gregory and J. Stevenson, *The Longman Companion to Britain in the Eighteenth Century* (Longman, London, 2000)

The website which accompanies this volume also contains substantial statistical and other factual information. It is designed to provide appropriate support for the themes developed here.

The Blackwell series of 'Companions' offers a lively series of up-to-date interpretative essays. The volumes covering the period of this book are:

H. T. Dickinson (ed.), *A Companion to Eighteenth-Century Britain* (Blackwell, Oxford, 2002)

C. Williams (ed.), *A Companion to Nineteenth-Century Britain* (Blackwell, Oxford, 2004)

C. Wrigley (ed.), *A Companion to Twentieth-Century Britain* (Blackwell, Oxford, 2002)

'The Short Oxford History of the British Isles' also comprises a series of substantial thematic essays which attempt to sustain a focus on Britain as a whole. The relevant volumes in this series are:

P. Langford (ed.), *The Eighteenth Century, 1688–1815* (Oxford University Press, 2002)

H. G. C. Matthew (ed.), *The Nineteenth Century, 1815–1901* (Oxford University Press, 2000)

K. G. Robbins (ed.), *The British Isles, 1901–1951* (Oxford University Press, 2002)

Two series, by Longman and by Arnold, have proved their value over a number of years:

G. Holmes and D. Szechi, *The Age of Oligarchy: Pre-Industrial Britain, 1722–83* (Longman, Harlow, 1993)

E. J. Evans, *The Forging of the Modern State: Early Industrial Britain, 1783–1870*, 3rd edn (Pearson Education, London, 2001)

K. G. Robbins, *The Eclipse of a Great Power: Modern Britain, 1870–1992*, 2nd edn (Longman, Harlow, 1994)

I. R. Christie, *Wars and Revolutions: Britain, 1760–1815* (Arnold, London, 1986)

N. Gash, *Aristocracy and People: Britain, 1815–65* (Arnold, London, 1979)

E. Feuchtwanger, *Democracy and Empire: Britain, 1865–1914* (Arnold, London, 1985)

Readers will find in C. Matthew, B. Harrison and L. Goldman (eds), *Oxford Dictionary of National Biography* (Oxford University Press, 2004) an invaluable new resource. It provides detailed information on about 60,000 significant individuals. Each entry contains extensive bibliographical information on its subject.

Ireland

Books

P. Bew, *Charles Stewart Parnell*, 2nd edn (Gill and Macmillan, London, 1991)

D. G. Boyce (ed.), *The Revolution in Ireland, 1879–1923* (Macmillan, Basingstoke, 1988)

D. G. Boyce, *The Irish Question and British Politics, 1868–1996* (Macmillan, Basingstoke, 1996)

D. G. Boyce and A. O'Day (eds), *The Making of Modern Irish History: Revisionism and the Revisionist Controversy* (Routledge, London, 1996)

P. Bull, *Land, Politics and Nationalism: A Study of the Irish Land Question* (Gill & Macmillan, Dublin, 1996)

F. Campbell, *The Irish Establishment, 1879–1914* (Oxford University Press, 2009)

L. M. Cullen, *The Emergence of Modern Ireland 1600–1900* (Batsford, London, 1981)

M. Elliott, *Partners in Revolution: The United Irishmen and France* (Yale University Press edn, 1990)

N. C. Fleming and A. O'Day, *The Longman Companion to Irish History since 1800* (Longman, London, 2005)

R. F. Foster, *Modern Ireland, 1600–1972* (Penguin, London, 1989)

P. Geoghegan, *The Irish Act of Union: A Study in High Politics, 1798–1801* (Gill & Macmillan, London, 2001)

K. T. Hoppen, *Elections, Politics and Society in Ireland, 1832–1885* (Oxford University Press, 1984)

J. Hutchinson, *The Dynamics of Cultural Nationalism: The Gaelic Revival and the Creation of the Irish Nation State* (Macmillan, Basingstoke, 1987)

J. Kennedy, *An Economic History of Ulster, 1820–1939* (Manchester University Press, 1985)

K. Kenny (ed.), *Ireland and the British Empire* (Oxford University Press, 2004)

J. Mokyr, *Why Ireland Starved: A Quantitative and Analytical History of the Irish Economy, 1800–1850* (Allen & Unwin, London, 1983)

J. Mokyr, *Why Ireland Starved: A Quantitative and Analytical History of the Irish Economy, 1800–1850* (Routledge reprint edn, London, 2006)

A. O'Day, *Irish Home Rule, 1867–1921* (Manchester University Press, 1998)

C. Ó Gráda, *Ireland: A New Economic History, 1780–1939* (Oxford University Press, 1994)

J. Smith, *Britain and Ireland: From Home Rule to Independence* (Longman, Harlow, 2000)

M. Vaughan (ed.), *A New History of Ireland: Vol. 5, 1801–70* and *Vol. 6, 1870–1921* (both Clarendon Press, Oxford, 1989 and 1996 respectively)

W. E. Vaughan and J. A. Fitzpatrick (eds), *Irish Historical Statistics: Population 1821–71* (Royal Irish Academy, 1978)

M. J. Winstanley, *Ireland and the Land Question, 1800–1922* (Routledge, London, 1984)

Articles

S. Connolly, 'Reconsidering the Irish Act of Union', *Transactions of the Royal Historical Society*, 6th series, 10 (2000), pp. 399–408

S. Daltrey, D. Dickson and C. Ó Gráda, 'Eighteenth-Century Irish Population from Old Sources', *Journal of Economic History*, 41 (1981), pp. 601–28

P. M. Geoghegan, 'The Catholics and the Union', *Transactions of the Royal Historical Society*, 6th series, 10 (2000), pp. 243–58

T. K. Hoppen, 'Tories, Catholics and the General Election of 1859', *Historical Journal*, 13 (1970), pp. 48–67

P. Jupp, 'Britain and the Union, 1797–1801', *Transactions of the Royal Historical Society*, 6th series, 10 (2000), pp. 197–219

C. Ó Gráda, 'A Note on Nineteenth-Century Emigration Statistics', *Population Studies*, 29 (1975), pp. 143–9

B. Walker, 'The 1885 and 1886 General Elections in Ireland', *History Ireland*, 13 (2005), pp. 36–40

Scotland

Books

T. M. Devine, C. H. Lee and G. C. Peden (eds), *The Transformation of Scotland: The Economy* (Edinburgh University Press, 2005)

I. Donnachie, *A History of the Brewing Industry in Scotland* (John Donald, Edinburgh, 1979)

W. H. Fraser and R. J. Morris (eds), *People and Society in Scotland: Vol 2, 1830–1914* (John Donald, Edinburgh, 1990)

R. A. Houston and I. D. Whyte (eds), *Scottish Society, 1500–1800* (Cambridge University Press, 1989)

I. Hutchinson, *A Political History of Scotland, 1832–1924* (John Donald, Edinburgh, 1986)

M. Lynch, *Scotland: A New History*, 2nd edn (Pimlico, London, 1992)

T. C. Smout, *A History of the Scottish People, 1560–1830*, 2nd edn (Fontana, London, 1998)

T. C. Smout (ed.), *Anglo-Scottish Relations from 1603 to 1900* (Oxford University Press, 2005)

H. Trevor-Roper, *The Invention of Scotland: Myth and History* (Yale University Press, London, 2008)

J. Wormald (ed.) *Scotland: A History* (Oxford University Press, 2005)

Articles

R. D. Anderson, 'Secondary Schools and Scottish Society in the Nineteenth Century', *Past & Present*, 109 (1985), pp. 176–203

C. Kidd, 'Race, Empire and the Limits of Scottish Nationhood', *Historical Journal*, 42 (2003), pp. 873–92

G. Pentland, 'The debate on Scottish parliamentary reform, 1830–32', *Scottish Historical Review*, 85 (2006), pp. 100–30

Wales

Books

J. Davies, *A History of Wales* (Allen Lane, London, 1993)

D. G. Evans, *A History of Wales, 1815–1906* (University of Wales Press, Cardiff, 1989)

G. Jenkins, *A Concise History of Wales* (Cambridge University Press, 2007)

K. O. Morgan, *Rebirth of a Nation: Wales, 1880–1980* (Oxford University Press, 1981)

G. A. Williams, *The Merthyr Rising* (Croom Helm, Beckenham, 1978)

G. A. Williams, *When Was Wales? A History of the Welsh* (Black Raven Press, London, 1985)

Articles

R. Quinault, 'The French invasion of Pembrokeshire in 1797', *Welsh History Review*, 19 (1999), pp. 618–41

G. W. Roderick, 'Education, Culture and Industry in Wales in the Nineteenth Century', *Welsh History Review*, 13 (1987), pp. 438–52

Political history and biography

Books

J. Belchem, *Orator Hunt: Henry Hunt and English Working Class Politics* (Oxford University Press, 1985)

J. Belchem, *Orator Hunt: Henry Hunt and English Working Class Radicalism* (Clarendon Press, Oxford, 1985)

J. Belchem, *Popular Radicalism in Nineteenth-Century Britain* (Macmillan, London, 1996)

M. Bentley, *Lord Salisbury's World: Conservative Environments in Late-Victorian Britain* (Cambridge University Press, 2001)

M. Bentley and J. Stevenson (eds), *High and Low Politics in Modern Britain* (Clarendon Press, Oxford, 1983)

E. Biagini, *Gladstone* (Palgrave Macmillan, Basingstoke, 2000)

J. Black, *British Foreign Policy in an Age of Revolutions, 1783–1793* (Cambridge University Press, 1994)

R. Blake, *Disraeli* (Eyre & Spottiswoode, London, 1966)

N. Blewett, *The Peers, the Parties and the People: The General Elections of 1910* (Macmillan, London, 1972)

J. Brewer, *The Sinews of Power: War, Money and the English State, 1688–1783* (Routledge, London, 1989)

M. Brock, *The Great Reform Act* (Hutchinson, London, 1973)

A. Burns and J. Innes (eds), *Rethinking the Age of Reform: Britain, 1780–1850* (Cambridge University Press, 2003)

M. Chase, *Chartism: A New History* (Manchester University Press, 2007)

B. Coleman, *Conservatism and the Conservative Party in the Nineteenth Century* (Hodder Arnold, London, 1988)

L. Colley, *Britons: Forging the Nation, 1714–1837* (Yale University Press, New Haven, 1992)

C. Cook, *The Longman Companion to Britain in the Nineteenth Century* (Longman, London, 1999)

M. Cowling, *1867: Disraeli, Gladstone and Revolution* (Cambridge University Press, 1967)

H. T. Dickinson, *British Radicalism and the French Revolution* (Wiley-Blackwell, Oxford, 1985)

H. T. Dickinson, *Caricatures and the Constitution, 1760–1832* (Chadwyck Healey, Cambridge, 1986)

H. T. Dickinson (ed.), *Britain and the French Revolution, 1789–1815* (Macmillan, Basingstoke, 1989)

M. Duffy, *The Younger Pitt* (Longman Pearson, Harlow, 2000)

D. Eastwood, *Governing Rural England: Tradition and Transformation in Local Government, 1780–1840* (Oxford University Press, 1994)

J. Ehrman, *The Younger Pitt, Vol. 1: The Years of Acclaim* (Constable, London, 1969)

J. Ehrman, *The Younger Pitt, Vol. 2: The Reluctant Transition* (Constable, London, 1983)

J. Ehrman, *The Younger Pitt, Vol. 3: The Consuming Struggle* (Constable, London, 1996)

J. Epstein, *The Lion of Freedom* (Croom Helm, London, 1982)

D. Epstein and D. Thompson (eds), *The Chartist Experience: Studies in Radicalism and Culture* (Macmillan, London, 1982)

E. J. Evans, *William Pitt the Younger* (Routledge, London, 1999)

E. J. Evans, *Chartism* (Longman, London, 2000)

E. J. Evans, *Parliamentary Reform, c1770–1918* (Pearson Education, Harlow, 2000)

E. J. Evans, *Sir Robert Peel: Statesmanship, Power and Party*, 2nd edn (Routledge, London, 2006)

E. J. Evans, *Britain Before the Reform Act: Politics and Society 1815–32*, 2nd edn (Pearson Education, London, 2008)

E. Feuchtwanger, *Disraeli* (Hodder Headline, London, 2000)

D. R. Fisher (ed.), *The House of Commons, 1820–32. Vol. 1* of *The History of Parliament* (Cambridge University Press, 2009)

N. Gash, *Politics in the Age of Peel: A Study in the Technique of Parliamentary Representation, 1830–50* (Longmans Green, London, 1953)

N. Gash, *Lord Liverpool: The Life and Political Career of Robert Banks Jenkinson, Second Earl of Liverpool* (Weidenfeld & Nicolson, London, 1984)

N. Gash, *Mr Secretary Peel: The Life of Sir Robert Peel to 1830*, 2nd edn (Longman, Harlow, 1985)

N. Gash, *Sir Robert Peel: The Life of Sir Robert Peel since 1830* (Longman, Harlow, 1986 edn)

N. Gash (ed.), *Wellington: Studies in the Military and Political Career of the First Duke of Wellington* (Manchester University Press, 1990)

R. A. Gaunt, *Sir Robert Peel: The Life and the Legacy* (I. B. Tauris, London, 2010)

D. Goodway, *London Chartism* (Cambridge University Press, 1982)

B. Gordon, *Economic Doctrine and Tory Liberalism, 1824–30* (Macmillan, London, 1979)

A. Grant and K. J. Stringer (eds), *Uniting the Kingdom: The Making of British History* (Routledge, London, 1995)

D. Green, *Great Cobbett, the Noblest Agitator* (Oxford University Press, 1983)

E. H. H. Green, *The Crisis of Conservatism: The Politics, Economics and Ideology of the British Conservative Party, 1880–1914* (Routledge, London, 1995)

W. Hague, *William Pitt the Younger* (Harper Perennial edn, London, 2005)

W. Hague, *William Wilberforce* (Harper Press, London, 2007)

H. J. Hanham, *The Reformed Electoral System in Great Britain, 1832–1914* (Historical Association, London, 1969)

P. Harling, *The Waning of 'Old Corruption', 1779–1846* (Clarendon Press, Oxford, 1996)

R. Harrison, *Before the Socialists* (Routledge, London, 1965)

A. Hawkins, *Parliament, Party and the Art of Politics in Britain, 1855–1859* (Macmillan, Basingstoke, 1987)

A. Hawkins, *British Party Politics, 1852–86* (Macmillan, Basingstoke, 1998)

A. Hawkins, *The Forgotten Prime Minister: Ascent, 1799–1851* (Oxford University Press, 2007)

A. Hawkins, *The Forgotten Prime Minister: Achievement, 1852–1869* (Oxford University Press, 2008)

W. A. Hay, *The Whig Revival, 1808–1830* (Palgrave Macmillan, Basingstoke, 2005)

A. B. Hilton, *The Age of Atonement: The Influence of Evangelicalism on Social and Economic Thought, 1785–1865* (Oxford University Press, 1992)

P. Hollis, *The Pauper Press: A Study of Working-Class Radicalism in the 1830s* (Oxford University Press, 1970)

P. Hollis, *Ladies Elect: Women in English Local Government, 1867–1914* (Clarendon Press, Oxford, 1989 edn)

P. Jalland, *The Liberals and Ireland: The Ulster Question in British Politics to 1914* (Harvester, Brighton, 1980)

R. Jenkins, *Mr Balfour's Poodle: Peers versus People* (Macmillan, London, 2001 edn)

T. A. Jenkins, *Gladstone, Whiggery and the Liberal Party, 1874–1886* (Oxford University Press, 1988)

T. A. Jenkins, *The Liberal Ascendancy, 1830–1886* (Macmillan, Basingstoke, 1994)

T. A. Jenkins, *Parliament, Party and Politics in Victorian Britain* (Manchester University Press, 1996)

C. Jones, P. Salmon and R. W. Davies (eds), *Partisan Politics, Principle and Reform in Parliament and the Constituencies, 1689–1880* (Edinburgh University Press, 2005)

P. J. Jupp, *Lord Grenville, 1759–1834* (Oxford University Press, 1985)

P. J. Jupp, *British Politics on the Eve of Reform: The Duke of Wellington's Administration, 1828–30* (Macmillan, Basingstoke, 1998)

P. J. Jupp, *The Governing of Britain, 1688–1848* (Routledge, London, 2006)

S. Kent, *Sex and Suffrage in Britain, 1860–1914* (Princeton University Press, 1987)

P. Langford, *Englishness Identified: Manners and Character* (Oxford University Press, 2000)

J. Lawrence and M. Taylor (eds), *Party, State and Society: Electoral Behaviour in Britain since 1820* (Scolar Press, Aldershot, 1997)

K. Laybourn, *A Century of Labour: A History of the Labour Party, 1900–2000* (Sutton, Stroud, 2000)

S. M. Lee, *George Canning and Liberal Toryism, 1801–27* (Royal Historical Society, Boydell Press, Woodbridge, 2008)

J. Liddington and J. Norris, *One Hand Tied Behind Us: The Rise of the Women's Suffrage*, 2nd edn (Rivers Oram Press, London 2001)

N. D. LoPatin, *Political Unions, Popular Politics and the Great Reform Act of 1832* (St Martin's, New York, 1999)

O. MacDonagh, *A Pattern of Government Growth* (MacGibbon & Key, London, 1961)

O. MacDonagh, *Early Victorian Government, 1830–70* (Weidenfeld & Nicolson, London, 1977)

I. Machin, *Disraeli* (Longman, Harlow, 1995)

I. Machin, *The Rise of Democracy in Britain, 1830–1918* (Macmillan, Basingstoke, 2001)

P. Mandler, *Aristocratic Government in the Age of Reform* (Clarendon Press, Oxford, 1990)

P. Mandler, *The English National Character* (Yale University Press, London, 2006)

P. Marsh, *Joseph Chamberlain: Entrepreneur in Politics* (Yale University Press, London, 1994)

H. G. C. Matthew, *Gladstone, 1875–1898* (Clarendon Press, Oxford, 1995)

N. McCord, *The Anti-Corn Law League* (Routledge, London, 1958 and e-edition, London, 2006)

L. G. Mitchell, *Charles James Fox* (Oxford University Press, 1992)

L. G. Mitchell, *The Whig World* (Hambledon, London, 2005)

I. Newbould, *Whiggery and Reform, 1830–41: The Politics of Government* (Stanford University Press, 1990)

F. O'Gorman, *Voters, Patrons and Parties: The Unreformed Electorate of Hanoverian England 1714–1832* (Clarendon Press, Oxford, 1989)

J. P. Parry, *The Rise and Fall of Liberal Government in Victorian Britain* (Yale University Press, 1993)

H. Pelling, *The Social Geography of British Elections, 1885–1910* (Macmillan, London, 1967)

J. A. Phillips, *The Great Reform Bill in the Boroughs: English Electoral Behaviour 1818–41* (Clarendon Press, Oxford, 1992)

P. Pickering and A. Tyrell, *The People's Bread: A History of the Anti-Corn Law League* (Leicester University Press, London, 2000)

B. Porter, *Britannia's Burden: The Political Evolution of Modern Britain, 1851–1990* (Arnold, London, 1994)

D. Powell, *Nationhood and Identity: The British State since 1800* (I. B. Tauris, London, 2002)

J. Prest, *Lord John Russell* (Macmillan, London, 1972)

J. Prest, *Politics in the Age of Cobden* (Macmillan, London, 1977)

J. Prest, *Liberty and Locality: Parliament, Permissive Legislation and Ratepayers' Democracies in the Mid-Nineteenth Century* (Clarendon Press, Oxford, 1990)

M. Pugh, *State and Society: A Social and Political History of Britain, 1870–1997*, 2nd edn (Arnold, London, 1999)

M. Pugh, *The March of the Women: A Revisionist Analysis of the Campaign for Women's Suffrage, 1886–1914* (Oxford University Press, 2000)

M. Pugh, *The Making of Modern British Politics, 1867–1945*, 3rd edn (Blackwell, Oxford, 2002)

M. Pugh, *Speak for Britain! A New History of the Labour Party* (Bodley Head, London, 2010)

J. Ramsden, *The Age of Balfour and Baldwin, 1902–1940* (Longman, London, 1978)

J. Rendall (ed.), *Equal or Different? Women's Politics, 1800–1914* (Wiley-Blackwell, London, 1987)

K. G. Robbins, *Nineteenth-Century Britain: Integration and Diversity* (Oxford University Press, 1988)

A. Roberts, *Salisbury: Victorian Titan* (Weidenfeld, London, 1999)

M. Roberts, *Political Movements in Urban England, 1832–1914* (Palgrave Macmillan, Basingstoke, 2009)

J. Robins, *Rebel Queen: How the Trial of Caroline Brought England to the Brink of Revolution* (Simon & Schuster, London, 2006)

E. Royle, *Chartism*, 3rd edn (Addison Wesley Longman, Harlow, 1996)

E. Royle, *Revolutionary Britannia: Reflections on the Threat of Revolution in Britain, 1789–1848* (Manchester University Press, 2000)

J. Saville, *1848: The British State and the Chartist Movement* (Cambridge University Press, 1987)

P. Scherer, *Lord John Russell: A Biography* (Associated University Presses, London, 1999)

J. Schwarzkopf, *Women in the Chartist Movement* (Palgrave Macmillan, Basingstoke, 1991)

G. R. Searle, *The Quest for National Efficiency* (University of California Press, 1971)

G. R. Searle, *Entrepreneurial Politics in Mid-Victorian Britain* (Oxford University Press, 1993)

R. T. Shannon, *The Age of Disraeli, 1868–81: The Rise of Tory Democracy* (Longman, Harlow, 1992)

R. T. Shannon, *The Age of Salisbury: Unionism and Empire, 1881–1902* (Longman, Harlow, 1996)

R. T. Shannon, *Gladstone: Heroic Minister, 1865–1898* (Allen Lane, London, 1999)

E. A. Smith (ed.), *Reform or Revolution? A Diary of Reform in England, 1830–32* (Alan Sutton, Stroud, 1992)

F. B. Smith, *The Making of the Second Reform Bill* (Cambridge University Press, 1966)

O. Smith, *The Politics of Language, 1791–1819* (Oxford University Press, 1984)

P. Smith, *Disraelian Conservatism and Social Reform* (Routledge, London, 1967)

P. Spence, *The Birth of Romantic Radicalism: War, Popular Politics and English Radical Reformism* (Scolar Press, Aldershot, 1996)

D. Steele, *Lord Salisbury: A Political Biography* (Routledge, London, 1999)

R. Stewart, *The Foundation of the Conservative Party, 1830–1867* (Longman, Harlow, 1978)

D. Tanner, *Political Change and the Labour Party* (Cambridge University Press, 1987)

M. Taylor, *The Decline of British Radicalism, 1847–60* (Clarendon Press, Oxford, 1995)

M. I. Thomis, *Threats of Revolution in Britain* (Macmillan, Basingstoke, 1977)

D. Thompson, *The Chartists: Popular Politics in the Industrial Revolution* (Temple Smith, London, 1984)

R. G. Thorne (ed.), *The History of Parliament: The House of Commons, 1790–1820* (Secker & Warburg, London, 1986)

A. Thorpe, *A History of the British Labour Party*, 3rd edn (Palgrave Macmillan, Basingstoke, 2008)

J. Tomlinson, *Government and the Enterprise since 1900: The Changing Problem of Efficiency* (Oxford University Press, 1994)

M. J. Turner, *Pitt the Younger: A Life* (Hambledon, London, 2003)

J. Vernon, *Politics and the People: A Study in English Political Culture, 1815–67* (Cambridge University Press, 1993)

J. Vernon (ed.), *Re-reading the Constitution* (Cambridge University Press, 1996)

A. Vickery (ed.), *Women, Privilege and Power: British Politics, 1750 to the Present* (Stanford University Press, 2001)

P. Waller (ed.), *Politics and Social Change c1860–1880* (Harvester, Brighton, 1987)

M. Wood, *Radical Satire and Print Culture, 1790–1822* (Clarendon Press, Oxford, 1994)

Articles

D. E. D. Beales, 'The Right to Vote and the Opportunity', *Parliamentary History*, 11 (1992), pp. 139–50

J. Belchem, 'Nationalism, Republicanism and Exile: Irish Emigrants and the Revolutions of 1848', *Past & Present*, 146 (1995), pp. 101–35

I. R. Christie, 'Economical Reform and the "Influence of the Crown" 1780', *Cambridge Historical Journal*, 12 (1956), pp. 144–54

S. Collini, 'The Idea of "Character" in Victorian Political Thought', *Transactions of the Royal Historical Society*, 5th series, 35 (1985), pp. 29–50

J. E. Cookson, 'The English Volunteer Movement of the French Wars, 1793–1815: Some Contexts', *Historical Journal*, 32 (1989), pp. 867–91

J. Davis and D. Tanner, 'The Borough Franchise after 1867', *Historical Research*, 69 (1996), pp. 306–27

D. Eastwood, 'Toryism, Reform and Political Culture in Oxfordshire, 1826–37', *Parliamentary History*, 7 (1988), pp. 98–121

S. Farrell, 'A First Step towards Democracy', *History Today*, 60 (2010), pp. 10–17

J. Fulcher, 'The Loyalist Response to the Queen Caroline Agitations', *Journal of British Studies*, 34 (1995), pp. 481–502

P. Ghosh, 'Disraelian Conservatism: A Financial Approach', *English Historical Review*, 99 (1984), pp. 268–96

P. Harling, 'Rethinking "Old Corruption"', *Past & Present*, 147 (1995), pp. 127–58

P. Harling and P. Mandler, 'From "Fiscal-Military" State to Laissez-Faire State, 1760–1850', *Journal of British Studies*, 32 (1993), pp. 44–70

R. Harrison, 'The British Working Class and the General Election of 1868', *International Review of Social History*, 5 (1960), pp. 424–55

S. Lee, '"A New Language in Politicks": George Canning and the Idea of Opposition', *History*, 83 (1998), pp. 472–96

J. C. Lowe, 'The Tory Triumph of 1868 in Blackburn and Lancashire', *Historical Journal*, 16 (1973), pp. 733–48

J. A. Phillips and C. Wetherell, 'The Great Reform Act of 1832 and the Political Modernization of England', *American Historical Review*, 100 (1995), pp. 419–22, 435

M. Philp, 'Vulgar Conservatism, 1792–3', *English Historical Review*, 110 (1995), pp. 42–69

J. G. A. Pocock, 'The Political Economy of Burke's Analysis of the French Revolution', *Historical Journal*, 25 (1982), pp. 331–49

R. Poole, '"By the Law or the Sword": Peterloo Revisited', *History*, 91 (2006), pp. 254–76

D. Tanner, 'Elections, Statistics and the Rise of the Labour Party, 1906–1931', *Historical Journal*, 33 (1991), pp. 893–908

M. Taylor, 'Rethinking the Chartists: Searching for Synthesis in the Historiography of Chartism', *Historical Journal*, 39 (1996), pp. 479–95

Diplomacy, foreign policy and empire

Books

C. A. Bayly, *Indian Society and the Making of the British Empire* (Cambridge University Press, 1988)

C. A. Bayly, *Imperial Meridian: The British Empire and the World* (Longman, Harlow, 1989)

C. A. Bayly, *Empire and Information* (Cambridge University Press, 1996)

C. A. Bayly and D. H. A. Kolff (eds), *Two Colonial Empires* (Springer, New York, 1986)

J. Belich, *Replenishing the Earth: The Settler Revolution and the Rise of the Anglo-World, 1783–1939* (Oxford University Press, 2009)

J. Black, *British Foreign Policy in an Age of Revolutions, 1783–93* (Cambridge University Press, 1994)

J. Black, *The War of 1812 in the Age of Napoleon* (Continuum International, London, 2009)

T. C. W. Blanning, *The French Revolutionary Wars, 1787–1802* (Arnold, London, 1996)

K. Bourne, *The Foreign Policy of Victorian England* (Clarendon Press, Oxford, 1970)

P. Brendon, *The Decline and Fall of the British Empire, 1781–1997* (Cape, London, 2007)

P. J. Cain and A. G. Hopkins, *British Imperialism: Innovation and Expansion, 1688–1914* (Longman, Harlow, 1993)

D. Cannadine, *Ornamentalism: How the British Saw their Empire* (Allen Lane, London, 2001)

G. Chakravarty, *The Indian Mutiny and the British Imagination* (Cambridge University Press, 2005)

M. E. Chamberlain, *British Foreign Policy in the Age of Palmerston* (Longman, Harlow, 1980)

M. E. Chamberlain, *Pax Britannica? British Foreign Policy, 1789–1914* (Longman, Harlow, 1988)

J. Charmley, *Splendid Isolation? Britain and the Balance of Power, 1874–1914* (Hodder & Stoughton, London, 1999)

L. Colley, *Captives: Britain, Empire and the World, 1600–1850* (Pantheon Books, New York, 2002)

S. David, *The Indian Mutiny: 1857* (Penguin edn, 2002)

J. W. Derry, *Castlereagh* (Allen Lane, London, 1976)

P. Dixon, *Canning: Politician and Statesman* (Weidenfeld & Nicolson, London, 1976)

S. Engerman, *Slavery, Emancipation and Freedom: Comparative Perspectives* (Louisiana University Press, 2007)

C. Esdaile, *The French Wars, 1792–1815* (Routledge, London, 2001)

C. Esdaile, *Napoleon's Wars: An International History, 1803–15* (Allen Lane, London, 2007)

N. Ferguson, *Empire: How Britain Made the Modern World* (Allen Lane, London, 2003)

D. Gates, *The Spanish Ulcer: A History of the Peninsular War* (Pimlico, London, 2002)

V. T. Harlow and F. Madden, *British Colonial Developments, 1774–1834* (Clarendon Press, Oxford, 1953)

P. Hayes, *The Nineteenth Century, 1814–80* (A. C. Black, London, 1975)

P. Hayes, *Modern British Foreign Policy: The Twentieth Century, 1880–1939* (Black, London, 1978)

R. B. Henig, *The Origins of the First World War*, 3rd edn (Routledge, London, 2002)

C. Hibbert, *The Great Mutiny: India 1857* (Penguin edn, 2002)

W. Hinde, *George Canning* (Collins, London, 1973)

H. Hook, *Empires of the Imagination: Politics, War and the Arts in the British World, 1750–1850* (Profile Books, London, 2010)

R. Hyam, *Britain's Imperial Century, 1815–1914: A Study of Empire and Expansion*, 3rd edn (Cambridge University Press, 2002)

R. Hyam, *Understanding the British Empire* (Cambridge University Press, 2010)

D. Judd and K. Surridge, *The Boer War* (Palgrave Macmillan, Basingstoke, 2003)

P. Kennedy, *The Rise of Anglo-German Antagonism, 1860–1914* (Ashfield, London, 1987)

P. Levine, *The British Empire: Sunrise to Sunset* (Pearson Education, Harlow, 2007)

T. O. Lloyd, *The British Empire, 1558–1983* (Oxford University Press, 1984)

J. Lowe, *Britain and Foreign Affairs, 1815–1885* (Routledge, London, 1998)

J. M. MacKenzie, *The Scramble for Africa* (Routledge, London, 1983)

J. M. MacKenzie (ed.), *Imperialism and Popular Culture* (Manchester University Press, 1986)

E. V. Macleod, *A War of Ideas: British Attitudes to the Wars against Revolutionary France* (Ashgate, Aldershot, 1998)

P. J. Marshall (ed.), *Oxford History of the British Empire. Vol. 2, The Eighteenth Century* (Oxford University Press, 1998)

R. Millman, *Britain and the Eastern Question, 1875–1878* (Clarendon Press, Oxford, 1979)

P. K. Monod, *Imperial Island: A History of Britain and its Empire, 1660–1837* (Wiley-Blackwell, Oxford, 2009)

K. Morgan, *Slavery and the British Empire* (Oxford University Press, 2007)

J. Mori, *William Pitt and the French Revolution* (Keele University Press, Edinburgh, 1997)

R. Muir, *Britain and the Defeat of Napoleon, 1807–15* (Yale University Press, London, 1996)

K. Neilson, *Britain and the Last Tsar: British Policy and Russia, 1894–1917* (Clarendon Press, Oxford, 1995)

A. Porter (ed.), *The Oxford History of the British Empire: Vol. 3, The Nineteenth Century* (Oxford University Press, 1999)

B. Porter, *Critics of Empire* (Macmillan, London, 1968)

B. Porter, *Plots and Paranoia: A History of Political Espionage in Britain, 1790–1988* (Routledge, London, 1992)

B. Porter, *The Absent-Minded Imperialists* (Manchester University Press, 2004)

B. Porter, *The Lion's Share*, 4th edn (Longman Pearson, London, 2004)

J. Ridley, *Lord Palmerston* (Constable, London, 1970)

P. Schroeder, *The Transformation of European Politics, 1763–1848* (Clarendon Press, Oxford, 1994)

H. M. Scott, *British Foreign Policy in the Age of the American Revolution* (Oxford University Press, 1990)

R. W. Seton-Watson, *Britain in Europe, 1789–1914* (Cambridge University Press, 1937)

J. Sherwig, *Guineas and Gunpowder: British Foreign Aid in the Wars with France, 1783–1815* (Cambridge, MA, 1969)

I. R. Smith, *The Origins of the South African War, 1899–1902* (Longman, London, 1996)

M. Swartz, *The Politics of British Foreign Policy in the Era of Disraeli and Gladstone* (Macmillan, Basingstoke, 1985)

H. Temperley and L. M. Penson (eds), *Foundations of British Foreign Policy from Pitt to Salisbury* (Cambridge University Press, 1938)

A. S. Thompson, *Imperial Britain: The Empire in British Politics, c1880–1932* (Pearson Education, Harlow, 2000)

J. Walvin, *Slaves and Slavery: The British Colonial Experience* (Manchester University Press, 1992)

J. Walvin, *Questioning Slavery* (Routledge, London, 1996)

A. Webster, *The Debate on the British Empire* (Manchester University Press, 2006)

H. L. Wesseling, *Divide and Rule: The Partition of Africa* (Praeger, London, English trans., 1996)

J. Williams, *British Commercial Policy and Trade Expansion, 1750–1850* (Clarendon Press, Oxford, 1972)

K. M. Wilson, *The Politics of the Entente: Essays on the Determination of British Foreign Policy* (Cambridge University Press, 1985)

M. E. Yapp, *Strategies of British India: Britain, Iran and Afghanistan, 1798–1850* (Clarendon Press, Oxford, 1980)

Articles

J. Darwin, 'Imperialism and the Victorians', *English Historical Review*, 112 (1997), pp. 614–42

D. French, 'Spy Fever in Britain, 1900–15', *Historical Journal*, 21 (1978), pp. 355–70

J. D. Hargreaves, 'Towards a History of the Partition of Africa', *The Journal of African History*, 1 (1960), pp. 97–109

A. Offer, 'The British Empire, 1870–1914: A Waste of Money?', *Economic History Review*, 2nd series, 46 (1993), pp. 215–38

J. Pebble, 'Resources and Techniques in the Second Maratha War', *Historical Journal*, 19 (1976), pp. 375–404

Social, cultural and religious themes

Books

G. Anderson, *Victorian Clerks* (Manchester University Press, 1976)

P. Bailey, *Leisure and Class in Victorian England* (Routledge, London, 1978)

J. M. Beattie, *Crime and the Courts in England, 1660–1800* (Oxford University Press, 1986)

D. W. Bebbington, *Evangelicalism in Modern Britain: A History from the 1730s to the 1980s* (Unwin Hyman, London, 1989)

D. W. Bebbington, *Religion and Political Culture in Britain and Ireland* (Cambridge University Press, 1996)

J. V. Beckett, *The Aristocracy in England, 1660–1914* (Blackwell, Oxford, 1986)

J. V. Beckett, *The East Midlands from AD1000* (Longman, Harlow, 1988)

J. Belchem (ed.), *Liverpool 800: Culture, Character and History* (Liverpool University Press, 2006)

P. Borsay, *The English Urban Renaissance: Culture and Society in the Provincial Town* (Oxford University Press, 1989)

P. Borsay (ed.), *The Eighteenth-Century Town* (Longman, London, 1990)

P. Brandon and B. Short, *The South-East from AD1000* (Longman, London, 1990)

J. Brewer and J. Styles (eds), *An Ungovernable People: The English and their Law in the Seventeenth and Eighteenth Centuries* (Hutchinson, London, 1980)

J. Burnett, *A Social History of Housing, 1815–1985*, 2nd edn (Methuen, London, 1986)

D. Cannadine, *Lords and Landlords: The Aristocracy and the Towns, 1774–1967* (Leicester University Press, London, 1967)

D. Cannadine (ed.), *Patricians, Power and Politics in Nineteenth-Century Towns* (Leicester University Press, 1982)

D. Cannadine, *The Decline and Fall of the British Aristocracy* (Yale University Press, London, 1990)

D. Cannadine, *Class in Britain* (Yale University Press, London, 1999)

J. Cannon, *Aristocratic Century* (Cambridge University Press, 1984)

A. Clark, *The Struggle for the Breeches: Gender and the Making of the British Working Class* (University of California Press, London, 1995)

J. S. Cockburn (ed.), *Crime in England, 1550–1800* (Methuen, London, 1977)

L. Colley, *Britons: Forging the Nation, 1707–1837*, 2nd edn (Yale University Press, 2005)

S. Collini, R. Whatmore and B. Young (eds), *History, Religion and Culture: British Intellectual History, 1750–1950* (Cambridge University Press, 2000)

R. Colls and P. Dodd (eds), *Englishness: Politics and Culture, 1880–1920* (Croom Helm, Beckenham, 1986)

P. Corfield, *The Impact of English Towns, 1700–1800* (Oxford University Press, 1982)

P. Corfield, *Power and the Professions in England, 1700–1850* (Routledge, London, 1995)

G. Crossick (ed.), *The Lower Middle Classes in Britain, 1870–1914* (Croom Helm, London, 1976)

M. Daunton (ed.), *The Cambridge Urban History of Britain, 1840–1950* (Cambridge University Press, 2000)

M. Daunton, *State and Market in Victorian Britain: War, Welfare and Capitalism* (Boydell Press, Woodbridge, 2008)

L. Davidoff and C. Hall, *Family Fortunes: Men and Women of the English Middle Class, 1780–1850*, 2nd edn (Routledge, London, 2002)

G. M. Ditchfield, *The Evangelical Revival* (Routledge, London, 1998)

M. Dresser, *Slavery Obscured: The Social History of the Slave Trade in an English Provincial Port* (Leicester University Press, 2001)

F. Driver, *Power and Pauperism: The Workhouse System, 1834–84* (Cambridge University Press, 1993)

C. Dyhouse, *Girls Growing Up in Late Victorian and Edwardian England* (Routledge, London, 1981)

C. Emsley, *Crime and Society in England, 1750–1900* (Longman, Harlow, 1987)

C. Emsley, *The English Police: A Political and Social History* (Longman, Harlow, 1996)

E. Englander, *Poverty and Poor Law Reform in Nineteenth-Century Britain, 1834–1914* (Addison Wesley Longman, Harlow, 1998)

E. J. Evans, *The Contentious Tithe: The Tithe Problem and English Agriculture, 1750–1850* (Routledge, London, 1976)

E. J. Evans (ed.), *Social Policy, 1830–1914: Individualism, Collectivism and the Origins of the Welfare State* (Routledge, London, 1978)

K. Gleadle, *British Women in the Nineteenth Century* (Palgrave, Basingstoke, 2001)

S. Gunn, *The Public Culture of the Victorian Middle Class: Ritual and Authority in the English Industrial City, 1840–1914* (Manchester University Press, 2007)

J. Harris, *Private Lives, Public Spirit: Britain, 1870–1914* (Penguin, London, 1993)

D. Hay, P. Linebaugh and E. P. Thompson (eds), *Albion's Fatal Tree: Crime and Society in Eighteenth-Century England* (Allen Lane, London, 1975)

E. Hellmuth (ed.), *The Transformation of Provincial Culture* (Oxford University Press, 1990)

D. Hempton, *Religion and Political Culture in Britain and Ireland* (Cambridge University Press, 1996)

D. Hempton, *The Religion of the People: Methodism and Popular Religion, c1750–1900* (Routledge, London, 1996)

E. P. Hennock, *Fit and Proper Persons: Ideal and Reality in Nineteenth-Century Urban Government* (Arnold, London, 1973)

D. Hey, *Yorkshire from AD1000* (Longman, Harlow, 1986)

A. B. Hilton, *The Age of Atonement. The Influence of Evangelicalism on Social and Economic Thought, 1785–1865* (Oxford University Press, 1988)

E. J. Hobsbawm and G. F. E. Rudé, *Captain Swing* (Lawrence & Wishart, London, 1969)

D. Hunt, *A History of Preston*, 2nd edn (Carnegie Publishing, Lancaster, 2009)

E. H. Hunt, *British Labour History, 1815–1914* (Weidenfeld & Nicolson, London, 1981)

J. S. Hurt, *Elementary Schooling and the Working Classes, 1860–1918* (Routledge, London, 1979)

P. Jalland, *Women, Marriage and Politics, 1860–1914* (Oxford University Press, 1986)

A. Kidd and D. Nicholls (eds), *Gender, Civic Culture and Consumerism: Middle Class Identity in Britain, 1800–1940* (Manchester University Press, 1999)

A. Kidd, *State, Society and the Poor in Nineteenth-Century England* (Macmillan, Basingstoke, 1999)

A. Kussmaul, *Servants in Husbandry in Early Modern England* (Cambridge University Press, 1981)

P. Levine, *Feminist Lives in Victorian England: Private Roles and Public Commitment* (Blackwell, Oxford, 1990)

J. Lewis, *Women in England, 1870–1950: Sexual Divisions and Social Change* (Prentice Hall, London, 1984)

N. Longmate, *The Workhouse* (Temple Smith, London, 1974)

R. W. Malcolmson, *Popular Recreations in English Society, 1700–1850* (Cambridge University Press, 1973)

P. Mathias, *The Brewing Industry in England, 1700–1830* (Cambridge University Press, 1959)

N. McKendrick, J. Brewer and J. H. Plumb (eds), *The Birth of a Consumer Society: The Commercialisation of Eighteenth-Century England* (Harper Collins, London, 1984)

R. J. Morris, *Class, Sect and Party: The Making of the British Middle Class, Leeds 1820–50* (Manchester University Press, 1990)

J. Neeson, *Commoners: Common Rights, Enclosure and Social Change in England* (Cambridge University Press, 1993)

A. Peacock, *Bread or Blood: The Agrarian Riots in East Anglia, 1816* (Gollancz, London, 1965)

H. J. Perkin, *The Origins of Modern English Society, 1780–1880* (Routledge, London, 1969)

H. J. Perkin, *The Rise of Professional Society: England since 1880* (Routledge, London, 1990 edn)

C. B. Phillips and J. H. Smith, *Lancashire and Cheshire from AD 1540* (Longman, Harlow, 1994)

D. Phillips and R. Storch, *Policing Provincial England, 1829–1856: The Politics of Reform* (Leicester University Press, London, 1999)

F. Prochaska, *Women and Philanthropy in Nineteenth-Century England* (Oxford University Press, 1980)

J. Purvis (ed.), *Women's History, Britain 1850–1914* (UCL Press, London, 1995)

A. Randall, *Before the Luddites: Custom, Community and Machinery in the English Woollen Industry, 1776–1809* (Cambridge University Press, 1991)

E. Richards, *Leviathan of Wealth: The Sutherland Fortune in the Industrial Revolution* (Routledge, London, 1973)

M. Rowlands, *The West Midlands from AD1000* (Longman, Harlow, 1987)

W. D. Rubinstein, *Men of Property: The Very Wealthy in Britain since the Industrial Revolution* (Croom Helm, Beckenham, 1981)

W. D. Rubinstein, *Elites and the Wealthy in Modern British History* (Palgrave Macmillan, Basingstoke, 1987)

W. D. Rubinstein, *Capitalism, Culture and Decline in Britain, 1750–1990* (Routledge, London, 1993)

W. D. Rubinstein, *Who Were the Rich? Vol. 1, 1809–39 A Biographical Dictionary of British Wealth Holders* (Social Affairs Unit, London, 2009)

J. Rule, *The Labouring Classes in Early Industrial England, 1750–1850* (Longman, London, 1986)

K. D. M. Snell, *Annals of the Labouring Poor: Social Change and Agrarian England* (Cambridge University Press, 1985)

R. A. Soloway, *Prelates and People: Ecclesiastical Social Thought in England, 1783–1852* (Routledge, London, 1969)

G. Stedman Jones, *Languages of Class: Studies in English Working-Class History, 1832–1932* (Cambridge University Press, 1983)

W. B. Stephens, *Education in Britain, 1750–1914* (Macmillan, Basingstoke, 1998)

J. Stevenson, *Popular Disturbances in England, 1700–1870*, 2nd edn (Longman, Harlow, 1992)

R. D. Storch, *Popular Culture and Custom in Nineteenth Century England* (Croom Helm, London, 1982)

R. Sweet, *The English Town, 1680–1840: Government, Society and Culture* (Longman, London, 1999)

R. Swift and S. Gilley (eds), *The Irish in Britain* (Pinter, London, 1989)

A. J. Taylor (ed.), *The Standard of Living Controversy in Britain in the Industrial Revolution* (Methuen, London, 1975)

M. I. Thomis, *The Luddites: Machine Breaking in Regency England* (David & Charles, Newton Abbot, 1970)

E. P. Thompson, *The Making of the English Working Class* (Penguin edn, London, 1968)

E. P. Thompson, *Whigs and Hunters: The Origins of the Black Act* (Allen Lane, London, 1975)

E. P. Thompson, *Customs in Common* (Merlin Press, London, 1991)

F. M. L. Thompson, *English Landed Society in the Nineteenth Century* (Routledge, London, 1963)

F. M. L. Thompson (ed.), *The Cambridge Social History of Britain, 1750–1950* (3 vols, Cambridge University Press, 1990)

F. M. L. Thompson, *Gentrification and the Enterprise Culture: Britain, 1780–1980* (Oxford University Press, 2001)

R. M. Trainor, *Black Country Elites: The Exercise of Authority in an Urban Area, 1830–1900* (Clarendon Press, Oxford, 1993)

M. E. Turner, *Parliamentary Enclosure: Its Historical Geography and Economic History* (Archon Books, Folkestone, 1980)

P. Virgin, *The Church in an Age of Negligence: Ecclesiastical Structure and Problems of Church Reform, 1700–1840* (Cambridge University Press, 1989)

D. Wahrman, *Imagining the Middle Class: The Political Representation of Class in Britain* (Cambridge University Press, 1995)

P. Waller, *Town, City and Nation: England 1850–1914* (Oxford University Press, 1973)

J. K. Walton (ed.), *Leisure in Britain, 1780–1939* (Manchester University Press, 1983)

J. K. Walton, *Lancashire: A Social History, 1558–1939* (Manchester University Press, 1987)

J. K. Walton, *Blackpool* (Edinburgh University Press, 1998)

J. T. Ward, *Popular Movements, 1830–50* (Macmillan, Basingstoke, 1970)

M. Watts, *The Dissenters. Vol. 2, The Expansion of Evangelical Nonconformity* (Clarendon Press, Oxford, 1995)

M. J. Wiener, *English Culture and the Decline of the Industrial Spirit, 1850–1980* (Cambridge University Press, 1981)

K. Williams, *From Pauperism to Poverty* (Routledge, London, 1981)

E. A. Wrigley, *People, Cities and Wealth: The Transformation of Traditional Society* (Wiley-Blackwell, Oxford, 1987)

Articles

L. Andrews, 'The School Meals Service', *British Journal of Educational Studies*, 20 (1972), pp. 70–5

J. V. Beckett, 'English Landownership in the Later Seventeenth and Eighteenth Centuries: The Debate and the Problems', *Economic History Review*, 2nd series, 30 (1977), pp. 567–81

M. Daunton, '"Gentlemanly Capitalism" and British Industry', *Past & Present*, 122 (1989), pp. 119–58

E. J. Evans, 'Some Reasons for the Growth of English Rural Anti-Clericalism', *Past & Present*, 66 (1975), pp. 84–109

J. Garrard, 'Urban Elites, 1850–1914: The Rule and Decline of a New Squirearchy', *Albion*, 27 (1995), pp. 583–621

W. Gibson, 'The Professionalization of an Elite: The Nineteenth-Century Episcopate', *Albion*, 23 (1991), pp. 459–82

H. J. Habbakuk, 'The Rise and Fall of English Landed Families', *Transactions of the Royal Historical Society*, 5th series, 29 (1979), pp. 187–207; 30 (1980), pp. 199–221; 31 (1981), pp. 195–217

S. Horrell and J. Humphries, 'Women's Labour Force Participation and the Transition to the Male-Breadwinner Family', *Economic History Review*, 48 (1995), pp. 89–117

P. Lindert and J. Williamson, 'English Workers' Living Standards during the Industrial Revolution: A New Look', *Economic History Review*, 2nd series, 36 (1983), pp. 1–25

P. Mandler, 'The Making of the New Poor Law Redivivus', *Past & Present*, 117 (1987), pp. 131–57

M. W. McCahill, 'Peers, Patronage and the Industrial Revolution, 1760–1800', *Journal of British Studies*, 16 (1976), pp. 84–107

J. Mokyr, 'Is There Still Life in the Pessimist Case? Consumption during the Industrial Revolution, 1790–1850', *Journal of Economic History*, 48 (1988), pp. 69–92

D. Porter, '"Enemies of the Race": Biologism, Environmentalism and Public Health in Edwardian England', *Victorian Studies*, 34 (1991), pp. 159–78

P. Thane, 'The Working Class and State "Welfare" in Britain, 1880–1914', *Historical Journal*, 27 (1984), pp. 877–900

J. Torrance, 'Social Class and Bureaucratic Innovation: The Commissioners for Examining the Public Accounts', *Past & Present*, 78 (1978), pp. 56–81

J. Walvin, 'The Slave Trade, Abolition and Public Memory', *Transactions of the Royal Historical Society*, 6th series, 19 (2009), pp. 139–49

Economic themes

Books

W. Albert, *The Turnpike Road System in England, 1663–1840* (Cambridge University Press, 1972)

D. Aldcroft and M. Freeman (eds), *Transport in the Industrial Revolution* (Manchester University Press, 1983)

D. Alexander, *Retailing in England during the Industrial Revolution* (Athlone Press, London, 1970)

R. C. Allen, *The British Industrial Revolution in Global Perspective* (Cambridge University Press, 2009)

T. S. Ashton, *The Industrial Revolution, 1760–1830*, 2nd edn (Oxford University Press, 1997, with introduction by P. Hudson)

P. Bagwell, *The Transport Revolution* (Routledge, London, 1988)

J. V. Beckett, *The Agricultural Revolution* (Wiley-Blackwell, Oxford, 1990)

J. D. Chambers and G. E. Mingay, *The Agricultural Revolution, 1750–1880* (Batsford, London, 1966)

M. Collins, *Banks and Industrial Finance in Britain, 1800–1939* (Cambridge University Press, 1995)

P. L. Cottrell, *Industrial Finance, 1830–1914: The Finance and Organisation of English Manufacturing Industry* (Routledge, London, 1980)

M. J. Daunton, *Progress and Poverty: An Economic and Social History of Britain, 1700–1850* (Oxford University Press, 1995)

M. J. Daunton, *State and Market in Victorian Britain: War, Welfare and Capitalism* (Boydell Press, Woodbridge, 2008)

R. Davis, *The Industrial Revolution and British Overseas Trade* (Cassell, London, 1979)

P. Deane and W. A. Cole, *British Economic Growth, 1688–1959* (Cambridge University Press, 1967)

H. J. Dyos and D. Aldcroft (eds), *British Transport* (Leicester University Press, London, 1969)

N. Ferguson, *The House of Rothschild: Money's Prophets, 1798–1848* (Penguin, London, 1998)

N. Ferguson, *The Ascent of Money* (Allen Lane, London, 2008)

M. W. Flinn, *The History of the British Coal Industry. Vol. 2, 1700–1830* (Clarendon Press, Oxford, 1982)

R. Floud, *The People and the British Economy, 1830–1914* (Oxford University Press, 1997)

R. Floud and P. Johnson (eds), *The Cambridge Economic History of Modern Britain. Vol. 1, 1700–1860* and *Vol. 2, 1860–1939* (Cambridge University Press, 2004)

R. Floud and D. McCloskey (eds), *The Economic History of Britain since 1700. Vol. 1, 1700–1860* (Cambridge University Press, 1981)

T. R. Gourvish, *Railways and the British Economy, 1830–1914* (Studies in Economic and Social History, Macmillan, London, 1980)

W. Hardy, *The Origins of the Idea of the Industrial Revolution* (Trafford Publishing, Oxford, 2006)

E. J. Hobsbawm, *Industry and Empire* (Penguin, London, 1968)

B. A. Holderness and M. E. Turner (eds), *Land, Labour and Agriculture, 1700–1920: Essays for Gordon Mingay* (Hambledon Press, London, 1991)

K. Honeyman, *Women, Gender and Industrialisation in England, 1700–1870* (Macmillan, Basingstoke, 2000)

A. Howe, *Free Trade and Liberal England, 1846–1946* (Clarendon Press, Oxford, 1997)

P. Hudson, *The Genesis of Industrial Capital: A Study of the West Riding Wool Textile Industry* (Cambridge University Press, 1986)

P. Hudson, *Regions and Industries: A Perspective on the Industrial Revolution in Britain* (Cambridge University Press, 1989)

W. P. Kennedy, *Industrial Structure, Capital Markets and the Origins of British Economic Decline* (Cambridge University Press, 1987)

S. King and G. Timmins, *Making Sense of the Industrial Revolution* (Manchester University Press, 2001)

D. Kynaston, *The City of London. Vol. 1, 1815–50* and *Vol. 2, 1890–1914* (Chatto & Windus, London, 1994 and 1995)

P. Mathias, *The First Industrial Nation: The Economic History of Britain, 1700–1914*, 2nd edn (Routledge, London, 1983)

P. Mathias (ed.), *Agriculture and Industrialization from the Eighteenth Century to the Present Day* (Blackwell, Oxford, 1996)

G. E. Mingay (ed.), *The Agrarian History of England and Wales. Vol. 6, 1700–1850* (Cambridge University Press, 1989)

G. E. Mingay (ed.), *The Agrarian History of England and Wales. Vol. 7* (Cambridge University Press, 2000)

J. Mokyr (ed.), *The Economics of the Industrial Revolution* (Allen & Unwin, London, 1985)

J. Mokyr, *The British Industrial Revolution: An Economic Perspective*, 2nd edn (Westview Press, Boulder, Colorado, 1999)

K. Morgan, *The Birth of Industrial Britain* (Longman, London, 1999)

A. E. Musson, *The Growth of British Industry* (Batsford, London, 1978)

H. J. Perkin, *The Age of the Railway* (Routledge, London, 1970)

R. Perren, *Agriculture in Depression, 1870–1940* (Cambridge University Press, 1995)

P. J. Perry (ed.), *British Agriculture, 1875–1914* (Routledge, London, 1973)

A. D. M. Phillips, *The Underdraining of Farm Land in England during the Nineteenth Century* (Cambridge University Press, 1989)

W. Reader, *Professional Men: The Rise of the Professional Classes in Nineteenth-Century England* (Weidenfeld & Nicolson, London, 1966)

G. Routh, *Occupation and Pay in Great Britain, 1906–60* (Cambridge University Press, 1965)

N. Tranter, *Population since the Industrial Revolution: The Case of England and Wales* (Barnes & Noble, London, 1973)

N. Tranter, *Population and Society, 1780–1940* (Longman, Harlow, 1985)

Articles

R. C. Allen, 'Tracking the Agricultural Revolution', *Economic History Review*, 2nd series, 52 (1999), pp. 209–35

M. Berg and P. Hudson, 'Rehabilitating the Industrial Revolution', *Economic History Review*, 2nd series 45 (1992), pp. 24–50

M. Collins, 'The Banking Crisis of 1878', *Economic History Review*, 2nd series, 42 (1989), pp. 504–27

N. F. R. Crafts, 'English Economic Growth in the Eighteenth Century: A Re-Examination of Deane and Cole's Estimates', *Economic History Review*, 2nd series, 29 (1976), pp. 226–35

N. F. R. Crafts and C. K. Harley, 'Output Growth and the British Industrial Revolution', *Economic History Review*, 2nd series, 45 (1992), pp. 703–30

C. H. Feinstein, 'Pessimism Perpetuated: Real Wages and the Standard of Living in Britain during and after the Industrial Revolution', *Journal of Economic History*, 58 (1998), pp. 625–58

V. A. C. Gatrell, 'Labour, Power and the Size of Firms in Lancashire Cotton in the Second Quarter of the Nineteenth Century', *Economic History Review*, 2nd series, 30 (1977), pp. 95–139

C. K. Harley and N. F. R. Crafts, 'Simulating Two Views of the British Industrial Revolution', *Journal of Economic History*, 60 (2000), pp. 819–41

E. Higgs, 'Women, Occupations and Work in the Nineteenth-Century Censuses, *History Workshop Journal*, 23 (1987), pp. 59–80

B. A. Holderness, 'The English Land Market in the Eighteenth Century: The Case of Lincolnshire', *Economic History Review*, 2nd series, 27 (1974), pp. 557–76

C. Hosgood, 'The "pigmies of commerce" and the Working Class Community: Small Shopkeepers in England, 1870–1914', *Journal of Social History*, 22 (1989), pp. 439–60

A. C. Howe, 'Free Trade and the City of London', *History*, 77 (1992), pp. 391–410

R. V. Jackson, 'Rates of Growth during the Industrial Revolution', *Economic History Review*, 2nd series, 45 (1992), pp. 1–23

D. Jeremy, 'The Enlightened Paternalist in Action: William Hesketh Lever at Port Sunlight before 1914', *Business History*, 33 (1991), pp. 58–91

E. L. Jones, 'The Changing Basis of Agricultural Prosperity, 1853–73', *Agricultural History Review*, 10 (1962), pp. 102–19

E. L. Jones, 'The Agricultural Labour Market, 1793–1872', *Economic History Review*, 2nd series, 18 (1964–5), pp. 332–8

D. McCloskey, 'Did Victorian Britain Fail?', *Economic History Review*, 2nd series, 23 (1970), pp. 446–59

M. Overton, 'Re-Establishing the English Agricultural Revolution', *Agricultural History Review*, 43 (1996), pp. 1–20

W. W. Rostow, 'The Take-Off into Self-Sustained Growth', *The Economic Journal*, 66 (1956), pp. 25–48

P. Sharp, '1846 and All That: The Rise and Fall of British Wheat Protection in the Nineteenth Century', *Agricultural History Review*, 58 (2010), pp. 76–94

Index

Magistrates, *see* Justice of the Peace
Malthus, Thomas, 14, 37
Manchester, 2, 36, 52, 54, 141, 168, 191,
    243, 248–9, 252–3, 267–8, 274, 284,
    305, 324, 343, 398, 400, 403, 407–8,
    428, 459
Margarot, Maurice, 110
Marshall, William, 67–8
Marx, Karl, 36, 79, 268–9, 429
master manufacturers, 58–9, 75–6, 211
medical profession, *see* doctors
Melbourne, Viscount, 205, 212–13, 225,
    228–31, 310, 342, 361, 460
merchants, 11, 35–6, 58, 79–80
Merthyr Tydfil, 2, 57, 81, 166, 326, 431
metals, *see* iron and steel industries
Methodism, 38, 57, 156–8, 256, 262
middle classes, 31–41, 73, 78–82, 84, 123,
    158, 211, 240–1, 243, 247, 251–2, 265,
    283–4, 292–3, 297–8, 342, 350, 359,
    378, 383–4, 395, 431, 462
Middlesborough, 57, 245
Middleton, Charles, 101–2
Midlothian Campaign (1879–80), 337–8,
    347, 391, 435, 437
Mid-Victorian Boom, 223, 239–40
migration, 6, 15–16, 54, 69, 77, 93, 138, 201,
    203, 222, 260–1, 288, 378
militia, 111
Mill, James, 20, 28, 180, 263
Mill, John Stuart, 20, 263, 402
missionaries, Christian, 353, 372
Molesworth, Sir William, 314
monarchy, institution and powers of, 45,
    85–92, 97–8, 151–3, 206–7, 228,
    258–9, 336, 343, 373, 377–8, 382, 441,
    460
money men, *see* banking
Monroe Doctrine (1823), 190–1
Moore, Sir John, 132–3
More, Hannah, 116–17
Morocco, 447–8, 452
motor-car industry, 278
Municipal Corporations Act (1835), 219,
    252, 268, 387, 461

music, 253, 283, 451
music halls, 306, 378

Nash, John, 24–5
Nasmyth, James, 244–5
National Debt, 3, 7–8, 35, 99, 106, 149, 163,
    273, 345
national identities/nationalism, 256–64,
    310, 436–7
National Union of Women's Suffrage Society
    (NUWSS), 404, 407, 409–10
naval mutinies (1797), 113, 124
Navigation Acts, 93, 173, 176, 194, 269,
    311–12
navy, British, 101, 113, 120, 121–9, 132,
    136–7, 155, 186, 191, 194, 273, 353,
    359, 362–3, 396, 399, 442, 444–7, 457
    Anglo-German naval rivalry, 446–7,
    450–1
Nelson, Admiral Horatio, 124, 130
Netherlands, the, 51, 93, 102, 118–22, 124,
    131, 134, 141, 149, 183, 185, 187,
    351–2, 373
New Zealand, 194, 196, 202, 327, 360, 371,
    379, 395, 456
Newcastle, 5th Duke of, *see* Lincoln, Earl of
Newcastle-upon-Tyne, 36, 42, 52, 57, 167,
    292, 357, 459
Newport Rising (1839), 221
newspapers, 36–8, 110, 115, 150, 165–6,
    169, 172, 211, 220–2, 244, 256, 269,
    276, 278, 299, 303, 319, 326, 328,
    356–7, 359, 364–5, 372, 376–7, 426,
    430, 443, 451–2, 454, 457
nonconformists/nonconformity, 37–8, 75,
    80, 156–8, 207, 215, 223, 228–9, 256,
    268, 293, 300, 303, 310, 312, 330, 365,
    387–8, 394, 397, 401
Nootka Sound incident (1789), 102–3
Norfolk, 59, 63, 67–8, 71, 109, 130, 156
Normanby, 1st Marquess of, 229
North, Lord, 5, 27, 85–91, 96–7, 100, 104,
    107, 112, 140, 151, 199
Northampton, 217, 326
Northamptonshire, 71